Evangelical News

Religion and American Culture

Series Editors
John M. Giggie
Charles A. Israel

Editorial Advisory Board
Catherine A. Brekus
Paul Harvey
Sylvester A. Johnson
Joel W. Martin
Ronald L. Numbers
Beth Schweiger
Grant Wacker
Judith Weisenfeld

Evangelical News

Politics, Gender, and Bioethics in
Conservative Christian Magazines
of the 1970s and 1980s

ANJA-MARIA BASSIMIR

The University of Alabama Press   Tuscaloosa

The University of Alabama Press
Tuscaloosa, Alabama 35487–0380
uapress.ua.edu

Copyright © 2022 by the University of Alabama Press
All rights reserved.

Inquiries about reproducing material from this work should be addressed to the University of Alabama Press.

Typeface: Minion and Plantin

Cover image: istockphoto.com; arthobbit
Cover design: Michele Myatt Quinn

Cataloging-in-Publication data is available from the Library of Congress.
ISBN: 978-0-8173-2124-6
E-ISBN: 978-0-8173-9400-4

To my parents, who set me on my path, and to Martin,
who decided to walk it with me

CONTENTS

List of Illustrations ix

Acknowledgments xi

Introduction 1

PART I
The 1970s

1 The 1970s: An Overview 19

2 Conversion Politics: From Countercultural Revolution to the Born-Again Presidency of Jimmy Carter 27

3 Feminist Challenges: Women and Gender Debates 75

PART II
The 1980s

4 The 1980s: An Overview 127

5 Christian America: The Era of the New Christian Right and the Reagan Revolution 137

6 Biomedical Challenges: From Abortion to Genetic Engineering 177

Conclusion 227

Notes 235

Bibliography 317

Index 353

ILLUSTRATIONS

Figure 2.1. ". . . and they crucified him." Cover of *Post-American*, Fall 1971 28

Figure 2.2. "Unfortunately, this is the only deadline we have in Vietnam." Cover of *Post-American*, Winter 1972 28

Figure 2.3. "God is an American and Nixon is his prophet." Cover of *Post-American*, Fall 1972 29

Figure 2.4. Illustration accompanying W. Glyn Evans, "Are We Living in Post-America?," in *Eternity*, December 1974 61

Figure 2.5. Charles Colson as President Nixon's unscrupulous henchman. Cover of *Christianity Today*, March 12, 1976 63

Figure 2.6. Illustrations accompanying Ronald D. Michaelson, "What Would an Honest Politician Look Like?," in *Eternity*, February 1976 66

Figure 3.1. "Hello, passion flower, your Total Man is home!" Cartoon in *Christianity Today*, July 18, 1975 95

Figure 3.2. "The Totaled Woman." Cover of *Wittenburg Door*, August/September 1975 97

Figure 3.3. "Are Women Human?" Cover of *Eternity*, February 1974 102

Figure 3.4. Illustrations accompanying William L. Coleman, "How to Be a Huggable Husband" and "How to Be a Wonderful Wife," in *Moody Monthly*, February 1973 116

Figure 4.1. "As an evangelical, who would I like to vote for in November? Has Dick Nixon shown any signs of repenting?" John Lawing, cartoon, in *Christianity Today*, July 18, 1980 129

Figure 4.2. "Sizing Up the Reagan Revolution." Cover of *Christianity Today*, October 21, 1988 132

Figure 4.3. "After Reagan: What's Left for the Religious Right?" Cover of *Moody Monthly*, February 1988 133

Figure 5.1. Christian Right activists drawn in a pose resembling the raising of the flag on Iwo Jima. Cover of *Wittenburg Door*, June/July 1980   138

Figure 5.2. "The Crusade for a Christian America." Cover of *Eternity*, May 1983   152

Figure 5.3. "HuMANism." Cover of *Moody Monthly*, September 1980   158

Figure 5.4. "Pat Robertson's Run: Going for It?" Cover of *Eternity*, September 1987   170

Figure 6.1. "The World's Leading Pediatric Surgeon on Society's Most Controversial Issue." Cover of *Moody Monthly*, May 1980   178

Figure 6.2. A single red rose and a full-page photograph of C. Everett Koop surrounded by young children. *Moody Monthly*, May 1980   179

Figure 6.3. "We thought we'd do for marriage what we've done for birth control." Cartoon in *Christianity Today*, December 9, 1977   182

Figure 6.4. "Where to, folks—the maternity ward or the abortion clinic?" Cartoon in *Christianity Today*, February 14, 1975   183

Figure 6.5. Stereotypical drawing of the abortion procedure, erasing the body and plight of the woman. *Christianity Today*, April 6, 1984   191

Figure 6.6. Unusual drawing of a fetus wearing glasses at different stages of gestation. *Christianity Today*, September 5, 1980   193

Figure 6.7. "If Not Abortion, What Then? Why Prolife Rhetoric Is Not Enough." Cover of *Christianity Today*, May 20, 1983   195

Figure 6.8. Black-and-white photograph of a decontextualized infant, reminiscent of antiabortion propaganda. *Christianity Today*, August 7, 1987   203

Figure 6.9. "A Legacy of Life." Cover of *Christianity Today*, January 18, 1985   209

Figure 6.10. "It's the surrogate mother . . . she wants you to know your labor pains are just two minutes apart!" Cartoon in *Eternity*, February 1987   222

ACKNOWLEDGMENTS

This book has been a long time in the making, and many people helped shape my thinking and supported me on the way. First of all, I want to thank my academic teachers whose respective disciplines make up the interdisciplinary scope of my work. I am especially thankful to Heike Bungert, professor of North American history at the University of Münster, for giving me my start in academics, taking on this project, and guiding me along to its finish. I want to thank Oliver Scheiding, professor of American studies at the University of Mainz, my boss for six years and my collaborator in several projects on religious periodicals. And I want to thank Annette Wilke, professor of religious studies at the University of Münster.

I also want to thank the University of Alabama Press and especially my editor Dan Waterman and the editorial team, as well as the external readers, for guiding me along the long path that is manuscript revision. I couldn't have done it without you! Thank you also to Sarah Watkins and her editing skills.

This book is based on extensive reading of evangelical magazines, and I am grateful for the institutions that provided access to those materials and other sources: the Wheaton College Library and Archives; the Billy Graham Center at Wheaton College; the University of California, Santa Barbara, Library; the Library of Congress, the University Library in Tübingen; and the Bethel University Library in Saint Paul, Minnesota. Thank you also to the staff of *Christianity Today* and former editor in chief Mark Galli for their willingness to talk to me in person. I am also grateful for the hospitality of Linda and Bill, with whom I lived while doing research in Wheaton. I am grateful for financial assistance from the Universities of Münster and Mainz and the German Research Foundation (DFG), as well as an archival scholarship from the German Historical Institute.

At the University of Münster, where I spent three years as a lecturer, I profited from the proximity to the Cluster of Excellence on Religion and Politics under the guidance of Professor Barbara Stollberg-Rilinger and the exchange with colleagues including Felicity Jensz, Manja Quarkatz, and Felix Krämer. I enjoyed the close collaboration within the field of North American history, especially with Jana Weiß, Charlotte Lerg (visiting from the University of Munich), Anne Overbeck, and Claudia Roesch. I want to thank my colleagues in the field of Latin American history, especially Professor Silke Hensel, Deborah Gerstenberger, and Barbara Rupflin, not only for joining study groups but also for sharing their work on Latin America and teaching me to say *United States* of America.

At the University of Mainz, I am especially thankful for the collaboration and support of my colleagues from the DFG research group UnDoing Differences, many fruitful discussions and conversations, working groups, and conferences. I want to thank all the colleagues by symbolically thanking our speaker, Professor Stefan Hirschauer, and moderator, Tobias Boll. In Mainz, I also profited from conversations and friendships with colleagues at the Obama Institute for Transnational American Studies, especially Damien Schlarb and Nele Sawallisch, new colleagues Professor Axel Schäfer and Torsten Kathke, former students turned colleagues like Julia Velten, former office neighbors René Dietrich, Johanna Seibert, and Maximilian Meinhardt, and student helpers Tanja Ebner and Sophia Eva Martin.

I profited from membership in the German Association of Religious Studies (DVRW) and especially from the working group on evangelical, Pentecostal, and charismatic movements under the leadership first of Sebastian Schüler and Martin Radermacher, then of Esther Berg-Chan. I am grateful for the collaboration with Swiss colleagues Andrea Rota and Fabian Huber. I enjoyed collaborating with Anna Neumeier, Kathrin Kohle, and Katharina Neef. Many thanks also to the members of the working group on religions and politics and my former cospeakers Hannah Müller-Sommerfeld, Karsten Lehmann, Ansgar Jödicke, Christian Meyer, and Ulf Plessentin. A shout-out also to the colleague I've known the longest, Carsten Ramsel, and our old mentor, Professor Günter Kehrer.

I am grateful for the international exchange and collaboration with scholars. I had the opportunity to speak about this project at many workshops and conferences worldwide and collaborate in some projects along the way. Thank you to the research group European Bible Belts, especially my Swedish colleagues Daniel Lindmark and Stefan Gelfgren. I am indebted to the participants in the Religious Press and Print Culture conference and several workshops I organized in Mainz and the many other colleagues I had the fortune to meet and learn from, including Candy Gunther Brown, Daniel Vaca, and Heidi Campbell. Thank you especially to Elesha Coffman for ongoing support and collaboration.

I am indebted to many teachers but especially to my mentors at Hobart and William Smith Colleges, Michael Dobkowski, Richard Salter, and Susan Henking, as well as Fay Botham, who passed away in early 2021 and is greatly missed. I am grateful for the opportunities provided by former president Mark Gearan, the friendship of his family, the friendship and advice of Chevanne

DeVaney and Alejandra Molina, and the many friendships that have nurtured me since college days, especially Felipe, Mavreen, Rafeek, and Erika. My good friend and colleague Jasmine Yarish has proven an indispensable sounding board and fount of advice. Thank you to my host family and many friends in the United States who provided a home away from home on my research trips. Thank you also to my friends and family at home. This book is dedicated to my parents, who encouraged me to explore the world and supported my academic endeavors. This book is also dedicated to my husband, Martin, who entered my life late in the writing process but has become indispensable in so many ways. He checked the punctuation in my footnotes when my eyes blurred, and he lifted up my heart when I would have despaired.

Evangelical News

Introduction

> Among the external resources available to the church, the
> printed page stands first.
> —Frank E. Gaebelein, "The Christian Use of the Printed Page"

In the late 1970s, Carl F. H. Henry wrote a series of articles collectively titled "In Search of Evangelical Identity" for *Christianity Today*, in which he described Evangelicalism as a "long-caged lion." Yet he complained that this lion, "while still on the loose, and still sounding his roar, . . . is nonetheless slowly succumbing to an identity-crisis."[1]

Henry and popular evangelist Billy Graham had been among those who in the 1940s and 1950s revived the category of Evangelical. Reacting to the public devaluation of the term Fundamentalism in the wake of the Scopes Trial of 1925, they waged an image campaign for their conservative Protestant movement, encouraging people to, among other things, self-identify as Evangelical. In the Fundamentalist-Modernist controversy, white Protestants debated whether new scientific findings could be reconciled with biblical faith. One faction insisted that the Bible contained irrevocable truths and thus adhered to the verbal inspiration and inerrancy of the Bible. They took their name—Fundamentalists—from a series of treatises, *The Fundamentals: A Testimony to Truth* (1910–15), in which they expounded the main tenets of their faith. The other faction, known as Modernists, applied new scientific findings to their faith, interpreting the Bible through methods like historical-critical exegesis. The Scopes Trial, a court case in Dayton, Tennessee, gained dubious fame as a showdown between Fundamentalism and Modernism. Five states, including Tennessee, had passed laws against teaching evolution in public schools. The American Civil Liberties Union (ACLU) wanted to challenge the constitutionality of these laws and sought a test case, recruiting teacher John Thomas Scopes of Dayton as a defendant. When William Jennings Bryan, populist and three-time Democratic presidential candidate, volunteered his services as plaintiff, Chicago lawyer Clarence Darrow volunteered to be the ACLU's defense lawyer, guaranteeing popular attention for the case. Formally, the prosecution won, and Scopes had to pay a fine for teaching evolution. But in the popular rendering of the case, journalists stylized the population of Dayton and others who were in favor of banning Darwin's theory from classrooms as ignorant country bumpkins and small-minded Fundamentalists. In the wake of the trial, the term Fundamentalism, "decouple[d] ... from the movement that had made it," degenerated into a pejorative term hurled at conservative political opponents.[2] The founding of new institutions like the National Association of Evangelicals (NAE, est. 1942) and Fuller Theological Seminary (1947), as well as the launch of the magazine *Christianity Today* (1956), served to recast and bolster the image of conservative Protestants. The term Evangelical proved to be so popular that *Newsweek* proclaimed 1976 the Year of the Evangelical, after Evangelical Jimmy Carter captured the presidency and a Gallup poll found that one-third of the US population claimed to identify with the labels "born again" or, in a general sense, "Evangelical." However, while the term Evangelicalism as used by Henry and Graham was meant to signify a distinct religious movement, the nuance of the term was weak. For one, the term had been used historically as a synonym for Protestantism (in the sense of the German *evangelisch*) as well as to describe various Protestant revivals in Great Britain and the United Sates. Furthermore, the Evangelicalism of Henry and Graham never became a denomination but is better characterized as a religious movement or faith tradition lacking formal traits of constitution like a creed, official membership, and administrative structure.[3] This movement underwent an internal process of diversification in the generations following Henry and Graham, with followers adhering to different theological traditions (most notably Wesleyan versus Reformed traditions) and splitting up into different age cohorts and sociopolitical camps.[4] Additionally, with the popularity of the term in the 1970s came its appropriation. People selectively claimed Evangelical language and symbols and started calling themselves Evangelical.[5] While never part of a clearly defined and bounded entity, Evangelicals, faced with developments that diluted the movement and pulled them apart, struggled to retain their identity.

Evangelical News traces the struggle of Evangelical magazines to meaningfully define the term Evangelical and outline Evangelical positions on contemporary social and political issues during the 1970s and 1980s.[6] Evangelical magazines labored to create shared visions—a common repertoire of perspectives, concepts, and rhetoric. Magazines often succeeded in coining terminology and pronouncing a broadly defined vision. Yet in their assemblage of contributions and contributors' points of view, the heterogeneity of Evangelical perspectives remained visible, exhibiting nuance and sometimes disagreement on the interpretation of particular issues. Magazines were but one platform where Evangelical entrepreneurs struggled to define the boundaries of Evangelicalism and set an agenda for the movement. Television, radio, and various organizations and political stages also provided settings for entrepreneurs to push their versions of and goals for Evangelicalism. Accordingly, *Evangelical News* tells only one part of the story. Magazines were not removed from other platforms for envisioning Evangelicalism. Both in their function of reporting and as an assemblage of various contributions, magazines incorporated a broad range of Evangelical issues, perspectives, and persons. However, as a whole, magazines were targeted at a reading audience of people educated, interested, and affluent enough to buy their product. Individually, magazines had particular foci and pet issues and thus appealed to particular audiences. Visions produced by Evangelical magazines were thus only representative of their self-selected crowd of readers, and ultimately failed to gain definitory power over the movement and its agenda.

Evangelical News argues that through discourse—the shared rhetoric, concepts, and perspectives that collectively form "visions"—religious community was created and sustained by Evangelicals during the 1970s and 1980s. By virtue of publication, statements become common good; they become knowledge that can be reproduced and marshaled by different people and in different contexts. Thus media language differs from private language not only in its reach and influence but also in quality: published statements take on facticity. In the process of publication media create that which they speak of. I argue that it fell to Evangelical entrepreneurs, whom I simply refer to as spokespersons, to form an Evangelical consensus—and therefore define the community—through their work (re)presenting Evangelicalism, for example in the pages of periodicals. Spokespersons are both the gatekeepers and innovators of Evangelicalism. As Evangelicals, they operate within a specifically Evangelical discourse that preconfigures what can be meaningfully said and sets the boundaries for what counts as Evangelical perspective. Yet as spokespersons, they are also in a unique position to push against and redraw these boundaries. Both tradition and innovation are necessary to keep Evangelicalism relevant. The "labour of representation," then, can be conceived of as an ongoing project that consists of perpetuating Evangelicalism by finding a balance between continuity and change, between orthodoxy and currentness, and between distinction and relatability.[7] Periodical publishing can be understood as one arena in which Evangelical spokespersons negotiated their positions and struggled to spell out a common vision and consensus.

During the 1970s and 1980s, a vibrant market of Evangelical magazines existed, including magazines for politically conservative (*Moody Monthly*), mainstream (*Christianity Today, Eternity*), and politically liberal audiences (*Other Side, Post-American/Sojourners*); magazines targeting students (*HIS*); feminist magazines (*Daughters of Sarah*); and satirical magazines (*Wittenburg Door*). A synoptic reading of these magazines reveals shared visions, showing how an Evangelical identity congealed at a certain time within the temporary consensus of a particular topic, only to then dissolve and be re-created again.[8]

During the 1970s and 1980s, radio and television were further vehicles for defining, refining, and spreading Evangelical convictions, and during the mid-1990s, the internet was added to this assemblage.[9] Yet, to Evangelicals, the printed word remained central. Frank E. Gaebelein, the founding headmaster of Stony Brook School on Long Island, New York—a prominent Evangelical educator, prolific author, and contributor to Evangelical magazines—believed that the written word would endure. In January 1970 in *Christianity Today*, Gaebelein pointed to the centrality of words for conveying ideas and feelings to others, both to communicate and to relate. Furthermore, he highlighted the advantage of published texts over fast-moving electronic media: they were repositories of knowledge that could be studied at leisure and consulted indefinitely.[10] Religion scholar Martin E. Marty concurred with Gaebelein's assessment. Describing religion as "one of the most vital concerns of individuals and social groups in America," he highlighted the importance of religious periodicals, stating that "periodicals are a most effective way of propagating ideas, witness, opinion."[11] Historian Daniel Vaca describes Evangelicals as "book people," pointing out that "the form and concept of the book complemented evangelical emphasis on individual authority and introspection," an observation that can be applied to periodicals as well.[12] Evangelical spokespersons during the 1970s and 1980s labored to form a consensus on contemporary social issues like feminism, abortion, and reproductive technologies, and debated Evangelical ways of participating in politics. Periodicals were one medium of Evangelical meaning making and provide one repository for tracing distinct meanings particular to the Evangelical community.

Defining the meanings of Evangelicalism and its place in the world became even more important after the tumultuous and sometimes violent 1960s.[13] Though the 1970s—a time when "nothing happened"—could never evoke the same levels of nostalgia as other historical periods, historian Peter N. Carroll emphasizes the importance of the decade for "confront[ing] long-building redefinitions of the national identity to include nonmainstream groups," especially women of all races and African Americans, but other marginalized ethnic and cultural groups as well.[14] While American society still has not achieved equality today, the rights of women and ethnic and racial minorities have become part of mainstream politics. Where Carroll focuses on the "changing national culture," Andreas Killen emphasizes the crises of the decade. He writes of the "specter of the 1970s," pointing to the Vietnam War, the war the United States lost; the economic crisis, a time when oil embargoes and so-called stagflation threatened the livelihood of Americans and disrupted everyday practices like driving to work; and the Watergate crisis, the political scandal that revealed corruption in the highest echelons of power.[15] For historian Sean Wilentz, "the Watergate scandal marked a break which hastened the collapse of the political center in both parties," making possible the rise of "the sunny, right-wing optimism of Ronald Reagan." Accordingly Wilentz understands the 1970s as the introduction to what he calls "the Age of Reagan."[16] Railing against the "welfare queen," Reagan, during his tenure as president of the United States, scaled back spending on social welfare programs, built up the defense sector, and steered a big business-friendly course that benefited corporations over labor.[17] The 1980s also saw the economic rise of the so-called Sun Belt, a region that stretches from the South across Texas to the Southwest.[18] Politically, this region tended to be conservative and increasingly shifted to the Republican Party. "The result was," in the words of historian H. W. Brands, "a two-party system that more clearly distinguished liberals from conservatives"—with liberals lining up with the Democratic Party and conservatives lining up with the Republican Party.[19] In the 1990s, sociologist James Davison Hunter popularized the phrase "culture wars" for the prevailing feeling of an increasingly polarized nation, one split between orthodox and progressive forces.[20] Indeed, the national newsmagazine *Time*, as early as 1972, portrayed the "two Americas," depicted in a cover illustration by the figures of Richard Nixon, the Republican presidential incumbent, and his Democratic contender, George McGovern. According to the author of the lead article, citizens divided into a conservative America associated with Nixon and a liberal America associated with McGovern.[21] Historians Maurice Isserman and Michael Kazin have employed the term "culture war" to describe the heated ideological battles fought over various social and political issues "left unresolved since the end of the 1960s."[22] If America during the 1970s and 1980s was in the midst of a battle over identity, Evangelicals had stakes in this struggle as well.

While generally rejecting the phenomenon of hyphenated identities, self-identified Evangelicals grudgingly allowed that an added adjective might clarify their positioning at a time when the definitional power of the term was under duress. Writing for *Christianity Today*, New Testament scholar Leon Morris in November 1971 asserted that most Evangelicals disliked hyphenating the word Evangelical. Yet, he went on to explain, "because names like 'liberal evangelical' or even 'catholic evangelical' are sometimes heard, those who adhere to historic evangelicalism have come to be called 'conservative evangelicals.'" From this statement, it can be inferred that for Morris there was one authentic Evangelical tradition that only needed additional markers because others—liberal believers and Catholics, for example—had started to appropriate the term. Morris could live with the description "conservative," in the sense of conserving the right tradition, as long as historical religious practices were the focus. However, "conservative" fell lamentably short when one took into account Evangelicals' social and political engagement.[23]

Self-identified Evangelicals included believers of different sociopolitical convictions, from conservative traditionalists like the stalwarts of Moody Bible Institute, to left-leaning draft evaders and social activists like Jim Wallis and his *Post-American* community. Print media was one of the predominant ways they not only communicated with and supported their own constituencies, but also talked with one another.

"Cutting across denominational barriers and furrowing into the hearts of millions throughout the world, the magazine has long been ranked among the most influential and important Christian periodicals published," wrote managing editor Jerry B. Jenkins on the occasion of *Moody Monthly*'s seventy-fifth anniversary in September 1975. With slightly different foci, Evangelical magazines emphasized their contribution to and importance for their interdenominational religious constituency. *Moody Monthly* highlighted its role in strengthening and enlarging Evangelicalism. In the words of Jenkins, "the magazine is designed to build and challenge churches to grow and to inspire believers to evangelize."[24] Similarly, Billy Graham thought of *Christianity Today* as an institution that provided guidance and continuity to an otherwise institutionless religion. Reflecting on his inspiration for founding the magazine, Graham wrote that he envisioned *Christianity Today* as a "standard" around which "men and women in virtually every denomination who were committed to the historic biblical faith" could gather.[25] And after twenty years of publishing the magazine *Sojourners*, the editors felt that their magazine had succeeded in fostering real belonging: "Around the world and throughout the years, the people who have been connected via the magazine have always been much more than just subscribers. We have felt and continue to feel part of a real community of faith and conscience."[26] In their self-understanding, then, editors understood Evangelical magazines as fostering Evangelical community.

Magazines, especially the most prominent, *Christianity Today*, are regularly described by scholars as a source of identification for those who call themselves Evangelicals.[27] According to Ken Waters, one of the foremost scholars on US Evangelical media, religious communities can be understood as distinct "tribes" that create and use vernaculars not only to distinguish themselves from other groups but also to transport values that might run counter to national sensibilities. Periodicals help demarcate the boundaries between one religious community and another by (re)inscribing a particular perspective, cultivating tradition and an imagined community, and nurturing an individual religious identity.[28]

Curiously, while histories have been written of specific religious periodicals and some excellent studies have focused on the importance of periodical writing for religious communities—like Candy Gunther Brown's *The Word in the World* and Gisela Mettele's *Weltbürgertum oder Gottesreich?*—case studies on religion are missing from periodical studies, and scholarship on religious periodicals is almost nonexistent in the field of religion and media studies.[29] For example, while the *Journal of Media and Religion*, founded in 2002, set out to address the lack in scholarship on religion and media, the journal has thus far focused primarily on new media. Periodical studies, for its part, is a relatively new field, its emergence facilitated by digitization.[30] Concentrated especially in the vicinity of literary studies, scholars have taken advantage of new databases that provide easy access to periodicals and make them searchable.[31] Many newspapers and magazines today keep their own digital archives, often going back to the 1990s and successively extending backward into their history, thus slowly closing the digitization gap of the mid-twentieth century. Yet Evangelical periodicals of the mid-twentieth century remain largely undigitized, perhaps accounting for the lack of scholarship.[32]

Despite their current shortcomings, periodical studies and studies of media and religion, read together, form the background for this study. I take from the study of media and religion an emphasis on religion as well as a culturalist approach that focuses on "religion as expressed and experienced," highlighting that "the objective of media scholarship must be to focus on meaning construction."[33] From periodical studies I take the seriousness with which its scholars approach the format. Periodical publications are a particular structure, "characterized by both seriality—single titles are instantiated across multiple issues—and periodicity—titles strive for, if they don't always achieve, a regular publication cycle that structures reader engagement."[34] Periodicals are thus both timely and enduring, and accordingly are able to bridge the tension between innovation and continuity important to keeping a religious identity salient and relevant. I agree with periodical studies scholars "on the value of reading across full issues and multiyear runs of serial texts," rather than cherry-picking single articles, illustrations, or the contributions of a specific author. Such an approach promises to put into focus periodicals as complex media.[35] In other words, rather than treating periodicals as containers of disparate pieces of information, I approach periodicals as specific cultural products, produced by particular people in a particular time and place and composed of heterogeneous materials. Furthermore, I take seriously the observation that periodicals "are frequently in dialogue with each other," following the debates not only through time but also across different Evangelical periodicals.[36]

Using as criteria that they are not affiliated with any denomination or missionary or evangelistic agency, I selected for *Evangelical News* the four best-known, nationally circulated Evangelical magazines from the 1970s and 1980s, with an eye to representing the sociopolitical spectrum from right to left: the conservative *Moody Monthly*, the Evangelical flagship *Christianity Today*, the mainstream *Eternity*, and the left-wing *Post-American/Sojourners*. I supplemented my comprehensive reading of these magazines with selected readings of four other periodicals: *HIS*, targeted at college-age students; the *Other Side*, a periodical sympathetic to the civil rights movement; *Daughters of Sarah*, the Evangelical feminist newsletter; and the *Wittenburg Door*, a humorist magazine.

I follow Bourdieu's theory as set forth in *Language and Symbolic Power*. Bourdieu was concerned with everyday linguistic exchanges. He argued against philosopher John L. Austin that it is not a word's power—its *illocutionary force*—that acts. Rather, words gain power only in historical and social context and are thus dependent on both the actor and the situation in which they are used.[37] Just as there are regional variations in speech—dialects, for example—one might say that different groups of people use different vernaculars. How people employ words depends on their socialization, and a word, for example "submission," may have a different meaning in a secular context than it does in a religious context.[38] Meaning making is neither arbitrary nor ex nihilo. It draws on a preexisting repertoire and thus perpetuates certain symbolic conventions as well as the social order connected to them. In *Evangelical News*, I argue that rather than saying one thing and doing something else, Evangelicals operate within a unique discourse and employ a particular vernacular. To illustrate this, I study public Evangelical narratives in the form of Evangelical periodical publishing.

Evangelical narratives congealed in certain terms like "civil religion" or "sanctity of life" that are related to and evoke a web of associations and ideals, implicitly linking to particular thought traditions or a previous argument. From the Latin verb *videre*, to see or perceive, vision here should first of all be understood as a way of looking at or perceiving something. Accordingly—and contrary to the term "image," which strongly emphasizes the artificial—the term "vision" conveys notions of immediate, unfiltered reality.[39] Additionally, vision conveys different aggregates of reality. While in a biological sense, vision refers to this-worldly sight, in a religious context, vision references the seeing and often experiencing or partaking of a supernatural reality. In the popular lexicon, the term is furthermore used to describe ideals and future plans. In the context of Evangelical periodical publishing, the biological aspect of vision corresponds to a magazine's function of reporting facts, the religious aspect corresponds to the mission of relating to and conveying higher truths, and the colloquial understanding of envisioning corresponds to the capacity of sketching out alternatives and dreaming up ideals. An Evangelical vision comprises all three aspects.

I understand vision as shorthand for a particular construct of ideas. Far from extinguishing differences, vision contains (both collects and curtails) competing notions. This allows a vision to be dynamic enough to become relevant for people of different backgrounds and ages. It also accounts for both the minute and huge changes in meaning a vision might undergo over time. However, it contains the danger that outsiders overemphasize a suppressed aspect of a vision (zeroing in, for example, on the aspect of theocracy contained in the vision of Christian America) or that different groups of adherents focus on different traditions contained in one vision (emphasizing, for example the complementary or the hierarchical aspect of the vision of submission). Accordingly, while a shared vision implies a shared Evangelical logic and identity, a tension between consensus and plurality of voices remains. Therefore, the project of defining Evangelicalism always refers to a struggle for interpretative control.

Vision in its active form of *envisioning* conveys the creative aspect, what Bourdieu subsumed under the term "labour of representation."[40] It presupposes actors: people who actively represent a group. I argue that Evangelicalism, lacking institutionalized forms of authority, was represented to a certain degree by those who wrote for Evangelical magazines. Writers become representatives through a twofold, dialectical process: a magazine chooses writers because they are assumed to be authentic Evangelical representatives, and writers become authentic Evangelical representatives because they write for Evangelical magazines. While this process is circular, it is legitimized by an Evangelical community consisting of subscribers and readers. Like the professional politicians described by Bourdieu, Evangelical spokespersons are in the business of "producing ideas capable of producing groups by manipulating ideas in such a way as to ensure that they gain the support of a group."[41] As long as their legitimacy was not in doubt, then, authors and editors became and remained representatives of Evangelicalism.

The Evangelical identity crisis Carl F. H. Henry detected during the 1970s can be understood as a consequence of disparate Evangelical voices and contested Evangelical authority. Not only did people from different backgrounds claim the Evangelical label, they also disagreed on its meaning and boundaries. Evangelical magazines and the spokespersons that used them as their platforms fought—and ultimately failed—to (re)assert a universal definition of Evangelicalism. Evangelical magazines both attest to the diversification of Evangelicalism—magazines catered to different audiences—and actively sought to bridge the differences by (re)producing a common Evangelical language and shared visions. Not only did Evangelical magazines during the 1970s and 1980s discuss the same topics, they also cited one another and shared a pool of writers. Evangelical magazines can be understood as products of the "labour of representation." Evangelical magazines publicly claimed to (re)produce Evangelical voices and arguments and differentiate authentic from illegitimate positions. Their struggle to reach and maintain audiences indicates a struggle to stay relevant, to maintain the power of representation, and, ultimately, to gain definitional power. Spokespersons thus used Evangelical magazines as a platform for producing Evangelicalism as a difference that matters, as a relevant marker that people chose to identify with, and that characterized them as a distinct religious movement.

Evangelical News is divided into two chronological parts that survey political and social concerns during the 1970s and the 1980s, respectively. I highlight Evangelical visions pertaining to politics, tracing a reawakened Evangelical political consciousness from the Watergate crisis through the new political savvy during the Carter presidency (chapter 2) to the challenges of the so-called New Christian Right during the Reagan years (chapter 5). Visions that emerge from the periodical discourse include civil religion, conversion politics, and Christian America. I trace notions of social concern from the gender debates of the 1970s (chapter 3) to the question of life itself in relation to new biomedical challenges in the 1980s (chapter 6). Evangelical spokespersons struggled to form a consensus concerning visions of submission and the sanctity of life. I highlight the character of the Evangelical movement by investigating both the heterogeneity and the unity of Evangelicalism, showing that unifying visions were at the same time producing consensus and remaining ambiguous enough to subsume a range of attitudes.

PORTRAYALS OF EVANGELICAL PERIODICALS
Christianity Today

Christianity Today, the flagship publication of Evangelicalism, was envisioned by popular evangelist Billy Graham (1918–2018) as the Evangelical pendant to the *Christian Century*.[42] When Evangelicalism (re)emerged after World War II, the religiously liberal *Christian Century* was the only religious magazine cited in the general press and lauded by *Newsweek* and *Times*. *Century*, which had a circulation of forty thousand in 1947, was called by *Newsweek* "the most important organ of Protestant opinion in the world today."[43] While the *Century*'s circulation since then has oscillated between thirty thousand and forty thousand, *Christianity Today* soon averaged three times that, reaching a circulation of 140,000 in 1962, and peaking at almost 200,000 in 1981.[44] In 1985, the Christianity Today Institute, a think tank, was founded to provide the magazine with scholarly thinking.⁴⁵ Christianity Today Inc. became a parent company, acquiring *Today's Christian Woman*, a magazine targeted at women, in 1988, and eventually housing several periodicals including *Leadership Journal*, the academic *Christian History*, and *Ignite Your Faith*, a magazine for teenagers.⁴⁶ *Christianity Today*, a trendsetter of religious publishing, went online in 1994 and has remained a vanguard in making use of technological innovations. After the financial crisis of 2008, *Christianity Today* was rebranded as *CT*, closed many of its side venues, and streamlined all other publications for crossover appeal and brand recognition. Today, there are nine print issues of *CT* per year, which, according to the website, reach an audience of 800,000 readers, supplemented by 100,000 podcast listeners and 2,500,000 targeted monthly online visitors.⁴⁷ *Christianity Today* is the best-known and most successful Evangelical periodical.

Christianity Today started publication in 1956. The brainchild of Billy Graham, it was supported by well-known neo-Evangelicals, including Graham's father-in-law, surgeon and former missionary to China L. Nelson Bell. It was financed with the support of well-disposed industry magnates J. Howard Pew of Sun Oil Company (now Sunoco) and W. Maxey Jarman of the General Shoe Company (now Genesco). The board of trustees was headed by pastor Harold John Ockenga (1905–85), and theologian Carl F. H. Henry (1913–2003) became the founding editor.⁴⁸ When Henry stepped down from the editorship in 1968 after twelve years, it marked the end of an era. Neo-Evangelicalism was no longer a reform movement of Fundamentalism but was recognized as a distinct religious community. A second generation of Evangelicals had come of age and was taking over leadership positions.⁴⁹

Moreover, *Christianity Today* not only weathered the founding period, but had become very successful. Henry was succeeded by Harold Lindsell (1913–98), who had been part of the founding faculty of the Evangelical Fuller Theological Seminary. With Lindsell born in the same year as Henry, his nomination symbolized a continuation rather than a fresh start or generational renewal. Indeed, Lindsell proved to be more traditionalist than Henry, taking a rigid stance on biblical inerrancy.⁵⁰ Paradoxically, Lindsell's editorship coincided with a climate favorable to socially and politically liberal Evangelicalism. Positioned between Fundamentalism and Modernism/liberal Protestantism, *Christianity Today* incorporated the voices of a new generation of Evangelicals, provided space for biblical feminists and social activists, and discussed conditions for political involvement. While the Evangelical Left has been retrospectively shown to be only a minority, in the 1970s, its positions appeared to be viable and influential.⁵¹ In his relatively short first period as editor, from 1978 to 1982, Kenneth S. Kantzer (1917–2002), a theologian and former president of the Evangelical Theological Society, published an increasing number of articles on social justice, nuclear disarmament, and anti-materialism.[52] At the beginning of his editorship, a statement of circulation announced that *Christianity Today* had averaged a paid circulation of 142,444 over the previous twelve months, with an average 349 copies sold over the counter. It additionally gave away an average of 8,570 copies per issue.[53]

Kantzer was succeeded by V. Gilbert Beers (b. 1928), a Christian author and educator. He was editor from 1982 to 1985. In 1985, the editorship ceased to be a position held by one person and instead became a board of senior editors. This first board included Kantzer, George K. Brushaber, Terry C. Muck, Dennis F. Kinlaw, and J. I. Packer. Early in 1986, Brushaber and Muck were elevated to positions of executive editors. While the composition of the board of senior editors occasionally changed, Brushaber remained in his position until 1990, and Muck remained until 1993. Brushaber also served as president of Bethel College and Bethel Seminary (1985–2004) and went on to become president of Bethel University (2004–8), located in Saint Paul, Minnesota. Muck, a theological educator and writer, went on to become executive director of the Louisville Institute, a Lilly Endowment–funded program training religious scholars and researchers. During the 1980s, despite the general political turn to the right, *Christianity Today* stayed the course, advocating social consciousness and maintaining distance from the conservative political activism of the New Christian Right.

Christianity Today has been described as "the scholar of Christian magazines."[54] In the era under study, it was characterized by well-written articles on a wide range of topics, concerning both contemporary (social and political) and eternal (theological) issues. During the 1970s and 1980s, the magazine was published semimonthly; starting in 1978, there was only one issue each month for July and August, but two issues for all other months.

Eternity

Another mainstream Evangelical magazine was *Eternity*, published from 1950 to 1989. Donald Grey Barnhouse (1895–1960), a visionary Christian leader and minister of the Tenth Presbyterian Church in Philadelphia, founded a Fundamentalist magazine, *Revelation*, in 1931. According to an *Eternity* tribute, Barnhouse "disliked being called a fundamentalist but always insisted he was faithful to the 'fundamentals.'" In 1950, after he lost the editorship of *Revelation* (which folded shortly thereafter), he founded *Eternity*. Three years later, Barnhouse suddenly but decisively pivoted in an Evangelical direction, taking the magazine with him.[55]

Another watershed moment in the history of the magazine was Barnhouse's death in 1960, which created concern among the staff about the survival of the magazine. Russell T. Hitt, who had been working for *Eternity* for seven years, took over the editorship and managed the transition. Between 1960, when he took over, and 1975, when he retired, circulation climbed from thirty thousand to fifty thousand copies. While the magazine was dedicated to analyzing contemporary issues from an Evangelical perspective and in light of eternity, during Hitt's editorship it also upheld the tradition of occasionally jolting readers with issues outside their comfort zone, like advocating leadership roles for women.[56]

Continuity was provided by columnist Joseph Bayly (1920–86), who had previously edited the InterVarsity magazine *HIS* (1952–60), and whose Out of My Mind column ran from 1960 almost until his death.[57] In 1975, the editorship passed on to William J. Peterson, another long-time veteran of the magazine. In September 1975, Stephen Board, another former editor of *HIS*, was introduced as new executive editor. This team led *Eternity* until the end of 1983, when Board moved on to a job with David C. Cook Publishing.[58] For a few issues, art director Deborah Barackman took over as executive editor, before Kenneth A. Mayers took on the executive editorship starting with the April 1984 issue. Peterson and Mayers, with Barackman in the position of managing editor, continued until the end of 1986. According to an overview of Mayers's career in the *Weekly Standard*, Mayers was fired by the board because he dedicated the magazine to "frivolous" topics of culture.[59] At the beginning of 1987, a new team took over, led by editor James Montgomery Boice (1938–2000), giving *Eternity* a new look and focus. The magazine attempted to be a Christian news provider and cultural commentator.[60] However, the last issue was published in January 1989.

Eternity was known for being "on the cutting edge of evangelical thought."[61] Its articles regularly both engaged with and formulated positions on current topics. The magazine also sported regular sections on contemporary culture in the form of film, music, and especially book reviews. It was known for its annual book poll. During the 1970s and 1980s, *Eternity* was published monthly.

Moody Monthly

Moody Monthly has the longest history of the magazines analyzed in this study. Its predecessors predated not only the moniker (neo-)Evangelical but also that of Fundamentalist. *Moody Monthly* was the magazine of the Moody Bible Institute in Chicago (founded in 1886), dating back to the activities of the evangelist Dwight L. Moody (1837–1899) at the turn of the twentieth century. In its first embodiment, as *Institute Tie* (1891–93), the magazine was an alumni newsletter, and it was revived in that format in 1900.⁶² It subsequently developed into a general religious news magazine, and it existed as a published magazine in various formats continuously to 2003.

While some Evangelicals considered *Moody Monthly* beyond the scope of Evangelicalism, it has also been pointed out that Moody Bible Institute was the place of early meetings of what adherents came call Evangelicalism.⁶³ Scholar Joel A. Carpenter argues that the magazine initially played a conciliatory role, mediating between the wings of separatist Fundamentalists and emerging neo-Evangelicals, but was well-disposed toward Evangelicalism, giving "glowing coverage" to the activities of evangelist Billy Graham.⁶⁴

William Culbertson III (1905–71), a Reformed Episcopal bishop, became president of Moody Bible Institute in the late 1940s and functioned as main editor of *Moody Monthly* until his retirement and death in 1971. During his tenure, the magazine established its focus on family issues. Furthermore, the magazine was increasingly shaped by contributions from professional journalists.⁶⁵ By 1971, when George Sweeting (b. 1924) took over as the new institute president and editor, *Moody Monthly* had become the conservative voice of Evangelicalism. *Moody Monthly* reported a circulation of approximately 250,000 copies per issue in 1974, bragging that "the traditional steady *Moody Monthly* was the fastest growing Christian periodical in the country."⁶⁶ Sweeting was succeeded in 1987 by Joseph Stowell, who was followed in 1989 by Jerry B. Jenkins (b. 1949), who would later coauthor with Tim LaHaye (1926–16) the enormously successful, twelve-volume *Left Behind* series (1995–2007), an apocalyptic thriller.⁶⁷

During the 1970s and 1980s, *Moody Monthly* advocated both social engagement and social conservatism. It tended to come down on the conservative side of issues, advocating traditional sexual roles, gender norms, and family relationships, largely favoring the conservative politics of Presidents Nixon and Reagan, and even defending the Vietnam War. Yet in good evangelical Christian tradition, it also sounded the warning not to confuse politics with religion. In 1991, *Moody Monthly* was refashioned as *Moody Magazine*, and it continued as the voice of conservative Evangelicalism until the end of its publication. In 2003, at a circulation of eighty-five thousand, the magazine was ended "due to increased media competition, a gradual decline in circulation, and the continuing need for significant subsidization."⁶⁸

Moody Monthly was known for its focus on personal spirituality and traditional family issues. A writer for the Evangelical youth magazine *HIS* judged that it made good, wholesome reading for the whole family: "from dad who wants to be a better Sunday-school teacher, to mom who's coping with depression, to the kids who read Gil Beers's 'muffin' stories."⁶⁹ *Moody Monthly* represented the conservative end of the Evangelical spectrum, especially with regard to moral issues and family affairs. During the 1970s and 1980s the magazine was published monthly.

Post-American/Sojourners

Post-American/Sojourners is the youngest of the magazines discussed in this study. First published as Post-American in 1971 and renamed Sojourners in 1975, it became the predominant magazine for the Evangelical Left and is closely associated with editor Jim Wallis (b. 1948). It evolved at the conjunction of student activism and Evangelical conviction in the late 1960s. Wallis, soon to be "one of the most important faces of the evangelical left," experimented with the activism of the counterculture and political ideas of the New Left before returning to his childhood faith and developing a socially conscious critique of contemporary Evangelicalism. He and fellow combatants like Bob Sabath were students at Trinity Evangelical Divinity School in Deerfield, Illinois, in the mid-1960s, when Kenneth S. Kantzer, who later served as editor of Christianity Today, was the dean of students. They initially launched criticism against the way the school dealt with student activism, but they soon attacked what they regarded as the Evangelical establishment as embodied by Kantzer.[70] The disgruntled students organized as the People's Christian Coalition, found mentors like theology professor Clark Pinnock (1937–2010), and, in 1971, started publishing the Post-American, critiquing the hypocrisy of Evangelical social ethics, advocating social justice, and loudly criticizing the war in Vietnam.[71]

Although Wallis was initially on good terms with Carl F. H. Henry, the relationship between the two soon soured. Instead, an unlikely but productive relationship developed between Wallis and the Evangelical senator Mark Hatfield (1922–2011).[72] In 1975, the community behind the magazine, which practiced communal living, moved to an impoverished, predominantly Black neighborhood in Washington, DC. The magazine, renamed Sojourners, was part of the community's broader mission of a socially engaged Evangelicalism that also included community service and political demonstrations.[73]

The People's Christian Coalition printed thirty thousand copies of the first issue of the Post-American and distributed them widely across the Chicago area, earning themselves an initial 225 subscriptions.[74] From humble beginnings the paid circulation of the magazine climbed steadily. From 1976 to 1979 Sojourners gained approximately ten thousand new readers annually, reporting a circulation of approximately ten thousand in 1976 and forty thousand in 1979. In the 1980s Sojourners' paid circulation climbed to and remained around fifty thousand.[75] While it was a young magazine with a relatively small circulation, *Sojourners*, according to scholar Ken Waters, "succeeded in nudging evangelicals to a broader understanding of their role in society."⁷⁶

Sojourners became the voice of the Evangelical Left. It published articles on issues like the arms race or poverty, and it generally denounced local and global injustices. It was not known to be placating. On the contrary, "*Sojourners* informs readers of worldwide social, political and religious hypocrisy. It challenges the reader to get moving and right these wrongs."⁷⁷ The *Post-American* was printed irregularly; it appeared quarterly, then bimonthly, and finally monthly, with combined issues for June/July and August/September.

Other Magazines

Besides the four main magazines, the study selectively draws on further magazines, namely the *Wittenburg Door*, the *Other Side*, *HIS*, and *Daughters of Sarah*. This last was an Evangelical feminist newsletter published from 1975 to 1990. Lacking representation, female Evangelical leaders who were present at the drafting sessions of the 1973 Chicago Declaration of Evangelical Social Concern founded the Evangelical Women's Caucus, which published the newsletter.⁷⁸ The *Wittenburg Door*, a magazine with "the look of an underground newspaper," was originally targeted at Evangelical youth workers but became known especially for its satire and in-depth interviews. It was more or less regularly published bimonthly beginning in 1971 by Youth Specialties, out of El Cajon, California, with editors Mike Yaconelli (1942–2003), Wayne Rice, Denny Rydberg (1945–2019), and Ben Patterson. They used humor as a form of internal Evangelical criticism and ultimately aimed at reform.⁷⁹ The magazine was sold to the Trinity Foundation in Dallas, Texas, in 1996, and it slowly deteriorated until it was closed in 2008. A rudimentary homepage was put up about the same time, and new content has been published here since late 2020.⁸⁰ The *Other Side* was a magazine associated with the Evangelical Left, published, edited, and in large part written by John F. Alexander from 1965 until 2004. It was known for its articles on social—especially racial—injustice.⁸¹ *HIS* was the magazine of the InterVarsity Christian Fellowship in the United States, an organization doing Christian outreach, Bible studies, and other forms of Christian activities on college campuses. The magazine was started in 1941, shortly after the US branch of the British organization was started.⁸² The magazine, aimed at college students, was published until 1986.

PART I
The 1970s

1
The 1970s
An Overview

POLITICS AND REVOLUTION

"The Bible Belt is in fact bursting the bonds of geography and seems on the verge of becoming a national state of mind," read *Time* magazine's cover story of December 26, 1977. "Encouraged by the presence of a born-again Southern Baptist in the White House, stirred by the widespread fear that modern man will not be able to make it to the end of the century without some spiritual help, the far-flung residents of the new Bible Belt are loosely lumped together under the name Evangelicals."[1] Until the mid-1970s, Evangelicals were almost invisible to the public, especially the national media. But with the presidential candidacy of born-again Jimmy Carter in 1976, media pundits rediscovered evangelical Christianity. Magazines from *Newsweek* to *Playboy* were suddenly interested in Carter's faith.[2] Adhering to a broad definition of Evangelicalism, the national media was especially interested in the combination of religion and political activism.

Evangelicals, in the 1970s, did not come out of nowhere. As Joel A. Carpenter has pointed out, conservative Protestantism did not simply disappear after the Scopes Trial of 1925; it merely retreated into its own institutions.[3] Known under changing names—the designation Fundamentalism was dominant before World War II, and the designation Evangelicalism became preeminent thereafter—conservative Protestants developed an extensive network of independent religious organizations (not associated with any denomination), most importantly Bible schools and colleges like Moody Bible Institute (est. 1886) and Fuller Theological Seminary (est. 1947), and they built on this infrastructure in the 1950s and beyond, often through periodicals.[4] While the media rediscovered Evangelicalism during the 1970s in conjunction with President Carter's faith, media accounts subsequently equated Evangelical politics with the New Christian Right. Writing in 1996, political science scholar Clyde Wilcox defined the New Christian Right as "a movement that attempts to mobilize evangelical Protestants and other orthodox Christians into conservative political action," but he warned not to overestimate its reach. He pointed out that "some white evangelicals oppose the Christian Right, many are neutral to the movement, a sizeable minority are supportive, and a much smaller number are active members."[5] The emergence of the New Christian Right—represented by organizations like the Moral Majority (est. 1979), Concerned Women for America (est. 1979), and the Christian Coalition (est. 1989)—has been understood as a defense of conservative Christianity.[6] Its lobbying for socially conservative political goals notwithstanding, the theory of a conservative backlash against the ideas of 1960s counterculture has been scrutinized by scholars like Axel Schäfer. Tracing Evangelical politics from the 1950s to the 1980s, Schäfer shows how conservative Christian activists appropriated and elaborated on countercultural language and demands.[7] Further, the notion that Evangelicals had "traditionally been less likely to participate in politics than other citizens" was challenged in the 2010s by scholars like Kevin M. Kruse and Matthew Avery Sutton, who recovered the long history of modern evangelical Christian politics.[8] Even though Evangelical political activism today has become associated with the conservative politics of the Republican Party and Christian Right activists, the example of Jimmy Carter shows that conservative faith and conservative politics did not necessarily go hand in hand. Indeed, during the 1970s, no inevitable connection between conservative Protestantism and conservative politics could be detected, and it was possible to imagine liberal views dominating Evangelical politics.[9] Realizing that before the presidency of Ronald Reagan conservative Protestants had largely been associated with the Democratic Party, scholars have further spoken of a "party realignment" of Evangelical Christians between 1976 and 1988, and set out to explain how the South, formerly a stronghold of both conservative Protestantism and the Democratic Party, became a power base of the Republican Party.[10]

Evangelical political activism and social initiative were not suddenly invented in the late 1970s; nonetheless this narrative was often employed in Evangelical accounts. For a generation of Evangelical scholars, writers, and other persons of public interest coming into their own in the 1970s and 1980s, the myth of their apolitical and socially segregated Fundamentalist forebears proved useful. Evangelical scholars like George M. Marsden (b. 1939) and Mark A. Noll (b. 1946), who decisively affected academic discussions, conventionalized the notion that social and political activism was the issue that divided Fundamentalists from Evangelicals.[11] According to this Evangelical historiography, Fundamentalists, in their search for ecclesiastic purity, practiced militant separatism by refusing to cooperate with less stringent believers. Evangelicals, conversely, sought social relevance and reached out to others.[12]

Historiography in the vein of Marsden located the beginning of a new religious movement, variously labeled "neo-evangelicalism" or "resurgent evangelicalism," in the 1940s and 1950s.¹³ Noll prominently recounted how Billy Graham, described by Joel A. Carpenter as "a fundamentalist favorite son," had been ousted from the Fundamentalist community for cooperating with mainline Protestant churches in his New York crusade of 1957.¹⁴ Searching for a starting point for their own religious tradition, these writers found in Graham a founding father. By building institutions like the National Association of Evangelicals (NAE, est. 1942), Fuller Theological Seminary (est. 1947), and the magazine *Christianity Today* (est. 1956), men like Harold John Ockenga, Billy Graham, and Carl F. H. Henry established a new Evangelicalism. Social concern was the overarching vision of Henry's 1947 book *The Uneasy Conscience of Modern Fundamentalism*, regarded as the founding "manifesto" of the new movement.¹⁵ In the book, Henry settled the score with the old Fundamentalists, blasting them for separatism and infighting, and lamenting their neglect of pressing social issues. In the introduction, Ockenga, then pastor of Park Street Church in Boston, proclaimed: "If the Bible-believing Christian is on the wrong side of social problems such as war, race, class labor, liquor, imperialism, etc., it is time to get over the fence to the right side."¹⁶ Marsden argued that the book showed that new Evangelicals "deplored fundamentalism's emphasis on personal ethical prohibitions at the expense of a positive social program."¹⁷ According to his reading, social concern prompted a new Evangelical political activism, and sociopolitical engagement was considered the hallmark of the new movement. Matthew Avery Sutton has debunked "the dubious postwar myth that earlier generations [of adherents of the Fundamentalist-Evangelical tradition] had been indifferent to politics."¹⁸ Yet for Evangelical intellectuals and leaders, this notion, which they helped create, served a decisive purpose: it provided a starting point for the movement in the 1950s, a nemesis against which Evangelicalism could be defined, and an impetus for a sociopolitical agenda that they started to follow in the 1970s.

Despite the importance of social concern in the founding narrative of Evangelicalism, "intellectually, social concern," in the words of Axel Schäfer, "remained the Cinderella of neo-evangelicalism throughout the 1950s and early 1960s."¹⁹ Hand in-hand with historiographical efforts of distancing Evangelicalism from Fundamentalism in the 1970s went renewed sociopolitical efforts, as Evangelical intellectuals and activists rediscovered their penchant for social issues. Sociologist James Davison Hunter points out that it was especially "the level of Evangelical rhetoric endorsing social ministry as *an end in itself*" that changed in the 1970s; according to his calculation, liberal and conservative Christians in this era appropriated approximately the same percentage of their budgets—18 percent—for social welfare.[20] Hunter's observation suggests that the sociopolitical focus was part of a discourse that sought to position Evangelicals as concerned and engaged citizens and thus distance them from Fundamentalism. Nonetheless, this rhetoric had tangible consequences, as existing Evangelical humanitarian organizations like World Relief (est. 1944) and World Vision (est. 1950), according to Hunter, "reported a surge of growth in the 1970s." Furthermore, younger Evangelical thinkers and activists, influenced by the countercultural movement and anti-Vietnam War protests, were concerned about social inequality and advocated social action. Known as the Evangelical Left, they disseminated their ideas through a slate of new publications like the *Post-American/Sojourners*, *Radix*, *Seeds*, and *Inside*, and "over thirty books."[21] This "revival" of social concern resulted in the Chicago Declaration of Evangelical Social Concern, which was signed by fifty-three leaders in 1973. The document pronounced an Evangelical commitment to social justice and condemned various -isms, from racism to materialism and militarism. These efforts were largely attributed to Evangelicals leaning toward progressive political positions.[22] But Evangelicals were by no means all politically progressive. Billy Graham's close relationship with President Nixon signaled an Evangelical defense of the political status quo. Historian Kevin M. Kruse argues that "the inauguration of Richard Milhous Nixon involved an unprecedented display of public prayer and formal worship."[23] The official inauguration festivities included, for the first time, a full church service. Aligning the new administration more closely with formal Protestant religion, Billy Graham's inauguration prayer was more sectarian than usual for these events: "Eschewing the ecumenical tones of past invocations, Graham specified that Americans needed to be 'born again' [through] a renewed faith in Jesus Christ." The new president also introduced a regular Sunday service at the White House, which was officiated by politically conservative religious leaders selected by Nixon and Graham.[24] The Watergate crisis put this conservative religiopolitical alliance into doubt, temporarily making progressive Evangelical critiques more attractive, but the appeal of the New Christian Right the following decade again drew on politically conservative sentiment.

Social Concern

One big social issue of the 1970s was women's liberation. The 1970s were a decade of conflicting activism by and on behalf of women, with the United Nations declaring 1975 the International Women's Year. The women's liberation movement had formed during the previous decade, with Betty Friedan's *Feminine Mystique* published in 1963, and the National Organization for Women founded in 1966. The movement, even though it never had large numbers of registered members, made inroads into US society. Feminist ideas became widely known, with demands like "equal pay for equal work" shared by many. According to historian Mary P. Ryan, it was correct to speak of a "feminist mass movement" in the 1970s because, "by 1975, no less than 80 percent of Americans were aware of feminism, and a slim majority actually registered support for its basic proposition of gender equality."²⁵ In 1973, the Supreme Court decision in *Roe v. Wade* legalized abortion, a ruling that was celebrated as a major feminist success.²⁶ Also, the Equal Rights Amendment (ERA), an amendment to the Constitution that would have ensured equal rights for women, passed Congress in 1972. However, it immediately provoked a countermovement. Catholic conservative activist Phyllis Schlafly founded STOP-ERA, an organization opposed to the ERA and feminist ideas, battling the amendment from 1972 until 1982, when ratification finally failed.²⁷

Evangelicals developed their own stance toward women's liberation. With the premise that Evangelicals denounced but did not fully reject "an earlier fundamentalist pattern of retreat from 'worldliness,'" historian Margaret Lamberts Bendroth argues that Evangelical negotiations of Christian womanhood "vacillated between nostalgia for a less secular past and a yearning for social relevance in the present."²⁸ According to her, Evangelical attitudes toward gender relations existed on a continuum, with a Fundamentalist penchant for Victorian gender norms on the one end, and uncritical Evangelical enthusiasm for contemporary society, including modern notions of gender equality, on the other. Religious studies scholar Betty A. DeBerg challenges the idea of apolitical Fundamentalism, arguing instead that the battles to uphold Victorian gender norms (which she sees as providing the founding impetus for Fundamentalism) were inherently political.²⁹ While they disagree as to whether Fundamentalism was political, Bendroth and DeBerg agree that Fundamentalists sought to preserve Victorian notions of family, gender relations, and sexual norms. Although they were never more than an ideal, Victorian gender concepts prescribed different "spheres" for men and women, with men working outside the home and women working at home. Connected to the idea of spheres was the ideal of a strict division of roles, with women being primarily defined as mothers and homemakers and men being primarily defined through their jobs and as breadwinners for their families. Because of their different functions, men and women were assigned different characteristics: men were active and strong and pursued economic and sexual conquests; women were passive and weak but also morally superior and caring. This Victorian heritage, combined with "the sharply conservative attitudes of the post–World War II era," formed the background for the subsequent development of Evangelical gender conceptions, including a "new emphasis on women's domestic role."³⁰ Yet, as will be shown in chapter 3, Evangelicals rejected the overtly misogynist predisposition of Fundamentalist leaders like

John R. Rice, editor of the magazine *Sword of the Lord*, or prolific writer Charles C. Ryrie, who insisted on women's inferiority.[31]

Accordingly, conservative attitudes toward women's place and role were not an uncritical subscription to Victorian ideals or the theories of Fundamentalist leaders; rather, in the 1970s, and in engagement with demands from the women's liberation movement, a conservative reenvisioning of gender ideals took place. Political scientist Robert Booth Fowler, who published one of the earliest studies on Evangelicalism and social and political thought, noted in 1982 that well-known Evangelicals like Billy Graham and Edith Schaeffer readily agreed that Jesus was "the world's greatest liberator of women" and that women should receive equal pay for equal work; nonetheless, they were strictly opposed to the women's liberation movement.[32] By accepting some feminist critique but dismissing the movement as a whole, Evangelicals like Graham and Schaeffer shored up a position that came to be known as traditionalist. Traditionalists emphasized the "order of creation," but they deemphasized notions of superiority and inferiority formerly connected with it.[33] Taking their cue from the second creation account (Gen. 2:21–22), traditionalists stressed the sequence of creation—man before woman—and combined it with an ideal of order, the notion that God had assigned each creature its place. Women who subscribed to the traditionalist view, like popular writer Marabel Morgan or former missionary Elisabeth Elliot, emphasized the harmony and order such a perspective conferred onto personal relations as well as society.[34] While putting new emphasis on biological differences between the sexes, this revision of gender ideals also empowered women by allowing them to "choose" their God-given role and defending their choice publicly. Historians like Lisa McGirr and Ruth Murray Brown emphasize the role that conservative women activists and their debates about women's liberation played in the emergence of new, politically right movements. McGirr analyzes grassroots organizations of suburban women in opposition to the liberal women's rights movement, while Brown traces the beginnings of the New Christian Right to discontent over the ERA.[35] While antifeminist activists rejected many claims of the women's liberation movement, McGirr's and Brown's accounts also show that conservative women took the initiative to transgress conventional roles, inventing new "traditional" roles for themselves.

Despite Evangelicals' conservative predisposition, an indigenous Evangelical feminism emerged, connected especially to new organizations like the Evangelical Women's Caucus and the newsletter *Daughters of Sarah*.[36] Historian Pamela D. H. Cochran has recovered the history of Evangelical feminism, which both appropriated secular feminist ideas and developed its own stance.[37] Although Evangelical feminists were few in number, Evangelical feminist ideas were widely discussed in Evangelical magazines; Bendroth points out that "undoubtedly many evangelicals first encountered feminism while browsing unwarily through Christian periodicals."[38] Evangelical feminists accepted the idea that men and women were equal. Rather than focusing on the question of what this would mean for the individual, however, Evangelical feminists focused on what equality would mean for relationships. Against their traditionalist coreligionists, they argued that the foundation of harmonious relations was not a clear order of commands but cooperation. The first Evangelical feminist articles to be printed—Letha Scanzoni's "Woman's Place: Silence or Service?" and "Elevating Marriage to Partnership," published in *Eternity* in 1966 and 1968, respectively—as well as the backlash against them have become canonical in the history of Evangelical feminism.[39] However, no study to date has brought into conversation the two sides of the traditionalist-feminist debate as it played out in Evangelical magazines during the 1970s.[40]

Visions

Intellectual Evangelicals during the 1970s and 1980s developed narratives about the origins and distinctiveness of their movement that were closely linked with notions of political and social thought. The magazine record reveals a distinctly Evangelical rhetoric that not only uses proper religious terminology but appropriates cultural language, adapting and sometimes inverting its meaning. Evangelical spokespersons invented political activism as a distinctly Evangelical practice and, as will be shown in the next chapter, borrowed countercultural language to define Evangelical goals and ideals. Condemning the abuse of political power, spokespersons in Evangelical magazines during the 1970s advanced an Evangelical discourse that inverted the meaning of civil religion to connote the idolatrous relationship of state and religion. Disillusioned by the abuse of political power, Evangelical spokespersons reenvisioned political engagement in religious terms, popularizing the notion of conversion as a legitimate basis for rehabilitating both individuals and institutions. Negotiating the proper attitudes of Evangelicals toward the society they lived in, Evangelical spokespersons grappled with the issues of the day, including the reorganization of society according to new conceptions of gender and gender relations introduced by feminists. Evangelical spokespersons discarded the older notion that women were naturally inferior to men and reenvisioned gender relations in more equal terms. Rejecting feminist ideas of self-actualization, Evangelical spokespersons reevaluated gender roles in the context of society, envisioning a God-created order within which every person had their own particular place. Taking up Pauline conceptions of corporate organization, both so-called Evangelical traditionalists and Evangelical feminists envisioned society as an organic whole. Traditionalists, on the one hand, emphasized hierarchy as the instrument that enabled the members of a body to function as a whole; feminists, on the other, regarded cooperation as the principle that allowed societies to run smoothly.

2

Conversion Politics

From Countercultural Revolution to the Born-Again Presidency of Jimmy Carter

In fall 1971, a new magazine commenced publication: the *Post-American*, a periodical started by Evangelical seminary students of Trinity Evangelical Divinity School in Deerfield, Illinois, around editor Jim Wallis. The cover illustration of the first issue suggested that people had wrapped Jesus in an American flag before they crucified him (figure 2.1). The cover of the second issue depicted a long row of gravestones with the explanation that "this is the only deadline we have in Vietnam" (figure 2.2).[1] A few issues later, commenting on the presidential election campaign between Richard Nixon, the Republican incumbent, and George McGovern, the Democratic contender, the *Post-American* printed a caricature of Nixon with the presidential seal as his halo, subtitled with the words: "God is an American and Nixon is his prophet" (figure 2.3). Taken together, these covers comprised a new and potent Evangelical critique of US politics and society, especially with regard to President Richard Nixon and the Vietnam War. Jim Wallis expressed the motivation for the new publication when he wrote: "We have unmasked the myth of the American Dream by exposing the reality of the American Nightmare."[2] It was the task of the *Post-American* and the community of Evangelicals it represented, the People's Christian Coalition, to reveal and combat not only US political transgressions but also the faith system that legitimated them. Wallis claimed that "there is a church whose god is American, white, capitalist, and violent; whose silent religion and imagined neutrality goes hand and hand with 'nigger' and 'napalm.'"[3] In the following issue, Wallis's fellow combatant Joe Roos called this religion—which he argued functioned to legitimize the status quo, valorize materialism, perpetuate racist prejudice, and justify brutal measures against Third World peoples—"civil religion."[4] The community writing for the *Post-American* believed that a majority of US citizens, including Christians, had been ensnared and were worshipping the false god of American power.

Figure 2.1. "... and they crucified him." Cover of *Post-American*, Fall 1971. Courtesy of Buswell Library Special Collections, Wheaton College, Illinois. Reprinted with permission from *Sojourners*, https://sojo.net.

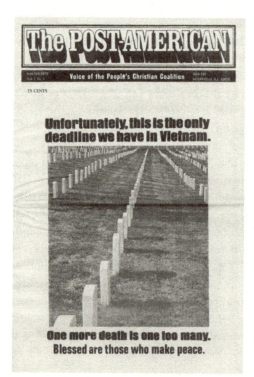

Figure 2.2. "Unfortunately, this is the only deadline we have in Vietnam." Cover of *Post-American*, Winter 1972. Courtesy of Buswell Library Special Collections, Wheaton College, Illinois. Reprinted with permission from *Sojourners*, https://sojo.net.

Figure 2.3. "God is an American and Nixon is his prophet." Cover of *Post-American*, Fall 1972. Courtesy of Buswell Library Special Collections, Wheaton College, Illinois. Reprinted with permission from *Sojourners*, https://sojo.net.

The Watergate scandal, which resulted in President Nixon's resignation on August 9, 1974, exposed corruption in the highest echelons of government and destroyed the illusion of American moral rectitude. Whereas Nixon's re-election revealed the Evangelical Left as, in the words of historian David R. Swartz, a "moral minority," Nixon's Watergate resignation exposed the mistake of equating access to the White House with moral influence.[5] The scandal prompted an Evangelical debate about national sin and individual responsibility, and for a brief time, jeremiads, the prophetic judgment pronounced over doomed nations, became attractive.[6] Dissatisfied with political elites, Evangelicals felt that Christianity had been abused to provide a moral veneer to hide immoral actions. Evangelicals diagnosed an American idolatry in which citizens worshipped not God but the state.

The French philosopher Jean-Jacques Rousseau coined the term *religion civile* (civil religion) in a theoretical discussion of what constituted a good society, and sociologist Robert N. Bellah introduced the term to the US context in the late 1960s.[7] In a speech to the American Academy of Arts and Sciences in 1966 and a subsequent *Daedalus* article, Bellah used the term "civil religion" to describe a generic religious dimension that he observed in US politics and society, focusing especially on the rhetoric used in presidential inaugural addresses.[8] Noting that civil religion took on a decisively negative meaning for Evangelicals, I disagree with scholarly accounts that use the term "civil religion" to describe Evangelical politics. I find it problematic to categorize expressions by religious spokespersons on behalf of their constituencies as civil religion, as sociologist Robert Wuthnow has done, and propose instead to take them seriously as *religious* expressions by leaders of faith traditions.[9] Evangelicals adopted and debated the term "civil religion" in the 1970s. As will be shown in this chapter, Evangelical discourse was not about the phenomenon that Bellah labeled civil religion. Indeed, Bellah himself largely abandoned the term, complaining that "civil religion was understood by many people to mean the idolatrous worship of the state."[10] This was certainly the case for Evangelicals who integrated the term (as an object of attack) into their debate about the proper relationship to the state. They envisioned themselves as a community of those who were "in but not of the world," and therefore were able to critically judge transgressions. Evangelical spokespersons agreed that there was a moral crisis in the United States and that God would judge the nation unless its people repented. Evangelicals saw themselves as the moral conscience of the country, responsible for revealing its transgressions and pointing out its national sin, civil religion: the hubris and hypocrisy of worshipping its own power.

In the wake of Watergate, Evangelical politics floundered, with spokespersons groping for adequate responses. Power and prestige looked suspicious, deterring Evangelicals from embracing political responsibilities. Demanding accountability, Evangelicals projected the religious formula of conversion onto the political realm: rehabilitation was possible by means of confession and conversion. Willing to give US democracy a second chance, Evangelicals demanded that politicians admit their wrongdoing and promise betterment before returning to or accepting jobs. This formula proved successful for Watergate culprits like former Nixon aide Charles W. Colson. Democratic contender Jimmy Carter further promoted the notion of being born again when he made his faith and conversion experience part of the 1976 presidential campaign. Indeed, pollster George Gallup Jr. revealed that a born-again experience was so common among US Americans that *Newsweek* pronounced 1976 the Year of the Evangelical. However, being born again became popular at the cost of diluting its Evangelical theological meaning.[11] At the end of the decade, the term "born-again politics" was associated not with self-identified Evangelicals but with political activists of Fundamentalist and Pentecostal backgrounds. In this sense, Evangelicals proved to be trailblazers for the New Christian Right, a religiously motivated political lobbying network that capitalized on a post-Watergate Evangelical notion of conversion as personal or political rehabilitation.

Pastors, Prophets, and Politics

Australian-born Leon Morris, who was a visiting professor at the Trinity Evangelical Divinity School in Deerfield, Illinois, observed changing Evangelical attitudes to social and political engagement in the 1970s. While he had the world at large in mind, he also highlighted the US scene, pointing especially at the student activities and social movements. In this regard, he concluded that "it seems idle to speak of evangelicals these days as conservative." On the contrary, there was "an eager search for new ideas and new methods."[12] He described innovation and pluralization within a community of believers that he characterized as theologically conservative. He also pointed to a reorientation of Evangelicals toward social and political engagement.

In stressing that the innovators were securely on Evangelical ground, Morris might have had a few specific faces in mind. Trinity Evangelical Divinity School, where he taught, was one of the foremost Evangelical institutions in the United States and produced many of the religiopolitical entrepreneurs of the rising generation. In 1970, some of these young people, including Jim Wallis, formed the People's Christian Coalition, which started publishing the magazine *Post-American* in fall 1971.[13] Writing that "the Scriptures are clear in condemning social and economic injustice, oppression, racism, hypocrisy, environmental destruction, and the kind of chauvinistic nationalism that gives rise to aggression, imperialism and endless war," the adherents of the People's Christian Coalition pointed to societal problems they thought Evangelicals had not paid enough attention to thus far.[14] The magazine became associated with the so-called Young Evangelicals or Evangelical Left, in opposition to the more traditional voices of so-called establishment Evangelicalism and the magazine *Christianity Today*.[15]

The People's Christian Coalition could not claim social action as an original idea, but its members helped instigate a new discussion of social and political involvement among Evangelicals in the early 1970s, one that would continue onward. On November 25, 1973, a group of visible Evangelical leaders adopted the Declaration of Evangelical Social Concern.[16] The original signatories included many second-generation and Young Evangelicals, among them Carl Thomas McIntire, son of Fundamentalist leader Carl McIntire; John F. Alexander and Jim Wallis, the founding editors of the *Other Side* and *Post-American*, respectively; peace activist Art Gish; young prolific writer Richard V. Pierard, whose book *The Unequal Yoke: Evangelical Christianity and Political Conservatism*, was published in 1970; and other illustrious Evangelicals born in the late 1930s and 1940s. But there were also Evangelicals from the founding generation, among them Carl F. H. Henry, the first editor of *Christianity Today*; Frank E. Gaebelein, sometime editor of *Eternity* and *Christianity Today*; Christian theologian and educator Vernon C. Grounds; and Joseph Bayly, whose column Out of My Mind ran from 1961 to 1986 in *Eternity* and who at one time was editor of *HIS*. The list also included Black Evangelical John M. Perkins, who had created the Voice of Calvary Bible Institute; female Evangelical writers Sharon Gallagher and Nancy Hardesty, who were early representatives of Evangelical feminism; and the Evangelical politician Mark Hatfield. This heterogeneous list of signatories points to the significance that spokespersons from across the Evangelical spectrum attributed to addressing the various crises of the times. Against the background of a creed-like statement of Evangelical convictions, they put out a call for action: "So we call our fellow evangelical Christians to demonstrate repentance in a Christian discipleship that confronts that social and political injustice of our nation."

Carl F. H. Henry took it on himself to describe the need for and reasons behind the Declaration of Evangelical Social Concern, doing so in the March 1, 1974, issue of *Christianity Today*. Henry envisioned Evangelical engagement as more than personal piety divorced from action (a criticism often leveled at Evangelicals) and more than social action divorced from biblical reasoning (a criticism often leveled at mainline Protestants). Instead, Evangelicals were to "focus on the divine demand for social and political justice, and to discover what the Kingdom of God requires of any contemporary option." Henry confirmed that currently Evangelicals were "more disposed to social involvement" than they had been in years. Yet he lamented the lack of leadership—a problem the Declaration and its proponents set out to remedy.[17] Despite the fact that this coalition of heterogeneous Evangelical signatories almost immediately fell apart, the revival of social concern and renewed emphasis on political involvement had long-lasting consequences. During the 1970s, Evangelicals rethought their attitudes toward politics and negotiated their religiopolitical stance, oscillating between pastoral and prophetic approaches.

In the early 1970s, two general templates for social and political involvement emerged. To draw from Evangelical terminology, these two styles can be labeled as "pastoral" and "prophetic."[18] Whereas the pastor is entrusted with the spiritual well-being of each member of their flock, the prophet decries the shortcomings and errors of a society. The former guides the spiritual development of their charge, hopefully to finally lead them to salvation. The latter judges society at large, predicting doom for all unless corporate changes are made. Accordingly, pastoral politics, as envisioned by Evangelical spokespersons, focused on transforming society by reforming individuals, and prophetic politics used social criticism in an attempt to bring about corporate change. At the beginning of the 1970s, establishment Evangelicals as well as the Evangelical Left laid claim to prophetic politics, with the former embracing the style of the prophet Daniel, who criticized the nation from the privileged position of the ruler's favorite counselor (Book of Daniel), while the latter embraced the style of Jeremiah, who called doom onto the nation (Book of Lamentations). The style of Daniel lost credibility in conjunction with the Watergate scandal, and Billy Graham, known for his close relationship to President Nixon, redefined and reinvented his style as pastoral politics, as spiritual counsel reinforcing individual growth.

Revolutionary Spirit

The pervasive atmosphere at the beginning of the decade was one of turmoil and upheaval. The editorialist of the conservative Evangelical, family-oriented *Moody Monthly* magazine observed, almost dazed: "And in the midst of the clamor even our Lord Jesus Christ has been cast into the role of a revolutionist."[19] At the end of the 1960s, many factors conspired to create a pervasive feeling of crisis.[20] The prevailing picture was one of social unrest and disintegration, complete with the assassinations of President John F. Kennedy and civil rights movement leader Martin Luther King Jr. People voiced their discontent by joining various insurgent movements, divided over issues such as the Vietnam War, and agonized over the impression of cultural, ethnic, and religious diversification after the immigration reform of 1965.[21] Historian Peter N. Carroll, while acknowledging that pluralism of a sort had always existed in the United States, points out that "the prime assumption before the 1960s involved some version of melting-pot change, the faith that cultural differences would bubble away into an assimilationist froth."[22] This assumption was challenged in the 1960s as US society appeared to be subdividing into multiple groups with divergent agendas, including feminism and the Black Power. The multiplication of religious worldviews became visible, for example, in the diversification of the sacral architecture that provide believers of immigrant religions and new religious movements with space to worship.[23] Especially disconcerting to Evangelicals were what they regarded as challenges to traditional morality and conservative Christian notions of order and decency. An editorial in *Christianity Today* described the 1960s in the following way:

> This was the decade of change and uncertainty, of unfaith and disorder. It was the decade of the Second Vatican Council, the new morality, the big plunge into secularity and secularization, the popularization of process theology, the death-of-God flap, and the rise of the so-called theology of hope. It was a decade of violence—in the cities and on the campuses, in Viet Nam and the Middle East. It was a decade of shifting political power, of repression in Czechoslovakia and China, of acute racial tension, of mushrooming population and urbanization, and of growing ecological anxiety.[24]

While the editorialist worried about violence, social unrest, and pollution, half the space was taken up by his concern over religious developments rang-ing from the liberalization of Catholicism, to the pessimistic death-of-God theology, to the purported increasing secularization of the United States.[25] Evangelicals feared that the nation was losing its religious and moral foundations and was thus slipping into violent chaos.

While the underlying problem appeared to be a loss of moral and religious values, the immediate danger was a potential eruption of violence. Vernon C. Grounds, president of the Conservative Baptist Theological Seminary in Denver, warned in a *Christianity Today* article that "the seriousness of our nation's situation at the beginning of 1971 can hardly be denied. The country is seething with the potential of revolution, a violent revolution, a bloody revolution, a revolution of guerilla terrorism, a revolution of sabotage and torture and chaos."[26] Published in January 1971, Grounds's depiction of the situation was more than a fever dream. On college campuses all over the country, student protesters clashed with President Nixon's law-and-order mentality. These rumblings would reach a terrible climax in what came to be called the Kent State massacre. In May 1970, National Guardsmen fired into a crowd of unarmed students at Kent State University in Kent, Ohio, killing four and wounding nine more.[27] In the light of rowdy revolts on college campuses and violent confrontations between students and law officers, Grounds's fears seem warranted. This, however, was no reason for resignation or withdrawal from society. Grounds postulated that people still had a choice between bombs and Bibles.[28]

The sentiment that despair was not an option, even in the face of such social unrest and chaos, was echoed elsewhere. In the same month that Grounds's article was published in *Christianity Today*, an editorial in *Eternity* proclaimed that there was still "Hope for the '70s," but that believers had to act now: "We cannot sit on our hands and wait for the Lord's return in some neutral corner of the world. We need to enlarge our perspective, remembering that there have been previous periods of revolution and social disruption, periods when history seemed as cataclysmic as ours is today. What if God's people had abandoned the world then?"[29]

Conveying a sense of urgency, the *Eternity* editorialist called people to action. The writer enlisted the New Testament Parable of the Talents (Matt. 25:14–30) and "Parable of the Sheep and the Goats" (Matt. 25:31–46) as evidence that God wanted believers to be involved in society and address the plight of the people. In the Parable of the Talents, servants are asked to take care of their master's money while he is away. Upon his return, the servant who has invested and thus increased his master's talents is rewarded, and the one who did not invest his talents is punished. The message the editorialist sent was that inaction was wrong, that God had given his followers a mandate to work on his behalf, and that it was a Christian duty to aim at improving the current situation. The "Parable of the Sheep and the Goats" reminded readers that "the righteous," who will "gain eternal life," are being separated from the rest, who will "gain eternal punishment." God meted out judgment according to the rule that "whatever you did for one of the least of these brothers and sisters of mine, you did for me [God]."[30] Using biblical examples, the editorialist argued that being God's stewards on earth meant that Christians must take an active role. Withdrawal from society or neutrality in the conflict, accordingly, were not options; rather, Evangelical magazines urged readers to engage with the social and political issues of the day.

With palpable grievances and revolutionaries all around them, Evangelical spokespersons felt the need to take a stand. The countercultural concept of revolution had great appeal and seemed to connect with Christian ideas of fighting for righteousness in a hostile world and preparing for the second coming of Christ. The biblical story of Jesus, too, could be read as a revolutionary tale. With the article "Christians and Revolution," *Christianity Today* addressed the issue head on. Linking activists' concerns to biblical ideals, the article recounted that "more and more Christians, especially young ones, are developing authentically biblical sensitivities that make them extremely uncomfortable with the same evils that have driven revolutionaries to reject the establishment." The author, Joel H. Nederhood, noted Evangelical sympathies for insurgents' grievances and acknowledged the legitimacy, for example, of fighting "racial injustice" and "the deficiencies of prevailing economic systems."[31] Even so, Nederhood—known to Evangelicals as a host of the radio show *Back to God Hour*—urged caution in the face of the Evangelical attraction to the revolutionary spirit of the age. He rejected the language of insurgent movements on the grounds that biblical concepts better conveyed Evangelical convictions. While Evangelicals during the early 1970s flirted with the notion of revolution, there were those—especially among socially and politically conservative Evangelicals, writing in magazines like *Moody Monthly* but also in *Christianity Today*—who warned of the dangers of revolutions, like violence and social anomie. Yet in the long run, Nederhood's was a losing position. As scholars like Axel Schäfer and Eileen Luhr have shown, countercultural vocabulary and ideas were eventually appropriated and domesticated by Evangelicals.[32] An analysis of Evangelical magazines shows how Evangelical spokespersons reenvisioned revolution in Christian terms and redirected revolutionary zeal.

The April 10, 1970, cover of *Christianity Today* showed a stylized red hand showing the victory sign, a common countercultural symbol of peace. The headline for the issue proclaimed "Evolution, Revolution, or Victory," with the index finger and middle finger substituting for the "V" of "Victory." While peace is a sentiment in keeping with Christian ideals, the cover portrayal was a surprising choice for an Evangelical magazine. Both the sign and the color were markers of counterculture, political insurgency, and left or communist affiliations. Yet the illustration was framed by the familiar title *Christianity Today*, and, similarly, the provocative content was contained in familiar Evangelical sentiments. The cover article, which presented the argument that neither societal evolution nor social revolution was an adequate answer to contemporary problems, was authored by Harvard-trained theologian and intellectual standard-bearer for the pro-life movement Harold O. J. Brown.[33] The same issue also included the first part of an article discussing how teachers could engage the present generation of politicized and critical students, written by Virginia Ramey Mollenkott, associate professor of English at secular Paterson State College in New Jersey, who would soon become a visible figure in the Evangelical feminist movement. Finally, the issue included an article on the civil rights movement by prominent Black evangelist Tom Skinner.[34] The April issue thus addressed various insurgent movements, and all three highlighted articles exhibited a certain degree of understanding of—even sympathy for or identification with—the demands of activists.

However, as Brown argued, the choice between evolution, defined as "gradual, evolutionary, non-violent process," and sudden, violent revolution "is not a true choice, at least not for the Christian, because *both* sides are drawn from the world's set of values."[35] Highlighting the example of the hippie movement, Brown argued that progress was not a value in itself and that the call to go "forward" was so imprecise as to be aimless. Instead, by reinterpreting countercultural symbolism, Brown claimed the victory sign for Christ: "we can choose obedience to the One who has gained the decisive victory, and who will make us victors with him." To take a Christian stance did not require withdrawal from society, he argued. Rather, the knowledge of assured victory—as foretold in the Gospel of John—freed Christians from fear and worldly delusions. Christianity thus constituted a third option, or, according to Brown, the only option: "The evil in the heart of man can be *overcome* by Christ, but it cannot be *outgrown* by evolution nor *outlawed* by revolution."[36] When confronted with the choice between society's offers of evolution or revolution, Evangelicals had the duty to reject both and proclaim the transformative power of the Gospel instead.

What looked rather impractical in Brown's theoretical deliberations was fleshed out in the article by Tom Skinner, who spoke as both an Evangelical observer and a Black liberation activist. Skinner affirmed that there was a Black revolution going on and that Black people in the United States had valid grievances that needed addressing. However, he disagreed with the form of the revolution. Speaking as an evangelist, someone whose job it is to proclaim the good news of the Bible, he translated the struggle into the metaphor of the well-known conflict between the Jews and the Roman occupancy during Jesus's days. In the passion of Christ, the biblical account of the end of Jesus's life from his entrance into Jerusalem to his crucifixion on Mount Calvary as described in the four Gospels, Barabbas was an insurrectionary who fought against the Romans and who was to be crucified with Jesus. But Pontius Pilate, the prefect of the Roman province of Judea, gave the people the choice to release one of them, and they chose to free Barabbas. In Skinner's rendering, Barabbas became a Black rights activist, and Jesus acknowledged the injustices Barabbas fought against: "Jesus would have agreed with Barabbas. He would have said, 'Barabbas, you are right. The Roman system stinks. It's racist, it's prejudiced, it's bigoted, it's militaristic, it's materialistic, it's polytheistic, it's godless.'" Yet burning down the existing system was no solution. Jesus, in Skinner's version, would have told the Black insurgent Barabbas: "Don't you understand, Barabbas, that you're going to replace that stinking Roman system with your own messed-up kind of system and that there is no difference between a corrupt white man and a corrupt black man?" Any human system must, according to Skinner, fall short because all humans were fallible, sinful creatures, no matter the color of their skin. As long as humans were motivated by their own hopes and grievances, all human effort was corrupt. The only durable system that could be envisioned thus had to be built on biblical foundations—had to be built on Jesus Christ. In Skinner's rendering, Jesus proclaimed to the insurgent: "I have come, therefore, to create a new kingdom. I've come to start a new race and, [sic] it's going to be built upon me, Barabbas."[37] Aside from discrediting parts of the Black liberation movement, Skinner prophesied a Christian transformation of society that had been started by Jesus Christ and would eventually result in a truly revolutionary society, or, in biblical imagery, a new heaven and earth. Skinner argued that human revolutions only succeeded in replacing one bad system with another, but that belief in Christ transformed the nature of humans. God would use these new creatures, Christians, to lay the foundation for a truly revolutionary community. Jesus, he explained, had instigated this movement not with weapons and threats but with something less tangible and more dangerous: the contagious vision of his own example and the promise of the kingdom of God.[38]

While acknowledging the grievances put forth by insurgent movements, the *Christianity Today* issue challenged the answers proposed by social activists. In the contributors' argumentation, it was hubris to assume that humans could independently conceive of a better system for society. Therefore, Christians could not support revolutions devised and commenced by humans. This, however, did not mean that Evangelicals advocated complacency or resignation. On the contrary, they insisted on the transformative power of Christianity, indeed defining Christianity as the only truly transformative power. In their vision, all human endeavors to change society were destined to fail. But if people submitted to the will of God, they would be able to build a better society, not by virtue of their own strength and wisdom but by the grace of God. While rejecting the revolutionary tendencies they observed within contemporary society, these authors ascribed a truly revolutionary quality to Jesus Christ and the future he stood for. Appropriating countercultural symbols and language, Evangelical spokespersons contained their disruptive social potential and added a transformative spiritual dimension, thus effecting a decisively Evangelical shift in meaning. In the course of the debate in Evangelical magazines, it became customary to speak of revolution as a Christian concept. However, there were nuances in how the formula was to be understood.

"Nineteen long centuries have passed," a subsequent *Christianity Today* article proclaimed, "but basically the question remains the same. Which revolutionary shall we choose—Barabbas or Jesus?"[39] Leighton Ford, who was brother-in-law to evangelist Billy Graham and at the time vice president of the Billy Graham Evangelistic Association, argued that the present was a revolutionary age and that the only choice people had was what kind of revolution they supported, a secular one or God's. Agreeing with the analysis of a society plagued by crisis, Ford believed that the cause was an individual one: "Sin ought to be spelled s-I-n, 'the big I.' This is what lies at the root of our problems." Even though he agreed that systemic evils like world hunger could not be solved by converting people to Christianity, he thought of conversion as "a platform from which we can begin to tackle those problems."[40] To him, revolution was something that happened within the individual; all else would follow. Ford advocated what historian Eileen Luhr identifies as the attempt to "confine the meaning of change and revolution along spiritual lines."[41] Ford's application of the word "revolution" allowed him to be in favor of it as a concept while condemning the actual tactics and practices of contemporary actors. Ford differentiated between "the revolution of hate and violence" on the one hand and "Christ's revolution of love and spiritual power" on the other, making clear that he disliked the former.[42] Ford "seized upon," to borrow Luhr's words, "the iconic language of the era to describe the promise of personal transformation."[43] Ford advocated the view that "our greatest need is for an inner revolution that can transform men's hearts," thus calling for a revolution, defined as individual, inner revival.[44] Ford thus subscribed to the view that the origin of all evil was individual sin. Political scientist Robert Booth Fowler found that this perspective was "characteristic of *Christianity Today*" in the 1960s and the first half of the 1970s: "It placed the blame on individuals and their sinful actions—and thus on all of us. The editors of *Christianity Today* were little inclined to the view that capitalism, or government, or one or another nation was at fault."[45] During the 1970s, however, other views of revolution and the origins of social injustices emerged.

Arguments for a revolution more in line with countercultural definitions of the term came from an unexpected source: Francis A. Schaeffer.[46] Schaeffer, in his early years, was the epitome of a separatist Fundamentalist. As a student, he was part of a faction that split from Westminster Theological Seminary, considered too compromising, and in 1937 he followed his mentor J. Gresham Machen to the newly established Faith Theological Seminary. The split mirrored the breaking away of the Bible Presbyterian Church (in which Schaeffer was ordained as a minister after graduating in 1938) from the Presbyterian Church in America. Schaeffer's life followed a separatist trajectory through several church splits and mergers, until, working for the mission board of the Reformed Presbyterian Church, Evangelical Synod, he was sent to Europe. His life took a major turn when he decided to stay in Europe, and in 1955 he started L'Abri, a conservative Christian community, in Huemoz, Switzerland. Opening their home to young spiritual seekers, Schaeffer and his wife, Edith, attracted youth from all over the world, especially from Europe and the United States. Engaging his young audience in Evangelical critiques of philosophy, art, and contemporary culture, Schaeffer paved the way for a new intellectual Evangelicalism. In the mid-1960s, Schaeffer received his first invitations to speak on Christian campuses back in the United States. Subsequently, he emerged as an inspiration for young and academically inclined Evangelicals.[47]

From his many encounters and work with young people, Schaeffer exhibited understanding and even sympathy for their discontent. In an assessment of US culture, published as *The Church at the End of the Twentieth Century* and printed in condensed form in *HIS*, the InterVarsity magazine targeted at college-age Evangelical readers, he agreed with the secular New Left's criticism of the United States as a "plastic culture."[48] He painted a bleak picture of a culture torn between two extremist positions—Left and Right—and he ultimately feared that Evangelicals, led by comfort, would side with the Right, which he called the "establishment":

> The result of all this present situation will, I believe, be this. As the New Left grows stronger and more violent and disruptive, and as the number of dropouts carried by society increases, society itself will move further toward chaos. The majority of the "Silent Majority" will then fight back and in doing so tend to accept the Establishment elite and solutions, namely a growing Establishment totalitarianism. At first this may not seem as serious as the totalitarianism of the New Left, but it is. Like its

counterpart, the Establishment elite lacks absolutes and will eventually be as oppressive though perhaps in a less open way. The danger is that the evangelicals being so committed to middle-class norms, and often even elevating these norms to an equal place with God's absolutes, will slide without thought into accepting the Establishment elite.[49]

Schaeffer criticized the complacency of the "silent majority" celebrated in the political rhetoric of President Nixon. Identifying Evangelicals as part of this imagined population of decent, law-abiding citizens, he feared that the radicalism of left-wing agitators would push them into the arms of the conservative elite of the "establishment." Schaeffer warned that the law-and-order mentality Nixon pursued and many Evangelicals found enticing would bring about a dangerous totalitarianism. Because of their contentment and indolence, Schaeffer continued his argument in the next issue of *HIS*, when the choice was between "revolution" and "reconciliation," Evangelicals were tempted to choose reconciliation. Reconciliation, Schaeffer explained, sounded like the peaceful choice, but Evangelicals who felt that way were wrong. Such rhetoric was deceitfully employed to hide the political aspirations of conservative elites. He warned that Evangelicals were also wrong to side with the radicals of the New Left. Rather than joining any existing movement, Schaeffer proclaimed, "we must have a Christian revolution." He emphasized that the starting point of such a revolution must be "love," and that at the center of structural change must be individual transformation, echoing the theme of individual transformation conservative Evangelicals like Leighton Ford advocated. However, he went one step further. Individual transformation was not enough. Schaeffer envisioned a communal solution to the cultural crisis, preferably in the form of tight-knit Christian communities.[50] Schaeffer not only translated the Christian concept of conversion into the countercultural language of revolution, he also provided Evangelicals with L'Abri, a working model of a Christian community and alternative to hippie communes.[51] By envisioning the transformative power of Jesus Christ as a communal project, he inspired a new generation of Evangelicals to think about corporate Christian activism for social justice.

The People's Christian Coalition, the community behind the new Evangelical magazine *Post-American*, was one group inspired by Schaeffer.[52] Toying with various terms of identification—Post-American Christianity, radical Christians, movemental church—Evangelicals around Jim Wallis published elaborate critiques of contemporary Christianity and its relationship to the state. In its founding document, the People's Christian Coalition advocated a "revolutionary" Christianity, claiming that "an orthodox Biblical theology and the total Gospel of Jesus Christ necessitate a radical commitment to and an activism for social justice."⁵³ Leon Morris, a New Testament scholar at Trinity Evangelical Divinity School in Deerfield, Illinois, where the People's Christian Coalition originated, characterized this new generation as people who, "while holding firmly to the basic evangelical position, . . . are refusing to be bound by the old evangelical shibboleths and are advocating radically new ideas and practices."⁵⁴ Inspired by the counterculture, writers for the *Post-American* embraced the concepts of revolution and social action.

In the second issue of the *Post-American*, Winter 1972, an unsigned article approvingly quoted Schaeffer with the words that "if we want to be fair we must teach the young to be revolutionaries, revolutionaries against the status quo."⁵⁵ Citing maxims of technological and economic progress that depleted natural resources, destroyed the environment, exploited people as cheap labor—especially in so-called Third World countries—and profited only those who were already prosperous, the article explained that the young had no choice but to be revolutionaries. According to the writer, America was a fallen nation. All that was left to do was to prophetically pronounce disapproval. The writer cast himself (or herself) in the role of the prophet Jeremiah, through which God spoke: "Shall I not punish them for these things?" But, all was not yet lost. The writer prayed that with God's help society might yet be reformed: "Jeremiah provides this lasting critique of the predicament of man as well as the formula of hope. He points toward man's reconciliation to God as the means whereby we may begin revolution—revolution away from exploitation toward discipleship and love for Christ and our fellow man."⁵⁶

Following Evangelical tradition, the article proclaimed that true transformation could only be brought about by God. The article also embraced the language and critique of the time, envisioning young Evangelicals as revolutionaries and including an explicit call to social action. In contrast to older forms of social concern, the *Post-American* article criticized structural injustices.

In the very first issue of the new publication, Clark Pinnock, a Canadian-born theologian teaching at Trinity Evangelical Divinity School, had set out guidelines for "the Christian revolution," surmised in four theses and two prescriptions. Pinnock affirmed in thesis 1 that Christianity was revolutionary, but he charged in thesis 2 that the Christian churches in the United States had become complacent. Initiative had thus passed to secular actors. Thesis 3 acknowledged that the student movements addressed "legitimate moral concerns," albeit displaying "weaknesses" in their approach. Finally, thesis 4 reaffirmed that Christianity provided a secure basis for bringing about revolutionary change. Two further points provided instructions for the Christian revolutionary, explaining that revolutions were only legitimate if they conformed to divine values and warning readers that "the real problem in our society is man himself."[57] While the article was a call to revolution, it also proclaimed that legitimate revolution was only possible by born-again Christians. Only converted believers—those through whom God acted—could be trusted to work for godly change and not start revolution for lowly ends.

In a further article, Pinnock elaborated on what a Christian revolutionary looked like. He explained that true Christians were revolutionaries by definition because their ultimate authority lay with God and not with the government or other authorities. As such, Christians were "subversives, a threat to the system." Indeed, the Bible called them "strangers and pilgrims" (Heb. 11:13, 1 Pet. 2:11). Pinnock thus characterized revolutionaries as radical agents, ultimately loyal to no earthly regime. True revolution never originated with humans; rather, it originated with God, who would, at the end of time, radically transform the world. Accordingly, a Christian was not the author of the revolution but only the "herald and harbinger of that revolution." Christians could never defend the status quo: they were looking forward to the kingdom of God. It was their duty to embody Christian values and divine love and thus make "visible as well as verbal" the good news of the New Testament.[58] Pinnock in his deliberations not only claimed the terms "revolution" and "revolutionary" for Christians, he also, conversely, defined Christians in terms of the counterculture as messengers and tools of radical transformation.

While the claims of the Evangelical Left went further than those of establishment Evangelicalism, Evangelicals generally agreed that the gospel had transformative power and that Jesus Christ had come to radically change the world. They agreed that as God's messengers they must embody his values, becoming visible examples for the revolutionary Christian lifestyle. Unanimity also existed in what positions Evangelical spokespersons rejected as un-Christian. In their deliberations on the right relationship between state and church, they used the vocabulary of the counterculture but adapted it to criticize both the secular Left and the politically conservative elites. Vernon C. Grounds summed up this perspective in a preview published in *Eternity* of his upcoming book, *Revolution and the Christian Faith: An Evangelical Perspective*: "we must help the church resist all pressures to abandon its own distinctive role, whether these pressures come from the right or from the left." The ultimate fear associated with either side was that extremism would ultimately lead to anarchy (by the Left) or to totalitarianism (by the Right). Advocating a middle position, Grounds addressed the Left, reminding them that God ordained order and governments and that worldly revolution always ended in a bloody mess. He also reminded the Right that it was godly to show "Christian courage and humility" and that "the American way of life is not to be treated idolatrously."[59]

At the beginning of the 1970s, the countercultural language of revolution was adapted by Evangelical spokespersons to describe the transformative power of the gospel and advertise Christianity as a revolutionary program to change corrupt society. To speak of revolution implied critique; indeed, Evangelicals agreed that there was a national crisis and urged social engagement. Yet they differed in their assessment of the present crisis and the question of whether the situation could be salvaged. To establishment Evangelicals, on the one hand, America was largely a righteous nation that had recently lost its path. They believed in the "silent majority" of decent, law-abiding citizens who could be inspired by the testimony of their Christian neighbors to fulfill their civil obligations and thus restore proper order. The Evangelical Left, on the other hand, found itself radically at odds with the government regarding fundamental issues such as war (especially the Vietnam War), economics (especially the gap between rich and poor in the United States and abroad), and human rights (regarding issues such as racism). To them, America had become Babylon, the biblical symbol of sin and pride, which they prophetically criticized and condemned.[60] No restoration was possible; radical reorientation was necessary. Accordingly, while Evangelicals shared a vision of Christian revolution, they disagreed about its precise nature, and they charted different ways for political involvement.

Honor America

"We find ourselves rich in goods, but ragged in spirit; reaching with magnificent precision for the moon, but falling into raucous discord on earth. We are caught in war, wanting peace. We are torn by division, wanting unity. We see around us empty lives, wanting fulfillment. We see tasks that need doing, waiting for hands to do them." With these words, Richard Nixon, in his 1969 inaugural address, pitted America's technical advances and material success against a crisis epitomized by war, disunity, and disillusionment. With overt religious overtones, he described this situation as a "crisis of the spirit," a phrase more generally associated with the evangelist Billy Graham.[61] Historian Steven Miller points out that "while the notion of 'crisis' permeated the public discourse of postwar America, it also had a strong evangelical pedigree."[62] For his part, Graham, speaking at the same event, intoned in his inaugural prayer: "As George Washington reminded us in his farewell address, morality and faith are the pillars of our society. We confess that these pillars are being eroded in an increasingly materialistic and pessimistic society."[63] The two speeches seemed to resemble each other. *Christianity Today*, the publication Graham helped found, noted that "Graham's prayer and Nixon's message sounded much the same tone, and some Washington newsmen began speculating that the evangelist might have been called in to help draft the speech."[64] The rhetorical similarities between Nixon and Graham, as well as the unprecedented prominence of religion in the Nixon White House indicated an alliance between conservative politics and conservative Christianity.

Writing in 2015, historian Kevin M. Kruse challenged the idea that the coalescences between conservative Christianity and conservative politics were a reaction to the communist scare of the 1950s. Instead, he convincingly argues that this coalition was forged in reaction to President Franklin D. Roosevelt's (1933–45) New Deal policy—and became more urgent in light of President Lyndon B. Johnson's (1963–69) Great Society—by "corporate titans" who feared for their influence. Kruse points out that

> when the Cold War era's religious nationalism took root during Dwight Eisenhower's administration, his vice president [Richard Nixon] and his favorite preacher [Billy Graham] had been key agents in the change. Nixon and Graham had front-row seats, often literally, for major developments in that transformational moment in American political culture, from the first inaugural prayer and first presidential prayer breakfast, through the adoption of the mottos "one nation under God," and "In God We Trust," and on to the era's wider embrace of religion in industry, advertising, and entertainment.[65]

When Nixon entered the White House in 1969, the fusion of God and country came of age. What Kruse called "public religion" and others referred to as "civil religion" was already enshrined in institutions like the National Prayer Breakfast (est. 1953 as the Presidential Prayer Breakfast), and the addition of the phrase "under God" to the Pledge of Allegiance and the phrase "In God We Trust" to paper stamps and money (both in 1954). Nixon further conflated church and state by instituting a regular Sunday worship in the East Room of the White House.[66] It might be futile to discuss whether Nixon used Billy Graham and religion out of political stratagem, or whether Graham used Nixon to gain political influence.[67] However, it is notable that the fusion of politics and religion at the turn of the decade coincided with a renewed Evangelical call for social action.[68] Graham and like-minded Evangelicals stressed the need to engage with social issues and politicians for the purpose of correcting national moral misdirection. Graham's infatuation with the powerful can be interpreted as one attempt to make Evangelicalism more relevant to US politics.

Billy Graham, embodying establishment Evangelicalism, thought the best strategy for social transformation was to rally the nation and have a public confession of sins and recommitment to traditional values. Honor America Day, the 1970 rally that he helped conceive and execute, was his answer to the national crisis. It can be interpreted as an occasion staged to prophetically criticize the nation and bring about collective repentance. To a younger generation of Evangelicals, however, events like this were part of the problem. In the *Post-American*, Honor America Day was explicitly reproved because, according to Joe Roos, "Graham not only fails to condemn American corporate sin with the same vigor that he condemns personal sin, but he frequently identifies with that American system which creates so much evil in the world."[69] To the Evangelical Left, Honor America Day, far from critical, was a celebration of the status quo.

Honor America Day was held on July 4, 1970, on the Mall in Washington, DC, between the Lincoln Memorial and the Washington Memorial, and was attended by a large crowd of people. The *New York Times* estimated that around 350,000 people attended the rally, while about 10,000 people attended Graham's interfaith prayer service.[70] Announcing the event, *Christianity Today* quoted the organizers Billy Graham and comedian Bob Hope with the words that with Honor America Day they "want[ed] the world to see that Americans can put aside their honest differences and rally around the flag to show national unity." More than that, Graham explicitly intended to use the event to "preach Christ as the way to heal America." Graham thus framed the event as a solution to national turmoil, as a way to unite the people, mend fissures between them, and demonstrate national strength. Accordingly, the event was advertised as nonpartisan. This intention was put in doubt, however, by the simultaneous wish, expressed by the organizers, that President Nixon would attend the event as a "guest star" (he did not).[71]

Contemporaries as well as historians observed that Graham's friendship with President Nixon cast into doubt any proclamation of nonpartisanship. To contemporary Evangelical historians Richard V. Pierard and Robert D. Linder, it is clear from Graham's connection with Nixon that the particular America Graham wanted to honor was synonymous with Nixon's government.[72] In *One Nation under God* historian Kevin M. Kruse reveals the close relationship between Graham and Nixon that had begun during Dwight D. Eisenhower's presidency (1953–61). He argues that Graham operated as an unofficial functionary of the Nixon administration, not only by advising Nixon on religious matters and working as his religious liaison, but also by creating opportunities and staging events that allowed Nixon to appear in a favorable light. One came when Graham invited Nixon to share his pulpit at his Billy Graham Crusade at the University of Tennessee in Knoxville on May 28, 1970, at the height of the controversy over the Vietnam War and not even a month after the fatal shootings at Kent State University. Another was Honor America Day.[73] The barely covered partisanship of the event notwithstanding, Honor America Day functioned as a form of prophetic counsel for the nation.

It seems obvious that Honor America Day was not as nonpartisan as the organizers claimed it was.[74] Nonetheless, in the eyes of establishment Evangelicals Honor America Day comprised a legitimate strategy of cautious public exhortation. While the social movements of the 1960s had jolted Evangelicals' social conscience, establishment Evangelicals emphatically opposed their approach. Born of a tradition of personal piety and the saving of individual souls, Graham and his like rejected strikes and protests. They favored events that highlighted the common good and appealed to the conscience on an individual level. This form of cautious prophetic counsel clashed with the ideas of the Evangelical Left, which wanted to combine prophetic judgment with a concerted effort to tackle systemic injustices. Faithful to the notion that worldly politics were secondary at best, establishment Evangelicals continued to prioritize spiritual salvation. In an article titled "Evangelical Responsibility in a Secularized World," theologian Klaas Runia lamented: "So often we have concentrated one-sidedly on purely spiritual activities and have left social problems, politics, education, and other important areas to their own fate."[75] Motivating large numbers of conservative believers to concerted political action was a fate later accomplished by the so-called New Christian Right, but it was still unthinkable at the beginning of the decade.

In his Honor America Day speech, printed in full in the July 31, 1970, issue of *Christianity Today* and published separately as a booklet by the Billy Graham Evangelistic Association, Graham spoke of "the dream that has become America."[76] After recounting the social goods the state provided for its citizens—most prominently summarized in the Declaration of Independence's "natural rights" to "life, liberty, and the pursuit of happiness"—Graham turned to more somber topics. He reminded his audience of prevailing social inequalities, injustices, and indecencies. Appealing to the mythical picture of "Betsy Ross sewing the first American flag," Graham urged people to "check the stitches" that held the country together, pointing out persisting problems of racism, poverty, foreign policy, pollution, moral permissiveness, and threats to freedom. Graham thus exhorted the people and asked them as citizens to recommit themselves and the nation to the "vision" of the founding fathers, making the "dream" come true that this was "one nation under God, where men can live together as brothers."[77] Graham used the event both to point out problems and to rally people to work together to overcome them. He emphasized grievances and divisions as well as commonalities, conjuring a strong and united nation. He put on the prophetic mantle by predicting doom if people stayed the course, promising a brighter future if only they repented and worked together. Yet, ultimately, his solution to contemporary social problems was a conservative one. Graham invoked a nostalgic vision of a better past, when the diligent work of women like Betsy Ross and men like George Washington forged a new nation out of the ragtag peoples who had settled in the American colonies. Meant to admonish listeners to honor the heroic efforts of their forebears, Graham's vision largely suppressed problematic aspects of the United States' founding history, like slavery and gender inequality. By invoking the fairy tale of the American dream—that all are equal and that hard work will lead to success—Graham dismissed social problems as the individual's problems. Graham's answer to contemporary challenges thus failed to satisfy social activists, who condemned the systemic injustices they encountered in American society.

Critics regarded the Honor America event as something that provided a religious smoke screen for the conservative politics of the Nixon administration, and they charged Graham with effectively acting as a court chaplain.[78] The July 20, 1970, cover of *Newsweek* showed a picture of Graham under a banner proclaiming him "The President's Preacher." The designation "civil religious" was attached to Honor America Day in the course of media coverage of the event.

In the wake of Honor America Day, this designation was attached to Graham as well. A *Newsweek* article stated that Graham's God resembled more the God of civil religion than that of any specific traditional religion. The article opened with the observations that "on the Fourth of July 1970, evangelist Billy Graham came closer as anyone has to adapting Rousseau's idea of a civil religion to the American experience."[79] Evangelicals also latched on to the term "civil religion." As David R. Swartz's discussion of the Evangelical Left's reaction to Honor America Day shows, Graham was disparaged for being uncritically supportive of the Nixon administration and confusing his patriotic and religious loyalties. Introduced by Graham's critics, the term "civil religion" in Evangelical magazines came to denote the illegitimate conflation of politics and religion.[80]

Graham himself knew about the accusations of civil religion. Whether reacting to the *Newsweek* article or internal, Evangelical critics, Graham felt the need to clarify his motivation for Honor America Day. In November 1970, *Christianity Today* writer David Kucharsky wrote a piece with the title "Billy Graham and 'Civil Religion,'" which gave Graham the space to respond to the charge. Relating a phone interview he conducted with the evangelist, Kucharsky explained that Graham found it ironic that he was facing criticism both for associating with political leaders and for not getting involved with politics. Graham's dilemma was how to balance politics and religion: how political could he become without losing his religious authority, and how involved in politics did he need to be to effect the social change his Evangelical faith dictated? He tried to resolve the conflict, he indicated to Kucharsky, by becoming a strong influence on the politically powerful, indirectly influencing the course of the nation. He carved out for himself the role of preacher to the powerful, and he had been a confidant to all US presidents starting with Harry S. Truman (1945–53). This, according to him, required finesse: "If I told them in public what I tell them in private, they would never listen to me again—in public or in private."[81] In his own view, then, his Evangelistic duty required him to minister to the powerful. Graham could not chastise political leaders publicly, he argued, because they would simply stop listening to his counsel altogether; he needed to be on good terms with them to continue to counsel them. Yet he felt public celebrations provided an adequate platform to gently point out general deficits and misdirection. In his opinion, Honor America Day was not civil religious, either in the sense of adhering to a generic civic faith or in the sense of abusing religion for political ends. Rather, he considered Honor America Day to be part of his missionary effort to proclaim God's truth and steer people toward biblical morality.

Graham's explanation did not satisfy politically left-leaning Evangelicals. They complained that Graham was cozying up to the powerful and illegitimately mixing political and religious motives. Graham's ingratiation with the powerful was unacceptable to them. In the new magazine *Post-American*, Graham was repeatedly lambasted for uncritically supporting existing power structures and elites. Alluding to Graham, Jim Wallis, *Post-American*'s editor, complained that "our leading evangelist plays golf with the corporate elite, opens his pulpit to the President's politics, presides over nation-worship ceremonies, and thinks the poor should kill their own rats."[82] Wallis thus accused Graham of brownnosing the wealthy, powerful elite and disrespecting the poor. Bill Pannell, a Black Evangelical and contributing writer, furthermore accused Graham and his ilk of hiding social problems through the use of meaningless symbolism. He wrote sarcastically that people were meant to believe that "with Mr. Graham's preaching, [US attorney general] John Mitchell's big stick, and Bob Hope's humor everything would be all right."[83] From his perspective, neither establishment Evangelicalism, nor the Nixon administration's law-and-order policy, nor the entertainment industry adequately addressed societal problems. On the contrary, in Pannell's rendering, events like Honor America Day distracted from the real problems or, worse, belittled them.

In this regard, the *Post-American* was on the same page as the somewhat older Evangelical left-wing magazine the *Other Side*. In its first issue in 1971, the *Post-American* republished a scathing satire by the *Other Side*'s editor, John F. Alexander. In this piece, Alexander, who was known for his social activism and especially for his support of racial equality, wrote a fictitious letter from the perspective of "white man's religion" to the "Madison Avenue Jesus."[84] With these labels, Alexander made clear that his text was a satirical critique of how the white privileged "Madison Avenue" business elite used religion as a prop. In this parody, the letter writer scolded Jesus for being too negative. Instead of always criticizing the culture, the writer proposed, Jesus should organize an "Honor Israel Day" and celebrate the nation's "glorious tradition," suggesting that it was easier to sell the gospel as nonthreatening ornament.[85] The parallels and reference to Honor America Day were obvious. Alexander indirectly criticized religious leaders for flattering the ruling class rather than delivering the biblical message. His scathing critique indicated that the organizers of Honor America Day had gotten their priorities wrong: instead of glorifying God and helping the poor, they glorified the rich and powerful. Associate editor Joe Roos in a subsequent issue spelled out the accusation: "Graham fails to distinguish between the God of American civil religion and the God of Judeo-Christianity."[86]

The problem of compatibility between Christianity and state governments is discussed in the Bible. The Synoptic Gospels record how the Pharisees asked Jesus whether they should pay taxes, whereupon Jesus answered: "Give to the emperor the things that are the emperor's, and to God the things that are God's" (Mark 12:17). However, things were never clear cut. Indeed, Billy Graham used this very passage (as it reappears in Matthew) to justify his involvement with Honor America Day.[87] The *Post-American* community, in contrast, argued that Christians had made too many concessions to the state, diagnosing an "American captivity of the church."[88] While both diagnosed a crisis and called for revolution, establishment Evangelicals and the Evangelical Left differed as to the remedy they proposed. Both envisioned Evangelicals as a community that was obedient to the commandments of God and that prophetically judged the nation. But establishment Evangelicals hoped to return America to Christian values through gentle guidance and individual conversions, while the Evangelical Left favored a radical revolution of society and advocated corporate action to combat structural injustices.

Watergate Crisis

President Richard Nixon was reelected on November 7, 1972. In *Eternity*'s first issue in 1973, an article looked back on the year 1972 and the recent news about government corruption, stating hopefully: "As four more years begin for President Nixon, evangelicals are also concerned that the President display the moral leadership that is necessary in leading this great country." The editorial expressed the "hope that the reelected President will not be known simply as a pragmatic politician who has achieved diplomatic success in thorny international issues, but one who by precept and example guided the nation out of its moral morass."[89]

Retrospectively, it appears naive for anyone to have placed trust in Richard Nixon to resolve his administration's quagmire. During his reelection campaign, on June 17, 1972, five men, allegedly plumbers, broke into the Democratic National Committee offices at the Watergate complex of buildings in Washington, DC. Their goal was to "bug" the offices to gain information with which to enhance the Republican Party's campaign strategy. The burglars were apprehended by plainclothes police officers. The event was reported to the press (and linked to the administration as early as August 1972), but the affair was initially regarded as a minor incident by individuals acting on their own accord. Richard Nixon was reelected and swore the oath of office on January 20, 1973. However, more details about the break-in and the subsequent White House cover-up reached the public, mostly because of the investigations of *Washington Post* journalists Carl Bernstein and Bob Woodward. In spring 1973, the Senate started investigations into the Watergate affair. A Senate Watergate Committee held televised hearings from May to August of that year. During the hearings, the public found out that Nixon had taped conversations in the Oval Office. A Supreme Court decision in July 1974 forced Nixon to release the tapes and brought to light incriminating material concerning Nixon's involvement in the Watergate affair. The House Committee on the Judiciary voted in August to impeach the president, who promptly resigned his office. Unrelated to the Watergate affair, vice president Spiro Agnew had resigned his office in October 1973 because of crimes committed during his time as governor of Maryland. Therefore, in July 1974 Gerald Ford, Agnew's replacement, suddenly found himself president of the United States.[90]

At the time of the 1972 election, Evangelicals largely supported Nixon, or, in the words of the *Eternity* editorial, "evangelicals, like the rest of the country, were strongly pro-Nixon." Yet there was also a vocal minority in opposition, who organized and lobbied as "Evangelicals for McGovern." According to *Eternity*, this was the first time Evangelicals officially organized to campaign for a presidential candidate.[91] As David R. Swartz has demonstrated, the arguments of socially and politically progressive coreligionists were reported favorably in Evangelical magazines, especially in the *Post-American* and the *Other Side*, yet monetary campaign contributions from this group made up only $5,762 (donated by 358 people).[92] Evangelical McGovern supporters were thus a small but vocal minority. At the same time, not all who voted for Nixon were ardent supporters. The *Eternity* editorial—dated the same month as Nixon's second inauguration—pointed out that many Evangelicals were concerned "that Nixon's image was seriously tarnished during the past few months," adding that "the unanswered questions of Watergate, campaign financing and wheat deals give the impression that the administration does not care about the morality and ethics of politics. All that counts is the final outcome."[93] A *Christianity Today* editorialist agreed, reporting that "throughout the election campaign a moral cloud hung over the White House."[94] Despite these concerns, many Evangelicals were convinced that Nixon stood above the corruption that shredded his administration. They based this fatally misguided conviction on the facts of Nixon's "close association with Billy Graham and his conservative Quaker upbringing."[95]

In the course of the revelations about the Watergate affair, Evangelicals were forced to revise their picture of Nixon. The Watergate scandal also brought into sharp relief the way Evangelicals had envisioned political action thus far. Whereas Nixon's reelection exposed the New Left as a minority position, Watergate destroyed Graham's approach of ingratiation with the powerful as a valid option. In Evangelical magazines, references to the Watergate crisis were sparse prior to the Senate's investigations. But substantial meditations on Watergate appeared in summer 1973, in conjunction with Senator Mark Hatfield's widely reported speech at a Mayor's Prayer Breakfast in Chicago.[96] Billy Graham only slowly distanced himself from President Nixon, still accepting an invitation from Mrs. Nixon to a private Christmas service at the White House in December 1973.[97] He held fast to his belief that Richard Nixon was not personally involved in the scandal until he could no longer deny the fact. Yet in conjunction with new revelations, Evangelicals across the political spectrum came to regard Watergate as the result of a misplaced faith in America, an idolatrous civil religion, shrouding a proper assessment of the political process.

In 1973, it was still possible to believe, as Billy Graham apparently did, that President Nixon had not been involved with the government transgressions now simply referred to as Watergate. In a *Christianity Today* interview published in January 1974, Graham explained that "in America a person is presumed innocent until proven guilty. As far as I know, the President has not been formally charged with a crime." He distinguished between the president and the administration, but he also admitted that "mistakes and blunders have been made." While he acknowledged the worrisome nature of known Watergate crimes, emphasizing that "some of them involve moral and ethical questions," he refrained from accusing Nixon. He insisted that "if I have anything to say to the President it will be in private."[98] His logic, thus, remained the same it had been in connection with Honor America Day. While he used the national stage to address what he considered a national crisis, he did not chastise leaders publicly. But he now vocally rejected being cast into the role of a prophet. According to the interview, Graham was no "Nathan," the prophet who called out King David's abuse of power (2 Sam. 12), nor was he an "Ambrose," referring to the bishop who banned Roman emperor Theodosius from the Milan Cathedral after the massacre of Thessalonica in 390. Graham rejected these comparisons as faulty. He firmly denied that he had a duty to castigate leaders. He further emphasized: "As I have already stated, I have no proof that the President did anything illegal, and I would have no ecclesiastical power over him to do anything about it if I did have proof."[99] He thus rejected the positive as well as negative roles ascribed to him, claiming that all he could and did do was offer spiritual counsel. In reaction to charges against the Nixon White House and his own proximity to the president, Graham thus envisioned a very narrow radius for Evangelical political action.

Graham walked a fine line, condemning known crimes as well as unbecoming behavior on an abstract level while remaining loyal to Nixon and depicting his own role as beyond reproach. Nonetheless, the suspicion of inappropriately mixing religion and politics remained. Asked by the interviewer whether he thought that Evangelicalism was now "America's civil religion," Graham responded with a resounding no. He rejected the allegation, explaining that all presidents had had ties to various Christian traditions and that Evangelicals were only now "targets of criticism" because of the public's recently rediscovered interest in Evangelicalism.[100] He thus argued that the present administration's ties to religion were no closer than previous administrations', and that there was nothing improper in the way religion and politics currently interacted. Graham emphatically denied that his continued presence at the White House "implies a kind of benediction on everything that happens at the White House," and he condemned what was known about the Watergate break-in thus far as "not only unethical but criminal."[101] In this interview, Graham carefully maneuvered between pitfalls, condemning known crimes but not the president, and disentangling himself from Washington politics without cutting his ties to Nixon. While he insisted that he acted in good conscience and to the best of his knowledge, others appraised the situation differently. They regarded Watergate as a sign that citizens had misplaced their trust in a corrupt system. This position was most effectively voiced by Mark Hatfield.

Senator Mark Hatfield, the former governor of Oregon, was not only a well-known politician but also a well-known Evangelical. A lifelong Republican, he adhered to the progressive wing of the party and was known for his bipartisanship. He was considered as a potential running mate by Republicans Nelson Rockefeller in 1964 (if he had become a presidential contender) and Richard Nixon in 1968, and even by Democrat George McGovern in 1972. Hatfield also became famous for casting the only vote against a resolution supporting the US military presence in Vietnam.[102] After Hatfield read the first issue of the *Post-American*, there developed, in the words of David R. Swartz, "a long and unlikely friendship between the long-haired radical [Jim Wallis] and the silver-haired politician voted the best-dressed man in government [Hatfield]."[103] But the connections between Hatfield and the *Post-American* community went deeper than that. Hatfield became a contributing editor, and Wes Granberg-Michaelson, his chief aide and ghostwriter of his 1976 autobiography *Between a Rock and a Hard Place*, became a contributing editor and later managing editor of the publication, then renamed *Sojourners*.[104]

Hatfield was invited to deliver a comment at the National Prayer Breakfast on February 1, 1973. While local prayer breakfasts had been started in various cities in the 1930s and 1940s, Congress started a prayer breakfast in 1942, after the bombing of Pearl Harbor, and the newly elected president Dwight D. Eisenhower started a National Prayer Breakfast in 1953, usually held in January. Organized by the clandestine nonprofit organization the Fellowship, the National Prayer Breakfast annually brings together the president and high-ranking members of government to rededicate themselves and the country to God.[105] Hatfield represented the Senate at the breakfast in 1973, following the conservative senator Strom Thurmond, who had addressed the breakfast congregation the previous year. In a hagiographic biography of Hatfield, published a few years later, the authors recalled the event and wrote that Hatfield's address had "stunned" the audience.[106] Contemporary journalists were impressed, too. The *New York Times* ran an article on the National Prayer Breakfast with long passages devoted to Hatfield's comments.[107] The *Post-American* also reported on Hatfield's performance in laudatory tones, claiming that "this year, in a conscientious break with the customary prayers pronouncing benediction upon the national cause, the speaker from the Senate Prayer Group raised the issue of moral culpability in the war on Indochina, calling for individual and national repentance."[108] Hatfield, using words that were, according to David R. Swartz, in part "taken almost word for word from a manuscript written by Wallis," warned of the "danger of misplaced allegiance, if not outright idolatry," if people "fail[ed] to distinguish between the god of the American civil religion and the God who reveals Himself in the Holy Scripture and in Jesus Christ."[109] The address earned Hatfield a place on President Nixon's infamous "enemy list" and a concerned letter from Billy Graham.[110]

With some delay—after some of Nixon's top aides resigned or were fired and the Senate Watergate Committee began its televised hearings on May 18, 1973—*Eternity* jumped on the bandwagon of Hatfield admirers with an editorial in its June 1973 issue, lauding Hatfield for his "brave words." Self-critically, the eminent Evangelical columnist Joe Bayly wrote: "Whether we like it or not, a major problem we face as evangelical Christians today is the identification in the popular mind of the religious position we represent with the Nixon administration and its actions. We are 'middle America,' the group sector that gave President Nixon his 'mandate.' We are the war party, the white backlash (if not racist) party, the Watergate scandal party."[111]

By their lack of criticism and opposition, Evangelicals had accepted and implicitly condoned political machinations. Americans, indeed, had become jaded about corruption in politics. An editorial from June 1973 recounted a new Gallup poll according to which people believed that the Watergate incident was symptomatic for politics in general and nothing out of the ordinary. Asking what the "big deal" was, the editorial answered: "Well, the big deal is that 'Righteousness exalts a nation, but sin is a reproach to any people' (Prov. 14:34)." Arguing not only that the Bible condemned national sin but that corruption mattered to those people who suffered its consequences, the editorial urged a return to morality and ethics: "The cure to Watergate lies in taking it seriously. We must begin by caring about integrity in all walks of life. We must demand integrity of ourselves and certainly of our leaders. Watergate with its many permutations is one of the worst reproaches America has ever suffered. Let us acknowledge the shame of it and make it clear that we care."[112]

Another editorial in the same issue describes the "Watergate Logic." It went like this: "Whatever I may have done, I did it in the belief that it was for the good of my country." Good intention thus absolved people from responsibility for horrible blunders. The editor blamed this sort of thinking for the concurrent corruption because anything could be justified "in the eye of the beholder." Linked to situational ethics (often decried as moral relativism), this way of reasoning heralded the downfall of nations, the editorialist argued. He illustrated this with the example of a biblical parallel: "The darkest pages of biblical history tell of the waning period of the judges, when 'every man did what was right in his own eyes.' The result was chaos."[113] In the perception of these Evangelical spokespersons, by summer 1973, Watergate was the very symbol of the crisis, indicating an idolatry of power.

When Mark Hatfield next spoke about the dangers of American civil religion, Evangelical magazines took note. The summer issues of *Christianity Today* (June), *Eternity* (July), and *Moody Monthly* (July/August) reprinted the full or excerpted text of his speech at the Chicago Mayor's Prayer Breakfast in May 1973.[114] The *Post-American* did not print Hatfield's speech that summer, but in its May/June 1973 issue it did print an article by Hatfield expounding the issue of "piety and patriotism."[115] *Moody Monthly*, the most conservative of these magazines, highlighted that Hatfield's speech had to be understood as a critique of Watergate. It printed the text over a stylized picture of the Watergate Hotel, from which the scandal took its name. In a pun on the wiretapping of the Democratic National Committee—the crime that the five burglars apprehended at the Watergate had committed—*Moody Monthly* also printed an editorial with the title "Watergate: Are We Listening?" The editorialist approvingly cited Hatfield's speech, reporting that "Oregon Senator Mark Hatfield recently laid it on the line."[116]

The topic of Hatfield's speech was political leadership. Rather than blame leaders for their abuse of power, however, Hatfield emphasized that all citizens were complicit in the corruption of political authority. Hatfield warned that "we have become adroit at manipulating religious impulses in our land to sanctify this political life."[117] Because religion was so closely entwined with the political status quo, any critique of government praxis was suspect. The logical conclusion of such thinking was an end to the democratic process and blind obedience to authority.[118] Therefore, he warned, "we run the risk of misplaced allegiances, if not idolatry, by failing to distinguish between the god of an American civil religion and the God who reveals himself in the Scripture and in Jesus Christ." In other words, Hatfield complained that people were worshipping not God but America, as embodied in its political representatives. In contrast to God, politicians were fallible. Yet in the political bid for votes and power, it had become anathema to admit mistakes. Reporting that "somehow it has become a political maxim to never admit that one is wrong," Hatfield judged: "that may be wise politics. But it is terrible Christianity." Hatfield acknowledged the strong temptations of power. He argued that power was morally destructive whenever it became an end in itself and advocated faith as an antidote. Christianity offered forgiveness and healing, but only after a confession of wrongdoings and repentance. Unfortunately, Christians, by "our worship of political power," were implicated in the insulation of politicians from responsibility, contributing also to an "idolatry of the Presidency."[119] Hatfield never attacked President Nixon outright; rather, he saw a collective problem, a national sin. Indeed, he argued that "in certain ways he [the president] is victimized by our idolatrous expectations." Government transgressions were more likely to happen when people held unfounded beliefs in the superiority of their leaders and their country, what Hatfield called "cultism." He rhetorically asked: "Why does each one of us want to believe that God blessed America more than any other land?"[120] In his *Post-American* article, Hatfield called this attitude "nationalistic, vain glory," and a sure sign of national sin, the collective adoration of the "small and very exclusive deity" of American "civil religion."[121] The whole nation was guilty of the attitudes that made possible corruption like Watergate and stood in need of repentance. In elaborate words, Hatfield thus urged his listeners to rethink their stance, detangle religion from politics, and return to true Christian values.[122] Hatfield also transformed the Evangelical notion of social concern from an individual's responsibility into a corporate affair.

New revelations about the Watergate scandal in summer 1973, including the existence of tapes recording everything in the Oval Office, brought an about-face in Evangelical spokespersons' assessments of Nixon and jump-started a reappraisal of Evangelical attitudes toward government. An editorial in *Eternity* in November 1973 reflected the fact that many Evangelicals had been lulled by the conviction that "the conservative politics of the administration, coupled with Mr. Nixon's religious roots and associations, pointed towards a high moral tone in government." The editorial, which was approvingly quoted in a *Christianity Today* article in March 1974, considered Watergate to be "a jolting reminder that no man, no party, no administration can give us assurance of righteousness in government."[123] In the *Christianity Today* article, the author, identified as a minister of the First Presbyterian Church of Pittsburgh, chided Evangelicals for their misplaced faith in a political system and in politicians.[124] *Eternity* columnist Joseph Bayly went even further, partially blaming fellow Christians for the current situation and scolding them for their underdeveloped democratic sensitivities. In acerbic words, Bayly criticized Christians who had "rallied to the support of President Nixon with religious fervor, with an 'attitude reflecting the divine rights of Presidents.'" In his opinion, this attitude was not only un-Christian: it reflected monarchic attitudes unbecoming of citizens of the United States. Combining the worst of religion and politics, "a cult of the Presidency" had developed. Bayly hoped that people would use the current crisis to counter the trend.[125] While not using the same word, these contributions echoed Mark Hatfield's criticism of American civil religion.

By summer 1974, with President Nixon implicated in the Watergate crimes, Evangelical spokespersons debated whether he should resign or be impeached. To the authors of a June 7, 1974, *Christianity Today* editorial, there was a qualitative difference between the two, and impeachment was preferable: "We think that the constitutional process should be followed, and followed with dispatch. Either Richard Nixon should be removed from office by the Senate or he should be acquitted." While they insisted on the proper course of the law, they did not think that wrongs could be rectified this way. Indeed, whether Nixon was proven guilty or not, they implored him to confess and seek forgiveness for his immoral transgressions uncovered by the Senate investigations: "In our judgment the President would be well advised to seek the forgiveness of God by repenting privately and then going to the people publicly and asking for their forgiveness."[126] The Christian sacrament of penance seemed to promise reconciliation not only to the individual sinner, President Nixon, but also to the nation. Impeachment would show that the American political system was able to rectify itself after a period of corruption and abuse, and a confession of guilt and display of remorse would go a long way toward restoring Nixon's damaged honor in the eyes of these editorialists. But their expectations were disappointed. Richard Nixon resigned his office on August 9, 1974, evading impeachment (the House Committee on the Judiciary had approved articles of impeachment by this time, but the full House had not yet voted). Another *Christianity Today* editorial saw Nixon's abdication as the pinnacle of a period of crises encompassing the last decade and a half. The question of justice was still unresolved, though, with the editorialists asking whether Nixon would be prosecuted; whether it was fair if others served prison sentences but not him; or, were Nixon to be pardoned, whether others should also be pardoned. Because Nixon refused to admit guilt, the American people were denied closure, and Evangelical hopes of justice, penance, and reconciliation were frustrated. The writers had lost all illusion about the virtues of America and American politics; all they could do was offer the new president, Gerald Ford, their prayers: "We wish him well and assure him of our prayers and, we hope, the prayers of the nation. With them the going will still be rough; without them he stands little chance of solving the grave problems that beset the American people."[127]

The abrupt but unsatisfactory end of the Watergate crisis cast doubt on both the American democratic process and the Evangelical project of political concern. Nixon had deceived the American electorate and disappointed Evangelical moral standards—and had gotten away with it. By evading impeachment and refusing to do penance, Nixon also evaded the cleansing and self-restoring functions politics and religion had to offer. Accordingly, he left both realms in tatters.

Watergate shocked the nation. In its wake, Evangelicals found that they were living in a democracy in which the new president had no democratic legitimation for the office, and in which laws applied to ordinary citizens but not to the former president.[128] Nixon's successor, Gerald Ford, granted him a full pardon, thus effectively aborting further investigations. The *Post-American* editor Jim Wallis was especially bitter, complaining that "even the presidents [sic] top advisors [were] under indictment or already convicted while the man who gave them their orders goes free."[129] In light of the Watergate revelations, Evangelical spokespersons exhibited distrust and weariness in regard to the US political system. *Christianity Today* columnist Carl F. H. Henry questioned whether democracy had "a future." Henry was not very enthusiastic but nevertheless clung to the notion that "democracy still has a great deal in its favor."[130] A *Moody Monthly* editorial, focused on the American founding fathers, similarly noted that "Americans have lost confidence in their institutions." Acknowledging the pervasiveness of government corruption, cumulating in the Watergate scandal, the *Moody Monthly* editorialist nonetheless insisted that "it is no time to throw out the baby with the bathwater," imploring readers that "we can still make the system work."[131]

While the scandal seriously damaged these writers' confidence in the US government, they yet regarded its principles as sound and hoped to salvage it. The experiences with the Nixon White House changed Evangelicals' attitude toward politics. Billy Graham was forced to distance himself from Nixon and would henceforth be more careful in how he portrayed his relations with the powerful. The critique of politics and power structures by the Evangelical Left appeared justified, and Senator Hatfield's prayer breakfast speech, in which he condemned civil religion, was widely circulated and approvingly cited. In the wake of the scandal, Evangelicals were careful to point out idolatry and national sin and keep away from association with it. While Evangelicals believed that they should contribute a unique perspective to politics, being able to judge society critically but compassionately as engaged outsiders, Watergate proved this vision to be more complex. Proximity to the powerful ensnared even the faithful. This meant they had to come up with a new concept for engaged political involvement. Watergate thus forced Evangelicals to revise their position on the relationship between politics and religion.

Politics after Watergate: From Post-American Dystopia to Born-Again Confidence

Jim Wallis and the community he gathered around himself were disillusioned by the political system in the United States and the systemic inequalities they encountered. Pointing out that even decent, churchgoing people were inadvertently complicit in economic and racial hierarchies, Wallis, who was emerging publicly as the figurehead of politically progressive Evangelicals concerned with issues of social justice, strove to free Evangelicalism from bad sociopolitical entanglements. He labeled his project "Post-American Christianity" and named both his fellowship and his magazine *Post-American*. While this was technically a hopeful endeavor, his analysis of the present situation was thoroughly negative. In 1971, Wallis characterized post-American Evangelicals as people "disillusioned, alienated, and angered by an American system that we regard as oppressive; a society whose values are corrupt and destructive."[132] Focusing his ire on President Nixon and the Watergate scandal, Wallis in editorials throughout 1974 appealed to Christians to create a new approach to politics. In January, Wallis called "the present 'law and order' administration the most lawless on record." He argued that Christians should not have been surprised by the revelation of corruption within the national government; indeed, the fact that Christians, too, "had come to closely identify with this administration" was part of the problem. He condemned the "uncritical allegiance with governmental power" and found the current talk about impeachment "uninspiring, late, and lacking in moral credibility."[133] In an editorial in April 1974, when some of Nixon's aides had already pleaded guilty or were indicted, Wallis called America "a fallen nation," alluding to the "fall" of humanity described in the biblical account of Genesis, in which Adam and Eve lose their innocence through an act of willful and corrupting disobedience. In Wallis's opinion, a radical separation of the faithful from contemporary politics was the only way to recover moral authority. In his words, "being separated from the world—a break with the prevailing idolatries and mythologies of American life and society [sic] is a necessary part of any responsible biblical action." He envisioned Christian politics as a counterweight to mundane politics, calling for a rediscovery of the church as a "counter-sign to the values of American society and power."[134] Regarding Watergate as only one indication of a thoroughly dysfunctional and corrupt system, Wallis lobbied for a radical overthrow of the current political system in the name of Christian justice and morality.

Nixon's resignation on August 9, 1974, marked the end of the national drama Watergate had become. Evangelicals were divided over the prospects of the new president, Gerald Ford. Whereas some, for example at *Moody Monthly*, found solace in the new president's apparently honest character, Wallis was disillusioned, not believing that US Americans had learned from Watergate or that there would be drastic changes under Ford's administration.[135] One sign that Ford would continue politics as usual was Ford's pardoning of Nixon on September 8, 1974. Whereas protestors in Pittsburgh, where Ford visited after he pardoned Nixon, booed the new President and carried signs stating "justice died," Wallis, in an editorial from October 1974, complained that justice had been dead for years. He pointed out the "double standard" of American justice that allowed amnesty for the rich and powerful but severely punished ordinary citizens.[136] To Wallis, the pardon was especially odious when one compared the "crimes" of draft evaders with the organization of illegal activities undertaken by Nixon. Citing the example of Steven, a young construction worker, Wallis illustrated how Christian accountability and honor could be modeled. Steven had refused to fight what he considered an immoral war in Vietnam, proposing to help build a hospital instead. His offer was rejected, he was convicted for dodging the draft, and he was sentenced to three years in prison. Honoring both his conscience and the law, Steven accepted his sentence.[137] The Watergate crimes, in contrast, were not so much addressed as swept under the rug. While Wallis was bitter that Nixon did not acknowledge his wrongdoings and accept punishment, he was galled by something else: in his words, "the nation did not deserve the right to cleanse itself in a dramatic act of purification."[138] The problem was bigger than Nixon, and the public outcry over Nixon's crimes and his subsequent pardon, while cathartic, did little to change that. Indeed, while Ford might provide a fresh face for the government, Wallis complained that the ruling machinery remained the same. His biggest concern was the nomination of economic powerhouse and business tycoon Nelson Rockefeller as vice president. As governor of New York, Rockefeller had presided over the 1971 "massacre at Attica," a prison riot he ended through lethal force. His legislative record, according to Wallis, attested to his condescension of ordinary people, and his business practices exploited people at home and abroad. To Wallis, the nomination of Rockefeller was symptomatic of the deeply ingrained inequities and corruption of the government and politics. Replacing one president with another, in Wallis's opinion, was little more than a sham; the system itself needed to be overhauled.[139]

In the wake of the Watergate scandal, Wallis's vision of a "fallen nation" and the call for a post-American Christianity gained currency with other Evangelical spokespersons. But whereas for Wallis the vision of post-American Christianity held out the hope of redemption, other writers conflated "post-America" with Wallis's dystopian description of the status quo. *Eternity* in December 1974 published an article asking whether we are "living in post-America." The article employed stark imagery that conveyed a doomsday feeling of destruction and hopelessness. A monochrome image of the Statue of Liberty sinking into the sea crowded out the text on a double-page spread (figure 2.4). The writer referenced the Old Testament prophet Jeremiah's "doleful message" to the fallen nation of Judah. Having thoroughly displeased God, Jeremiah announced God's imminent judgment, clarifying that even prayer and fasting would not sway God (Jer. 14:11). The *Eternity* writer wondered whether this was the situation the contemporary United States found itself in. Linking historical events with the Apocalypse and the second coming of Christ—the belief, based on the Gospel of John, that eventually a battle of good versus evil would be fought and Jesus Christ would return to earth—the writer suggested that incidents like the Watergate scandal might be signs of the approaching end times.[140] Until God, like in Judah, ordered Americans to stop praying, however, there was still time to repent and work to redeem the nation. Believers needed to acknowledge that religion and culture had become so entwined that it was "difficult to separate the Gospel from American culture," cut the comforts that seduced and ensnared them, live God-fearing and righteous lives, and try to reform the nation by example.[141] The writer asked: "Has America passed its peak as a nation and is it ripening for judgement?" Admitting that he did not know, he nonetheless asserted that "the nation is at the crossroads" and implored Evangelicals to work for change.[142] Ultimately, the writer thus held on to a vision of hope even in the face of a post-American dystopia understood as assured doom.

In a *Christianity Today* column, Carl F. H. Henry similarly linked the United States to lost nations of the past. Starting with a reminiscence of a trip taken to the Holy Land decades earlier, Henry observed that the collapse of nations throughout history should be a warning to America. Meshing with the negative mood of the moment, he stated that "even before Watergate, I was convinced that America as a nation has already passed its spiritual and

Figure 2.4. Illustration accompanying W. Glyn Evans, "Are We Living in Post-America?," in *Eternity*, December 1974. Courtesy of Buswell Library Special Collections, Wheaton College, Illinois.

moral peak. That is still my view." Enumerating countless ills including social inequities, immorality, and wars, and approvingly citing Peruvian theologian Samuel Escobar's condemnation of the United States and empathetic plea to worship God, not mammon, Henry argued that "socially sensitive evangelicals need to make such musings their own in these dark times."[143] While ostensibly in agreement with Wallis, Henry asked: "Is the *Post-American* right in its judgment that the structure and exercise of American power must be viewed negatively, that American institutions are past redemption's point, and that an authentically biblical attitude ... demands a post-American perspective?"[144]

Henry argued that ultimately, the *Post-American* perspective demanded that Evangelicals "overthrow" the system and "renounce their [US] citizenship." Yet Henry berated the *Post-American* for such all-encompassing claims, pointing out that it would take "omniscience" to know for sure. Meanwhile, Henry advocated a position that steered clear of the two extremes (blind patriotism or doomsday despair), proclaiming that "the truths seems to me to lie somewhere between a super-Americanism that adulates our national institutions and Jim Wallis's *post*-American requiem."[145] While sharing many of the concerns voiced by Wallis, Henry rejected the post-American conclusion. Whereas Wallis's analysis resulted in a call to discard a corrupted system, Henry hoped yet to save it. Rather than take a position for or against the system, Henry wanted to change it from within.

Because of the Watergate scandal, the *Post-American*'s radical criticism of contemporary US politics became temporarily attractive beyond its ordinary audience. While the doom and gloom pronounced by editor Jim Wallis suited the mood of some Evangelicals right after Nixon's resignation, writers were reluctant to embrace his positions outright. Not even the Post-Americans themselves could maintain their radical position of judging America for long. When the community and the magazine moved to Washington, DC, in 1975, they also changed their name to Sojourners.[146] According to researcher David Kling, the Post-Americans had always attempted to be a "community that seeks to live out what it boldly espouses in print," and the name change "illustrates this connection."[147] Retrospectively, Wallis explained that by changing their name, they deemphasized prophetic criticism and focused on changing society through social involvement.[148] By and large, Evangelicals were no Jeremiahs, pointing out only the shortcomings and failures of the nation and announcing impeding disaster without hope for redemption. Yet as Henry's assessment indicated, the position of enthusiastic patriotism, what he called "super-Americanism," was also discredited.[149]

Politics of Conversion: From Colson . . .

People in Washington, DC, were prominently introduced to the Evangelical conversion experience in December 1973, when it was described in a *Washington Post* article as "a great inner serenity, a great relief in a sense, really a new life."[150] The reason a statement like that made front-page news was who had said it: Charles Colson, former special adviser, or "hatchet man," to President Nixon. Just months later, on March 1, 1974, Colson, one of the "Watergate Seven," a group of presidential advisers and aides involved in the Watergate crimes, was indicted on criminal conspiracy charges. Unlike President Nixon, who was pardoned by his successor, Colson (who pleaded guilty to the lesser charge of obstruction of justice) served seven months in prison, from July 7, 1974, to January 31, 1975.[151] Upon regaining his freedom, in 1976, he founded Prison Fellowship, dedicating his life to evangelizing and ministering to the prison population.[152] By the late 1970s "Chuck" Colson had become the poster boy for the regenerated Evangelical life.

The conversion experience had always been central to Evangelical faith; now, in the mid-1970s, it became the foundation for Evangelical politics. Em-

Figure 2.5. Charles Colson as President Nixon's unscrupulous henchman. Cover of *Christianity Today*, March 12, 1976. Courtesy of Buswell Library Special Collections, Wheaton College, Illinois.

phasizing the sinful nature of all human beings, Evangelicals expected politicians to admit their shortcomings before they (Evangelicals) were ready to bestow their trust. Politics and political ambition had become tainted by the Watergate scandal. People expected signs that politicians were not merely returning to business as usual, and politicians were eager to reassure their constituencies. Accordingly, Senator Mark Hatfield's proposal for a national Day of Repentance during the height of the Watergate investigations was accepted by Congress, and the initiative was lauded in Evangelical magazines.[153] Moreover, one aspect about the aftermath of Watergate that troubled Evangelical spokespersons was the fact that Richard Nixon never admitted guilt or repented for wrongdoings.[154] Evangelicals were ready to embrace reformed sinners; there was almost nothing that could not be forgiven if the culprit only admitted guilt and exhibited a proper degree of remorse and humility. This pattern of rehabilitation dominated the scandal's aftermath, culminating in 1976 in born-again Jimmy Carter's election as president of the United States and George Gallup Jr.'s proclamation of the Year of the Evangelical.[155]

Charles Colson's preconversion attitude was summed up in a *Christianity Today* cover surmising the notion that Colson would have done anything, including walking over his own grandmother, to ensure Nixon's reelection (figure 2.5). Therefore, his conversion, which became public while he was being investigated for alleged Watergate crimes, seemed, depending on one's perspective, either suspect or very dramatic.¹⁵⁶ Well-known and well-respected Evangelicals like Democratic senator Harold Hughes vouched for Colson's sincerity and changed nature.¹⁵⁷ Colson's Watergate notoriety contributed to the popularity that the concept of born-again Christianity subsequently gained with the public at large.¹⁵⁸ Colson's book about the Watergate scandal and his conversion, *Born Again*, not only became a best seller but was also made into a movie.¹⁵⁹ Billy Graham, too, contributed to the born-again hype, publishing his own book on the topic in 1977. In time, public figures from former Nixon aide Jeb Stuart Magruder to former Black Panther Eldridge Cleaver publicly announced that they had committed their lives to Jesus Christ, and their stories were eagerly printed in Evangelical magazines.¹⁶⁰ The notion of being born again, of being able to start over, became attractive to US Americans, so much so that when Gallup introduced the question "have you been born-again" to a survey in 1976, a third of all respondents claimed the label.¹⁶¹

While theologically intricate, a simplified and popularized notion of conversion found public favor because it charted a way out of the crisis, allowing people in general and Evangelicals in particular to continue individual and national life without overthrowing the existing system.¹⁶² In his best-selling book *How to Be Born Again*, Billy Graham wrote: "The Bible teaches that the person who is born again has a changed will, changed affections, changed objectives for living, changed dispositions, new purpose. He receives a new nature and a new heart. He becomes a new creation."¹⁶³ Conversion was an individual, inner revolution that refined sinners and helped them lead new and transformed lives. This change was so incredible that theologian Millard J. Erickson in a 1974 *Christianity Today* article insisted that it was "incomprehensible to unregenerate man."¹⁶⁴ To be "made new in Christ" required the death of the old persona. In a 1979 article in *Christianity Today*, the author in martial language declared that "the loss of the old Self" was central to gaining new life, "for it acknowledges that it has been judged, deemed worthy of death, and slain."¹⁶⁵ While the idea of dying was drastic, the promise of a new life proved attractive, not least to politicians tainted by scandal. Simplified, conversion implied a change of heart accompanied by a changed lifestyle that resulted in a restart of one's life. Conversion as a formula of regeneration and rehabilitation gained wide approval as a template for restituting politicians and the political system.¹⁶⁶

Conversion promised an unbloody revolution, change without the necessity of replacing government personnel and structures. Lit-Sen Chang, a lecturer at Evangelical Gordon-Conwell Theological Seminary, wrote an article lambasting the social activism of the New Left; yet, in conformance to findings presented earlier in this chapter, he claimed revolution as an original Christian concept. He explained that "since the weapons of the Christian's warfare are not carnal, his strategy of revolution cannot be in the form of frontal assault upon the world or its governments, nor can it employ violence." While acknowledging the need for social change, he insisted that "Christian revolution should be primarily a revolution of the 'inner man' (Eph. 3:15) 'by the renewing of the mind' (Rom. 12:2)." This was an individualistic act, and national renewal, indeed, depended on the conversion of individuals: "Real social uplift and enduring national renovation," according to Chang, "can be achieved only through the regeneration of individuals."[167] Individual conversion could thus be a political act.

Congressman John B. Anderson, an Evangelical and a Republican from Illinois, connected the idea of national renewal to regenerate individuals in an address at the Moody Bible Institute, published in *Moody Monthly* in 1975. Lamenting recent scandals and current problems, Anderson nonetheless assured his audience that "after fifteen years in Washington, I still believe in representative democracy." While, in his opinion, democracy still represented the best system of government humans had come up with, Anderson agreed with Daniel Patrick Moynihan, former ambassador to India, that "government cannot provide values to people who have none, or who have lost those they had." This perspective implied that the nation could only be as good as its people. The nation was exactly the sum of its people. While Anderson implored his fellow Evangelicals "to build in our midst a true spirit of Christian community," other spokespersons more explicitly called for individual and national conversion.[168]

Moody Bible Institute president George Sweeting's formulation was most pointed. On the occasion of Independence Day 1975, he observed that historically, nations cyclically rose to and fell from greatness. To him, the cause of decline was obvious: "According to the Bible, nations fall because they turn from God and His law." He implied that the United States was approaching collapse. However, there was a way to prevent such a fate, as shown by biblical Israel: "To the nation Israel, God said, 'If my people, which are called by my name, shall humble themselves, and pray, and seek my face, and turn from their wicked ways; then will I hear from heaven, and will forgive their sin, and will heal their land' (2 Chron. 7:14)."[169]

The formula for preventing national decay was conversion in the sense of reversal; people had to change their habits and turn away from their former ways. According to Sweeting, "God's cure works for nations because it is formulated to meet the needs of the individual. *What, after all, are dying civilizations but the sum total of dying individuals?*"[170] Whether the problem was individual corruption or the systemic corruption of a nation, the answer was the same: it required individual repentance and an about-face of attitudes and behavior.

Figure 2.6. Illustrations accompanying Ronald D. Michaelson, "What Would an Honest Politician Look Like?," in *Eternity*, February 1976. Courtesy of Buswell Library Special Collections, Wheaton College, Illinois.

Turning a page was an act required of readers by one *Eternity* article in February 1976 (figure 2.6). Titled "What Would an Honest Politician Look Like?," the article began with the drawing of the back of a person on its first page. When readers turned the page, they were faced with the well-known likeness of Abraham Lincoln, the president who turned the country around by fighting the Civil War and putting an end to slavery. Despite this historic example, the author, Ronald D. Michaelson, warned that "our ancestors were probably not as good as we nostalgically like to think," urging readers to look not to the past but to the future.[171] Playing on the theme of reversal, Michaelson insisted that morality, despite an abundance of examples to the contrary, should have its place in politics. He suggested that strong personal values and integrity of citizens were foundational for holding the president to moral standards. According to him, "politics and morality may at times seem strange bedfellows, but that is only because we get the kind of public morality we ask for." An honest president required an upright citizenry that held him accountable. By reassessing their own priorities, Evangelicals had their part to play in "[restoring] our public sense of right and wrong and [learning] from what has happened."[172]

In the wake of Watergate, Evangelical spokespersons emphasized personal repentance and conversion as a formula for reestablishing trust in individuals and in the political system. They translated the notion of religious conversion to the realm of public life, molding a template for the restitution of fallen leaders and national transformation. They thus combined a pastoral emphasis on the individual with prophetic concern for the social, envisioning the ideal nation as one led by reformed individuals. A community of steadfast moral citizens would hold their leaders accountable.

Politics of Conversion: . . . to Carter

In the mid-1970s, Evangelicals felt that they were making an impact, that in the United States "religiously, the climate of opinion is going evangelical." An indication that the notion of conversion, borrowed from evangelical Christianity, became attractive to large numbers of US Americans was the 1976 presidential election campaign. One *Christianity Today* columnist judged that "the most dramatic illustration of the new wave of evangelical influences lies in the American presidential campaign arena."[173] Indeed, all major candidates—incumbent Gerald Ford, Republican contender Ronald Reagan (whom Ford bested in the primary), and Democratic contender Jimmy Carter—claimed to be evangelical Christians and sought Evangelical endorsement. Carter, according to one report, had "blurted" out that he was a born-again Christian, provoking other candidates to speak candidly about their faith.[174] The *Christianity Today* columnist, however, warned that "the degree to which an evangelical president would influence the country toward biblical ideals would not be simply a function of his 'conversion experience': it would depend on whether his theological head was screwed on straight."[175]

Nonetheless, reversal, in the sense of a moral turnaround of the country, was something Evangelical spokespersons looked for in the campaign promises of candidates, as can be seen from cross sections of the published hopes and expectations of Evangelical spokespersons. In preparation for the election, the editors of *Eternity* asked well-known Evangelical spokespersons to share their thought process on how they planned to vote. *Eternity* collected the short essays in spring 1976 but only published them on the eve of the election: the article appeared in the September issue; Election Day was November 2.[176] The assessments from Evangelical leaders from across the political spectrum revealed the longing for a new era of moral leadership.

Eternity editor Russell T. Hitt's opinion illustrated disappointment with past political performances and the yearning for something new. In a statement that was printed last in the collection of opinions, Hitt admitted: "I'm a registered Republican. In fact, I voted twice for Nixon!" Yet this admission turned out to be a confession rather than an indication of future voting behavior. Hitt explained that "Watergate was a traumatic experience and it still colors my thinking. I was very upset when President Gerald Ford pardoned Richard Nixon." After weighing the different options (and marveling "that a far-right Republican like Ronald Reagan could make such a showing against an incumbent President"), Hitt concluded: "It will be difficult for a life-long Republican to do it, but I may jump the traces and vote for enigmatic Jimmy Carter."[177] While most other statements were not explicit in naming a favorite candidate, the gist of all the essays was hope for a return of values to politics.[178]

The essayists roughly divided into two categories: those who envisioned a new, Christian morality in politics, and those who, skeptical of the efficacy of (Christian) morality in politics, nonetheless hoped that the new president would be both competent and moral. In the first category was, for example, Margaret N. Barnhouse, the widow of *Eternity* founder Donald Grey Barnhouse. After painting a picture of her ideal America, she asked: "What kind of leadership on all levels could accomplish all this?" and answered: "Born again, ideally."[179] Similarly, James B. Irwin, a former astronaut and now president of a Christian organization, stated: "I will vote for a candidate who can lead our country with God-directed wisdom. This country was clearly founded upon godly principles and we desperately need a person at the helm that can receive godly guidance."[180] These statements reveal the wish for a literal conversion politics by a born-again leader.

Other writers, however, while attracted to the idea of a Christian president, warned that Christian convictions alone were not enough for political office. Wes Pippert, United Press International Washington correspondent was in this second category. He believed that "we evangelicals have tended to make decisions about politicians largely on whether we think they have made a personal commitment to Christ." He empathized with and understood this attitude especially in light of recent political scandals: "In the wake of Richard Nixon, Spiro Agnew, Wilbur Mills, and Wayne Hays [the last two being Democratic congressmen whose sex scandals broke in the 1970s], the United States desperately needs leadership of exemplary personal character." However, he warned, a good Christian did not necessarily make a good politician. He announced that he would gladly vote for a candidate who combined good character with political savvy.[181] Author Gladys Hunt stated bluntly: "It's unrealistic to hope that any candidate can be an ultimate Deliverer." Nonetheless, she, too, wished to see morality returned to politics, stating that "as a responsible citizen I want to elect to office—whether in the presidency, the Congress, or local government—people who have a basic sense of morality, who grapple with what is good and what is evil, rather than submitting to what is politically expedient."[182] Most explicitly, Vernon C. Grounds, president of the Conservative Baptist Theological Seminary, envisioned an ideal president as one who embodied political competence tempered with moral conscience. With the example of Senator Mark Hatfield in mind, he wrote: "My ideal candidate would be a man of unblemished integrity, social sensitivity, legislative know-how, well-informed intelligence, historical perspective, and moral courage, i.e., the stomach and backbone to espouse unpopular causes and stand the heat of caricature and vilification. If at the same time that candidate were an authentic Christian, he would be even more ideal."[183]

Buzzwords found in the various essays, besides "morality" and "values," were "justice," "honesty," and "integrity." Evangelicals were clearly ready to leave political scandals in the past and were looking forward to a new era of, if not Christian values, then at least morality in politics. They put emphasis on good character rather than political shrewdness or experience. While some advocated an explicit politics of conversion by calling for a converted president, others envisioned a broader politics of conversion by casting it as a return of values and moral standards to the political sphere.

In *Christianity Today*'s first issue after the election, editor Harold Lindsell observed tersely that the prayers of Evangelicals had been heard: God had said yes to those who had wanted Carter as president and no to those who had wanted Ford as president.[184] Generally, though, Evangelical spokespersons were enthusiastic about having a born-again president. Moody Bible Institute president George Sweeting published an open letter to Carter, assuring the new president of the prayers of "like-minded citizens" and emphasizing their shared faith, if not party loyalties.[185] A *Christianity Today* editorial congratulated the president-elect but also sounded a warning. The editorialist reminded Carter that people were now watching for him to fulfill his campaign promises, not least his assurance of honesty and his image as an outsider untainted by Washington scandals.[186] In the same issue, David Kucharsky, who later authored a Carter biography, published a flattering account of Carter, "the man from Plains," and his faith and status as a Washington outsider.[187] While some Evangelicals did not support Carter, there was a strong hope that he would turn out to be the born-again president Evangelicals envisioned.[188] This hope was eloquently expressed by Stephen V. Monsma, professor of political science, who charted three possible stances a Christian president could adopt: He could adopt the "civil-religion model" that most of his predecessors had adhered to and that was toothless at best and idolatrous at worst. He could adopt a "personal-morality model," as with candidates who explained that they personally held certain opinions but would not impose them on the citizenry. Or, in the option that Monsma favored, he could adopt the "policy-transformation model." This model basically called for a conversion of the nation by a converted president through faithful application of his convictions to all areas of political decision-making.[189] These deliberations displayed an Evangelical vision of an ideal president as one guided by his personal conversion experience and accountable to values and morals derived from his faith and shared by the Evangelical citizenry. It revealed the conviction that individual moral rectitude was able to transform society. With Carter's election, the formula of conversion politics had proved successful, both in the sense that the country now had a born-again leader and in the sense that Carter had promised to transform the country and discontinue the immoral practices that tainted Washington politics. The difficulty for Carter was living up to expectations.

Born-Again Politics and the New Christian Right

Christianity Today observed in 1976 that Carter's election was both his "political peak" and also its "brink." This observation might well be applied to Evangelicals, too.[190] The year 1976 had been both the year of Carter's election and the Year of the Evangelical. Yet it was impossible for Carter to sustain this high and fulfill the expectations placed in him; and Evangelicals quickly found that popular notions of conversion were so successful as to wrest control of the term away from them. The formula of conversion as means of rehabilitation and a new start was readily adopted and adapted to American popular culture. Columnist Joseph Bayly complained that in its popularity, "born again" could now be used to describe a medical miracle or a change of political affiliation.[191] A couple of years into his presidency, Jimmy Carter received low public ratings for his political performance. But his popularity received a boost after the so-called Camp David talks, secret negotiations between Egyptian president Anwar el-Sadat and Israeli prime minister Menachem Begin. The talks, hosted by Carter, paved the way for a peace treaty between Egypt and Israel.[192] This increased Carter's popularity, a fact noted by *Newsweek*, which depicted the president as politically born again. The newsmagazine put a drawn likeness of a toothy Carter on its cover with "BORN AGAIN" printed in bold letters, yet here the term applied not to Carter's faith but to "the President's rising polls and refurbished image."[193] In a way, then, Evangelicalism was incredibly successful—and a failure at the same time. The crux with the terms Evangelical and "born again" was that they simultaneously became almost omnipresent and very imprecise. In a poll in 1976, Pew, the leading pollster firm in the United States, defined "evangelicals" as born-again Christians, a category that encompassed many more conservative Christians than simply self-identified Evangelicals and that proved rather popular.[194] Furthermore, as a versatile signifier, the term "born again" allowed some to describe a particular religious experience and identify with a religious community and others to describe cathartic if mundane moments from medical recoveries to political victories.

At the end of the 1970s, new actors appeared on the scene and forged an alignment between conservative religion and conservative politics: the New Christian Right. Secular journalists initially labeled this new brand of religiously motivated political lobbying as "born-again politics," another sign that Evangelicals had lost the power of definition over the term.[195] What started as a loose coalition of people (as described in a *Newsweek* article) would soon be known as the New Christian Right. Its most prominent spokespersons were Fundamentalist Jerry Falwell and charismatic Pat Robertson. Depending on the definition, Fundamentalists, Evangelicals, and Pentecostals are all generically counted as evangelicals; yet there are some traits that distinguish them as different subsets of conservative Protestants. Believers who retained the name Fundamentalists, even after the term was mostly used pejoratively by commentators, insisted on theological purity and tended to be separatists. Adherents of Pentecostalism focused their faith on the Holy Ghost, the third person of the godhead, and practiced speaking in tongues and faith healing. These distinct practices were generally rejected by Evangelicals, who emphasized the conversion experience and a personal relationship with Jesus Christ.[196] While the New Christian Right recruited followers from across the spectrum of conservative Christianity, eventually branching out to be, at least nominally, open to conservatives of all faith traditions, it is wrong to equate these political entrepreneurs with Evangelicalism.

In 1977, *Newsweek* asked whether the country was taking a political turn to the right. Painting a complex picture of recent developments, the authors of the article judged that it was more correct to speak of "shifting political alliances and a search for new political definitions."[197] An information box set within the article reported on the "new activists" of the Far Right, from STOP-ERA founder Phyllis Schlafly, who lobbied against the ratification of the Equal Rights Amendment; to Paul Weyrich, a conservative lobbyist and figurehead of the emerging New Christian Right. According to the authors, "most moderate observers tend to dismiss the possibility of a popular front forming behind the activist right." Mark Siegel, political scientist and adviser to President Jimmy Carter, was quoted with the words: "All their programs are negative: stopping this, stopping that ... in the long term, I don't think they'll be successful."[198] Only a few years later, the perception had dramatically changed. In 1980, *Newsweek* ran a cover-story on "born-again politics," the political activism of conservative Christians like Jerry Falwell and his Moral Majority. Reporting on findings from a Gallup survey that there was a large pool of conservative Christians who thus far had shied away from politics, *Newsweek* speculated that "born-again politics could well play a decisive role in this year's Presidential race."[199] The authors noted that this constituency was traditionally apolitical, believing that "the road to salvation lies in the Bible—not the ballot box." Yet they predicted that this was about to change, judging that conservative Christians "have clearly become convinced that their fiercely held conservative values of God, country, and family are threatened by a rising tide of what they call 'secular humanism' sweeping through government."[200]

Writers for Evangelical magazines were initially wary of and distanced themselves from the self-proclaimed conservative politics of the New Christian Right. In 1981, in a *Christianity Today* book review, author Richard V. Pierard, professor of history at Indiana State University, tried to distance Evangelicalism from this political movement. The article favorably spoke of one book, Robert E. Webber's *The Moral Majority: Right or Wrong?*, where Jerry Falwell's organization was criticized for "propagating a moralistic, conservative secular humanism that glorifies capitalism, portrays America as a Christian nation, and draws its ethics from the American civil religion." Erling Jorstad, the author of another book, *The Politics of Moralism: The New Christian Right in American Life*, was chided for "neglect[ing] the crucial element of civil religion in shaping rightist thinking." The reviewer warned that the New Christian Right needed to be "feared." He lauded Jorstad for warning readers of the New Right's "moralism," and Webber for encouraging Evangelicals to distance themselves from "extremism" and instead move "to the center." The review emphasized civil religion—shorthand for the wrong relationship to the state—as one of many faults of the New Christian Right.[201] This accusation indicated idolatry, branding some of the New Christian Right as heretical. Evangelical spokespersons tried to convey the fact that it was not correct to conflate Evangelicals with the New Christian Right; neither did the New Christian Right necessarily represent Evangelicals politically. Yet in the long run, many aspects of New Christian Right politics proved attractive, and the borders between religious spokespersons and political activists, blurry to begin with, became all but invisible.

Conclusion: Politics and Conversion

During the 1970s, spokespersons debated the form Evangelical social and political activism should take. They envisioned Evangelicals as a community of believers whose social concern prompted them to participate in politics. Whether they prophetically chastised leaders or pastorally encouraged leaders to take certain positions, Evangelical spokespersons envisioned political engagement as altruistic service for society. The perception of crisis, already present at the outset of the decade, was amplified by the Watergate affair, and roused a desire for national repentance and reform, or, in other words, conversion. Imagining a society of transformed and refined individuals, Evangelical spokespersons redefined conversion as a political act. They envisioned Evangelicals not as the remnant but as the seed of moral sincerity and accountability in public life.

The challenges of the previous decade—sharpening of social inequities and liberalization of social and moral norms—spurred Evangelical political awareness but provoked different forms of involvement. At the beginning of the decade, divergent forms of prophetic politics were practiced. Embodied by Billy Graham and Jim Wallis, respectively, one emulated the prophet Daniel and his role of a privileged adviser to the powerful, while the other emulated the prophet Jeremiah and his radical criticism of society.

In the words of historian Axel Schäfer, "pairing a critique of civil religion with a demand for structural socioeconomic change, radical evangelicals challenged conservative orthodoxies particularly regarding race, gender, warfare, anti-communism, and capitalism."[202]

While a minority, this Evangelical Left succeeded in finding a hearing for these issues across the spectrum of Evangelicalism, contributing to an Evangelical self-conception as a community of socially engaged, politically critical conservative believers. The Watergate affair unsettled Evangelical spokespersons' trust in the US political system, momentarily leaving them with jeremiads as the only possible Evangelical response. At this point, however, the vision of socially and politically caring citizens had become such an integral part of Evangelicals' self-portrayal that a complete withdrawal from society was unthinkable.

While Evangelical spokespersons were not ready to give up on politics, they demanded reform, and especially demanded a return of morality and values to politics as a sign of national recovery. Turning around one's life was a common theme in Evangelical faith, and the religious tenet of conversion proved a successful template for the political realm. Exemplary was the conversion of Watergate culprit Charles Colson. His private experience of being born again was followed by a public confession of sins and reversal of his activities. Previously a lawyer and political adviser, Colson started a prison mission after his conversion, supporting and evangelizing a neglected segment of the population. Evangelical spokespersons reenvisioned the private act of conversion as a political act: by converting to Christianity, an individual could do their part to contribute to the betterment of society. The vision of conversion politics that developed in the aftermath of the Watergate affair was two-pronged: it could be understood literally as politics by a converted Christian, or it could be understood figuratively as the politics of moral reversal. Understanding conversion figuratively opened the way for the restitution of leaders tainted by scandal and of the US political system in general. It also allowed Evangelicals to envision themselves as responsible citizens who were simultaneously part of the system and aloof from its scandals.

Untainted by scandals, the Washington outsider Jimmy Carter won the presidential election of 1976. His election promised to introduce a breath of fresh air to the moral quagmire of national politics; more than that, though, as a born-again Christian he fit into Evangelicals' literal vision of conversion politics. With Carter, Evangelicals had arrived not only in the American mainstream but in the seat of political power. Axel Schäfer argues that "Jimmy Carter embodied the moderate, Niebuhrian, neo-evangelical orientation of 1970s conservative Protestantism."[203] Yet neither Carter nor Evangelicals retained their position for long. In the face of national and international crises, Carter's approval rates plummeted. And Evangelicals, in politics, were soon upstaged by the more boisterous activists of the New Christian Right.

At the end of the decade, then, there were important political developments. Ronald Reagan, who had been dismissed by some Evangelicals as too far right in the previous presidential election, had become a valid, if not favored, contender.[204] After struggling for at least a decade for a valid approach to bringing their faith into politics, Evangelicals had developed the successful formula of conversion politics. The template became not only popular but popularized, and at the end of the decade it became associated with the New Christian Right. These new activists hijacked the discussion of concern for the family, turning it into a moralistic crusade for "family values."[205] While historian J. Brooks Flippen argues that "Carter had unintentionally magnified the issues that drove the Religious Right," this chapter shows that Evangelical spokespersons had been political pioneers not only for the Christian Right but also for Jimmy Carter.[206] By envisioning Evangelicals as Christian citizens—understanding their Christian duty as both loyalty toward God and active and caring involvement in the politics of their country—Evangelical spokespersons had fostered acceptance for religiously inspired politics. In the following decade, the New Christian Right came to be associated with issues dear to Evangelicals—God, country, and family. Media attention focused almost exclusively on the New Christian Right, obscuring both the political forays by self-identified Evangelicals during the 1970s and the internal Evangelical identity politics of the 1980s, which, as we will see in chapter 5, largely functioned by distancing Evangelicals from the New Christian Right.

3
Feminist Challenges
Women and Gender Debates

Here also is a paradigm for both of you, Margie and Mark, in your Christian marriage. Work to make your love so total that you keep the other spotless and perfect by the strength of your love. Such a love doesn't need someone in charge. It shuns both manipulation and individualization. You are one flesh fused together by your love. Don't coerce; serve. Don't worry about your freedom; seek to liberate your mate. As you do, you will be free. Moreover, your relationship will serve as a model of God's love for us—both to your friends, your family, your future children, your future parishioners, and yourselves. Amen.
—Robert K. Johnston, "Submission, a Wedding Meditation"

In his wedding sermon for Margaret Turbyfill and Mark Ogren on May 22, 1976, Robert K. Johnston meditated on the words of Ephesians 5. Whereas this Bible passage, in which the apostle Paul talks about submission, was often used to remind brides of their wifely duties, often in conjunction with an oath to "love, honor, and obey" the husband, Johnston stressed the couple's mutual love and service for each other. This wedding homily was printed in *Daughters of Sarah*, a newsletter by and for Evangelical feminists, published since 1975. Ascribing to feminist ideas, the *Daughters* eschewed the notion that women were inferior to men or should take a submissive role in relations with men. Yet the term "submission" was not deleted from Margie and Mark's wedding sermon; on the contrary, Johnston stressed that "the husband's love, like the wife's, is based on submission." In an interpretation favored by Evangelical feminists, Johnston stressed the mutuality of the relationship: as a man and a woman gave up their individual lives to become spouses they also gave up their individual desires to *instead* serve each other. In Johnston's words: "What Paul is saying is that becoming one flesh means surrender for both husband and wife as they build a new relationship."[1] In marriage, individual lives were dissolved to bring forth something new, the wedded couple. Selfless dedication to each other, mutual submission, was considered an expression of God's love and an incorporation of his heavenly order.

The women's liberation movement, which challenged sex-based social hierarchies and asked for recognition of women's talents beyond their roles as housewives and mothers, also affected Evangelicals.[2] During the 1970s—"the woman's decade"—Evangelicals, too, revised their attitudes toward women and male-female relations.[3] While most Evangelical spokespersons were united in their opposition to more radical forms of feminism, they also disavowed the patriarchal idea that women were inferior by *nature*.[4] They debated the question of whether there was a God-given hierarchy of gender roles in society. Some insisted on hierarchical gender relations (referred to as the traditionalist view), while others advocated gender equality (referred to as the feminist view).[5] The debate continues, but the main positions and arguments were formed during the 1970s. In 1973, Evangelical women started building their own support system, culminating in the foundation of the Evangelical Women's Caucus and the newsletter *Daughters of Sarah*. Both seem to have been unintended outcomes of an Evangelical workshop on social concern attended by some fifty Evangelical intellectuals in Chicago around Thanksgiving in 1973.[6] The concern for greater social and political involvement brought together a heterogeneous group of leaders from left and left-leaning, but also traditional and establishment, backgrounds in Chicago. As a result of this workshop, on November 25, 1973, the group adopted the so-called Declaration of Evangelical Social Concern. In the declaration, which was written like a confessional, the signers professed their faith, admitted neglect of social concerns, and vowed to fight injustices like racism.[7] Against the background of a statement of Evangelical convictions, they put out a call for action: "So we call our fellow evangelical Christians to demonstrate repentance in a Christian discipleship that confronts the social and political injustice of our nation." A statement on sexism, too, made it into the declaration: "We acknowledge that we have encouraged men to prideful domination and women to irresponsible passivity. So we call both men and women to mutual submission and active discipleship."[8] Historian Margaret Lamberts Bendroth, a self-identified Evangelical, pointed out that this was a "relatively mild admission," and Ron Sider, the workshop coordinator, later stated that "looking back, the Chicago Declaration sounds pretty tame . . . [but] it was new and powerful in 1973."[9] While not an outright call for women's liberation, the declaration denounced the way women were generally treated. The dissemination of the declaration and the list of signers in Evangelical magazines, furthermore, ensured that the community of Evangelicals took note.[10]

Evangelicals for Social Action, which was created after the workshop, initially gave both progressive Evangelicals and emerging Evangelical feminists a home.[11] As discussed in chapter 2, however, the unity demonstrated in the declaration soon fractured, epitomized by a public quarrel between the eminent Carl F. H. Henry, founding editor of *Christianity Today*, and Jim Wallis, the young founding editor of *Post-American/Sojourners*.[12]

Only three women—Nancy Hardesty (then assistant editor of *Eternity*), Sharon Gallagher (part of the commune Christian Liberation Front in Berkeley, California, and editor of its tabloid, *Right On!*), and Ruth L. Bentley (director of supportive services at the University of Illinois Medical Center)—were invited to the 1973 Chicago meeting. But additional "uninvited" women, the wives of workshop participants, were present. They went further than pressing for the inclusion of the short paragraph on women in the declaration.[13] Recognizing the need for a network of contacts, support, and information, a group of academically oriented women around Nancy Hardesty and Lucille Sider Dayton (assistant director of the Urban Life Center in Chicago, sister of workshop organizer and Messiah College dean Ron Sider, and wife of Donald Dayton, another workshop participant and later theology and ethics professor) founded the *Daughters of Sarah*.[14] Evangelicals for Social Action proved hospitable to the concerns of Evangelical women and spawned an independent women's association, the Evangelical Women's Caucus.[15] Through this emerging network, Evangelical feminists jockeyed for recognition of their concerns.

The founding of the newsletter *Daughters of Sarah* was one expression of a new confidence among Evangelical women leaders. But their ideas and concerns were also discussed across the spectrum of Evangelical magazines. Advocates and opponents of feminist ideas started an intense reexamination of biblical texts and Christian history. Women were the foremost authors of texts in support of gender equality as well as in support of so-called traditional marriages and gender hierarchies. Authors grappled with ambiguities in the Bible like the dual creation accounts of Genesis.[16] They debated whether God had destined the relationship between men and women to be equal (the "feminist" position), or whether he intended there to be a hierarchical order (the "traditionalist" position). Both positions, feminist and traditionalist, were decisively Evangelical and new; they clashed with older notions of Christian womanhood.[17] Traditional Christian models of womanhood are usually traced back to early church fathers like Tertullian, who described women as the "devil's gateway." In this view, women were of inferior nature because they were created from man (Gen. 2) and were thus a lesser reflection of the image of God. Because Eve was tempted by the serpent in the Garden of Eden, women were thought to be more easily tempted, and because Eve made Adam eat of the forbidden fruit (Gen. 3), women were also seen as temptresses. Accordingly, women were considered to be incomplete or defective men. They were thought of as weak and emotional. They were thus inferior in nature. The misogynist tradition included Greco-Roman church fathers like Tertullian, Ignatius, Aquinas, and Augustine. Similarly, the fathers of Protestantism, Martin Luther and John Calvin, held negative views of women. Until the 1960s, such arguments were used to explain the subjugation of wives to husbands.[18] Evangelical revisions of gender roles developed within the framework of devout belief and in negotiation with demands made by the women's liberation movement. What came to be known as the traditionalist and feminist positions marked opposite ends of the Evangelical spectrum, but they developed in tandem and grappled with the same issues. Accordingly, both used scriptural concepts and developed a shared rhetoric. However, because their answers to questions regarding gender relations varied, ideas and biblical terms like "submission" came to mean different things in different contexts. While not feminist in a secular sense, both traditionalist and feminist revisions of older forms of gender norms were liberating and empowering in affording women agency and affirming their intrinsic value.

Calls for social action as well as realization of feminist goals came to be associated largely with the Evangelical Left, while mainstream and conservative Evangelicals generated a traditionalist (but no less innovative) vision of womanhood.[19] Feminist ideals were embraced by magazines like the *Other Side* and *Post-American/Sojourners*, while middle-of-the-road magazines like *Christianity Today* cautiously endorsed women's rights but remained opposed to what was regarded as feminist radicalism.[20] *Christianity Today* and other mainstream magazines like *Eternity* perpetuated a double vision by printing both feminist and traditionalist views, often side by side, like when *Eternity* printed book reviews of Marabel Morgan's *Total Woman* and Nancy Hardesty and Letha Scanzoni's *All We're Meant to Be* on the same two-page spread, or when *Eternity* introduced a spectrum of Evangelical opinions in its forum on women, discussed later.[21] Conservative Evangelicals were opposed to feminism. Yet *Moody Monthly*, the magazine that ostensibly catered to this segment of Evangelicalism, sported just as many if not more women writers as other magazines. These women, prominent among them Winnie Christensen and Zeda Thornton, penned advice columns for women readers, and in so doing helped shape a new, self-assertive traditionalist vision of women and gender relations.[22] Moreover, during the 1970s *Moody Monthly* was fairly open-minded and presented articles by Evangelical feminists like Patricia Gundry, becoming more restrictive only with the 1980s emergence of the New Christian Right and its political Christian conservatism.[23] The 1970s was an era rich with debate about women's role and design and the way that men and women were to relate to each other. While those issues were controversial, debates crossed boundaries, with Evangelical feminist and traditionalist voices granted hearing and being discussed across the spectrum of Evangelical magazines. Lacking a consistent gender theology, Evangelicals in the 1970s developed visions of Evangelical womanhood, starting with a definition of women.

REVISIONS OF EVANGELICAL WOMANHOOD

In a study published in 2000, sociologist Christian Smith found that evangelical Christians often embraced conservative concepts, like the idea that the husband was to be the "head" of the household, but that they barely differed in their lifestyles from the general US public.[24] Between 1995 and 1997, Smith and his colleagues interviewed 130 "ordinary" evangelical Christian Protestants in an attempt to find out "what evangelicals really want." Smith contrasted the radical statements of some evangelical Christian leaders and the fears of liberal media pundits with the answers given by these "ordinary" believers. In conclusion he wrote that the worldview of those interviewed for the study neither conformed to the liberal-secular worldview of critics nor matched their fears. Rather, Smith found "complexities and incongruities" in evangelical Christians' attitudes toward societal issues like politics or gender relations, concluding that they, like other groups of people, were "diverse, complex, ambivalent, and inconsistent for that."[25] In a chapter on marriage that Smith cowrote with Melinda Lundquist, the authors formulated the puzzling findings as questions: "Marriage relationships in which the husband is the 'head' are also equal? Wives defer to husbands a final authority in decisions that husbands do not exercise? Husbands may not rule their families, but are still ultimately entirely responsible for them?"[26] Smith and his colleagues documented this apparently contradictory attitude. They reasoned that evangelical Christians were more liberal in practice than in ideology because of the influence of the women's rights movement on society at large and because economic necessity forced some women to work outside the home. They thus suggested that social realities encroached on Christian ideals. Nonetheless, the authors insisted: "we think it would be a misinterpretation to argue that an essential evangelical patriarchy has been corrupted by entirely external cultural and social forces, pushing evangelicals toward a more egalitarian practice that is in fact alien to their true faith."[27]

Liberalizing gender norms and relations were not necessarily forced on evangelical Christians; indeed some egalitarian notions developed indigenously within evangelical Christianity. Smith and Lundquist point to Nancy Hardesty, Letha Scanzoni, and Patricia Gundry as examples of Evangelical feminism.[28] The study neatly documents many instances in which interviewees used terms in ways contrary to the intuitive meanings expected by interviewers. While the study compellingly illustrates that evangelical Christians adhered to apparently hierarchical concepts like "male headship" while simultaneously embracing more egalitarian practices in their personal relationships, it does not try to resolve the ostensible discrepancy between language and practice. This is the starting point for the current study, which emphasizes that this discrepancy is not merely a case of saying one thing and doing another.[29] This chapter investigates the genesis of gendered visions within Evangelical magazines, asking what specific meanings terms like "male headship" or "submission" took on within the Evangelical debate about gender roles and relations during the 1970s.

Women? The Eternity Forum

In 1971, *Eternity* printed an article by former assistant editor Nancy Hardesty assessing the contemporary situation for women in US society and reevaluating the women's liberation movement from an Evangelical perspective.[30] *Eternity* acknowledged the need for an Evangelical discussion of the role of women and provided the space for it. The editors came up with a unique design to ensure that the debate was more than a rebuttal of second-wave feminism. The *Eternity* editors printed a lengthy introduction, explaining the need for an earnest study of what the Bible and Christian tradition had to say about women. Pointing out that "the Christian woman's place in the world is a delicate matter," the editors invited Hardesty to provide a critical reading of women's roles from her unique position as both a devout Evangelical with proven credentials and an advocate for women's liberation. The editors, accordingly, wanted to discuss the pressing societal question of the role of women, but they wanted an Evangelical perspective on it. Therefore, not only was an Evangelical writer, Hardesty, invited to expound her position on the issue, but her article functioned as a backdrop for a forum of responses from eleven "distinguished men and women." Also, readers were invited to send in their own responses.[31] The magazine thus provided a forum where the gamut of Evangelical views on women could be presented.

Rather than criticize traditional Evangelical assumptions about women's roles outright, Hardesty's article started out with an attack on feminists who saw women's liberation and religion as incompatible or even blamed religion for misogyny. After thus deflecting the charge that she was just another "libber," Hardesty counseled that Evangelicals had not always been champions of geniality, especially with regard to women. She pointed out that many Evangelical statements seemed to affirm secular feminist suspicions that Christians were inimical to their cause, and she cited advice for women printed in various Evangelical magazines, including statements calling for women's "subordination and honor in the home, silence and helpfulness in the church."[32] Despite this record, Hardesty insisted that "I believe that Scripture does have some good news for women." She depicted her position as Evangelical, firmly grounded in the Bible and Christian history. The "good news for women," she continued, "cannot be found from a few select verses taken out of context but is based on principles found throughout the Bible and on the passages as a whole that deal with women."[33] Hardesty thus highlighted her biblicism and criticized the prevailing practice of quoting individual biblical passages to prove that women's place was one of inferiority. A case in point was the creation account in Genesis, which could be used to demean women: a selective reading could lead to the conclusion that "woman was made by God as an afterthought, to be Adam's servant." This, she argued, contradicted the account as a whole: when the passage is read in context, taking into account both Genesis 1 and Genesis 2, it becomes clear that "man and woman were created equals.... The order of creation was full equality and partnership of the sexes, both charged with care of the earth and animal life."[34] Similarly, the most famous passages quoted in support of women's subordination—Paul's statement that the husband was the head of the wife (1 Cor. 11) and his admonition that women were to be silent in church (1 Tim. 2)—needed to be considered in the biblical context and the historical situation in which they appeared. In the first case, Paul's apparent hierarchical expression that "the head of the woman is man," she argued, was mitigated by the injunction that "Christ is the head of the church." In Hardesty's reading, this passage was meant not as an instruction for dominance and rulership but as an injunction of mutual and sacrificial love. In the second case—Paul's admonition, "I do not permit a woman to teach or to assume authority over a man"—Hardesty employed historical criticism to show that Paul addressed "specific situations in particular churches," and that he was "concerned about the church's reputation among and witness to unbelievers." Hardesty pleaded for Evangelicals to take the biblical record as well as the historical circumstances seriously in assessing the proper role for contemporary women. She argued that the Christian message was one of liberation for both men and women and challenged her readers that if "we really believe ... shouldn't it make some difference in our attitudes and in our actions?"[35]

Eternity surrounded Hardesty's article with responses from well-known Evangelicals, spanning the spectrum from patriarchal to egalitarian points of views. In providing readers with such a range of opinions, the forum thus tested their feelings on the matter. On one end of the spectrum was Charles C. Ryrie, a famous theologian and author who was known for his Fundamentalist stance and defense of premillennial dispensationalism. He had written *The Place of Women in the Church*, which expounded a patriarchal and Victorian view of women.³⁶ Unsurprisingly, Ryrie was opposed to the women's liberation movement and critical of Hardesty's feminist approach to the Bible. In his response, Ryrie lamented that "once again it has been demonstrated that you can prove most anything you want from the Bible by telling the truth but not the whole truth." Focusing on technicality rather than content, Ryrie employed the strategy of putting into doubt Hardesty's biblical knowledge, suggesting that she had no authority to speak on such matters. He accused Hardesty of poor exegetical skills, listing Bible passages that she had either failed to consider or, in his opinion, interpreted wrong.³⁷ Engaging with Hardesty's arguments but rejecting her position was Elisabeth Elliot, a former missionary. She had become famous when her husband and other missionaries were killed in Ecuador in 1956 by a group of Huaorani, an Indigenous tribe they attempted to convert to Christianity. Elliot and her ten-month-old daughter stayed on and continued the missionary work until 1963, when they returned to the United States. Despite her independent missionary work and subsequent work as an author and speaker, Elliot disavowed women's equality and passionately disapproved of Hardesty's position. She stated that she "could not disagree more heartily" with Hardesty's article and went on to explain that hierarchy was part and parcel of the created order. Attempts at equality between the sexes were therefore "rebellion against God," on par, indeed, with Adam and Eve's original sin and therefore decisively un-Christian.³⁸

On the opposite end of the spectrum were those who agreed with Hardesty, like Janet Rohler Greisch, an assistant editor for *Christianity Today*, who declared: "Bravo to Nancy Hardesty!" Recalling that Christian colleges generally did not discriminate against students based on their sex but allowed them to thrive and compete, she complained that women then "'graduated' to church nurseries, where a math degree is unlikely to sooth a crying baby." Criticizing the squandering of talent, she asked: "Really, does God give women brains and then declare their use beyond college years unfeminine and unChristian?" She thought not and hoped that the article would help others come to the same conclusion.³⁹ Similarly, Harold Barnes Kuhn, professor at Asbury Theological Seminary, wrote that he "finds himself in agreement with [Hardesty] in most important respects." In his contribution, he provided further biblical evidence that women and men should be equal. He added testimony from the Song of Solomon on the love of spouses and cited 1 Peter 3:7 ("being heirs together") in support of a reciprocal spousal relationship. He admitted that women were treated badly in the current "fallen order," but argued that Christianity could help correct the grievances.⁴⁰

Other commentators also urged distinguishing between the practices of the "world" and Christian ideals, arguing that degradation of women was a secular disease rather than a Christian principle. One respondent, like Hardesty, explicitly criticized feminist prejudice against Christians. The commentator instead highlighted ways in which Christianity, in his opinion, had furthered women's rights.[41] Several respondents argued that the situation for women in biblical times had been even worse than described by Hardesty and that Jesus and later Paul displayed attitudes toward women that were significantly at odds with Jesus's contemporary culture: whereas Jewish men thanked God for their not having been born as women, the New Testament afforded women dignity and respect. These commentators, including the theologian Bernard Ramm, agreed with Hardesty that "the Scriptures do not teach the servility of women." However, they did not necessarily conclude that this made women equal. Old Testament scholar Marvin Wilson asserted that "in light of the nature of sexuality, full equality will never be possible," and Ramm added that Hardesty's article did not suffice as a treatise on the biblical view of the sexes.[42] According to these commentators, Christians, because of the biblical record and Jesus's example, should treat women better than did unbelievers. This, however, did not mean that the commentators approved of the demands of the women's rights movement.

Even though Hardesty's article did not explicitly deal with this matter, many commentators were careful to point out that they believed in biblical differences between men and women. Commentators held fast to innate distinctions between the sexes—reminiscent of the Victorian idea of different spheres and functions—and fended off any suggestion that men and women might be interchangeable. English professor Elva McAllaster used the metaphor of poplars and oaks to make her point: neither tree is better than the other, but they are different, and this difference is good. She feared that the women's liberation movement wanted to erase women of all their differences and countered that the goal should be "fulfillment of her feminine personhood, not a renunciation." Similar concerns led Bernard Ramm to conclude that "the categories 'superior' and 'inferior' are secondary"; he explained that because male and female were inherently different forms of being, male and female roles "do not and should not compete."[43] Edith Deen, a prolific author and former editor with Fort Worth Press, concluded that because women were different from men, they necessarily have different functions in society. She conceded that women might have to lead nations in times of crisis, yet she insisted that they would do it differently: it was man's nature to command, and woman's nature to influence.[44]

The readers' letters that *Eternity* printed were also mixed, revealing disunity on the question what role women should have. One reader, in disguised critique of Hardesty's article, expressed appreciation for Elisabeth Elliot's contribution. More outright condemnation of Hardesty's view was voiced by Betty Lou Nordeen, identified as a housewife from Madison, Wisconsin, who expressed the opinion that "if more of my sisters would let Him [God] fill their lives, we would not be worrying about our citizenship," effectively rendering the issue of women's rights negligible. In contrast, Gladys Hunt, a prolific Evangelical author, wrote in to point out reprovingly that *Eternity*'s contributing editors were still all men, even though "you are out front discussing the matter-of [sic] women's lib." Finally, a male respondent and clergyman agreed with Hardesty's positions and thought he might "go even further than she did."[45]

The *Eternity* forum recorded a moment in time when most Evangelical spokespersons did not yet have glib prefabricated answers to the woman question. The spokespersons were searching for a place that adequately represented their high regard for both the biblical record and the value of women. While Elliot and Hardesty put down stakes on opposite ends, both women confidently used the space of the magazine to make public their views. Evangelicals agreed that women should be treated with respect—and the majority agreed that the way women were treated in contemporary society needed to be improved. On the conservative end of the Evangelical spectrum were those, like Elliot, who believed that God had instituted an order and that women who strove to be equal destroyed such an order. On the opposite end were those who argued for full equality. Given how ingrained Victorian views of women still were (among Evangelicals and society at large), it is striking how many contributors generally agreed with Hardesty that women should not be treated as "second-class citizens." Yet the primary concern for Evangelicals was not, as Bernard Ramm phrased it, a demonstration that "the Scriptures do not teach the servility of women"; rather, it was an investigation into the "biblical view of human sexuality."[46] Spokespersons thus acknowledged that notions of male superiority and dominance were outdated. Yet, rather than adhering to feminist talking points, they wanted to broaden the conversation, focusing not on women's individual rights but on the role of sex and sexual distinctions in God's created order more generally.[47] The forum attests to a general confusion over such concepts as sex versus gender, and innate qualities versus social roles.[48] Discussants spoke of male and female "functions" and were divided over the question of whether they were innate or culturally conditioned. The title of Hardesty's article—"Women: Second-Class Citizens?"—missed the main concern of most contributors. Whether women should have political and social "rights" was secondary to the question of what was the God-created "design" of women and their part in the Christian community. The *Eternity* forum revealed the need for an Evangelical (re)vision of what women were and how they fit into created order. During the 1970s, Hardesty's and Elliot's positions would become more elaborate, evolving respectively, into the Evangelical feminist and Evangelical traditionalist visions of gender roles and relations.

"The Feminists and the Bible": Letha Scanzoni's 1973 Christianity Today *Article*

Letha Scanzoni was a young Evangelical writer who had published two books for youth, *Youth Looks at Love* (1964) and *Why Am I Here? Where Am I Going? Youth Looks at Life* (1966), when her first article in favor of gender equality, "Woman's Place: Silence or Service?" appeared in *Eternity* in 1966.[49] Hardly known outside of Evangelical circles, Scanzoni was one among a group of Evangelical women—which also included Nancy Hardesty, Sharon Gallagher, Virginia Ramey Mollenkott, and Lucille Sider Dayton—who criticized customary gender roles and became strong advocates of biblical feminism. In her article, Scanzoni challenged gender inequality by questioning why women could take on leadership roles in evangelism but were barred from teaching mixed (male and female) Sunday school classes. The 1966 article provoked mostly negative reactions. In the wake of this article, she and others published a few more articles in support of gender equality, which were all framed by a "stream of negative letters, editorials and articles."[50] But at the beginning of the new decade, more articles authored by women appeared, and appeals to gender equality were slowly gaining support in some Evangelical circles. Liberalized gender views were widely circulated throughout the articles of Evangelical magazines. In February 1973, for example, Scanzoni published "The Feminists and the Bible," a biblical argument for gender equality, in *Christianity Today*.[51] Although *Christianity Today* at this time—as Robert Booth Fowler points out—"was inclined to the critical side of the controversy" and was never "a natural home for evangelical feminists and their cause," the magazine's editors were willing to publish articles by Scanzoni and critically engage with her proposals and the arguments of emerging Evangelical feminism. Scanzoni's article laid out what came to be staple arguments in favor of a biblically grounded, Evangelical plea for gender equality.[52]

Scanzoni, in her *Christianity Today* article, argued that "the vision of men and women as co-sharers of God's grace and co-workers in Christ's kingdom is a timely message for the 1970s." She connected the contemporary women's rights movement to the struggle for civil rights and suffrage a century earlier: "Often rebuffed and ridiculed in their efforts to secure freedom for slaves, women were jolted into a realization that blacks were not the only ones whose individual rights and human dignity were being ignored."[53] She connected feminism to abolitionism, which by then was undisputedly a worthy cause. She reproved the general dismissal of women's rights by pointing out that some people had ridiculed the fight against slavery, just as they now ridiculed the fight for women's rights. Through this rhetorical sleight she elevated feminism from an egotistical complaint to a human rights issue. She enlisted the arguments of nineteenth- and early twentieth-century Christian women reformers in support of feminism: they had shown that Bible accounts from Genesis to the writings of Saint Paul, as well as the example of Jesus Christ's treatment of women and "the general spirit of Christianity," demonstrated the equality of women. These women did not challenge their traditional roles hastily, she claimed; rather, they "had wrestled with this challenge for a long time, and they knew the matter must be settled in their own mind as well as public debate."[54] Scanzoni thus answered critics who saw women's liberation as a fad. She put herself and other biblical feminists into a long tradition of deeply religious women who had grappled with the biblical record before publicly pleading for equal rights. She presented her arguments in favor of women's rights as the result of this tradition of feminist Bible study: Genesis 2, which states that Eve was created from Adam, did not make men superior; when this passage is read in context with Genesis 1, the creation account shows that God created both man and woman in his image and that they were both given dominion over the Earth. Moreover, the idea that men were superior to women because man was created first was put into doubt by interpretations that claimed that whatever God created last was most important—in which case women, not men, might be the pinnacle of creation. While the epistles of Saint Paul were often cited to relegate women to an inferior place, Scanzoni pointed out that early feminists had already shown that in the biblical record both man and woman depended on God (rather than woman simply depending on man, as 1 Corinthians 11 was sometimes understood). Indeed, passages like Galatians 3:28 ("there is neither male nor female") indicated that sexual distinctions did not matter to God. Nineteenth-century feminists had furthermore pointed out that some biblical notions—like Paul's injunction that women cover their head or keep silent in church—were owed to culture and custom and should not be binding in a different time and cultural context. Sometimes, also, a male bias had tarnished Bible translations, for example when English translations referred to Phoebe (Rom. 16:1) as a "servant," whereas the same Greek word in other contexts was translated as "minister" or "deacon." Indeed, the Bible portrayed a number of women—Miriam, Deborah, and Priscilla, among others—that "had *public* ministries, and duties in church and state," contradicting the notion that women were unfit for office. While Jesus did not give "specific instructions on such things as women's suffrage," early feminists felt that the example of how Jesus treated women nonetheless provided useful guidance. Against Victorian ideals, nineteenth-century women argued that men and women shared the same humanity—they were "CREATED EQUAL"—and they should use their God-given longings and drives to the best of their abilities. They also rejected the Victorian notion that male characteristics ("ambition, reason, debate, . . . physical force") differed from female ("peace and love, . . . gentleness and benevolence"), arguing instead that all Christians should be distinguished by displaying virtues like "love, peace, meekness, and kindness."[55] Scanzoni cast her argument in favor of women's rights as the findings of intense Bible study commenced a decade earlier. She took into consideration not only the Bible but also Christian tradition and history. She started out with the creation account, worked her way through the teachings of Paul, considered the cultural and historical context of Bible narratives, gave examples of female leadership in the Bible, highlighted Jesus's attitude toward women, looked at the notion that in a final analysis man and woman were both human, and concluded with a survey of the general spirit of Christianity. While she lamented that feminist arguments had not much changed the situation for nineteenth-century women, Scanzoni hoped that the time was now ripe for a transformation of society. With the outline of biblical and Christian arguments in favor of women's rights, Scanzoni helped develop what came to be known as the Evangelical feminist position.

Scanzoni's arguments—even the exact wording—were taken up in a subsequent issue of the magazine: an editorial in March 1973 started out with the closing sentence of Scanzoni's article, claiming that it was time for women to come into their own as "co-sharers of God's grace and co-workers in Christ's kingdom." In support of Scanzoni's position, the editorialist argued that it needed to be possible for women to follow their divinely appointed calling. Yet the editorialist rephrased her demands in language that simultaneously acknowledged and curtailed those demands. The editorial can thus be read, in part, as prototypical for the Evangelical traditionalist stance, which developed through confrontations with the secular women's liberation movement and Evangelical feminism. The author took women's grievances seriously and highlighted women's intrinsic potential and value to society. Advocating a reconsideration of the role of women in contemporary society, however, the editorialist insisted that the gender debate was "a task of eternal significance" not because women needed to claim certain rights, but "because evangelical women are engaged in God's business, not just their own. They do not struggle for their freedom only but for the opportunity for all human beings to find freedom through enslavement to Christ."[56] The editorialist rejected the feminist "rights" discourse focused on individual fulfillment in favor of a religious discourse that stressed the communal ideal of God-created harmonious order. In language inverting intuitive meanings, the editorialist described true liberation as radical submission, indeed "enslavement," to the will of God. This was true for all humans but for women in particular. Women's liberation, rightly understood, so the argument went, was the freedom to submit themselves to their God-appointed place. While this sounds like hairsplitting, the difference between succumbing to one's fate and choosing the place one was destined for was vital to the argument. It presupposed free will and the capacity of women to analyze the situation, realize that God-created order was the best possible order, and thus choose their right place. While this approach did not necessarily change anything about a woman's place in her family or her day-to-day work, it changed the thinking about women. Women were no longer passive creatures, simply put into their place for protection or natural belonging. Rather, women had agency and cognitive skills, allowing them to choose their own fate. Going one step further, the editorialist argued that it would be wrong for the body of Christ, the church, to squander the capital God had placed at its command. To ignore women's innate potential was to reject God's provisions—and dismiss a significant part of the human resources available for church work and evangelism. Accordingly, a woman's place might not be restricted to the home: it might, for example, entail a leadership position in the church. Cautiously advocating stronger roles for women, the editorialist pointed out the necessity of creating an infrastructure that would enable women to network with and educate one another. In the editorialist's words: "Perhaps it is time—though we wish it were unnecessary—for evangelical women to band together to encourage one another to fulfill themselves as human beings with God-given abilities. A forum, a newsletter, a job referral service, a permanent organization are possibilities in the task of encouragement and education."[57]

While this was no call for an Evangelical women's movement, it was an acknowledgment that for "it [the Church] to be faithful to its calling," women needed help and support.[58] This editorialist, then, advocated, albeit somewhat reluctantly, organizational structures for the benefit of Evangelical women as both legitimate and timely (incidentally, the Evangelical Women's Caucus was founded in the fall of the same year).

Even though it was partly a response to the women's liberation movement, the debate in Evangelical magazines was not primarily about women's rights. Evangelicals were concerned about God's design for the world, and the women's rights movement prompted them to ask whether they adhered to divine principles in gender norms or needed to adjust their behavior. They tried to distinguish between the practices common in society and the proper gender relations prescribed by the Bible. This distinctly theological approach showed that for Evangelicals the woman question was not merely anthropological—that is, concerned with *anthropos*, the human—but that anthropology was always a matter of trying to understand God and God's created order. Evangelicals easily agreed that women should be treated well and that attitudes toward women could be improved. However, they were wary about women's rights, fearing that feminists provoked war between the sexes and subverted the order. Yet acknowledging that women had legitimate grievances, they searched the Bible for help, redetermining what they knew about its precepts for women. The debate quickly expanded to include deliberations about the nature and purpose of women and men and their relation to each other and society. Contributions in Evangelical magazines throughout the 1970s reenvisioned women, defining women and men as cosharers of the image of God and part of the God-created order.

The Feminist Position: Scanzoni and Hardesty

Letha Scanzoni and Nancy Hardesty finished their draft of *All We're Meant to Be*—a distinctly feminist and Evangelical approach to gender issues—in 1971, but it took several years for a publisher to accept the book, which was not released until 1974.[59] Despite these initial difficulties, the book had an immense impact on the Evangelical debate of women's roles. In 2006, it was named the twenty-third most influential book for Evangelicals by *Christianity Today*. Influential, however, does not mean universally lauded. Rather, the comment in *Christianity Today* read that *"for better or for worse*, no evangelical marriage or institution has been able to ignore the ideas in this book."[60] The book affected the Evangelical community by introducing the ideal of gender equality and discussing the role of women from a rigorously Christian perspective. In *All We're Meant to Be*, Hardesty and Scanzoni reconsidered women's roles by systematically tackling all biblical passages relevant to the question. They used classical hermeneutics as well as historical context, church history, and everyday experience in their theological reinterpretation of critical passages. They refuted the patriarchal view that women were inferior and embraced the vision of full equality for women. Both Scanzoni and Hardesty had some standing within Evangelical circles, with Hardesty having been an editor for *Eternity* and Scanzoni having published books as well as articles for Evangelical audiences.[61] The two women thus found Evangelical magazines to be open to their perspective, although not unreservedly so: legend has it that one of Scanzoni's earlier articles only accidentally bypassed editorial review, while *Eternity* printed a caveat in connection with one of Hardesty's articles. Even so, magazines from across the sociopolitical spectrum (all but *Moody Monthly*) eventually printed their contributions. Various magazines printed previews of *All We're Meant to Be* as well as advertisements and reviews.[62]

Letha Scanzoni's 1973 *Christianity Today* article "The Feminists and the Bible," discussed above, can be read as a summary of the book's argument. The article carried a preface that announced the forthcoming book, then tentatively titled "The Christian Woman's Liberation." Scanzoni lamented that "the [negative] image of women's lib is unfortunate; it misses the whole point of the movement and encourages the widespread suspicion that Christianity and feminism are incompatible."[63] She countered that not only were feminism and Christianity compatible, but the original concern for women's rights had been religiously motivated. The article was a call for Evangelicals to engage more seriously with Christian mandates for women. *Christianity Today* published one letter to the editors in response to the article. The positive assessment from a female reader concluded with the words "Thank you for this start toward peace in the seventies!"[64] While the article, like the book (which references women's liberation in its subtitle), clearly sympathized with and drew inspiration from feminism, Scanzoni's position differed from mainstream feminist writings in that she did not reject but grappled with biblical precepts for women. Scanzoni upheld the ultimate authority of Scripture but argued that, understood correctly, the biblical account supported the equality of women and men.[65]

The left-leaning magazine the *Other Side* also provided space for previews of the book's arguments. Scanzoni and Hardesty each had an article in the July/August 1973 issue dedicated to the woman question. Here, Scanzoni developed the argument that beyond biological differences, male and female behavior was conditioned rather than inborn. She did not attempt to reassign to women traits traditionally described as male (active, competitive, strong, decisive, etc.), or to men traits traditionally described as female (passive, caring, weak, sensitive, etc.); instead, she advocated adopting a different list of traits to characterize all Christians: "Love, joy, peace, patience. . . . You recognize them, of course; they're qualities that according to the New Testament should characterize *every* Christian as an outflowing of new life in Christ."[66] According to her, ideas of proper behavior for men and women were cultural rather than Christian and therefore not compulsive. Hardesty, in her article, added that women often had to suppress their God-given talents to adjust to cultural expectations. Starting with the biblical Parable of the Talents, in which servants are expected to return investments with interest (Matt. 25:14–30), she argued that God had charged His followers with developing their talents. She added a fictional version of what that effort looked like in contemporary society: "When I went to study business administration, the dean denied my admission. When I went to apply for a business loan, the banker said he would need my husband's permission. In the marketplace I was paid only half what my talent was worth. When I went to my pastor, he told me I had no business working. I tried to start a small business in my home, but my husband complained that I should concern myself solely with house and children."[67]

She thus accused contemporary society of obstructing women's development of God-given talents. Hardesty then combed through the biblical account and church history to show that God bestowed women with "gifts," and that women throughout the ages had used and developed these gifts in his service. She concluded that it was wrong to exclude women from full participation in society but also that it was a grave negligence for women not to try to develop their talents.

Even though the topic was contentious, reviews in *Christianity Today*, *Eternity*, and the *Post-American* positively appraised Hardesty and Scanzoni's book. *Christianity Today* printed an assessment of the book by assistant editor Cheryl Forbes, who called *All We're Meant to Be* "one of the finest books to come out on the controversial subject of women's liberation." She highlighted the notion that God-given talents should not be denied, writing that "Scanzoni and Hardesty want to waken more Christian women to the possibilities and responsibilities of fully using their God-given talents and gifts."[68] In the *Post-American*, Boyd Reese, the associate editor, and in *Eternity*, Nancy Barcus, a contributor and assistant professor of English, similarly praised the book. Barcus pointed out that Scanzoni and Hardesty challenged many taken-for-granted assumptions about men and women. Accordingly, this was "a book that cannot be ignored. It is a powerful book and a painful book."[69] Reese lauded the book as important reading not only for women. He described the challenges the book presented to audiences, particularly to men. He found it "necessary to add that women's liberation is not just a women's issue. It is fundamentally a human issue. Men need to be liberated as well as women."[70] The reviewers thus acknowledged the importance of Scanzoni and Hardesty's contribution to the gender debate, even when they did not fully accept or agree with all the writers' arguments.

Reese's personal testimony is indicative of expectations that clashed with notions of women's liberation. He confessed: "When I was in college, I expected to be married and that my wife's vows would include the words 'love, honor, and obey,' because that's the way it's supposed to be." However, since then, his views had changed considerably, and he now regarded "marriage as an egalitarian partnership," noting that "I feel [egalitarian marriage] can really free me and others to realize our fullest potential and dynamic maturity."[71] Reese thus approved of the book's notion of an egalitarian relationship. Barcus generally agreed with the idea of gender equality but issued a warning. She alleged that Scanzoni and Hardesty advocated "role interchangeability," or the idea that, were it not for cultural conditioning, men and women would be equally good in any role. Barcus, however, was convinced about "*her* uniqueness, *his* uniqueness," emphasizing essential differences between the sexes. She pointed out that the question "what is maleness and femaleness in relation to humanness"—and therefore also the question of what "we're meant to be"—

had not been comprehensively answered.[72] To Forbes and Reese, one asset of the book was that *All We're Meant to Be* grappled not just with the role of married women but also with the needs and talents of single women, providing a more holistic vision of womanhood. All three reviews included the caveat that not every Evangelical would agree with Scanzoni and Hardesty's exegesis in every case. Nonetheless, Scanzoni and Hardesty's ideas found kindly disposed reviewers who saw the book as an important contribution to recovering a vision of women as "full persons."[73] All this guaranteed that the Evangelical feminist perspective represented by Hardesty and Scanzoni was widely disseminated during the 1970s. Yet even these positive reviews did not fully embrace Hardesty and Scanzoni's position, highlighting the fact that wide circulation and critical appraisal did not equal endorsement. If Evangelical magazines were not eager to embrace Evangelical feminism, they also seemed reluctant to engage with all aspects of an opposing vision of women: Marabel Morgan's "total woman."

The Reception of Marabel Morgan's Total Woman

On June 9, 1974, a "Book Ends" article in the *New York Times* reported that "feminism isn't totally sweeping the country." On the contrary, a book with a "distinctly pro-homebody stance" was selling at a rate of thirty five thousand copies a week: Marabel Morgan's *The Total Woman*. With barely veiled glee, the article described the book as a cross between a sex advice manual and a child-raising manual for married housewives of a Christian bent.[74] Many liberal observers regarded Morgan's book with ridicule and were startled by its popularity. Contemporary critics from religion scholar Martin E. Marty to sex researchers Virginia Johnson and William Masters decried Morgan's backward attitude toward sex and the role of women.[75] The Total Woman workshops that had spawned the book were popular with conservatives and numbered among their graduates the conservative singer, antigay activist, and former Miss America Anita Bryant.[76] But as the *New York Times* review added, the book didn't just appeal to women in the Bible Belt: it sold well in supposedly liberal New York City. *The Total Woman* was the bestselling book of 1974, outselling even *All the President's Men*, Carl Bernstein and Bob Woodward's chronicle of their investigation of the Watergate scandal.[77] Marabel Morgan provided practical and spiritual advice on how to improve one's marriage. She wrote from the perspective of a white, middle-aged, middle-class housewife, and she sprinkled her account with personal testimonies. Echoing some feminist grievances, she recounted that she had been a frustrated wife and mother, fighting a lot with her husband, Charlie. But then one simple realization changed all that: she realized that it was biblical for the wife to submit to the husband's leadership. Contrary to feminist wisdom, happiness lay not with self-actualization but with acceptance of one's God-given place in the family and in society. Once she submitted voluntarily, she lived a happy life. Banking on newfound sexual frankness and a celebration of marital sex in Evangelicalism, Morgan also provided her readers with dress-up tips and advice to instigate sexual encounters.[78] She promised that this would not only please the husband but also predispose him to spoil the wife with goodies. Because of its enormous success, *The Total Woman* defined the public image of Evangelical gender roles and sexuality, obscuring the debates that raged within Evangelical circles about the book and gender roles more generally. The cynical treatment afforded the book also hid a new self-assertion of Evangelical women. The "total woman" depicted by Morgan was a deviation from the "traditional" Christian model of womanhood, affording choice and agency to women.

Marabel Morgan was initially unknown in Evangelical circles, and as sociologist Robert Booth Fowler observed, religious bookstores at first did not carry her book. Her arguments were indeed impoverished from an Evangelical point of view: "Morgan rarely was specific about where the Bible supported her ideas and she never entered the controversies over biblical interpretations regarding the proper roles for men and women." Rather, the book fit into the emerging market of marriage counseling books and sex manuals. But contrary to liberal discourses, she propagated sex and marriage advice for "the woman, or perhaps especially the man," according to Fowler, "for whom the question [of women's liberation] was completely closed."[79] Her arguments, then, focused on improving spousal relationships and spicing up sex lives within the given parameters of traditional gender norms. Accordingly, her book was initially discussed in Evangelical magazines in women's columns and under the rubric of self-help literature.

The first review of the book in *Moody Monthly*, in December 1973, only a month after publication, regarded the book as an answer to deteriorating marriages fueled by ideas disseminated by secular feminists. Assistant managing editor Zeda Thornton, a self-described "single girl," focused on the chapters of *The Total Woman* that discuss how communication between husband and wife could be reestablished and improved, recommending the book as worthwhile reading material on marriage for both married and single women. She mentioned that there were also chapters on sex and child-rearing, but she did not discuss these in the review. After highlighting Morgan's advice to women to take a look at their own lives to find out what they wanted and how they could organize and economize their schedules, Thornton summarized the "four A's" of Morgan's recommendation with regard to husbands: "1. Accept your husband. . . . 2. Admire your husband. . . . 3. Adapt to his way of life. . . . 4. Appreciate all he does for you." The book review presented Morgan's precept of changing oneself to appeal to the husband as a good formula for creating a more harmonious relationship.[80] Thornton also marshaled the courses that predated the book as evidence for the success of the total woman concept, asserting that "testimonies from the students verify that the principles work." She explicated: "Ten wives of the Miami Dolphin football players attended one of the first classes. They really tried to put their husbands first and bring out the best qualities in them. I guess you can't determine how much the course had to do with it, but it may not be mere coincidence that the next season the team won every game. It was the first undefeated season in the history of professional football, including play-off games and the Super Bowl."[81]

Thornton seemed to say that by becoming total women, wives not only improved their marriage but bolstered their husbands' successes. She neither scrutinized the vision for women espoused by the book nor questioned the book's advice on how wives could become more attractive to their husbands. Instead, Thornton focused on results. Her appraisal of the book was based on a pragmatic argument: floundering relationships had been improved by Morgan's formula.

The first mention of *The Total Woman* in *Christianity Today*, in its March 1974 special issue on books, similarly stressed the book's value for improving marriages. The book warranted a paragraph in the section on "Counseling and Psychology of Religion" under the subhead "For Women Only," classifying it, effectively, as a self-help book for women. The author judged that "the reasonably well-adjusted woman whose marriage is mediocre and dull is likely to react with productive enthusiasm to the wealth of practical ideas [proposed in the book] for generating happy sparks in her marriage." The format for the review articles in the *Christianity Today* books issue provided little space for details and discussion. The description remained necessarily short and vague. Accordingly, the reader was left to wonder whether she was a "reasonably well-adjusted woman," what constituted a "mediocre and dull" marriage, and which aspects of the relationship could be improved by Morgan's advice. While the book review clearly located Morgan within the genre of advice literature, a preface to the section singled out the book as an answer to "the modern woman's question about her identity, purpose, and function."[82] With this sentence, the book was additionally characterized as one response to the contemporary debates about a woman's role in society sparked by the liberation and feminist movements. Yet early descriptions of *The Total Woman* focused primarily on its usefulness as a self-help book. They hardly engaged with the portrayal of a woman's role and gender relations as envisioned by Morgan. These reviews also skipped the passages that dealt with sex and seduction.

FEMINIST CHALLENGES 95

Figure 3.1. "Hello, passion flower, your Total Man is home!" Cartoon in *Christianity Today*, July 18, 1975. Courtesy of Buswell Library Special Collections, Wheaton College, Illinois.

This reception changed as the book drew attention outside of Evangelical circles, as with the *New York Times* book review cited above. As Fowler pointed out, "no evangelical could avoid the fact that Morgan claimed to be an active ally."[83] Evangelical magazines started printing their own critical and often satirized commentaries, distancing themselves from Morgan. In July and September 1975, respectively, *Christianity Today* and *Moody Monthly* published pieces that addressed the outlandish seduction advice provided in *The Total Woman*, which was such a source for glee for non-Evangelical commentators. *Christianity Today* responded to Morgan's sex advice with humor and let a cartoon speak for itself. The magazine published a satirical rendering of the "total man" (figure 3.1). In a witty counterpoint to the tips for seduction provided by Morgan—advising the wife to greet her husband at the door in revealing costumes like lingerie and high heels—the artist provided a sketch of a man greeting a woman at the doorstep with only his briefcase to cover him. It is interesting to note that the picture still showed the woman with a broom inside the house as the man was approaching the door, likely returning home from work. Clearly, the artist was not attempting to ridicule the domestic arrangement of breadwinning husband and stay-at-home wife. Rather, the cartoon rendered ridiculous the scene of a naked and a clothed person meeting on the doorstep. By reversing not the domestic arrangement but the naked and clothed individuals, the illustrator made clear that the whole concept of seduction at the doorstep was inappropriate.

Morgan's emphasis on sex was not a laughing matter for David R. Douglass, who wrote an opinion piece for *Moody Monthly*. Douglass grumbled that it was no wonder that liberal journalists were "taught" by *The Total Woman* "to have a clean conscience while being sex-obsessed." He decried the "'anything-goes' in the marriage bed (or under the dining room table)" approach to sex advocated by Morgan. While he also criticized the unconditional obedience to husbands Morgan advertised as a perversion of the biblical principle that God was the true lord and sovereign, his main critique centered on the portrayal of sex and seduction. To Douglass, the gravest fault of *The Total Woman* was lending a Christian veneer and therefore legitimation to sexual practices borrowed from a corrupt culture.[84] Both the *Christianity Today* cartoon and the *Moody Monthly* opinion piece rebutted Morgan's ideas on sex and seduction, which had become a source of hilarity for liberal observers. They did not, however, question the underlying view of what role a woman was supposed to play. This task was left to the makers of the satirical *Wittenburg Door*.

The *Wittenburg Door*, which specialized in humor and wit, dedicated its August/September 1975 issue to "The Totaled Woman"—using a similar play on words to the opinion piece in the more conservative *Moody Monthly*, which was called "*The Total Woman*: Totaled." While the expression "totaled" can indicate the summing up of a topic, in combination with the cover image, it conjured the image of a totaled or wrecked car—or in this case, a wrecked woman. The cover showed an elderly woman with her hair in rollers sitting in an easy chair, soaking her feet, scratching her leg, and reading Morgan's *The Total Woman* (figure 3.2). A couple of magazines, including an issue of *Moody Monthly*, were carelessly strewn around the room, and a bottle of Pepto-Bismol and a set of false teeth were positioned within reach. The woman vaguely resembled Marabel Morgan, visible on the back of the book sleeve, as both were sitting in about the same position in a dark recliner in their living rooms. With the hair rollers, the woman might even have been attempting to copy Morgan's hairstyle. The picture can be interpreted in several ways. It might be ridiculing the sort of woman that reads Morgan's book; it might be contrasting the glamorous housewife ideal embodied by Morgan with a satirized version of reality; or it might show a woman in the process of transformation from her disgruntled former self to the ideal of the "total woman" reached and modeled by Morgan. The magazine cover has the effect of distancing observers from the ideal of *The Total Woman*, making them question whether Morgan's ideal of womanhood was practical, and whether it

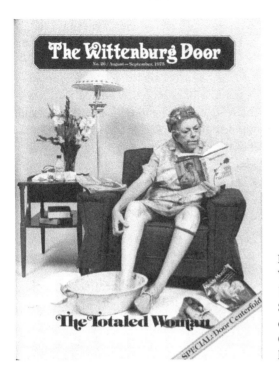

Figure 3.2. "The Totaled Woman." Cover of *Wittenburg Door*, August/September 1975. Courtesy of Buswell Library Special Collections, Wheaton College, Illinois.

was an aspirational ideal. Accordingly, the satire of the *Wittenburg Door* went beyond the ridicule of Morgan's seduction advice. However, a reference to the sexualized notions of womanhood depicted by Morgan was not completely missing, either. A banner in the lower-right corner of the page announced a "centerfold"—the sort of foldout poster of scantily clad women known from men's magazines like *Playboy*—linking Morgan's sexual advice for women directly to voyeuristic and pornographic aspects of secular society usually condemned by Evangelicals. In an interesting twist, there actually was a centerfold, but it consisted of a picture of the (fully clothed) Evangelical feminist Letha Scanzoni who was extensively interviewed in the following pages. With a few well-arranged signs, then, the *Wittenburg Door* managed to satirize the ideal of the total woman, provoking readers into thinking about what life as a stay-at-home wife and mother was actually like. It also criticized the degradation of women as sexual objects. Furthermore, it succeeded in placing the book in the context of the debate about a woman's role in society and portraying the full spectrum of Evangelical visions by integrating the perspective of Evangelical feminists represented by Scanzoni. Finally, the vision of women represented by *The Total Woman* was not only summarized, but was also dismissed as both unattainable and undesirable: real women were closer to the *Wittenburg Door* cartoon than to the Marabel Morgan ideal, and the ideal itself was false because the total woman let herself be made into a sex object.

For all their discomfort with Morgan's sexual advice, Evangelical spokespersons and magazines did not summarily reject her gendered worldview. Rather, as evidenced by both the review published by *Moody Monthly* and *Christianity Today*'s cartoon, some felt that the ridicule Morgan's book drew threatened to discredit the ideal of working husband and stay-at-home wife. While others have argued that Morgan's book was part of an emerging Evangelical literature that celebrated sex within marriage and prepared the way for "politicization of family life," the magazine record shows that Evangelical elites were initially embarrassed by Morgan's style.[85]

Clashing Gendered Visions:
The Wittenburg Door *and Definitions of Submission*

While Marabel Morgan came down on the conservative, hierarchy-affirming side of the debate, Evangelical feminists lobbied for equality in all matters, including household chores and ordination. *The Total Woman* stole the limelight in terms of overall popularity, but Letha Scanzoni and Nancy Hardesty's Evangelical feminist treatise *All We're Meant to Be* won the praise of Evangelical elites, including taking *Eternity*'s book award for the most influential book in 1975.[86] In *Christianity Today*'s 1975 special issue on books, Carol Prester McFadden, editor of Canon Press, cited *The Total Woman* and *All We're Meant to Be* as "opposite poles" within the Evangelical debate on gender roles. She judged that "*All We're Meant to Be* (Word) by Letha Scanzoni and Nancy Hardesty, is a well-informed, scholarly, if at times arbitrary analysis of multifaceted womanhood." She was not so generous in her judgment of "the other book," writing that "*The Total Woman* (Revell) by Marabel Morgan, regrettably a best seller, takes some sound principles, bows them before the great god sex, and wraps them in pink baby-doll pajamas for delivery to the unsuspecting as an alternative to hard-core Woman's Liberation."[87]

The most thorough examination of Morgan's and Scanzoni/Hardesty's different visions of womanhood—the traditionalist and the feminist stances, respectively—took place in the *Wittenburg Door*. The magazine dedicated its August/September 1975 issue to the "sober reflection on the meaning of the sexes from a Christian perspective."[88] While the *Wittenburg Door* showed more sympathy for the positions of Evangelical feminists like Scanzoni—and in an aside implied that Evangelicals who read Morgan's *The Total Woman* also subscribed to their conservative nemesis *Moody Monthly*—it nonetheless provided space for both Morgan and Scanzoni to explicate their views on the role of women and gender relations.[89] The magazine printed long interviews with both authors, presenting them as opposite ends in this "male/female controversy" within Evangelicalism.[90] The editors asked both women detailed questions about how they came to write their books and the ideas they presented therein. Despite their differences, both women emphasized the concept of submission. While the use of the same term in the first instance masks differences, how they used and understood the term illustrates the disparity of their positions. Morgan advocated a hierarchical relationship, arguing that the woman needed to adapt to her husband's needs and work hard to make the relationship work; Scanzoni, conversely, propagated an egalitarian view, espousing equality as the only way spouses could be friends and therefore have a meaningful relationship.[91]

The interview with Morgan commenced with the question of how she "got started with the Total Woman." Morgan recalled the bad state her marriage was in, emphasizing that there had been "no communication" between her and her husband, Charlie. But when she changed her routine, doing "silly little things" like cooking his favorite meal or dressing up for him, Charlie opened up to her. She told her friends, and they observed similar changes in their husbands after attempting similar steps.[92] She thus focused on the pragmatic approach that put the book in the self-help category. While Morgan's advice to "give 100%" with no expectation of a return from the husband sounded unfair even to her, she insisted that it worked, and it was a God-given principle.

When the *Door* asked Morgan, "So your feeling is that when a woman becomes married, she's placed herself in a subservient position?" Morgan answered that she did not like the term "subservient" but would use "submissive." She explained: "Subservient puts me on a slave basis where the man could wipe his feet on me. . . . Submissive is my willingness to obey. And to place myself under his leadership." The slight variance here mattered quite a lot: Morgan's point was that the woman had a choice. She could fight her husband, as Morgan claimed she had. But for the relationship to be "harmonious," the wife needed to "adapt to his way of life." In Morgan's way of thinking, a woman who submitted did not resign herself to an unfair power structure but chose the place God had intended for her. By willingly acquiescing to an inferior position, a woman accepted her place in God's created order, and her marriage would be happier because of it—it was "a God-given principle."[93] Religion scholar Ruth Marie Griffith, who encountered similar arguments while studying charismatic Protestants in the 1990s, highlights the internal, empowering logic of this argumentation. She also points out that it could be explained as a coping strategy for women in bad situations: "While many outsiders might assume that the conservative Christian women in Aglow [the community Griffith studied] are merely participating in their own victimization, internalizing patriarchal ideas about female submission that confirm and increase their sense of personal inferiority, the women themselves claim the doctrine of submission leads both to freedom and to transformation, as God rewards His obedient daughters by healing their sorrows and easing their pain." Yet the point is well taken that the rhetorical strategy subverts a degrading concept into one that allows for agency.[94] In another study, scholar Christine J. Gardner found that Evangelicals adopted the liberal language of choice as a rhetorical strategy. Studying the rhetoric of abstinence campaigns, Gardner argued that "evangelicals are co-opting forms of secular culture to make chastity sexy."[95] Adopting the feminist slogan "my body, my choice," abstinence campaigns encouraged young women to choose not to have sex before marriage. In this case, too, an apparently illiberal command was reinterpreted in empowering terms as choice. While purporting to represent the traditional position, then, Morgan's argumentation exhibited an innovative strain, "emancipating" women and making "submission" a conscious choice. Through this rhetorical strategy, women like Morgan achieved a sense of agency. This rhetorical shift reenvisioned the concept of submission without succumbing to the secular culture from which the language was borrowed. Morgan continued to advocate a traditional and hierarchical relationship wherein the wife was secondary to the husband.

Scanzoni's use of the term "submission" could not have been more different. Scanzoni insisted that "submission, of course, is Biblical because all Christians are told to submit to each other. Submitting means giving up one's rights for the rights of the other and for the mutual well-being of any relationship." She explicitly rejected submission as a "one-way street" and stressed the mutuality of the principle. Submission was not something asked of women only, and if it was, it corrupted its purpose. Scanzoni mentioned Jesus Christ as the ultimate example of submission: he sacrificed himself for others. Accordingly, "all Christians are told that greater love hath no one than this: to lay down his life for his friends."[96] Submission, understood this way, was a godly principle, and it was asked of all Christians regardless of their sex. Scanzoni thus advocated an egalitarian ideal of marriage, couched in traditional biblical language and justified by biblical exegesis.

Morgan, as well as Scanzoni and Hardesty, understood themselves to be operating on biblical principles and tackling the problem of a woman's place in society from a biblical perspective. Both Morgan's traditionalist and Scanzoni and Hardesty's feminist perspectives constituted reinterpretations of a woman's place. Morgan's perspective granted women agency by making gendered submission a deliberate choice; Scanzoni and Hardesty broke with hierarchical gender models and affirmed the equality of the sexes and the mutuality of gender relations. Yet both sides employed the term "submission" to describe their vision, thus defining opposite ends of what Evangelicals could mean when they used the term: a hierarchical relationship with wives submitting to husbands, or an equal relationship with spouses submitting to each other for the sake of friendship and the greater good. Submission thus became a vision Evangelicals across the spectrum ascribed to but one that had decisively different meanings depending on the context. Writers for Evangelical magazines tended to favor one side over the other, while subscribing wholeheartedly to none. They mixed traditionalist and feminist arguments depending on the issue at hand. Indeed, language and ideas were borrowed from both camps, mixed, and often had shifting meanings.

Vision of Gender Relations

Prompted by the feminist movement, Evangelicals took up the debate about women but took it into a very different direction. Evangelical spokespersons did not conceive of the woman question as a rights discourse or as a matter of individual fulfillment. Rather, the magazine record of the 1970s shows that Evangelicals attempted to reevaluate God's design for women. Revisiting the question of what it means to be human, they sought biblical answers to what it meant to be female. They stressed the biblical account that God created humans as male and female, insisting both on innate differences between the sexes and on the complementary nature of men and women. Evangelicals stressed the relationship between humans, mirroring a theological development. According to Roger E. Olson, "toward the end of the twentieth century a popular interpretation gaining ground among evangelical theologians was that the image of God refers to relationality; humans are created for relationships, just as God exists in community as three persons united in a single essence."[97] One could thus only be meaningfully female in relationships, and the primary relationship was that of marriage.

Are Women Human?

An *Eternity* cover in February 1974 asked the disturbing question "are women human?" (figure 3.3). The cover showed a drawing of a woman's face. It looked like a child's arts and crafts project: A simple color-pencil drawing of a woman's face on a piece of cardboard, complete with actual hoop earrings pierced through the cardboard. This mixed-media artwork had been photographed against a pale background. This technique removed the viewer from the object of discussion—women. The viewer was presented with a representation of a representation that was at once familiar and unrealistic: one could recognize a woman and at the same time know that this was not a woman but a drawing. Moreover, the drawing offered a distorted representation—a large face with huge eyes and a kissing mouth framed by curly side bangs. This face disappeared seamlessly—without a neck—into a white lace collar atop

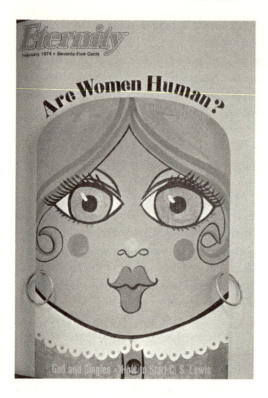

Figure 3.3. "Are Women Human?" Cover of *Eternity*, February 1974. Courtesy of Buswell Library Special Collections, Wheaton College, Illinois.

a hinted-at blue blouse. The drawing was by no means detailed or exacting. Rather, it was reminiscent of the scheme of childlike characteristics, or "cuteness," first proposed by zoologist and behavioral scientist Konrad Lorenz: a large head, large round eyes, a little nose, round cheeks, and retreating chin. According to Lorenz, this scheme, found especially in newborn humans and other mammals, arouses protective feelings in the viewer.[98] The cover, then, managed to introduce women as something at the same time familiar and unknown and in need of protection. Accordingly, the image of women presented here, especially in connection with the question whether women were human, was reminiscent of the portrayal of an exotic and endangered species. The cover thus invited viewers to review what they really knew about women.

The question on the cover—are women human?—was borrowed from a 1938 presentation by Dorothy L. Sayers, a Christian scholar, author, and contemporary of Oxford luminaries J. R. R. Tolkien and C. S. Lewis. *Eternity* printed excerpts from Sayers's presentation, announced by the editors as "pungent prophetic words about a still explosive issue, women in a male-dominated society."[99] In the excerpt, originally delivered as an address to a women's society, Sayers proclaimed that "a woman is just as much an ordinary human being as a man, with the same individual preferences, and with just as much right to the tastes and preferences of an individual"—an observation the editors of *Eternity* apparently felt worth republishing in 1974.[100] *Eternity* took up the question again some time later, with another magazine issue dedicated to the woman question in March 1975. This one was prefaced with the following words: "Thirteen months ago *Eternity*'s cover asked, 'Are Women Human?' Obvious as the answer is, somehow the question won't go away."[101] These two covers implied that women's nature was a matter of debate. The first step in the negotiation of gender relations among Evangelicals in the 1970s thus needed to be an understanding of women's humanity.

John F. Alexander echoed Sayers's question when he asked in the *Other Side*'s 1973 issue on women: "Are women people or not?" While this might look like a rhetorical question with the self-evident answer that, of course, women are people, Alexander retorted that "most of us have decided that they are not." Explaining his counterintuitive answer, he pointed out that in contemporary society women were regarded merely as "sex objects, household servants, typists, or anything else useful to men." Far from rhetorical, then, the question whether women were human was a serious one. Some Evangelical observers found that in society at large women were treated not as people but as assets to men. Alexander took issue with this situation. He recounted that women were often asked not to compete against men. The reason for this admonition was not that they would fail but that they might surpass and thus threaten the men. Alexander found this logic indefensible and inhumane.[102] He called this perspective "thinking male" but cautioned that a lot of women did it, too, because, "raised in a male-dominated society, most women have bought a bill of goods." Echoing feminist complaints, Alexander thus affirmed that men had not only come to dominate society, they had also come to define humanity, and mechanisms were in place, perpetuated by men as well as women, that made and kept women in a less-than-human category. Alexander presented both the strategy of continuing male hegemony and the opposite strategy, that of "thinking female." The latter was introduced as a tool employed by some extreme feminists and some radical Evangelicals to reverse the power structure, making men subservient. Alexander concluded that neither attitude was particularly Christian.[103] Alexander, then, was opposed to defining humanity either as solely male or as solely female and objected to practices whereby either men or women dominated society. Instead, he reminded readers that humanity was both male and female.

In the same issue, author Judith Sanderson offered a vision that transcended the examples of contemporary male dominance or proposed feminist female dominance: the biblical example of how Jesus treated women, a popular strategy employed in defense of Evangelical feminism.[104] In her article

"Jesus and Women," Sanderson affirmed that "He showed respect for each woman as a unique individual whom He loved as a person and in whom He recognized special needs and special gifts."[105] This example was heralded as an alternative vision, an ideal that affirmed women's humanity and individuality. Jesus, according to this reading, had treated women not as women but as human beings. Accordingly, the *Other Side* contrasted the role of women in society with a biblical vision, arguing that the contemporary, inhumane treatment of women was a deviation from God's plan.

There is no evidence in the magazines in the 1970s of authors who argued that women were not human or were created as inferior creatures. Yet the frequent affirmation that women were created equal suggests that this was a point in need of repetition. The argument that women were as human as men was made most often through the analogy of the creation account. A contributor to *Christianity Today*, for example, described humanity as a "double image": God created both man and woman in his image. The writer evoked Genesis 1:27—"God created man in his own image, in the image of God he created him; male and female he created them"—to show that both sexes bore the image of God.[106] Similarly, author Winnie Christensen in an article in *Moody Monthly* explained that "men and women were created in the image of God with a joint responsibility over all the earth." Therefore, woman was "his [man's] equal," "a total human being," and "a unique person."[107] The author thus made an argument for the personhood of women, the idea that humans shared the image of God, distinguishing them from the created material world. Human life becomes precious because it partakes in the image of God—an argument that comes up again in the debates on abortion and biomedical advances during the 1980s.

While being modeled in the image of God made men and women equally worthy, Carl F. H. Henry, the founding editor of *Christianity Today*, argued that the Pauline record also showed that the divine image was what made humans special, no matter whether they were male or female: "in Galatians 3:29 he [Paul] affirms that in Christ there is neither 'male nor female,' a reminder that Christian realities turn not on gender but on the divine image." Because men and women were both created in God's image, therefore, it was wrong to degrade women. In Henry's words, "his [Paul's] position can hardly be that the male is superior to the female of the species. Not an iota in Paul's writings suggests any sympathy for the prevalent ancient view that women and slaves are inferior creatures."[108] Henry thus identified the opinion that women were inferior as both "ancient" and "prevalent," suggesting that a misogynist image had been passed down through time to haunt contemporary society with false references. This supposedly distorted vision of women was countered in Evangelical magazines throughout the 1970s by the repeated affirmation that both men and women reflected God's image.

There seemed to be a need, while never explicitly stated, for refuting positions that described women as less than human. A first step in the Evangelical renegotiation of gender roles and relations, then, was to affirm women as human beings. For Evangelicals, this went hand in hand with the theological affirmation that women, just as well as men, were created in the image of God. They were not defective men or secondary images of God, but equal counterparts. It seemed to be necessary to establish this point before any discussion remotely concerning women's rights could take place. Some articles—like Sayer's "Are Women Human?"—asked the question deliberately; others repeated the point that women were also made in the image of God almost like a reflex whenever women were discussed. The magazine record of the 1970s shows Evangelicals at pains to affirm the full humanity of women. However, authors were careful to point out, also, that to be created equal did not mean to be created the same. Uncomfortable with feminist notions of gender but concerned for the dignity of women, Evangelicals thus reenvisioned women in explicitly theological terms. Griffith's conclusion might fit here as well: "Both conservative evangelical women and feminists, then, want to see women's cultural and social labor revalued, celebrated, and elevated in status; the basic difference between their images is that they ascribe contrary meanings to the substance of womanhood."[109]

Equal but Different: Gendered Personhood

The obstacle that feminism—and, to a degree, Evangelical feminism—presented for many Evangelicals was that by advocating equality of the sexes, they challenged gender identity. This was poignantly expressed by *Eternity*'s longtime columnist Joseph Bayly in a discussion of "sexist" language in the Bible. Presenting an oversimplified and nostalgic notion of the past, he proclaimed that "up to the present time, men have pretty well known who they were, and women have known who they were." Yet feminists seemed to be "blurring the lines between the sexes," making men and women interchangeable. The breaking down of distinctions between the sexes was often criticized as the "androgynous" feminist ideal. While some scholars have considered this a rhetorical strategy, in the internal discourse in Evangelical magazines it marked a position of concern about identity. Revealing his confusion, Bayly lamented that in the past, "nobody felt the need of unisex or bisexuality."[110] Discussions of gender equality thus conjured up fears of the interchangeability of the sexes and of sexual practices marked as deviant. Clearly, the idea that men and women could fill the same roles had Evangelicals questioning the *nature* of men and women and the purpose of God creating Adam and Eve. If they were essentially the same, why did God bother with creating two different humans in two different ways? Evangelicals pondered the question of whether men and women were essentially the same.

The fear that some strove for the interchangeability of men and women was not completely unwarranted because feminists did use the term "androgyny" regarding gender relations. In Evangelical circles, this terminology was introduced by Virginia Ramey Mollenkott. A professor of English literature, Mollenkott received her BA from Fundamentalist Bob Jones University but adopted progressively more radical perspectives, eventually moving beyond the bounds of Evangelicalism. During the 1970s, Mollenkott understood herself as an Evangelical feminist and was referenced as such in Evangelical magazines.[111] In one article in *Sojourners*, Mollenkott explained what biblical feminists meant when they spoke of androgyny. Criticizing hegemonic male interpretations of the Bible, she argued that "traditionalists tend to fall into unconscious idolatry when they operate on the assumption that the male relates to God directly while the female relates to God through the authority of the male." She rejected the idea that women had to defer to male authority because they were women. Indeed, she challenged common notions of male and female. Interpreting the creation account of Genesis 1:27, Mollenkott agreed that there were sexual distinctions, writing: "Whatever else that may mean [Gen. 1:27], it certainly *must* mean that there is a feminine aspect as well as a masculine aspect in the nature of God."[112] However, she challenged the idea that male and female aspects had to fall neatly in place in male and female bodies. Rather, God embodied male and female aspects (and might embody other unknown aspects), and humans, to a degree, reflected both. Accordingly, she explained that

> when biblical feminists call for psychological androgyny, we are not talking about becoming hermaphrodites or homosexuals, and we are not talking about unisex; we are talking about developing all aspects of God-given male and female personalities, so that each person becomes a unique and unstereotyped harmony of male and female components. Biologically, we remain male and female and relate to each other in that fashion; but we are basically persons, whole beings, made in the image of a God whose being apparently mingles what society has defined as masculine and feminine components.[113]

Mollenkott challenged the idea that biological differences between male and female bodies neatly aligned with distinct male and female traits. Instead, she advocated "psychological androgyny," a view that celebrated personal growth and the development of all talents as a reflection of bearing the image of God, an image that was not limited to sex-specific characteristics. Therefore she also rebutted the notion that mixing male and female characteristics was a sign of homosexuality or hermaphroditism, or that it heralded the end of all sexual distinctions. "Psychological androgyny," according to her, had nothing to do with sexual preferences, with the biological condition where an individual is born with ovarian and testicular tissue, or with the social aspiration of removing sexual distinctions from public life. Yet these fears persisted, and in the mid-1980s conservatives felt their theories confirmed when artists like Boy George and Michael Jackson as well as fashion designers embraced cross-dressing, gay tropes, and unisex styles.[114] Mollenkott's stance that men and women equally exhibited male and female psychological characteristics went well beyond what most Evangelicals were willing to accept.

Wittenburg Door editor Ben Patterson expressed simultaneous confusion and contempt regarding the contemporary gender debate: "We have men and we have women, right? See how different they are. Wrong! Oh, they are 'different'—but only because we have crammed persons with penises into one cultural model and persons with vaginas into another cultural model."[115] Whereas in scientific parlance "sex" came to constitute inborn, or biological, traits, and "gender" came to encompass culturally conditioned traits like behavior, attire, and "roles," Evangelicals did not always accept this logic. Following in the tradition of C. S. Lewis, the preeminent Oxford novelist, some Evangelicals claimed that gender was indeed more concrete than sex. *Christianity Today* in 1973, for example, printed an analysis of C. S. Lewis's view of sexuality by Joan Lloyd, then a senior at Gordon College in Wenham, Massachusetts. Concurring with his point of view, Lloyd quoted from Lewis's *Perelandra*: "Gender is a reality and a more fundamental reality than sex. Sex is, in fact, merely the adaption to organic life of a fundamental polarity which divides all created beings."[116] She thus accepted Lewis's conviction that masculinity and femininity were transcendent realities. While not everyone subscribed to this notion and many did accept the common distinction between sex and gender, many spokespersons preferred to use terms like "function" and "design" either exclusively or alongside the terms "sex" and "gender."

The challenges presented to Evangelicals by feminist thinking were best expressed by Ben Patterson. He claimed: "The axe being ground here is the question of the relative fluidity or rigidity of the sexuality. Should we adopt the more androgynous term 'person' to speak of human beings? Or do we stick with humans as male and female?"[117] Some clearly feared the dissolving of distinctions and blamed all kinds of social ills on it. One example was *Wittenburg Door* contributor Rod Rosenbladt. He complained about "the fouled-up exchange of roles," blaming it for problems in the family and church community, including homosexuality, which was regarded as a sin against God's created order. In his opinion, "the daughters who come from such atmospheres become suicidally promiscuous and controllingly castrating toward men. The sons search for frigid women to marry, and warm accepting women to function as mistresses." In the writer's opinion, the reason for this distortion of family life through sexual deviance was an emotionally repressive atmosphere that permeated Evangelicalism, coupled with taboos surrounding sex and sexuality. His advice was to embrace "the truth that we are created sexual and that this is good." More than sexual beings, humans were, indeed, distinctly different. Rosenbladt urged: "When are we going to start acting as though we believed that God intended to create us male and female?"[118] For Rosenbladt, then, sexual distinctions were basic—it had been God's intention to create two distinct sexes—and distinct roles for men and women needed to be embraced as a remedy against emotional deprivation and sexual deviance.

Against the apparent dissolving of distinctions, Evangelical spokespersons defended a conviction in basic differences between men and women. Nancy B. Barcus, assistant professor of English at Houghton College in Houghton, New York, writing in one of *Eternity*'s special issues on women, argued that the biblical concept of submission illustrated God's design for the sexes: "[the Bible] says there *is* a difference, and that the difference is so recognizable that women, all women . . . , are happy only when they go as far as to do something which the Bible calls 'submit.'"[119] Barcus denied the idea "that there should be *no distinction*" and emphatically affirmed differences between the sexes, claiming that "any woman, married or single, needs to know that besides being a human being (created in the image of God), she is a woman. . . . God made it that way, and it is good." Yet this did not mean that women were inferior. On the contrary, Barcus affirmed: "Yes, they are equal. (We can thank the Bible and women's lib for that understanding.) But women are not *the same* as men."[120] Therefore Barcus acknowledged some accomplishments of the women's movement and thought them in keeping with the Bible. What she rejected was the idea that men and women were interchangeable. She argued, based on a reading of the creation account in Genesis, that God had destined men and women for different "functions:" "Scripture says Eve was made to be a 'help-meet' to Adam, each to supply what the other lacked—but not in the same way." Sexual distinction was a basic division and not something that had been corrupted, as some biblical feminists argued, by sin entering the world: "God put the differences there way back before the fall. That it was there *before* the fall is very important. That means this is how God meant it to be, whether Adam and Eve had sinned or not."[121] Sexual differences were thus basic and essential, and humans would only be happy if they acknowledged this and "submitted" to God's design. This, then, was true freedom: to find oneself fulfilling the function God had created one for. Barcus extolled: "Let us prize our freedom in Christ, and enjoy our God-created differentness. It was a splendid idea!"[122]

The formula that the sexes were "equal but different" was bluntly stated and embraced by Evangelicals across the spectrum.[123] For example, author Rolf E. Aaseng poignantly proclaimed in a contribution for *Christianity Today*: "To say that the sexes are equal is not to say that they are the same. Vive la différence! . . . we don't have to be alike to be equal."[124] In his column, Carl F. H. Henry, former editor of *Christianity Today*, called women and men "identical yet different by creation."[125] *Moody Monthly* assistant editor Zeda Thornton also affirmed that in the Bible "the distinction of the sexes is delineated" and went on to describe just how they were different.[126] *Eternity* columnist Joseph Bayly proclaimed: "Thank God for making women different from men."[127] And as already pointed out, several contributors to the *Eternity* forum on women also emphasized that men and women were essentially different. In the words of Ben Patterson, "our personhood is grounded in our sexuality—the polarity of male and female."[128] Evangelical magazines, also, carried advertisements for study books that promised to "teach boys to be manly for Christ" and to "teach girls to be lovely for Christ," indicating a basic distinction between boys and girls.[129] Evangelicals envisioned sexual distinctions to be intrinsic to human nature and foundational for auspicious human relations. Indeed, Evangelical spokespersons stressed the relational aspect in the dual creation of humanity as male and female.

Better Together

Evangelicals explained the conviction that men and women were simultaneously equal and different with the idea that they reflected different aspects of God. Therefore, taken together, they more closely reflected God's image. Starting with the creation account, *Moody Monthly*'s Winnie Christensen explained: "Man alone was incomplete. So God created woman. . . . She was not made to duplicate the male. . . . They were to work together as a unit fulfilling God's design for their lives."[130] Men and women, in this reading, embodied complementary functions, both in society and in private lives. This attitude went contrary to notions like women's liberation and individual fulfillment. In the Evangelical vision, an individual was by definition deficient, and fulfillment could never be a solitary program. While Evangelicals were at pains to make the single life meaningful, the ideal was the unity of married spouses.[131] Instead of working for male realization or female liberation, then, the goal was to attain complementarity of male and female. The pinnacle of this relation was holy matrimony, in which individuals dissolved into a more perfect union. For Evangelicals, men and women each reflected only one aspect of the divine image and were therefore better together.

The ideal of marriage was highlighted in the idea that Adam and Eve as the prototypical man and woman were made for each other. One example will demonstrate the argument. Thomas Howard, professor of English at Gordon College in Wenham, Massachusetts, published an article in *Christianity Today* in which he responded to the demands of the women's rights movement by describing "the yoke of fatherhood." He countered feminist claims that people should be primarily regarded as "persons"—what he decried as the "androgynous ideal"—with a vision of the "splendid and dual modality of male and female."[132] In scathing language he admonished readers to try to understand the Bible before "we replace it all with our sociology texts." He took up the argument that men and women reflected different aspects of God's image. These two were "made for each other": by uniting they became whole, and "this wholeness turns out to be . . . fruitful." According to Howard, it was God's plan for these two equal but different creatures to unite, both because together they more perfectly reflected God and because together they could conceive children. By invoking a chain of descent from creation to today, he dismissed homosexuality and highlighted the fundamental fact that it took a woman and a man for procreation. Accordingly, "one will want to have this Edenic picture at the bottom of his imagination, in which the Adam and the Eve—me and my wife, now, ten thousand generations later—enact the human mystery in which the image of God, under the dual modality of man and woman, appears in its wholeness." Being a woman or being a man was thus a limitation. But communities needed both aspects, male and female. Marriage was the pinnacle of uniting differences and creating a more perfect whole. It was also a realm where the purpose of differences was testified by biology: "The very biology attests to the theological mystery: I, a man, am made for the other; but not just any other. I am made for the other who is also the image of God, but *not me*." It followed that the very limitation of the sexes was a gift, allowing men and women to offer to each other what the other lacked and therefore complete each other. Sexual union and procreation affirmed not only that it took two but that there were different designs for the sexes, as mothers and fathers: "She was made to be a mother. Her womb awaits the fructifying seed. I was made to be a father. My loins offer that seed to the only matric that will receive and vivify it." Consequently, Howard attested that "it is my appointed gift, or burden, or yoke, to *be* husband and father, precisely because I am a man, it would seem."[133] Men were designed to be husbands and fathers, while women were designed to be wives and mothers. Sexual differences were not only part of the divine order; the language of sexual differences directly illustrated divine order. Jesus Christ was referred to as the bridegroom, while the church was called his bride. Evangelicals, therefore, not only followed a set plan when they married and took on the roles of husband and wife, but also embodied divine order and Jesus Christ's sacrificial love. Living as husbands and wives was thus a form of testimony, one that Evangelical children observed at home: "our vision of Christ and his Church is to be attributed very heavily to what we witnessed of this man and this woman enacting year after year before our eyes the corresponding (not interchangeable) roles of husband and wife."[134] Howard argued that it was good that there were differences between the sexes. As husbands and wives, men and women complemented and completed each other and more perfectly reflected the image of God. Moreover, holy matrimony transcended mundane marriage by representing Christ's relationship to the church.

Difference, for Evangelicals, was a constitutive element in sexual relations. Rolf E. Aaseng, associate editor of the *Lutheran Standard*, explained in *Christianity Today*: "Sexual union between male and female is one means of attaining a part of the completeness that was intended."[135] In an article directed at teenagers in *Moody Monthly*, C. Fred Dickason, chair of the department of theology at Moody Bible Institute, proclaimed that "the plan for sex came from the Creator of sex."[136] And in an interview with the *Wittenburg Door*, Charlie and Martha Shedd, successful authors of Christian self-help literature, declared that a robust sex life was vital for a good, Christian marriage.[137] During the 1960s, in response to liberalizing attitudes toward sex in US culture, Evangelicals had started developing a theology of sex, tackling the subject more frankly than ever before. Starting a whole industry of Christian sex guides and sex education manuals, Evangelical authors proclaimed the univocal message that premarital sex was wrong but that sex within marriage should be joyous.[138] Reflecting on recent Evangelical history, Charlie Shedd feared that "the church has sort of put a shamey-shamey on sex," that was responsible not just for boring sexual practices but for deteriorating marriages. Yet he insisted that "sex is beautiful and from the Lord." Evangelical authors like the Shedds downplayed procreation and emphasized the benefit of mutual sexual satisfaction for Christian marriages.[139] *Christianity Today* dedicated one issue in 1975, displaying the drawing of a double bed on its cover, to the argument that sex within marriage was a pure and beneficial thing.[140] Falling into a time when sex was discovered as a topic for evangelical Christians and self-help books and manuals for this audience were published, Evangelical spokespersons stressed the idea that heterosexual intercourse, based on sexual distinctions between male and female, was stipulated in God's original design for humans.

Evangelical authors agreed that God had intended sexual differences and therefore heterosexual sexual relations.[141] The fact that these might lead to the conception of children was one sign that these relations were good. Sex was indeed the foundation for familial relations. For C. Fred Dickason, this was a basic conviction and constituted a certain order. He wrote: "Our bodies are a gift from the Creator, but sex is more than a bodily function. Sex has to do with differences in personality, with roles in life. It involves the whole spectrum of relationships between people of the opposite sex—masculinity and femininity, leading and following, being a father to a daughter, being a son to a mother, being a husband to a wife, being a grandmother to a grandson."[142]

On the other end of the spectrum, Evangelical feminist Letha Scanzoni stressed the social dimension of marriage, insisting that "no one is really married unless at least one other person knows about it." She therefore defined marriage in this way: "Marriage is the socially permitted cohabitation of male and female."[143] Because Evangelical spokespersons envisioned differences between the sexes to be building blocks in human relationships, merging a man and a woman into a couple and relating all human beings, sexual differences were foundational for social life.

Evangelical spokespersons stressed the point that marriage needed a man and a woman. "God's creatures," according to Rolf E. Aaseng, "are interdependent."[144] Letha Scanzoni wrote: "God made man and woman to complement and supplement one another and to experience in marriage a closeness which in itself may be a reflection of God's image."[145] While C. Fred Dickason believed that there was a divinely implemented hierarchy, he also stressed companionship and completeness as two main reasons why God had instituted marriage.[146] Marriage thus emerged as the most important social institution. A plethora of advice literature existed, counseling couples to "save" their marriage. *Moody Monthly* regularly printed advice columns—like those by the Christensens—and articles with titles like "Things Women Should Know about Men," "Give Your Wife a Happy Husband," "Ten Guidelines for a Happy Marriage," or "What God Says about Remarriage."[147] Carl F. H. Henry summed up the prevailing view in one of his *Christianity Today* columns by calling for "a new theology of marriage—one that ignores neither the importance of sexual commitment and family responsibility nor the importance of the wife's gifts as a career woman alongside her domestic role."[148] For Evangelicals the liberation of women was not an individual's choice or a problem concerning women only. Rather, the question affected communities and therefore needed to be discussed in context with social relations.

Liberated Mothers: Gender Roles between Hierarchy and Equality

The one question that remained was the one most fiercely disputed between the traditionalist and the feminist camps. As the examples of Marabel Morgan's *The Total Woman* and Nancy Hardesty and Letha Scanzoni's *All We're Meant to Be* demonstrate, both the traditionalist and the feminist camps employed the biblical language of submission. However, the former interpreted the concept to constitute a hierarchical order of the sexes, while the latter read into it the mutual servanthood of men and women. Conservative spokespersons tended to favor the order provided by the concept of male headship, while liberal spokespersons tended to favor the justice provided by the concept of mutual submission, findings that concur with studies undertaken in related areas.[149] The debate came to a head especially when it came to the question of how men and women should relate to each other in their private lives as spouses and parents. The language of either traditionalists or feminists was not self-contained but influenced the arguments of the other side; there were even contributions that borrowed from both traditions, mixing arguments. Furthermore, spokespersons, whether they favored hierarchy or equality, agreed that the issue of gender relations should not be viewed in light of a dichotomy of superiority and inferiority. Contrary to what observers usually attest, from the standpoint of Evangelical spokespersons the debate was not about power but about the means of achieving harmonious relations.[150] The magazines' selection of contributions and subsequent discussions resulted in a vision of gender relations that allowed women to embrace both feminist and traditionalist notions—sometimes at the same time.

While Evangelical spokespersons agreed that men and women were equal but different, they disagreed on how these distinctions expressed themselves. Concerning gender relations, the most basic and most immediately affected unit was the married couple and, by extension, the family. At the most extreme, one side argued that God's plan was a hierarchical order that appointed every creature, including men and women, a specific place in God's design with a specific role to play; the other side argued that beyond biological conditions, men and women could play interchangeable roles in society. However, the positions of Evangelical traditionalists and Evangelical feminists were not so far removed from each other as some combatants claimed.[151]

The controversy was heated, yet there was also common ground. Spokespersons by and large agreed that women had legitimate grievances that needed to be addressed.[152] Evangelical spokespersons also agreed that women and men fulfilled different functions as mothers and fathers, and, by extension, as daughters and sons, sisters and brothers, grandmothers and grandfathers, and so on.[153] While there were some, like Virginia Ramey Mollenkott, who believed that sexual differences transcended human bodies and male and female characteristics could be developed in women and men alike, these spokespersons by the 1980s were considered—and considered themselves—to be beyond the Evangelical fold.[154]

In contrast, Letha Scanzoni, whose name became synonymous with Evangelical feminism, embraced a complementarian view of the sexes that emphasized the different-but-equal formula. Her discussion of the creation account did not sound so different from that of traditionalist writers like *Moody Monthly*'s Winnie Christensen. Scanzoni read the biblical creation account in the following way: "God gave woman to man to be his counterpart, his 'other half' in a very real sense—like him in spirit, though different in body, and perfectly suited for the partnership God intended husband and wife to experience together in the presence of Him who gave them to each other."[155] Christensen's take on the same text read as follows: "Man was created first; woman was made for man. And the man is head of his wife. Because God places man in authority does not mean that woman is less than man. Just as you wouldn't try to place two riders side by side up front on a horse, the Lord doesn't give a family two heads."[156]

Both writers pointed out that according to the biblical account, woman was made for man. Curiously, Scanzoni, the feminist, emphasized that these two complemented each other, while Christensen, the traditionalist, emphasized that they were equal. The two writers came to different conclusions about what the particularity of creation meant for life. Whereas Scanzoni stressed the partnership, Christensen stressed the aspect of order. In one account, complementary partners strove for an egalitarian relationship, while in the other account equal partners submitted to a hierarchical order. The controversy between Evangelical feminists and Evangelical traditionalists, accordingly, was about principles of order. Could life be negotiated democratically, or did order presuppose that the final decision was delegated to a representative, a *primus inter pares*?

Conservative spokespersons argued that sexual differences logically implied a hierarchy of different roles for men and women. This meant prescriptions not only for women but also for men. In February 1973, *Moody Monthly* published two complementary articles by Evangelical author William L. Coleman, titled "How to Be a Huggable Husband" and "How to Be a Wonderful Wife." The drawings accompanying the articles showed (1) a woman with flying skirt throwing herself at a man in a suit, and (2) a woman modeling her apron, while in the background a man sat in a recliner reading a paper. The message was that when people were fulfilling their roles as husbands and wives, their spouses were content. The proper husband got a hug; the proper wife got a happy husband (figure 3.4). The author urged men to consider the following three questions before they proposed marriage to a woman: "1. Do I promise to love her real good? 2. Do I promise to lead her, not drive her? 3. Do I promise to leave everything else but God in second place?"[157] Women, on the other hand, were encouraged not to be misled by the feminist movement but to hold on to the following "rights": "1. Protect your right to be beautiful.... 2. Protect your right to be a woman.... 3. Protect your right to be a mother." The gist of the articles was that it was masculine to be a leader and that a woman should be feminine. Femininity was first and foremost defined as not male: "If God made you a woman, why would you ever stoop to be a man?" It was further defined by physical beauty and the biological ability to become a mother. While this sounds patriarchal, certain elements indicate a more complex vision. Most importantly, the husband was described not as a sovereign ruler but as someone who loved and guided. Furthermore, the author assured readers that the essential difference between the sexes was not "superior" and "inferior," but "feminine" and "masculine." His was an argument for God-created order: the key passage for the proper order of relationships was Proverbs 31 ("The Wife of Noble Character"), and the key term was "submission." This meant, according to Coleman, that God had appointed "husbands as the heads of families," and wives were to acknowledge the man's "authority in the home."[158] While Coleman insisted that men and women were equal, he nonetheless emphasized a hierarchy within marriage. The wife was to "yield" to her husband, love and respect him—even if she was a "valedictorian" and he was "an academic dummy"—avoid gossip, "know what to wear" and how to make herself beautiful, and be "meek."[159] The point of the articles was that men were not *natural* leaders, and women were not inferior by *nature*. Indeed, men had to work hard to lead successfully, and women had to make a conscious effort to follow their husband's lead. By nature, they were equal—women could be just as intelligent, or even smarter, than men. Yet the Bible set forth a certain hierarchy to which all humans had to yield. For the sake of order, men were to lead and women to follow. Coleman thus adopted a theology of created order, yet he took great pains to assure readers that the woman's was by no means an inferior position.

That roles and hierarchical relations were not natural and did not come easy was attested to by the amount of advice literature aimed at making men successful husbands and women successful wives. *Moody Monthly* regularly printed such articles. The December 1975 issue as well as the January 1976 issue, for example, carried special sections for men. George Sweeting, president of Moody Bible Institute and editor in chief of *Moody Monthly*, wrote an article advising men to "give your wife a happy husband." His argument was that the husband and father needed to be the leader of the household because the tone he set was decisive for his whole family. Sweeting painted a traditionalist picture of family life with a strong, breadwinning husband. He was to be the "provider," and it was his "privilege to protect, and if need be, to suffer for his bride." The man represented his family in society (and, if they went wrong, he was punished on their behalf).[160] More than that, though,

Figure 3.4. Illustrations accompanying William L. Coleman, "How to Be a Huggable Husband" and "How to Be a Wonderful Wife," in *Moody Monthly*, February 1973. Courtesy of Buswell Library Special Collections, Wheaton College, Illinois.

he also represented God to his family: he was to be "the priest of his home," and he was to "lead in spiritual matters" because "the husband and father is God's deputy invested to carry out God's government in the home." This, according to Sweeting, meant not arbitrary power over family members, but self-sacrificing love. Indeed, a "man sins if he neglects his family. His wife and children should not be forced to compete with the newspaper or television for attention." Being a husband and father was a "big job" with lots of responsibilities, and it was vitally important for men to take the job seriously for the well-being of the family.[161] This point was driven home in a contribution by Gordon MacDonald, a pastor and author, who called husbands and fathers "pacesetters." Using the biblical examples of Mordecai and Eli, MacDonald demonstrated the divergent outcomes of a having a successful leader for a father versus a father who failed to exercise leadership over his sons. According to the account in the Book of Esther, Mordecai had adopted his cousin Esther and raised her well. She became King Ahasuerus's wife. Eli, on the other hand, failed as a father. Eli was a high priest of Shiloh, but his sons, Hophni and Phinehas, were spoiled and defiled the sanctuary of the temple. Because Eli failed to punish them, God punished him and his family (1 Sam.). MacDonald thus admonished fathers to exercise foresight and leadership. Moreover, elsewhere, he identified these traits as characterizing the "effective father."[162] While some texts seemed to indicate that men and women had *naturally* different inclinations, advice literature exposed role differences and gender hierarchies as ideals. The authors of these articles assumed that men had to be taught to be leaders.[163] These are examples of the traditionalist vision. They prescribed a hierarchical order of the sexes but described it not as natural but rather as a God-given design that, if followed, proved beneficial to individual men and women as well as society.

Whereas traditionalists insisted that God intended a hierarchical order that made men leaders at home, feminists demurred, arguing that an egalitarian vision was in keeping with the Bible. Letha Scanzoni advocated marriage as a mutually beneficial partnership: "they [husband and wife] can work together for *mutual profit* rather than going in separate directions out of self-interests. A tremendous sense of colleagueship can be built up in a truly egalitarian marriage." Echoing secular feminist sentiments, she saw traditional roles as restrictive for both women and men. She complained that a "woman's occupational choices have either been limited to one option only (homemaking) or else have been circumscribed by the expectation that any job will be considered secondary to family interest." Accordingly, women were severely restricted in their personal development. But men also suffered from this arrangement. They were not given "the option of *not* working," and it was none too easy for them to take off time for a new baby or a sick child. She considered restrictive norms to be culturally constructed, not biblically prescribed. She pointed to the biblical example of Priscilla and Aquila, a missionary couple traveling with the apostle Paul, as a model for Christian couples to share their lives and ministry.[164] Because of biblical examples like this—Paul acknowledged their work (Rom. 16:3-4) and therefore seemed to approve of egalitarian marriage—Scanzoni and other feminists believed that Paul's expression that the husband was the "head" of the wife had been misinterpreted by adherents of patriarchal and traditionalist persuasion.

When Berkeley and Alvera Mickelsen, he a professor of the New Testament and she an assistant professor of journalism, discussed the passages where Paul talked about man's "headship" (1 Cor. 11:3 and Eph. 5:23) in one of their Bible study groups, they found that the translator had prescribed a patriarchal view by the choice of words.[165] In an article for *Christianity Today*, the Mickelsens reported that they had intended to discuss Paul's use of the term "head," only to find that in the study Bible the group was using the passage had been translated to read: "the husband is supreme over his wife." They lamented that in this instance, "male dominance" had "tarnished our translation," seriously impeding their ability to grapple with what the Bible had to say on "the strategically important issue of men-women relationships."[166] The term "head" seemed problematic enough. Nancy Hardesty complained that many "read into the words an inequality," yet she insisted that the passage implied not "a one-way street but a reciprocal relationship." She compared Paul's notion of headship to the example of Jesus Christ. According to her, people submitted to him not because he forced them to but because he loved them so much. Similarly, the husband was asked to love his wife.[167] The passage, in her reading, purported a mutual relationship. Other readings stressed the body metaphor, explaining that Paul had not intended a hierarchy but had meant to express the idea that women and men in marriage became different parts of the same "body," or unit: the Mickelsens, for example, were convinced that "'head' is used in a head-body metaphor to show the unity of husband and wife and of Christ and the church."[168] For Evangelical feminists the idea of "headship" was a metaphor that emphasized the symbiosis of wife and husband.

While traditionalist positions could be recognized by the emphasis on order and the feminist position by the emphasis on mutuality, many articles about the woman's role were concerned with neither. In an instance of wordplay on feminist demands, one female contributor to *Christianity Today* defended the right of "Liberated Mothers" as the right of women to feel liberated as mothers and homemakers. While she allowed that if a woman was so inclined and had time to spare, she could work outside the house, she insisted: "there is one job for which wives and mothers are uniquely qualified. By making our homes heavens for our husbands, our children, and those around [us] in need, we can serve Christ in a way that is ours alone."¹⁶⁹ Echoing the language of liberation but evoking a different sentiment, *Moody Monthly*'s assistant editor Zeda Thornton encouraged women to "dare to be liberated." Thornton agreed with those who called for women's rights that women should be able to develop their talents. Indeed, women were to "glorify God" by using all the "gifts" God had bestowed on them, and the claim that they were too busy with housework was no excuse. It was a woman's duty to develop her full potential, not only for her own sake but the sake of her family: "The woman who is knowledgeable and confident as well as gracious and loving will be a pride to her husband and children. Her happiness and fulfillment as a person, a wife and a mother will spill over and add the warmth and joy that every Christian home should have."¹⁷⁰

Both accounts borrowed language from the liberation movement and subscribed to the idea of liberation and self-fulfillment. They claimed the right for women to develop their talents, framing that right as, moreover, a God-given duty. Yet the authors applied these notions to the traditional roles of motherhood and homemaking. They insisted that it was possible to be both liberated and maternal, and indeed to be liberated *as* mother. Both the *Christianity Today* article and the *Moody Monthly* article illustrate the creative power of Evangelicals to envision women at the same time as liberated and traditional.

Notions of order and mutuality became secondary in discussions affirming women's rights as "liberated" wives and mothers. Both spokespersons who emphasized the notion of order and those who emphasized the notion of mutuality could embrace the concept. Carl F. H. Henry, in one of his columns, proposed that women who felt called to be mothers could open their families to provide assistance for working mothers: "Can it be that Christian women who delight in homemaking as a divine calling can fill a role also as godparents to the children of others who are divinely gifted and burdened to pursue a career alongside motherhood?"¹⁷¹ Henry, who in another column defended "the order that God intends between man and woman in the home and in the church," thus accepted that God might lead some women to dedicate their lives to their families, and others to seek occupations outside the home.¹⁷² On the other end of the spectrum was Evangelical feminist Renee J. Hermanson, who, in *Daughters of Sarah*, proclaimed that she finally felt liberated when "this night I was happy to leave the men to their talk while I did my own thinking over the dishwater."¹⁷³ In her eyes, it was a sign of liberation that she could embrace doing housewifely chores without becoming defensive about it or feeling insecure about her status. In biblical imagery (Luke 10:38–42), women could be both Martha, the woman who cooked for Jesus and his disciples, and Mary, the woman who sat at Jesus's feet and listen to his teaching—and they were liberated because it was their choice to be either or both women, depending on the circumstance.[174]

The discussion about gender in Evangelical magazines in the 1970s revolved around questions of order. Evangelical spokespersons wondered whether the most basic unit of society—the married couple—should be organized in an egalitarian or hierarchical manner. Evangelicals believed that men and women had different but equally important strengths. However, they drew different conclusions from this conviction. Feminists, on the one hand, believed that men and women complemented each other and should therefore make decisions together, as equal partners. Traditionalists, on the other hand, concluded that because men and women complemented each other, one needed to lead and the other needed to follow. Because the man and woman were of equal value—and in most cases, neither was a natural-born leader—God had instituted an order. These two positions revealed not so much a different attitude toward women (even though personal biases might have played a role, as a different outlook on humanity and social order. The feminists generally had a positive view of humanity and believed that Christians could come to mutual conclusions, making a chain of command superfluous. In contrast, the traditionalists had a negative view of humanity and believed that a hierarchical order with clearly defined roles for all individuals, however arbitrary, was necessary to prevent chaos. Beyond these differences in outlook, however, Evangelical spokespersons agreed that women should be liberated. But their vision of what liberation meant differed from secular expectations. As Nancy B. Barcus pointed out, the secular notion of liberation "isn't freedom," as Evangelicals understood it.[175] In Evangelical discourse, liberation came to take on the meaning of the freedom to submit to God and thus realize one's true destiny. Regarding women's roles, this could mean either the liberation of wives and mothers or the liberation as wives and mothers—Evangelical women could realize themselves either in the role of Martha or Mary.

Conclusion: Women and Submission

The Evangelical vision that developed in magazines during the 1970s depicted women as liberated wives and mothers. In this context, terms like "submission" came to carry complex connotations. When employed by traditionalists, submission implied a hierarchical gender order, and when employed by feminists it implied egalitarian decision-making. Whereas spokespersons who ascribed to one view rejected the other, the fact that eminent Evangelical spokespersons could be found in either camp made both of them legitimate Evangelical views. Moreover, both camps agreed on the centrality of the Bible and understood freedom as submission to the will of God. Liberation, accordingly, was not an individualistic project or something that released one from community bonds and obligations. On the contrary, freedom could be realized by becoming a servant of God and embracing the role and relations God had destined one for. Evangelicals across the board agreed that God had designed women to become wives and mothers, and men to become husbands and fathers. By accepting their assigned places, people would experience fulfillment. Liberation was to embrace one's God-ordained purpose and become who God destined one to be. Whereas spokespersons for the traditionalist or the feminist position differed in their opinion how gender roles were to be practically arranged in society, other spokespersons embraced the idea that women could be Marthas as well as Marys. Depending on the preference of a particular woman, or depending on her inclination given a particular situation, she could choose to realize herself as a homemaker, catering to her husband and family; or she could choose to develop her talents as a disciple of Christ and serve society by embracing a career.

Submission in an Evangelical context carried all these connotations— liberation as servanthood to God, service to fellow humans, individual realization through submission to His purpose and design, as well as a God-ordained order, either hierarchical or egalitarian. This explains why "ordinary" evangelical Christians interviewed by sociologist Christian Smith in the 1990s could simultaneously be in favor of women's liberation and traditional roles, and embrace hierarchical and egalitarian notions of decision making. Smith concluded that a statement like "marriage should be an equal partnership involving mutual submission between husbands and wives in all things" would have been just as likely to have been signed by "ordinary" evangelical Christians as the *Baptist Faith and Message Statement*, which requested women to "submit herself graciously" to her husband and asked him to "provide for, protect, and lead his family."[176] Evangelical convictions about gender roles were renegotiated during the 1970s, resulting in the rejection of patriarchal views. Both feminist and traditionalist views constituted new attitudes that allowed for female agency. As R. Marie Griffith found, women who adhered to the traditionalist view could also feel "empowered."[177] The fact that conservative Evangelical women could *choose* to submit to a family arrangement that placed them below the man in the hierarchy meant that they could feel liberated because they embraced their God-given role. Accordingly, notions of liberation and emancipation informed conservative Evangelical thinking, albeit in different ways than envisioned by secular feminists. The findings of this chapter concur with Gallagher's conclusion that "explicitly feminist perspectives remain marginalized within evangelicalism because gender persists as a central, salient and effective element of the boundary work that maintains evangelical subculture and identity."[178] Both traditionalist and feminists accepted the idea that God had created men and women as equal yet different beings, and that men and women, in their family roles and relations, had different functions. This served to distinguish Evangelical views on gender relations, and therefore Evangelicals as a community, from US American society.

However, I take issue with Gallagher's claim that Evangelical renegotiations of gender roles and relations did not result in changes of the concept of headship. Gallagher asked: "given the influence of second wave feminism on gender norms within American culture, and given the availability of a discourse of mutuality and partnership within evangelical subculture, and given the pragmatic egalitarianism of most ordinary evangelicals, the question remains: why have the ideals advocated by evangelical feminists thus far failed to transform the culture of husband's headship among American evangelicals?"[179]

My analysis shows that "headship" went through a transformation when Evangelical spokespersons across the board rejected the idea that men were superior to women or that they were naturally better leaders. Rather, Evangelical traditionalists developed the idea that a man was the nominal head of the household, destined to be *primus inter pares*, a leader not by nature but through training, installed in this position by God not because he was better suited or more deserving but because there needed to be some kind of order.

In the 1970s, language of submission, previously used to explain women's inferiority, changed to become a positive marker of willing and in some cases mutual servanthood. At the end of the decade, the notion of submission and the biblical exegesis of passages connected with the term, was no longer used to prove women's inferiority. Rather, men and women were attributed equal value because they were equally created in God's image. Being created specifically as male or female, men and women were also essentially different, making them complementary creatures. Magazine contributors shared the vision that men and women completed each other; ideally they paired off and constituted life-long, dedicated units as a married couple. In the ideal marriage, the spouses were subsumed into one unity, making a discussion about headship and submission superfluous. But in a fallen world, frictions remained and problems had to be negotiated. In this case, the Evangelical debate on gender relations in the 1970s created a dual vision that validated both the idea that spouses were to submit to each other and the idea of headship or, in other words, the demand that wives submitted to their husbands. As Christian Smith's study demonstrated, Evangelicals in the 1990s drew on both argumentations in their daily decision-making.[180] Evangelical magazines thus helped to shape the language and acceptable views on gender relations. Drawing on feminist and traditionalist ideas, the vision of submission as a positive concept of biblical servanthood granting agency to all parties bridged disparate positions.

Yet the concept of family was increasingly embattled, not least because of changing roles of men and women in society, and the changing political atmosphere in the US. Historian Mary Ryan found that "whatever way the political winds blew, and there would be a decided shift to the right [in the 1980s], the deeply rooted changes in the meaning of male and female that surfaced in the 1960s and 1970s would not be easily reversed."[181] Women had become a fixture in the social and political arena, entering the work force, and lobbying for various concerns.

These changes prompted President Jimmy Carter, during his election campaign, to promise a White House conference dedicated to the concerns of the contemporary family. He made good on his promise in 1980. The title of the conference was changed to White House Conference on *Families* (WHCF) [my emphasis] because, so it was argued, there were multiple forms of families. This, however, enraged conservatives who saw the "traditional" family under attack. The WHCF—three conferences in Baltimore, Minneapolis, and Los Angeles during the summer of 1980—was used by activists as a platform to promote either the still pending Equal Rights Amendment or opposition against abortion.[182] The debacle surrounding the WHCF was one more crisis in Carter's Presidency, precluding his reelection and it attested to the heated controversy surrounding family issues in society at large.

Moreover, as historian Leo Ribuffo notes, "family policy became an ideal vehicle for the new Christian right to ride into the political mainstream."[183] The New Christian Right came to be a shrill voice in favor of so-called traditional family values. Continuing the gender controversy, these conservative Christians made family the focus of their political activism. Eithne Johnson has identified the transmission of traditionalist arguments into the setting of the New Christian Right as the "Dobson discourse." Analyzing the advice literature for women that James Dobson, of the New Christian Right organization Focus on the Family, published, she asserted: "Rooted in conservative Christian beliefs, the Dobson discourse is fundamentally devoted to framing gender identities and their proper relationships in a hierarchical pattern: God is to man as man is to woman as woman is to child."[184] During the 1980s, then, the controversy shifted away from women to center on children. Considered a conservative decade, the 1980s were characterized by the presidency of Ronald Reagan and the political activism of the New Christian Right. Even though abortion had been legalized with the *Roe v. Wade* decision in 1973, it was only in conjunction with the emergence of the New Christian Right in the 1980s that antiabortion activism became a broad phenomenon, no longer confined to Catholics. It predominated the discussion of family throughout the decade, until, in the early 1990s, antiabortion activism escalated into extremism and violence with a series of terrorist attacks, starting with the murder of Dr. David Gunn in Pensacola, Florida, in March 1993.

The Evangelical debates on abortion and new biomedical advances during the 1980s echoed some of the arguments about women in the 1970s. Deliberating the questions of when human life started and what made it sacred, Evangelical spokespersons drew heavily on the vision of personhood—the idea that all humans share aspects of the image of God. The notion of personhood prompted Evangelical spokespersons to adopt a pro-life stance that was not only opposed to abortion but also encompassed the plight of the living and the fatally ill. But scientific advances muddied the waters, complicating definitions of human life and pitting the inviolability of life against the imperative to heal.

PART II
The 1980s

4
The 1980s
An Overview

CITIZENSHIP, MORALITY, AND POLITICS

In the 1970s, Evangelicals, especially those of politically and socially liberal persuasion, were politically active. At the close of the decade, Evangelical spokespersons expected this trend to continue. Exemplary was an assessment in *Eternity* by author Russell T. Hitt in early 1980. Hitt pointed out that social concern had long been on the Evangelical agenda, especially for such politically liberal groups as Evangelicals for Social Action. Yet he knew that relief efforts were not confined to sympathizers of *Sojourners* and the *Other Side*. He also cited World Vision as the biggest relief agency and pointed out that the National Association of Evangelicals (NAE), too, had comparable agencies, for example World Relief. He believed that such efforts, generally from the Evangelical Left, would continue in the 1980s.[1] When *Christianity Today* reported on the New Christian Right, it tended to include references to the political activities of the Evangelical Left as well. In November 1979, for example, *Christianity Today* printed a lengthy news account on the New Christian Right. An information box was inserted into the article informing readers how Evangelicals for Social Action, described as "a small group of moderate-to-liberal Christians," started "stacking sandbags against the conservative flood."[2] And in September 1980, just six weeks before the presidential election (November 4), *Christianity Today* editorialized on "getting God's kingdom into politics" by pointing at examples from both the Moral Majority and Evangelicals for Social Action.[3] The next few pages were given over to an essay on biblical principles for political action, written by staffers of Evangelicals for Social Action.[4] Accordingly, political engagement was conceivable as a liberal or conservative undertaking (neither side had a monopoly on it). Furthermore, Evangelical magazines allowed that any one of the major presidential candidates was a legitimate choice for Evangelicals. This showed that the New Christian Right did not have a monopoly on religiously inspired political lobbying, and that self-identified Evangelicals did not ascribe to a homogeneous political viewpoint. Indeed, spokespersons envisioned Evangelicalism as a politically heterogeneous community.

During the 1980 election season, *Eternity* printed an article that compiled the personal views of Evangelical leaders on how they planned to vote and what their thoughts on religion and politics were. None of the ten people showed particular enthusiasm for any one candidate, and some were still undecided on whom to vote for, but there were voices in favor of every candidate—the current president, Jimmy Carter, a Democrat; former California governor Ronald Reagan, a Republican; and former congressman John B. Anderson, an independent.[5] A month later, *Moody Monthly* published an article entitled "Why Vote?" It was a lukewarm plea for political engagement, arguing that even though Christians could be assured that God's plan would be fulfilled independent of human activity, Christians had a duty to further God's work on Earth, and part of that was fulfilling their civic duty of voting.[6] A general Evangelical disinterest in current politics and choice of candidates was expressed in a cartoon published in *Christianity Today*. Satirizing the deterioration of conversion politics, as described in chapter 2, the artist depicted a man being polled at his doorstep (figure 4.1). The caption under the drawing gave the man's answer as follows: "As an evangelical, who would I like to vote for this November? Has Dick Nixon shown any signs of repenting?" The *Other Side*'s John F. Alexander went even further by proclaiming that he was going to vote for Donald Duck—arguing that it was important to exercise the right to vote but also to register one's discontent with the available choices.[7] In the last *Christianity Today* issue before the election, Carl F. H. Henry pointed out that "by remarkable coincidence, all three presidential candidates claim to be evangelical Christians." He used this example to refute the idea that there was one clearly discernible Christian position in politics. He also rejected being born again as a litmus test for political office. He chided clergymen who endorsed candidates and criticized the political agenda of the New Christian Right as too narrow.[8] Instead of advocating for or against one particular candidate, Henry advised readers to inform themselves and vote for whomever they considered politically and morally best qualified for the presidency.[9] The idea that political qualifications should be the hallmark for the office of president was echoed by Stephen V. Monsma. The former science professor and Michigan state senator wrote an article in *Eternity*, providing information on what Christians should pay attention to when voting. A test of faith was not on the list. Rather, presidential candidates, according to Monsma, should exhibit "personal morality," "proper attitudes," "expert knowledge," and "political skills."[10] Spokespersons thus ideally envisioned Evangelicals as informed and politically mature citizens who did not let themselves be co-opted by the

Figure 4.1. "As an evangelical, who would I like to vote for in November? Has Dick Nixon shown any signs of repenting?" John Lawing, cartoon, in *Christianity Today*, July 18, 1980. Courtesy of Buswell Library Special Collections, Wheaton College, Illinois.

New Christian Right but rather exercised political rights according to their own faith-based convictions.

While before the election, magazines might have been careful of their words for the purpose of unbiased campaign reporting, immediately after the election there was no discernible enthusiasm for Ronald Reagan either. Accordingly, the title of a *Christianity Today* editorial on Reagan's election—"Just Because Reagan Has Won . . ."—did not read like an endorsement. As if in response to unrecorded claims, the editorialist wrote that "Ronald Reagan is President-elect of all Americans, not just evangelicals. He gained that office by the votes of a majority of American people, not just of evangelicals. And not all evangelicals voted for Mr. Reagan." The author thus cautioned that neither would Reagan be the Evangelicals' president, nor would he be a president for the Evangelicals. The *Christianity Today* editorial credited the New Christian Right with helping get Reagan elected and lauded its members for their general effort of registering Christians to vote. This praise, though, was conditional: insisting that evangelical Christians were a "minority in a pluralistic society," the editorialist warned New Christian Right leaders and activists against "triumphalism." Concluding that Reagan was not the ultimate solution to all problems, the editorialist debunked some of the more audacious hopes proclaimed by the New Christian Right: "Reagan will not bring the millennium to America, nor will he restore an imaginary golden age of an earlier day." In this vein, he also warned that "certainly they [the New Christian Right leaders] need to make plain they are not seeking a theocratic kingdom or a return to the Massachusetts Bay Colony of three centuries ago." Rather than celebrating Reagan's election, the editorial welcomed the new religious interest in politics and admonished readers not to let this opportunity pass them by. Criticizing the narrow focus of the New Christian Right—as well as its misguided criteria for evaluating the fitness of officeholders—the editorialist called for a holistic Evangelical approach to politics.[11]

John F. Alexander of the *Other Side* pointed out that the Reagan victory was not so great, after all: "In this election 52 percent either stayed at home or voted for third-party candidates. In this right-wing landslide," Alexander ridiculed, "Reagan got the support of a grand total of 26 percent of the potential voters. And a good many of those were not voting for Reagan but against Carter."[12] At a time when New Christian Right leaders were congratulating themselves for getting Reagan elected—and national media followed suit by reporting on the influence of this supposedly massive new voting bloc—evaluations like Alexander's, while cynical, turned out to be more accurate.[13] Historian Patrick Allitt sums up the backlash against Carter that prompted conservative Christians to support Reagan: "The sexual revolution, feminism, legalized abortion, easily accessible pornography, the homosexual rights movement, church-state separation, high rates of violent crime, and declining standards of public and political morality—all these things they interpreted as signs of a national moral crisis, which they believed Carter had done too little to oppose."[14]

Protest against Carter, in combination with low voter turnout and votes for third-party candidates, was one explanation why Reagan had won the election, and some Evangelical spokespersons used it as an argument in their attempt to distance themselves from being co-opted by the New Christian Right or the so-called Reagan Revolution. These examples show that Evangelical spokespersons were reluctant to be uniformly associated with conservative politics and sought to retain an independent identity.

Whether or not Evangelical spokespersons agreed with or welcomed the activism of the New Christian Right and the election of Ronald Reagan, their arrival signaled the beginning of a politically conservative period. Stating it negatively, Russell T. Hitt, in *Eternity*, noted drily and with an eye on the machinations of the New Christian Right: "As the hour approaches when Ronald Reagan will be inaugurated as the nation's fortieth President, there is no question that we have come to the end of a liberal era."[15] This was the situation with which Evangelicals subsequently had to contend. While they welcomed many aspects of the politically conservative turnabout, Evangelical spokespersons demarcated a border between conservative politics and conservative religion, envisioning the Evangelical community as a distinct entity.

Throughout the Reagan years, spokespersons in Evangelical magazines maintained a critical distance. Yet they acknowledged that Reagan found the right choice of words to appeal to Evangelicals. According to one account of Reagan's 1983 speech to the NAE, "whether one agrees with Ronald Reagan's politics and policies, the typical Christian would not disagree with him that 'the rule of law under God' undergirds much of the stability of the nation."[16] Reagan succeeded in adopting Evangelical language and thus in appealing to this constituency; he helped make religious matters part of the political debate. During the 1984 election campaign, *Christianity Today* reporter Beth Spring recounted that "Reagan's moral vision, his determination to translate rhetoric into legislative offices, and his unabashed courting of conservative Christians . . . , have all worked to turn the matter of church and state into an incendiary campaign issue this fall."[17]

While this made Reagan popular with many Evangelicals, Spring reported that it was a mistake to consider Evangelicals a homogeneous voting bloc. Yet when he was reelected, a writer for *Christianity Today* also admitted that "Evangelicals have helped elect a president they overwhelmingly favored."[18] Thus, while spokespersons emphasized Evangelicalism as a separate religious community, many Evangelicals came to support Reagan politically.

Reagan's presidency came to denote an important era in Evangelical historiography. In 1988, articles and even cover stories in Evangelical magazines retrospectively evaluated the Reagan Revolution. *Christianity Today*, for example, ran a cover illustration with Reagan astride an elephant and the slogan "Sizing Up the Reagan Revolution," and *Moody Monthly* similarly featured a cover illustration with Reagan atop a horse and the question "After Reagan: What's Left for the Religious Right?" (figures 4.2 and 4.3).[19] This singular effort to appraise the president attested to his significance for Evangelicals. By this time, Evangelical magazines were regularly and seriously reporting on political developments, providing readers with enough information to form their own opinions. Indeed, there were critical assessments of President Reagan and his achievements. For example, Charles W. Colson, in his column in *Christianity Today*, reflected on the evening of Election Day 1980, when Reagan was named as winner and Christians became enthusiastic about politics. He cited one commentator with the words, "Welcome to the Great Awakening of 1980." However, Colson lamented, despite Reagan's pious promises, many of the problems Evangelicals were concerned with, like abortion, school prayer, and the national deficit, had not been resolved under his

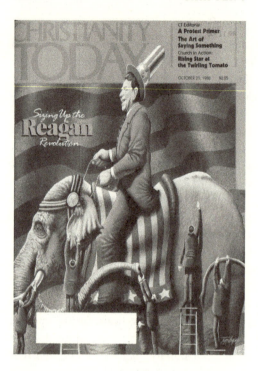

Figure 4.2. "Sizing Up the Reagan Revolution." Cover of *Christianity Today*. October 21, 1988. Courtesy of Buswell Library Special Collections, Wheaton College, Illinois.

aegis: "Now, nearly eight years later, the sun is setting on the Reagan years—and the hopes of once-euphoric evangelicals as well. Despite unprecedented access to the Oval Office, most items on the evangelical social agenda have been either defeated or shelved."[20] Even while paying tribute to Reagan, Colson introduced a note of criticism. He thus marked the Evangelical position as one apart from Reagan's politics, from where it was possible to assess his achievements critically.

To gain perspective on the Reagan years, *Moody Monthly* and *Christianity Today* both opened their pages to forums of commentators, inviting both insiders and outsiders to their own respective readership circles to evaluate this era. Whereas *Moody Monthly* printed commentaries by three spokespersons generally associated with the Evangelical Left and one spokesperson from the New Christian Right, *Christianity Today* invited five nationally renowned cultural commentators of various religious backgrounds to assess the situation.[21] These reviews revealed a professional approach to politics, inviting critical assessment and heterogeneous opinions as enriching rather than threatening to the Evangelical community and their self-understanding. But they also fulfilled the purpose of celebrating a new political savvy among politically active conservative believers. Despite their heterogeneous backgrounds, the commentators generally agreed that during the Reagan era religious voices had

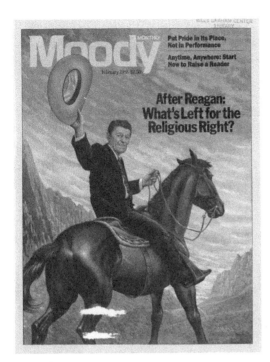

Figure 4.3. "After Reagan: What's Left for the Religious Right?" Cover of *Moody Monthly*, February 1988. Courtesy of Buswell Library Special Collections, Wheaton College, Illinois.

gained hearing in politics and that political rhetoric had accommodated religious sensibilities publicly.

Not surprisingly, Tim LaHaye, a former spokesperson for Moral Majority and founder of the American Coalition for Traditional Values, was mostly positive about the achievements of the New Christian Right. Not mentioning Reagan at all, he lauded New Christian Right activists for mobilizing conservative Christians, yet admitted that "we could not turn the country around quickly."[22] All other commentators, whether non-Evangelical or Evangelical Left, agreed with this point, arguing that the biggest achievements of the New Christian Right were symbolic rather than concrete. Evangelical Vernon C. Grounds credited the New Christian Right with having "revealed the need and legitimacy of evangelical political involvement."[23] Evangelicals Richard V. Pierard and Jim Wallis generally agreed but sounded a note of warning, fearing that Christians let themselves be used by politicians.[24] Joseph Sobran, a syndicated national columnist and an editor of *National Review* magazine, emphasized that religion had arrived again as a player in national politics: "Reagan has used the bully pulpit of the presidency to reinforce the legitimacy of political participation by religious people. As a result, even their enemies no longer deny their right to play the game."[25] Similarly, Robert Coles, professor of psychiatry and medical humanities at Harvard Medical School, while skeptical about the actual achievement of politically active Christians during the Reagan years, welcomed the "religiously suggestive rhetoric" as "a nice feeling, given some of the agnostic, secular idolatries we have to endure constantly."[26] Most poignantly, Martin E. Marty, professor at the University of Chicago and senior editor of the liberal Protestant *Christian Century*, declared that "the Reagan Revolution in religion leaves America feeling different, talking different, and acting pretty much as it did before."[27] These assessments supported the Evangelical vision that religious voices in politics were important. They also supported the conclusion that the Reagan Revolution had largely succeeded in integrating religious voices into politics but had not changed the political game.

In their cover stories, *Moody Monthly* assessed the Reagan era and the New Christian Right, and *Christianity Today* assessed the Reagan era and the relationship between religion and politics. Writing for *Christianity Today*, David Aikman, a veteran *Time* magazine correspondent, voiced disappointment about the Reagan years and the lack of results. According to him, "the hopes of many conservative Christians that the Reagan administration would see the implementation of a pro-evangelical agenda of social issues have obviously not been borne out."[28] He partially blamed Moral Majority and other New Christian Right organizations, which had less of a following than initially thought and deterred many by their shrill rhetoric. Elwood McQuaid, an instructor at Moody Bible Institute and *Moody Monthly* contributing editor, came to a similar conclusion. He observed that "clear-cut accomplishments from the 10-year tryst with conservative politics seem few and far between."[29] All in all, Evangelical spokespersons throughout the Reagan years retained a minimal critical distance from Reagan and the New Christian Right, acknowledging the allure but never completely endorsing either. They carefully described Evangelicals as a religious community that welcomed many initiatives of the New Christian Right and the Reagan administration, but could not be conflated with either.

Social Concern

One issue dear to the New Christian Right was the fight against abortion. During the 1980s—which were bookended by the 1980 White House Conference on Families (WHCF), which provided antiabortion activists with a national stage, and the 1992 election of Bill Clinton to the presidency, which shelved hopes for a ban on abortion—the battle over abortion became more inflamed, marked in particular by a rise in antiabortion terrorism.[30] It also provided a pivotal impetus for Evangelical spokespersons to think through the issues of childbirth and life.[31] While single-issue pro-life activists were often accused of not caring for the life of the mother or the life of the child once it was born, spokespersons in Evangelical magazines saw the pro-life stance as part of a larger concern for humanity. Similarly to debates about the role of women in the 1970s, Evangelical spokespersons tackled the issue of abortion by asking whether embryos were human. Taking up theological discussion of humanity, which distinguished between "the human *constitution*, that is, what uniquely marks human nature, and the human *condition*, that is, the actual life of humanity," Evangelical spokespersons embedded the abortion question in a debate about the sanctity of life.[32] Arguing that human life, imbued with the image of God, was holy, they also reasoned that it was worth protecting, nurturing, and healing. Evangelical spokespersons developed a notion of responsibility for life, based on a vision of "being partners with God in the mystery of procreation."[33] Also similarly to the debate about women, they stressed the interrelatedness of human life in the context of the abortion issue. Distinguishing themselves from single-issue antiabortion activists, Evangelical spokespersons analyzed abortion within the societal context in which it happened. They focused not only on the crime against the unborn but on the effects of abortion on mothers, fathers, the family, and society. They envisioned a society in which all humans were cared for and abortions became unnecessary. The value of children was emphasized in the vision that Christians constituted a new family: through conversion humans became children of God and siblings of Jesus Christ and one another. Being pro-life became a marker for the high esteem of God's creation—which became complicated in the context of new biomedical developments.

While a public discussion on genetics arguably became virulent only in 1996 with the case of Dolly, the cloned sheep, genetic medicine and new reproductive technologies like in vitro fertilization and prenatal genetic diagnosis became available during the late 1970s.[34] During the 1980s, they prompted an Evangelical debate about the beginning and end of human life and the ways that biomedical advances convoluted what it meant to sustain and heal human life. These debates were more than an extension of the abortion debate. I argue that the issues of abortion, genetic research, and new reproductive technologies were but visible examples of a larger Evangelical discourse on what constituted human life and what made it precious. An analysis of the debate surrounding issues of abortion, new reproductive technologies, and biomedical developments within Evangelical magazines reveals an Evangelical vision of the sanctity of life in which children function as a symbol for life itself and an integral part of the human and divine family.

VISIONS

During the 1980s, Evangelical spokespersons were preoccupied with questions of morality. The New Christian Right entered the scene, embracing both conservative politics and conservative religion and thus offering a compelling form of morality politics. Evangelical magazine editors and authors endeavored to dissect the politics and issues of the New Christian Right for their readers. The New Christian Right both served as an Other against which Evangelical spokespersons, especially historians, defined Evangelicalism, and became a religiopolitical pacesetter and instigator for new ideas. While Evangelical spokespersons were at pains to differentiate simple slogans promoted by the New Christian Right, they also concurred with many of its leaders' analyses. Accordingly, Evangelicalism and the New Christian Right drew slowly nearer and, in the minds of many observers, converged.

Evangelical spokespersons engaged the ideal of a Christian America put forth by the New Christian Right. While the myth proved attractive, Evangelicals carefully showed that there was no historical basis for it. Furthermore, they distanced themselves from any theocratic aspirations. Instead they formulated a citizenship ideal that postulated Evangelicals as both good Christians and good Americans. They envisioned themselves as mature citizens, participating in politics and making good use of their democratic rights, including the freedom of religion.

During the 1980s, Evangelical spokespersons were preoccupied with questions about the meaning of human life, prompted by antiabortion activism and new biomedical possibilities. Building on the notion of *imago dei*, the image of God, they emphasized that every individual life was sacred. At the same time, because they believed in the triune God, they stressed the interrelatedness of all human life. The vision of the sanctity of life congealed in the image of the innocent child that was both precious in itself and a symbol for humanity at large.

5
Christian America
The Era of the New Christian Right and the Reagan Revolution

The June/July 1980 cover of the *Wittenburg Door* shows a group of five men raising a US flag (figure 5.1). At least two men, dressed in clerical collar and robe, one of them holding a Bible, can be identified as religious officials. The features of the man in front resemble those of James Robison of the Religious Roundtable but might have been intended to resemble Tim LaHaye, another New Christian Right leader, interviewed within the pages of the magazine. The drawing was obviously modeled on the historical photograph of the raising of the flag on Iwo Jima, or the war memorial of the same at Arlington National Cemetery in Washington, DC. By citing this famous and widely known image, the magazine depicted the New Christian Right activists as war heroes defending their country's freedom, revealing in satirical manner the inflated perception of importance some activists had of themselves and their cause. At the turn of the decade, the New Christian Right arrived on the scene with a bang and the message that Christian morality was the last thing that propped up an otherwise corrupt country. Notions of a long-lost, original, intended, or future Christian America permeated the discourse, a promise to some and a source of dread to others.

The emergence of religiously inspired conservative political lobbying was cause for Evangelical spokespersons to reexamine their beliefs on the proper relationship of religion and politics. Whereas a young and outspoken Evangelical Left during the 1970s gave the impression that Evangelicalism might well be a socially and politically liberal phenomenon, during the 1980s a boisterous Christian Right emerged and clamored for media attention.[1] Observers, confounded by these conservative religious activists, suddenly detected an enormous evangelical voting bloc. Because some confused the political lobbyists with the religious constituencies from which they recruited, inflated numbers about the might of New Christian Right organizations like the Moral Majority circulated.[2] A Gallup poll in summer 1982 somewhat corrected the picture with the finding that few people had heard of the Moral

Figure 5.1. Christian Right activists drawn in a pose resembling the raising of the flag on Iwo Jima. Cover of *Wittenburg Door*, June/July 1980. Courtesy of Buswell Library Special Collections, Wheaton College, Illinois.

Majority, and even fewer liked it.³ Subsequently, media accounts oscillated between portraying the New Christian Right as a small and extreme movement and rediscovering it as the orchestrator of a massive voting bloc.⁴ Not only did observers have a hard time differentiating between religious ministries and religiously inspired political organizations (especially when figures like Jerry Falwell simultaneously headed both), they also often conflated the different types of conservative Christians within political coalitions. Pollsters conflated the numbers by defining evangelicals as white Christian Americans. The New Christian Right adopted many of the concerns dear to Evangelicals, and since the fact that it had begun to found institutions suggested that it was here to stay, Evangelical magazines needed to evaluate its propositions and find a proper stance on the new Christian lobbyists. The initial appraisal in Evangelical magazines was not necessarily favorable, but the positions of the New Christian Right would take up regular space in their pages.

Jerry Falwell, pastor of the Thomas Road Baptist Church in Lynchburg, Virginia, and head of the Moral Majority (est. 1979), became one of the most prominent figures of the New Christian Right.⁵ In an interview with *Eternity* in 1980, he justified his political involvement: "Back in the sixties I was criticizing pastors who were taking time out of their pulpit to involve themselves in the Civil Rights Movement or any other political venture. I said you're wasting your time from what you're called to do. Now I find myself doing the same thing and for the same reasons they did."[6]

Reckoning with his apolitical past and adversarial stance toward the civil rights movement, Falwell now struggled to legitimize Christian political activism. Falwell's turnabout is emblematic of the New Christian Right. In an interview with the *Wittenburg Door*, Moral Majority spokesperson Cal Thomas summarized the goals of the organization in four slogans: "pro-life, pro-traditional family, pro-morality and pro-America."[7] Evangelical magazines shared many of these concerns but remained critical of the new movement. While in Evangelical magazines space was dedicated to introducing the goals and spokespersons of the New Christian Right, it was regarded as an external phenomenon that could be welcomed or rejected but that needed to be critically assessed.

Discontent with society was not new: Evangelicals had observed with concern the countercultural upheavals of the 1960s and had been disillusioned with government after the Watergate scandal of the 1970s. At the outset of the 1980s, the New Christian Right drew on this history, portraying the United States in stark terminology as a country that had lost its path. The historian and Evangelical spokesperson Mark A. Noll summarized its motivation: "Part of the animus behind evangelical political mobilization is the deep conviction that the United States was once a Christian country that in the fairly recent past has been hijacked by secularists in a great conspiracy to negate that historical reality."[8] In nostalgic yearnings, New Christian Right leaders conjured up an idealized past and plan for the future—a Christian America. This vision proved attractive to conservative believers from all sorts of Christian backgrounds, and Evangelicals in particular were recruited to the New Christian Right's political agenda. Exemplary is the story of Francis A. Schaeffer, who started out as a separatist Fundamentalist, became a prominent Evangelical figure and the inspiration for intellectually engaged Evangelicals during the 1970s, and, during his last years, the 1980s, sympathized with and was a spokesperson for the New Christian Right.[9] The notion of Christian America introduced by New Christian Right activists proved attractive, but Evangelical magazines were initially wary. Employing up-and-coming historians George M. Marsden and Mark A. Noll, Evangelical magazines challenged the freewheeling versions of Christian America but eventually adopted a subdued version of the vision.

A plethora of articles in Evangelical magazines assessed whether the United States ever was a Christian country, in what regard one could speak of Christian America (and whether it was even desirable to do so), and what was the Christian's role as a citizen.[10] They used historical and legal arguments, decried the moral crisis, and rallied in defense of religious freedom. While personal attitudes toward the New Christian Right varied, Evangelical spokespersons generally agreed that a Christian theocracy never existed nor should exist in the United States.[11] Rather, spokespersons defended the concept of constitutional democracy and a pluralistic society as the best conditions for the freedom of religion and therefore for a true and uncoerced expression of faith. They critically engaged the New Christian Right's vision of a Christian America and appropriated it. In their discourse, Christian America came to connote a country undergirded by and favorable to Christian ideas, with laws that prevented government from interfering with religion and that allowed for the free expression and exercise of that religion. In arguing that this was the best environment for fostering "true" evangelical Christianity, Evangelical spokespersons could be patriotic and embrace notions of a Christian America. Evangelical spokespersons developed their ideas of Evangelical political involvement into a vision of Christian citizenship.

Crisis for Christians in America

Evangelical spokespersons did not unconditionally embrace the New Christian Right when it first formed, but neither did they agree with recent societal transformations. They shared the feeling that the United States was in a state of crisis. *Christianity Today* dedicated its January 4, 1980, issue to looking back on the 1970s and looking forward to the 1980s.[12] In their contributions, both Carl F. H. Henry and Billy Graham spoke of a contemporary crisis. Henry concluded that "Evangelicals have failed to penetrate the public mood and conscience," and Graham reported that "many feel only a miracle will prevent a serious crisis."[13] Societal change was leading away from treasured traditions and values. *Moody Monthly*'s George Sweeting judged: "The key to a nation's greatness is the combined character of all its people. Unfortunately, our combined character is not good." In his opinion, the present situation called for "a spiritual awakening."[14] Many Evangelical spokespersons shared the fear that the wrong people were shaping the overall mood and outlook of US society. The Evangelical Left was concerned with issues like world hunger, poverty, the arms race, war, and the threat of nuclear bombs. Conservative Evangelical spokespersons were preoccupied with the legalization of abortion, which they considered murder, and gay rights, which they considered a perversion, as well as issues like gambling, pornography, and the substitution of science for religion in schools. A *Christianity Today* cartoon summed up this divide, claiming that "social issues" were associated with the Democrats (or the Left), and "moral issues" were associated with the Republicans (or the Right).[15] All these issues were of general concern to Evangelicals across the spectrum, but the Left and the Right set different priorities, as can be seen from the frequency with which topics were discussed in different

Evangelical periodicals and the choice of topics that made it onto the cover. Carl F. H. Henry summed up the different emphases when he complained that "*Sojourners* [formerly known as *Post-American*], whose point of view reflects a minority of the evangelical constituency, . . . almost never speaks on abortion, promotes military disarmament, and tends to blame America for the ills of the world. . . . *Christianity Today*, the established evangelical voice, on the other hand . . . , did not even probe the two questions—military disarmament and nuclear power. . . . *Eternity* magazine tried to rise above evangelical divergence by a series of panel discussions . . . , but with qualified success."[16] Evangelical spokespersons counted a plethora of grievances yet were divided on the question of which wrong was the worst and needed attention first.

Evangelical spokespersons agreed that the dismal situation had been caused by an erosion of values. One writer in *Christianity Today*, for example, spoke of a "values crisis," lamenting that "we can no longer assume a consensus on basic beliefs and values."[17] This destruction of common foundations led to a dangerous moral relativism. Without a shared ethical code, the common good would be destroyed and egotistical self-interest would rule. Joseph Bayly, in *Eternity*, linked the erosion of values to the fall of nations, arguing that "Rome fell while moralists slept," and likening the historical example to the present-day United States.[18] *Christianity Today*'s editor Kenneth S. Kantzer went so far as to ask for the reaffirmation of some American civil religion to save the nation. Agreeing that civil religion among Evangelicals was generally understood as "blatant idolatry," he revived the term to describe the "cement that holds a nation together," leaning on what he saw as a sociological definition according to scholars like Émile Durkheim.[19] These descriptions illustrate how dire the situation was in the minds of Evangelical spokespersons. Doom was imminent if a moral consensus could not be restored.

The pervasive feeling among these spokespersons was that the traditional Christian values that once sustained society were now eroding and were sometimes consciously erased. They perceived a direct connection between the loss of religious values and the loss of freedom. Kantzer editorialized that "for the health of the nation, it is imperative that we do not seek to dam up these spiritual forces," because if religious expression was curtailed, religious freedom was endangered, and soon all other freedoms were at risk.[20] Some at *Moody Monthly* felt that the process was already far advanced, and in 1982 the magazine printed a three-part series on the loss of religious freedoms. The magazine's Washington correspondent Martin Mawyer recounted long lists of grievances endured by churches, church officials, and individual believers: churches' and church-run institutions' tax-exempt status being revoked by the IRS, church-run schools being closed because of building code violations, laypeople being imprisoned for public witnessing, students being forbidden to pray in school. The collage of petty and major incidents that he assembled added up to an atmosphere inimical to Christianity.[21]

Evangelical spokespersons appreciated the forays that religious activists made into politics and welcomed the reintroduction of moral themes and a moral tone into politics. While many Evangelicals supported President Ronald Reagan, Evangelical magazines kept a critical distance from the activists of the New Christian Right, reiterating that Evangelicals were not to be co-opted by political actors.

New Christian Right

Martin E. Marty—a Lutheran, a renowned scholar of religion, and the liberal editor of the mainline Protestant flagship magazine *Christian Century*—might be credited for inadvertently popularizing the label New Christian Right. In winter 1979, he had been approached by the *Saturday Review* to write an article about the phenomenon of conservative religious politics worldwide. Marty's article, "Fundamentalism Reborn: Faith and Fanaticism," was published in May 1980, just when information was being sought about domestic organizations that blended politics and religion.[22] A follow-up that contextualized the US Christian phenomenon was printed in July in *Context* and reprinted approvingly in the Evangelical *Wittenburg Door*. Marty considered the phenomenon in terms of a renewed Fundamentalism, yet he also referred to it as a "new Christian right wing."[23] When *Newsweek* put Jerry Falwell on its September 1980 cover and printed an article on "born-again politics," it identified and started to refer to the movement as a "new Christian right," a term that it attributed to Marty.[24] Yet this label was and is by no means the obvious choice. A news article in *Christianity Today* spoke of "new Christian lobbies," an opinion piece in *Moody Monthly* labeled the phenomenon a "new Christian crusade," and in one article, Richard John Neuhaus, the eminent Lutheran pastor and author, used Moral Majority, the name of Jerry Falwell's organization, to refer to the whole movement.[25] Activists themselves often stressed that they counted supporters of various religious backgrounds among their ranks and accordingly preferred the term Religious Right as a label.[26] Even though some conservative Jews aligned themselves with this movement and activists learned to speak of "our Judeo-Christian tradition," it remained a predominantly Christian affair.[27] Accordingly, Religious Right and New Christian Right came to be used interchangeably to refer to a loose coalition of lobbying organizations and activists that aimed at mobilizing conservative believers for political goals.[28]

The one face most often associated with the New Christian Right was that of Jerry Falwell, who identified himself and was recognized by other Christians as a Fundamentalist.[29] While the lines between conservative Protestant movements were blurry at best, Fundamentalists appeared to be outside the Evangelical fold at the beginning of the 1980s. Some spokespersons used the apparent differences between Evangelicals and Fundamentalists to distance Evangelicals from the New Christian Right. Evangelical scholars emphasized the Fundamentalism-Evangelicalism controversy in their historiography. Corwin E. Smidt, for example, pointed out that Evangelicals and Fundamentalists differed on various political issues.[30] Some Evangelicals were suspicious of the New Christian Right precisely because of its Fundamentalist leaders. This was exacerbated by Jerry Falwell's choice to stress Fundamentalism rather than some ecumenical spirit in the title of his 1981 book *The Fundamentalist Phenomenon*, prompting the *Wittenburg Door* to dedicate one issue to Fundamentalism so as to explain this movement to its readers.[31] Even though people would identify as one or the other, the line between Evangelicalism and Fundamentalism was not clearly demarcated. Inconveniently, the label Fundamentalism could be either worn as a badge of honor or applied to demean someone else. This point was vividly illustrated by Evangelical historian George M. Marsden. Asked by the *Wittenburg Door* to define Fundamentalism, he replied:

> Generally, people use the term fundamentalism to refer to someone who is religiously to the right of wherever they happen to be. People think that someone like myself from Calvin College is a fundamentalist. But at Calvin College, you won't find anyone who is willing to admit that he/she is a fundamentalist. They believe the real fundamentalists are at Wheaton College. But at Wheaton College they believe the fundamentalists are all at Moody Bible Institute. Go to Moody Bible Institute and they believe all the fundamentalists are at Bob Jones University. And when you get to Bob Jones University they say, "Yes, we are fundamentalists and you'd better believe it."[32]

This explanation highlights the complexities involved in identifying Fundamentalists and reveals the Evangelical aversion to Fundamentalism, which was treated as something just beyond the realm of comfort.

That the Evangelical intelligentsia was slightly uncomfortable with Fundamentalism also had biographical reasons. At the beginning of the twentieth century, Fundamentalism was the main expression of evangelical Christianity, and many of those who later called themselves Evangelical grew up in Fundamentalist households. In the *Wittenburg Door* a whole slate of Evangelical luminaries recounted their Fundamentalist upbringings.[33] According to their own historiography, Evangelicals separated from Fundamentalism, but not on account of theology and doctrine. Rather, in the words of Smidt, "they were critical of their fundamentalist brethren on at least three points: 1) they objected to the anti-intellectualism which they viewed to be associated with fundamentalism; 2) they rejected the total otherworldliness concern which they believed characterized fundamentalism; and 3) they rejected the extreme ecclesiastical separation frequently practiced by fundamentalists."[34]

While distinctions appeared to be mostly of an emotional nature as people identified with one or the other, suspicions between the two strands of conservative Protestantism continued. These suspicions accounted for some of the Evangelical wariness of the New Christian Right. Cal Thomas, in an interview with the *Wittenburg Door*, found it necessary to emphasize that "the Moral Majority is not, as you always see mentioned in the papers, a rightwing, fundamentalist Christian organization." Nonetheless, the interviewers inquired: "Are you a fundamentalist?" and "Is Jerry Falwell a fundamentalist?" Thomas affirmed that they were Fundamentalists but insisted that Fundamentalism was not characterized by "polyester suits, white socks, know-nothingism, anti-intellectualism and a whole host of other baggage," leaving the reader with exactly this cliché in mind.[35]

The *Wittenburg Door*, while making clear that its editors disagreed with the approach and many of the positions of the New Christian Right, opened its pages to Tim LaHaye, a spokesperson for the Moral Majority, so he could depict the goals of his organization and fellow activists. LaHaye stated his conviction that the United States was currently ruled by godless liberals actively endeavoring to make immorality the law of the land: "We have been led to Sodom and Gomorrah by a hardcore group of committed humanists who set out over a hundred years ago to control the masses." He also expounded the inspiration for the name Moral Majority, stating that "we believe we represent the overwhelming majority of the American people. More importantly, we represent the minimum moral desires of the majority of the people."[36] The *Door* interviewers were confounded by some things LaHaye passed off as Christian consensus. When LaHaye affirmed the suspicion that he would rather vote for a guy who had accepted a bribe of $25,000, like Florida Republican Richard Kelly, than for a professing Christian with a clean record who did not vote against abortion, like Illinois Democrat Paul Simon, the interviewer exclaimed: "You can't be serious." LaHaye retorted: "I'm dead serious."[37]

However, as little as the Evangelical Left liked the New Christian Right, they disliked the political Left just as strongly. Richard John Neuhaus, in an article in *Christianity Today*, for example, exclaimed: "If our only choice is between the militant fundamentalism of Moral Majority and the militant secularism of the American Civil Liberties Union (ACLU), the outlook is not encouraging."[38] Ben Patterson, the editor of the *Wittenburg Door*, conceived of the New Christian Right and its secular foes in terms of a John Wayne movie: "There is a symbiotic relationship between John Wayne and the outlaw. Neither exists without the other. Absolute Evil calls forth Absolute Good in this Manichean system. Enter the Humanist/liberals; behold the Moral Majority."[39] Accordingly, spokespersons located toward the left of the Evangelical spectrum acknowledged that the emergence of the New Christian Right had been provoked by a similarly radical secular force, a specter that they labeled "secular humanism."[40] They considered the New Christian Right and secular humanism to be two sides of the same coin, one presupposing the other. In this regard, they generally agreed with the analysis of the New Christian Right that the political Left was bringing about evil. Yet far from embracing the swaggering heroics and noisome rhetoric of the New Christian Right, the Evangelical Left was weary of the coalition and its proclaimed absolutes. Rather than siding with one against the other, spokespersons felt that both sides needed dismantling. Said Patterson: "We need government to protect us from [feminist] Betty Friedan and from Jerry Falwell."[41]

Despite a long tradition of political involvement and recent forays into politics during the Nixon, Ford, and Carter administrations, a weariness as to the wisdom of political involvement remained.[42] Indicative was the reaction of readers to an opinion piece on the New Christian Right in *Moody Monthly*. In the article, Ted Miller, a journalist from Wheaton, Illinois, asked whether Evangelicals should join "the new Christian crusade." Careful not to condemn political involvement per se, Miller argued that the primary focus for Evangelicals should be religion, not politics. He was also critical of the idea that there was always a clearly discernable Christian position on political issues and that Christians should be united in their political goals.[43] The letters to the editors about this piece ranged from the opinion that Christians should not involve themselves in politics to an outspoken approval of the new political activism. Seven letters were printed. One Warren Wiersbe simply stated that he agreed with Miller, while Tom Friez took the opposite position, exclaiming, "let's join the 'Christian Crusade.'" Of the remaining five letters, two argued against political involvement, and three welcomed it. While one side counseled that the work of Christians was within the church and political involvement would "weaken" this work or waste energies on "unprofitable confrontations," the other side saw Christianity and morality under attack by hostile forces and argued that it was "time to take a stand." Most interesting were two long letters, one seemingly agreeing and one disagreeing with Miller: both, despite their opposing perspectives, essentially argued for individual political engagement, like voting, but counseled against being co-opted by politics.[44] This sample shows that conservative Evangelicals were skeptical of political activism that went beyond basic involvement like voting.

Surveys from the time indicate that conservative Christians were generally opposed to religious officials' political activism.⁴⁵ This view was expressed, for example, in a *Moody Monthly* column entitled From Pastor to Pastor. Erwin Lutzer, the senior pastor of Moody Memorial Church in Chicago, pointed out that "some fundamentalist preachers have jumped into the political arena with both feet." While he affirmed that "Americans are entitled to work through the political process to effect change," he nonetheless was "troubled when I see ministers speak out on matters that would better be left to the politicians." He feared that political issues would be confused with biblical ones and that Christians would be led to substitute the political transformation for a spiritual one. Also, by Evangelicals' joining forces with unbelievers, the biblical message might be diluted.⁴⁶ Implicitly, Lutzer accused politically active pastors of getting their priorities wrong. He reminded readers that "our message is not a political agenda but the full biblical mandate of submission to the will of God." It was not the Evangelicals' duty to resolve political wrongs; it was their job to work for the salvation of people and the nation through the church. Lutzer resolved: "If our problems were political, a political solution would be all that is needed. But if they are spiritual, they must be addressed from that vantage point."⁴⁷ At the beginning of the 1980s, thus, some Evangelicals were unconvinced about the wisdom of joining politics; some, while advocating voting, were weary of active political involvement; and some spoke out against the political activity of pastors.

At the time that the New Christian Right emerged, Evangelical spokespersons regarded it as a force external to their own community. Although the progressive wing of the Evangelical spectrum advocated political involvement, the conservative wing was somewhat skeptical of it. Yet conservatives were more likely to agree with the overall positions of the New Christian Right than were liberal Evangelicals. Initially, the approach toward the New Christian Right, therefore, was one of critical observance.

The Turn Right and the Reagan Revolution

The New Christian Right and the Reagan Revolution are often seen in conjunction. Throughout the 1980 presidential campaign and right after the election, media reports largely credited Ronald Reagan's success to the mobilization efforts of New Christian Right leaders and activists.⁴⁸ Some were surprised by the relationship between Reagan and conservative believers. As historian H. W. Brands points out, "Reagan was possibly the least pious of America's postwar Presidents, which made it ironic—his opponents called it hypocritical—that he leaned so heavily on supporters for whom religion was the most important thing in life."⁴⁹ Yet the New Christian Right clearly favored Reagan. His Dallas appearance before a group of conservative Christians in August 1980 has become legendary. Invited by James Robison of the New Christian Right organization Religious Roundtable, Reagan told the gathering of approximately fifteen thousand people: "I know you can't endorse me, but I want you to know that I endorse you and what you are doing." Observing that "Reagan had the hearts and the votes, if not the formal endorsement, of the new religious right," Bruce Buursma, in his report for *Christianity Today*, spoke of the event, tongue in cheek, as "a 'non-partisan' stump" for Reagan.[50] Accordingly, even though the New Christian Right organizations were officially nonpartisan, it was an open secret that leaders and activists were working toward Reagan's election. While Reagan's victory was sometimes celebrated as an Evangelical success, not all Evangelicals were on board with the New Christian Right, conservative politics, or Reagan. As early as April 1976, *Sojourners* published an article revealing "an alarming political initiative by the evangelical far right," pointing at the outpouring of religio-patriotic writing prompted by the bicentennial celebrations.[51] Also, Ben Patterson, in his editorial in the *Wittenburg Door*, took issue with Jerry Falwell for insinuating that in this election there was only one choice for conservative Christians. Patterson wrote that if Falwell was not so convinced of himself, "perhaps then the significance of the fact that all three major presidential contenders claim to be born again Christians, would not be lost on him."[52] Whereas it was expected that spokespersons of the Evangelical Left, like those writing for *Sojourners* and the *Wittenburg Door*, would be critical of conservative politics, the record of Evangelical magazines shows that support for Reagan and the New Christian Right agenda was by no means obvious or inevitable.

The Christian as Citizen

The increasing prominence of the New Christian Right at the beginning of the 1980s prompted scholars to analyze the political orientation of conservative Christians. Sociologists asserted that religion continued to play a decisive role in political orientation and voting behavior but that the denominational tradition and heritage played a diminishing role.[53] Writing in 1991, James Davison Hunter described this trend as "culture wars," detecting a society split into the two camps of orthodox believers and progressives.[54] While his thesis has since been questioned, it highlighted two general developments: that political allegiances formed between believers from different religious backgrounds; and that conservative religion had come to be associated with conservative politics, just like liberal religion had with liberal politics.[55] This trend, however, was complicated by studies focusing on the convictions of small groups and individual believers. Sociologist Irene Taviss Thomson, in a 2010 revision of the culture war thesis, argued that while the image of the culture wars persists, "American public opinion is considerably more ambivalent and internally inconsistent."[56] Self-identified Evangelicals generally welcomed the turn to conservative politics but maintained the stance that Evangelicals were politically heterogeneous. Furthermore, Evangelicals fought the subordination of their political approach to the politics of the New Christian Right. Indeed, Evangelical spokespersons developed a vision of Evangelical politics that decisively differed from that of the New Christian Right.

The emergence of the New Christian Right confounded many observers who feared that religiously inspired politics were intolerant.[57] While *Newsweek* in September 1980 reported that there was opposition to the New Christian Right, not only from the political Left but also from conservative Christians, the election of President Reagan fired the fear of the new political players.[58] When Jerry Falwell and the Moral Majority, after the election, put on a celebratory display complete with flag-waving and a marching band on the steps of the New Jersey State House, the *New York Times* reported that the spectacle reminded the writer of "the beginning of Fascism back in the 1930s."[59] Sociologist Sara Diamond surmises the prevailing feeling, defining the New Christian Right as "a political movement rooted in a rich evangelical subculture, one that offers participants both the means and the motivation to try to take dominion over secular society."[60] While conflations of the New Christian Right and evangelical Christianity were common, some studies sought to distinguish them and examined the relation of religious and political convictions. Noting that reactions to the New Christian Right in general had been "strongly negative," James Davison Hunter, in a study published in 1984, investigated the political orientation of evangelical Christians. Using the term "evangelical" to refer to conservative Protestants, he asked whether this group was a threat to democratic values and tolerance. He insisted that conservative Christians had to be differentiated from the New Christian Right, but he nonetheless found that in general, this group was politically more conservative than the average US population. He also acknowledged that evangelical Christians, especially the elites, were pushing for a hearing of religion in the public square and argued that "in this sense, Evangelicals, at least by what they say, do violate dominant cultural (though not legal) norms concerning the role of religion in the public sphere." He studied survey findings concerning the positions of the coming generation, focusing on students at Christian colleges and seminaries, concluding that "it would appear that Evangelicals in general, but the coming generation particularly, are firmly committed to the liberal traditions of social and political tolerance."[61] He summarized that conservative moral positions helped distinguish and identify religious communities—providing "a sense of social solidarity, moral unity, and ideological cohesiveness," but that the behavior of people in these communities matched that of average Americans, showing that they "embraced the ethic of civility," findings since then reiterated by sociologists like Alan Wolfe and Christian Smith.[62] To self-identified Evangelical spokespersons, the activists of the New Christian Right were newcomers to political activism. While they lauded the energy that activists invested into lobbying for themes dear to religious conservatives, they chided these activists for their oversimplified views and disregard for facts. To Evangelical spokespersons, the New Christian Right provided a foil against which they could define their own vision of religious politics. In this vision, Evangelicals were mature and savvy political participants, Christian citizens.

The Search for Christian America

Moody Monthly opened its pages early to guest contributions from New Christian Right writers. In summer 1981, an article by John W. Whitehead summarized the argument of his forthcoming book, *The Second American Revolution*.[63] Whitehead, an attorney and New Christian Right activist who in 1982 would found the Rutherford Institute to provide legal counsel in defense of religious freedom, understood the present situation as characterized by a reinterpretation and ultimate perversion of constitutional rights by liberals, especially in the courts. This required a "second American revolution." In a mixture of historical and legal interpretation, Whitehead argued that the United States was founded on a "Christian base," built on Christian principles that were essential to its composition. Separation of church and state was to be understood as a separation of the institutions, preventing the state from dictating the one legitimate expression of Christianity by establishing a state church. The original meaning of pluralism was therefore the freedom to practice different styles of confessing Christianity. Only liberal reinterpretations had given it a new meaning, enforcing tolerance of unacceptable worldviews: "The Christian community, however, should denounce pluralism when it is used to justify non-Christian or inhumane acts. There is truth and there is non-truth; there is good and evil. Christianity is truth." Since anything non-Christian must be false, according to this point of view, it was not only permissible but necessary to fight the "secularization of America." In conclusion, he wrote: "We need to repel the secularization process by recalling that American history is on the Christian's side."[64] In other words, according to this New Christian Right writer, a proper interpretation of history would prove that America was historically and intentionally a Christian nation and that it was the duty of Christians to restore the nation to its Christian base.

By tracing the Protestant quest for a Christian America, church historian Robert T. Handy showed that the idea was not new. Focusing on denominational history since colonial days, he argued that Protestantism, while not the official religion, was the established American faith, encouraging spokespersons to envision the coalescence of state and religion. However, according to his study, Protestantism became disestablished during the early twentieth century, giving way to de facto religious pluralism, and ending Protestant aspirations of turning America into a Christian nation. In the last chapter of the second edition of his book, printed in 1984, Handy focused on the contemporary scene and found that a "new crusade to make America a Christian nation had not only been launched but had gathered considerable political cloud."[65] Handy speculated that this new crusade would differ decisively from older quests because it originated outside denominational structures and was not supported by the denominations. Furthermore, he pointed out that conservative believers, too, took issue with the new movement, which they denied "represent[ed] 'biblical morality.'" According to Handy, the new crusaders had to reckon with religious pluralism, separating religion from morality to be successful.[66]

Studies of the New Christian Right stress that its politics were moralistic and not, for example, economic.[67] However, Handy's observation that the New Christian Right had to renounce the right to speak in the name of any particular faith community has been largely obscured. Indeed, a popularization of the term "evangelical" has led to the conflation of the political activism of the New Christian Right with a diffuse evangelical Christianity. Clyde Wilcox has pointed out that "media accounts frequently equate the Christian Right with all born-again Christians, and these stories greatly exaggerate its strength." In reality, Wilcox continues, "some white evangelicals oppose the Christian Right, many are neutral to the movement, and a much smaller number are active members."[68] Indeed, while the vision of a Christian America had a particular allure, Evangelical spokespersons tried to distance themselves from ideas of the New Christian Right and define their own version of Christian America.

While most Evangelical writers would not follow New Christian Right argumentations like Whitehead's in detail, the idea of a Christian America proved popular.[69] The feeling that there was a moral crisis was pervasive, and the vision of Christian America seemed to provide an antidote. Richard John Neuhaus, for example, was disillusioned with the lack of moral leadership in US society. He believed that "the leadership of mainline Protestantism has abdicated that culture-forming responsibility," making way for a secular worldview. While not wholly welcoming of the New Christian Right, Neuhaus considered it the answer to and replacement of "the 200-year hegemony of the secular Enlightenment in Western culture." Despite his disregard for New Christian Right leaders like Jerry Falwell, he nonetheless agreed with them that "the puzzling thing is not that some people still talk about Christian America, but that talk about Christian America is thought to be un-

American." He insisted "that America was as Christian as it was a republic was self-evident throughout most of our history."[70] *Christianity Today*'s chief editor, Kenneth S. Kantzer, agreed with the assessment that the substitution of man-made measures for God-given truths was a problem. Yet he was not ready to blindly subscribe to the notion of a Christian America, writing, in the same issue as Neuhaus, that "whether or not America was ever in any legitimate sense a Christian nation is open to debate."[71] Debates soon ensued in Evangelical magazines about precisely this question.

Because the New Christian Right blended ideological and historical argumentations, Evangelical magazines printed articles investigating US history and assessing the manner in which it was appropriate to speak of a Christian America. The Evangelical intelligentsia, which fought for academic recognition of Evangelical scholarship, was embarrassed by some of the undifferentiated, sweeping historical claims of New Christian Right activists. Evangelical historians felt a special duty to set the record straight—to correct the glaring misappropriations of historical argumentation without necessarily opposing the general gist of the argumentation. Well-established scholars like Mark A. Noll, Nathan O. Hatch, and George M. Marsden not only published for an academic audience but also wrote pieces for general Evangelical consumption in Evangelical periodicals. Also, Noll and Hatch were listed as contributing editors to *Christianity Today* from September 2, 1983, into at least the 1990s.[72] They provided significant historical material for a discussion of Christian America within the Evangelical community.

Marsden was especially concerned with what he once referred to as the "Politicization of Francis Schaeffer & Co." He approached Stephen Board of *Eternity* for the publication of a so-titled article. He saw Francis A. Schaeffer's 1981 *A Christian Manifesto* as one of a triad in conjunction with his son Franky Schaeffer's *A Time for Anger* and Whitehead's *The Second American Revolution* because "the authors praise each others [sic] works extravagantly and their arguments are so much of one piece that clearly they are meant to be a concerted statement." Marsden found their argumentation that America was built on a Christian base problematic from a historian's perspective and suspected that their solution to the contemporary moral crisis was the "old Calvinist ideal" of making "the law of God . . . the basis for the law of the land."[73] Far from dismissing the three books outright, though, Marsden spent the last paragraph of the proposal asking for better solutions to current problems. *Eternity* reacted positively to Marsden's article outline, yet cautioned: "A lot of the criticism of Schaeffer reminds me of someone stopping a fireman on his duties to correct his grammar."[74] The makers of the magazine were reluctant to criticize those who spoke out against what most Evangelicals agreed was a contemporary values crisis. Even so, *Eternity* was ready to

Figure 5.2. "The Crusade for a Christian America." Cover of *Eternity*, May 1983. Courtesy of Buswell Library Special Collections, Wheaton College, Illinois.

dismantle the vision of a Christian America as a viable political goal and, in May 1983, published Marsden's revised article as the feature story. The published article was entitled "Quest for a Christian America." The subtitle clarified the author's position—"Why American Christians Cannot Re-Establish a Christian Nation"—and the article put forth an alternative vision, or "suggestions of where we can go from here."[75]

The cover of the May 1983 issue showed a drawing of the Statue of Liberty with Bible and cross in hand and was titled "The Crusade for a Christian America" (figure 5.2). The preview to the issue read: "One problem for active Christians won't go away: How can we see Christian standards of justice and morality upheld in our society in a way that preserves the freedoms of non-Christians?" As if expecting objections to Marsden's article, the writer pointed out that *Eternity* routinely printed articles on this subject and challenged readers to decide for themselves whether they agreed more with Marsden or with the people he criticized. To this end, the issue also included a response by John W. Whitehead.[76]

Investigating the arguments of New Christian Right leaders like Jerry Falwell and Tim LaHaye, as well as writers like Francis A. Schaeffer and John W. Whitehead, Marsden, in the feature article, stated that "historical perceptions are especially important, since the goal is to return America to a lost heritage." He criticized the New Christian Right's conflation of the Reformation and the founding of the United States, pointing out that historically the two were based on very different ideals regarding the relationship of church and state. Whereas the former took for granted established state churches, the latter repudiated them.[77] Accordingly, Marsden asked whether a Christian America would not mean repudiating the founding ideals of the United States. Yet he opted for a "middle way," finding it possible to preserve Christian values without cementing them in an established church or theocracy, or turning over the polity to antireligious secularists. Turning again to history, he showed that while there was a strong Christian influence in eighteenth- and nineteenth-century America, Christianity was not deliberately integrated into the political system. He did allow that "this might seem like a major compromise" but pointed out that "compromise is the genius of the American political system."[78] Marsden's alternative vision to Christian America was a democratic, pluralistic America governed by political compromise. Although he agreed that there were problems marring US society and that Christians had the right and duty to speak out and join politics to work on solving these problems, he emphasized that "while the Bible does not err, its interpreters do," arguing that it was humanly impossible to determine the one true Christian position on all issues.[79]

The relationship between Christianity and the state proposed by Marsden stood in stark opposition to the notion of Christian America advocated by New Christian Right writers like John W. Whitehead. Indeed, Whitehead called Marsden's conception a "doctrine of neutrality and compromise," judging that "men like Marsden inevitably find themselves standing with the secularists who oppose Christian involvement in the totality of life." Painting an alarming picture, he disparaged Marsden's faith as "diluted Christianity" and "philosophy" and compared it to the attitude of the "pre-Nazi Germany church."[80] With a few quick lines, Whitehead made lackluster German Christians responsible for the genocide of the Jews, called abortion the contemporary Holocaust, and equated Nazi Germany with the situation of the contemporary United States, which people like Marsden, duped by the "secularists" of the ACLU and the like, were helping bring about.

Interestingly, the two readers' letters that *Eternity* printed in the July/August issue were by Carl F. H. Henry, the former editor of *Christianity Today*, and Ray Joseph, the editor of the *Christian Statesman*, a magazine dealing with civil government published by the National Reform Association. This group, which traced its origins to 1861, was trying to include a "Christian amendment," incorporating the name Jesus Christ and the law of God, into the US Constitution.[81] Not surprisingly, Joseph sided with Whitehead, while Henry wrote quite bluntly: "Marsden is right in this debate (Schaeffer and

Whitehead wrong, and Rushdoony more so)."[82] Whether putting these letters side by side was deliberate or accidental, the names of these two men and the respective periodicals they were associated with indicated that Marsden's position was Evangelical, while Whitehead's was, at best, on the fringes. Yet later letters to the editor still showed "no consensus" on the debate about Christian America. One writer sided with Marsden and thought that Whitehead's response attested to the "close-mindedness" of the New Christian Right; the other found that Marsden "misses the point Schaeffer, Falwell, Whitehead, and LaHaye are making," reiterating the idea that government could once rely on a now lost "Christian consensus."[83] Since the feeling of a moral crisis was pervasive, the vision of a Christian America proved attractive, even when careful historical arguments showed that things had never been as simple as the New Christian Right writers indicated.

Nonetheless, the effort to keep the historical record straight continued. Marsden and other historians kept contributing articles with historical assessments to Evangelical magazines.[84] Furthermore, in a September 1982 letter to Lane Dennis of Crossway Books, Mark A. Noll proposed a book-length historical investigation into the claims of a Christian America. He emphasized that "there does seem to be a need for such a project (whether by this group of people or not)."[85] He proposed a book of essays by George M. Marsden, Nathan O. Hatch, and himself, with an integrating introduction, an idea readily accepted by Crossway Books and printed as *The Search for Christian America* in 1983.[86] The book was positively reviewed in *Eternity* by James A. Keim, identified as a professional legal assistant. Convinced by their historical argument and accessible writing style, Keim found that "the historical conclusions seem unavoidable" and predicted that "*Search* may well bring the midcourse correction its authors seek." The book won third place in *Eternity*'s annual book poll in 1984.[87]

Admitting in his introduction "the polemical nature of this book," Noll stressed that "our intent in making this rebuttal, however, is not vindictive. It is meant as a positive contribution to responsible Christian action." Accordingly, while the authors argued that in the final analysis, America never was a Christian nation, Noll emphasized that the authors yet shared many concerns about contemporary society.[88] They also endorsed biblically motivated political action. In this sense, they were interested in bridging the differences between themselves and some of those writers they criticized, most notably the Schaeffers.[89] Yet while they lauded Christian social concern, they feared that the populist idea of a Christian America was misguided and ultimately detrimental—both in terms of politics and that of the Christian cause. Noll argued that the confusion of US history with scriptural revelation "leads to idolatry of our nation and an irresistible temptation to national self-righteousness."

Furthermore, this conflation of America and Christianity precluded the development of an "independent scriptural position" from which Christians could criticize culture. Providing Evangelical readers with a proper historical account, in contrast, would enable them to operate on a sound basis. In the authors' opinion, correcting "the distorted and overinflated view of America as a distinctively Christian nation" was no pedantic motion distracting from the bigger cause, but the very foundation that made Christian politics possible.[90] They saw themselves not as "stopping a fireman on his duties to correct his grammar," to repeat the worry of the *Eternity* editor, but as handing the fireman the proper equipment and pointing him in the right direction.[91]

Evangelical historians intervened in the debates about Christian America, interjecting historical argumentation in an attempt to correct simplified accounts. They did nothing to diminish the allure of the concept or deny that the Christianization of the United States was an ideal. But they relegated this ideal to a time after the second coming of Christ, pointing out that fallible humans could not usher in the kingdom of Christ and that any legal or forced conflation of state and religion was ultimately corrupt. Accordingly, they helped shape a notion of Christian America that envisioned Evangelicals as the spiritual community of true believers laboring within the confines of the democratic system to uphold biblical morality and convert others to this vision.

Christian Foundations

What Noll, Marsden, and Hatch did not contest was that there had been times in the history of the United States when Christians and Christianity had been influential in public life. Noll wrote that "one of our auxiliary purposes is to show that Christians in the history of America have often displayed a genuine and sincere faith, and that this faith has played an important role in American history."[92] Abbreviating the historical argument, Evangelical spokespersons liked to speak of Christian values that had once undergirded official decision-making processes and that they wished to see again in contemporary politics. It was generally assumed that people acted according to certain values, Christian or otherwise. However, recent developments, especially in the courts, seemed to preclude Christian argumentation from the political process, thus implicitly favoring value systems inimical to Christianity. The antagonistic worldview seen as dominating contemporary society was labeled "secular humanism." This system was considered to be atheistic and oriented on the human being as the measure of all things. Because Evangelicals considered humans fallen and fallible creatures, and because secular humanism lacked any external standard, it was regarded as dangerously arbitrary and relativistic, ultimately leading to moral anomie. Where some saw a concerted conspiracy to oust Christianity, others, more sedately, saw an unfortunate political development. Articles in Evangelical magazines urged Christian political engagement, arguing that Christianity was not only a legitimate but the most important source for social concern.

Secular humanism in this sense was a term coined by Francis A. Schaeffer. He traced its origins to the Renaissance, a time when humans, in Schaeffer's reading, had considered themselves gods. In his 1976 book *How Should We Then Live?*, the popular theologian and philosopher discussed Michelangelo's *David* (1504) and called it "the statement of humanistic pride in the Renaissance." He described the statue: "As a work of art it has few equals in the world. . . . But let us notice that the David was not the Jewish David of the Bible. David was simply a title. Michelangelo knew his Judaism, and in the statue the figure is not circumcised. We are not to think of this as the biblical David but as the humanistic ideal. Man is great!"[93]

Even in his 1968 book *The God Who Is There*, Schaeffer argued that Western culture had crossed what he called "the line of despair," beyond which no certainties existed: at an earlier time, people had absolutes; now the very meaning of truth was being challenged. He introduced humanism as one of the philosophical concepts deteriorating Christianity. He explained: "Humanism . . . is the system whereby man, beginning absolutely by himself, tries rationally to build out from himself, having only man as his integration point, to find all knowledge, meaning and value."[94] Humanism, according to Schaeffer, had existed even before people crossed the line of despair, but it had provided them with an optimistic outlook. When all the philosophical concepts did not provide ultimate answers, humanists disregarded the very rules of logic, crossing the line of despair and landing in relativism.

In his book, *How Should We Then Live?*, he illustrated this shift by comparing the image of man as depicted in Michelangelo's *David* with the image of humanity depicted in Michelangelo Antonioni's 1966 film *Blow-Up*: "Antonioni was portraying how, in the area of non-reason, there are no certainties concerning moral values, and no human categories either. *Blow-Up* had no hero. Compare this with Michelangelo's *David*—the statement of humanistic pride in the Renaissance. Man had set himself up as autonomous, but the end result was not Michelangelo's David, but Antonioni's non-hero. All there is in the film is the camera which goes 'click, click, click,' and the human has disappeared."[95] This new humanism, therefore, was pessimistic and ultimately inhuman.

The threat of humanism thus was not only that it provided an alternative, non-Christian worldview but that it seemed to be the polar opposite of Schaeffer's Evangelicalism; the two conceptions of the world canceled each other out and could not coexist. This as well as Schaeffer's attempt to refute humanism is illustrated in a quote from an interview printed in *Christianity Today* in October 1976: "Mathematically, beginning from a finite person you cannot project an absolute. So all humanism is mathematically projected to fail. There is only one basic issue, and that is whether there is another source of knowledge which can tell us what we can't find out for ourselves. Historic Christianity believes there is. We believe the Bible and the revelation of God in Christ are united and give us knowledge, not only 'religious' knowledge but a key to understanding the universe and history. The Bible gives us absolutes by which to help and by which to judge society."[96] The specter of secular humanism comprised the fear of atheistic anomie that was the negative of Christianity.

New Christian Right writers readily adopted the term "secular humanism." Tim LaHaye, for example, in his 1980 book *The Battle for the Mind*, drew much of his argumentation from Schaeffer, contending that there were two diametrically opposed worldviews for humans: humanism or Christianity. Somewhat missing the point of Schaeffer's use of the *David* example, but harping on moral issues dear to the New Christian Right, LaHaye wrote: "The giant replica of Michelangelo's magnificent David stands nude, overlooking that beautiful city [Florence, Italy]. Quite naturally, this contradicts the wisdom of God, for early in Genesis, the Creator followed man's folly by giving him animal skins to cover his nakedness. Ever since, there has been a conflict concerning clothes, with man demanding the freedom to go naked. The Renaissance obsession with nude 'art forms' was the forerunner of the modern humanist's demand for pornography in the name of freedom."[97]

Where Schaeffer's accounts can be read as engaging Christian critiques of culture, LaHaye's was, in the words of one reviewer for the Evangelical magazine *Eternity*, "at best a passionate book and at worst an often illogical diatribe."[98] While LaHaye in particular and the New Christian Right more generally oversimplified and overstated arguments, the pictures they painted, bromidic and boorish as they might be, were also catchy and made for good copy in the media. But even though the review of LaHaye's *The Battle for the Human Mind* in *Eternity* was harsh, the author did not challenge LaHaye's argument as such. Rather than dismissing the whole book, he concluded that the argument needed more careful stating: "In a time when the Christian faith is challenged by a formidable foe, I cannot see the wisdom of using overstatement and faulty logic in a battle for truth."[99]

Whereas the approaches of Schaeffer and LaHaye arguably differed, the two authors shared an underlying argument: if God was taken out of the picture, if man was taken as the measure of all things, absolutes became arbitrary and could disappear altogether. This argument was received in and spread through Evangelical magazines. Through Evangelical thinkers like Schaeffer

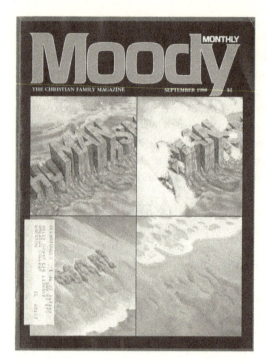

Figure 5.3. "HuMANism." Cover of *Moody Monthly*, September 1980. Courtesy of Buswell Library Special Collections, Wheaton College, Illinois.

and Christian political pundits like LaHaye, as well as through magazines and other forms of media, this understanding of humanism was made accessible to a wide evangelical Christian constituency.

A *Moody Monthly* cover story in September 1980 dealt with humanism and depicted the idea that it was a worldview built out of and on sand (figure 5.3). The cover illustration was divided into four panels, each showing the same section of shoreline. In the first panel the word "humanism" appeared. The drawing indicated that the word had been built out of sand, much like a sandcastle. "Man," as part of the word "huMANism," was elevated, suggesting the importance of man or the man-made nature of the sand sculpture. In the succeeding panels, a wave crashed over the beach, progressively erasing the sand sculpture. This depiction suggested that humanism, as a man-made worldview, could not withstand the forces of nature. The cover article introduced humanism as the worldview inimical to and opposing Christianity. An excerpt from the 1973 Humanist Manifesto II, the new and updated version of the original manifesto (1933) that outlined the humanist worldview, served to illustrate this (in the eyes of the Evangelical commentators) godless system of thought.[100] Nancy B. Barcus and Dick Bohrer explained that "the humanist builds his house upon the sand," but also warned that humanists had set out to convert the public to their worldview. They understood their article as a manual for recognizing and combatting secular humanism, countering each of the secular tenets they introduced with a Christian answer.[101] The article suggested that this system, while unsound, was steadily undermining Christianity.

The sentiment that Christianity had once been the foundation of society was best expressed by *Christianity Today*'s editor Kenneth S. Kantzer, who wrote: "In the past, these values were central in our society. Today many of us are fearful that they are being pushed to the periphery of American life." He continued: "Certainly evangelicals are not seeking a return to a New England–type theocracy. Nor do they wish to support the establishment of religion—either their own or some innocuous civil religion."[102] While emphasizing that Evangelicals were not looking for a religious establishment of whatever kind, Kantzer nonetheless advocated the consideration and acknowledgment of Christian values in public life. His fear was that if it were not Christian values that sustained decision-making, it would be other, possibly less clearly identifiable and likely more destructive worldviews that would take their place.

One of the most elaborate treatises on the expulsion of religious values from public life was Richard John Neuhaus's 1984 book *The Naked Public Square*.[103] Standing on its head the usual complaint about the transgressive politics of Christian America, Neuhaus, a Lutheran pastor, pleaded: "Whatever our political persuasion, if we care about a democratic future, we have a deep stake in reconstructing a politics that was not begun by and cannot be sustained by the myth of secular America."[104] The book's argumentation was that the rules of public decision-making were changing, excluding religion and religious argumentations from the process. A long excerpt was printed in *Christianity Today*, and the book won fourth place in 1984 in *Eternity*'s annual book poll. A note accompanying the list of winners pointed out that this was "a book that should probably also win a special award for Books Whose Titles Coin a New and Popular Phrase in Current Debate."[105] In an interview with the *Wittenburg Door*, Neuhaus explained the title: "The Naked Public Square means that, in the last three or four decades, it has been increasingly assumed, and in some places explicitly articulated, that religion or religiously 'tainted' values should be systematically and constitutionally excluded from American public life."[106]

Accordingly, the public square was being stripped of values and moral underpinnings grounding the common rules for society. Neuhaus considered secularism to be the worldview demanding such an erosion of common foundations. However, there was no such thing as a conspiracy of secularists (here he clearly disagreed with New Christian Right writers). If it were so, he wrote in *Christianity Today*, "they could be exposed and driven from their positions of influence, perhaps." But, indeed, "our difficulty is greater than that. It is the pervasive influence of ideas about a secular society and a secular state, ideas that have insinuated themselves also into our religious thinking and that have been institutionalized in our politics." The danger was that secularism had become the official attitude despite the fact that the people of the United States were more religious than ever before. Therefore, he agreed to a certain extent with the New Christian Right and welcomed its activism as a necessary corrective: "The democratic vitalities of America are today being stirred by those who were not consulted when it was decided that this is a secular society. Groups like the Moral Majority come to the public square not with the political religion of the republic but with the revivalist politics of the camp meeting."[107]

While Neuhaus's basic argument was that secularism was banning moral arguments from public discourse, he also claimed that ultimately this situation could not be sustained. In 1991, Neuhaus retrospectively summarized this point in an interview printed in an ecumenical magazine: "My argument is that the naked public square is an impossibility, that it will inevitably be filled with something."[108] While he seemed to think of secularization predominantly as a process of emptying, he suspected that it also introduced some basis for decision-making. In 1984, he still wrote prospectively that civil religion or some belief system would fill the void.[109] By 1991, he seemed to be more convinced that secularism itself constituted an alternative worldview: "At present, it [the public square] is primarily filled with an obsession with rights language and entitlements premised upon the assumption of the autonomous self." Yet this self-centered perspective, while established, was at odds with the values most US Americans held dear: "it has not pervaded the entirety of the culture by any means. It lives in enormous tension with what is still, for the great majority of Americans, a biblical understanding of the moral basis of the social order."[110] He thus eventually saw an egocentric, human-centered worldview taking the place of moral argumentation.

In an article in *Eternity*, Mark A. Noll called Richard John Neuhaus a neoconservative, explaining that neoconservatives were disillusioned liberals criticizing the loss of values in society. He placed Neuhaus in the context of other well-known religious spokespersons of various backgrounds who ten years earlier first called attention to the deterioration of social norms. While in the mid-1970s, little attention had been paid to such concerns, now their time had come. Reviewing the Hartford Appeal—a document prepared by Richard John Neuhaus and Peter L. Berger and discussed with and signed by a slate of leaders of various religious backgrounds in 1975—Noll pointed out that current critiques, like Neuhaus's *The Naked Public Square*, "received serious attention because they come from individuals and groups who had themselves been certified by the liberal establishment."[111] But Neuhaus was not only able to speak to the general public; he was also able to bridge some of the differences between liberal and conservative Evangelicals. His unique background allowed him to speak to and be understood by the Left as well as the Right. While Neuhaus had turned to the Right, welcoming the activism of the New Christian Right, he stressed that the Hartford Appeal for him still had the "ring of truth."[112]

Neuhaus's argumentation corresponded with fears of other Evangelical spokespersons who considered the present situation to be one of a values crisis. They feared the deterioration of society because decisions were based on the wrong values or no values at all. Carl Horn, for example—an Evangelical attorney who worked for the Reagan administration but resigned to run for Congress (and failed to be elected)—thought the fate of the nation lay in how US Americans answered one important question, namely: "What is the *source of values*, religious or otherwise, in contemporary American life?"[113] Similarly, for William E. Dannemeyer, a US representative from California, the ultimate question that "no man or woman, whether a private citizen or an elected official, can escape" was: "Do we follow God or man?" With different emphases and degrees of vehemence, Evangelical spokespersons reproved societal developments that they saw as leading away from tradition, morals, and norms. They believed that all decision-making was based in some worldview and that the current trend of excluding values could not be sustained. It was suspected that the attempt to exclude values constituted a new worldview—what some called secular humanism. In its negativity, it was antithetical to Christianity—it was considered to be not only atheistic but anti-religious and hubristic to make the human the measure of all things. Dannemeyer explained: "Humanism proclaims its own set of self-serving, unproved dogmas as replacement for the tenets of traditional religion. It asserts that the universe is 'self-existing and not created.' It says man is the product of evolution and that the 'joy of living' and the 'satisfaction of life' are the supreme goal of men. Ethics come from 'human experience,' not from God."[114]

Not only was it dangerously wrong, it was also destined to fail because without external authority, it was a system built on sand, as the *Moody Monthly* cover indicated. Accordingly, religious involvement in politics was not only legitimate but necessary, and the goal was not only to integrate a Christian point of view but to maintain the US system of government as such. Kenneth S. Kantzer pointed out that "most Americans are convinced not only that religion and religious values are basic to the social structure of our society, but that they are essential to the preservation of our American freedoms as well."[115] It was thus necessary to show that affirming religious values in the public square was in keeping with both the original intention of the founders and the best interest of all citizens.

Evangelical spokespersons lobbied for including religious motivation and values in politics, arguing that an external authority was needed lest politics as a guideline of human life became relativistic and eventually irrelevant, pitching society into moral pandemonium. They agreed, to a certain extent, with New Christian Right activists, on combating secular humanism. Spokespersons not only depicted religion as an integral part of politics, but envisioned Evangelicals as ideally equipped for participation in politics.

The Christianity Today Institute and the Vision of Christian Citizenship
Feeling the need to investigate issues more thoroughly, *Christianity Today* established an institute where questions could be discussed with more academic rigor. Run by the outgoing editor Kenneth S. Kantzer, the institute engaged a variety of different Evangelical thinkers and scholars, depending on the topic.[116] The results of the institute's discussion were published as special installments in the magazine. The elder statesman of Evangelicalism, Carl F. H. Henry, explained the need for a Christian think tank like the Christianity Today Institute in an interview. Complaining that intellectual discourse was not always well-regarded in Evangelical circles, he insisted that there was a need for discerning Evangelical positions that went beyond "hot rhetoric or the simplistic one-liner." Evangelicals not only needed well-thought-out positions on crucial issues; they also needed to formulate them well in order to gain hearing beyond the Evangelical community.[117]

Significantly, the first installment from the Christianity Today Institute, published in April 1985, was dedicated to an analysis of "The Christian as Citizen."[118] In a dig at the New Christian Right, Henry, in his contribution, wrote: "Ecclesiastics who cannot agree on basic principles of church dogma suddenly become specialists in deriving from whatever doctrines they choose to retain a list of legislative options. Meanwhile, the views of highly informed and experienced political statesmen, who are also church affiliated, are overlooked and even disparaged by self-declared omnicompetent clergy who speak outside their field of learning."[119] In the announcement of this institute installment, it was pointed out that "Christians are awakening to political issues." Since they felt that there were many leaders but little thoughtful information on how contemporary Christians should relate to the state, the fellows of the institute dedicated themselves to this issue. The Evangelical experts developed and presented their vision of Christian citizenship. Announcing the institute supplement, Tom Minnery warned that the insights these Evangelical scholars were going to present, were "not likely to make either the Religious Right or Left completely happy."[120]

Nonetheless, the voices from the Right and the Left were represented in interviews with Moral Majority leader Jerry Falwell and *Sojourners* editor Jim

Wallis. The "view from the Evangelical center" was represented in the interview section by Charles Colson, the former Nixon adviser and now chairman of Prison Fellowship Ministries. All three of them agreed that Christians ought to be involved in politics and that the Bible should inspire the way Christians did so. Colson stated that "in being involved, we need to be free to pursue biblical righteousness as we're best able to understand it."[121] To Wallis, this meant a very particular perspective: "If we want to be biblical, our views and politics should be profoundly shaped by the priority of the poor."[122] Falwell was more concerned with moral issues and especially the prevention of abortions.[123] Both Wallis and Falwell, however, based their activism on their faith and believed that the Bible dictated this particular priority. Wallis, in his seminary days, had cut out of the Bible all the parts that dealt with the poor to demonstrate that if you ignored this topic there was hardly anything left in the Bible.[124] Colson, though he had different priorities, sympathized with and explained this stance: "If as Christians we privately believe something but it has no effect on our actions, we have a dreadful denial of the lordship of Christ." Accordingly, he thought that an issue like abortion should be "at the top of everyone's list." Yet he also pointed out that there was a whole range of issues that concerned Christians. He warned that "Christian political movements . . . tend to make the gospel hostage to a particular political agenda. You may wrap the cross in the flag and make God a prop for the state. This is a grave danger." This did not mean withdrawal from politics—Colson rejected the "mindset . . . that says the church doesn't have any relevance to how people live"—but rather participation in an informed and discerning Christian politics.[125] Representing the evangelical Christian spectrum from Fundamentalism to the Evangelical Left, these three spokespersons thus agreed that faith should inspire action and therefore that religious convictions did and should play a role in politics. They emphasized their personal faith as foundation for political action. Christians were not to be co-opted by majority opinion or party loyalties, but were individually accountable to God. An individual component, the personal relationship between a believer and God, was thus the basis for political behavior.

The reason for organizing this installment of the institute ("The Christian as Citizen") was, according to Kantzer, that Evangelicals were "lacking a well-thought-out philosophy of government" and "theology of citizenship." While not denying that personal knowledge of God was the basis for all Evangelical deportment, he implied that individual feeling was not enough for responsible political involvement. He advocated a vision of the Christian citizen as one acting not on gut feeling but on political knowledge and theology. The Christianity Today Institute took up issues regarding religion and politics already debated in Evangelical circles and used experts to summarize, rectify, and present how they envisioned Christian citizenship. Canadian theologian J. I. Packer discussed the characteristics that distinguished the Christian citizen, Carl F. H. Henry wrote a plea for religious political involvement, political scientist and former state politician Stephen V. Monsma argued for the permeability of Jefferson's wall of separation, and David L. McKenna, a local politician and seminary president, analyzed the extent to which churches could and should get involved in local politics. The assumption for all four contributions was, as Kantzer stated, that "if religion is our ultimate concern and we love people, we clearly cannot escape the overlap and intertwine of such crucial issues as religion and politics." Pointing out that Americans were a religious people, he determined that "good religion and good politics ought to mix."[126] The installment was an illustration of how he and other Evangelical spokespersons envisioned the intersections of "good religion" and "good politics" to be.

J. I. Packer's contribution was to emphasize that the Christian was also a citizen.[127] As trivial as this observation might seem, it was foundational for Evangelicals because Christianity's otherworldly orientation meant that social engagement was not a given. In this sense Packer continued age-old Christian arguments as to what their role in society was, emphasizing the idea that Christians were citizens of the world as well as of heaven.[128] He discerned three fallacies in connection with political involvement: relativism, absolutism, and imperialist biblicism. As relativists he identified those who adapted biblical principles to societal situations. To him this was a violation of revealed truth because essentially this meant "the heart is cut out of the gospel." He saw liberals, especially those Christians organized in the World Council of Churches, as guilty of this aberration. In contrast, Christian absolutists were hindered by their excessive religiosity. Those Christians, conservatives of various Catholic, Orthodox, and Protestant backgrounds, tended to withdraw from society and declined political involvement.[129] While some conservative evangelical Christians were among this group, Packer judged that "pietistic passivity cannot be justified, and its present practitioners need to be educated out of it." The last aberration he identified was the "imperialism of some Christian biblicists." This was the fallacy some activists of the New Christian Right were guilty of: a "fundamentalist" or "uncompromising fighting stance." Not only was "holy war ... no part of God's plan for the church," it was also detrimental to the democratic process and therefore not a commendable form of political involvement in the United States.[130]

Democracy was not only the political system US American Evangelicals were necessarily required to operate in, it was also one, according to Packer, that Christians could and should support: "from a Christian standpoint it is a fitter and wiser form than any other." Democracy was not perfect. It required compromise, and it defied easy, black-and-white answers, something that Christians, with their concept of revealed truth and moral absolutes, struggled with. But these characteristics reflected human fallibility. All human knowledge, including the knowledge that professing Christians possessed, was partial, and people approached the same issue from different perspectives and calculated different consequences. Democracy required participation, and Christian citizens had the opportunity to help shape their society. Accordingly, Packer advocated Evangelical participation in politics. In his opinion, all Evangelicals should inform themselves, vote, and pray for politicians. Beyond this basic democratic involvement, some—those who felt this to be God's calling for them—should become more active in politics, as critics or as politicians.[131] A Christian citizen was thus someone who neither compromised his faith nor shrugged off his political duties. The Christian citizen sought to represent the biblical position on issues but was also aware of the nature of politics and acted accordingly. He neither tried to force his beliefs on others nor let his beliefs be compromised or used for political agendas.

The Christian citizen was thus at home in both his religious community and in the polity. Carl F. H. Henry argued that it was theoretically possible to distinguish between political and religious spheres but that, in practice, both religion and politics were essential to people's lives and were thus hard to separate. Indeed, "both [the religious and the political sphere] are indispensable aspects of a faithful Christian calling, and each renders service to the other." According to Henry, both spheres rendered irreplaceable service to private and communal life and should be thought of as complementary and reinforcing. Whereas God ordained both church and state as human institutions in this world, a separation of these institutions was necessary to ensure true freedom. Freedom of religion was not just a political quirk or a pragmatic tool to prevent religious war; it reflected godly principles: "it is a God-given virtue rooted in the character of true religion." Likewise, the disestablishment of religion was not a bad thing; Henry argued against a theocracy and for democracy and freedom of religion because he saw these as requirements for an expression of true religion: "By its very nature authentic religion demands religious freedom. Coerced spiritual decision is worthless both to God and to man. In view of its emphasis on the indispensability of personal decision, evangelical Christianity should in fact be seen as the champion of voluntarism."[132]

The institutions of church and state in the United States both supported religious freedom. More than that, from an Evangelical perspective, freedom of religion protected freedom itself: The Bible demanded that the Christian "render to Caesar what is Caesar's," but it also prescribed that the highest authority was God. If the state encroached on religious right, exceptions could be made for believers, and if the state overstepped its jurisdiction, it was biblically legitimate for a Christian to refuse the state. In this sense, "religious freedom shelters all other freedoms."[133] In a happy coincidence, then, Christians could not only arrange themselves within the US political system but embrace it; the system was not only ordained by God (like all but the most inhumane states), it also exhibited Christian truths.

This situation, however, was not to be taken for granted, and it did not come for free. Presently, as Henry saw it, forces from the political Left and the Christian Right were shaking the foundation of religious freedom, with the Left moving toward an abolition of religion in the public realm and the Right moving toward a theocratic establishment.[134] If Evangelicals took their citizenships seriously—both in this world and in heaven—it was their duty to counter both trends. Christians had a responsibility toward the state, and it was up to them to protect religious freedom. The US political system not only allowed for but was built on active participation, and if Evangelicals got involved, they could help shape society. However, "Christians know that the penalty for withholding exemplary guidance and involvement for the social common good is to surrender the political arena by default to non-Christian alternatives." The United States offered Evangelicals the opportunity to influence society through the democratic process, but it was up to them to do so. In this view, noninvolvement was not only a wasted opportunity but also a sin. According to Henry, "lack of public engagement in the world is tantamount to defection from the Redeemer's army of occupation and liberation."[135] The United States granted the privilege of religious freedom and the opportunity of democratic political involvement; to waste this opportunity to advance God's cause was a grave failure. Christian citizenship was thus active service to God and society.

Stephen V. Monsma pointed out that there were "windows and doors in the wall of separation."[136] He argued that this was necessary for the state to protect itself from actions "destructive of good social order in the name of the free exercise of religion." It was therefore in no one's (and decidedly not in the state's) interest that the so-called wall separating the religious from the political sphere be absolute. The point was not to enforce some strict separation but to determine "by what principles [we can] sort out the permissible from the impermissible activities of government that regulate or limit the actions of religion."[137] Echoing widespread fears propagandized by the New Christian Right, Monsma counseled that religious freedoms were currently eroding because of a too-strict interpretation of the idea of separation of church and state. The contemporary problem, therefore, was not state interference in religious matters but the opposite: even "nonpreferential aid to religion" was now considered unconstitutional. A too-strict interpretation had another negative consequence: the exclusion of religious and religiously based moral arguments from the political decision-making process. Monsma discussed civil disobedience as a last resort against inhumane and opportunistic decisions born of this situation. He pointed to the legalization of abortion and decisions against the picketing of abortion clinics as situations in which Evangelicals currently debated civil disobedience. While asking for restraint and the maximum exhaustion of legal options, he nonetheless advocated that civil disobedience was "an option we believe the evangelical church should more frequently debate, weigh, and consider in the face of clear and severe injustices."[138] The right of religious freedom and the therein implied freedom of conscience granted by the US Constitution were privileges that needed exercising: "Our joy and thankfulness for this uncommon religious freedom requires that we defend and strengthen the daily application of it."[139] According to Monsma, then, the Christian citizen was one who exercised his rights and defended them by protesting against their violation. Civic duty required keeping abreast of current political developments, examining them in light of the Bible, and making one's position public. While the state had a viable right to curtail legal transgression in the name of religion, religious freedom remained the highest good. This right could and should be employed to counter political aberrations.

David McKenna brought the debate to a close with a discussion on what people could do at the local level to do their part as Christian citizens. The precept for political involvement, for McKenna, was biblical soundness and political effectiveness. He insisted that the church's role was foremost religious: "politics is not the primary task of the church." Even so, however, politics was "a part of [the church's] public witness."[140] While he did not consider politics to be the church's main concern, then, he nonetheless underscored the arguments of the previous writers that political involvement was a Christian duty. He specified that political activism was an individual rather than a corporate undertaking, by which he meant that Christians should not be aligned with parties but should retain their independent voices. Concerted action from believers, too, should be reserved for exceptional problems concerning one of three issues: "religious liberty," "social equality," or "moral order." He described the "biblical church" as defined by three main functions, namely "prayer, preaching, and teaching." For McKenna, "to pray for government is to participate in politics." This was the main duty of individual Evangelicals and Evangelical churches. Preaching was a prophetic function but not the place to analyze political details. Rather, "the pulpit is where a prophetic voice is heard proclaiming the biblical vision of justice." Preaching should thus chart the general parameters for biblically inspired political action, but not prescribe a specific political agenda. Teaching, finally, was more explicitly political because teaching meant that Evangelicals could lead by example and persuasion. Here, McKenna credited the Moral Majority for reminding Christians of their political duties. Yet he warned his readers about demagogy and insisted that involvement presupposed "political literacy," which required people to inform themselves—a task that could be fulfilled by local churches.[141] While not categorically refusing political involvement by clergy, McKenna made clear that their main obligation lay elsewhere. McKenna's contribution focused on the role of local churches in politics. He emphasized that political action should be foremost thought of as an individual exercise but added that Christian communities could be political especially by praying together and by teaching one another. In exceptional cases, a pastor could also be a politician, but it was generally better to keep the two functions apart.

Christian citizenship, as a vision of how Evangelicals were to conduct themselves in their dual roles as Christians and US citizens—"citizens of two kingdoms," as they liked to put it—took up many of the characteristics that connoted ideas of Christian America without conflating the two spheres.[142] Writers celebrated the political system of the United States as the best humanly created model of governing so far.[143] Accordingly, the Christian could be happily patriotic.[144] But they also took seriously concerns about the loss of the moral and religious foundation of the government and the political decision-making process. Rather than conjuring up Christian roots or some original Christian intent, they emphasized religious freedom as the highest good. This argument reintroduced Christian principles through the back door: if laws violated basic Christian convictions, then Evangelicals could claim the right to follow their religious convictions rather than the law. Unlike those who argued that America was essentially Christian, Evangelicals affirmed religious freedom as a universal (not Christian) right. This universality was considered positive because it made an uncoerced decision and therefore "true" faith possible. Religious freedom was not to be taken lightly; it was a privilege that needed to be cultivated. Evangelicals needed to take seriously their political duties as Christian citizens. Only then could religious freedom be perpetuated, free from the attempts of co-optation by the political Left or Christian Right. It was an Evangelical duty to be informed—both politically and theologically—and to participate in society. Political engagement was broadly defined: the most basic activity was praying. Spokespersons emphasized that all Evangelicals needed to fulfill their obligations as citizens, which generally meant obeying the laws, keeping informed, and possibly voting in elections. Spokespersons were generally wary of advocating active political involvement. They pointed out that while "some should seek political influence" and "some should accept a political vocation," this was not a general obligation, and not everyone was fit for it.[145] They were especially suspicious of clergy becoming politically active. Christian citizenship was primarily understood as an individual right and duty, and politically active pastors could be mistaken for speaking for the church. Yet writers reserved for all Evangelicals the right to "salt" society by introducing Christian values and convictions into the political process—through voting, lobbying, participating in grassroots campaigns, seeking office, and, ultimately—but as a last resort—engaging in protest and civil disobedience.[146] The state was a God-ordained institution and generally deserving of Christians' obedience. More than that, because the US government exhibited characteristics compatible with biblical principles, exercising one's citizenship was a service not only to society but to God. Exemplary Christian citizenship—exhibiting both democratic and Christian values—could be understood as a form of teaching and witnessing and had the power to transform society for the better.

Pat Robertson and the Presidential Campaign of 1988

The rare form of Evangelical political engagement described by the Christianity Today Institute fellows was that of a calling to political office. While not categorically against such engagement, the fellows were skeptical as to the wisdom of a preacher becoming a politician. Yet this was the aspiration of televangelist Marion Gordon Robertson, better known as Pat Robertson, who felt "called by God" to enter the bid for the office of US president in the election of 1988.[147] His campaign spotlighted the New Christian Right, for whom it proved to be both a high and a low. On the one hand, because Robertson was a viable candidate for a large number of US Americans, it demonstrated that religiously and politically conservative activists had to be taken seriously.[148] On the other hand, it also brought to light misconducts and scandals committed by New Christian Right leaders. Ultimately, Robertson's campaign revealed the differences that continued to exist between evangelical Christian traditions. Robertson's following consisted mainly of Pentecostal and charismatic believers and his TV audience.[149] Evangelicals in general were as likely to vote for him as they were to vote for one of the other candidates, like the conservative Jack Kemp or the middle-of-the-road contender George H. W. Bush. Hurtful to Robertson's campaign were televangelist scandals like the one engulfing Jim Bakker and his Praise the Lord (PTL) imperium in 1987.[150] Jim and his wife, Tammy Faye Bakker, were superstars in the televangelist universe and appealed, like Robertson, to a Pentecostal following. The media coverage of Jim Bakker's sexual and financial misconduct destroyed the virtuous image of televangelists and put into doubt the high moral standards they preached, and by extension negatively affected the Robertson campaign. Evangelical magazines reported on both the Robertson campaign and the televangelist scandals and saw a correlation between televangelism's

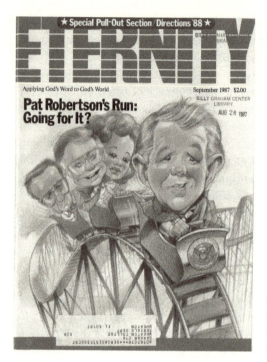

Figure 5.4. "Pat Robertson's Run: Going for It?" Cover of *Eternity*, September 1987. Courtesy of Buswell Library Special Collections, Wheaton College, Illinois.

increasingly negative image and Robertson's ultimate loss of the nomination. The September 1987 cover of *Eternity*, for example, depicted the Robertson campaign as a roller-coaster ride, with the Bakkers riding along in the car behind Robertson (figure 5.4). Riding in the last car was Oral Roberts, another televangelist who created negative publicity in 1987 (he announced that God would strike him dead if his ministry was not able to raise $5.4 million by the end of March). Evangelical spokespersons generally supported Robertson's right to enter the race for the presidency but did not endorse him or any other candidate.[151] Yet, ultimately, they positively evaluated Robertson's race for the presidency, regarding it as a sign that Christians had returned to the public square and that Christian language and concerns were once again part of public life.

Speculations about Pat Robertson's potential run for the presidency started shortly after Ronald Reagan's second inauguration in January 1985. According to an article in *Christianity Today*, rumors had first been reported in March 1985 in the *Saturday Evening Post*.[152] By the end of 1985, Robertson's deliberations about a bid for the presidency were being reported and commented on in Evangelical magazines. Introducing the preacher, his television empire (the Christian Broadcasting Network, CBN, with its central program, *The 700 Club*), and his New Christian Right activism, Beth Spring in *Christianity Today* commented: "Running for President will not guarantee Robertson a term in the White House, but it will almost certainly mean that the Presidential candidates in 1988 will not be able to dismiss moral issues that matter to Christians."[153] While she was optimistic about the moral tone the televangelist would introduce into politics, Joseph Bayly, writing in *Eternity*, was warier. In his column, he connected rumors about Robertson's potential run for president with a report about Jerry Falwell's visit to South Africa. In a notorious incident, for which he had to apologize, Falwell had called Desmond Tutu, the Anglican bishop, social activist, and opponent of South African apartheid, a "phony." Bayly used this example to point out the dangers of self-aggrandizement and hypocrisy. Falwell had accused Tutu of claiming to speak for Black South Africans when he was not democratically legitimated, yet he failed to be as critical about his own person. Pointing out that Falwell was in no way democratically legitimated in either his position as Christian spokesperson or that of self-proclaimed leader of the Moral Majority, Bayly claimed: "I would be willing as being quoted as saying that the Rev. Jerry Falwell does not represent me, even though I am evangelical and try to be moral." Responding to the rumors about a bid from Robertson, Bayly warned, "I hope that Robertson does not encourage the press to call him the 'evangelical candidate.'" He continued by pointing out that Robertson would leave the religious sphere and enter the political one, where he would represent not evangelical Christians but the Republican Party. Bayly's remarks revealed a pessimistic view. As the Falwell anecdote illustrates, he expected not righteousness but self-righteousness when religious leaders became political. Furthermore, he rejected the conflation of religion and politics in a single candidate, insisting that any tentative claim of religious representation Robertson had would not carry over into the political realm: if he entered the presidential race, "he is a Republican seeking office . . . , just as Robert Dole or anyone else."[154]

The hope that moral concerns would be taken seriously by contenders for the presidency and the fear that Christian sensibilities would be abused for political gain were the two themes that continuously came up whenever Evangelical spokespersons argued for or against Robertson's entering the presidential race.[155] Both views came together in an assessment by Charles W. Colson. In November 1986, before Robertson had officially declared his candidacy, Colson, at this point a regular columnist for *Christianity Today*, warned that "winning isn't everything." He recounted that since Jimmy Carter's presidency, some Christians had enthusiastically plunged into politics. Yet he also pointed out the pitfalls of political engagement, especially the damage to Christian reputation caused by hypocrisy and double standards. Colson attested that Robertson had a clean bill, stating that "Robertson . . . with but a few slips has avoided triumphal language." However, according to Colson, "Robertson has inherited the sum of ten years of excessive rhetoric and thus draws fire on all sides from secular critics." Other New Christian Right leaders, according to this assessment, had destroyed the reputation of politically inclined Christians. Winning the presidency, accordingly, was not the only or even the most important goal. Colson stated that "the Robertson campaign puts evangelicalism to its toughest test in decades," predicting that "if the triumphalism continues, the backlash will intensify, diminishing Christian influence in society."[156] The task was to restore credibility and dignity to Christian political engagement. This would be the true accomplishment of the presidential campaign, and this was the task he now assigned to Robertson:

> It is a heavy responsibility, but Pat Robertson, who is intelligent and articulate, can do it, if:
> - He steps out of the pulpit and drops the 'Reverend.' . . . Not only is there a deeply ingrained tradition against clergy in politics, but for Robertson to run as a reverend creates the impression that he represents the church as a corporate body.
> - He makes clear that he is running on his abilities, not on divine mandate. . . .
> - He articulates a responsible Christian view of justice, which is little understood by the secular world. He must make clear to both his supporters and his detractors the distinction between the responsibilities of Christians as private citizens and Christians as office holders.[157]

Colson thus articulated a vision of the Christian politician as engaged in this-worldly politics while embodying otherworldly, Christian virtues, yet without playing one against the other. Because Robertson was not a religious authority in the political realm, according to Colson, he was not to rely on his religious virtuosity or create the impression that he was representing a religious community. Rather, he had to conform to the rules of the political game and convince voters by his political capabilities. His faith would inform his actions but only as an example of justice, not as a template to which others had to conform. If he accomplished this task, "it may be a far greater contribution than anything he could achieve if he won the Oval Office."[158]

Robertson's chances at winning the election—or even the nomination of the Republican Party—were greatly diminished by scandals that wreaked havoc on the televangelist scene. Most prominently, in 1987, it was uncovered that televangelist Jim Bakker had had an extramarital affair and paid off the woman to keep it quiet.[159] As if this was not enough, further investigations revealed the financial fiasco of Bakker's PTL imperium, with, at first count, $69 million missing.[160] The scandal negatively affected Robertson both because he also was a televangelist and because, like the Bakkers, he catered to a Pentecostal audience. More than that, though, Robertson was directly and personally associated with the Bakkers. Robertson had hired Jim and Tammy Faye Bakker in 1965 for his fledgling television network, CBN. Not only had *The Jim and Tammy Show* been one of the most popular shows on the network, but Robertson had also made Jim Bakker host of *The 700 Club*, Robertson's own signature television program. In 1973, the Bakkers had left CBN, first to cofound the Trinity Broadcasting Network, and then to start their own PTL Network.[161] *Eternity* magazine, which chronicled the Robertson run for the presidency as a roller-coaster ride, cited a June 1987 admission from Robertson that "the PTL scandal has hurt the evangelical world" and reported that it had also hurt his campaign.[162] Moreover, the scandal highlighted the tension between evangelical Christian traditions. In an attempt to save PTL, Fundamentalist televangelist Jerry Falwell took over the network.[163] Yet in October 1987, Falwell suddenly departed. *Christianity Today* speculated that the tension between PTL's original Pentecostal workforce and audience and Falwell's new Fundamentalist board of directors had caused the rupture.[164] Evangelical magazine reports of the scandal and its consequences were matter-of-fact, casting themselves in the role of outside observers and thus emphasizing their distance from both the scandals and the televangelism. Yet *Eternity*'s executive editor, Don McCrory, highlighted a positive aspect of the scandal. According to McCrory, the media coverage of Jim Bakker's affair proved that religious language and concerns had been reinstated in public life: "Suddenly, a one-night stand in a Florida hotel room is viewed for the thing it really is—*sin*."[165] While the scandal spelled disaster for Robertson's campaign, articles in Evangelical magazines were more concerned with the human tragedy of fallen leaders than with the New Christian Right's sinking political aspirations.[166] Indeed, the fact that this incident was discussed in terms of sinful behavior, even outside of evangelical Christian circles, was interpreted by some as a success of Christian values being reacknowledged in public life.

After Super Tuesday—March 8, 1988—it was clear that Pat Robertson had no chance of winning the Republican nomination.[167] The coverage of Robertson's campaign in Evangelical magazines up to this point had been predominantly in the style of reported facts rather than expressions of emotional attachment, let alone endorsement. Rather than seeing Robertson's run as a fulfillment of the Evangelical political impetus, Evangelical spokespersons used his campaign to further develop their vision of Evangelical political involvement. Reporting on a conference on this theme in October 1986 at Calvin College, in Grand Rapids, Michigan, Beth Spring summarized: "Pat

Robertson's likely presidential bid has infused discussions of Christians in politics with a new dimension of enthusiasm and concern."[168] Now that Robertson's race was all but over, Evangelical spokespersons were not enthusiastic about either the Democratic nominee, Michael Dukakis, or the Republican nominee, George H. W. Bush. One report called them political technocrats and (because of their apparent similarities) compared them to Tweedledum and Tweedledee, the twins from *Alice in Wonderland*.[169] But there was no bitterness or disappointment over Robertson's failure, either. Indeed, the debates over how Evangelicals should conduct themselves in politics continued, and some voices even suggested that through Robertson's campaign Evangelicals had become more "sophisticated" in the political arena.[170] Articles by Evangelical spokespersons throughout the presidential race can be interpreted as an exercise in demonstrating that Evangelicals did not want to dictate their values to society or install the New Christian Right version of righteousness, but that they were eager all the same to participate in politics. Through their reporting they cast themselves in the role of professional political observers and engaged, responsible citizens. They envisioned themselves as exercising their democratic right in a pluralistic society and electing not a Christian candidate but whomever they considered to be the fittest choice politically.

Conclusion: Christian and American

The end of the Robertson campaign also drew a line under a decade of New Christian Right activism. Chronicling the ups and downs of New Christian Right activities, some Evangelical spokespersons concluded that while it might be premature to call it quits on the New Christian Right, the movement was at least in a transitory state.[171] Pat Robertson's bid for the presidency in this sense was the culmination—both a high point and a (preliminary) final point—for the New Christian Right and especially for Evangelicals' fascination with its vision of America. In early 1987, a book review of Robertson's 1986 book *America's Date with Destiny* had pointed out that "Robertson's vision of America as a New World Zion is a beautiful myth, and not without appeal, nor some accuracy. It is certainly more appealing to evangelical Christianity than the false secularist vision of America as a libertarian, progressive utopia." Yet the reviewer ended with an open question, stating that "whether Robertson can persuade American voters of this vision is another matter."[172] Robertson not only failed to convince the US electorate, he failed to convince a more narrow audience of Evangelicals. At the end of a decade of flirting with New Christian Right notions of a Christian nation, Evangelical magazines were outgrowing the myth. Writing in the Speaking Out column, a *Christianity Today* installation that allowed diverse opinions from guest contributors, Rick McKinniss argued, "it is time to stop trying to save the America of yester-year—the America often referred to as 'a Christian nation.' It is time to give up that expression and come to grips with the America of today and tomorrow. To do that, we must dispel the faulty notion that America ever was a Christian nation."[173] To some observers, the Robertson campaign was a pinnacle of Evangelical political maturation precisely because it helped emancipate them from a beguiling mirage. In the end, Evangelicals seemed to have accepted what Evangelical spokespersons like Mark A. Noll had tried to teach them throughout the 1980s, namely that "no nation, including the United States, can be God's 'new Israel.' . . . It is in fact idolatry to think that our nation has received those special dispensations Scripture declares God has reserved for the church."[174] Whereas at the beginning of the decade, a black-and-white view of history and easy answers to complex problems had seemed to be the pull of the New Christian Right, during the Robertson campaign observers noticed that Evangelicals were no longer satisfied with simplistic slogans. Nor were they willing to let themselves be boxed into but one "Christian" choice. Carl F. H. Henry reported on Evangelicals' "growing resentment of major movements that rally believers to a specific political program, that pressure Christians to line up for or against a particular political agenda as a test of orthodoxy, that oblige them to choose for or against particular candidates for office as a matter of religious preference."[175]

It was obviously two different things to either freely support a Christian candidate or be told that the Christian had but one choice. Henry had predicted that this would be an issue deterring people from voting for Robertson. The ultimate failure of Robertson's bid for the candidacy was not regarded as a failure of Evangelical politics because Evangelical spokespersons had never fully identified with the New Christian Right or with Robertson's campaign. Conversely, the fact that Evangelicals were supporting a variety of different candidates was considered to be an indication of their political coming-of-age. Evangelical spokespersons had countered the New Christian Right myth of Christian America with their own vision of Christian citizenship; they could be proudly Christian and American and embrace both religious and political liberty.

Political scientist Michael Lienesch argues that the New Christian Right created something new, "a highly charged hybrid—part religious politics, part political religion."[176] Some Evangelical spokespersons would have agreed, chastising the New Christian Right for transforming and ultimately reducing Christianity to a political entity. *Christianity Today* editor Terry Muck warned that "whenever the church has functioned primarily as a political force, the gospel has been compromised" and criticized those New Christian Right leaders who "have succumbed to the temptation to reduce the church to political party status."[177] While Evangelical spokespersons were in favor of a Christian presence in politics, they charged the New Christian Right with getting the priorities wrong: the first duty was always the church; the state was only second. Mark A. Noll wrote: "For Christians, the kingdom of God must always take priority over deference to country." This, however, never meant a withdrawal from politics because "where it is possible to shape the course of a country by the values of the kingdom, Christians enjoy a wider opportunity for serving their king."[178] Political involvement was a divine duty because it presented Christians with the opportunity to infuse society with biblical values. Evangelical spokespersons insisted that faith must be the basis for their political engagement, arguing that all decision-making was based in values. In their worldview, "true" values were based on the Bible.[179] Yet they also embraced democracy and a pluralistic society, considering these the basis for independent decision-making and freedom. Evangelical spokespersons called out and rejected New Christian Right activists' romance with theocratic notions. As Carl F. H. Henry saw it, the New Christian Right leaders were latecomers to the idea of religious freedom. In his opinion, the "freedom test" was the benchmark for Christian citizenship. Religious freedom was considered to be the highest political good, sheltering all other rights and guaranteeing universal freedom. The New Christian Right was often only interested in "Christian freedom"—not religious freedom as such—thus perverting the idea of freedom and finally "stifling" the biblical message.[180] Yet freedom and individual choice were the basis for authentic confession, both religious and political. Accordingly, Evangelicals supported the US democratic and pluralistic political system as the best one conceived by humans so far and one amenable to and accommodating of Christianity. Yet after a decade of New Christian Right politics, Evangelicals had lost any romantic notions about their political involvement and had learned political savvy. In the words of Charles W. Colson, "Christians belong in the political arena, working for both morality and justice in public policies—but without illusions." He emphasized that "there are no quick fixes" and asked his readership to "dig in for the long haul."[181] Whereas what the New Christian Right had to offer at times was highly appealing, Evangelical spokespersons during the 1980s consistently rejected the conflation of the political lobbying of the New Christian Right with the religious category of Evangelicalism, and therefore they kept a critical distance. They rejected the simplistic myth of Christian America, emphasizing that a "greater cause beckons: that of actually *saving* America." Politics was not a cure-all but only one aspect of Evangelicals' mission of evangelizing the world. Their vision of Christian citizenship was one of transforming America by example, individually and voluntary, but decisively: "It is not 'America, a Christian nation,' that we are trying to save, it is Christ's kingdom that we are seeking to establish."[182]

6
Biomedical Challenges
From Abortion to Genetic Engineering

In 1980, *Moody Monthly* ran heavy advertisements for its May issue, announced in its editorial as possibly "the most important issue *Moody Monthly* ever published." This was "admittedly a strong statement after 80 years of publishing," but, according to editor Jerry B. Jenkins, the topic discussed was so important as to warrant this preamble. The topic was: "The death of the unborn." He meant abortion. Not mincing words, Jenkins pronounced that "the non-accidental death of an innocent whose conception may have been accidental or even criminal does nothing to remedy the cause of that conception. The elimination of one of the innocent parties is a 'wrong' that will not make a 'right.'"[1] Prenatal life was portrayed as a distinct human life-form, innocent and in need of protection. No matter how bad the circumstances, then, abortion would always be seen as wrong.

The cover of the issue showed a picture of C. Everett Koop, a stern-looking man in a white medical gown, with a toddler on his arm. The headline introduced Koop as "the world's leading pediatric surgeon" (figure 6.1). With Koop thus established as a medical authority, the main article recounted his observations and opinion on abortion as told to *Moody Monthly* journalist Dick Bohrer.[2] The topics discussed in the text—abortion in conjunction with rape, incest, deformation and disability, and infanticide—contrasted with a full-page picture of Koop surrounded by young children of both sexes and various ethnic backgrounds (figure 6.2). The images of young children implicitly equated prenatal life with children. Moreover, the article was interspersed with pictures of a single red rose, a heady Christian symbol. In Christian traditions, the rose is generally associated with love, passion, and sacrifice, with a white rose symbolizing purity, while a red rose symbolizes martyrdom and blood. The rose is also the flower and symbol of the Virgin Mary, often described as a rose without thorns to symbolize a state free of sin.[3] On a symbolic level, then, *Moody Monthly* approached the topic of abortion by playing on notions of life and death, purity, and ultimate sacrifice. The composition

Figure 6.1. "The World's Leading Pediatric Surgeon on Society's Most Controversial Issue." Photograph of C. Everett Koop holding a baby. Cover of *Moody Monthly*, May 1980. Courtesy of Buswell Library Special Collections, Wheaton College, Illinois.

of the articles and illustrations revealed the underlying fear that prompted condemnation of abortion: abortion was not only the killing of unborn life; it was the murder of a child, an unspeakable crime.

During the 1980s, abortion, if not "the most important issue," became a hotly debated issue in the United States.[4] Observers spoke of a "crisis of the American family," and throughout the 1980s, the battle over abortion became one of its most visible symbols. Jimmy Carter's White House Conference on Families (WHCF), rather than relieving the situation, became a debacle; the New Christian Right emerged fighting for "traditional" Christian families; and Ronald Reagan adopted a language of values that cherished the family and appealed to conservative Christians.[5] Beyond the country, the plights and rights of children were highlighted in 1979 when UNESCO named it the International Year of the Child, and again in 1989, when the United Nations held its Convention on the Rights of the Child. At the same time, abortion was the rallying cry for both liberal-feminist and conservative-traditionalist activists in the United States, with one side fighting for a women's right to bodily autonomy (the right to choose whether to have a baby or an abortion), and the other side fighting against abortion or for the protection of unborn life.[6] While abortion was legalized in 1973, substantial Evangelical opposition to it only formed in the early 1980s. *Moody Monthly* registered its opposi-

Figure 6.2. A two-page spread with a single red rose inset into the text (*left*) and a full-page photograph of C. Everett Koop surrounded by young children. Illustrations accompanying C. Everett Koop and Dick Bohrer, "Deception-On-Demand," in *Moody Monthly*, May 1980. Courtesy of Buswell Library Special Collections, Wheaton College, Illinois.

tion to abortion with its May 1980 issue; *Christianity Today* and *Eternity* followed suit with their issues of May 20, 1983, and January 1986, respectively. Furthermore, the question of when human life started and required legal protection was complicated by new reproductive, medical, and genetic technologies. These options challenged Evangelicals' notion that children should be the offspring of marital intercourse (or else come into the family through adoption). These new technologies required thinking about what constituted life and what qualities made a life that was worth living. Whereas "embryonic discourse"—the notion that conception equals the creation of a human life—is well established in the literature, the complexity and intersections of the Evangelical discourses on reproduction, sanctity of life, family values and child-rearing, and new biomedical advances are understudied.[7]

Sociologist John H. Evans is one of few scholars to have investigated the attitudes of Christians about the issues of abortion and reproductive genetics in this era.[8] In a study published in 2002, he found that whereas evangelical Christians in 1974 had held the second-most liberal attitude toward abortion out of four religious groups, they had become the most conservative by the mid-1980s.[9] He would later call this finding the "best historical example of an organized religious elite changing the views of the average members of their tradition."[10] In 2010, he noted (echoing an observation from others) that the debate over abortion was characterized by "a lack of integrative complexity," resulting in a "black-and-white discourse." As he demonstrated, the bottom line of the pro-life discourse was that life began at conception and that all life was worthy of protection, culminating in the slogan that abortion is murder.[11] Sociologists John P. Hoffmann and Sherrie Mills Johnson have pointed out that most people differentiate between abortion for "elective" and for "traumatic" reasons.[12] Writing in 2005, and controlling survey data accordingly, they corroborated Evans's finding that evangelical Christians out of all surveyed religious groups were becoming increasingly opposed to abortion. They looked at the responses to the six questions about abortion consistently asked in the University of Chicago's General Social Survey between 1972 and 2002. Three of these questions presented elective reasons for abortion, and the other three presented traumatic reasons.[13] They found that all religious groups generally opposed abortion for elective reasons but that evangelical Christians increasingly and categorically opposed abortion no matter the circumstance. In other words, while the survey showed that Christian believers opposed abortion as a method of birth control, many allowed for abortion in circumstances like rape, a threat to the mother's life, or predicted deformity of the child. Yet evangelical Christians were increasingly opposed to abortion even in these traumatic situations. Hoffmann and Johnson speculated that "strong opposition allows the Evangelical community to demonstrate its distinctiveness from the rest of a society seen as experiencing moral decline."[14] Indeed, a particular attitude toward abortion and corresponding vision of life distinguished the Evangelical community from other Christian groups. Yet my analysis of the debate in Evangelical magazines in the 1980s shows that opinion was more differentiated, that elective and traumatic reasons for abortion were not clearly distinguishable, and that abortion was seen not as the cause but as the symptom of a problem. Criminalization of abortion was not the goal: rather, the goal was rectification of whatever circumstances led to abortion.

In 2007, on the assumption that embryonic life discourse would also color conservative Christians' attitudes toward reproductive genetics, John H. Evans and Kathy Hudson published the first sociological study on this topic. They assumed that the logic of pro-life discourse would cause Christians to avoid a deeper examination of ethical issues involved in new biomedical developments, in favor of only considering the question of whether embryos were destroyed in the process. This line of argumentation was true for some respondents, as Evans elaborated in one chapter of a later published book. Yet, generally, the hypothesis did not hold: other factors, such as religious teachings on the meaning of suffering, also played a key role. Evans and Hudson concluded that "beliefs about embryonic life do not wholly explain attitudes towards reproductive genetic technologies."[15] The debate within Evangelical magazines during the 1980s helps nuance Evans and Hudson's findings, showing that reproductive and new medical technologies were not categorically opposed, and that notions of sexuality and a vision of what constituted a family played a decisive role in Evangelical attitudes toward biomedical developments. Evangelical attitudes toward practices of abortion and new reproductive technologies were part of an Evangelical vision that celebrated human life and treasured the child as a faint reflection of the divine image.

THE PRO-LIFE STANCE

The Supreme Court's 1973 decision in *Roe v. Wade* (and the companion case of *Doe v. Bolton*, decided the same day) legalized abortion in the United States.[16] Directly after the decision, *Christianity Today* published an editorial in which associate editor Harold O. J. Brown stated: "it appears doubtful that unborn infants now enjoy any protection prior to the instant of birth anywhere in the United States."[17] This position notwithstanding, William Martin, a professor of religion and public policy, judged that while abortion would become a "litmus test of extraordinary importance" for conservative Protestants, they initially had "little to say about it one way or another."[18] Indeed, some conservative Protestant denominations initially approved of legalized abortion. Most notably, the Southern Baptist Convention, generally considered to be the largest evangelical Christian denomination, had looked favorably on legalized abortion, but "in 1980 they rescinded their former attitude and in 1984 passed a strict resolution against abortion," as Kenneth S. Kantzer recounted in *Christianity Today*.[19] Nonetheless, it would be inaccurate to say that there was no Evangelical antiabortion activism before the 1980s. Two years before the *Roe v. Wade* decision, in 1971, *Eternity* dedicated one issue to the question of abortion.[20] And in connection with the 1973 *Roe v. Wade* decision and throughout the 1970s, *Christianity Today* published several contributions on the issue, including cartoons that decried the practice of abortion as a too-easy, selfish, unnatural choice (figures 6.3 and 6.4).[21] Moreover, some Evangelicals, most notably Harold O. J. Brown, also lobbied against abortion. Brown, in conjunction with Billy Graham and C. Everett Koop, founded the Christian Action Council in 1975, which published a newsletter

Figure 6.3. "We thought we'd do for marriage what we've done for birth control." Cartoon in *Christianity Today*, December 9, 1977, reprinted on May 25, 1979. Courtesy of Buswell Library Special Collections, Wheaton College, Illinois.

with information on abortion legislation and lobbied Congress.[22] But a cohesive Evangelical position on abortion only developed in the 1980s, alongside a significant increase in magazine contributions on the topic. This Evangelical antiabortion activism was kick-started in the late 1970s by Francis A. Schaeffer and C. Everett Koop's *Whatever Happened to the Human Race?*, a book and film series.[23] Both Evangelical luminaries, philosopher-theologian Schaeffer and pediatric surgeon Koop took a firm stance against abortion and popularized this position among evangelical Christians.[24] *Christianity Today* previewed the film series *Whatever Happened to the Human Race?*, and advertisements for the book, the films, and the film and speaking tour were printed in various Evangelical magazines. *Christianity Today* also gave out the book as a free gift to new subscribers.[25] Koop was consulted on the abortion issue, and articles were published in conjunction with the release of the book.[26] Because of such coverage, Schaeffer and Koop's opposition to abortion was suddenly ever-present in Evangelical magazines. As William Martin has pointed out, "the combination of the film and book, together with the extensive promotional tour in which both men participated, is often credited with having been the single most important factor in bringing evangelicals into the fight against abortion."[27]

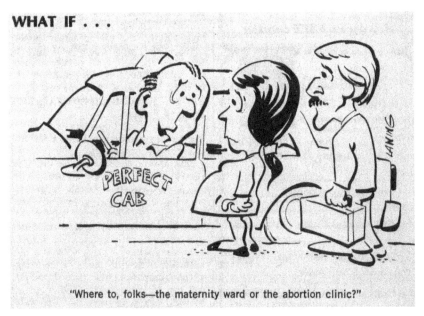

Figure 6.4. "Where to, folks—the maternity ward or the abortion clinic?" Cartoon in *Christianity Today*, February 14, 1975. Courtesy of Buswell Library Special Collections, Wheaton College, Illinois.

Whatever Happened to the Human Race?

While Francis A. Schaeffer and C. Everett Koop were friends and coauthors, they were of different temperaments. Koop was a doctor who spoke out of experience; Schaeffer took an approach that was philosophical and more abstract. These differences were obvious to Bruce H. Palmer, who reviewed the book *Whatever Happened to the Human Race?* for *Eternity*.[28] Over time, Schaeffer became more ideological, while Koop remained pragmatic and adhered to scientific facts. As scholars James Risen and Judy L. Thomas point out, *Whatever Happened to the Human Race?* could be understood as the second step in a three-step process for Schaeffer. In 1976, Schaeffer had published *How Should We Then Live*, a tirade against the evils of secular humanism. In the 1979 *Whatever Happened to the Human Race?*, he continued the argument, highlighting abortion as the greatest calamity caused by secular humanism. Both publications were accompanied by films produced by Schaeffer's son, Franky Schaeffer. Finally, in his 1981 book *A Christian Manifesto*, Francis A. Schaeffer concluded that civil disobedience was a justified method in the fight against abortion. While *Whatever Happened to the Human Race?* prompted Evangelicals to adopt a pro-life attitude, it also inspired single-issue antiabortion activists (like Randall Terry, the founder of Operation Rescue, whose members practiced civil disobedience through sit-ins at clinics) and extremists (including Lutheran pastor and abortion clinic bomber Michael Bray).[29] *Whatever Happened to the Human Race?* equated the embryo and fetus with a human child. Consequently, Schaeffer and Koop described abortion as murder and portrayed it as an American Holocaust.[30] Given this drastic rhetoric, people like Bray arrived at the conclusion that killing one (the abortion doctor) to prevent the killing of many (the "unborn children") was justified.[31] Schaeffer, whose death in May 1984 spared him from witnessing how his arguments were adopted by antiabortion terrorists, progressively moved away from a self-identified Evangelical mainstream and toward New Christian Right ideology.[32] Koop, in contrast, seemed to take the opposite trajectory. Koop never embraced a strict prohibition on abortion and, as US surgeon general under the Reagan administration, actually muted his antiabortion rhetoric.[33] Contrary to the fears of the political opposition, he did not use his government position to lobby against abortion. On the contrary, he eventually took on issues like finding treatment for patients with AIDS at a time when many conservative Christians considered the infection to be God's just punishment for the sin of homosexuality.[34] While doing so lost him his status as an icon of the New Christian Right, he remained an authority on abortion and infant care in Evangelical magazines. At the end of his eight-year term as surgeon general, he was honored in *Christianity Today* with an article and interview reflecting on his career.[35]

Asked in *Eternity* to answer the book's title question, Koop answered: "The current scene brings into focus three life issues which we have to contend with now. One is abortion, the second is infanticide, and the third is euthanasia." This list already suggests that among Evangelicals, abortion was discussed as a life-and-death question in the context of the allegedly inviolable right to human life. Referring to the *Roe v. Wade* Supreme Court decision, Koop stated that "abortion fell with a loud boom in this country, and it separated our citizens as no other issue has since the days of slavery." In Koop's estimation, abortion was the first step on a slippery slope, making killing of unwanted life acceptable: "I think because of the fact that life has become cheapened by the killing in the womb . . . our society is willing to take the next step and look at the born baby, eliminating him if he is not perfect. . . . I suspect the next category of our citizens to be categorized as nonpersons will be the elderly."[36]

While the killing of burdensome old people was still a distant threat, the killing of unwanted infants was a topic dear to Koop. In his 1980 *Moody Monthly* cover article, he submitted that "infanticide was the second domino, and it fell very silently. . . . It is still illegal in every state in the union; yet for some reason when a newborn baby is starved or in some other way allowed to die, the law turns its back."³⁷ Koop was one of the country's leading pediatric surgeons and pioneered the field of neonatal care in the United States. He was surgeon-in-chief at Children's Hospital of Philadelphia, where he set up the country's first neonatal care unit and specialized in surgery on premature and malformed infants. One of his celebrated feats was the separation of conjoined twins in 1974.³⁸ Relating experiences from his body of work, he told both *Eternity* and *Moody Monthly*'s Dick Bohrer that it was the practice in some hospitals to "allow" malformed children to die by withholding life-saving measures or letting them starve. He could not condone the practice and testified that the disabled infants who had been his patients grew up appreciating life and often became productive members of society. In his words: "I never had a family come to me and say, 'Why did you try so hard to save the life of our child?' nor have I ever had a grown child come to me and say, 'Why did you try so hard to save my life?'" He continued, emphasizing, "these youngsters become loved and loving children. They become productive members of society."³⁹ Because of this experience, Koop dismissed the argument that life with severe disabilities was not worth living. The cool economic calculation that the care of such infants cost society too much he found frightening and inhumane. Such arguments, however, let him to speculate that the termination of economically unproductive people, especially the elderly, would be next. He told *Eternity*: "Newborn babies are allowed to die for the very symptoms which affect a considerable number of elderly people who find their quality of life right now to be very precious."⁴⁰ Koop's professional concern was for premature and malformed neonates. Working in this field, he knew how parents worried for the life of their newborns and how children fought to stay alive. In his experience, the value of life depended neither on the sound condition of an infant's body at birth nor on their mental condition or capacity; a disability did not necessarily spoil a child's or a family's happiness. Furthermore, given that he had personally developed methods to fix various birth defects, he knew that some deformations could be repaired, and some impairments could be improved. Accordingly, Koop abhorred the idea of letting an infant die if a medical procedure could save its life. His rejection of abortion was essentially a rejection of a predetermined notion of what sort of life was worth living and whose life was valuable. This concern was also obvious in his fear that the socially unproductive elderly would soon be targeted by euthanasia programs.⁴¹

Koop's medical argument was that there was no qualitative difference between the life growing inside the womb and the one outside of it, especially since technologies existed that could sustain premature infants. The dichotomy between one's trying to save a premature neonate in one wing of the hospital at the same time that a doctor in another wing was aborting a fetus was a tension not only felt by Koop but also played up in the film series *Whatever Happened to the Human Race?*[42] One early scene in part 1 showed Koop answering a phone at the hospital. The next scenes showed how a newborn was rushed to the hospital, where surgical staff prepared the tiny infant for surgery. This hospital scene in which many people were involved in caring for one infant was the visual opening for the film series on abortion. In a voice-over, Francis A. Schaeffer asked, "Why is human life worth saving?" While a large surgical team in blue scrubs, hairnets, and masks started operating on the infant, the voice-over explained that according to the concept of the sanctity of human life every life was valuable. The camera was then trained on Schaeffer, who lectured the viewer that Western society had forgotten its Judeo-Christian roots and fallen into the traps of humanism and materialism, valuing human life no longer for itself but only for its productivity. In the course of the film, Schaeffer argued that this shift in perspective had made the practice of abortion possible.[43] Abortion, according to Schaeffer, ultimately was not a legal problem but rather a theological and even ontological one. In answer to the question of why the infant should not be left to die and why the time and effort of a medical team should be wasted on one baby, he stated that the Christian worldview prescribed that every single human life was valuable and therefore worthy of protection. By showing that medical assistance was without question extended to a premature baby, he visually challenged the assumption that prenatal life was not yet human or deserving of protection. In the movie, the drama underscored this point, keeping the audience enthralled in fear and hope for the infant's survival. By equating the fetus with the baby via the link of the premature neonate, Schaeffer could call abortion a form of murder legalized by a state deprived of its Christian sense of right and wrong. The film painted the dystopian vision of a society ruled by immoral legalism, in which abortion was the door that opened the way for other forms of legal killings.

Lauding the film's "strong, prophetic statement," David Singer, in the *Christianity Today* film preview, judged that "humanists have been given notice on the impending moral chaos that faces a society divested of its Judeo-Christian foundations."[44] Schaeffer and Koop did not consider abortion to be a remedy to a bad situation, for example the physical, emotional, or economic hardship of the mother. These aspects played at best a minor role in the two men's thinking. Rather, the doctor and the philosopher asked questions pertaining to the meaning and value of life. As Koop bluntly stated: "If you believe the universe came about by chance, that you and I evolved from primordial ooze, then there is no unique dignity to human life. Why worry about it?" Thus, a purely scientific explanation for life provided no moral guidelines, and without them, according to Koop and Schaeffer, humans were not truly human, and society would plunge into inhumane anomie. However, "if you believe that man was created in the image of God and that he has total, unique, specific specialness, then he should be protected to the best of our ability for all of his lifetime."[45] In Koop and Schaeffer's perspective, the abortion issue illustrated a particular vision of life; the question was thus whether people wanted to live in a world that came about by chance and in which life could therefore be dispensed of indiscriminately, or whether they wanted to live in an ordered, meaningful universe in which each life was unconditionally valuable and worthy of protection. For Koop and Schaeffer, it was obvious which vision was the right one. Yet they saw society progressively undermining its own foundations by dismissing its morals. One scene in the film especially impressed the reviewer, Singer: "The camera wanders above a seemingly endless expanse of hot, white sand strewn with hundreds of 'dead' dolls," eventually finding Koop standing at the shore of the Dead Sea surrounded by the dolls. Against this graphically memorable backdrop, Koop recounted conservation statistics for endangered species. The juxtaposition of image and text made viewers wonder what sort of society protected animals yet aborted human life. More than that, according to Singer, "we live in a schizophrenic society concerned about the increasing rate of child abuse, while it licenses doctors to kill the unborn."[46] *Whatever Happened to the Human Race?* accordingly did not address abortion for its own sake but considered it symptomatic of a society gone astray. Koop had identified abortion as the first "domino," evoking a particular Cold War image that suggested an imminent chain reaction of falls, unless there was an intervention. The dominos were the scruples protecting the lives of weak members of society. In Koop and Schaeffer's portrayal, the abortion issue showed that society no longer regarded life as a gift to be cherished and protected but rather saw it as an accident to be exploited, disposed of, or otherwise treated as seen fit. Prenatal life had already lost protection, and they wondered what category of humans would become fair game next. The offered solution, then, according to the *Eternity* book review, was not primarily the overturning of abortion legislation but rather "a rededication by committed Christians to involvement in society."[47] As the title of the book and film series indicate, for Schaeffer and Koop abortion was not simply an issue that concerned the life of one fetus/child or many fetuses/children; the legalization and subsequent demand for the practice of abortion, to them, signaled the decaying of the "human race."

Embryonic Life Discourse and the Focus on the (Unborn) Child
Evangelical readers reacted vehemently to *Whatever Happened to the Human Race?* and the portrayal of the antiabortion argument in *Moody Monthly*, making abortion one of the lead issues in Evangelical magazines during the

1980s.[48] *Sojourners* received numerous letters pressuring it to take a stand on abortion, and it printed a special issue on the topic in November 1980. Editor Jim Wallis explained that the *Sojourners* community had been put off by the antiabortion activism of the New Christian Right yet affirmed that a stance against abortion fit well with *Sojourners*' overall outlook: "Our deepest convictions about poverty, racism, violence, and the equality of men and women are finally rooted in a radical concern for life—its absolute value and the need to protect it. It was only a matter of time before the spiritual logic of these other commitments would lead us to a 'pro-life' response to abortion as well."[49] *Christianity Today* dedicated its May 20, 1983, issue to abortion. The latest but most strident positioning came from *Eternity*, which only in January 1986 addressed the issue of abortion but then took a firm stand against it.

Sociologist John H. Evans used the term "embryonic life discourse" to refer to what became the established argumentation among pro-life advocates. This discourse focused on the life of the unborn, highlighting that "'life begins at conception' and to destroy such life is therefore wrong."[50] The main strategies employed in the fight against abortion were (1) a technical-biological description of fetal development and definition of life that appeared to be scientifically objective, and (2) a clinical but brutal description of the process of abortion that played on the audience's emotions. Political scientist and reproductive rights activist Rosalind Pollack Petchesky in the mid-1980s wondered how the image of the fetus had become such a powerful pro-life argument. She traced the standard representation of the fetus back to a 1962 *Look* photo series that introduced a new book, Geraldine Lux Flanagan's 1962 *The First Nine Months of Life*. She described that series as typical for all following fetal representations:

> In every picture the fetus is solitary, dangling in the air (or its sac) with nothing to connect it to any life-support system but "a clearly defined umbilical cord." In every caption it is called "the baby" (even at forty-four days) and is referred to as "he"—until the birth, that is, when "he" turns out to be a girl. Nowhere is there any reference to the pregnant woman, except in a single photograph at the end showing the newborn baby lying next to the mother, both of them gazing off the page, allegedly at "the father." From their beginning, such photographs have represented the fetus as primary and autonomous, the woman as absent or peripheral.[51]

The strategy of "teaching" viewers to recognize abortion as a violent procedure, especially for the fetus, was described by Petchesky using the example of the 1984 short film *The Silent Scream*. Ultrasonic images here supposedly provided medical evidence for the moralistic message that abortion was wrong.

Communications scholar Celeste Michelle Condit describes how the visual argument presented in pictures and films was metonymically reduced and metaphorically charged to become a potent, persuasive trope: the fetus as unborn child.[52]

Schaeffer and Koop had facilitated this particular line of argumentation, but pro-life activists adopted and perfected it.[53] Evangelical magazines, however, did not promulgate this abbreviated and one-sided argument; they rarely presented abortion without discussing the plight of mothers, families, and society. Even though most Evangelical spokespersons eventually took a stance against abortion, they saw the simplistic conviction that abortion was the murder of an unborn child—far from self-evident—as resulting from complex theological and ethical considerations. Yet, once the notion of the sanctity of life was established, it found a potent symbol in the vision of the (unborn) child.

In Koop and Schaeffer's argument, the pregnant woman hardly played a role. On the rare occasion when they did refer to women who considered an abortion, they could be shockingly insensitive. Koop mentioned rape and incest as two reasons brought forth by abortion advocates to justify the legalization of abortion. While he called incest "the most common untalked-about crime in this country," he dismissed rape rather offhand. One letter writer called Koop out on this omission, writing: "Dr. Koop sweeps the whole rape issue away by saying, 'Rape practically never results in pregnancy.'" Koop's argument had been somewhat more circumspect—he had also pointed out that "even if a child is conceived through rape, destroying it does not end the trauma. It does not deter the rapist. It does not blot out the woman's memory of the assault. It does not change her degradation in any way." Yet he spared no thought for what a nine-month-long pregnancy might mean for a woman so treated. An anonymous letter writer asked: "How can you say that a baby conceived through rape or incest should always be kept and not aborted? Would you want something in you that wasn't of God and made in a horrible manner?" Koop seemed to somewhat contradict himself: on the one hand, he described rape as not much of an issue in the context of abortion because, according to him, it did not often result in pregnancy; but, on the other hand, he discussed incest almost exclusively in terms of a young girl being raped by a family member, thus becoming a young, unwed teenage mother. The one sentence in this discussion that most upset *Moody Monthly* readers was Koop's affirmation that "if a girl is old enough to conceive, she is old enough to have the baby."[54] One of the aforementioned letter writers called it a "gross insensitivity." Another letter writer, identified as a "Christian Family Practitioner," pointed out that a girl in search of an abortion—whether the "victim of rape, incest, or just ignorance or carelessness"—had to be in serious distress to confess that "I know I'd be killing my baby but I just can't bear the anguish of carrying it in me for nine months and then giving it up."[55] The vehemence of the reactions toward Koop's insensitivity regarding women showed that for some Evangelicals the fate of the fetus could not be divorced from the expectant mother's situation. Yet Koop and Schaeffer's rather cursory treatment of women was deliberate. As Koop later admitted, he believed that focusing on the woman's plight weakened the argument against abortion.[56] While he thought that abortion should be an option for extreme cases, he nonetheless advised pro-life activists to bring forth the strongest case possible against abortion by focusing on the life of the unborn. Accordingly, part of the short shrift women received in *Whatever Happened to the Human Race?* and Koop and Schaeffer's discussion of abortion during that time might be considered tactical. Their focus was on a particular vision of life: in their narrative the "unborn child" (the weakest member of society) symbolized the necessity to return to a meaningfully ordered society.

The embryonic life discourse was strategic: if the mother was not mentioned, the abortion issue could simplistically be portrayed as a matter of whether an embryo would be allowed to fully develop and be born as a human child. Images supported these discourses, selectively portraying a fetus in the absence of the mother or the womb, and providing supposedly accurate information and visual confirmation of the "baby's" development.[57] Consistently portraying the embryo or fetus as a child not yet born, as demonstrated in the literature, became the main tactic in the fight against legalized abortion. Once a fetus was established as a miniature person, it had to have individual rights and legal protection.[58] This discourse was also present in Evangelical magazines. However, while pro-life leaders instructed their activists not to divert from the issue by considering adjacent concerns, in Evangelical magazines, the issue of abortion was always embedded in a larger context. While focusing on the unborn child, the discourse was always relational, considering also the familial relationships. Also, biomedical knowledge alone, for Evangelicals, could not conclusively confer notions of personhood or the sanctity of life. Evangelical spokespersons thus tackled the questions of when life began and what constituted the value of life. The embryonic life question in Evangelical magazines was not only technical-biological but also, and primarily, moral, theological, and social.

This does not mean that the strategy of employing pictures supposedly showing gruesome details from the process of abortion was absent. Images carried a potent emotive message, strongly suggesting the humanity of unborn life. In her analysis of the use and influence of the fetal image in the abortion controversy, political scientist and reproductive rights activist Rosalind Pollack Petchesky has shown that images were not objective evidence but rather

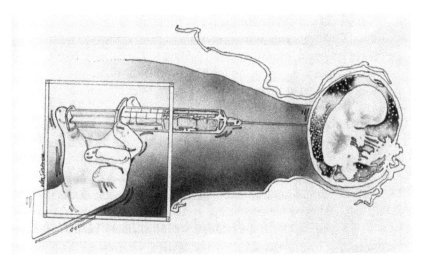

Figure 6.5. Stereotypical drawing of the abortion procedure, erasing the body and plight of the woman. Illustration accompanying Carl Horn, "How Freedom of Thought Is Smothered in America," in *Christianity Today*, April 6, 1984. Courtesy of Buswell Library Special Collections, Wheaton College, Illinois.

"cultural representations," used by pro-life activists "to make fetal personhood a self-fulfilling prophecy."[59] One example in Evangelical magazines was an illustration accompanying a long article in *Christianity Today* by Carl Horn, an attorney who had recently resigned from the Reagan administration to run for Congress. Horn assembled divergent examples to demonstrate that in the United States, Christian values were excluded from public life and replaced with ones inimical to Christianity. When he turned to abortion, he cited lengthily from Magda Denes's 1976 report of her observations in an abortion clinic. Even though Denes had been in favor of legalized abortion, Horn used detailed and shocking passages from her account to argue that abortion was wrong and un-Christian. One quote from a "distressed doctor," for example, read: "with the needle, I have harpooned the fetus. I can feel the fetus move at the end of the needle just like you have a fish hooked on a line."[60] A few artistic drawings illustrated the article. One sketch depicted the aforementioned scene: a schematically drawn fetus in a hinted-at uterus was speared by a long, handheld needle (figure 6.5). The woman inside whom the drama played out was nowhere to be seen in this depiction. The combination of text and image created the impression that a human child was killed like a lowly animal, a drastically un-Christian practice. This sort of scientifically inclined argument was not often found in the Evangelical magazine context. Scientific "facts" like the observation that embryos moved around and felt pain could bolster an argument but did not determine the status of prenatal life for Christians. Accordingly, biblical exegesis was necessary to "prove" prenatal personhood.

British theologian John R. W. Stott, writing in *Christianity Today*, set out to answer the question of whether life begins before birth. He used biological evidence but arrived at his conclusion—that, indeed, human life begins before birth—via the Bible. To him, "the biblical evaluation of the humanness of the fetus is confirmed by modern medical science." He then continued with a scientific description: "In the 1960s the genetic code was unraveled. We now know that from the moment the ovum is fertilized by the penetration of the sperm, the zygote has a unique genotype distinct from both parents. The 23 pairs of chromosomes are complete. The sex, size, and shape, the color of skin, hair, and eyes, the intelligence and temperament of the child are already determined." While this, to Stott, was confirmation, the main evidence that human life began at conception was biblical. He enlisted the following points in favor of his argument: (1) Psalm 139, in which the writer reflects on his own prenatal life; (2) Luke 1:41–44, in which the pregnant Elizabeth and the pregnant Mary meet, and the prenatal John the Baptist leaps in his mother's womb in recognition of the prenatal Jesus; and (3) the example of Jesus himself, who was both God and human as soon as he entered Mary's womb. Accordingly, scientific findings confirmed what Christians already knew about prenatal life from biblical accounts. Therefore, Stott argued, the fetus was not "a lump of jelly or a blob of tissue" but "actually a 'he' or 'she,' an unborn child."[61]

The picture inserted into Stott's article did not so much show an anatomically correct fetus as illustrate the qualities of the human being it would grow into (figure 6.6). The monochrome pencil drawing showed a progression of four humanlike figures, suggesting the development of a fetus into a born baby. The rough sketches showed hardly any variation between the first three, supposedly prenatal fetuses, other than that the drawings increased in size. The most distinct difference between the sketches of the fetuses and the sketch of the baby was that this last had hair and open eyes. While the lack of detail for the first three sketches indicated a lack of effort to depict an anatomically correct fetus with reference to gestational stage, the most obvious feature that highlighted the figurative rather than literal nature of the illustration was a pair of glasses that accompanied the child in each sketch. This detail might represent something like the child's shortsightedness or bookishness, since Stott suggested that a person's characteristics and dispositions were already present in the early stages of fetal development. Whatever it was supposed to represent, this impossible pair of prenatal glasses forced the observer to regard the drawing from a figurative plane of interpretation. The picture emphasized Stott's point that it was not biological, material evidence

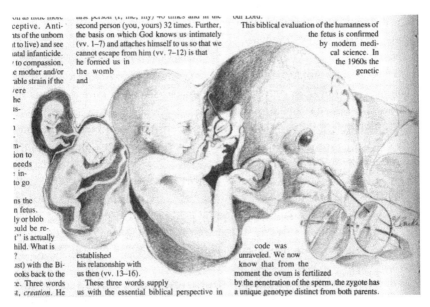

Figure 6.6. Unusual drawing of a fetus wearing glasses at different stages of gestation Illustration accompanying John Stott, "Does Life Begin before Birth?," in *Christianity Today*, September 5, 1980. Courtesy of Buswell Library Special Collections, Wheaton College, Illinois.

but rather immaterial, theological evidence that forced Evangelicals to regard abortions as the murder of unborn children.

The figure of C. Everett Koop seemed better suited for medical-scientific embryonic discourse than for theological discourse. He could authoritatively talk about fetal development. In his contribution to *Moody Monthly*'s abortion issue, he delivered a scientific description of the fetus: "Many of our people [i.e., Evangelicals] don't realize that by the twenty-first day—before most women even know they are pregnant—the baby's heart demonstrates its first feeble beats. A child's fingerprints are indelibly in place by the twelfth week."[62] The description suggested (albeit implicitly) that even before a woman knew she was pregnant, a fully formed child was awaiting birth in her womb. Scientific "facts" seemed to establish that the fetus was but an unborn child.[63] Yet, to Koop, as already pointed out, a biological description of life did not confer any value on that life. If life came about by chance, as a secular and scientific worldview seemed to suggest, no moral judgment could be attached to its destruction. It took a theological notion for human life to become special and therefore worthy of protection. The sacredness of all human life, to Koop, was patently obvious: "Of all people, the evangelical should best know that man is unique because he has been created in the image of God and is precious to Him."[64] For Evangelicals, the special place of humans in God's creation was a basic conviction, hardly in need of repetition.

What was encompassed in this Evangelical vision of the "sanctity of life" was explicated by Doug Badger, director of the Christian Action Council, in *Sojourners'* special issue on abortion: "Yahweh fashioned human beings in God's image [Gen. 1:26–28]. Each person thus is vested with an inviolable dignity on the basis of his or her creation." Accordingly, only because humans were created in God's image was the killing of another human being wrong. But the notion entailed more. As Badger wrote: "the Torah's sixth commandment [Exod. 20:13] . . . functions not only as a prohibition of murder, but as a positive injunction to respect human life."[65] Because of the way humans were created, then, human life was to be held in high esteem. Evangelicals extended the dignified position of humanity to the unborn. Yet in this case, too, scientific observations served as confirmation rather than evidence. In much the same way, even though he used elaborate scientific descriptions on fetal development, Koop turned to Christian teachings to secure a special status and therefore protection for the fetus. Koop argued that when God became man in Jesus Christ he was human not from birth but from conception: "The story of the incarnation leaves no room for doubt. The angel told Joseph, 'That which is conceived in her is of the Holy Spirit.' From the moment of conception God had entered human life."[66] Accordingly, from the moment of conception, developing life was human and as such was entitled to protection. Koop combined medical-scientific and religious argumentation in his plea against abortion—but scientific "facts" only took on meaning within the religious framework.

A strong theological argument for the personhood of the fetus, as just shown, was that God himself had become human and Mary had been pregnant with him for nine months. Mary had been crucial for the incarnation, the central tenet of Christian faith. In the Evangelical worldview, the fetus could not be considered independent of its familial relations. Indeed, *Moody Monthly* editor Jerry B. Jenkins stressed the importance of discussing the topic of abortion in "a Christian family magazine": abortion was a family problem.[67] In *Moody Monthly*'s abortion issue, Koop's testimony on abortion, accordingly, was surrounded by other articles discussing abortion in the context of families, like writer Lucibel Van Atta's contribution addressing the opinion that "this is no time to have a baby," a not-uncommon justification for couples considering abortion.[68] Chuck and Winnie Christensen regularly provided advice on family issues to *Moody Monthly* readers in their column, and in this issue, they addressed women who had had abortions. They felt sure that among their readers were converted Evangelical women who regretted having had an abortion: "You have admitted to yourself and to God

BIOMEDICAL CHALLENGES 195

Figure 6.7. "If Not Abortion, What Then? Why Prolife Rhetoric Is Not Enough." Cover of *Christianity Today*, May 20, 1983. Courtesy of Buswell Library Special Collections, Wheaton College, Illinois.

that you were wrong." Under these circumstances, the Christensens' women could rest assured that God had forgiven them and that they were allowed to continue with their lives: "If God has forgiven you, why keep punishing yourself?"[69] Contributions like those by Van Atta and the Christensens showed that neither was abortion unknown to Evangelicals, nor did it concern only the developing unborn life. The composition of articles in this issue reveals that for *Moody Monthly* abortion was a family issue that affected not just the unborn but its expectant mother and further relatives. Furthermore, there were Evangelicals who had had abortions, and those who had considered doing so. It was a pervasive practice with complex reasons that concerned all.

This trend of discussing abortion as a familial and societal issue could be observed in other treatments of the topic as well. *Christianity Today*'s May 1983 issue is a case in point. The cover displayed a naked newborn baby held in front of a black background by two adult hands (figure 6.7). Like with the pictures used in antiabortion propaganda as studied by Petchesky, the focus was squarely on the baby, not the parent. And yet, hands held the child in the photograph. While only the hands and lower arms were visible, this detail illustrated that children did not exist on their own; they needed adults to hold them. This was the first time abortion made it onto the cover of *Christianity Today* in the 1980s, and the issue's objective was neither to categorically proscribe abortion nor to equip readers with pro-life rhetoric to fight it. Rather, the issue was dedicated to finding alternatives to abortion. The headline asked "If Not Abortion, What Then?" and promised answers to "Why Prolife Rhetoric Is Not Enough."

A story titled "Willa's Dilemma" in this issue of *Christianity Today* introduced a situation in which a woman was forced to consider an abortion, which was cast as a viable option and possibly the lesser of two evils. The fictional account empathetically described a situation in which it was hard to condemn a woman for choosing an abortion. Willa was depicted as a model citizen of poor origins. She and her husband had worked their way out of an impoverished neighborhood, but then, with two children and a third on the way, the husband had a fatal accident. Willa was forced to move back into her old neighborhood because she could no longer afford to pay for her own apartment. Worse, because of the pregnancy she was about to lose her job and therefore the sole income for her family. A friend provided temporary babysitting services for the two children but would not be able to do so indefinitely and certainly not for an infant. The apartment they were forced to move to had a hole in the wall, and it was suggested that the previous tenant had smacked around her child so hard that it left that hole. It was indicated that another mouth to feed when the situation was already bleak was something that led mothers to turn violently against their own children. The friend brought up the idea of an abortion. Willa did not want an abortion, but there seemed to be no other option.[70] The message of the story was that it was not enough to carry a child to term—it then had to be cared for, both physically and emotionally. In the worst scenario, not only was there no money and no love to spare for the newborn, its arrival would also draw precious resources away from older siblings. The baby's birth would be, at least figuratively speaking, the death of its family.

In this story, neither is the woman absent, nor were so-called traumatic reasons for abortion given: no injury or deformity to the unborn child was mentioned, the mother's life was not endangered because of the pregnancy, and she did not conceive the child through rape or incest. All of the reasons why Willa considered an abortion were supposedly elective or therapeutic.[71] Yet they added up to constitute quite a dilemma, indeed. The author seemed to indicate that given the circumstances, abortion was really the only plausible option for Willa. Of course, the author did not advocate abortion. A postscript in another article expressed the hope that Christians would knock at Willa's door and show her a way out of her dilemma.[72] Apparently, the goal of the story was to provoke readers into considering what circumstances led women to have abortions and how such situations could be improved— or more precisely, what Evangelicals could do to remedy bad situations that forced women into having abortions. In the lead article, Scott Reed and Paul Fromer explained: "Moved by compassion and conscience to demand that every woman carry her baby to birth, we find ourselves also urged by the same motives to help that woman and child to find life of some quality. We say that the aborter rejects the child, but if we were indifferent to the kind of life the child would be forced into, in some sense we too would be rejecting him. We want to join right-to-birth with right-to-life, meaning quality-of-life."[73]

These authors suggested that all those who did not help women and families in need were indirectly complicit in the practice of abortion. If Evangelicals wanted to reduce the number of abortions, they had to become active in their churches, their neighborhoods, their cities. If they wanted to claim the right to denounce the practice of abortion, they had to offer alternatives and assist those in need, including taking responsibility for the quality of life of the child once it was born.[74] The authors envisioned the question of whether to have an abortion as one that might decide the welfare of a whole family. Accordingly, they argued, abortion was a problem that concerned everyone, and everyone, to a degree, shared responsibility.

This aspect of the issue, that devastating social circumstances pressured women into having abortions, was also highlighted by articles in *Sojourners*. Generally concerned with protesting the nuclear arms race and the country's overseas wars, *Sojourners* also fought social and racial injustices at home. Poverty, especially in deprived, Black, inner-city neighborhoods, was a topic discussed intermittently.[75] In July 1981, for example, a long interview with Marian Wright Edelman, a lawyer with the NAACP Legal Defense and Educational Fund and the founder of the Children's Defense Fund, was published. Entitled "Suffer the Little Ones," the article focused on how poverty hurt children and disproportionately affected Black children.[76] In *Sojourners*' 1980 abortion issue, race and poverty were linked to abortion by the civil rights leader Jesse Jackson. He complained that experts were calling for "population control" precisely at a point in time "when black people in America and people of color around the world were demanding their rightful place as human citizens." Accordingly, he condemned people who advocated abortion only because "they do not want to spend the necessary money to feed, clothe, and educate more people," and he deplored the practice of cutting social services that benefited poor children.[77] That the antiabortion movement was largely regarded as a white phenomenon was attested to by the Black Evangelical Spencer Perkins in an article in *Christianity Today*. He explained why Black people were reluctant to join the movement by pointing out that many of the activists had also opposed Black liberation. He related the question of "a black single mother" who had asked him: "Do you think they would care if only black babies were aborted?" While he did not embrace the practice of abortion, Spencer pointed to the vicious cycle of poverty and violence in impoverished areas that would be perpetuated indefinitely if a "zero abortions policy" were to be enforced.[78] These articles show that race as a factor in abortions was largely ignored in the argumentation of the general pro-life movement but was (to a certain, albeit minimal degree) presented in Evangelical magazines. The inclusion of race in these conversations highlighted the point that abortion was a practice that hit the most vulnerable ones—not just the "unborn child" but also impoverished Black women, for whom abortion was often the only way to prevent the decline of an already dire situation. That abortion was intrinsically related to the question of "welfare" was argued by freelance writer Elizabeth Moore. She pointed out the double-edged nature of abortion and poverty: it could either be argued that abortion was the solution to the problem of poverty, or that abortion was forced (through the withholding of adequate social services) onto a particular segment of the population that happened to be poor.[79] Accounts like this show that for many Evangelical spokespersons, abortion was but a symptom of larger issues like poverty and social injustice.

The Evangelical embryonic discourse focused on the "unborn child" as a human being that was created in the image of God and was therefore worthy of protection. Yet the fetus was not seen isolated from familial relationships. Evangelicals acknowledged both that children needed caring adults to live good lives, and that parents, especially women carrying unwanted life or women in hard economic situations, needed assistance. Evangelicals envisioned the unborn child as part of a complex web of relationships that ultimately represented life itself. Accordingly, every human bore responsibility for creating conditions that made raising children, and continuing the circle of life, desirable. In their vision, the question of abortion would be obsolete in a perfect Christian community because no circumstances would force women to have abortion, and the high esteem for all human life would prevent anyone from voluntarily choosing to abort.

Vanishing Children

The issue of abortion was only one aspect of the discussion concerning children in Evangelical magazines. Spokespersons diagnosed a situation that was increasingly inimical to the raising of children.[80] In 1984, *Christianity Today* ran a two-part story from Rodney Clapp called "Vanishing Childhood." The gist of the articles was that childhood was a culturally created concept had shifted through time and was about to change again. Clapp, in the second part of the report, spoke of a new "era of the wanted child."[81] While this sounded positive—after all, wanted children were planned and cared for—the author actually judged that "things are happening in our society that could mean that adults generally like children less." Children, according to him, were no longer regarded as a natural part of life. Rather, they had become a choice, a commodity rivaling other commodities like cars. The title, then, referred to the idea that childhood was no longer an unburdened, taken-for-granted period of time because the birth of a child was no longer a natural event, a gift of God to be accepted as it happened. The common practices of abortion and infanticide, according to the author, ensured that parents could choose not only whether to have a child but which child they kept (aborting, for example, one with chromosomal abnormalities). Additionally, Clapp charged, "people openly describe children as brats, eels, piranhas," disparaging them when they did not turn out as planned.[82] The first part of the story was given over to an analysis of children being expected to act more and more like adults. While Clapp generally welcomed the children's rights movement, he saw this trend in behavioral expectations as social regress rather than progress.[83] The "wanted child" in his story sounded more like the outlaw of the "wanted" posters than longed-for offspring. By attempting to improve the conditions for children, society, in his view, was actually on its way to outlawing and eradicating childhood altogether. Accordingly, Clapp exhorted parents: "To be created in God's image means, above all and uniquely among his creation, to be a responsible creature. It means to be capable of choice and to be held liable for our decisions and the actions that flow from them." The solution was not to deal with children by doing away with them—literally through abortions or figuratively by redefining them legally as adults—but to accept one's God-given role as a parent. Rightly understood, parenthood was a privilege, and it could be the most consequential and fulfilling of tasks: "And so parenthood, comprehended, means not only shaping individual children, it means shaping tomorrow." Clapp described two clashing trends in contemporary society: a concern for the well-being of children as epitomized in the growing field of expert literature on child-rearing, and the rise in practices inimical to children.[84] In Evangelical magazines, these two apparently opposing trends resulted in debate about wanting and rejecting children, cumulating in the question of what God's design for children and parenthood was.

While not opposed to methods of birth control per se, Evangelicals were wary of the societal trends that were leading to a decrease in the number of children: a general reduction in the number of children per family, and growing numbers of couples choosing to delay pregnancy or simply to avoid having children at all. Former *Christianity Today* editor and antiabortion activist Harold O. J. Brown promulgated the most drastic of arguments, predicting that societies that allowed legal abortions were aborting themselves. He argued that abortion and the choice to have fewer or no children was leading to a fatal population reduction—not only in the United States but also in places like Germany and Switzerland. He called this trend "collective suicide."[85] While other spokespersons did not subscribe to Brown's reissuing of the idea of race suicide, reminiscent of earlier eugenic discourses, they shared his worry about a society apparently inimical to children. A general ill feeling about an apparent cultural trend against children permeated Evangelical magazines. For example, Chuck and Winnie Christensen, in their family advice column in *Moody Monthly*, responded in April 1986 to a concerned letter writer. The expectant mother was disturbed by the warnings of her church friends that a cute baby would soon turn into a nuisance. While allowing that the friends were merely trying to correct her "rose-tinted" perspective of parenthood, the Christensens also suspected that the general society's negative attitude toward children was penetrating Christian communities. They reported that according to a recent poll, 70 percent of respondents would decide against children if they could retract their decisions.[86] Evangelicals' bewilderment regarding conscious and rationalized decisions against children was expressed by Robert C. Roberts in *Christianity Today*: "These days, couples who have decided against having children are often strikingly candid about it. We may be shocked at the casual way they measure the value of children against winter sports, trips to Europe, and careers." Roberts rejected this commodification of children and argued that the value of children was incomparable and could and should not be measured against "ski trips and flexibility of schedule and career continuity."[87] Similarly, Pamela P. Wong, in an *Eternity* article, analyzed the new generation's changed attitudes. She stated: "They're marrying later—if they do marry. They are putting off having children—if they ever do. In a variety of ways, they are choosing to pursue more self-oriented, 'I-deserve-the-best' images, rather than the formerly-valued, family-oriented, 'our-kids-deserve-the-best' images." Not all of these changes were bad. After all, Wong argued, if couples only postponed becoming parents, they might be more mature once they started having children. Rather than condemning all developments, she wished to combine the best: "The challenge, it appears, is to promote the positive strengths of the new images, while preserving the strengths of the old values."[88] However, decisions against children were still suspect. Whereas secular reproductive rights activists usually considered parenthood a choice—and tended to see contraceptives, family planning, and abortion as a triad of rights that made it a choice— Evangelicals understood family planning more literally as making provisions for a family.[89] In a companion to Wong's article, assistant professor of Biblical studies John H. White discussed the biblical mandate to marry and procreate. While he acknowledged that God charged some people with tasks that were best undertaken without children, he nonetheless insisted that this was the exception. He judged: "But if a couple desires not to have children for clearly selfish reasons—that is surely wrong!" Contraception, in this view, was a legitimate method of family planning but should not be used to prevent the birth of children altogether. Even though parenthood could be a challenge, "the great vision set before Christian couples is the inestimable privilege of nurturing children."[90]

Children were considered both a gift and a charge from God. It was a biblical mandate to procreate, yet children were a reward in themselves. More than that, children both imbued life with value and embodied the value of life. Children reminded Roberts, for example, "of the fundamental importance of love, of our kinship with every human being, and of our need for eternity." And, "to love children," according to him, was "to love life, not like an egoist who cringes in the face of his own annihilation, but like a connoisseur who appreciates the treasure for its intrinsic worth."[91] Contemporary social trends threatened this vision. The conscious decision against children was regarded as unnatural and against God's design. Children were life and future, both literally and figuratively. Their commodification robbed them of that value and made them a lifestyle choice among others. A decision against children was a decision against life and, in the last consequence, meant the end of humanity itself.

Adoption

The most pivotal contrast evoked in Evangelical magazines was that of infertile couples longing for children, on the one hand, and women aborting unwanted babies, on the other.

Associate editor of *Today's Christian Woman* Kelsey Menehan, for example, in a *Christianity Today* article titled "Where Have All the Babies Gone?," argued that abortion was the prime reason why fewer babies (especially desirable, healthy "blond-blue-eyed babies") were available for adoption.[92] What was an unwanted pregnancy to one couple could be a blessing to another. In reaction to articles on abortion, readers wrote in, commenting that they would not have had a now dearly loved child if its mother had not gone through with the pregnancy and given up the baby for adoption.[93] Some advocated adoption as an alternative to abortion. Accordingly, "Alternative to Abortion" hotlines and centers, like those started by the Christian Action Council, generally also helped with the process of adoption.[94] Such a matchup between prospective parents and pregnant woman—in this case, the Bynums (a pastor and his wife) and a pregnant teenager—was described in Menehan's article. The young woman, called by the pseudonym Karen, almost fit the cliché of irresponsible and immoral behavior: she was a sixteen-year-old unwed pregnant teenager with a family history of abortion (her older sister) and marital problems (her parents). Yet Karen had become a Christian and believed that abortion was murder. She found Christians who supported her through her pregnancy and helped her find a Christian couple, the Bynums, to adopt the baby. Menehan considered it "ironic" that each year, approximately the same number of couples sought a child through adoption as abortions were performed. She introduced several crisis pregnancy centers that also counseled women to give up their baby for adoption, highlighting the work of the Catholic Pearson Foundation and pointing out that the Christian Action Council had been criticized for not pushing adoption hard enough. Not only could "children" be saved from abortion through adoption, these children, she suggested, would be better off in adopted families than in the low-income, crime-ridden, single-parent households of their birth mothers. Menehan and others suggested that poor Black neighborhoods, in particular, reproduced their plight because it was "taboo" to give up children for adoption.[95] This opinion was made explicit in an *Eternity* editorial called "Babies Having Babies," where the vicious circle of one generation after another of Black children being raised in poverty by teenage mothers was decried.[96] According to Menehan, then, not only could adoption be the answer to the problem of abortion, it could also alleviate some social inequalities and injustices by providing children with better homes. In this scenario, abortion was unsatisfactory to more than the parties involved: it not only killed a child and made the mother an unwitting murderer, it also "frustrated" infertile couples.[97] In Evangelical accounts, the notion of having an abortion and that of wanting an adoption were starkly contrasted, pitting a vision of doom and death against a vision of life and hope. Menehan's report suggested, although did not state outright, that there really were no unwanted children and that if only God's plans were followed, all children would find loving, adoptive homes.[98]

Infertility Treatments

Christianity Today's Washington editor Beth Spring published a book on contemporary Christian attitudes toward infertility, and a long article detailing the argument was printed in the magazine.[99] Barrenness or unwanted infertility were described as devastating problems faced by a significant number of couples. The article was illustrated by a photograph of a newborn infant, apparently floating in space, reminiscent of pro-life illustrations (figure 6.8). To the outside observer, the established repertoire of images thus suggested another discussion of abortion. Instead, the reader found the story of Barb and Paul and their unfulfilled longing for a child. Infertility was described like a trauma with stages of denial, acceptance, and eventual overcoming. Whereas other couples found medical help and used new reproductive tech-

Figure 6.8. Black-and-white photograph of a decontextualized infant, reminiscent of antiabortion propaganda. Illustration accompanying Beth Spring, "When the Dream Child Dies," in *Christianity Today*, August 7, 1987. Courtesy of Buswell Library Special Collections, Wheaton College, Illinois.

nologies or adopted a child, Barb and Paul "remain child-free." While their path was painful and required work, they finally accepted that they were not meant to be parents and found other meaningful tasks within their church community.[100] The article developed the vision that children (biological or adopted) were not necessary for a "family"; rather, Evangelicals themselves were children of God.

This largely narrative text was theologically contextualized by Ray S. Anderson. In a box set within the larger article, Anderson, professor of theology and ministry at Fuller Theological Seminary, summarized the biblical teachings on children, the childless, and the Christian family. He argued that in the Old Testament, barrenness was a punishment by God. However, the concept of what it meant to be a family changed in the New Testament context: "Marriage and childbearing are still recognized as valuable, but not exclusive or necessary, experiences." Now, all true believers were God's children, constituting a covenant family in which they were brothers and sisters to one another; the New Testament family was the chosen, adopted family.[101] Family, according to this vision, required no parenthood; instead all believers made up God's family.

While Spring and Anderson argued that unwanted infertility was no curse or punishment, Spring acknowledged that many couples who longed for children initially regarded it that way. The story of Barb and Paul thus took seriously the hardship and emotional stress experienced by the infertile couple. Yet the story also demonstrated the pacification and satisfaction experienced by accepting one's fate and finding other outlets for one's love and energy. Spring suggested that God had destined infertile couples for other tasks, as with Barb and Paul, who opened "a retreat center in rural Ohio for former members of religious cults."[102] As children of God, infertile couples thus had their place in God's family and in their church communities. Yet to "remain child-free" was not acceptable to all Christian couples, as other examples mentioned in the article showed. Another info box set within the text provided further information on "alternatives to infertility." Points six and seven offered adoption and the choice to remain without children as answers to infertility, while the first five points listed methods of reproductive medicine. Spring was clearly wary of such options, but since infertile couples often wanted children and adoption had become a hassle with long waits and too few available children, new reproductive methods seemed to offer relief.[103]

In Evangelical accounts, children came to signify life itself. To reject children—either by opting to remain without children in the absence of infertility issues or by aborting unwanted life—was a grave offense. To reject children seemed especially contemptuous given the plight of infertile couples. Not only did abortion mean the murder of a child (in the Evangelical view), it also meant that couples who could not conceive were denied the option of adoption. Evangelicals trusted that to live the life God had destined one for would work best and to everyone's satisfaction. Unwanted children, in this vision, would be cared for by others who longed for them. Evangelicals saw the situation as exasperated by the atmosphere in the contemporary United States, which appeared hostile to children: people's selfish attitude actually devalued the quality of life. Evangelical spokespersons juxtaposed this situation with a vision of a covenant family in which all humans were children of God and everyone would find a loving, adoptive family.

SCIENCE, SUFFERING, AND THE SANCTITY OF LIFE

The Evangelical concept of the divine family was thus imagined as God being parent to everyone and to all the different human families. In the words of Ray S. Anderson, "God's family is formed through all of us becoming children, and then becoming brothers and sisters. In this way, the situation of every person—single, married, with or without children—is enhanced and blessed."[104] Despite this sentiment, the longing for children often remained. New scientific advances and reproductive technologies seemed to be the answer to such longings. In many ways, the benefit of new medical methods seemed obvious. Evangelicals lauded the care that doctors like C. Everett Koop provided for premature and malformed infants. Through prenatal medicine and genetic research the conditions of many infants could be improved. Medical apparatuses and procedures that saved and kept the life of premature infants delivered earlier and earlier even seemed to annul legalized abortion. Because a provision in the *Roe v. Wade* decision restricted legalized abortion to the time before a fetus became viable—that is, able to survive outside the womb—research seemed to promise a future when every fertilized ovum was viable. Yet all these technologies and methods were also problematic. They raised questions about what constituted life, whether humans could and should improve what God had created, and how life should be reproduced. Every technological advance also seemed to have a negative side: While medical developments promised relief, they also raised the fear of new, dictated norms that precluded deviation. While reproductive medicine offered answers to infertility, it raised the fear of breeding and preselecting perfected human beings. While genetic research promised cures to severe illnesses and deformities, it also conjured up the specter of creating monsters. All these technologies and methods raised questions not only about what people could do but about what they should do. For Evangelicals, these questions were ethical and theological and touched on the ultimate questions of life, namely, the meaning and value of life, and the purpose of procreation and family. By responding to the challenges of medical developments, Evangelicals were forced to grapple with the purpose of life.

Baby Doe Cases: The Value of Life and the Imperative to Heal
Arguing that all life was sacred, Evangelicals overwhelmingly considered themselves pro-life. Their high regard for life fit well with the Hippocratic Oath, the physician's vow to heal and do no harm. In many ways, they seemed to be natural allies of the medical profession. Yet medical practices were increasingly seen not as saving but as threatening life. One (generally) socially accepted reason for seeking an abortion was a deformation of the fetus and expected physical and/or mental disability. Evangelicals abhorred the practice of abortion as eugenics, a means of producing only perfect human beings. New scientific advances, however, provided tools to save, or at least prolong, the life of infants born so severely disabled or ill that only years before they would not have survived. This situation confronted Evangelicals with a new conundrum, namely whether it was ever right to terminate a life, if only by not providing medical assistance. The general attitude prescribed by Evangelical spokespersons in these situations was compassion. However, given the

complexity of the issue, even compassion was ambiguous. Compassion could mean allowing a child to die. In some instances, then, the imperative to heal and the dictum of compassion were in conflict.

One hotly debated issue—both in Evangelical magazines and among the general public—was that of the so-called Baby Doe cases. These involved infants who had been born with both physical and mental defects and been left to die, most notably Baby Doe in 1982 in Bloomington, Indiana, and Baby Jane Doe in 1983 in New York City.[105] According to one reading, these were cases where the predicted value of life was so dismal that it rendered moot the medical imperative to heal. According to another reading, these were cases of legal infanticide and apparently proved a fear long postulated by Evangelicals, namely that abortion opened the door to other legal killings. There was another connection between the Baby Doe cases and the practice of abortion: had the birth defects been detected earlier, the fetus would have been aborted, and there would have been no public record and no public outcry. The cases, therefore, seemed to illustrate the blurry and artificial lines between a fetus and a child. The cases raised questions of when life was worth living and whether birth defects were grounds enough to morally justify abortion or the withholding of medical assistance—and if yes, whether this was true in all cases.

In March 1982, *Christianity Today* published an editorial on a Baby Doe case in Britain, before the topic had become an issue at home (the first Baby Doe in Bloomington, Indiana, was born on April 9 of that year). A British surgeon had been charged and acquitted for letting a three-day-old baby with Down syndrome and other complications die. While recognizing the "anguish" felt by doctors and parents in a situation with a severely disabled infant, the writer insisted not on the imperative not to kill but on the imperative to keep alive. The editorialist insisted on Evangelicals' opposition to mercy killings and abortions and charged that there were two main reasons why Evangelicals no longer trusted medical authorities: "First, they are disturbed by the rapid shift away from extraordinary measures to preserve life to ordinary measures, to no measures at all, to positive action to destroy unwanted human life. . . . A second cause of evangelical unease relates to the increasing, and increasingly more trivial, grounds for 'mercy killing': the effect of 'defective' children on a marriage, the cost of keeping them alive, the psychological damage on brothers and sisters, the quality of life of the disabled or the parents of the disabled." Accordingly, the editorialist—besides condemning an increasingly egotistical attitude of people in general—accused medical professionals of betraying their oath to heal and sustain life. It was feared that "more and more, human life may be terminated when convenient. The sacredness of human life becomes a myth of the past."[106] Just as in the question of abortion, the issue boiled down to whether life, any human life, was sacred and therefore should be protected.

Philosophical Debate of Personhood

For some, the notion of personhood, linked to the notion of *imago dei* (the image of God), was central to the question of the sacredness of human life. The *Christianity Today* editorialist argued that "to take a human life made in the image of God is to take what belongs to God."[107] But whether the fetus, a malformed infant, an adult with disabilities, or a debilitated elderly person was actually made "in the image of God" was contested. Some Evangelicals adopted a distinction between "human" and "person" common in philosophy; others argued that to make such a distinction was to open the door and invite disaster. This was the position taken by the makers of *Eternity*. The dilemma surrounding the question of personhood was introduced in the 1986 issue on abortion. *Eternity* entered the debate over abortion late but then took a decisive and categorical stand against it.[108] In this issue, Terri Graves Taylor, an instructor of philosophy at Temple University, Philadelphia, recounted the dilemma she faced before there was a strong Protestant pro-life movement: in her junior year at a Christian college she overheard a dorm mate planning to have an abortion. She felt abortion was wrong and wanted to confront the woman but did not know how. She sought advice, and when the pastor was unhelpful she found it with a philosophy professor. He pointed at his three-month-old son and asked her whether it would be right to kill the boy. He argued that the baby could not talk or walk, let alone reason—and therefore the baby was closer to the fetus than to a fully developed person. Yet the infant, and by extension the fetus, was a "potential person" and should therefore be protected. Taylor was convinced and confronted the dorm mate. The anonymous woman was not convinced and had an abortion. While the idea of gradually developing personhood appeared to be a way to extend protection backward to the life of the fetus, in this case the argument failed. Indeed, to establish a similitude between infants and fetuses on the grounds of their shared "potential personhood" was dangerous. While Taylor had attempted to use the argument for the protection of the unborn, others might use it to take away the rights of the newborn. The logic was the same. Taylor wrote: "But fetuses don't start down the birth canal as potential persons and pop out at the other end as actual ones. In fact, like my professor's son, they spend most of their childhood years developing the capacities requisite for personhood."[109] If personhood was a prerequisite for the sanctity of human life, then it applied neither to the fetus nor the infant.

Similar considerations led Peter Leithart, reviewing pro-choice and Evangelical pro-life literature for *Eternity*, to conclude with scathing sarcasm:

"These Christian writers have adopted arguments which fail to recognize what [Michael] Tooley and [Peter] Singer recognize: birth is not a morally significant event in the life of an individual."[110] He called this the "good news, bad news" scenario. The good news was that many intellectuals now admitted that there was basically no distinction between the fetus and the newborn baby. The bad news was that rather than dismissing the human/person distinction and fiercely protecting the life of the fetus, some pro-choice intellectuals concluded that the life of newborns was not protected either. Leithart feared that Evangelical writers who adopted the argument of personhood to allow for abortion in certain extreme cases were proceeding down a "slippery slope" that opened the door to other forms of mercy killings. Logically, if some human was only a potential person because he or she lacked something substantial for granting personhood and therefore legal protection, it was alright to kill that human—whether a fetus, a newborn, a disabled adult, or a debilitated senior. Leithart singled out the eminent Evangelical intellectual Carl F. H. Henry, who, in one of his books, had written: "The fetus seems less than human, moreover, in cases of extreme deformity in which rational and capacities integral to the *imago Dei* are clearly lacking."[111] Leithart fiercely rejected the idea that only persons were made in the image of God, while potential persons were still lacking certain necessary features— or lacking them again, as in the case of the elderly. Taylor similarly rejected the logic of the human/person distinction. She pointed out that "not only fetuses but all humanity are in some sense only potential bearers of the image of God." This meant that "our philosophers must either deny everyone the right to life or else extend it to anyone who is potentially in the image of God—even the fetuses."[112] Accordingly, she rejected the human/person and potential/actual distinctions in favor of the sanctity and protection of all human life. These authors rejected the notion of "personhood" as a criterion in deciding whether someone was made in the image of God and therefore deserving of protection. Others used it, especially in the complicated situation of deciding whether and when to let someone die, because the argument of diminished personhood legitimated the humane act of allowing a severely injured or terminally ill human to die.

Letihart's deliberations about the use of the philosophical concept of personhood had been prompted by the fact that the infants in the Baby Doe cases had been born with birth defects. The possibility that eugenic notions may have played a role in withholding crucial treatment from infants prompted Evangelical and public uproar. The Baby Does, the one in England as well as the one in Indiana, had been born with Down syndrome and physical birth defects; Jane Doe in New York City had spina bifida and other complications. Surgeon general C. Everett Koop, who reviewed the US cases for the gov-

Figure 6.9. "A Legacy of Life." Cover of *Christianity Today*, January 18, 1985. Courtesy of Buswell Library Special Collections, Wheaton College, Illinois.

ernment, concluded that the physical complications could and should have been addressed.[113] Politicians also reacted, and in 1984 Congress amended the Child Abuse Prevention and Treatment Act of 1974 in order to require hospitals and doctors to provide care for impaired infants, except in very specific circumstances. Signed into law by president Ronald Reagan on October 9, 1984, this Baby Doe Law was the first attempt by the government to regulate treatment for neonates with birth defects.[114] Because Down syndrome is not life threatening, and with medical treatment, the other defects would not have been either, Beth Spring, in a report on the case in Indiana, summarized the fear that "the practice [of allowing Baby Does to die] is ridding parents of unwanted handicapped children."[115] Indeed, Koop counseled that the question in need of clarification was "when we say 'Baby Doe has a life that's not worth living,' are we not really saying, 'It's not worth our effort to take care of him'?"[116] The cases raised questions about the value and quality of life, especially for children with disabilities.

Christianity Today reacted to the Baby Doe cases with a cover story in 1985. The cover showed an infant from the side, medical tubes attached to its body (figure 6.9). It seemed to be gazing out through the clear plastic walls of a hospital crib at a hospital room and a group of vaguely visible hospital staff. The scene seemed to suggest that an indefensible child was helplessly awaiting whatever decision the doctors would pronounce over its life. The reader's perspective was that of the infant, looking over its shoulder at the medical team and thus anticipating with it. The picture—and the accompanying title, "A Legacy of Life"—was open to interpretation as to whether the "right" decision was the imperative to heal and thus sustain the baby's life, or whether it would be more compassionate to let the child die. Whatever decision the doctors made would constitute the legacy of their lives, too.

In the pages of the magazine issue, Thomas Elkins, a physician at the neonatal intensive care unit at the University of Tennessee Medical Center, was introduced as one who "has devoted himself to developing a case for Christian ethics in newborn situations where parents are faced with the reality of a handicapped infant."[117] But Elkins was not only a medical expert. His own daughter, Ginny, had Down syndrome, making him a personal witness. Using Ginny as his example, Elkins discussed the difficulties of life with a disabled child but ultimately stressed its rewards. He affirmed that "with a child like Ginny, we learn that love is deeper. It's love because of the personal qualities of the child and because of something of the spirit of God that's within that child—what we term personhood." He thus affirmed that disabled humans, too, had personhood and bore the image of God, arguing both in favor of treatment for disabled newborns and against abortion in cases of physical or mental defects. Yet he took no strict antiabortion view; he allowed for abortions in cases when the mother's life was threatened. Moreover, he recounted cases in which he found abortion to be the more compassionate avenue. He recalled the case of a mother being repeatedly forced to give birth to babies with anencephaly (a condition in which the baby is born without a brain and dies shortly after birth). Under such circumstances, he felt it would be humane to allow for abortion.[118] Similarly, he felt that in certain rare cases, nontreatment of severely impaired infants was defensible, even compassionate. Elkins considered it a gracious and Christian act to allow a terminally ill newborn to die rather than to prolong its life for the few days it could be medically sustained. He looked favorably at the practice of keeping a terminally ill newborn alive for a short time only to allow the parents to bond and then grieve for it. He considered this the right thing to do for the family, "but to prolong an agonizing, painful situation for two, three, or four days for the sake of some group's political agenda is inhumane." Accordingly, Elkins tried to square his medical imperative to heal with his ethical responsibility not to prolong suffering. He took a pro-life stance that was contextual rather than categorical; it took into account the specific situation in order to find "a loving, compassionate approach" for both the infant and the family.[119]

Elkins's contribution in *Christianity Today* was contextualized by a short statement on the Baby Doe cases by C. Everett Koop and a forum discussion on medical decision-making. Koop's position, excerpted from a speech he had given on September 19, 1984, to the Committee on Hospital Care of the American Academy of Pediatrics, was on par with Elkins's stance. Addressing the ethical dilemma faced by doctors in cases like the Baby Does (and worse), the surgeon general issued the dictum that "we ought to do those things that give a person all the life to which he or she is entitled, but not to do anything that would vainly extend that person's act of dying."[120] The two medical practitioners thus agreed that it was not enough to sustain a life just because doing so was medically possible; rather it was an ethical decision whether the more compassionate choice was to sustain life or to let an infant die.

While generally advocating a pro-life stance, the distinguished Evangelical spokespersons on the forum assembled by *Christianity Today* largely agreed with this position. Lewis B. Smedes, professor of theology and ethics at Fuller Theological Seminary, agreed that abortion should generally be disallowed but should be permitted in certain dire situations, like when a child would be born without a brain. Accordingly, he argued that "in our decision making, we must have a passion for life, but a compassion for the living."[121] Staunch pro-life activist Harold O. J. Brown also agreed with Elkins's account, yet he argued that while the gracious choice in a few, severe cases was to let an infant die, it was wrong to speed up death. Life and death, according to him, were to be in God's hands. Therefore, he also argued that decision-making should flow out of a Christian ethic that guided the use of technology—rather than technology influencing ethics.[122] Norman B. Bendroth, director of communications for the Christian Action Council, the largest Protestant pro-life organization at the time, agreed with what Elkins said but further emphasized the new consensus among pro-life and disability-focused organizations. He reported that both groups supported the new legislation in connection with Baby Doe. He noted positively that the legislation provided malpractice standards, which were a type of guideline familiar to physicians. This afforded some protection to people with disabilities, a group Bendroth described as facing discrimination and often considered unproductive by society.[123] The *Christianity Today* forum, thus, did not categorically insist on saving and prolonging any life indiscriminately. The spokespersons employed a restricted version of the quality-of-life argument, advocating for a compassionate stance toward life that allowed for the nontreatment of infants and others when treatment would but prolong suffering. The contributors acknowledged the difficulties faced by doctors in deciding when it was right to let a neonate die but lauded the fact that the Baby Doe Law now made it malpractice to withhold critical medical treatment in all but some rare cases when treatment was deemed futile. They articulated clear support for disability rights. They would have well agreed with a statement by Koop, pronounced years earlier:

"Like it or not, God makes the imperfect. And you and I as His stewards have no more right to destroy the imperfect than we have the right to destroy the perfect."[124] The spokespersons in this *Christianity Today* issue acknowledged that medical advances complicated life-and-death decisions. They rejected fast and easy answers to complex situations. They allowed that sometimes it was compassionate to let a patient die, but they wanted medical practitioners to grapple hard with their conscience before withholding treatment.

New scientific advances in medicine confounded Evangelicals because, as much as they welcomed the ability to save lives, they realized that technologies created new problems: there was a fine line between saving a life and prolonging the process of dying. Evangelical spokespersons quarreled with the medical community, accusing them of betraying the Hippocratic Oath by too easily giving in to the demand to withhold treatment from the physically or mentally incapacitated. They envisioned all humans to be children of God and therefore sacred, no matter their ability to reason, walk, or work. This revealed a vision of human value divorced from social and economic productivity. Accordingly, nontreatment of infants with disabilities and repairable birth defects particularly offended their moral sensibilities. Surprisingly, in light of the fact that they held all life in high esteem, Evangelical spokespersons granted that there were cases in which nontreatment was defensible. In the debates in the magazines, spokespersons envisioned Evangelicals as those who sought compassionate solutions that served the best interest of every individual patient.

Genetic Engineering, Biomedical Decision-Making, and the Question of Life

The imperative to heal was further complicated by new biomedical advances and genetic research. In early 1988, an editorial in *Christianity Today* presented a tremendous ethical dilemma to Evangelicals' perspective of the sanctity of life in the context of new medical technologies, namely the question of whether the life of an infant with anencephaly be prolonged so that its organs could be donated to another baby. Such an extension of life, just to harvest the organs, could be considered inhumane. But enhancing the life of another suffering child was a worthwhile undertaking, and there were precedents of artificially sustaining one life to help another—for example with brain-dead pregnant women who were kept alive for the sake of their fetuses. While the donation of organs could be considered Christian, the infant had no means of consenting or dissenting. Because, from an Evangelical perspective, the lives of two children were involved—the infant with anencephaly and the infant in need of an organ transplant—new medical technologies that allowed doctors to help one through the other presented an ethical conundrum.[125]

Given the rapid advances of scientific developments, the ethical dilemmas, it was predicted, would not lessen but increase. And these advances could be regarded, according to an *Eternity* article, from one of two essential perspectives: "One side might state it this way: Is it right—is it safe?—to monkey with the genetic makeup that we assume was placed in us by an omniscient God? The other side might put it: If we have the God-given ability through genetic engineering to heal and improve humanity's lot in life, how can we possibly not promote the use of it?"[126] Thus, rapid scientific advances led to ambiguous situations that muddled a clear identification of the sanctity-of-life position. There was no established Christian teaching answering the question of whether it was a holy duty or whether it was blasphemous to use new technologies to improve on the human condition. Complicating the issue was that genetic and biomedical developments could not have been foreseen in biblical times, leaving Evangelicals without biblical instructions. Furthermore, research was ongoing, steadily adding to the information that had to be considered and fueling unwarranted expectations and dystopian fears.

Throughout the 1980s, Evangelical magazines were fascinated with genetic and biomedical research.[127] The first adult cell had been cloned in 1952, but research activity became virulent in the 1980s, when first the cloning of a yeast cell (1980) and then the cloning of cells of a golden carp (1981) and a sheep (1984) were successful. The term "genetic engineering" also became popular, especially in conjunction with the 1980 Supreme Court ruling in *Diamond v. Chakrabarty*, which allowed the patenting of genetically altered organisms, and with the commercialization of insulin-producing bacteria in 1982.[128] In conjunction with the 1980 Supreme Court decision, an editorial in *Christianity Today* called on Evangelicals to enter the debate and pronounce a Christian position on genetic engineering. The editorialist, recalling legalized abortion and developments in gay rights, lamented that "in recent years, however, evangelicals all too often have forfeited any leadership and simply reacted to the decisive direction of the secular world." The issue of genetic research was important because, while still in the very early stages, scientists were attempting to "manipulate life." But there were also no easy, ready-formed answers to the questions posed by the new science. Therefore, "Evangelicals must be dead sure of all the facts before they say this is 'the' Christian position on genetic engineering. They need the best informed, most judicious Christian opinions before attempting to influence public policy. They must be as sure as it is humanly possible to be that wherever they draw the line, this is indeed where God draws the line." To come up with a comprehensive Evangelical position, the editorialist insisted that "we need [to] carefully ascertain scientific, biblical, ethical, and theological facts."[129] Evangelical magazines, indeed, kept up with scientific developments; *Christianity Today* dedicated one magazine issue each to genetic engineering and medical research, and it held a Christianity Today Institute forum on biomedical decision-making.[130]

One striking observation about contributions on genetic and biomedical research in Evangelical magazines was how evenhanded they were. An exception was the reporting in the magazine *Sojourners*: only a few articles grappled with questions of biomedical decision-making, but the makers of the magazine were strictly opposed to genetic engineering.[131] Feature articles in *Christianity Today*, *Eternity*, and *Moody Monthly* all approached the topic by listing threats as well as benefits, and arguments for positive as well as negative reception of the new technologies. As benefits they listed factors such as increasing knowledge that would lead to more precise diagnoses and new technologies resulting in better treatment or prevention of genetic defects. As threats they recounted fears about the safety of the research (the purposeful or accidental creation of deadly mutant genes or their weaponization) and fears regarding the eugenic use of new findings (not only the screening for harmful genetic defects but the eradication of defective life and creation of a "superhuman race"). Accordingly, there were both pessimistic and optimistic attitudes toward the new research. A reason to be pessimistic, according to these articles, was the fear that research could lead in directions that threatened basic assumptions about the creation and value of life, namely that God was the author of all life and that life had an intrinsic value of its own. The Christian view of the sanctity of life seemed to be cheapened by artificial creation of life in the laboratory, and by the creation of life merely as material to sustain the life of another, or even to satisfy scientific curiosity. On the other hand, an optimistic perspective highlighted the research as a validation of God's providential care for the world. In this view, God, as the author of all life, had also equipped humans with the tools to improve on their own conditions. Taken together with a biblical mandate to heal, biomedical advances could be regarded as affirming the value of life by enhancing it and repairing genetic defects.[132]

The ambivalence about genetic and biomedical developments was also attested to by the subtitles of the feature articles—things like "Genetic Engineering: Promise and Threat" and "Genetic Engineering: Good and Harmful?"— and titles of further articles like "Curses or Prayers for Genetic Engineers?" and "The Promise and Perils of Genetic Meddling."[133] Yet Evangelical spokespersons generally affirmed the right of scientific research, and, moreover, they were cautiously optimistic about genetic and biomedical research.[134] They found biblical grounds for pursuing research and employing the findings: V. Elving Anderson, the assistant director of the Dight Institute for Human Genetics at the University of Minnesota, affirmed, "God's charge to Adam included the basis for science (to study, name, and classify) and for technology (to subdue)."[135] And David B. Fletcher, assistant professor of philosophy at Wheaton College, legitimated scientific research based on its medical benefits: "Christians are committed to the biblical mandates to be stewards over the earth and to heal—mandates which give us a theological basis for science." He judged that the benefits of genetic engineering probably outweighed the dangers of tampering with the DNA code.[136] Yet the crucial determining factor for Evangelical spokespersons as to whether new technologies proved harmful or helpful was, according to Anderson, the question of "what it means to be human."[137] David Boehi, a writer for the Family Ministry of Campus Crusade for Christ, concurred. In his words, "what's needed is a clearly articulated Christian world view that explains what makes man unique, why life is sacred, the proper way to view death, and what decisions we should leave in the hands of God."[138]

A particular vision of human life was also at the center of the Christianity Today Institute's forum on biomedical decision-making. When Kenneth S. Kantzer asked the forum about the foundations for making difficult medical decisions, Paul Brand, one of the three eminent Evangelical spokespersons participating in the discussion, responded: "The basic question for the Christian is, What is man? The answer: Man is qualitatively different from the rest of creation. Therefore, man is sacred."[139] While this statement was undisputed, the panelists had diverse opinions on what exactly made humans different. Brand, a doctor, considered it to be the human mind and potential for reasoning. Accordingly, a brain-dead patient to him was no longer human, and the very young and the very old might only possess human traits to a certain degree. For ethicist Hans Tiefel this description was too narrow, as he insisted that the *imago dei* could not be reduced to the mind but also included the human body.[140] The two men approached the subject from two different perspectives: the doctor primarily searched for signs of when to stop treatment and how to distribute scarce resources, whereas the ethicist searched for answers to explain compassion toward family members who did not live up to standards of economic productiveness or intellectual standards of personhood—like the very young, the disabled, or the elderly. Kenneth S. Kantzer summarized that Evangelicals readily agreed on the principle of the sanctity of human life but said that there were no easy answers when it came to applying this principle to biomedical decision-making. He diplomatically formulated a statement that "conscious human beings are a sacred treasure. Merely to preserve the physical human body alive would not have high priority among biblical values."[141]

Evangelicals did not demonize biomedical advances. Rather, scientific knowledge and technologies were considered neutral, only becoming good or evil in connection with how they were used. According to Dennis Chamberland, an Evangelical science writer and nuclear engineer, "the evil we face, therefore, is not from the tools of life but from the minds that made them."[142] Moreover, as the forum found, the situations in which biomedical decision-making became relevant confronted people with "impossible decisions, those with seemingly no right answer; where the decision maker is confronted with choosing between the 'lesser of two evils.'"[143] New technologies created part of the problem. New technology that could sustain a life that would otherwise fail caused the dilemma of having to decide whether it was more humane to treat or not to treat a patient. Despite these complications, Evangelical spokespersons during the 1980s did not reject scientific developments.[144] The high regard for human life and the imperative to heal led Evangelicals to be positively disposed to medical advances and cautiously optimistic about the value of genetic and biomedical technologies. However, new technologies were not categorically good, either. Even though Evangelical spokespersons longed for a clear position, they had to admit that questions of genetic engineering and biomedical developments were too complex for black-and-white answers. Further, the variables involved in bioethical decisions were so variegated and the biblical guidelines so meager, that fallible humans were bound to go wrong. In the words of Hans Tiefel, "You make your decision as best as you can in the light of what you know about God—and with a lot of prayer."[145] Accordingly, the intentions with which new technologies were applied played a decisive role. Spokespersons envisioned the right Evangelical position as one made in light of all the technological information and biblical guidelines available. The new technologies, thus, were not evil or good per se but could be used for better or worse by fallible humans. Yet there was one area where Evangelical judgment was less ambiguous: new reproductive technologies.

New Reproductive Technologies as Assaults on the Traditional Family
During the 1980s, new reproductive technologies like in vitro fertilization, sperm donation, and surrogate motherhood became available. Genetic screening techniques helped doctors and pregnant women find out whether the fetus had or was likely to have a genetic defect. Ultrasound imaging, furthermore, allowed doctors and expectant parents to "see" inside the womb. All these advances helped couples realize their desire for a child and facilitated the birth of a healthy child.[146] Yet while Evangelicals were favorably disposed toward children and subscribed to the Hippocratic Oath, they were skeptical of, if not outright opposed to, new reproductive technologies. Many Evangelical spokespersons argued that the human regulation of and techno-medical interference in procreation was unnatural and possibly uncouth. Furthermore, while they happily embraced genetic and biomedical advances to alleviate or repair physical and genetic defects, they wondered whether the pre-

natal screening and engineering of "healthy" life was not hubris. Did these technologies really fix medical problems, or were humans tampering with God's design? Furthermore, the issue touched on an Evangelical vision of the meaning of sex and raised the question of what constituted family.

The best documented opposition to new reproductive technologies involved the embryonic life discourse: Evangelicals opposed in vitro fertilization because in this procedure more embryos than needed were created and destroyed.[147] In September 1982, *Moody Monthly* published an article on "test-tube babies." Martin Mawyer asked "how [anyone could] be against the humanitarian objective behind test tube babies," referring to the goal of helping couples conceive a child. He answered: the problematic ethical issues involved in the practice included the "deaths of many human embryos unsuccessfully implanted."[148] Opposition to the practice was an extension of the opposition to abortion. If a fertilized egg was considered to be a human baby, then the destruction of surplus embryos was murder, and experimentation with embryos was evil. In vitro fertilization included both, and by one count, "almost 95 percent of all test-tube babies die sometime during the process."[149] For the same reason, ovum transfer, a method through which an ovum was implanted into an otherwise infertile woman's womb, was dismissed as an option for Christian couples by one Evangelical doctor. After reviewing the procedure for *Christianity Today*, the obstetrician and gynecologist concluded: "I cannot endorse the process because it necessarily, though incidentally, involves what I believe are abortions."[150]

A variation of this narrative was the baby-for-spare-parts narrative. Biomedical research had found that fetal tissue transplants helped patients with life-threatening and chronic diseases, like Parkinson's. The use of body parts of a fetus to help a grown-up, according to Dave Andrusko, the editor of *National Right to Life News*, presupposed the legalization of abortion and the incidental denial of personhood to the unborn. He feared the practice of creating embryos solely for the purpose of harvesting tissue, and eventually other body parts like organs. Andrusko saw a precedent for such a practice in the push of some clinics to use newborns with anencephaly as donors. He argued that such practices violated the Hippocratic Oath, "making one person the means to another person's ends."[151] Practices like in vitro fertilization and fetal/newborn tissue transplantation were suspect because they, in the view of Evangelical spokespersons, violated the sanctity of life and the rights of the unborn or terminally ill newborn.

Whereas Mawyer reported that the practice of in vitro fertilization currently increased the chance of defects in fetuses (he reported disapprovingly that some clinics required women to abort the fetus in such a case), other authors feared that reproductive technologies could be used to create "super humans."[152] One article in *Christianity Today*, for example, affirmed the "mandate to heal," while warning that this notion could be taken too far: "We ought to endorse techniques that will prevent or repair the effects of genetic disease, while rejecting the idea of genetically creating superior individuals in order to transcend the limitations of our finitude."[153] Alan Verhey, assistant professor of religion at Hope College, in Holland, Michigan, thought through the argument for genetically engineering life to conclude that this notion could lead to a demand of only giving birth to "a perfect child or a dead child." He arrived at this dire conclusion by a variation of the "slippery slope" argument, predicting that "technologies . . . introduced as options . . . can quickly become socially enforced." He used the example of the car to illustrate his point: "The automobile was introduced as an option—but try to ride a horse home on the interstate!" His argument was that once a technology became available, its internal logic demanded its use. Furthermore, while many scientific developments were positive, in the case of reproductive medicine it was too early to bless all advances indiscriminately. He chided: "We are seizing control of reproduction, gaining power to intervene purposefully in the genetic endowment of our children precisely when we are more confused about parenting than ever." Screening the fetus to ensure the birth of a healthy child was no guarantee for the happiness of the parents, and it seemed cruel irony to try to ensure the happiness of the child by aborting the defective fetus.[154] The fear that new reproductive technologies would be used to produce a perfect child or even lead to laws criminalizing the birth of disabled children was shared by other Evangelical spokespersons. While deplorable in itself, this threatening practice also raised questions about what counted as "normal" and who got to decide.[155] One editorialist spoke of a "feminist boomerang" when he noticed that screening techniques also led to gender preselection, making the "normal" child a healthy boy.[156] Evangelical spokespersons thus feared that reproductive technologies would lead to a devaluation, if not eradication, of natural and naturally imperfect human life. The debate revealed that Evangelical spokespersons were conflicted about the promises and threats of medical advances gained from genetic research. Yet it also showed that spokespersons adhered to a vision of humans being created in the image of God, no matter their defects.

The question about the perfectibility of human life raised additional questions about the authorship of life. One editorialist wrote: "To ally the word engineering to genetics means that certain skilled humans can change other humans. . . . Does this also mean that God, in one respect at least, has in fact relinquished his role as creator and sovereign over man's destiny?"[157] The unanswered question pitted God against the scientist. A most vehement argument against genetic engineering, indeed against genetic research, was put forth by author Jeremy Rifkin in *Sojourners*. He linked genetic research to eugenics by describing his fear that humans would create new people in their own image and try to produce the "perfect human being." Accordingly, he called genetic engineering a "Faustian bargain," a deal with the devil that was by definition evil. Rifkin concluded the article with the appeal: "we must say no to the genetic age."[158]

Most spokespersons were not so quick to condemn genetic research, yet the questions they asked revealed skepticism about genetically engineered humans: Lewis B. Smedes, professor of theology at Fuller Theological Seminary, implored readers to think through three related issues: whether there was some essence that made humans human and should therefore not be altered, whether it was morally acceptable that some humans change other humans (and even remake humanity), and whether it was acceptable that those who economically profited from the new technologies currently also dictated the rules.[159] The question of whether "mankind [has] any business in the area of generating new life" was raised by William Colliton Jr., an obstetrician and gynecologist at Holy Cross Hospital in Silver Spring, Maryland, cited at length in a *Moody Monthly* article on "test-tube babies." He wondered: "Is this not an undertaking that really should be in God's hands?"[160] These spokespersons were wary of genetic research and sounded an alarm against the aggrandizement of researchers. In their opinion it was wrong for any human to assume the position of God by artificially creating new life or (potentially) tampering with the genetic makeup of a human embryo to such a degree that it might result in the birth of a new type of human being. Ultimately, they envisioned God as the author of all life; to create something new or significantly deviate from the blueprint, so to speak, was a violation against the authority of God.

Evangelical spokespersons rejected any form of reproductive medicine that destroyed embryos and opposed technologies that artificially created life or caused the birth of artificially altered human beings. Yet they also felt uneasy toward new reproductive technologies for other reasons. This was obvious especially in the debate about surrogate motherhood, prompted by the case of Baby M, born March 27, 1986.[161] Elizabeth Stern suffered from a medical condition that made pregnancy a potentially life-threatening situation. Therefore, she and her husband, William Stern, hired a surrogate mother, Mary Beth Whitehead, to carry their child. Whitehead was artificially inseminated with Stern's sperm and gave birth to a baby girl. Mary Beth Whitehead and William Stern were the biological parents, but Whitehead had given up her rights over the child contractually. Yet even though she initially handed the child over to the Sterns, Whitehead felt she could not give up her baby and kidnapped the child. Lengthy legal procedures ensued, and in the end, custody was awarded to the Sterns, while Whitehead received visitation rights.

To Evangelicals, this case illustrated the heartache brought about by messing with traditional family concepts and proved the harmful nature of new reproductive technologies that involved third parties.[162] Accordingly, two major points of concern largely led Evangelical spokespersons to reject such types of new reproductive technologies: their vision of human sexuality, and their vision of the traditional family.

New reproductive technologies introduced an artificial element into the process of procreation. They thus seemed to challenge the purpose of sex. This was most acutely felt by the Catholic Church. In early 1987, the Vatican released a document in which new reproductive techniques were discussed and summarily rejected.[163] Evangelical spokespersons welcomed yet critiqued this statement. In an article in *Christianity Today* the document was criticized on two accounts: its restricting of the purpose of sexual intercourse to procreation, and its prohibiting of all forms of reproductive technology. Stanley J. Grenz, associate professor of systematic theology and Christian ethics at North American Baptist Seminary in Sioux Falls, South Dakota, insisted that reproductive medicine was not inherently bad: "a fuller understanding of the meaning of the sex act within the marital bond would welcome as God's gift, and not discourage, technological assistance in procreation."[164] In connection with the Baby M case, Beth Spring collected the attitudes of Evangelical intellectuals toward the matter. She reported that "ethicist Lewis Smedes of Fuller Theological Seminary wonders whether surrogacy 'violates the kind of relationship that ought to exist between marriage and child bearing.'"[165] While Evangelical spokespersons tended to agree that surrogate motherhood, artificial insemination, and other artificial methods of conception did not constitute adultery because no lust was involved, they did regard these as a breach of the sanctity of marriage.[166] According to one article printed in *Eternity*, "just as it is wrong for a married person to 'give' himself or herself in sexual union to a non-spouse, that is, to commit adultery, so it is wrong for a married person to 'give' himself or herself to another procreatively, that is, to share with someone other than his or her spouse the power to generate human life."[167] Methods of artificial procreation could thus be seen, like adultery, as a violation of the sanctity of marriage, begging the question, "what is sex for?" Grenz set out to answer that question, listing three main points: "First, the act is an expression of the self-giving of the marriage partners. . . . Second, in the context of marriage the sex act is a spiritual metaphor. As an expression of the giving [of] oneself for the other, this act is a vivid reminder of the self-giving love of Christ for the church. . . . Finally, the sex act may be seen as the 'sacrament' of the marriage covenant. . . . Sexual intercourse is an outward act that seals and signifies an inward commitment."[168] Sexual intercourse, according to this perspective, was neither simply nor predominantly a means for procreation. Rather, it was an expression of the sacrificial, unconditional, and holy union of the married couple, of two people giving up individual rights and desires to become one. Intercourse, it could be said, sealed the deal. To turn to outside help for the intimate purpose of procreation was a violation of this union.

For most couples, nonetheless, children eventually tended to be the outcome of sexual intercourse, and so the desire for children was regarded as natural. Therefore, most Evangelical spokespersons did not categorically reject reproductive medicine. Lewis B. Smedes pointed out that seeking to become pregnant was the opposite desire of wanting to attain an abortion.[169] Furthermore, it seemed to be not only a most basic human desire and affirmation of life but also a validation of marriage.[170] Within narrow parameters, therefore, Evangelicals did consider medically facilitated reproductive means. Grenz affirmed: "For some infertile couples, the desire to experience the joy of being partners with God in the mystery of procreation may be a divinely given impulse, which ought to be facilitated when morally and technologically feasible." The one type of new reproductive medicine generally acceptable to Evangelicals was the artificial insemination of the wife with her husband's sperm. Indeed, "AIH [artificial insemination by husband] assists in the formation of new life—the natural offspring of the marital union—giving expression to the creative love present in the union of husband and wife."[171] To sum up, sexual intercourse, in the vision painted in these accounts, was an expression of love and partnership between spouses and could (but did not need to) result in offspring. Procreation was an act of participation in God's design for the world and was therefore held in high esteem—but only within the bounds of holy matrimony. The desire to become parents was considered natural and life-affirming, and seeking reproductive assistance was therefore acceptable.

Introducing a third party into the process of procreation, however, was a problem because it interfered with what Evangelicals regarded to be essential traits of parenthood and family. Beth Spring, reporting on the Baby M case, pointed out that "stepping outside the boundaries of marriage to create a child—as opposed to adopting a child whose conception was not premeditated—presents scores of relational dilemmas." One obvious problem was that Mary Beth Whitehead had bonded with the baby she was carrying and was loath to give it up. Health issues like depression and a suicidal tendency resulted, indicating that it was unnatural and cruel to ask a mother to give up her child.[172] The very concept of motherhood seemed to be challenged by surrogacy, with the biological mother consciously forgoing parenting and another woman agreeing to raise a child that had been contractually obtained by her husband.[173] While writers agreed that surrogacy could be a selfless act,

Figure 6.10. "It's the surrogate mother . . . she wants you to know your labor pains are just two minutes apart!" Cartoon in *Eternity*, February 1987. Courtesy of Buswell Library Special Collections, Wheaton College, Illinois.

they worried that it would attract a certain type of immoral woman—willing to sell her child, or at least rent out her womb—or result in destitute women being press-ganged into becoming "breeders" for the rich.[174] The practice was thus seen as degrading to women, asking them to render a service that Evangelical spokespersons considered unnatural and cruel.

Moreover, involving another woman in conceiving a child meant inviting another party into the confines of the family. According to one cartoonist in the February 1987 issue of *Eternity*, this essentially meant inviting another woman into the marital bed: the cartoon showed a man and woman in bed, presumably in the early morning. The man held a phone receiver in one hand and was looking at the woman with large eyes, his mouth open as if he was screaming. The caption recorded his words: "It's the surrogate mother . . . she wants you to know your labor pains are just two minutes apart!" (figure 6.10). The cartoon illustrated the disjunction involved in surrogacy. Procreation and giving birth became mediated acts that were far removed from the expectant adoptive mother: she learned of her imminent motherhood from her husband, who heard it—mediated through the phone—from the biological mother. Yet despite this disconnection between the birth mother and the couple raising the child, the biological mother would always be, if unwittingly, a component of the new family. This fact posed new questions. Paige Cunningham, in an opinion piece in *Moody Monthly*, asked: "How will the adoptive parents tell the child about his origins, or should they? Since the adoptive mother is not genetically related to the child, will she blame the husband for the child's negative traits? What if the biological father dies before birth? His wife is not party to the contract, so to whom does the child 'belong'? Should the child have access to information about his natural mother?"[175]

Surrogacy legally and emotionally complicated the notion of who was family.[176] This left children vulnerable to becoming pawns in custody battles, as was the case with Baby M. Cunningham also asked what would happen if a child was born with a disability and all parties disowned it, arguing that a practice like surrogacy, which potentially exposed children to such threats, "smacks of selfishness. The focus is not on the child, but on meeting the parents' needs."[177]

Surrogacy was therefore a practice that hurt all parties involved: it degraded the surrogate mother, it violated the sanctity of marriage, it introduced an alien party into the family, and, most importantly, it left children exposed. The debates showed that Evangelicals envisioned the family as a sanctum and refuge for all members, especially children, and that this vision was threatened by the practice of surrogacy.

Conclusion: Children and the Sanctity of Life

A synoptic reading of the debates in Evangelical magazines during the 1980s about abortion and new genetic and biomedical developments demonstrates a strong Evangelical concern for individual human life as well as families. Because every individual human life was sacred to them, issues of abortion and reproductive methods could not focus singularly on the (unborn) child. Rather, a focus on the plight of the (unborn) child, to Evangelicals, highlighted the interconnectedness of all human life. They envisioned all humans as children of God and potential brothers and sisters in Christ. Accordingly, they advocated for treating every individual as a patient and providing that individual with all the physical and medical, as well as emotional and spiritual, care that was needed. They thus envisioned Evangelicals as a caring and compassionate community that upheld the sanctity of individual but interconnected human life.

The Evangelical conviction that the destruction of human life was wrong was neither self-evident nor self-explanatory. The magazine records of the 1980s show that Evangelical spokespersons were busy establishing that the embryo/fetus was a human person as much as an adult was a human person, and that all human life was created in the image of God and was therefore sacred. Based on their reading of the Bible, human life began with conception: Jesus Christ had entered the world not as a baby but as an embryo growing in Mary's womb. Evangelicals believed that human life was sacred because God had created humans in his own image. The philosophical argument that some people were only potential persons, and the parallel religious argument that some persons only carried the potential to reflect aspects of the image of God, allowed spokespersons to justify discontinuing life-saving measures in certain situations. This position, however, was fiercely debated by Evangelical spokespersons, who feared that the introduction of the notion of potential had opened the door to legal killings. In the course of the debate, Evangelical spokespersons confirmed the inviolability of all human life. But extreme situations, like multiple babies born with anencephaly, confounded Evangelicals. While medical emergencies swayed Evangelicals to consider that the plight of a mother might trump the fate of her unborn child in certain, dire circumstances, they decried social circumstances that forced women to have abortions. Although they sympathized with the woman seeking an abortion because the birth of another child would mean that she would lose her job and therefore the livelihood for her family, they argued that such situations should not exist, and that Evangelicals needed to work to eliminate them. Accordingly, while they fiercely opposed the practice of abortion as the murder of a child, they considered it a symptom of a larger, societal problem.

Evangelical spokespersons criticized the commodification of children, upholding a vision of procreation as a natural process of life, and relegating it to the confines of marital relations. They imagined a perfect society, in which every person was materially and emotionally cared for. All humans would realize that they were children of God and, converting to Christianity, would form one community, the family of God. There would be no unwanted children because good, adoptive parents would be found for everyone. Accordingly, they envisioned the Evangelical community as those working toward such a heavenly community, alleviating the suffering of the impoverished and providing shelters for women in dire situations, and generally providing physical but especially spiritual care to those in need.

During the 1980s, Evangelicals grappled with questions of genetic research and biomedical advances, yet they remained undecided as to the merits and dangers of these technologies. While they took a stance against abortion (albeit allowing the practice in certain, extreme cases), their judgment on genetic and biomedical developments remained situational. The complexity of the issue was reflected in the complexity of the debates, and spokespersons generally agreed not to make any categorical pronouncements. Their high regard for life demanded they take seriously the circumstances defining a situation in which genetic and biomedical research was to be employed. They adhered to the imperative to heal and therefore cautiously embraced new technologies. Yet they were not blind to the ethical dilemmas caused by new procedures and possibilities. The dangers and benefits of biomedical interventions, like tampering with one's life to improve the condition of another, had to be considered and weighed according to the circumstance. Evangelical spokespersons envisioned the responsible doctor to be one who weighed all options and made a decision that was (in the doctor's judgment) both in keeping with the Bible and in the patient's best interest. The consensus of the debate is best summarized in the words of surgeon general C. Everett Koop, who pronounced that doctors should strive to save lives whenever possible but without unnecessarily extending a "person's act of dying."[178] In these debates, spokespersons envisioned Evangelicals to be a community of compassionate people, concerned with the unique needs and well-being of the individual as someone who was created in the image of God and was therefore a child of God and potentially a brother or sister in Christ.

To Evangelical spokespersons, the benefits of genetic and biomedical research, like treatments for diseases and new reproductive technologies that helped married couples conceive, were obvious. Yet they condemned many of its developments and consequences. "The vivid drama of Baby M," in the words of law professor Elizabeth S. Scott, "came to symbolize the pernicious threat that commercialization of reproductive technology posed to conventional understandings of family and of motherhood"—something Evangelicals and feminists agreed on during the 1980s.[179] Asking a mother to give up her baby seemed unnatural and unloving, and was regarded as the exploitation of psychically or economically vulnerable women. Surrogacy was also harmful to the child, exposing it to personal and potentially legal crises of identity and belonging. Conceiving a child in this manner, to Evangelicals, was a selfish act disconnected from any notion of what family was supposed to be. In the vision of Evangelicals, parenthood was intrinsically linked to matrimony. Evangelical spokespersons held fast to a theological vision that confined procreation to intercourse sanctioned by marriage. To procure a child in any other manner, except adoption, was, varying in degrees depending on the method, more or less objectionable.

Because children constituted a very high good in the Evangelical worldview—representing life itself—the longing for a child was considered natural and positive. Accordingly, medical assistance, even the use of some new reproductive technologies like artificial insemination, was acceptable, as long as no embryos were destroyed in the process. But to introduce a third party into parenthood (as in the case of surrogacy) or to divorce procreation from the intimacy of family (as in the artificial creation of life in the laboratory) was denounced as evil. The debate about new reproductive technologies revealed Evangelicals' high regard for the sanctity of human life and the centrality of the family.

Conclusion

In a book published in 2010, Evangelicals Steve Wilkens and Donald A. D. Thorsen argued that Evangelicalism "offers empirical evidence of something that looks impossible in theory," namely the unity of disparate people: "In evangelicalism today, we find Pentecostals at dispensationalist colleges. A rainbow of denominations shows up at Billy Graham crusades. . . . All this is at the heart and soul of evangelicalism, and it happens without requiring that one be an inerrantist, Calvinist, premillennialist, Republican, or a well-to-do citizen of the United States."[1]

In *Evangelical News*, I asked what allowed Evangelicals to conceive of an Evangelical community, given the fact that institutional ties, creed, and theology all held little sway. I followed the notion that a particular vernacular allowed Evangelicals to envision themselves as a distinct religious community. I studied nondenominational Evangelical magazines, paying attention to how writers and editors created and perpetuated Evangelical perspectives in both idiom and content, what I call visions. By coining the terms used in these discussions and delimiting Evangelical visions, these spokespersons thus engaged in defining Evangelicalism. In this process, Evangelical spokespersons, in the words of Pierre Bourdieu, "[brought] into existence groups by establishing the common sense, the explicit consensus, of the whole group." In doing so, they (re)produced the community of Evangelicals.[2]

While the topic of crisis was present in public discourse throughout the 1970s and 1980s, in the 1990s, US Americans became embroiled in a struggle over what sociologist James Davison Hunter described as "competing systems of moral understanding."[3] After two terms in office, President Ronald Reagan was succeeded by fellow Republican George H. W. Bush. Issues like the role of women, abortion, and homosexuality increasingly divided people, so much so that the incumbent president Bush was challenged from the left by Democrat Bill Clinton and from the right by conservative Republican Pat

Buchanan. Buchanan rallied a sizable following but ultimately lost in the primaries. Believing in the greater cause, Buchanan then pledged his support to Bush and delivered the opening night address to the 1992 Republican National Convention. In this speech, Buchanan coined the term "cultural war," pointing out the irreconcilable worldviews of the contemporary Democratic and Republican Parties. He warned: "There is a religious war going on in our country for the soul of America. It is a cultural war."[4] Hunter adapted the term "culture war" to refer to the battle between two camps—progressive and orthodox—that he detected in the contemporary United States. While this rendering might have been too schematic, with martial language that overstated the issue, he acutely observed that different groups "do not operate on the same plane of moral discourse."[5] In *Evangelical News*, I have argued that knowing a group's frame of reference matters enormously to understanding that group (in this case Evangelicals) and unpacking its vision, or the layers of meaning concealed in the key concepts and terms of its discourse (here, such terms as "civil religion" and "submission").

Whether or not a culture war really existed, during the 1990s the language used by pundits and activists became more divisive. Scholars like Alan Wolfe challenged Hunter's analysis, but journalists readily appropriated the term to talk about current issues.[6] In March 1995, *Christianity Today* put "Fighting Words" on its cover, adding the subtitle, "How Culture War Rhetoric Hurts the Work of the Church." While the lead article was dedicated to "Culture War Casualties," it seems that the topic was tedious to managing editor Michael Maudlin, who simply reminded readers that it would be more salutary to do battle against sin.[7] In the lead article, church historian John D. Woodbridge acknowledged that "the metaphor of 'culture war' reflects the reality of the conflict." While agreeing with James Davison Hunter that America was torn by a battle between liberal secular forces on the one side and conservative religious forces on the other side, he nonetheless cautioned against using bellicose rhetoric. In his opinion, for Evangelicals a more helpful metaphor than warfare was "America . . . as a mission field."[8] In the same vein, a twenty-five-year-old essay by well-loved Evangelical philosopher Francis A. Schaeffer (now dead for more than ten years), reprinted in the same issue, argued that the true "mark of the Christian" was neither a physical sign nor a rigid doctrinal stance, but compassion, or Jesus's command to "love one another" (John 13:34).[9] The *Christianity Today* issue testifies to a war of words in US culture but also highlights the reluctance of the combatants.

Indeed, Woodbridge was afraid that culture war rhetoric would spook a large group of Americans at the center, aligned with neither the Left nor the Right. Characterizing this sector of the populace as people "concerned about . . . the imposition of moral teachings by law," he pointed out that their private beliefs might none the less conform to Evangelical convictions. Conceiving of them, in culture-warrior style, as the "enemy" would hurt the greater cause. Woodbridge used the example of abortion, one of the most controversial issues in the culture wars, to illustrate his point: if many people, as Hunter had found, privately believed abortion to be wrong even if they opposed a top-down legal prohibition on abortion, then they were potential allies in the protection of unborn life—as long as culture war rhetoric did not alienate them from this cause.[10] Abortion remained a hotly debated issue during the 1990s, increasing, even, in fervor. While a *Time* cover in May 1992 proclaimed "Why *Roe v. Wade* is Already Moot," with these words printed over a picture of a judge's robe hanging in an otherwise-empty wardrobe, for antiabortion activists the fight had only started. Violent antiabortion activism found a first dramatic climax in the fatal shooting of Dr. David Gunn in Pensacola, Florida, in March 1993. It spiraled out from there, with attacks on clinics and clinic staff continuing into the 2010s and beyond.[11] Antiabortion activists adopted the slogan "abortion is murder," which rang true with many Evangelicals but was far from self-evident. Rather, particular narratives and arguments congealed in this slogan, their presence evident only to people steeped in the pro-life discourse.

Christianity Today is a case in point. Throughout the 1990s, the magazine followed the changing abortion legislation, reported on politicians' positions on abortion, and followed the story of Norma McCorvey, the "Roe" plaintiff from the *Roe v. Wade* Supreme Court case who later turned into a pro-life activist. The magazine even made abortion the cover story in January 1995.[12] In all these contributions, Evangelical spokespersons did not question that abortion was fundamentally wrong. The issue had been settled in the 1980s, when abortion had been one component of the discussion on the sanctity of life. In this vision, spokespersons produced Evangelicalism as the community of those who judged society according to how they treated their weakest members, especially those who could not speak for themselves, like the (unborn) child or the debilitated elderly person. The (unborn) child took on special meaning as the most innocent and indefensible part of humanity. In the context of this life discourse, abortion became an absolute evil. While the pro-choice movement framed abortion in terms of the rights of individual women, Evangelical spokespersons envisioned abortion against a web of familial and societal relations. It is only natural, then, that in the 1990s, *Christianity Today* focused on relatives who had been hurt by abortion and the loss of unborn life. Most poignantly, contributing editor Frederica Mathewes-Green wrote in 1998: "Abortion has been a disaster, first for the children who died and second for those who survived to grieve a lost child, grandchild, or sibling. It has damaged us all. How can we even measure the spiritual cost levied on a country that pronounces the killing of its own children a celebrated right?"[13] While clear in its antiabortion message, this article (and others like it) also reveals that enough women within the Evangelical community had had abortions for this issue to matter. Accordingly, the sanctity-of-life vision also covered up temporary defectors. Mathewes-Green gave voice to the notion that through abortion people hurt themselves. This resonates with other strains in the sanctity-of-life vision, those that concerned end-of-life treatment. Legal and medical developments during the 1980s had complicated the notion of what constituted life and how much humans could and should interfere with life. These deliberations led Evangelical spokespersons to a re-vision of the Hippocratic Oath. Rather than keeping a dying person alive as long as possible to satisfy the wishes of relatives, the doctor had to consider the patient's situation. While Evangelical spokespersons prescribed that everything should be done to save a person's life, they also believed that a person's act of dying should not be unnecessarily prolonged, proving that an apparently unequivocal dictum like the sanctity of life subsumed multiple aspects and tensions.

That Evangelical spokespersons generally privileged relationships over individual rights can also be seen in the discussion of the role of women. "Headship," for example, did not denote male dominance or superiority for Evangelicals but rather, in the magazine discourse of the 1970s, took on relational notions. To speak of headship was thus to emphasize the interconnectedness of all human life and to stress, depending on the situation and the person, either the need for a hierarchical order or the symbiotic relationship between different parts as suggested by the organic metaphor of head and body. Similarly, the term "submission," which has negative connotations of "yielding," "giving in," or "being made subject to some else's whims" in mainstream discourse, took on a different meaning in the Evangelical vernacular. More in line with "presenting someone else with one's unique skills and qualities," submission in the magazine discourse came to denote a conductive and altruistic service, in line with the notion of "loving your neighbor as yourself" (Lev. 19:18). While the feminist movement fought for the individual rights of women as independent, sovereign beings, Evangelical spokespersons rejected this vision of autonomous individuals. Instead, they stressed the interdependent and cooperative character of human relations, carrying in terms like "headship" and "submission" a vision of community as entangled human relationships. Such Evangelical visions thus allowed Evangelicals to distinguish themselves as people who put the harmonious relationship of married spouses, integrated in a larger human family, above the aspirations of disconnected individuals as expressed in rights discourses. Nonetheless the heated and often antithetical arguments within Evangelical magazines reveal that common visions only barely contained conflicts between feminist and traditionalist Evangelicals, and that disparate voices always threatened the tenuous Evangelical unity.

The debates about a woman's role in Evangelical magazines during the 1970s took place in the broader context of questions about God's design for men and women and led to general agreement in the magazines on the fundamental difference and compatibility of the sexes and the notion that the *imago dei* (image of God) required both male and female aspects. This history makes self-evident why, in the 1990s, Evangelicals viewed homosexuality as wrong. Homosexuality exploded as a topic of popular discourse during the 1990s, with news magazines printing coming-out stories, reporting on the AIDS crisis, depicting the ex-gay movement, wondering about the possibility of marriages between same-sex partners in the future, and finally reporting the gruesome crimes committed against gay and lesbian people during this period.[14] *Christianity Today*'s reporting was surprisingly muted on this topic.[15] Even so, the notion that homosexuality was sinful remained a bottom-line issue that distinguished Evangelicals from more liberal believers.[16] While sociologist Alan Wolfe, critical of the culture war thesis, proclaimed in 1999 that America was "one nation, after all," he nevertheless pointed out that if there was one topic Americans were divided over, it was homosexuality. He affirmed that "the question of gay rights is important to a discussion of religious toleration, for it is over this question that the more liberal and more conservative religious believers have had their most persistent clashes."[17] During the 1990s, when words themselves were contested, Evangelical spokespersons would have disagreed with Wolfe—if not with the sentiment of his statement, then with his choice of words—as tolerance became another problematic concept to them.

The topic of tolerance made it onto the cover of *Christianity Today*'s January 1999 issue. In the lead story, literary scholar Daniel Taylor deconstructed the popular use of the term, arguing that a more accurate meaning was not the celebration of difference but a sufferance of positions and lifestyles one deemed wrong. The cover illustration depicted twelve minimalist sketches of topics that liberals and conservatives disagreed on, including "divorce," "abortion," "pornography," "homosexuality," and the "prodigal president [Bill Clinton]." In the article, Taylor stressed the point that tolerance required objection, explaining: "Most social liberals, for instance, cannot rightfully be said to be tolerant regarding homosexual behavior since they have no objection to it." Accordingly, Taylor accused liberals of being the real intolerants. He argued that liberals required from conservatives that they embrace positions and lifestyles they did not agree with, while they, the liberals themselves, were not tolerant but merely morally indifferent.[18] Apparently, this way of thinking still holds sway. In March 2015, Mike Pence, then governor of Indiana, became embroiled in a controversy after signing a bill (later retracted) that would have allowed business owners to refuse to serve gay and lesbian patrons in certain circumstances. In a TV interview with George Stephanopoulos, Pence defended the bill by rhetorically asking whether "tolerance [was] a two-way street or not?"—suggesting that if Evangelicals tolerated gay people, liberals should tolerate a conservative refusal to do business with those gay people.[19] To Mike Pence in 2015, as to Daniel Taylor in 1999, tolerance did not mean giving up either the truth claim of the Bible or the rigidity of morality codes derived from it. Indeed, Taylor explained that God was both morally uncompromising *and* lenient and forgiving. Accordingly, he defended the Evangelical maxim, most often employed with regard to gay people, of "hate the sin, love the sinner."[20] It was consistent with this vision that Evangelicals could condemn homosexuality at the same time that C. Everett Koop, surgeon general under President Reagan as well as an outspoken Evangelical and antiabortion activist, could become the leading force in the fight against AIDS, showing again that a particular Evangelical vernacular and vision could both distinguish the Evangelical community and be ambiguous enough to contain a variety of attitudes.[21]

An analysis of how Evangelical spokespersons treated various issues of social concern in periodical contributions shows the complexity and layers that apparently simple slogans like "abortion is murder" or "homosexuality is sin" carry and reveals how multifaceted Evangelical visions continue to be effective. At the same time, the example of conversion politics shows how religious bodies lose control over the meaning of their own visions when nonreligious politicians and right-wing Christian pundits alike appropriate and redefine religious concepts in radically different ways. Decrying corruption in politics during the early 1970s as "civil religion," Evangelicals found in conversion a concept that not only allowed them to continue their political involvement but proved successful in rehabilitating fallen leaders. While the idea of conversion politics and moral leadership were utilized during the 1980s by the up-and-coming religiopolitical entrepreneurs of the New Christian Right, the movement was soon embroiled in scandals. First, televangelist empires like Jimmy Swaggart's and Jim Bakker's fell, then the New Christian Right organization Moral Majority disintegrated in the late 1980s, and finally Pat Robertson's run for president in 1988 failed. In the 1990s, political activists like Ed Dobson and Cal Thomas, disappointed by the meager political gains, prophesied the end of the New Christian Right. While particular religiopolitical movements have come and gone, morality politics continues today. Some Evangelicals celebrate the appropriation of Evangelical visions and vernacular as success; others lament it. Most poignantly, Evangelical believers were divided over the presidency of Donald Trump, with some Evangelical spokespersons outraged at his blatant immorality and others enamored with their unprecedented access to the White House.[22]

During the 1970s and 1980s, a vibrant magazine market existed. Established Evangelical magazines like *Moody Monthly*, *Eternity*, and *Christianity Today* flourished, and new Evangelical magazines like the *Post-American/ Sojourners* and *Daughters of Sarah* added to the spectrum of Evangelical periodicals. Special issue magazines, targeted at church leaders, missionaries, women, teenagers, and other groups, not investigated in this study, added to the diversity of the Evangelical periodical market.[23] Yet during the 1990s, there were distinct changes to this market. One was that some notable Evangelical magazines folded, most prominently, perhaps, *Eternity* in 1989.[24] A second change was the fact that during the mid-1990s the internet emerged as a new medium for communication and reshaped the publishing business, including the Evangelical periodical market.[25] *Christianity Today* was among the pioneers of online journalism, maintaining an online presence as early as 1994, providing content for the religion section for the software suite of America Online.[26] The internet offered advantages but also presented hazards, further reconfiguring religious periodical publishing in the new millennium, as yet an uncharted field of study.

During the new millennium, magazines like *Moody Monthly* and the *Wittenburg Door* capitulated in the face of internal and external developments and folded, but other magazines thrived. *Sojourners* survived the disintegration of the Sojourners community, adding a professional online site that provides subscription access to the magazine as a flip-book and also offers online-only content.[27] *Relevant*, an edgy periodical targeted at an audience of high school and college-age students, was launched online in 2002 and published online for a year before a print version was added. Described as a "trendsetter among a new generation of evangelicals," *Relevant* was started by Cameron Strang, the son of Stephen Strang, the publisher of the successful Pentecostal magazine *Charisma*. In 2005, InterVarsity discontinued its successful print publications, substituting an online site, showing that the internet offered attractive prospects for some Evangelical organizations. As Ken Waters pointed out in 2008, Evangelical periodicals today "have to compete with television, films and now visually entertaining websites like YouTube."[28] While some failed in the face of such competition, others rose to the challenge, producing print and online magazines of attractive graphic design and stimulating content. Today, there is a broad, as yet unstudied, range of magazines both in print and online.

In *Evangelical News*, I stressed the labor of representation, or, in sociologist Rogers Brubaker's words, "group-making as a project."[29] In the article "Ethnicity without Groups," Brubaker laments the practice of mistaking categories for groups, especially in the case of ethnicity. He criticizes the way that observers, by using the common-sense language of groups, helped reify what they sought to describe and moreover treated "the social and cultural world as a multichrome mosaic of monochrome ethnic, racial or cultural blocs."[30] Religion should be added to this list. Observers still largely treat religious communities as homogeneous, identifiable via institutionalized membership and a priori defined by common creeds.[31] Such assumptions also lead political observers to postulate an evangelical voting bloc, a notion that has been discredited scholarly but is still popular. Brubaker argues that "cohesiveness" and "collective solidarity" are not "constant, enduring, or definitionally present." Rather, moments of what he calls "groupness" are produced by conjuring the group, which is the work of spokespersons who have a vital interest in producing the group they represent.[32] Whereas Brubaker is sociologically interested in instances in which actors act in cohesion, in this study I have focused on how spokespersons in a particular historical context reified a particular group, Evangelicalism.

In *Evangelical News*, I have argued that knowing a group's frame of reference matters enormously to understanding *them*, that is, to unpacking their visions and translating their vernacular. During the 1970s and 1980s, Evangelical magazines were one space for Evangelical meaning making and facilitated continuous conversation and negotiation. Evangelical spokespersons—those who lived off of as well as for Evangelicalism—not only represented but created the community for which they spoke. Through the labor of representation they struggled to produce and maintain an Evangelical common sense, consisting of a particular vernacular and visions. Visions contained shared logics and curtailed conflicts and thus proved ambiguous enough to signal belonging to the heterogeneous group of Evangelical believers. They were flexible enough to develop and change throughout time and according to context and circumstance. While always in flux and always challenged, visions served to mark Evangelicals as a community apart.

NOTES

INTRODUCTION
1. Carl F. H. Henry, "Wavering Evangelical Initiative," *Christianity Today*, January 16, 1976, 32; Henry, "In Search of Evangelical Identity: A Ten-Piece Series," *Christianity Today*, January to October 1976.
2. Matthew Avery Sutton, *American Apocalypse: A History of Modern Evangelicalism* (Cambridge, MA: Belknap Press of Harvard University Press, 2017), 169–70. Compare Michael Hochgeschwender, *Amerikanische Religion: Evangelikalismus, Pfingstlertum und Fundamentalismus* (Frankfurt: Verlag der Weltreligionen, 2007), 15. For a history of the Scopes Trial (also known as the Scopes Monkey Trial), see Edward J. Larson, *Summer for the Gods: The Scopes Trial and America's Continuing Debate over Science and Religion* (New York: Basic Books, 1997).
3. Evangelicalism lacked institutional structures generally associated with a "church" (in the European context) or "denomination" (in the US context). In 1942, Evangelical activists founded the NAE as an umbrella organization and in competition to the liberal National Council of Christian Churches and the Fundamentalist American Council of Christian Churches. The NAE could have become an institution formalizing and structuring Evangelicalism, but it failed in this regard. See Axel R. Schäfer, *Countercultural Conservatives: American Evangelicalism from the Postwar Revival to the New Christian Right* (Madison: University of Wisconsin Press, 2011), 55–64. Whereas self-identified Evangelicals insist that Evangelicalism transcends denominational boundaries, sociologists regularly reintroduce the question of membership by equating evangelical Christianity directly with a group of conservative Protestant denominations. To pick but one recent example: sociologist Corwin E. Smidt approaches evangelical Christianity as a "tradition," using membership (i.e., affiliation with particular religious organizations) as the basis for his definition. Smidt, *American Evangelicals Today* (Lanham, MD: Rowman and Littlefield, 2013), xii.
4. For example, Evangelical theologian Donald G. Bloesch in 1973 spoke of an "Evangelical renaissance" and argued that "this movement is wider and deeper than the original surge of 'neo-evangelicalism.'" Bloesch, *The Evangelical Renaissance* (Grand Rapids, MI: Eerdmans, 1973), 30. Nearly two decades later, Donald W. Dayton complained about the predominance of the Reformed tradition within Evangelicalism. He also wondered whether, given the diversity of Evangelicalism, it was proper to subsume all under one term. See Dayton, "Some Doubts about the Usefulness of the Category 'Evangelical,'" in *The Variety of American Evan-*

gelicalism, ed. Donald W. Dayton and Robert K. Johnston (Knoxville: University of Tennessee Press, 1991), 245-51.

5. The complaint of misappropriation of the term can be found in many definitions of Evangelicalism put forth by participant-observer scholars. For example, Joel A. Carpenter complained that "Evangelicalism has been so pervasive in American culture that its tenets often show up in folk piety here." See Carpenter, introduction to *Twentieth-Century Evangelicalism: A Guide to the Sources*, ed. Edith L. Blumhofer and Joel A. Carpenter (New York: Garland, 1990), x. Roger E. Olson distinguished Evangelicalism proper from cultural evangelicalism in his multipoint definition of the term: "The seventh definition of *evangelical* and *Evangelicalism* is popular rather than scholarly or historical. One often hears or reads the adjective *evangelical* used by journalists to describe anyone or any group that seems particularly (by the journalist's standards) enthusiastic, aggressive, fanatical, or even simply missionary-minded. True fundamentalists (militant, separatist, ultraconservative Protestants) are often described in the media as evangelical; sometimes Roman Catholic missionaries and even Muslim groups that engage in missionary endeavors are labeled evangelical by journalists. This seventh use cannot simply be rejected; it has caught on in contemporary language. Jehovah's Witnesses, considered a cult by many conservative Protestants, are often called evangelical simply because of their door-to-door witnessing techniques." Olson, *The Westminster Handbook to Evangelical Theology* (Louisville, KY: Westminster John Knox Press, 2004), 6. Randall Balmer suggested pronunciation as the litmus test for "true" Evangelicals, stating that "although this rule is not universal, people who call themselves 'evangelical' generally pronounce the word with a short 'e' (the first two syllables rhyme with 'leaven'), while people who are not evangelicals use a long 'e' (ee-van-gel-i-cal)." Balmer, *Encyclopedia of Evangelicalism* (Waco, TX: Baylor University Press, 2004), s.v. "Evangelical." For more on participant-observation, see Douglas A. Sweeney, "The Essential Evangelicalism Dialectic: The Historiography of the Early Neo-Evangelical Movement and the Observer-Participant Dilemma," *Church History* 60, no. 1 (1991): 70-84.

6. There are at least two inflections of Evangelicalism in use today: the religious label refers to a specific subset of conservative Protestants; another inflection, the sociological category developed by polling institutes like Pew, more generally refers to conservative white Protestants. Since this book is concerned with the religious inflection, not the sociological one, I capitalize the term Evangelical.

7. For "labour of representation," see Pierre Bourdieu, *Language and Symbolic Power*, ed. John B. Thompson, trans. Gino Raymond and Matthew Adamson (Cambridge: Polity Press, 2008), 130, 234.

8. In focusing on Evangelical narratives of this era, this study pushes back on findings from sociologists' opinion polls and surveys of the time, which detected a discrepancy between what evangelical Christians said and what they did. A three-year project funded by the Pew Charitable Fund between 1995 and 1997 studied evangelical Christians across the States and from heterogeneous denominational and nondenominational backgrounds. The numerous sociologists in-

volved focused on "ordinary" believers, arguing that the perceived discrepancy could be explained by the gap between what elites proclaim and what ordinary believers appropriate in their own lives. However, researchers were still left with the paradox that ordinary believers subscribed to ideas like "Christian America" or "male headship" but manifested a desire neither for theocracy nor for male domination in their lives. Rather than dismiss words as empty rhetoric, I trace the genesis of such terms in Evangelical magazines, revealing the boundaries of what ideas were conceivable within Evangelical discourse. For the Pew study, see Christian Smith, *Christian America? What Evangelicals Really Want* (Berkeley: University of California Press, 2002); Sally K. Gallagher and Christian Smith, "Symbolic Traditionalism and Pragmatic Egalitarianism: Contemporary Evangelicals, Families, and Gender," *Gender and Society* 13 (1999): 211–33; Sally K. Gallagher, *Evangelical Identity and Gendered Family Life* (New Brunswick, NJ: Rutgers University Press, 2003); Melinda Lundquist Denton, "Gender and Marital Decision Making: Negotiating Religious Ideology and Practice," *Social Forces* 82, no. 3 (2004): 1151–80.

9. On the electronic church and televangelism, see, for example, Robert Abelman and Stewart M. Hoover, *Religious Television: Controversies and Conclusions* (Norwood, NJ: Ablex, 1990); Steve Bruce, *Pray T.V.: Televangelism in America* (London: Routledge, 1990); Shane A. Hipps, *The Hidden Power of Electronic Culture: How Media Shapes Faith, the Gospel, and Church* (Grand Rapids, MI: Zondervan, 2005); Stewart M. Hoover, *Mass Media Religion: The Social Sources of the Electronic Church* (Newbury Park, CA: Sage, 1988); Quentin J. Schultze, *Televangelism and American Culture: The Business of Popular Religion* (Grand Rapids, MI: Baker Books, 1991); Felix Krämer, *Moral Leaders: Medien, Gender und Glauben in den USA der 1970er und 1980er Jahre* (Bielefeld, Germany: Transcript, 2015).

On radio ministries, see, for example, Daniel P. Fuller, *Give the Winds a Mighty Voice: The Story of Charles E. Fuller* (Eugene, OR: Wipf and Stock, 2014), in which the author gives an account of the lives and ministry of his parents, including Charles Fuller's radio ministry (especially the "Old Fashioned Revival Hour"). See also Howard Dorgan, *The Airwaves of Zion: Radio and Religion in Appalachia* (Knoxville: University of Tennessee Press, 1993); Tona J. Hangen, *Redeeming the Dial: Radio, Religion, and Popular Culture in America* (Chapel Hill: University of North Carolina Press, 2002).

On religious communities and the internet, with examples occasionally borrowed from evangelical Christianity, see Heidi A. Campbell, *Exploring Religious Community online: We Are One in the Network* (New York: Peter Lang, 2005); Campbell, *When Religion Meets New Media: Media, Religion and Culture* (London: Routledge, 2010); Campbell, "Understanding the Relationship between Religion Online and Offline in a Networked Society," *Journal of the American Academy of Religion* 80, no. 1 (2012): 64–93.

10. Frank E. Gaebelein, "The Christian Use of the Printed Page," *Christianity Today*, January 30, 1970.

11. Martin E. Marty, "The Protestant Press: Limitations and Possibilities," in *The Religious Press in America*, ed. Martin E. Marty (New York: Holt, Rinehart and Winston, 1963), 8–9, 16. Despite their ubiquity, Protestant periodicals remained, as Marty noted, "largely invisible." While this review was published in 1963, the situation has not changed much. Marty's complaint was repeated in 1995 by P. Mark Fackler and Charles H. Lippy and P. Mark Fackler, and again in 2001 by Ken Waters: while a prolific industry, religious periodicals are largely overlooked as objects of scholarly analysis. See Fackler and Lippy, eds., *Popular Religious Magazines of the United States* (Westport, CT: Greenwood Press, 1995), xi; Waters, "Vibrant, but Invisible: A Study of Contemporary Religious Periodicals," *Journalism and Mass Communication Quarterly* 78, no. 2 (2001): 307–20.

12. Daniel Vaca, *Evangelicals Incorporated: Books and the Business of Religion in America* (Cambridge, MA: Harvard University Press, 2019), 12, 13.

13. See, for example, Maurice Isserman and Michael Kazin, *America Divided: The Civil War of the 1960s* (New York: Oxford University Press, 2000).

14. Peter N. Carroll, *It Seemed Like Nothing Happened: America in the 1970s* (New Brunswick, NJ: Rutgers University Press, 2000), xii.

15. Carroll, xiii; Andreas Killen, *1973 Nervous Breakdown: Watergate, Warhol, and the Birth of Post-Sixties America* (New York: Bloomsbury, 2006), 2.

16. Sean Wilentz, *The Age of Reagan: A History, 1974–2008* (New York: Harper Perennial, 2008), xv.

17. See Wilentz, 127–287; H. W. Brands, *American Dreams: The United States since 1945* (New York: Penguin Books, 2010), 213–62.

18. Elizabeth Tandy Shermer, *Sunbelt Capitalism: Phoenix and the Transformation of American Politics* (Philadelphia: University of Pennsylvania Press, 2015).

19. Brands, *American Dreams*, 231.

20. James Davison Hunter, *Culture Wars: The Struggle to Define America* (New York: Basic Books, 1991). For various critiques of the concept, see Alan Wolfe, *One Nation, After All: What Middle-Class Americans Really Think about God, Country, Family, Racism, Welfare, Immigration, Homosexuality, Work, the Right, the Left, and Each Other* (New York: Penguin Books, 1999); Dale McConkey, "Whither Hunter's Culture War? Shifts in Evangelical Morality, 1988–1998," *Sociology of Religion* 62, no. 2 (2001): 149–74; James Davidson Hunter and Alan Wolf, "Is There A Culture War?," mod. Michael Cromartie (conversation at the Pew Forum Faith Angle conference, Key West, FL, May 23, 2006), https://www.pewforum.org; Irene Taviss Thomson, *Culture Wars and Enduring American Dilemmas* (Ann Arbor: Michigan University Press, 2010).

21. "The Two Americas. Is It Still a Contest?," *Time*, October 2, 1972; "The Confrontation of the Two Americas," October 2, 1972.

22. Isserman and Kazin, *America Divided*, 4.

23. Leon Morris, "Conservative Evangelicals?," *Christianity Today*, November 19, 1971, 50.

24. Jerry B. Jenkins, "75 Years at Moody Monthly," *Moody Monthly*, September 1975, 29.

25. Billy Graham, "Standing Firm, Moving Forward," editorial, *Christianity Today*, September 16, 1996, 14.
26. "Inside Story," *Sojourners*, August/September 1991, 3.
27. For example, Joel A. Carpenter wrote, "this loose coalition that calls itself 'evangelicalism' is in fact less dependent on denominations than on a network of parachurch agencies such as InterVarsity Christian Fellowship, *Christianity Today* magazine, World Vision, Campus Crusade for Christ, Moody Bible Institute, Seattle Pacific University, Trinity Evangelical Divinity School, The 700 Club, and the Billy Graham Evangelistic Association." Carpenter, introduction to Blumhofer and Carpenter, *Twentieth-Century Evangelicalism*, ix. On the occasion of *Christianity Today*'s twenty-fifth anniversary, religion scholar Martin E. Marty enthused about the magazine: "*Christianity Today* has been the prime agent in demarcating, informing, and providing morale for the neo-evangelical, now evangelical, movement, at least in North America." Marty, "The Marks and Misses of a Magazine," *Christianity Today*, July 17, 1981, 48.
28. See Ken Waters, "Pursuing New Periodicals in Print and Online," in *Understanding Evangelical Media: The Changing Face of Christian Communication*, ed. Quentin J. Schultze and Robert H. Woods Jr. (Downers Grove, IL: InterVarsity Press, 2008), 78–79; Waters, "The Evangelical Press," in *The Oxford Handbook of Religion and the American News Media*, ed. Diane Winston (New York: Oxford University Press, 2012), 551–64; Waters, "Evangelical Magazines," in *Evangelical Christians and Popular Culture: Pop Goes the Gospel*, ed. Robert Woods, vol. 3 (Santa Barbara, CA: Praeger, 2013), 195–211; Waters, "Religious Magazines: Keeping the Faith," in *The Routledge Handbook of Magazine Research: The Future of the Magazine Form*, ed. David Abrahamson and Marcia R. Prior-Miller (New York: Routledge, 2015), 308–22. See also Robert H. Krapohl and Charles H. Lippy, *The Evangelicals: A Historical, Thematic, and Biographical Guide* (Westport, CT: Greenwood Press, 1999), 185; Stewart M. Hoover, *Religion in the News: Faith and Journalism in American Public Discourse* (Thousand Oaks, CA: Sage, 1998).
29. Candy Gunther Brown, *The Word in the World: Evangelical Writing, Publishing, and Reading in America, 1789–1880* (Chapel Hill: University of North Carolina Press, 2004); Gisela Mettele, *Weltbürgertum oder Gottesreich? Die Herrnhuter Brüdergemeine als globale Gemeinschaft, 1760–1857* (Göttingen, Germany: Vandenhoeck and Ruprecht, 2009). For histories of periodicals, see Elesha J. Coffman, *The Christian Century and the Rise of the Christian Mainline* (New York: Oxford University Press, 2013); Oliver Scheiding and Anja-Maria Bassimir, eds., *Religious Periodicals and Publishing in Transnational Contexts: The Press and the Pulpit* (Newcastle upon Tyne, UK: Cambridge Scholars, 2017).
30. Daniel A. Stout and Judith M. Buddenbaum, "Genealogy of an Emerging Field: Foundations for the Study of Media and Religion," *Journal of Media and Religion* 1, no. 1 (2002): 6; Sean Latham and Robert Scholes, "The Rise of Periodical Studies," *PMLA* 121, no. 2 (2006): 517–31.
31. Examples are the Modernist Journals Project (http://modjourn.org) and two databases from ProQuest: British Periodicals and American Periodicals Se-

ries. Endeavors like Northeastern University's Viral Texts Project (https://viraltexts.org) and Regesta Imperii of the Akademie der Wissenschaft und der Literatur Mainz (http://www.regesta-imperii.de) make available public-domain texts, thus avoiding the copyright laws that complicate digitization projects of more contemporary periodicals.

32. At one point, the *Wittenburg Door* sold a DVD with PDFs of its back issues through its (now-defunct) online store. The entire archive of *Christianity Today*, dating back to its 1956 founding, is available online to subscribers (https://www.christianitytoday.com), but this is a relatively recent development. As late as 2017, when I was researching this book, the website only had issues dating back to 1994.

33. Stewart M. Hoover, "The Culturalist Turn in Scholarship on Media and Religion," *Journal of Media and Religion* 1, no. 1 (2002): 28, 29.

34. Faye Hammill, Paul Hjartarson, and Hannah McGregor, "Magazines and/as Media: Periodical Studies and the Question of Disciplinarity," *Journal of Modern Periodical Studies* 6, no. 2 (2015): v.

35. Hammill, Hjartarson, and McGregor, v.

36. Latham and Scholes, "The Rise of Periodical Studies," 529.

37. Bourdieu, *Language and Symbolic Power*, 117–26.

38. In addition to building on Bourdieu, this study draws on the constructivist theory of sociologists Peter L. Berger and Thomas Luckmann. This approach insists that all that can be communicated is necessarily constructed. Following this approach, I do not make any claims about the "nature of things" or question whether something is true outside or independently of its social construction. Rather, I argue that context matters because it preconfigures what can be said (discourse) and how words are being used (vernacular), delimiting how people perceive reality and experience the world. See Berger and Luckmann, *The Social Construction of Reality: A Treatise in the Sociology of Knowledge* (Garden City, NY: Anchor Books, 1967).

39. I acknowledge this notion of immediate reality for those who experience it while at the same time studying the construction of visions as signifiers whose meaning is contingent on a certain time and context. While I prefer the term "vision," this notion of a community portrait also aligns with Benedict R. Anderson's "imagined community"; see Anderson, *Imagined Communities: Reflections on the Origin and Spread of Nationalism* (London: Verso, 1991).

40. Bourdieu, *Language and Symbolic Power*, 130, 234.

41. Bourdieu, 182.

42. See, for example, Douglas A. Sweeney, "Christianity Today," in Fackler and Lippy, *Popular Religious Magazines*, 145–46; Kenneth W. Shipps, "Christianity Today," in *The Conservative Press in Twentieth-Century America*, ed. Ronald Lora and William Henry Longton (Westport, CT: Greenwood Press, 1999), 171.

43. Coffman, *The Christian Century and the Rise of the Protestant Mainline*, 6.

44. Coffman, 221–22; Shipps, "Christianity Today," 171, 173; "CTAdvertising," *Christianity Today*, accessed December 1, 2014, http://www.christianitytodayads.com.

45. Sweeney, "Christianity Today," 148.

46. Glenn Arnold, "Today's Christian Woman," in Fackler and Lippy, *Popular Religious Magazines of the United States*, 463–68; "What We Do," Christianity Today, accessed June 10, 2021, http://www.christianitytoday.org.

47. "CT Advertising," *Christianity Today*, accessed August 10, 2021, https://www.christianitytodayads.com. See Anja-Maria Bassimir, "Evangelical Magazines in a Digital Age," in Scheiding and Bassimir, *Religious Periodicals and Publishing in Transnational Contexts*, 145–67; Anja-Maria Bassimir, "Combating Caustic Communication with Truth and Beauty: Christianity Today, Beautiful Orthodoxy, and US Culture," in *Strong Religion and Mainstream Culture: Opposition, Negotiation, and Adaption*, ed. Stefan Gelfgren and Daniel Lindmark (Basingstoke: Palgrave, 2021), 213–37; Anja-Maria Bassimir, "Religiöse Zeitschriften am Beispiel von Christianity Today," in *Zeitschriftenforschung: Eine Einführung*, ed. Oliver Scheiding and Sabina Fazli (Leiden: Brill, forthcoming).

48. See Shipps, "Christianity Today."

49. Sweet described this group as children of "the first generation of new evangelicals, who were themselves second generation fundamentalists." He had historians like George Marsden, Mark Noll, Joel Carpenter, Nathan Hatch, Harry Stout, and Grant Wacker in mind; but besides historians other young Evangelical leaders—working as writers, editors, and educators and in other capacities—could be added to the list. See Leonard I. Sweet, "Wise as Serpents, Innocent as Doves: The New Evangelical Historiography," *Journal of the American Academy of Religion* 56, no. 3 (1988): 401. Matthew Avery Sutton recently argued that the clear break between the Fundamentalists and neo-Evangelicals, often described in the literature, is mostly a fiction of Evangelical elites; see Sutton, *American Apocalypse*, 286, 294–95. Yet, Molly Worthen has shown how important Fundamentalism was as a foil from which the neo-Evangelicals set themselves apart; see Worthen, *Apostles of Reason: The Crisis of Authority in American Evangelicalism* (New York: Oxford University Press, 2016).

50. Harold Lindsell is best known for his book *The Battle for the Bible* (Grand Rapids, MI: Zondervan, 1976).

51. See Schäfer, *Countercultural Conservatives*; David R. Swartz, *Moral Minority: The Evangelical Left in an Age of Conservatism* (Philadelphia: University of Pennsylvania Press, 2012).

52. See Shipps, "Christianity Today," 175.

53. "Statement of Circulation," *Christianity Today*, October 20, 1978.

54. Carolyn Nystrom, "*HIS* Presents . . . the Competition! Other Christian Magazines You Should Know about," *HIS*, May 1979, 21.

55. Russell T. Hitt, "Barnhouse of Philadelphia," *Eternity*, April 1975, 16. See also William J. Petersen, "25 Years of *Eternity*," *Eternity*, April 1975; Balmer, *Encyclopedia of Evangelicalism*, s.v. "Barnhouse, Donald Grey (1895–1960)"; Michael T. Girolimon, "Eternity," in Fackler and Lippy, *Popular Religious Magazines of the United States*, 221–26.

56. William J. Petersen, "The Magazine That Lived," *Eternity*, May 1975.

57. See "Joe Bayly: Editor, Author, Humanist Dies at 66," *Christianity Today*, September 5, 1986.

58. Foretaste, *Eternity*, September 1975; Foretaste, *Eternity*, December 1983.

59. Andrew Ferguson, "Pop Goes the Culture: One Man's Quest to Preserve and Defend the Good, The True, and the Beautiful," *Weekly Standard*, January 14, 2013.

60. "Celebrating a New Beginning," *Eternity*, January 1986.

61. Nystrom, "*HIS* Presents . . . the Competition!," 21.

62. See Joel A. Carpenter, "Moody Monthly," in Lora and Longton, *The Conservative Press in Twentieth-Century America*, 103–11.

63. For the former view, see Timothy L. Smith, "The Evangelical Kaleidoscope and the Call to Christian Unity," *Christian Scholar's Review* 15 (1986): 130–31. For the latter, see Sweeney, "The Essential Evangelicalism Dialectic," 79n44, where Sweeney describes the Moody Bible Institute as "the location where the neoevangelical founders first strategized."

64. Carpenter, "Moody Monthly," 107.

65. Carpenter, 107–9.

66. Jenkins, "75 Years at *Moody Monthly*," 29.

67. See Paul C. Gutjahr, "The Perseverance of Print-Bound Saints: Protestant Book Publishing," in *A History of the Book in America*, vol. 5, *The Enduring Book: Print Culture in Postwar America*, ed. David Paul Nord, Joan Shelley Rubin, and Michael Schudson (Chapel Hill: University of North Carolina Press, 2009), 386–88.

68. Todd Hertz and Stan Guthrie, "Moody Closes Magazine, Restructures Aviation Program," *Christianity Today*, February 1, 2003, http://www.christianitytoday.com.

69. Nystrom, "*HIS* Presents . . . the Competition!," 21.

70. Swartz, *Moral Minority*, 48, and see 49–53.

71. The original seven Trinity Evangelical Divinity School students in this coalition were: Jim Wallis, Glen Melnik, John Topliff, Boyd Rees, Herb McMillan, Bob Sabath, and Barry Turner. "Founding Document," c. 1971, Sojourners, records (SC-023), series 4 (administrative records), box 58, folder 5, Buswell Library Special Collections, Wheaton College, Wheaton, IL. See also David Kling, "Sojourners," in *Religious Periodicals of the United States: Academic and Scholarly Journals*, ed. Charles H. Lippy (Westport, CT: Greenwood Press, 1986), 479–82.

72. Swartz, *Moral Minority*, 68–69. The relationship between Henry and Wallis deteriorated in 1974 in the aftermath of a joint project, the Chicago Declaration of Evangelical Social Concern.

73. See "Inside Story," *Sojourners*, August/September 1991 (the twentieth-anniversary issue).

74. Swartz, *Moral Minority*, 54.

75. In 1976, *Sojourners* printed an average of 10,267 copies per issue, of which an average of 8,877 went to paid subscribers. In 1977, *Sojourners* printed an average of 22,847 copies per issue, of which an average of 17,699 went to paid sub-

scribers. In 1978, *Sojourners* printed an average of 30,849 copies per issue, of which an average of 29,061 went to paid subscribers. In 1979, *Sojourners* printed an average of 39,099 copies per issue, of which an average of 36,977 went to paid subscribers. Paid circulation peaked at an average of 56,063 copies per issue in 1983. "Circulation Reports, 1976–1987," Sojourners, records (SC-023), series 4, box 58, folder 5. For an overview of the first twenty years of *Sojourners*, see Joe Roos, "Keeping the Vision Afloat," *Sojourners*, August/September 1991.

76. Waters, "The Evangelical Press," 556.

77. Nystrom, "*HIS* Presents . . . the Competition!," 23.

78. For brief information on the newsletter, see Joseph B. Modica, "Daughters of Sarah," in Fackler and Lippy, *Popular Religious Magazines of the United States*, 202–6.

79. Richard A. Morrow, "Door," in Fackler and Lippy, *Popular Religious Magazines of the United States*, 213.

80. See the tenth- and fifteenth-anniversary issues of *Wittenburg Door* (June/July 1981, and April/May 1986, respectively). Also see Ted Olsen, "Close the Door," *Christianity Today*, April 1, 2002, http://www.christianitytoday.com; and the *Wittenburg Door* home page, accessed June 10, 2021, http://www.wittenburgdoor.com.

81. See Swartz, *Moral Minority*, 26–46.

82. On InterVarsity, see "InterVarsity and IFES History," InterVarsity, accessed June 10, 2021, https://intervarsity.org.

Chapter 1

1. "Back to That Old Time Religion," *Time*, December 26, 1977, 53.

2. See, for example, Kenneth L. Woodward, John Barnes, and Laurie Lisle, "Born Again," *Newsweek*, October 25, 1976; "Jimmy Carter on Politics, Religion, the Press, and Sex," *Playboy*, November 1976.

3. Joel A. Carpenter, "Fundamentalist Institutions and the Rise of Evangelical Protestantism, 1929–1942," *Church History* 49, no. 1 (1980): 62–75.

4. On Fuller, see George M. Marsden, *Reforming Fundamentalism: Fuller Seminary and the New Evangelicalism* (Grand Rapids, MI: Eerdmans, 1995). On Moody Bible Institute, see Timothy E. W. Gloege, *Guaranteed Pure: The Moody Bible Institute, Business, and the Making of Modern Evangelicalism* (Chapel Hill: University of North Carolina Press, 2017).

5. Clyde Wilcox and Carin Robinson, *Onward Christian Soldiers? The Religious Right in American Politics* (Boulder, CO: Westview Press, 1996), 1, 6.

6. See, for example, Robert C. Liebman and Robert Wuthnow, *The New Christian Right: Mobilization and Legitimation* (New York: Aldine, 1983).

7. Axel Schäfer, *Countercultural Conservatives: American Evangelicalism from the Postwar Revival to the New Christian Right* (Madison: University of Wisconsin Press, 2011).

8. Wilcox and Robinson, *Onward Christian Soldiers?*, 102; Kevin M. Kruse, *One Nation under God: How Corporate America Invented Christian America* (New York: Basic Books, 2015); Matthew Avery Sutton, *American Apocalypse: A His-*

tory of Modern Evangelicalism (Cambridge, MA: Belknap Press of Harvard University Press, 2017).

9. See Robert Wuthnow, "Religious Commitment and Conservative: In Search of an Elusive Relationship," in *Religion in Social Perspective: Essays in the Empirical Study of Religion*, ed. Charles W. Glock (Belmont, CA: Wadsworth, 1973), 117–32; Woodward, Barnes, and Lisle, "Born Again"; Compare David R. Swartz, *Moral Minority: The Evangelical Left in an Age of Conservatism* (Philadelphia: University of Pennsylvania Press, 2012), 2.

10. See, for example, K. Jill Kiecolt and Hart M. Nelsen, "Evangelicals and Party Realignment, 1976–1988," *Social Science Quarterly* 72, no. 3 (1991): 552–69; Steven P. Miller, *Billy Graham and the Rise of the Republican South* (Philadelphia: University of Pennsylvania Press, 2009). Darren Dochuk has also traced the genesis of the alliance between conservative Protestantism and the Republican Party, but he does so via the transplantation of Southerners to California; see Dochuk, *From Bible Belt to Sunbelt: Plain-Folk Religion, Grassroots Politics, and the Rise of Evangelical Conservatism* (New York: W. W. Norton, 2012).

11. Darren Dochuk, Thomas S. Kidd, and Kurt W. Peterson, eds., *American Evangelicalism: George Marsden and the State of American Religious History* (Notre Dame, IN: University of Notre Dame Press, 2014).

12. See, for example, George M. Marsden, *Understanding Fundamentalism and Evangelicalism* (Grand Rapids, MI: Eerdmans, 1991), 1–4; Mark A. Noll, *American Evangelical Christianity: An Introduction* (Oxford: Blackwell, 2001), 18–22.

13. According to Christian Smith, resurgent Evangelicals focused in particular on (1) evangelizing, (2) making Evangelicalism intellectually compatible with secular scholarship, and (3) becoming socially and politically active. Smith, *American Evangelicalism: Embattled and Thriving* (Chicago: University of Chicago Press, 1998), 9–10. See also Robert D. Linder, "The Resurgence of Evangelical Social Concern," in *The Evangelicals: What They Believe, Who They Are, Where They Are Changing*, ed. David F. Wells and John D. Woodbridge (Nashville, TN: Abingdon Press, 1975), 200–202.

14. Carpenter, "Fundamentalist Institutions and the Rise of Evangelical Protestantism," 63; Noll, *American Evangelical Christianity*, 49.

15. Peter A. Huff, *What Are They Saying about Fundamentalisms?* (Mahwah, NJ: Paulist Press, 2008), 73; Carl F. H. Henry, *The Uneasy Conscience of Modern Fundamentalism* (Grand Rapids, MI: Eerdmans, 1947).

16. Harold John Ockenga, introduction to C. Henry, *The Uneasy Conscience of Modern Fundamentalism*, 13–14.

17. Marsden, *Understanding Fundamentalism and Evangelicalism*, 72.

18. Sutton, *American Apocalypse*, 308, and see xiii, 285, 294–95. Sutton regards the division between Fundamentalism and Evangelicalism as a marketing ploy meant to soften the premillennialism and the more esoteric thought of some of the movement. Nonetheless, differences existed between those who continued to call themselves Fundamentalists (like Carl McIntire or Bob Jones Sr. and Jr.) and the new Evangelical intellectuals (like those associated with *Christianity Today*)

who wanted the movement to be more broadly socially acceptable. See, for example, Robert Booth Fowler, *A New Engagement: Evangelical Political Thought, 1966–1976* (Grand Rapids, MI: Eerdmans, 1982), 11.

19. Schäfer, *Countercultural Conservatives*, 75, and see 72–76.

20. James Davison Hunter, *Evangelicalism: The Coming Generation* (Chicago: University of Chicago Press, 1987), 42 (emphasis in original).

21. Hunter, 257n35, 42.

22. Linder, "The Resurgence of Evangelical Social Concern," 204–5; and see Schäfer, *Countercultural Conservatives*; Swartz, *Moral Minority*.

23. Kruse, *One Nation under God*, 244.

24. Kruse, 246, and see 249–57. See also Ben Hibbs, ed., *White House Sermons* (New York: Harper and Row, 1972).

25. Mary P. Ryan, *Mysteries of Sex: Tracing Women and Men through American History* (Chapel Hill: University of North Carolina Press, 2006), 261–62.

26. Evangelical reaction to the legalization of abortion lagged behind the court decision; a major discussion of abortion took place during the 1980s and will be discussed in chapter 6. On the conflict between advocates and opponents of abortion immediately following the Supreme Court decision, see, for example, Pamela Johnston Conover and Virginia Gray, *Feminism and the New Right: Conflict over the American Family* (New York: Praeger, 1983); Kristin Luker, *Abortion and the Politics of Motherhood* (Berkeley: University of California Press, 1984).

27. See Donald T. Critchlow, *Phyllis Schlafly and Grassroots Conservatism: A Woman's Crusade* (Princeton, NJ: Princeton University Press, 2005).

28. Margaret Lamberts Bendroth, "The Search for 'Women's Role' in American Evangelicalism, 1930–1980," in *Evangelicalism and Modern America*, ed. George M. Marsden (Grand Rapids, MI: Eerdmans, 1984), 123.

29. Betty A. DeBerg, *Ungodly Women: Gender and the First Wave of American Fundamentalism* (Macon, GA: Mercer University Press, 2000).

30. Margaret Lamberts Bendroth, *Fundamentalism and Gender, 1875 to the Present* (New Haven, CT: Yale University Press, 1993), 119, 105; and see Alan G. Padgett, "The Bible and Gender Troubles: American Evangelicals Debate Scripture and Submission," *Dialogue* 47, no. 1 (2008): 22–23.

31. See, for example, John R. Rice, *Bobbed Hair, Bossy Wives and Women Preachers. Significant Questions for Honest Christian Women Settled by the Word of God* (Wheaton, IL: Sword of the Lord, 1941); Charles C. Ryrie, *The Place of Women in the Church* (New York: Macmillan, 1958); see also David H. Watt, *A Transforming Faith: Explorations of Twentieth-Century American Evangelicalism* (New Brunswick, NJ: Rutgers University Press, 1991), 96–99.

32. Fowler, *A New Engagement*, 55, and see 54, 74–75.

33. Bendroth, "The Search for 'Women's Role' in American Evangelicalism," 131. I follow here the argument of theologian Alan G. Padgett, who argues that the so-called complementarian view was "not the same as the traditional Christian patriarchal viewpoint." Padgett, "The Bible and Gender Troubles," 21.

34. Confusingly, Pamela D. H. Cochran and others have used the term "tra-

ditionalist feminists" to refer to those feminists that remained within the folds of Evangelicalism in the 1980s, when activists associated with the Evangelical Women's Caucus (EWC) and *Daughters of Sarah* went beyond its scope and started referring to themselves more broadly as biblical or Christian feminists. Cochran identifies as traditionalist feminists Catherine Kroeger, who founded Christians for Biblical Equality (CBE) in 1986, as well as other members of CBE and the Council on Biblical Manhood and Womanhood (founded 1987). See Cochran, *Evangelical Feminism: A History* (New York: New York University Press, 2005); see also Roger E. Olson, *The Westminster Handbook to Evangelical Theology* (Louisville, KY: Westminster John Knox Press, 2004), s.v. "Gender Roles: Complementarianism/Egalitarianism," 311–14.

35. Lisa McGirr, *Suburban Warriors: The Origins of the New American Right* (Princeton; NJ: Princeton University Press, 2001); Ruth Murray Brown, *For a "Christian America": A History of the Religious Right* (Amherst, NY: Prometheus Books, 2002).

36. Reta Halteman Finger and S. Sue Horner, "Euro-American Evangelical Feminism," in *Encyclopedia of Women and Religion in North America*, ed. Rosemary Skinner Keller and Rosemary Radford Ruether, vol. 1 (Bloomington: Indiana University Press, 2006), 467–76. For a short overview of the history of women in Evangelicalism, see Jane Harris, "American Evangelical Women: More Than Wives and Mothers—Reformers, Ministers, and Leaders," in Keller and Ruether, *Encyclopedia of Women and Religion in North America*, vol. 1, 447–57.

37. Cochran, *Evangelical Feminism*.

38. Bendroth, *Fundamentalism and Gender*, 121.

39. Letha Scanzoni, "Woman's Place: Silence or Service?," *Eternity*, February 1966; Scanzoni, "Elevating Marriage to Partnership," *Eternity*, July 1968. See also Bendroth, *Fundamentalism and Gender*, 121–22; Sally K. Gallagher, "The Marginalization of Evangelical Feminism," *Sociology of Religion* 65, no. 3 (2004): 222–23; Cochran, *Evangelical Feminism*, 22–24; Finger and Horner, "Euro-American Evangelical Feminism," 468–69.

40. The most helpful work on Evangelical feminism is Cochran, *Evangelical Feminism*. Now a professor of theology, Cochran focuses on the theological ramifications of Evangelical feminism but also provides a history of the activists and institutions connected with it. For the roots of Evangelical feminism, namely discussions of Fundamentalism and women, see DeBerg, *Ungodly Women*. Margaret Lamberts Bendroth also looks at the history of women in Fundamentalism and provides a useful perspective on how these ideas influenced the younger Evangelicalism; see Bendroth, *Fundamentalism and Gender*. Julie Ingersoll analyzes institutions and individuals associated with what Cochran had called "traditionalist feminism," namely Evangelical feminists who organized during the 1980s and struggled to be feminists while staying within the Evangelical fold, especially Christians for Biblical Equality; see Ingersoll, *Evangelical Christian Women: War Stories in the Gender Battles* (New York: New York University Press, 2003). From a sociological perspective, Sally K. Gallagher analyzes Evangelicals' attitudes toward feminism and gender relations; see Gallagher, *Evangelical Identity and Gen-*

dered Family Life (New Brunswick, NJ: Rutgers University Press, 2003); Gallagher, "The Marginalization of Evangelical Feminism." While these are scholarly contributions, all these authors have roots in Evangelicalism. Conversely, Rebecca Merrill Groothuis attempts to intervene directly in the Evangelical "culture war between traditionalism and feminism" by showing through a grand tour of church history that both the traditionalist view (which she conflates with the patriarchal view) and the feminist view are culturally conditioned and fairly new. She argues that it is wrong to assume that the traditionalist view was historical and therefore correct; rather, in her opinion, the feminist view (as she defines it) reflects biblical precepts more closely. See Groothuis, *Women Caught in the Conflict: The Culture War between Traditionalism and Feminism* (Grand Rapids, MI: Baker Books, 1993). The literature on the traditionalist view generally focuses on organizations and spokespersons associated with the New Christian Right, which emerged in the 1980s. For example, on Focus on the Family's treatment of questions regarding women, see Eithne Johnson, "Dr. Dobson's Advice to Christian Women: The Story of Strategic Motherhood," *Social Text* 57 (1998): 55–82. On women in the New Christian Right, see Leslie Dorrough Smith, *Righteous Rhetoric: Sex, Speech, and the Politics of Concerned Women for America* (New York: Oxford University Press, 2014); Brown, *For a "Christian America."*

Sociologist John P. Bartkowski undertook an analysis related to my own by comparing thirty family manuals published by evangelical Christian leaders, including Christian feminists and leaders of the New Christian Right. He found that the manuals ascribed to one of two contrasting perspectives, what he termed the "hegemonic" (hierarchical, male headship) and "counterhegemonic" (egalitarian, mutual submission) "discourses." Bartkowski, "Debating Patriarchy: Discursive Disputes over Spousal Authority among Evangelical Family Commentators," *Journal for the Scientific Study of Religion* 36, no. 3 (1997): 393–410. Bartkowski suggested that further studies should look at "the relationship between the prevailing gender *attitudes* and the actual *practice* of gender in conservative Protestant households" (406, emphasis in original). I find this direction of investigation misleading because it assumes a division between language and practice that I reject—saying (or believing) one thing and doing another. I am more intrigued by Bartkowski's observation that hegemonic discourses also "interjected egalitarian rhetoric" (397). While he did not investigate this finding any further, my study suggests that many Evangelical spokespersons envisioned gender relations in a complex way that did not neatly divide into the categories proposed by Bartkowski.

CHAPTER 2

1. The first several issues of the *Post-American* were irregularly published. After the inaugural, issue, dated fall 1971, the second issue was dated as winter 1972 but published at the beginning of the year, and the third was published in spring 1972. Starting in January/February 1973, the *Post-American* appeared regularly six times a year, and the issues were more clearly labeled by months and year.

2. Jim Wallis, "Post-American Christianity," *Post-American*, Fall 1971, 2.

3. Jim Wallis, "The Movemental Church," *Post-American*, Winter 1972, 2; and see "What Is the People's Christian Coalition?," *Post-American*, Fall 1971.

4. Joe Roos, "American Civil Religion," *Post-American*, Spring 1972, 8.

5. David R. Swartz, *Moral Minority: The Evangelical Left in an Age of Conservatism* (Philadelphia: University of Pennsylvania Press, 2012).

6. Jeremiads refer to a form of prophetic judgment associated with the prophet Jeremiah and the biblical Book of Jeremiah and Book of Lamentations. Jeremiah lamented the immorality and wickedness of people and proclaimed doom over the kingdom of Judah. Jeremiah is special among the prophets because "though a prophet is normally supposed to intercede (Gen. 20:7, 20:17), Jeremiah is told [by God] not to" and instead prophesies disaster. S. David Sperling, "Jeremiah," in *The Encyclopedia of Religion*, ed. Mircea Eliade, vol. 8 (New York: Macmillan, 1987), 5. Jeremiads were introduced to North America by the Puritans. Jeremiads are a literary form lamenting moral conditions and prophesying drastic consequences. In their extreme and most literal form, they refer to nations that are beyond redemption, which even repentance will not save. In popular form, jeremiads can refer to political sermons. See also Andrew R. Murphy and Thomas Wortmann, "Jeremiad," *Encyclopedia of the Bible and Its Reception*, accessed June 10, 2021, https://doi.org/10.1515/ebr.jeremiad. The most influential work on jeremiads in colonial America is Sacvan Bercovitch, *The American Jeremiad* (Madison: University of Wisconsin Press, 1978).

7. Jean-Jacques Rousseau, *The Social Contract* (1762; New York: Wallachia, 2015). According to Rousseau, in pagan societies only theocracies existed: every people had its own god, and when fighting one another, different peoples also fought different religions. This changed with the advent of religions that claimed universal truth, like Christianity. Rousseau lamented that Christianity, "by separating the theological from the political system, destroyed the unity of the state" (68). It was suddenly possible that different people all claiming Jesus Christ as their savior could fight against one another. Worse, ultimate authority would always reside with God, not with rulers, therefore potentially pitting Christians against their own nation and government. Rousseau sought a solution to this problem: how was it possible to ensure citizens' loyalty and forge national unity in an age when the state no longer represented divine authority to all its citizens? Civil religion was Rousseau's answer. According to him, each person had two religions: private faith and civic convictions. The former was adherence to Christianity, or any other religion. The latter was singular to a country and involved the basic tenets that everyone had to adhere to as citizens: "its dogmas, its rites, and its external forms of worship prescribed by law" (70). Rousseau defined civil religion as those basic convictions without which a society could not exist. See Günter Kehrer, "Bürgerliche Religion/Civil Religion," in *Handbuch Religionswissenschaftlicher Grundbegriffe*, ed. Hubert Cancik, Burkhard Gladigow, and Matthias Laubscher, vol. 2 (Stuttgart, Germany: Kohlhammer, 1990), 176–80.

In bringing Rousseau's concept to the US context, Bellah found that politicians and other leaders throughout US history appealed to transcendental notions in their description of the United States—the destiny of America, its God-ordained purpose and mission to the world, and the like—and he called this common system of beliefs "civil religion." See Robert N. Bellah, "Civil Religion in America," *Daedalus* 96, no. 1 (1967): 1–21. While Rousseau's concept had been prescriptive—a manual for how to build a society—Bellah claimed to be descriptive. In his wake, civil religion became a successful concept in academic discourse even beyond the US context. German scholar Thomas Hase, for example, has pointed out the frequent use of the term "Zivilreligion" in German daily and weekly newspapers; see Hase, *Zivilreligion: Religionswissenschaftliche Überlegungen zu einem Theoretischen Konzept am Beispiel der USA* (Würzburg, Germany: Ergon Verlag, 2001), 13–15. For discussions of civil religion, see, for example, Ronald C. Wimberley et al., "The Civil Religious Dimension: Is It There?," *Social Forces* 54, no. 4 (1976): 890–900; Wimberley, "Testing the Civil Religion Hypothesis," *Sociological Analysis* 37, no. 4 (1976): 341–52; Robert N. Bellah and Phillip E. Hammond, *Varieties of Civil Religion* (New York: Harper and Row, 1980). For an updated definition, see Heike Bungert and Jana Weiß, "Die Debatte um 'Zivilreligion' in Transnationaler Perspektive," *Zeithistorische Forschung/Studies in Contemporary History* 7, no. 3 (2010): 454–59. For recent applications of the concept, see Raymond J. Haberski, *God and War: American Civil Religion since 1945* (New Brunswick, NJ: Rutgers University Press, 2012); Morton Brænder, "Justifying the Ultimate Sacrifice: Civil and Military Religion in Frontline Blogs" (PhD diss., Aarhus University, 2009); Jana Weiß, *Fly the Flag and Give Thanks to God: Zivilreligion an U.S.-Amerikanischen, Patriotischen Feiertagen, 1945–1992* (Trier, Germany: Wissenschaftlicher Verlag Trier, 2015).

8. Bellah, "Civil Religion in America." Thomas Hase describes how Bellah, whose expertise was Japanese studies, was "arm-twisted" by sociologist Talcott Parsons to substitute for him at a conference dedicated to American religion; Hase, *Zivilreligion*, 57.

9. Robert Wuthnow, *The Restructuring of American Religion: Society and Faith since World War II* (Princeton, NJ: Princeton University Press, 1988), 241–67.

10. Robert N. Bellah, "Habits of the Heart: Implications for Religion" (lecture, St. Mark's Catholic Church, Isla Vista, California, February 21, 1986), Robert N. Bellah (website), Hartford Institute for Religion Research, accessed June 10, 2021, http://www.robertbellah.com.

11. See Kenneth L. Woodward, John Barnes, and Laurie Lisle, "Born Again," *Newsweek*, October 25, 1976. See also Joel A. Carpenter, introduction to *Twentieth-Century Evangelicalism: A Guide to the Sources*, ed. Edith L. Blumhofer and Joel A. Carpenter (New York: Garland, 1990), ix–xv. See also Roger E. Olson, *The Westminster Handbook to Evangelical Theology* (Louisville, KY: Westminster John Knox Press, 2004), 6, where Olson discusses the popularized definition of evangelical, as that "used by journalists to describe anyone or any group that seems particularly (by the journalist's standards) enthusiastic, aggressive, fanatical, or even simply missionary-minded."

12. Leon Morris, "Conservative Evangelicals?," *Christianity Today*, November 19, 1971, 51.

13. "Founding Document," c. 1971, Sojourners, records (SC-023), series 4

(administrative records), box 58, folder 5, Buswell Library Special Collections, Wheaton College, Wheaton, IL. The original members of this new organization were Jim Wallis, Glen Melnik, John Topliff, Boyd Reese, Herb McMillan, Bob Sabath, and Barry Turner. In full, the original title of their magazine was the *Post-American Voice of the People's Christian Coalition*. Other notable alumni of the school from this era include historian Mark Noll, who received his MA in church history and theology there in 1972, and Dennis P. Hollinger, since 2008 president of Gordon-Conwell Theological Seminary, who received his MDiv there in 1975.

14. "Founding Document," c. 1971, Sojourners, records (SC-023).

15. On the Evangelical Left, see, for example, David R. Swartz, "The Evangelical Left and the Move from Personal to Social Responsibility," in *American Evangelicals and the 1960s*, ed. Axel R. Schäfer (Madison: University of Wisconsin Press, 2013), 211–30; Swartz, *Moral Minority*. On the Young Evangelicals, see especially Richard Quebedeaux, *The Young Evangelicals: Revolution in Orthodoxy* (New York: Harper and Row, 1974).

16. The text of the Declaration of Evangelical Social Concern and a report were published in *Christianity Today*, December 21, 1973. Carl F. H. Henry also wrote a defense of the Declaration for the magazine; C. Henry, "Evangelical Social Concern," Footnotes, *Christianity Today*, March 1, 1974. His son, Paul B. Henry, wrote a guest editorial on the Declaration for *Eternity*; P. Henry, "Evangelicals of America, Arise!," *Eternity*, February 1974. The text was also published in *Post-American*, January 1974. See also Robert D. Linder, "The Resurgence of Evangelical Social Concern," in *The Evangelicals: What They Believe, Who They Are, Where They Are Changing*, ed. David F. Wells and John D. Woodbridge (Nashville, TN: Abingdon Press, 1975), 189–210; Swartz, *Moral Minority*, 170–84.

17. C. Henry, "Evangelical Social Concern," 99–100.

18. In one article, Mark O. Hatfield, an Evangelical and politician, articulated the wish that Evangelicals would "recover the picture of Jesus as both 'pastor' and 'prophet.'" Hatfield, "Pastors and Prophets," *Post-American*, October 1974, 14. Sociologist Max Weber distinguishes between priest and prophet in a different way: "The personal call is the decisive element distinguishing the prophet from the priest. The latter lays claim to authority by virtue of his service in a sacred tradition, while the prophet's claim is based on personal revelation and charisma." This definition, while useful in other contexts, does not apply here. Weber, *Economy and Society: An Outline of Interpretative Sociology*, ed. Guenther Roth and Claus Wittich (1922; Berkeley: University of California Press, 1978), 440.

19. "Was Jesus a Revolutionary?," editorial, *Moody Monthly*, January 1970, 22.

20. On the occasion of July 4, 1970, *Newsweek* diagnosed America as in a state of crisis and dedicated that week's issue to "The Spirit of '70" by having six historians express their views of the future. The six historians were Richard Hofstadter, Andrew Hacker, Eugene D. Genovese, Daniel J. Boorstin, Staughton Lynd, and Arthur M. Schlesinger Jr. See Peter Goldman, "The Spirit of '70: Six Historians Reflect on What Ails the American Spirit," *Newsweek*, July 6, 1970. That same day, the newsmagazine *Time* asked "who owns the stars and stripes?" ob-

serving that "it is as if two cultures, both of them oddly brandishing the same banner, were arrayed in some 18th century battle painting, the young whirling in defiant rock carmagnole against the panoplied Silent Majority." Lance Morrow, Jason McManus, and Marion Knox, "Who Owns the Stars and Stripes?," *Time*, July 6, 1970, 8. The writers were highlighting the apparent generational culture war. Young people were listening to rock music, growing out their hair, and wearing strange attire, and some moved to communes and experimented with sex and drugs. There were revolts on campuses, young men burned their draft cards, and demonstrations took place for Black rights, for women's rights, and against the war in Vietnam. On the other side of the divide, the older generation of Nixon's "silent majority" was longing for law and order, a return to the status quo, respect for authority, and adherence to conservative morality. On this history, see, for example, Maurice Isserman and Michael Kazin, *America Divided: The Civil War of the 1960s* (New York: Oxford University Press, 2000); Robert C. Cottrell, *Sex, Drugs, and Rock 'n' Roll: The Rise of America's 1960s Counterculture* (Lanham, MD: Rowman and Littlefield, 2015). The Evangelical community seemed to mirror this division of the generations exactly, with a young generation looking to overturn society and an older generation eager to return it to its old values. See, for example, Quebedeaux, *The Young Evangelicals*.

21. On the diversification of US culture after the Immigration and Nationality Act of 1965, see Charles B. Keely, "Effects of the Immigration Act of 1965 on Selected Population Characteristics of Immigrants to the United States," *Demography* 8, no. 2 (1971): 157–69; Isserman and Kazin, *America Divided*, 241–59; Diana L. Eck, *A New Religious America: How a "Christian Country" Has Now Become the World's Most Religiously Diverse Nation* (San Francisco: Harper San Francisco, 2001); Martin E. Marty, "Pluralism," *Annals of the American Academy of Political and Social Science* 612 (2007): 23.

22. Peter N. Carroll, *It Seemed Like Nothing Happened: America in the 1970s* (New Brunswick, NJ: Rutgers University Press, 2000), xii.

23. Diana L. Eck highlights the architectural dimension of religious pluralism in her study of religious diversification after 1965. She writes: "The religious landscape of America has changed radically. . . . Not all of us have seen the Toledo mosque or the Nashville temple, but we will see places like them, if we keep our eyes open. . . . They are the architectural signs of a new religious America." Eck, *A New Religious America*, 1.

24. "Farewell to the Sixties," *Christianity Today*, December 19, 1969, 21.

25. The Second Vatican Council (1962–65) made visible changes to Roman Catholic liturgy. Mass began to be celebrated in vernacular languages with the priest facing the congregation (rather than in Latin, with the priest facing the altar), and the liturgical calendar, clerical regalia, music, and church art were all adjusted or transformed. See, for example, Knut Wenzel, *Kleine Geschichte des Zweiten Vatikanischen Konzils* (Freiburg im Breisgau, Germany: Herder, 2005). On an Evangelical (and *Christianity Today*) assessment of the Second Vatican Council, see Neil J. Young, "'A Saga of Sacrilege': Evangelicals Respond to the

Second Vatican Council," in Schäfer, *American Evangelicals and the 1960s*, 255–79. Young argues that the council gave Evangelicals an opportunity to lambast Roman Catholicism for its pomp and ritualism. And yet, the council also "complicated, if not chastened, some of those [Evangelical] critiques": Evangelicals concluded that the council provided an impetus for individual Catholics to undergo "their own personal reformations," even as while they "maintained their historical reproaches for the institution [of the church]" (257, 274).

Originating in the 1960s, the death-of-God theology postulated that the increased secularity of the era arose because God had died. See, for example, Patrick Gray, "'God Is Dead' Controversy," *New Georgia Encyclopedia*, April 1, 2003, https://www.georgiaencyclopedia.org.

The term *secularization* has been used in Western societies since the Peace of Westphalia in 1648, when it was invoked to distinguish between secular and sacred spheres. The term evolved to describe a differentiation of secular and sacred institutions and functions. In the twentieth century, secularization came to denote a diminished "religious consciousness" in many societies worldwide. Bryan R. Wilson, "Secularization," in Eliade, *The Encyclopedia of Religion*, vol. 13, 162. For an overview of the major debates about secularization in sociology, see Rob Warner, *Secularization and Its Discontents* (New York: Continuum, 2010).

26. Vernon C. Grounds, "Bombs or Bibles? Get Ready for Revolution!," *Christianity Today*, January 15, 1971, 4.

27. See, for example, Rodney P. Carlisle and J. Geoffrey Golson, *America in Revolt during the 1960s and 1970s* (Santa Barbara, CA: ABC-CLIO, 2008), 121–34; Peter B. Levy, ed., *America in the Sixties—Right, Left, and Center: A Documentary History* (Westport, CT: Greenwood Press, 1998); David R. Farber and Beth L. Bailey, *The Columbia Guide to America in the 1960s* (New York: Columbia University Press, 2001).

28. Grounds, "Bombs or Bibles?"

29. "Hope for the '70s," *Eternity*, January 1971, 11.

30. "Hope for the '70s," 11.

31. Joel H. Nederhood, "Christians and Revolution," *Christianity Today*, January 1, 1971, 7.

32. Schäfer, *Countercultural Conservatives*; Eileen Luhr, "A Revolutionary Mission: Young Evangelicals and the Language of the Sixties," in Schäfer, *American Evangelicals and the 1960s*, 61–80.

33. Harold O. J. Brown, "Evolution, Revolution or Victory," *Christianity Today*, April 10, 1970. On Harold O. J. Brown and antiabortion activism, see chapter 6.

34. Virginia Ramey Mollenkott, "Teachers, Students, and Selfishness in the Seventies," *Christianity Today*, April 19, 1970; Tom Skinner, "Evangelicals and the Black Revolution," *Christianity Today*, April 19, 1970. On Mollenkott and Evangelical feminism, see chapter 3. On Skinner, see Edward Gilbreath, "A Prophet Out of Harlem," *Christianity Today*, September 16, 1996.

35. Brown, "Evolution, Revolution or Victory," 4 (emphasis in original).

36. Brown, 6 (emphasis in original).
37. Skinner, "Evangelicals and the Black Revolution," 12.
38. Skinner, 14. To Skinner, this was also the reason why the crowd wanted Jesus crucified. An ordinary insurrectionist like Barabbas, after all, could be put down, time and again, by ordinary means like police forces. "But how do you stop a man who's got no guns, no ammunition, no guerillas?" Skinner asked (14). While Skinner, like Brown, proposed Christianity as an alternative to revolution for the Black community, he also accused white Evangelicals of reducing the transformative power of Black Evangelicalism to ordinary revolt. According to him, whenever white people moved out of neighborhoods after Black neighbors moved in, and wherever schools and churches remained segregated, white people were saying "give us Barabbas" (14). They thus cast Black Evangelicals as ordinary insurrectionists who could be put into place by ordinary means, rather than fellow Christians with whom they might enter into a truly transformative fellowship.
39. Leighton Ford, "Revolution for Heaven's Sake," *Christianity Today*, December 4, 1970, 16.
40. Ford, 16, 15.
41. Luhr, "A Revolutionary Mission," 78.
42. Ford, "Revolution for Heaven's Sake," 16.
43. Luhr, "A Revolutionary Mission," 63.
44. Ford, "Revolution for Heaven's Sake," 14.
45. Robert Booth Fowler, *A New Engagement: Evangelical Political Thought, 1966-1976* (Grand Rapids, MI: Eerdmans, 1982), 36.
46. On Schaeffer, see Balmer, *Encyclopedia of Evangelicalism* (Waco, TX: Baylor University Press, 2004), s.v. "Schaeffer, Francis A(ugust)"; Barry Hankins, *Francis Schaeffer and the Shaping of Evangelical America* (Grand Rapids, MI: Eerdmans, 2008).
47. While he was a hero to the Young Evangelicals, inspired the Evangelical Left, and is credited with instigating a move toward academic Evangelicalism, Schaeffer remained politically conservative. Toward the end of his life, Schaeffer sided with the positions of the New Christian Right. See chapter 5.
48. Francis A. Schaeffer, "Shattering the Plastic Culture," *HIS*, October 1970; and see Schaeffer, *The Church at the End of the Twentieth Century* (London: Norfolk Press, 1970).
49. Schaeffer, "Shattering the Plastic Culture," 8.
50. Francis A. Schaeffer, "Christian Revolutionaries," *HIS*, November 1970, 27.
51. Changing culture by living transformed, communal lives was an approach of the Young Evangelicals as well. Christian communes that arose in this era included the Christian World Liberation Front in Berkeley, California. See, for example, Swartz, *Moral Minority*, 86-110. *Eternity* also published a report on Christian communes: Neta Jackson, "Living in Community," *Eternity*, August 1972.
52. The People's Christian Coalition also experimented with different forms of communal living. In summer 1975, the community moved to Washington,

DC, to live in an impoverished neighborhood inhabited predominantly by Black people. See Jim Wallis, "The Move," *Post-American*, August 1975; Balmer, *Encyclopedia of Evangelicalism*, s.v. "Sojourners Community."

53. "Founding Document," c. 1971, Sojourners, records (SC-023); and see Wallis, "The Movemental Church."

54. Morris, "Conservative Evangelicals?," 50–51.

55. "Man and Technocracy," *Post-American*, Winter 1972, 4.

56. "Man and Technology," 5.

57. Clark Pinnock, "The Christian Revolution," *Post-American*, Fall 1971, 10–11.

58. Clark Pinnock, "The Christian as a Revolutionary Man," *Post-American*, Summer 1972, n.p.

59. Vernon C. Grounds, "Revolutions Brewing," *Eternity*, March 1971, 13; and see Grounds, *Revolution and the Christian Faith: An Evangelical Perspective* (Philadelphia, PA: Lippincott, 1971).

60. Thomas W. Davis, "Babylon," in *Baker's Evangelical Dictionary of Biblical Theology*, ed. Walter A. Elwell (Grand Rapids, MI: Baker Books, 1996), Bible Study Tools, accessed June 10, 2021, https://www.biblestudytools.com; Jim Wallis, "Babylon," *Post-American*, Summer 1972.

61. Richard Nixon, "Inaugural Address," January 20, 1969, The American Presidency Project, accessed June 10, 2021, https://www.presidency.ucsb.edu.

62. Steven Miller, *Billy Graham and the Rise of the Republican South* (Philadelphia: University of Pennsylvania Press, 2009), 137.

63. "The 1969 Protestant Inaugural Prayers," *Christianity Today*, February 14, 1969, 27. This article includes the full text of the inaugural prayers offered by Billy Graham and Rev. Charles Ewbank Tucker, bishop in the African Methodist Episcopal Zion Church.

64. William Willoughby, "Inauguration amid Religious Trappings," *Christianity Today*, February 14, 1969, 31.

65. Kevin M. Kruse, *One Nation under God: How Corporate America Invented Christian America* (New York: Basic Books, 2015), 242.

66. For "public religion," see Kruse, 292; for "civil religion," see Andrew Preston, *Sword of the Spirit, Shield of Faith: Religion in American War and Diplomacy* (New York: Anchor Books, 2012), 14, 541. On the White House religious services, see Robert E. Friedrich Jr., "Sunday at the White House: Watchers and Worshippers," *Christianity Today*, August 22, 1969; Kruse, *One Nation under God*, 249–57; Gary Scott Smith, *Religion in the Oval Office: The Religious Lives of American Presidents* (New York: Oxford University Press, 2015), 271–77. In 1972, a book containing transcripts of White House sermons from the years 1969 and 1970 was published. In the introduction, President Nixon explained, "when I was elected to the highest office in the land, I wanted to do something to encourage attendance at services and to emphasize this country's basic faith in a Supreme Being." He also reiterated the line from his inaugural address, where he stated that "to a crisis of the spirit, we need an answer of the spirit," and he conceptualized

the East Room services as part of that "answer of the spirit." See Ben Hibbs, ed., *White House Sermons* (New York: Harper and Row, 1972), vi–vii. Nixon was also the first president to end a speech with the words "God bless America," the signature sign-off of President Ronald Reagan. Nixon used these words on April 30, 1973, in one of his speeches during the Watergate scandal. See David Domke and Kevin M. Coe, *The God Strategy: How Religion Became a Political Weapon in America* (New York: Oxford University Press, 2010), 61–64.

67. On the one hand, historian Andrew Preston writes that Nixon's "displays of piety rang hollow to those who were closest to him," and that "he also was fairly aggressive in trying to co-opt Graham's name for political purposes." Preston, *Sword of the Spirit, Shield of Faith*, 541. On the other hand, historian Steven P. Miller argues that "Graham was a public agitator in his own right. . . . In engaging political leaders and the pressing issues of his time, he made important decisions that, while always weighted against his higher priorities as an evangelist, reflected his own values, his own notion of the social and spiritual good. Graham's power, that is, was simultaneously readily visible and more than what met the eye." Miller, *Billy Graham and the Rise of the Republican South*, 3. And in a twist on the question, law scholar Leslie C. Griffin asks "whether Graham's career as America's pastor harmed or compromised the state in any way." Griffin, "Religious Sanctity and Political Power," in *The Legacy of Billy Graham: Critical Reflections on America's Greatest Evangelist*, ed. Michael G. Long (Louisville, KY: John Knox Press, 2008), 108.

68. Axel Schäfer has noted that "the 1969 Congress on Evangelism . . . put the emphasis on social action." Schäfer, *Countercultural Conservatives*, 80. Reporting on the congress, David Kucharsky related in *Christianity Today* that "secular newsmen were surprised to learn the degree of social concern on the part of evangelicals." Kucharsky, "U.S. Congress on Evangelism," *Christianity Today*, September 26, 1969, 40. Following the motto "Much Given . . . Much Required," the congress, held in Minneapolis, Minnesota, was one of several regional evangelization congresses initiated and organized by the Billy Graham Evangelistic Association; see Erhard Berneburg, *Das Verhältnis von Verkündung und Sozialer Aktion in der Evangelikalen Missionstheorie* (Wuppertal, Germany: R. Brockhaus Verlag, 1997), 61–68. In its report on the congress, the *Chicago Tribune* emphasized Graham's efforts to reach the hippie culture; see "Graham Kicks Off Evangelism Congress after Seeing Hippies," *Chicago Tribune*, September 9, 1969.

69. Roos, "American Civil Religion," 9.

70. "Honor America Day Cost Nation $68,770," *New York Times*, July 11, 1970; David Kucharsky, "Super Salute to God and Country," *Christianity Today*, July 31, 1970. For an analysis of newspaper reports on the event and an interpretation of the event as civil religion, see Weiß, *Fly the Flag and Give Thanks to God*, 157–64.

71. "Honor America Day," *Christianity Today*, July 3, 1970, 33.

72. Richard V. Pierard and Robert D. Linder, *Civil Religion and the Presidency* (Grand Rapids, MI: Academic Books, 1988).

73. Kruse, *One Nation under God*, 260–72. On the Billy Graham Crusade at the University of Tennessee, see, for example, Roger A. Bruns, *Billy Graham: A Biography* (Westport, CT: Greenwood Press, 2004), 119–22.

74. See Miller, *Billy Graham and the Rise of the Republican South*, 143; Swartz, *Moral Minority*, 83.

75. Klaas Runia, "Evangelical Responsibility in a Secularized World," *Christianity Today*, June 19, 1970, 11.

76. Billy Graham, "The Unfinished Dream," *Christianity Today*, July 31, 1970; Graham, "Honor America," Billy Graham Evangelistic Association pamphlet, 1970, Minnesota, MN, Billy Graham ephemera (CN-074), box 1, folder 1, Billy Graham Center Archives, Wheaton College, Wheaton, IL.

77. Graham, "The Unfinished Dream," 21.

78. Already in 1969, a *New York Times* article described Graham as "the closest thing we have to a White House chaplain." Edward B. Fiske, "The Closest Thing to a White House Chaplain," *New York Times*, June 8, 1969.

79. Kenneth L. Woodward, "Billy Graham and the Surging Southern Baptists," *Newsweek*, July 20, 1970, 50.

80. Swartz, *Moral Minority*, 85. After Evangelicals took up the term *civil religion*, Robert N. Bellah (who had first theorized the term in English) largely abandoned it, complaining that "civil religion was understood by many people to mean the idolatrous worship of the state." Bellah, "Habits of the Heart."

81. Graham, quoted in David Kucharsky, "Billy Graham and 'Civil Religion,'" *Christianity Today*, November 6, 1970, 56; and see "Billy Graham: Pastor to Presidents," Billy Graham Evangelistic Association, May 17, 2021, http://billygraham.org.

82. Wallis, "The Movemental Church," 2.

83. Bill Pannell, "Lawlessness American Style," *Post-American*, Fall 1972, 6.

84. John F. Alexander, "Madison Avenue Jesus," *Post-American*, Fall 1971, 14–15, first published in the *Other Side*, January/February 1971. On Alexander, see Swartz, *Moral Minority*, 26–46.

85. Alexander, "Madison Avenue Jesus," 14–15.

86. Roos, "American Civil Religion," 10.

87. "Many people have asked me why I, as a citizen of Heaven and a Christian minister, join in honoring any secular state. Jesus said, 'Render unto Caesar the things that are Caesar's' (Matthew 22:21). The apostle Paul proudly boasted that he was a Roman citizen (Acts 22:25–28). The Bible says, 'Honor the nation.'" Graham, "The Unfinished Dream," *Christianity Today*, July 31, 1970, 20. Matthew 22:21, Luke 20:25, and Mark 12:17 are all parallel passages; Mark 12:17 as quoted in the text is from the New Revised Standard Version (NRSV).

88. Wallis, "Post-American Christianity," 3.

89. "72's History, 73's Issues," *Eternity*, January 1973, 7.

90. On the Watergate scandal, see, for example, Carl Bernstein and Bob Woodward, *All the President's Men* (New York: Simon and Schuster, 1974); Keith W. Olson, *Watergate: The Presidential Scandal That Shook America* (Lawrence: Uni-

versity Press of Kansas, 2003); Stanley I. Kutler, *Watergate: A Brief History with Documents* (Malden, MA: Wiley-Blackwell, 2010).

91. "72's History, 73's Issues," 7.

92. Swartz, "The Evangelical Left and the Move from Personal to Social Responsibility," 222–23.

93. "72's History, 73's Issues," 7.

94. "Politics on the Ethical Periphery," *Christianity Today*, November 24, 1972, 29.

95. "72's History, 73's Issues," 7.

96. See, for example, Marjorie Hyer, "Confess Sins, Don't Implore God, Sen. Hatfield Tells Leaders," *Washington Post*, May 4, 1973.

97. Billy Graham, "Watergate," interview, *Christianity Today*, January 4, 1974.

98. Graham, "Watergate," 9.

99. Graham, 10.

100. Graham, 14. Furthermore, in an interview with the *Wittenburg Door* this same year, Graham explicitly distanced himself from what he called "Americanism," explaining that "our Gospel is not Americanism." He emphasized: "I'm an American citizen, yes, but I am not an American ambassador. I'm primarily a citizen of the kingdom of God and I'm representing the kingdom of God." Billy Graham, interview, *Wittenburg Door*, June/July 1974, 6.

101. Graham, "Watergate," 9, 12.

102. Swartz, *Moral Minority*, 68–85; see also Balmer, *Encyclopedia of Evangelicalism*, s.v. "Hatfield, Mark O(dom)."

103. Swartz, *Moral Minority*, 68. The second issue of the *Post-American* included a laudatory letter to the editor from Hatfield. Mark O. Hatfield, "Feedback," letter to the editor, *Post-American*, Winter 1972.

104. Hatfield and Michaelson were both introduced as contributing editors in the *Post-American*'s first issue of 1973. "Introducing the Contributing Editors," *Post-American*, January 1973. For more on Hatfield, see Robert Eells and Bartell Nyberg, *Lonely Walk: The Life of Senator Mark Hatfield* (Chappaqua, NY: Christian Herald Books, 1979); Mark Hatfield, *Between a Rock and a Hard Place* (Waco, TX: Word Books, 1976).

105. Balmer, *Encyclopedia of Evangelicalism*, s.v. "Prayer Breakfasts"; Swartz, *Moral Minority*, 78. Historian Steven P. Miller called the Fellowship a "publicity-shy but well-connected political outreach organization"; Miller, *The Age of Evangelicalism: America's Born-Again Years* (Oxford: Oxford University Press, 2014), 38. Investigative journalist Jeff Sharlet has published two books on the Fellowship: Jeff Sharlet, *The Family: The Secret Fundamentalism at the Heart of American Power* (New York: HarperCollins, 2008); Sharlet, *C Street: The Fundamentalist Threat to American Democracy* (New York: Little, Brown, 2010).

106. Eells and Nyberg, *Lonely Walk*, 83.

107. James T. Wooten, "Nixon Hears War Called a 'Sin,'" *New York Times*, February 2, 1973.

108. "Signs of a New Order," *Post-American*, March 1973, 13.

109. Swartz, *Moral Minority*, 78; "Signs of a New Order," 13.

110. Eells and Nyberg, *Lonely Walk*, 83–84. According to Robert Eells and Bartell Nyberg, in the letter to Hatfield, Graham, who had also been present at the breakfast, "praised the senator for boldly proclaiming the name of Christ and suggested that some civil religion practices at such functions had departed from the original Prayer Breakfast format," yet chided Hatfield for his choice of words, which had been interpreted by the press as a "personal rebuke to President Nixon" (84).

111. Joseph Bayly, "Senator Hatfield's Brave Words," *Eternity*, June 1973, 39. Nixon aides who departed at this time include White House staffers R. Haldeman and John Ehrlichman and attorney general Richard Kleindienst, all of whom resigned on April 30, 1973, and White House counsel John Dean, who was fired.

112. "Does Corruption Matter?," *Eternity*, June 1973, 8.

113. "Watergate Logic," *Eternity*, June 1973, 8, 10. A later article in *Christianity Today* explicitly linked this "Watergate logic" to the situational ethics of Joseph Fletcher; see Erwin W. Lutzer, "Watergate Ethics," *Christianity Today*, September 13, 1974.

114. Mark O. Hatfield, "The Vulnerability of Leadership," *Christianity Today*, June 22, 1973; Hatfield, "Crisis in American Leadership," *Eternity*, July 1973; Hatfield, "Begin with Repentance," *Moody Monthly*, July/August 1973. *Christianity Today* and *Eternity* printed the full text, while *Moody Monthly* only printed excerpts.

115. Mark O. Hatfield, "Piety and Patriotism," *Post-American*, May/June 1973.

116. "Watergate: Are We Listening?," *Moody Monthly*, July/August 1973, 20–21.

117. Hatfield, "The Vulnerability of Leadership," 4.

118. Compare to Hatfield, "Piety and Patriotism."

119. Hatfield, "The Vulnerability of Leadership," 4.

120. Hatfield, 5.

121. Hatfield, "Piety and Patriotism," 1.

122. "I know of no other formula for overcoming the corrupting influences of the world's power than to give our lives over to a higher power, the power of God's love. This can seem foolish in the eyes of the world. But there are times when each of us must choose where we give our final allegiance. The one who follows Christ is a citizen of a different kingdom; he has another Master; his allegiance is to a new order from which he derives his way of thinking, feeling, and judging. He therefore cannot give ultimate allegiance to the world and its way of operating. His first duty is to be faithful to the Lord." Hatfield, "The Vulnerability of Leadership," 5.

123. "Back to Reality," *Eternity*, November 1973, 8.

124. John A. Huffman Jr., "Biblical Lessons from Watergate," *Christianity Today*, March 15, 1974.

125. Joseph Bayly, "How Do We Want to Be Ruled?," *Eternity*, November 1973, 60, 62.

126. "Should Nixon Resign?," *Christianity Today*, June 7, 1974, 29.

127. "Fifteen Turbulent Years," *Christianity Today*, August 30, 1974, 25.

128. President Nixon had appointed Gerald Ford as vice president when Spiro Agnew resigned after facing federal charges. An editorial in *Moody Monthly* highlighted the fact that Ford was the first person appointed rather than elected as vice president, and *Moody Monthly* reiterated this fact when Ford was sworn in as president after Nixon's resignation. "Are We Praying for Our Leaders?," *Moody Monthly*, February 1974; "Honesty Does Pay," *Moody Monthly*, October 1974.

129. Jim Wallis, "The New Regime," *Post-American*, October 1974, 3. In one *Post-American* article, G. Clark Chapman Jr., associate professor of religion at Moravian College in Bethlehem, Pennsylvania, argued that the pardon was "favoritism," exempting the privileged from due process of law. Chapman, "Who Pays for Pardons?," *Post-American*, December 1974. A *Christianity Today* editorialist judged that "unless there were overriding reasons of which we have no present knowledge, it would appear that President Ford was mistaken in granting the pardon when he did." "The Pardon of Richard Nixon," *Christianity Today*, September 27, 1974, 37. A news report in the same issue showed, however, that Evangelicals were split on the issue of the pardon, with some in favor of it. Edward E. Plowman, "Ford's First Month: Christ and Conflict," *Christianity Today*, September 27, 1974.

130. Carl F. H. Henry, "Has Democracy a Future?," *Christianity Today*, July 5, 1974, 27. In November 1974, Henry repeated his fear that Watergate and other political scandals had made "the American variety of democracy . . . less than desirable." Henry, "The Judgment of America," *Christianity Today*, November 8, 1974, 22.

131. "The Makers of America," *Moody Monthly*, September 1974, 22.

132. Wallis, "Post-American Christianity," 2.

133. Jim Wallis, "The Lesson of Watergate," *Post-American*, January 1974, 1.

134. Jim Wallis, "Biblical Politics," *Post-American*, April 1974, 3-4.

135. See, for example, "Honesty Does Pay"; "Fifteen Turbulent Years"; Wallis, "The New Regime."

136. Wallis, "The New Regime," 3.

137. Wallis, 30.

138. Wallis, 3.

139. Wallis, 30.

140. W. Glyn Evans, "Are We Living in Post-America?," *Eternity*, December 1974, 25.

141. Evans, 55.

142. Evans, 25.

143. Henry, "The Judgment of America," 22, 24.

144. Henry, 22.

145. Henry, 24 (emphasis in original).

146. Wallis, "The Move."

147. David Kling, "Sojourners," in *Religious Periodicals of the United States: Academic and Scholarly Journals*, ed. Charles H. Lippy (Westport, CT: Greenwood Press, 1986), 480.

148. Jim Wallis, "Ten Years," *Sojourners*, September 1981.

149. Henry, "The Judgment of America," 22.

150. Charles W. Colson, quoted by William Greider, "Colson, 'Mr. Tough Guy,' Finds Christ," *Washington Post*, December 17, 1973, A1.

151. Colson was indicted for his role in events that preceded the Watergate scandal but did not come to light until Watergate broke. On September 3, 1971, burglars broke into the office of psychiatrist Lewis Fielding to obtain material for a smear campaign on his patient Daniel Ellsberg, a military analyst who had released to the press secret government documents relating to decision-making in the Vietnam War, the Pentagon Papers. Nixon considered Ellsberg's action a threat to national security and ordered the break-in as a covert operation, and Colson helped recruit the perpetrators and facilitate the smear campaign. In an interview with *Moody Monthly*, Colson explained that his newfound Christian faith informed him that he was a wicked man with much to repent, yet he felt he was not guilty of the conspiracy charge with which he was charged. Accordingly, he incriminated himself of a crime he felt he was guilty of, namely spreading false information about Ellsberg. See Charles W. Colson, interview by Shirl Short, *Moody Monthly*, February 1976; Howard Chua-Eoan, "The Watergate Dirty Trickster Who Found God: Charles Colson (1931–2012)," *Time*, April 21, 2012; Michael A. Genovese, *The Watergate Crisis* (Westport, CT: Greenwood Press, 1999), 15–18; Tom Wells, *Wild Man: The Times and Life of Daniel Ellsberg* (New York: Palgrave, 2001).

152. See Prison Fellowship (home page), accessed January 25, 2014, http://www.prisonfellowship.org; James C. Hefeley, "Colson, Cons, and Christ," *Christianity Today*, July 4, 1975; Shirl Short, "Former Nixon Aide Heads Prison Ministry," *Moody Monthly*, January 1976; Charles W. Colson, "Who Will Help Penitents in Penitentiaries?," *Eternity*, May 1977.

153. *Moody Monthly* reprinted the congressional record of the event as well as editorialized on it: "A National Day of Prayer," *Moody Monthly*, April 1974; "A National Day of Prayer," *Moody Monthly*, May 1974. *Eternity* editorialized that Hatfield had gotten the idea for the Day of Prayer from Abraham Lincoln. "Lincoln Inspired Hatfield's Day-of-Prayer Idea," *Eternity*, May 1974.

154. Jim Wallis lamented that "the full and unconditional pardon given by Gerald Ford and accepted by Richard Nixon came with still no admission of guilt or wrongdoing, much less repentance, on the part of the former president." Wallis, "The New Regime," 4.

155. Woodward, Barnes, and Lisle, "Born Again."

156. *Eternity* editor Russell T. Hitt admitted his initial disbelief when he heard of Colson's conversion. Hitt, "Editor's Ink," *Eternity*, September 1974.

157. Hughes, whose political positions were often diametrically opposed to Colson's, served as a spiritual mentor to Colson and assisted him in early interviews, including one on the CBS show *60 Minutes*. Marion Goldin, prod., *60 Minutes*, season 6, episode 19, "Charles Colson's Conversion," aired May 26, 1974, on CBS, transcript in Charles Wendell Colson papers (CN-275), box 11, folder 5, Billy Graham Center Archives.

158. In a 1977 installment of his Out of My Mind column in *Eternity*, Joseph Bayly lamented the "deterioration" of the term "born again" as a viable marker for the Christian conversion experience. Nonetheless, he grudgingly admitted that "Charles Colson's use of the term made many people aware of its religious usage." Bayly, "The Definition Drain," Out of My Mind, *Eternity*, January 1977, 73.

159. Charles W. Colson, *Born Again* (Old Tappan, NJ: Chosen Books, 1976). Colson's new Christian life was closely monitored by Evangelical magazines. *Christianity Today* reported on the Colson conversion as early January 1974 and cited from Greider's December 1973 *Washington Post* article: Edward E. Plowman, "News/Religion in Washington: An Act of God," *Christianity Today*, January 4, 1974. *Eternity* reprinted long excerpts from Colson's book, which also won first place in *Eternity*'s annual book poll: "Under Conviction: Charles Colson's Damascus Road," *Eternity*, March 1976; "'Hatchet Man' Dominates Annual Poll," *Eternity*, December 1976. Interviews with Colson appeared in *Moody Monthly* and *Christianity Today*: Colson, interview by Shirl Short; Charles W. Colson, "Watergate or Something Like It Was Inevitable," interview, *Christianity Today*, March 12, 1976. The movie *Born Again*, released in 1978, was directed by Irving Rapper and produced by AVCO Embassy Pictures. For a disparaging Evangelical critique of the movie, see Chuck Fager, "The Blast at *Born Again*," *Sojourners*, December 1978.

160. See, for example, Billy Graham, *How to Be Born Again* (1977; Dallas, TX: Word, 1989); Jeb Stuart Magruder, *From Power to Peace* (Waco, TX: Word Books, 1978). *Christianity Today* printed an excerpt from Mark O. Hatfield's foreword to Magruder's book: Hatfield, "Watergate: A Different View," *Christianity Today*, May 5, 1978. Cleaver was interviewed by *Eternity*: Cleaver, "Soul on Grace," interview, *Eternity*, May 1977.

161. Pollster George Gallup Jr. pronounced 1976 the Year of the Evangelical after the Gallup survey reported that 34 percent of Americans had had a "born-again experience." The following year, he founded the Princeton Religion Research Center with Miriam Murphy. See "Counting Souls," *New York Times*, October 4, 1976; Woodward, Barnes, and Lisle, "Born Again"; Kate Zernike, "George Gallup Jr., of Polling Family, Dies at 81," *New York Times*, November 22, 2011.

162. According to Roger E. Olson's *Westminster Handbook to Evangelical Theology* (Louisville, KY: Westminster John Knox Press, 2004), Evangelical theologians differentiated between different stages in the process of salvation. Salvation, literally "to be made whole," denoted "a right relationship with God that resulted in everlasting life in heaven" (260). While some stages leading to salvation were believed to happen simultaneously (and theologians disagreed somewhat about their order), the *ordo salutis* generally included: "election, calling, conversion, regeneration, justification, sanctification, and glorification" (248). Central to Evangelical faith was the need to be "born-again," a term that denotes regeneration (161). Conversion, the human act of repentance and renunciation of old and sinful ways, and regeneration, God's rehabilitation and restarting of one's life, could be understood as two sides of one coin (261). According to Olson, "conversion is salvation's initial or crucial event. It is the event—evangelical theologians agree—

in which an individual responds to the call of God with repentance and faith and receives from God regeneration (being 'born-again') and justification (forgiveness and declaration of righteousness)" (161). In Olson, see especially "Conversion" (160–63), "Regeneration" (248–50), and "Salvation" (260–63). For a discussion of conversion throughout time and in different contexts, see David W. Kling et al., "Conversion," *Encyclopedia of the Bible and Its Reception*, accessed June 10, 2021, https://doi.org/10.1515/ebr.conversion.

163. Graham, *How to Be Born Again*, 151.

164. Millard J. Erickson, "The New Birth Today," *Christianity Today*, August 16, 1974, 9.

165. Calvin D. Linton, "Dying to the God Who Is Me," *Christianity Today*, February 16, 1979, 21. Human nature was corrupted by sin and pride and thus needed to die for something new to take its place. Citing from the Gospel of Luke (Luke 9:23–24: "23 Then he said to them all, 'If any want to become my followers, let them deny themselves and take up their cross daily and follow me. 24 For those who want to save their life will lose it, and those who lose their life for my sake will save it.'"), Millard J. Erickson insisted that losing one's life to Christ meant finding true life: "'The real you' is not submerged in this experience; it most fully appears here and only here." Erickson, "The New Birth Today," 9. The mystery of the logical inversion that losing was gaining, and dying was living, was not so much resolved as embraced. Even though believers gave themselves up to Christ, being dissolved in this union with Christ meant not losing one's identity but rather realizing one's true design. Conversion, to Evangelicals, meant giving up everything one knew to gain everything that truly was.

166. Colson's well-published account illustrates the Evangelical conversion experience. After the disclaimer that words did not do justice to the experience itself, Colson recounted the steps that led to his conversion: he reported that he had been impressed with the example of a converted friend, Tom Phillips, who inspired him to investigate the possibility of a Christian life. He recalled how, through Tom's example, he came to acknowledge the sinfulness of his own life. Recognizing his wretchedness, he cried and prayed to God, promising betterment. He then retreated for a few days, studying the Bible and C. S. Lewis's *Mere Christianity*. While he had always found Christian doctrine unbelievable, he suddenly found Christianity not only plausible but so compelling that it was impossible not to believe. He had been born again and saw the world from a new perspective. Colson's conversion narrative included the following stages: an active search for God, a confession of sinful life, the offering or surrendering of his life to God, and a palpable change of heart and perspective. See Colson, *Born Again*; Colson, interview by Shirl Short; "Under Conviction: Charles Colson's Damascus Road."

167. Lit-Sen Chang, "Old Serpent; New Strategy," *Christianity Today*, May 23, 1975, 18.

168. John B. Anderson, "What America Needs Now," *Moody Monthly*, July 1975, 36 (including quote from Moynihan).

169. George Sweeting, "Happy Birthday, America," *Moody Monthly*, July 1975, 5.

170. Sweeting, 5 (emphasis added).
171. Ronald D. Michaelson, "What Would an Honest Politician Look Like?," *Eternity*, February 1976, 22.
172. Michaelson, 58.
173. John Warwick Montgomery, "Will an Evangelical President Usher In the Millennium?," *Christianity Today*, October 22, 1976, 65.
174. Peter Goldman opened a *New York Times* article with this observation. The article was republished in excerpts in *Moody Monthly* "for its informational value, and because it deals with the candidate's faith." Goldman, "The Rebirth of Hopeful Jimmy Carter," *Moody Monthly*, October 1976. *Moody Monthly* also invited several Evangelical spokespersons (including a *Christianity Today* editor and the president of the National Association of Evangelicals) to witness an interview with Gerald Ford on his faith, printed in a subsequent issue: "President Confers with Evangelicals," *Moody Monthly*, November 1976. The faith of presidential candidates was also the topic of other articles, including Edward E. Plowman, "An Election Year to Remember," *Christianity Today*, May 7, 1976; Forrest Boyd, "Do We Really Want a Saint in the White House?," *Moody Monthly*, September 1976.
175. Montgomery, "Will an Evangelical President Usher In the Millennium?" 65–66. Montgomery also proposed that Evangelicals should look at the issue of abortion as a benchmark for judging the new president. Abortion would become a major issue during the 1980s; see chapter 6.
176. "How I Think I'll Vote," *Eternity*, September 1976. Among *Eternity*'s eleven respondents were editors of the *Wittenburg Door*, the *Other Side*, and *Eternity* itself, as well as academics, authors, a journalist, and the president of a Christian organization.
177. Russell T. Hitt, "How I Think I'll Vote," *Eternity*, September 1976, 31; for an analysis of Evangelical attitudes toward President Reagan in the 1980s, see chapter 5.
178. Two respondents did name a favorite candidate: conservative author H. Edward Rowe announced that he would most likely vote for Ronald Reagan, and the editor of the *Wittenburg Door*, Denny Rydberg, a registered Republican, ventured that he would probably vote for Jimmy Carter. H. Edward Rowe, "How I Think I'll Vote," *Eternity*, September 1976; Denny Rydberg, "How I Think I'll Vote," *Eternity*, September 1976.
179. Margaret N. Barnhouse, "How I Think I'll Vote," *Eternity*, September 1976, 29.
180. James B. Irwin, "How I Think I'll Vote," *Eternity*, September 1976, 29.
181. Wes Pippert, "How I Think I'll Vote," *Eternity*, September 1976, 27. *Wittenburg Door* editor Denny Rydberg agreed: "At this time in our nation's history, I think we need a person who combines dynamic leadership ability with high moral values. After Watergate, Wilbur (Mills), and Wayne (Hays), in addition to the dirt that's been kicked up in the FBI and the CIA investigations, we need moral leadership." Rydberg, "How I Think I'll Vote," 30.
182. Gladys Hunt, "How I Think I'll Vote," *Eternity*, September 1976, 28.

183. Vernon C. Grounds, "How I Think I'll Vote," *Eternity*, September 1976, 31.
184. Harold Lindsell, editor's note, *Christianity Today*, November 19, 1976.
185. George Sweeting, "An Open Letter to President Carter," *Moody Monthly*, January 1977, 1.
186. "The Political Peak Is Also the Brink," *Christianity Today*, November 19, 1976.
187. David Kucharsky, "The Man from Plains," *Christianity Today*, November 19, 1976, 49.
188. The anti-Carter voice is exemplified, for example, in a *Christianity Today* article that reported that Carter's most ardent opponents had also been Christians. Arthur H. Matthews, "Crusade for the White House: Skirmishes in a 'Holy War,'" *Christianity Today*, November 19, 1976.
189. Stephen V. Monsma, "The Oval Office: Three Models for a Christian," *Christianity Today*, January 21, 1977, 28–29.
190. "The Political Peak Is Also the Brink," *Christianity Today*.
191. Bayly, "The Definition Drain." Similarly dissatisfied was Evangelical scholar Joel A. Carpenter, who lamented that the media's discovery of the Evangelical phenomenon in the 1970s had the unintended effect of popularizing the terms "evangelical" and "born-again" almost to the point of uselessness. Carpenter, introduction to Blumhofer and Carpenter, *Twentieth-Century Evangelicalism*, ix–xiv.
192. See J. Brooks Flippen, *Jimmy Carter, the Politics of Family, and the Rise of the Religious Right* (Athens: University of Georgia Press, 2011), 155, 159, 177–79, 214–15, 235.
193. Tom Mathews, "Born Again!," *Newsweek*, October 2, 1978, 24.
194. Anja-Maria Bassimir, "Definition—Macht—Evangelikal: Standortbestimmung zum Gegenwärtigen U.S.-Amerikanischen Evangelikalismus," *Amerikastudien/American Studies* 63, no. 3 (2018): 397.
195. Allan J. Mayer, "A Tide of Born Again Politics," *Newsweek*, September 15, 1980.
196. An appeal to differentiate between the political positions of Evangelicals and Fundamentalists was published by Corwin E. Smidt, "Evangelicals within Contemporary American Politics: Differentiating between Fundamentalist and Non-Fundamentalist Evangelicals," *Western Political Quarterly* 41, no. 3 (1988): 601–20. And between Evangelicals and Pentecostals: Smidt, "'Praise the Lord' Politics: A Comparative Analysis of the Social Characteristics and Political Views of American Evangelical and Charismatic Christians," *Sociological Analysis* 50, no. 1 (1989): 53–72.
197. David Gelman, "Is America Turning Right?," *Newsweek*, November 7, 1977, 36.
198. Richard Boeth, "The New Activists," *Newsweek*, November 7, 1977, 41 (including quote from Siegel). On Paul Weyrich and the role he played in instigating the New Christian Right, see William Martin, *With God on Our Side: The Rise of the Religious Right in America* (New York: Broadway Books, 1997), 169–75.

199. Mayer, "A Tide of Born Again Politics," 31.
200. Mayer, 29. And see chapter 5 for discussion on the New Christian Right.
201. Richard V. Pierard, "Should We Fear the New Right?," book review, *Christianity Today*, October 2, 1981, 96–97; and see Robert E. Webber, *The Moral Majority: Right or Wrong?* (Saint Louis, MO: Cornerstone, 1981); Erling Jorstad, *The Politics of Moralism: The New Christian Right in American Life* (Minneapolis: Augsburg, 1981).
202. Schäfer, *Countercultural Conservatives*, 103.
203. Schäfer, 111. By "Niebuhrian," Schäfer is referring to Reinhold Niebuhr (1892–1971), the theologian, writer, and political activist. Shaped by the Cold War experience, Niebuhr was a leading figure in Protestant social ethics and the theological school known as Christian Realism. See, for example, Robin W. Lovin, "Reinhold Niebuhr (1892–1971)," in *Makers of Christian Theology in America*, ed. Mark G. Toulouse and James O. Duke (Nashville, TN: Abingdon Press, 1997), 413–19.
204. See, for example, Hitt, "How I Think I'll Vote." Speaking of conservative Christians more generally, *Newsweek* reported, "Though as a group they are somewhat more conservative than the nation as a whole, the majority of the registered voters among them nonetheless identify themselves as Democrats, and they favored Jimmy Carter by a wide margin over Ronald Reagan. What's more, a majority (53 per cent) support ERA, and only 41 per cent favor the extreme position of banning abortion entirely." Mayer, "A Tide of Born Again Politics," 31.
205. See chapter 3 and 5.
206. Flippen, *Jimmy Carter*, 22.

CHAPTER 3

1. Robert K. Johnston, "Submission, A Wedding Meditation," *Daughters of Sarah*, January 1977, 4.
2. For a history of the women's liberation movement in the United States, see, for example, Kathleen C. Berkley, *The Women's Liberation Movement* (Westport, CT: Greenwood Press, 1999); Carol Giardina, *Freedom for Women: Forging the Women's Liberation Movement, 1953–1970* (Gainesville: University Press of Florida, 2010); Sylvia Engdahl, ed., *The Women's Liberation Movement* (Detroit, MI: Greenhaven Press, 2012). In her study of the historical meanings of "man" and "woman" in the United States, Mary P. Ryan finds that "fundamental rearrangements of all the coordinates of gender (asymmetry, the relations of the sexes, and hierarchy) were getting underway in the 1960s and had acquired enough coherence by the year 2000 to justify a declaration of the end of the modern gender regime." Ryan, *Mysteries of Sex: Tracing Women and Men through American History* (Chapel Hill: University of North Carolina Press, 2009), 247.
3. Political scientists Pamela Johnston Conover and Virginia Gray open their classic study *Feminism and the New Right* with this sentence: "The decade of the 1970s was the woman's decade. It began with thousands of women marching in

the streets to protest sexism, most notably on August 26, 1970, the fiftieth anniversary of women's suffrage." Conover and Gray, *Feminism and the New Right: Conflict over the American Family* (New York: Praeger, 1983), 1.

4. Ronald W. Pierce, "Contemporary Evangelicals for Gender Equality," in *Discovering Biblical Equality: Complementary without Hierarchy*, ed. Ronald W. Pierce and Rebecca Merrill Groothuis (Downers Grove, IL: InterVarsity Press, 2005), 58. I use "patriarchal" in reference to the view that women were inferior to men, or that God created women as inferior helpers to men. This view was held by many of the church fathers. John Chrysostom and Augustine, for example, believed that women were inferior to men. Tertullian saw women as "the devil's gateway." The foundational figures of Protestantism, Martin Luther and John Calvin, also held patriarchal views, believing that it was a woman's place to be a wife and mother. Feminist theologian Rosemary Radford Ruether discusses women's history of being regarded as the seat of evil by the church: Ruether, *Sexism and God-Talk: Toward a Feminist Theology* (Boston: Beacon Press, 1993), 165–73.

5. See Peter Gardella, "Sex and Submission in the Spirit," in *Religions of the United States in Practice*, ed. Colleen McDannell, vol. 2 (Princeton, NJ: Princeton University Press, 2002), 173–93; Roger E. Olson, *The Westminster Handbook to Evangelical Theology* (Louisville, KY: Westminster John Knox Press, 2004), s.v. "Gender Roles: Complementarianism/Egalitarianism." For a recent compilation of the egalitarian view see Pierce and Groothuis, *Discovering Biblical Equality*. Women's struggle with complementarian views of gender roles has been described, for example, by Sally K. Gallagher, *Evangelical Identity and Gendered Family Life* (New Brunswick, NJ: Rutgers University Press, 2003); Alan G. Padgett, "The Bible and Gender Troubles: American Evangelicals Debate Scripture and Submission," *Dialogue* 47, no. 1 (2008): 21–26.

6. Pamela D. H. Cochran, *Evangelical Feminism: A History* (New York: New York University Press, 2005), 12–14.

7. "A Declaration of Evangelical Social Concern," November 27, 1973, Evangelicals for Social Action collection (CN-037), box 1, folder 9, Billy Graham Center Archives, Wheaton College, Wheaton, IL; and see Schäfer, *Countercultural Conservatives*, 82–84; David R. Swartz, *Moral Minority: The Evangelical Left in an Age of Conservatism* (Philadelphia: University of Pennsylvania Press, 2012).

8. "A Declaration of Evangelical Social Concern." The statement of convictions read: "As evangelical Christians committed to the Lord Jesus Christ and the full authority of the Word of God, we affirm that God lays claim upon the lives of his people. We cannot, therefore, separate our lives in Christ from the situation in which God has placed us in the United States and the world."

9. Margaret Lamberts Bendroth, *Fundamentalism and Gender, 1875 to the Present* (New Haven, CT: Yale University Press, 1993), 122; Ron Sider, "Historical Context for the Declaration," on the homepage of Evangelicals for Social Action, accessed July 16, 2009, http://www.evangelicalsforsocialaction.org (site discontinued). Evangelicals for Social Action has since been renamed Christians for Social Action and has a new internet domain, https://christiansforsocialaction

.org. Sider's comments on the declaration, along with a companion piece called "A Reflection" that he authored, no longer appear on the organization's homepage.

10. A transcript of the declaration was published, for example, in *Christianity Today*, December 21, 1973; *Post-American*, January 1974; and the *Other Side*, March/April 1974. See chapter 2 for more on this declaration and the list of original signatories.

11. Evangelicals for Social Action met informally for workshops in 1974, 1975, and 1976. Only in 1978 did it formally organize, coming to be associated with the Evangelical Left. See Randall Balmer, *Encyclopedia of Evangelicalism* (Waco, TX: Baylor University Press, 2004), s.v. "Evangelicals for Social Action."

12. See especially Carl F. H. Henry, "Revolt on the Evangelical Frontiers," *Christianity Today*, April 26, 1974; Jim. Wallis, "'Revolt on Evangelical Frontiers': A Response," *Christianity Today*, June 21, 1974; and letters provoked by the exchange: "Young and New," letters to the editor, *Christianity Today*, June 7, 1974.

13. The phrasing of this paragraph was introduced by Nancy Hardesty. See Reta Halteman Finger and S. Sue Horner, "Euro-American Evangelical Feminism," in *Encyclopedia of Women and Religion in North America*, ed. Rosemary Skinner Keller and Rosemary Radford Ruether, vol. 1 (Bloomington: Indiana University Press, 2006), 470; Cochran, *Evangelical Feminism*, 12.

14. Cochran, *Evangelical Feminism*, 15–16. For more on Ron Sider, and on Sharon Gallagher, see Swartz, *Moral Minority*, 86–112, 153–69. Contemporary occupations of workshop participants can be found in the invite list for the second workshop of the Evangelicals for Social Action: "Invited Participants, Thanksgiving Workshop, Evangelicals for Social Action, Nov. 29–Dec. 1, 1974," Evangelicals for Social Action collection (CN-037), box 3, folder 1, Billy Graham Center Archives.

15. Bendroth, *Fundamentalism and Gender*, 122–23; Finger and Horner, "Euro-American Evangelical Feminism."

16. Genesis 1:26–27: "Then God said, 'Let us make mankind in our image, in our likeness. . . .' So God created mankind in his own image, in the image of God he created them; male and female he created them." Genesis 2:21–22: "So the Lord God caused the man to fall into a deep sleep; and while he was sleeping, he took one of the man's ribs and then closed up the place with flesh. Then the Lord God made a woman from the rib he had taken out of the man, and he brought her to the man." These two quotations are from the New International Version (NIV). For a theological discussion of this dual tradition in Christian history, see, for example, Georg H. Tavard, *Women in Christian Tradition* (Notre Dame, IN: University of Notre Dame Press, 1996).

17. On Evangelical feminism, see especially Cochran, *Evangelical Feminism*. For an overview of traditionalist, or "counterfeminist," positions, see David H. Watt, *A Transforming Faith: Explorations of Twentieth-Century Evangelicalism* (New Brunswick, NJ: Rutgers University Press, 1991), 119–36.

18. See Ruether, *Sexism and God-Talk*, 165–73; Padgett, "The Bible and Gender Troubles," 22–23.

19. Young Evangelicals across the country had been influenced by the 1960s liberation and countercultural movements and, stirred by current issues like civil rights and opposition to the Vietnam War, emerged as a visible faction within Evangelicalism. Loose groups like the Jesus People or locally concentrated groups like the Christian World Liberation Front in Berkeley, California, spearheaded a movement that came to be labeled the Evangelical Left or—as Richard Quebedeaux, himself part of this movement, dubbed it—Young Evangelicalism. As historian David R. Swartz has demonstrated, the counterculturally inspired Evangelicals, particularly the Sojourners fellowship, underwent a change from "personal to social responsibility" that prompted them to advocate political involvement. See Swartz, "The Evangelical Left and the Move from Personal to Social Responsibility," in *American Evangelicals and the 1960s*, ed. Axel R. Schäfer (Madison: University of Wisconsin Press, 2013), 211–30; Swartz, *Moral Minority*; Richard Quebedeaux, *The Young Evangelicals: Revolution in Orthodoxy* (New York: Harper and Row, 1974); my discussion of the Evangelical Left in chapter 2.

20. See Bendroth, *Fundamentalism and Gender*, 123.

21. Nancy B. Barcus, "A Milestone for Christian Women: Letha Scanzoni and Nancy Hardesty, *All We're Meant to Be*," *Eternity*, March 1975; Miriam G. Moran, "Marabel's Guide: Good despite Some Faults," *Eternity*, March 1975. *Eternity*'s forum on women appeared in its January 1971 issue.

22. Thornton served on the staff for nine years until the end of 1974, when she left *Moody Monthly* (and her role of managing editor) "to marry Gary Leonard." Robert G. Flood, "Behind the Scenes," *Moody Monthly*, December 1974, 23. In October 1975, *Moody Monthly* announced the hiring of another female assistant editor, Shirl Short. Jerry B. Jenkins, "Behind the Scenes," *Moody Monthly*, October 1975. In its "women's issue" of January 1971, *Eternity* published an editor's note in response to complaints that it did not have more women writers, proudly proclaiming that in this issue 50 percent of the writers were female, noting further: "We didn't look so good in 1960, with only 3% female bylines; but the ladies had increased to 11% by 1965, and in 1970 in was 30%." The note quipped: "if the trend keeps up, by 1995 we'll be known as the *Christian Ladies Home Journal*." Foretaste, *Eternity*, January 1971, 2. One disgruntled reader of *Christianity Today* canceled his subscription in 1978 because, in his opinion, the magazine had succumbed to women. *Christianity Today* printed his letter: "Is it now *Christianity Today*'s 'evangelical conviction' that women are to take over the leadership in shaping world opinion—even in Christian magazines? In the September 8 issue three of the four lead articles were by women. . . . I love women. I married one. But it doesn't mean I have given up the authority in my house, nor the leadership of shaping the opinions of my household. I take seriously the Scripture which placed me in that responsibility. Moreover, because I love my wife, it does not mean that I read *Woman's Day*, nor that I am, or ever will be, interested in receiving spiritual guidance and instruction from it for my life. If *CT* is to become the *Woman's Day* of the Christian world, you can count me out. I will not pay to receive it in my house." M. J. Michaux, "Female Takeover," letter to the editor, *Christianity Today*, October 20, 1978, 9.

23. For example, Patricia Gundry, "Perhaps We Should Take a Second Look," *Moody Monthly*, May 1975. Gundry was the author of the classic Evangelical feminist book *Woman Be Free: Biblical Equality for Women* (Grand Rapids, MI: Ministry Resources Library, 1977). Her husband, Stan Gundry, was professor of theology at Moody Bible Institute (1968–79), and during the 1970s, she was occasionally invited to speak at the institute and on its radio programming. In 1979, however, Stan Gundry was forced to resign from Moody because of his wife's egalitarian views, attesting to an end of the tolerance formerly exhibited there. See Patricia Gundry, "Woman Be Free!," interview by Jon Trott, *Blue Christians on a Red Background* (blog), September 25, 2006, http://bluechristian.blogspot.com; Cochran, *Evangelical Feminism*, 46.

24. Christian Smith, *Christian America? What Evangelicals Really Want* (Berkeley: University of California Press, 2000). Smith's arguments were based on a Pew-funded three-year survey (1995–97) of evangelical Christians across the United States. Others studies that drew on the findings included Sally K. Gallagher and Christian Smith, "Symbolic Traditionalism and Pragmatic Egalitarianism: Contemporary Evangelicals, Families, and Gender," *Gender and Society* 13 (1999): 211–33; Gallagher, *Evangelical Identity and Gendered Family Life*; Melinda Lundquist Denton, "Gender and Marital Decision Making: Negotiating Religious Ideology and Practice," *Social Forces* 82, no. 3 (2004): 1151–80.

25. Smith, *Christian America?*, 189, 194.

26. Smith, 188–89. Other sociologists have similarly found that evangelical Christians increasingly appreciated egalitarian spousal relations. See John P. Bartkowski, *Remaking the Godly Marriage: Gender Negotiations in Evangelical Families* (New Brunswick, NJ: Rutgers University Press, 2001); Gallagher, *Evangelical Identity and Gendered Family Life*.

27. Smith, *Christian America?*, 190.

28. Smith, 190.

29. In 1999, Sally K. Gallagher and Christian Smith spoke of "symbolic traditionalism and pragmatic egalitarianism" to explain the discrepancy between language and practice; Gallagher and Smith, "Symbolic Traditionalism and Pragmatic Egalitarianism." "Pragmatism" was also the explanation Gallagher used in 2003 to describe her findings in an investigation into "this tension between competing evangelical ideals of family and what evangelicals say they actually do in families." Gallagher, *Evangelical Identity and Gendered Family Life*, 4. Elsewhere, interpreting the results of a survey from 1996, she argued that "the majority of self-identified evangelicals affirm *both* the ideal of husbands' headship and the ideal of partnership in marriage." Gallagher, "The Marginalization of Evangelical Feminism," *Sociology of Religion* 65, no. 3 (2004): 228 (emphasis in original). I take issue not with these findings but with the implicit suggestion that Evangelicals say one thing and do another. Anneke Stasson explicitly took this position on "male headship" when she claimed that "there was a considerable divergence between evangelical rhetoric and practice during the 1990s and 2000s." Stasson, "The Politicization of Family Life: How Headship Became Essential to Evangelical Identity in the Late Twentieth Century," *Religion and American Culture* 24,

no. 1 (2014): 115. Rather than showing that Evangelical practice is at odds with the intuitive meaning outsiders assign to such terms, my study demonstrates how terms came to take on specific, sometimes counterintuitive meanings. In certain contexts, apparently degrading language like "submission" could have empowering and even egalitarian meanings.

30. Nancy Hardesty, "Women: Second-Class Citizens?," *Eternity*, January 1971. Hardesty was introduced as former assistant editor and current assistant professor of English at Trinity College in Deerfield, Illinois, and it was mentioned that she was working on a book on Christian women's liberation together with Letha Scanzoni. On Hardesty, see Balmer, *Encyclopedia of Evangelicalism*, "Hardesty, Nancy A(nn)."

31. Editors' note to Hardesty, "Women: Second-Class Citizens?," 14.
32. Hardesty, 14.
33. Hardesty, 15.
34. Hardesty, 16.
35. Hardesty, 28–29.
36. See Pierce, "Contemporary Evangelicals for Gender Equality," 59; Charles C. Ryrie, *The Place of Women in the Church* (New York: Macmillan, 1958).
37. Charles C. Ryrie, "Must Examine Scripture," *Eternity*, January 1971, 24.
38. Elisabeth Elliot, "Rebellion against God's Order," *Eternity*, January 1971, 25.
39. Janet Rohler Greisch, "From College to Nursery," *Eternity*, January 1971, 16.
40. Harold Barnes Kuhn, "Reciprocal Relationship," *Eternity*, January 1971, 29.
41. Stuart Barton Babbage, "Differences of Functions," *Eternity*, January 1971; and see also Thorwald W. Bender, "Joint Heirs of Grace," *Eternity*, January 1971.
42. Bernard Ramm, "A Total Way of Existing," *Eternity*, January 1971, 15; Marvin Wilson, "What D'ya Say, Dear?," *Eternity*, January 1971, 28; and see also Frank Stagg, "Keep Pace with Jesus," *Eternity*, January 1971.
43. Elva McAllaster, "Stunted Poplars," *Eternity*, January 1971, 24; Ramm, "A Total Way of Existing," 15.
44. Edith Deen, "To Influence, not Command," *Eternity*, January 1971.
45. Letters referenced are from, respectively, R. D. Erickson, Betty Lou Nordeen, Gladys Hunt, and Kenneth D. MacDonald, *Eternity*, March 1971, 4.
46. Ramm, "A Total Way of Existing," 15.
47. The notion of the individual and individualism played an important role in (secular) feminist positions, as political scientist Anne Phillips notes: "Much of the personal impetus towards a feminist politics is to do with claiming the space to choose who and what your are—not to be defined, contained, and dictated by notions of 'woman.'" Phillips addresses the uneasy relationship between equality and difference in feminist thinking, as well as the changing feminist stance on individuality. Phillips, *Democracy and Difference* (Oxford: Oxford University Press, 1993), 43, and see 36–54.
48. The term "gender," now well established, only became popular among feminists in the 1970s, when it was indicative of a break with an older politics. Mary P. Ryan writes, "The explosion of the new language and concepts of women's libera-

tion around the year 1970 marked a critical break with the women's politics of the past. Women's liberation burst out of the social movements of the 1960s, demanding a wholesale revolution in human thought and behavior." Ryan, *Mysteries of Sex*, 256. For an overview of the development and use of the term "gender" in scholarly discourse, see Jürgen Martschukat and Olaf Stieglitz, *Geschichte der Männlichkeiten* (Frankfurt, Germany; Campus Verlag, 2008), 12–32.

49. Letha Scanzoni, *Youth Looks at Love* (Westwood, NJ: Revell, 1964); Scanzoni, *Why Am I Here? Where Am I Going? Youth Looks at Life* (Westwood, NJ: Revell, 1966); Scanzoni, "Woman's Place: Silence or Service?," *Eternity*, February 1966. On Scanzoni, see Balmer, *Encyclopedia of Evangelicalism*, s.v. "Scanzoni, Letha Dawson."

50. Gallagher, Marginalization of Evangelical Feminism, 223; and see Bendroth, *Fundamentalism and Gender*, 121.

51. Letha Scanzoni, "The Feminists and the Bible," *Christianity Today*, February 2, 1973, 10–15.

52. Robert Booth Fowler, *A New Engagement: Evangelical Political Thought, 1966–1976* (Grand Rapids, MI: Eerdmans, 1982), 205–6, and see 201–4.

53. Scanzoni, "The Feminists and the Bible," 15, 10.

54. Scanzoni, 11–12.

55. Scanzoni, 12–13 (emphasis in original).

56. "First at the Cradle, Last at the Cross," editorial, *Christianity Today*, March 16, 1973, 26, 27.

57. "First at the Cradle, Last at the Cross," 26–27.

58. "First at the Cradle, Last at the Cross," 26.

59. Letha Scanzoni, "Coauthoring *All We're Meant to Be*—Getting Published," *Letha's Calling* (blog), March 21, 2011, http://www.lethadawsonscanzoni.com; Cochran, *Evangelical Feminism*, 11; Letha Scanzoni and Nancy Hardesty, *All We're Meant to Be: A Biblical Approach to Women's Liberation* (Waco, TX: Word Books, 1974).

60. "The Top 50 Books That Have Changed Evangelicals," *Christianity Today*, October 6, 2006, 51 (emphasis added).

61. After receiving a master's degree in newspaper journalism in 1964, Nancy Hardesty worked for the mainline Protestant magazine *Christian Century* before joining the editorial staff of the Evangelical *Eternity* magazine, which she left for a teaching position in 1969. See Margaret Lamberts Bendroth, "In Memoriam: Nancy A. Hardesty," American Academy of Religion, accessed July 9, 2015, http://rsnonline.org; Alison J. Killeen, "Finding Aid for the Nancy A. Hardesty Papers," Archive of Women in Theological Scholarship, Burke Library, Union Theological Seminary, accessed July 9, 2015, http://library.columbia.edu. Besides her two books for youth, Scanzoni had also written *Sex and the Single Eye* (Grand Rapids, MI: Zondervan, 1968) prior to approaching Hardesty with the suggestion that they author a book together. She had also published two articles in *Eternity* by this time (the February 1966 article "Woman's Place" and one in July 1968 titled "Elevating Marriage to Partnership"). Letha Scanzoni, "Backstory: 'Elevate

Marriage to Partnership (1968 *Eternity* article)," *Letha's Calling* (blog), April 14, 2010, http://www.lethadawsonscanzoni.com; Scanzoni, "Coauthoring *All We're Meant to Be*—The Beginning," *Letha's Calling*, January 7, 2011, http://www.lethadawsonscanzoni.com.

62. According to Margaret Lamberts Bendroth, Scanzoni's July 1968 *Eternity* article "Elevating Marriage to Partnership" had "slipped past editorial scrutiny," and the editors had added a photograph of Scanzoni with her husband to defuse the potentially controversial text. Bendroth, *Fundamentalism and Gender*, 121–22. In a similar move, the *Eternity* editors added a note to Hardesty's January 1971 article "Women: Second-Class Citizens?" Advertisements for Hardesty and Scanzoni's book appeared in both *Christianity Today*, September 13, 1974, and *Eternity*, September 1974.

63. Scanzoni, "The Feminists and the Bible," 10.

64. Roberta Gunner, "Well Done," letter to the editor, *Christianity Today*, March 2, 1973, 44.

65. See Cochran, *Evangelical Feminism*, 25–31.

66. Letha Scanzoni, "Mystique and Machismo," *Other Side*, July/August 1973, 38 (emphasis in original).

67. Nancy Hardesty, "Gifts," *Other Side*, July/August 1973, 23.

68. Cheryl Forbes, "God and Women: *All We're Meant to Be*," *Christianity Today*, December 6, 1974, 36.

69. Barcus, "A Milestone for Christian Women," 40.

70. Boyd Reese, "Letha Scanzoni and Nancy Hardesty, *All We're Meant to Be*," book review, *Post-American*, August/September 1975, 27.

71. Reese, 27.

72. Barcus, "A Milestone for Christian Women," 40 (emphasis in original).

73. Barcus, 40.

74. "Book Ends: Call Me Mrs.," *New York Times*, June 9, 1974, 375; and see Marabel Morgan, *The Total Woman* (Old Tappan, NJ: Revell, 1973).

75. See Gardella, "Sex and Submission in the Spirit," 173–74. In 1977, a *Time* article quoted several unflattering comments that non-Evangelical observers had made about Morgan's books *The Total Woman* and its follow-up, *Total Joy* (Old Tappan, NJ: Revell, 1977). New York psychiatrist Julianne Densen-Gerber called the books "hogwash and bullshit," religion scholar Martin E. Marty used the word "sick," and sex researcher William Masters reportedly described the books as "inaccuracies . . . clichés . . . a patchwork quilt of impressions, intuitions and out-of-style dogma." "The New Housewife Blues," *Time*, March 14, 1977. Marty joked in the liberal Protestant *Christian Century* that he would like to see Evangelicals raptured in their sex costumes. Martin E. Marty, "Fundies and Their Fetishes," *Christian Century*, December 8, 1976.

76. The Total Woman workshops, which were run by Morgan and female teachers she trained, constituted a "small Christian industry" in the early 1970s. Because the workshops included a "call to Christ," or conversion, they were a form of evangelism. Gardella, "Sex and Submission in the Spirit," 172.

77. Gardella, 173. According to Peter Gardella, even after the book had sold 1.5 million copies (which it did by 1975), sales continued at a rate of ten to twenty thousand copies per week (172).

78. See Daniel K. Williams, "Sex and the Evangelicals: Gender Issues, the Sexual Revolution, and Abortion in the 1960s," in Schäfer, *American Evangelicals and the 1960s*, 101–4.

79. Fowler, *A New Engagement*, 209. On sex manuals, see, for example, Anna E. Ward, "Sex and the Me Decade: Sex and Dating Advice Literature of the 1970s," *Women's Studies Quarterly* 43, no. 3–4 (2015): 120–36; Amy DeRogatis, "What Would Jesus Do? Sexuality and Salvation in Protestant Evangelical Sex Manuals: 1950 to the Present," *Church History* 74, no. 1 (2005): 97–137. DeRogatis points out that "Evangelical sex manuals followed the general publishing trend of secular sex manuals and also became bestsellers in the 1970s" (106).

80. Zeda Thornton, "*The Total Woman*: An In-Depth Look at the Recently Released Book," *Moody Monthly*, December 1973, 49. In an interview with the *Wittenburg Door*, Morgan would more explicitly call this strategy one of submission; Marabel Morgan, interview, *Wittenburg Door*, August/September 1975. In other contexts, scholars have described submission as a coping strategy and sometimes a subversive method for "asserting power over bad situations, including circumstances over which one may otherwise have no control." Ruth Marie Griffith, for example, undertook fieldwork in the mid-1990s in female prayer circles, the charismatic Women's Aglow Fellowship, in order to study "evangelical women and the power of submission." She found that within these circles, "submission works as a valuable tool for containing husbands and thereby regulating the home, and may be subtly modified or subverted, so that the women retain a kind of mediated agency through their reliance on the omnipotent God. Out of a doctrine that would seem to leave them helpless, evangelical women have generated a variety of substantial yet flexible meanings through which they experience some degree of control, however limited it may often appear." Griffith, *God's Daughters: Evangelical Women and the Power of Submission* (Berkeley: University of California Press, 2000), 179, 183.

81. Thornton, "*The Total Woman*," 48.

82. Lawrence J. Crabb, "Counseling and Psychology of Religion," *Christianity Today*, March 1, 1974, 25–26.

83. Fowler, *A New Engagement*, 209.

84. David R. Douglass, "*The Total Woman*: Totaled," *Moody Monthly*, September 1975, 107.

85. Stasson, "The Politicization of Family Life," 102.

86. "Poll Puts Women First," *Eternity*, December 1975; "The Top 25 Books: How They Ranked in *Eternity*'s Poll," *Eternity*, December 1975.

87. Carol Prester McFadden, "Ethics and Discipleship," *Christianity Today*, March 14, 1975, 19.

88. Ben Patterson, "May They Twain," *Wittenburg Door*, August/September 1975, 3.

89. Among the items surrounding the female reader of *The Total Woman* in the illustration on the cover of the August/September 1975 issue of *Wittenburg Door* was a well-worn copy of *Moody Monthly*, located at the lower-right corner of the page, near the woman's feet.

90. Patterson, "May They Twain," 3.

91. Morgan, interview, *Wittenburg Door*, esp. 9–11; Letha Scanzoni, interview, *Wittenburg Door*, August/September 1975, esp. 23.

92. Morgan, interview, *Wittenburg Door*, 7.

93. Morgan, 10–11.

94. Griffith, *God's Daughters*, 179, and see 4–5, 178–79, 181–82. Focusing on the popular writings of New Christian Right leaders, Michael Lienesch described this subversive phenomenon as "the paradox of power through powerlessness." Lienesch, "Family," in *The New Christian Right: Political and Social Issues*, ed. Melvin I. Urofsky and Martha May (New York: Garland, 1996), 308–10.

95. Christine J. Gardner, *Making Chastity Sexy: The Rhetoric of Evangelical Abstinence Campaigns* (Berkeley: University of California Press, 2011), 18.

96. Scanzoni, interview, *Wittenburg Door*, 23.

97. Olson, *The Westminster Handbook to Evangelical Theology*, s.v. "Humanity."

98. Konrad Lorenz, "Die angeborenen formen möglicher Erfahrung," *Zeitschrift für Tierpsychologie* 5, no. 2 (1943): 235–409.

99. Foretaste, *Eternity*, February 1974, 2.

100. Dorothy L. Sayers, "Are Women Human?" *Eternity*, February 1974, 15.

101. Foretaste, *Eternity*, March 1975, 2.

102. John F. Alexander, "Thinking Male," *Other Side*, July/August 1973, 3.

103. Alexander, 44.

104. See Fowler, *A New Engagement*, 201–2.

105. Judith Sanderson, "Jesus and Women," *Other Side*, July/August 1973, 36.

106. Rolf E. Aaseng, "Male and Female Created He Them," *Christianity Today*, November 20, 1970, 6.

107. Winnie Christensen, "What Is a Woman's Role?," *Moody Monthly*, June 1971, 23.

108. Carl F. H. Henry, "Further Thoughts about Women," Footnotes, *Christianity Today*, June 6, 1975, 36.

109. Griffith, *God's Daughters*, 208–9.

110. Joseph Bayly, "Revise Our 'Sexist' Scriptures?," Out of My Mind, *Eternity*, September 1974, 63; for an example of scholarship that treats this gender breakdown as a rhetorical strategy, see Gallagher, "The Marginalization of Evangelical Feminism."

111. Mollenkott's book *Women, Men and the Bible* (Nashville, TN: Abingdon Press, 1977) was positively reviewed in *Christianity Today*: Philip Siddons, "Paul's View of Women," book review, *Christianity Today*, February 10, 1978. Mollenkott, however, was one of those who, on closer inspection, had moved outside the confines of Evangelicalism. Interestingly, it was the liberal-leaning magazine *Sojourners* that solicited a critical review of Mollenkott's writings. Sharon Gallagher,

an Evangelical feminist and cofounder of the Bay Area chapter of the Evangelical Women's Caucus, criticized Mollenkott's arguments dismissing certain Pauline passages and therefore no longer fitting with an Evangelical reading of the Bible. Gallagher, "More on Women and Biblical Authority," *Sojourners*, March 1976. Indeed, Mollenkott embraced a broader understanding of Christianity and, in the 1980s, preferred the label biblical feminism, distancing herself from the more narrowly defined Evangelicalism. Cochran, *Evangelical Feminism*, 53–58.

112. Virginia Mollenkott, "A Challenge to Male Interpretation: Women and the Bible," *Sojourners*, February 1976, 23 (emphasis in original).

113. Mollenkott, 23–24; see also Mollenkott, "The Androgyny of Jesus," *Daughters of Sarah*, March 1975.

114. Reporter Roberta Green expressed her incredulity and shock of this phenomenon in an *Eternity* article. Green, "Gender Chameleons," *Eternity*, February 1985.

115. Patterson, "May They Twain," 3.

116. Joan Lloyd, "Transcendent Sexuality as C. S. Lewis Saw It," *Christianity Today*, November 9, 1973, 7. *Perelandra* is the second book in Lewis's *Space Trilogy*. It discusses Adam and Eve's seduction by Satan and subsequent banishment from paradise through the medium of a science fiction story. C. S. Lewis, *Perelandra: Voyage to Venus* (London: Harper Collins, 1943).

117. Patterson, "May They Twain," 3.

118. Rod Rosenbladt, "Deprivation within the Evangelical Family and Church," *Wittenburg Door*, June/July 1973, 15–16.

119. Nancy B. Barcus, "Liberation Isn't Freedom," *Eternity*, March 1975, 21–22 (emphasis in original).

120. Barcus, 21 (emphasis in original).

121. Barcus, 22 (emphasis in original).

122. Barcus, 23.

123. Barcus, 22.

124. Aaseng, "Male and Female Created He Them," 6.

125. Carl F. H. Henry, "The Battle of the Sexes," Footnotes, *Christianity Today*, July 4, 1975, 45.

126. Zeda Thornton, "Dare to be Liberated," *Moody Monthly*, November 1972, 82.

127. Joseph Bayly, "Revise Our 'Sexist' Scriptures?," Out of My Mind, *Eternity*, September 1974, 64.

128. Patterson, "May They Twain," 3.

129. Such advertisements appeared, for example, in *Christianity Today*, March 28, 1975; and *Moody Monthly*, May 1975.

130. Christensen, "What Is a Woman's Role?," 23.

131. During the 1970s, the single life, especially for women, was addressed by an emerging category of literature. Nancy Hardesty, herself a single woman, wrote extensively on the topic, as did Letha Scanzoni. See, for example, the chapter on single women in Scanzoni and Hardesty, *All We're Meant to Be*; Hardesty, "Marital Status: Single," *Daughters of Sarah*, January 1976; Scanzoni, *Sex and the*

Single Eye. Articles in Evangelical magazines included Frances Nordland, "A Look at the Single Woman," *Moody Monthly*, January 1970; Lois Thiessen, "What If You Don't Get Married . . . ," *Moody Monthly*, April 1974; Barb Sroka, "The Single, and Living Happily Ever After," *Moody Monthly*, December 1976; John MacArthur, "Singleness as a Gift of the Spirit," *Moody Monthly*, January 1977; "Serving Singles—Don't Play Mix and Match," *Christianity Today*, June 4, 1976; Richard L. Strauss, "The Family Church: Any Place for Singles?," *Christianity Today*, July 29, 1977; Margaret Clarkson, "Singleness: His Share for Me," *Christianity Today*, February 16, 1979; Cheryl Forbes, "Let's Not Shackle the Single Life," *Christianity Today*, February 16, 1979.

132. Thomas Howard, "The Yoke of Fatherhood," *Christianity Today*, June 23, 1978, 10.

133. Howard, 12–13 (emphasis in original).

134. Howard, 14.

135. Aaseng, "Male and Female Created He Them," 6.

136. C. Fred Dickason, "Where Do You Fit in the Sex Revolution," *Moody Monthly*, February 1974, 105.

137. Charlie Shedd and Martha Shedd, interview, *Wittenburg Door*, August/September 1974. At the time of the interview, the Shedds had developed the idea that praying together would lead to a better sex life, which, in turn, was constitutive for a good marriage. They eventually published books on the topic, including *Celebration in the Bedroom* (Waco, TX: Word Books, 1979); *How to Stay in Love* (Kansas City, KS: Andrews and McMeel, 1980); and *Praying Together: Making Marriage Last* (Grand Rapids, MI: Zondervan, 1985).

138. See, for example, DeRogatis, "What Would Jesus Do?"; Williams, "Sex and the Evangelicals." The Evangelical press took note of the rise in such manuals; the cover story for *Christianity Today*'s 1976 book issue, for example, was Donald Tinder, "Sexuality: A New Candor in Evangelical Books," *Christianity Today*, March 18, 1977.

139. Charlie Shedd and Martha Shedd, interview, *Wittenburg Door*, 14. Christian marriage-improvement manuals stressed the benefit of a fulfilled sex life. For example, Colleen Townsend Evans and Louis H. Evans's book of marital advice *My Lover, My Friend* (Old Tappan, NJ: Revell, 1976) was celebrated by a review in *Eternity* as "a mutual celebration of love and life." This same review lamented that Marabel Morgan's "advice for rekindling sexual desire" in her 1976 book *Total Joy* was "bizarre and silly." Deborah Barackman, "Strange and Sane Marriage Customs," *Eternity*, March 1977, 64–65.

140. The cover story was M. N. Beck, "The Bed Undefiled," *Christianity Today*, October 10, 1975. Another cover story a few years later was dedicated to debunking the "myth" of a boring and frigid puritan sex ethic, arguing that "far from minimizing the importance of sex in marriage, the Puritans flaunted their enthusiasm for married sex." Leland Ryken, "Were the Puritans Right about Sex?," *Christianity Today*, April 7, 1978, 14.

141. Sexual differences were considered to be natural, the basis for a sexual re-

lationship. Therefore, homosexuality was considered a deviation. A 1977 *Christianity Today* cover made this abundantly clear—not only in the cover article by John M. Batteau, a doctoral student in theology, but also by the picture on the cover. It depicted a pair of peacocks with the differences between male and female strikingly obvious, driving home the argument that sexual distinctions were foundational. John M. Batteau, "Sexual Differences: A Cultural Convention?," *Christianity Today*, July 8, 1977. Evangelical magazines printed a variety of articles discussing homosexuality, from Letha Scanzoni's treatment of "the homosexual" as a friend, to a description of the psychological ramifications of a male Christian college student who was raped by a man. Letha Scanzoni, "On Friendship and Homosexuality," *Christianity Today*, September 27, 1974; Jason Townder, "Single Men and Hasty Conclusions," *Eternity*, January 1979. Homosexuality was always considered aberrant. It was treated as a disease, lamentable behavioral flaw, or chosen lifestyle. As religious studies scholar Amy DeRogatis has shown, a whole body of anti-homosexual evangelical Christian literature existed. DeRogatis, "What Would Jesus Do?," 111.

142. Dickason, "Where Do You Fit in the Sex Revolution," 105.

143. Letha Scanzoni, "What Is Marriage?," *Wittenburg Door*, August/September 1974, 20.

144. Aaseng, "Male and Female Created He Them," 6.

145. Scanzoni, "What Is Marriage?," 23.

146. Dickason, "Where Do You Fit in the Sex Revolution," 106.

147. Clyde M. Narramore, "Things Women Should Know about Men," *Moody Monthly*, May 1974; George Sweeting, "Give Your Wife a Happy Husband," *Moody Monthly*, December 1975; Mildred Tengbom, "Ten Guidelines for a Happy Marriage," *Moody Monthly*, October 1977; George W. Peters, "What God Says about Remarriage," *Moody Monthly*, July/August 1978.

148. Carl F. H. Henry, "Reflections of Women's Liberation," Footnotes, *Christianity Today*, January 3, 1975, 25.

149. See, for example, the study of family manuals by sociologist John P. Bartkowski, "Debating Patriarchy: Discursive Disputes over Spousal Authority among Evangelical Family Commentators," *Journal for the Scientific Study of Religion* 36, no. 3 (1997): 393–410.

150. For examples of the opposing understanding here, see Bartkowski; Gallagher and Smith, "Symbolic Traditionalism and Pragmatic Egalitarianism"; Smith, *Christian America?*

151. *Moody Monthly* contributor Diane Litfin, for example, claimed that "the theological ramifications of a confrontation between evangelical feminists and traditionalists are so far-reaching that they extend to the fundamental aspects of a biblical view of men and women and their world." Litfin, "Do Biblical Feminists Have a Point?," *Moody Monthly*, December 1979, 20. While my study is not concerned with theological-methodical development, Pamela Cochran has pointed out that the 1970s were also marked by a controversy about biblicism, one of the pillars of Evangelical theology. She shows that theologians associated with

the Evangelical Left in conjunction with Evangelical feminists were at the fore of adapting critical methods to the Evangelical interpretation of the Bible. In this regard, then, the fear that feminists were changing the Evangelical understanding of the Bible was warranted. Cochran, *Evangelical Feminism*, 64–69. For a discussion of the biblicism debate, see, for example, Olson, *The Westminster Handbook to Evangelical Theology*, s.v. "Scripture: Inerrancy/Infallibility."

152. Diane Litfin, for example, admitted: "Women have often been short-changed and every Christian needs to be aware of it." Litfin, "Do Biblical Feminists Have a Point?," 23.

153. This point was made, for example, by Thomas Howard in "The Yoke of Fatherhood," *Christianity Today*; by Nancy Barcus in "Liberation Isn't Freedom," *Eternity*; and by C. Fred Dickason in "Where Do You Fit in the Sex Revolution," *Moody Monthly*.

154. Much of what Diane Litfin criticized about Evangelical feminism was based on a reading of Mollenkott's *Women, Men and the Bible*. Litfin, "Do Biblical Feminists Have a Point?" Reta Halteman Finger and S. Sue Horner note that feminists associated with *Daughters of Sarah* and the Evangelical Women's Caucus eventually went beyond the scope of Evangelicalism. In their chapter "Euro-American Evangelical Feminism," Finger and Horner, both former editors of *Daughters of Sarah*, attest that in the 1980s, they started referring to their movement as "biblical feminism" or "Christian feminism" (473). The Evangelical Women's Caucus also changed its name, becoming the Evangelical and Ecumenical Women's Caucus in 1990, to account for its wider audience. This biblical feminism, as Finger and Horner describe it, was part of a "penumbra evangelicalism," "with one foot in the evangelical world and another closer to mainstream church traditions" (469, 472). At the same time, Evangelical feminists who stayed within the Evangelical fold more narrowly defined also organized, as for example in Catherine Kroeger's Christians for Biblical Equality, founded in 1986 (471, 473–74).

155. Scanzoni, "What Is Marriage?," 22.

156. W. Christensen, "What Is a Woman's Role?," 23, 81.

157. William L. Coleman, "How to Be a Huggable Husband," *Moody Monthly*, February 1973, 30.

158. William L. Coleman, "How to Be a Wonderful Wife," *Moody Monthly*, February 1973, 33.

159. Coleman, 33, 46–47.

160. George Sweeting, "Give Your Wife a Happy Husband," *Moody Monthly*, December 1975, 38–39. God, according to Sweeting, judged not just the children but the "house" and admonished the father who did not keep them in check.

161. Sweeting, 39.

162. Gordon MacDonald, "You're the Pacesetter, Dad," *Moody Monthly*, January 1976, 31–32; and see MacDonald, "How to be an Effective Father," *Moody Monthly*, March 1976.

163. C. Fred Dickason exemplified the descriptive approach when he insisted

that "men and woman have very definite differences that distinguish and complement one another. Man has a basic need for respect and love. The woman has a need for security and a sense of being wanted. Generally, most men have a desire to rule and most women have a desire to follow." Dickason, "Where Do You Fit in the Sex Revolution," 105. Conversely, advice literature for women exemplified the prescriptive approach in that it aimed to teach women to become better wives, mothers, and homemakers. See, for example, Ella May Miller, "Housework Doesn't Come Naturally," *Moody Monthly*, January 1976.

164. Letha Scanzoni, "Feminism and the Family," *Daughters of Sarah*, May 1975, 2–3 (emphasis in original).

165. The Greek word used in the relevant passages is *kephalē* (head). The German translation is Haupt. For a theological overview of the use of the word in the Bible, see Peter Hofrichter, "Haupt," in *Bibeltheologisches Wörterbuch*, ed. Johannes Baptist Bauer (Graz, Austria: Styria, 2001), 285–87.

166. Berkeley Mickelsen and Alvera Mickelsen, "Does Male Dominance Tarnish Our Translations?," *Christianity Today*, October 5, 1979, 23–24, 25.

167. Hardesty, "Women: Second-Class Citizens?" *Eternity*, January 1971, 28.

168. Berkeley Michelsen and Alvera Mickelsen, "The 'Head' of the Epistles," *Christianity Today*, February 20, 1981, 22.

169. Mary Bouma, "Liberated Mothers," *Christianity Today*, May 7, 1971, 6.

170. Thornton, "Dare to be Liberated," 84, 86.

171. Henry, "Reflections of Women's Liberation," 26.

172. Henry, "The Battle of the Sexes," 45.

173. Renee J. Hermanson, "How Do You Know When You're Liberated?," *Daughters of Sarah*, January/February 1978, 10.

174. In one article in *Moody Monthly*, Mary and Martha were described as two different "temperaments": Martha, who cooked for Jesus, was "logical," while Mary, who listened to his teachings, was "emotional." J. Oswald Sanders, "Mary and Martha: A Study of Temperaments," *Moody Monthly*, April 1979.

175. Barcus, "Liberation Isn't Freedom."

176. Smith, *Christian America?*, 160, 191.

177. Griffith, *God's Daughters*.

178. Gallagher, "The Marginalization of Evangelical Feminism," 216.

179. Gallagher, 216.

180. Smith, *Christian America?*, 160–91.

181. Ryan, *Mysteries of Sex*, 276.

182. J. Brooks Flippen, *Jimmy Carter, the Politics of Family, and the Rise of the Religious Right* (Athens: University of Georgia Press, 2011), 272; Leo P. Ribuffo, "Family Policy Past as Prologue: Jimmy Carter, the White House Conference on Families, and the Mobilization of the New Christian Right," *Review of Policy Research* 23, no. 2 (2006): 328.

183. Ribuffo, "Family Policy Past as Prologue," 311.

184. Eithne Johnson, "Dr. Dobson's Advice to Christian Women: The Story of Strategic Motherhood," *Social Text* 57 (1998): 57.

CHAPTER 4

1. Russell T. Hitt, "They Come in Many Different Styles," *Eternity*, January 1980.

2. Edward E. Plowman, "Is Morality All Right?," *Christianity Today*, November 2, 1979; "Stacking Sandbags against the Conservative Flood," *Christianity Today*, November 2, 1979, 76-77. I use the term New Christian Right rather than Religious Right or another variant because the new religio-political activism flowering in the 1980s was dominated by conservative Protestant leaders.

3. "Getting God's Kingdom into Politics," editorial, *Christianity Today*, November 2, 1979.

4. Evangelicals for Social Action, "Can My Vote Be Biblical?," *Christianity Today*, November 2, 1979.

5. "How I Think I'll Vote," *Eternity*, October 1980.

6. Bruce Dunn, "Why Vote?," *Moody Monthly*, November 1980.

7. John F. Alexander, "Did We Blow It?," *Other Side*, February 1981, 10.

8. Carl F. H. Henry, "Evangelicals Jump on the Political Bandwagon," *Christianity Today*, October 24, 1980, 21.

9. Carl F. H. Henry, "Pull the Lever Knowing Why," *Christianity Today*, October 24, 1980.

10. Stephen V. Monsma, "What Makes an Ideal President?," *Eternity*, March 1980.

11. "Just Because Reagan Has Won . . . ," editorial, *Christianity Today*, December 12, 1980, 14-15.

12. Alexander, "Did We Blow It?," 11.

13. Stephen D. Johnson and Joseph B. Tamney, "The Christian Right and the 1980 Presidential Election," *Journal for the Scientific Study of Religion* 21, no. 2 (1982): 123-31.

14. Patrick Allitt, *Religion in America since 1945: A History* (New York: Columbia University Press, 2003), 151.

15. Russell T. Hitt, "Capital Clout: Now What?," *Eternity*, January 1981, 12.

16. "The President and Nebuchadnezzar," *Eternity*, May 1983, 21.

17. Beth Spring, "Republicans, Religion, and Reelection," *Christianity Today*, October 6, 1984, 54.

18. Robert P. Dugan Jr., "Election '84: Some Surprising Winners and Losers," *Christianity Today*, January 18, 1985, 44.

19. For its part, *Eternity* interviewed three Evangelical spokespersons to gain insight into their assessment of the Reagan Revolution: "Armstrong, Colson, and Noll: Reviewing the Reagan Revolution," *Eternity*, November 1988.

20. Charles W. Colson, "So Much for Our 'Great Awakening,'" *Christianity Today*, May 13, 1988, 72.

21. *Moody Monthly*'s February 1988 issue included commentaries from Richard V. Pierard, a history professor; Jim Wallis, the editor of *Sojourners*; and Vernon C. Grounds, president of Evangelicals for Social Action. Both *Sojourners* and Evangelicals for Social Action were considered institutions of the Evangelical Left, and

Wallis was the most prominent face of the Evangelical Left. Pierard and Grounds were more temperate but sympathized with the Evangelical Left. The feature also included commentary from Tim LaHaye, a spokesperson for the New Christian Right. See Elwood McQuaid, "What's Left for the Religious Right?," *Moody Monthly*, February 1988. *Christianity Today*'s October 21, 1988, issue included the following commentaries: Joseph Sobran, "Bully for the Bully Pulpit"; Robert Coles, "The Dangers of Idol Gazing"; George Weigel, "The Public Square Is Still Naked"; Martin E. Marty, "Adapting to the Age of Greed"; Richard John Neuhaus, "The Culture War Will Continue."

22. Tim LaHaye, "What's Left for the Religious Right?," *Moody Monthly*, February 1988, 17.

23. Vernon C. Grounds, "What's Left for the Religious Right?" *Moody Monthly*, February 1988, 16.

24. Richard V. Pierard, "What's Left for the Religious Right?," *Moody Monthly*, February 1988; Jim Wallis, "What's Left for the Religious Right?," *Moody Monthly*, February 1988.

25. Sobran, "Bully for the Bully Pulpit," 18.

26. Coles, "The Dangers of Idol Gazing," 19.

27. Marty, "Adapting to the Age of Greed," 20.

28. David Aikman, "Washington Scorecard," *Christianity Today*, October 21, 1988, 22.

29. McQuaid, "What's Left for the Religious Right?," 13.

30. James Risen and Judy L. Thomas, *Wrath of Angels: The American Abortion War* (New York: Basic Books, 1998), 373; Carol Mason, *Killing for Life: The Apocalyptic Narrative of Pro-Life Politics* (Ithaca, NY: Cornell University Press, 2002); Alesha E. Doan, *Opposition and Intimidation: The Abortion Wars and Strategies of Political Harassment* (Ann Arbor: University of Michigan Press, 2010); Jennifer L. Jefferis, *Armed for Life: The Army of God and Anti-Abortion Terror in the United States* (Santa Barbara, CA: Praeger, 2011).

31. The specifically religious connotation to pro-life activism has been noted. Early books focused especially on Roman Catholic activism. One of the foremost sociological accounts of the pro-life and pro-choice movements, Kristin Luker's *Abortion and the Politics of Motherhood* (Berkeley: University of California Press, 1984), overlooked the emerging Protestant activism but offers an exemplary description of Catholic activism in California. Kerry N. Jacoby's *Souls, Bodies Spirits: The Drive to Abolish Abortion since 1973* (Westport, CT: Praeger, 1998) argued that the antiabortion movement was more religious than political and traced its developments from the *Roe v. Wade* decision and the Catholic opposition to abortion, through the engagement of Fundamentalist and Evangelical Protestants in the 1980s (and the subsequent religious revivalism), to the 1996 election. Similarly, James Risen and Judy L. Thomas's 1998 *Wrath of Angels* linked the "abortion war" to the mobilization of evangelical Christians in the 1980s and credited it with a revival of the church-and-state debate. From a sociological perspective, Ziad W. Munson's *The Making of Pro-Life Activists: How Social Movement Mo-*

bilization Works (Chicago: University of Chicago Press, 2008) found "(not surprisingly) that pro-life activists are more religious on the whole than the general population" (8). While religious convictions motivated pro-life activists, Munson emphasizes that religious backgrounds were varied and often—as in Catholics and conservative Protestants—in conflict with one another. Furthermore, he points out that religious institutions were reluctant to mobilize or join the movement, and that being part of the movement affected religious convictions just as much as religious convictions affected activism. Journalist William Saletan's *Bearing Right: How Conservatives Won the Abortion War* (Berkeley: University of California Press, 2003) demonstrated "how the politically defeated extremes of the debate—on one side, opposition to legal abortion, and on the other, insistence on abortion rights with public funding and without parental control—faded away during the 1992 election year. Pro-choice politicians, led by Clinton and Senator Al Gore, converged with pro-life politicians, led by President George H. W. Bush, in a 'middle ground' of restricted choice, consecrated by the Supreme Court's decision in *Planned Parenthood v. Casey*" (5-6). John Dombrink and Daniel Hillyard's *Sin No More: From Abortion to Stem Cells, Understanding Crime, Law, and Morality in America* (New York: New York University Press, 2007), explored Supreme Court justice Sandra Day O'Connor's retirement in the year 2004 and the role abortion played in the political negotiations for finding her replacement (53-92). John P. Hoffmann and Sherrie Mills Johnson's 2005 article "Attitudes toward Abortion among Religious Traditions in the United States: Change or Continuity?," published in *Sociology of Religion* 66, no. 2 (2005), reviewed survey data from 1972 to 2005 and found that "controversy over abortion in the United States continues virtually unabated" (177).

32. Roger E. Olson, *The Westminster Handbook to Evangelical Theology* (Louisville, KY: Westminster John Knox Press, 2004), s.v. "Humanity" (emphasis in original).

33. Stanley J. Grenz, "What Is Sex for?," *Christianity Today*, June 12, 1987, 23.

34. See John H. Evans, "Religion and Human Cloning: An Exploratory Analysis of the First Available Opinion Data," *Journal for the Scientific Study of Religion* 41, no. 4 (2002): 747. In this study, the first of its kind, Evans analyzed attitudes of religious people toward human cloning, using data collected through a 2001 Pew survey.

CHAPTER 5

1. On the 1970s, see David R. Swartz, *Moral Minority: The Evangelical Left in an Age of Conservatism* (Philadelphia: University of Pennsylvania Press, 2012),

2. On the 1980s, see William Martin, *With God on Our Side: The Rise of the Religious Right in America* (New York: Broadway Books, 1996); Linda Kintz and Julia Lesage, eds., *Media, Culture, and the Religious Right* (Minneapolis: University of Minnesota Press, 1998); Ruth Murray Brown, *For a "Christian America": A History of the Religious Right* (Amherst, NY: Prometheus Books, 2002); Clyde Wilcox and Carin Robinson, *Onward Christian Soldiers? The Religious Right in American Politics* (Boulder, CO: Westview Press, 2011).

2. See Brown, *For a "Christian America,"* 158; Wilcox and Robinson, *Onward Christian Soldiers?*, 6.

3. "Unfavorable Views of Moral Majority Outweigh Favorable by 2:1," in "Religion in America," special issue, *Gallup Report*, nos. 201-2 (June/July 1982): 72. Compare the findings by sociologists James L. Guth and John C. Green in "The Moralizing Minority: Christian Right Support among Political Contributors," in *Religion and the Culture Wars: Dispatches from the Front*, ed. John C. Green et al. (Lanham, MD: Rowman and Littlefield, 1996), 30-43.

4. See, for example, Wilcox and Robinson, *Onward Christian Soldiers?*, 6-7. Some scholars pronounced the demise of the New Christian Right; see, for example, Steve Bruce, *The Rise and Fall of the New Christian Right: Conservative Protestant Politics in America, 1978-1988* (New York: Oxford University Press, 1988). Yet New Christian Right organizations were "marching to the millennium" and have been active beyond. See John C. Green, Mark J. Rozell, and Clyde Wilcox, eds., *The Christian Right in American Politics: Marching to the Millennium* (Washington, DC: Georgetown University Press, 2003); Clyde Wilcox, "Premillennialists at the Millennium: Some Reflections on the Christian Right in the Twenty-First Century," in *The Rapture of Politics: The Christian Right as the United States Approaches the Year 2000*, ed. Steve Bruce, Peter Kiviston, and William H. Swatos Jr. (New Brunswick, NJ: Transaction, 1995), 21-40.

5. On Falwell, see Randall Balmer, *Encyclopedia of Evangelicalism* (Waco, TX: Baylor University Press, 2004), s.v. "Falwell, Jerry." Anthropologist Susan Friend Harding studied the language and rhetorical appeal of Jerry Falwell during the 1980s; see Harding, *The Book of Jerry Falwell: Fundamentalist Language and Politics* (Princeton, NJ: Princeton University Press, 2000).

6. Jerry Falwell, "Where Is Jerry Falwell Going?," interview William J. Petersen and Stephen Board, *Eternity*, July/August 1980, 18.

7. Cal Thomas, interview, *Wittenburg Door*, December 1983/January 1984, 24.

8. Mark A. Noll, "Evangelicals Past and Present," in *Religion, Politics, and the American Experience: Reflections on Religion and American Public Life*, ed. Edith L. Blumhofer (Tuscaloosa: University of Alabama Press, 2002), 111.

9. Barry Hankins, *Francis Schaeffer and the Shaping of Evangelical America* (Grand Rapids, MI: Eerdmans, 2008). See also the Evangelical discussion of the Schaeffer legacy in light of the activism of Francis's son, Franky Schaeffer; *Wittenburg Door*, April/May 1984.

10. While political scientist Michael Lienesch commendably analyzed the discourse of the New Christian Right in popular books, so far no comparable study has been published analyzing the reception of the New Christian Right and its ideas and agendas in Evangelical discourse. This chapter addresses this gap by focusing on Evangelical spokespersons' reaction to and involvement with the political activism of the New Christian Right and the pervasive idea of a Christian America. Lienesch, *Redeeming America: Piety and Politics in the New Christian Right* (Chapel Hill: University of North Carolina Press, 1993).

11. This statement refers to the national level. Evangelical scholars sometimes referred to early colonial communities like the Massachusetts Bay Colony as

theocratic—and insisted that Evangelicals did not want to return to such a state. See, for example, Carl F. H. Henry, "Church and State: Why the Marriage Must Be Saved," *Christianity Today*, April 5, 1985.

12. "Gaining Perspective after a Decade of Change," editorial, *Christianity Today*, January 4, 1980.

13. Carl F. H. Henry, "Out of the Closet but Going Nowhere?," *Christianity Today*, January 4, 1980, 17; Billy Graham, "An Agenda for the 1980s," *Christianity Today*, January 4, 1980, 23.

14. George Sweeting, "Talking It Over: Godly Citizenship," *Moody Monthly*, August 1980, 1.

15. "Political Cross Bearing," *Christianity Today*, April 5, 1985, 15.

16. Carl F. H. Henry, "Evangelicals Jump on the Political Bandwagon," *Christianity Today*, October 24, 1980, 22.

17. Carl Horn, "How Freedom of Thought Is Smothered in America," *Christianity Today*, April 6, 1984, 14.

18. Joseph Bayly, "Rome Fell While Moralists Slept," *Eternity*, January 1986.

19. Kenneth S. Kantzer, "American Civil Religion," editorial, *Christianity Today*, July 13, 1984, 14.

20. Kenneth S. Kantzer, "The 'Separation' of Church and State?," editorial, *Christianity Today*, May 18, 1984, 10–11.

21. Martin Mawyer, "Are We Losing Our Religious Freedoms?," 3 parts, *Moody Monthly*, March to May 1982.

22. Martin E. Marty, "Fundamentalism Reborn: Faith and Fanaticism," *Saturday Review*, May 1980.

23. Martin E. Marty, "Points to Consider about the New Christian Right Wing," *Wittenburg Door*, June/July 1980 (reprinted from *Context*, July 15, 1980).

24. Allan J. Mayer, "A Tide of Born Again Politics," *Newsweek*, September 15, 1980, 28.

25. Edward E. Plowman, "Is Morality All Right?," *Christianity Today*, November 2, 1979; Ted Miller, "Shall We Join the 'New Christian Crusade'?," *Moody Monthly*, September 1980; Richard John Neuhaus, "Who, Now, Will Shape the Meaning of America?," *Christianity Today*, March 19, 1982.

26. See, for example, Wilcox and Robinson, *Onward Christian Soldiers?*, 8. Cal Thomas, speaking in an interview on behalf of Moral Majority, stated that "we even have conservative Jews and Mormons." Thomas, interview, *Wittenburg Door*, December 1983/January 1984, 24.

27. As late as 1980, Jerry Falwell denied that God heard the prayers of Jews (a position he quickly learned to revise). See, for example, Marjorie Hyer, "Evangelist Reverses Position on God's Hearing Jews," *Washington Post*, October 11, 1980.

28. For a definition of the New Christian Right/Religious Right, see, for example, Wilcox and Robinson, *Onward Christian Soldiers?*, 8.

29. In the early 1980s, Falwell's name and picture were ubiquitous in discussions of the New Christian Right. Randall Balmer writes: "Jerry Falwell's formation of Moral Majority in 1979 was perhaps the most visible eruption of Religious

Right impulses." Balmer, *Encyclopedia of Evangelicalism*, s.v. "Religious Right." See also Wilcox and Robinson, *Onward Christian Soldiers?*, 43.

30. Corwin E. Smidt, "Evangelicals within Contemporary American Politics: Differentiating between Fundamentalist and Non-Fundamentalist Evangelicals," *Western Political Quarterly* 41, no. 3 (1988): 601–20. While Smidt set out parameters to disambiguate Fundamentalism and Evangelicalism, he also suggested that the personal act of identifying with one or the other was important and indicative of certain attitudes.

31. Jerry Falwell, *The Fundamentalist Phenomenon* (Garden City, NY: Doubleday, 1981); *Wittenburg Door*, December 1982/January 1983. Additionally, first place in *Eternity*'s 1981 Book of the Year poll went to George Marsden's treatment of Fundamentalism. See "1981: The Winning Books," *Eternity*, December 1981; George M. Marsden, *Fundamentalism and American Culture* (Oxford: Oxford University Press, 2006).

32. George M. Marsden, interview, *Wittenburg Door*, December 1982/January 1983, 21. Yet the problems did not stop there. While Jerry Falwell identified as a Fundamentalist, Bob Jones ousted him as only a pseudo-Fundamentalist (23).

33. "I Was a Teenage Fundamentalist," *Wittenburg Door*, December 1982/January 1983.

34. Smidt, "Evangelicals within Contemporary American Politics," 603.

35. Thomas, interview, *Wittenburg Door*, December 1983/January 1984, 24–25.

36. Tim LaHaye, interview, *Wittenburg Door*, June/July 1980, 9.

37. LaHaye, 11. An interview with Paul Simon himself was printed in the following pages. Even though the congressman was clearly not favored by the Moral Majority, Simon agreed with it in one regard: "it [the Moral Majority] is right in sensing that the Christian mandate is to get involved." But he tempered this sentiment: "It is wrong in jumping to quick, easy solutions and it is wrong on the issues with which it judges people." Paul Simon, interview, *Wittenburg Door*, June/July 1980, 19.

38. Neuhaus, "Who, Now, Will Shape the Meaning of America?," 17. Neuhaus does not neatly align with either the Left or the Right. He was active in the anti-Vietnam movement but became disillusioned with liberal politics. The confusion about him was captured by the *Wittenburg Door*: "You probably think we interviewed Richard John Neuhaus because he's a scholar, or because he's a liberal—well, he's not really a liberal, he's actually very conservative on some issues, but on the other hand, lots of liberals don't like him, but, then, neither do a lot of conservatives." Neuhaus, interview, *Wittenburg Door*, February/March 1985, 17. Neuhaus continued to defy categorization: in the 1990s, he converted to Catholicism. Subsequently, he became an unofficial adviser to President George W. Bush and was voted by *Time* magazine among the twenty-five most influential Evangelicals. "Richard John Neuhaus," *Time*, February 7, 2005.

39. Ben Patterson, "John Wayne Lives," editorial, *Wittenburg Door*, June/July 1980, 4. John Wayne was the stage name of actor Marion Mitchell Morrison (1907–79), who was famous for playing the hero in Westerns.

40. Martin E. Marty warned in 1980 that "humanism" would be the watchword and target of the New Christian Right. Marty, "Points to Consider about the New Christian Right Wing." During the 1980s, "secular humanism" became a catchall for perceived social ills.

41. Patterson, "John Wayne Lives," 4.

42. On the history of evangelical politics, see Matthew Avery Sutton, *American Apocalypse: A History of Modern Evangelicalism* (Cambridge, MA: Belknap Press of Harvard University Press, 2017); Kevin M. Kruse, *One Nation under God: How Corporate America Invented Christian America* (New York: Basic Books, 2016). And see chapter 2.

43. Miller, "Shall We Join the 'New Christian Crusade'?"

44. "Crusaders," letters to the editor, *Moody Monthly*, November 1980, 5. Quoted letters are from, respectively, Warren Wiersbe, Tom Friez, Merle T. Huffmaster, Jack Dortignac, Olive M. Strout, Brenda Long, and Jack Dortignac.

45. Sociologist James L. Guth reported that "organizers and scholars alike identify several limits to pastoral leadership in the political kingdom," highlighting the idea that pastors should be primarily concerned with matters of salvation. However, in his study of political activism among Southern Baptist clergy, he somewhat refuted these claims, showing that clergy became "steadily more interested and psychologically engaged in political life." Guth, "The Bully Pulpit: Southern Baptist Clergy and Political Activism, 1980-92," in Green et al., *Religion and the Culture Wars*, 146, 168. Evangelical spokespersons like Charles W. Colson continued to warn activists against confusing their priorities by becoming entangled in politics. Colson, *Kingdoms in Conflict* (Grand Rapids, MI: Zondervan, 1987).

46. Erwin W. Lutzer, "The Preacher and Politics," From Pastor to Pastor, *Moody Monthly*, June 1983, 101.

47. Lutzer, 103.

48. This picture painted by the media was the starting point for sociologists Stephen D. Johnson and Joseph B. Tamney to investigate the influence of the New Christian Right on the election of 1980 in Muncie, Indiana. They found that New Christian Right mobilizing had made no difference. Johnson and Tamney, "The Christian Right and the 1980 Presidential Election," *Journal for the Scientific Study of Religion* 21, no. 2 (1982): 123-31.

49. H. W. Brands, *American Dreams: The United States since 1945* (New York: Penguin Books, 2010), 223.

50. Bruce Buursma, "Evangelicals Give Reagan a 'Non-Partisan' Stump," *Christianity Today*, September 19, 1980, 50 (including Reagan quote).

51. Jim Wallis and Wes Michaelson, "The Plan to Save America," *Sojourners*, April 1976.

52. Patterson, "John Wayne Lives," 4.

53. See, for example, James L. Guth, *The Bully Pulpit: The Politics of Protestant Clergy* (Lawrence: University Press of Kansas, 1997).

54. James Davison Hunter, *Culture Wars: The Struggle to Define America* (New York: Basic Books, 1991).

55. A similar trend has been observed by sociologist Robert Wuthnow; see his *After Heaven: Spirituality in America since the 1950s* (Berkeley: University of California Press, 1998). Some of those who have questioned his thesis include: Alan Wolfe, *One Nation, After All: What Middle-Class Americans Really Think about God, Country, Family, Racism, Welfare, Immigration, Homosexuality, Work, the Right, the Left, and Each Other* (New York: Penguin Books, 1999); Nancy J. Davis and Robert V. Robinson, "Religious Orthodoxy: An Army without Foot Soldiers?," *Journal for the Scientific Study of Religion* 35, no. 3 (1996): 249–51; Dale McConkey, "Whither Hunter's Culture War? Shifts in Evangelical Morality, 1988–1998," *Sociology of Religion* 62, no. 2 (2001): 149–74.

56. Irene Taviss Thomson, *Culture Wars and Enduring American Dilemmas* (Ann Arbor: University of Michigan Press, 2010), 1.

57. This is a common theme in literature. See, for example, Stephen Bates, *God's Own Country: Religion and Politics in the USA* (London: Hodder, 2008); Sara Diamond, *Not by Politics Alone: The Enduring Influence of the Christian Right* (New York: Guilford Press, 1998); Charles March, *Wayward Christian Soldiers: Freeing the Gospel from Political Captivity* (Oxford: Oxford University Press, 2007); Earl Shorris, *The Politics of Heaven: America in Fearful Times* (New York: W. W. Norton, 2007).

58. Mayer, "A Tide of Born Again Politics," 29.

59. Joseph F. Sullivan, "Falwell Warns Jersey Liberals at Capitol Rally," *New York Times*, November 11, 1980.

60. Diamond, *Not by Politics Alone*, 1,

61. James Davison Hunter, "Religion and Political Civility: The Coming Generation of Evangelicals," *Journal for the Scientific Study of Religion* 23, no. 4 (1984): 375.

62. Hunter, 376. Alan Wolfe wrote that "in every aspect of the religious life, American faith has met American culture—and American culture triumphed." Wolfe, *The Transformation of American Religion: How We Actually Live Our Faith* (Chicago: University of Chicago Press, 2003), 3. Christian Smith found that while Evangelicals were more conservative than the general population, their practices matched those of average Americans. Smith, *Christian America? What Evangelicals Really Want* (Berkeley: University of California Press, 2000).

63. John W. Whitehead, *The Second American Revolution*. Elgin, IL: D. C. Cook Publications, 1982.

64. John W. Whitehead, "The Secularizing of America," *Moody Monthly*, July 1981, 21; and see Whitehead, *The Second American Revolution* (Elgin, IL: D. C. Cook, 1982). Michael Lienesch, who analyzed the thought of New Christian Right writers via their popular book publications, pointed to the dualistic nature of arguments like this one from Whitehead as their most significant characteristic: "These writers see the polity in dualistic terms, as a place of good and evil, right and wrong, allies and enemies." Lienesch, *Redeeming America*, 193.

65. Robert T. Handy, *A Christian America: Protestant Hopes and Historical Realities*, 2nd ed. (New York: Oxford University Press, 1984), 204.

66. Handy, 208 ("biblical morality" is quoted from Carl F. H. Henry).
67. See, for example, Lienesch, *Redeeming America*, 11.
68. Wilcox and Robinson, *Onward Christian Soldiers?*, 9.
69. For an analysis of the New Christian Right vision of Christian America, see Lienesch, *Redeeming America*, 139-94.
70. Neuhaus, "Who, Now, Will Shape the Meaning of America?," 17-18.
71. Kenneth S. Kantzer, editor's note, *Christianity Today*, March 19, 1982, 4.
72. "Contributing Editors," *Christianity Today*, September 2, 1983. Hatch was still listed as contributing editor in 1994 but was not listed anymore as of 2010. Noll was listed as contributing editor until the July/August 2013 issue. After that, the rubric "contributing editor" was dropped from the published information. For an assessment of self-identified Evangelical historians, see Maxie B. Burch, *The Evangelical Historians: The Historiography of George Marsden, Nathan Hatch, and Mark Noll* (Lanham, MD: University Press of America, 1996).
73. George Marsden, letter to Stephen Board of *Eternity*, October 18, 1982, Mark A. Noll papers (SC-116), series 2, box 4, folder 2, Buswell Library Special Collections, Wheaton College, Wheaton, IL. The referenced texts include Francis A. Schaeffer, *A Christian Manifesto* (Westchester, IL: Crossway Books, 1981); Franky Schaeffer, *A Time for Anger: The Myth of Neutrality* (Westchester, IL: Crossway Books, 1982); and Whitehead, *The Second American Revolution*. For an analysis of these books in the context of New Christian Right writing on the state, see Lienesch, *Redeeming America*, 139-94. A discussion and excerpt from *A Christian Manifesto* were printed, for example, in *Moody Monthly*: McCandlish Phillips, "Francis Schaeffer: The Man behind the Manifesto," *Moody Monthly*, January 1982; Francis A. Schaeffer, "A Christian Manifesto," *Moody Monthly*, January 1982.
74. William J. Peterson and Stephen Board, letter to George Marsden, November 2, 1982, Mark A. Noll papers (SC-116), series 2, box 4, folder 2.
75. George M. Marsden, "Quest for a Christian America," *Eternity*, May 1983.
76. Foretaste, *Eternity*, May 1983, 1; and see John W. Whitehead, "A Response," *Eternity*, May 1983.
77. Marsden, "Quest for a Christian America," 19.
78. Marsden, 20.
79. Marsden, 22.
80. Whitehead, "A Response," 22.
81. "Friendly Persuasion," letters to the editor, *Eternity*, July/August 1983. For information on the National Reform Association and the *Christian Statesman* up to 1920, see Gaines M. Foster, *Moral Reconstruction: Christian Lobbyists and the Federal Legislation of Morality, 1865-1920* (Chapel Hill: University of North Carolina Press, 2002). In the introduction, Foster links the National Reform Association to the New Christian Right in the late 1970s. The *Christian Statesman* appears to have gone defunct around 2008.
82. Carl F. H. Henry, "Friendly Persuasion," letter to the editor, *Eternity*, July/

August 1983, 48. R. J. Rushdoony was a Calvinist theologian and philosopher and an influential theorist for the New Christian Right. He developed a school of thought known as Reconstructionism. His writings were judged to be racist and anti-Semitic and advocated the establishment of a theocracy. See Balmer, *Encyclopedia of Evangelicalism*, s.v. "Rushdoony, Rousas John." Henry apparently mentioned the name Rushdoony to point out the sources from which New Christian Right writers were drawing.

83. "No Consensus," letters to the editor, *Eternity*, September 1983, 87.

84. See, for example, Nathan O. Hatch, "Yesterday: The Key That Unlocks Today," *Christianity Today*, August 5, 1983; George M. Marsden, "Current Religious Thought: America's 'Good Old Days,'" *Christianity Today*, November 25, 1983; Mark A. Noll, "When 'Infidels' Run for Office," *Christianity Today*, October 5, 1984; Geoffrey W. Bromiley, "Church Members First, Citizens Second," *Christianity Today*, May 16, 1986; Noll, "Is This Land God's Land?," editorial, *Christianity Today*, July 11, 1986; Noll, "The Constitution at 200: Should Christians Join the Celebration?," *Christianity Today*, July 10, 1987; Daniel Ritchie, "Created Equal," *Eternity*, November 1985.

85. Mark Noll, letter to Lane Dennis, September 7, 1982, Mark A. Noll papers (SC-116), series 2, box 4, folder 2.

86. Mark A. Noll, Nathan O. Hatch, and George M. Marsden, *The Search for Christian America* (Westchester, IL: Crossway Books, 1983).

87. James A. Keim, "The Search for a Christian America," book review, *Eternity*, April 1984, 49–50; "The Winning List," *Eternity*, December 1984. First and second place in the *Eternity* list went to Charles W. Colson's *Loving God* and *Eerdmans' Handbook to Christianity in America*, edited by Noll, Hatch, and Marsden, along with David F. Wells and John D. Woodbridge.

88. Noll, Hatch, and Marsden, *The Search for Christian America*, 26, 22.

89. Letters indicate that the Evangelical historians were shocked by the sweeping, sometimes erroneous historical claims made by Francis A. Schaeffer; his son, Franky Schaeffer; and associates like John Whitehead. See, for example, Mark Noll, letter to Lane Dennis, September 7, 1982, and George Marsden, letter to Stephen Board, *Eternity*, October 18, 1982, both in Mark A. Noll papers (SC-116), series 2, box 4, folder 2. Yet the historians were also keen to maintain a good relationship with the much esteemed Francis Schaeffer. They acknowledged the Schaeffers in their book, pointing out that while the "Schaeffers will not agree with everything here," their opinions had been taken to heart and "this book has benefited from an exchange of correspondence with Francis and Franky Schaeffer." Noll, Hatch, and Marsden, *The Search for Christian America*, 12. Maxie B. Burch also analyzed the correspondence between Noll, Marsden, and Francis Schaeffer from November 1982 to July 1983, discussing specifically the tension between the opposing roles of evangelist and historian on the one hand, and Marsden and Noll's self-identification as Evangelical historians on the other. Burch, *The Evangelical Historians*, 56–83.

90. Noll, Hatch, and Marsden, *The Search for Christian America*, 22-23.

91. William J. Peterson and Stephen Board, letter to George Marsden, November 2, 1982, Mark A. Noll Papers (SC-116), series 2, box 4, folder 2.

92. Noll, Hatch, and Marsden, *The Search for Christian America*, 17-18.

93. Francis A. Schaeffer, *How Should We Then Live? The Rise and Decline of Western Thought and Culture* (Old Tappan, NJ: Revell, 1976), 202, 71-72.

94. Francis A. Schaeffer, *The God Who Is There* (Downers Grove, IL: InterVarsity Press, 1968), 15, 17.

95. Schaeffer, *How Should We Then Live?*, 201-2.

96. Francis Schaeffer, "How Should We Then Live?," interview, *Christianity Today*, October 8, 1976, 25.

97. Tim LaHaye, *The Battle for the Mind* (Old Tappan, NJ: Revell, 1980), 30.

98. Paul Jensen, "Humanism's Indigestion: Plop and Fizz," *Eternity*, April 1981, 46.

99. Jensen, 47.

100. "What the Humanists Believe," *Moody Monthly*, September 1980.

101. Nancy B. Barcus and Dick Bohrer, "The Humanist Builds His House upon the Sand," *Moody Monthly*, September 1980.

102. Kantzer, "The 'Separation' of Church and State?," 10.

103. Richard John Neuhaus, *The Naked Public Square: Religion and Democracy in America* (Grand Rapids, MI: Eerdmans, 1984). Neuhaus was active in the anti-Vietnam and pro-life movements. He became ordained as a Catholic priest in 1990, and he also founded the ecumenical magazine *First Things*. He worked on fostering relations with other conservative believers, as evidenced by *Evangelicals and Catholics Together* (Nashville, TN: Thomas Nelson, 1994), which he coedited with Charles W. Colson. He died in 2009. See Neuhaus, "How I Became the Catholic I Was," *First Things* 22 (2002): 14-20.

104. Richard John Neuhaus, "The Naked Public Square," *Christianity Today*, October 5, 1984, 32.

105. "Books of the Year 1984," *Eternity*, December 1984, 42; and see "The Winning List," *Eternity*.

106. Richard John Neuhaus, interview, *Wittenburg Door*, February/March 1985, 19.

107. Neuhaus, "The Naked Public Square," 31-32.

108. Richard John Neuhaus, "Christianity and Pluralism in America," interview, *Touchstone*, September 1991, 15.

109. Neuhaus, "The Naked Public Square," 29.

110. Neuhaus, "Christianity and Pluralism in America," 15.

111. Mark A. Noll, "Counterstrike at Secularized Religion," *Eternity*, May 1985, 39. The Hartford Appeal was written in 1975 at the Hartford Seminary Foundation in Hartford, Connecticut. The appeal, which was issued by theologians of different religious backgrounds, challenged thirteen trends in contemporary religion and society. See "The Hartford Appeal," *Eternity*, May 1985.

112. Richard John Neuhaus, "Ring of Truth," *Eternity*, May 1985. Noll pointed out that by no means everyone who signed the Hartford Appeal adapted a con-

servative political outlook or underwent a similar transformation as Neuhaus. Noll, "Counterstrike at Secularized Religion."

113. Horn, "How Freedom of Thought Is Smothered in America," 12 (emphasis in original).

114. William E. Dannemeyer, "Who Turned the First Amendment Upside-Down?," *Christianity Today*, June 18, 1982, 34.

115. Kantzer, "The 'Separation' of Church and State?," 10.

116. The last *Christianity Today* issue published under Kantzer's editorship was October 22, 1984. Kantzer handed over the reins to Gilbert Beers. Kenneth S. Kantzer, editor's note, *Christianity Today*, October 22, 1982; "Introducing: *CT*'s Fourth Editor," *Christianity Today*, October 22, 1982.

117. "Why We Need Christian Think Tanks," editorial, *Christianity Today*, March 15, 1985, 14–15.

118. Christianity Today Institute, "The Christian as Citizen," *Christianity Today*, April 19, 1985.

119. Henry, "Church and State: Why the Marriage Must Be Saved," 13.

120. Tom Minnery, "Christianity Today Institute Focuses Evangelical Thought on the Christian as Citizen," *Christianity Today*, April 5, 1985, 48.

121. Charles W. Colson, "A View from the Evangelical Center," interview, *Christianity Today*, April 5, 1985, 25.

122. Jim Wallis, "A View from the Evangelical Left," interview, *Christianity Today*, April 5, 1985, 26.

123. Jerry Falwell, "A View from Fundamentalism," interview, *Christianity Today*, April 5, 1985.

124. Wallis, "A View from the Evangelical Left."

125. Colson, "A View from the Evangelical Center," 24.

126. Kenneth S. Kantzer, "The Issue at Hand: 'The Christian as Citizen,'" *Christianity Today*, April 5, 1985, 2.

127. J. I. Packer, "How to Recognize a Christian Citizen," *Christianity Today*, April 5, 1985.

128. The two-kingdom doctrine was introduced by Martin Luther and became part of Protestant thinking more generally. See, for example, Harold J. Berman, "Law and Religion in the West," in *The Encyclopedia of Religion*, ed. Mircea Eliade, vol. 8 (New York: Macmillan, 1987), 472–75; David VanDrunen, "The Two Kingdoms Doctrine and the Relationship of Church and State in the Early Reformed Tradition," *Journal of Church and State* 49, no. 4 (2007): 743–63.

129. Packer, "How to Recognize a Christian Citizen," 5.

130. Packer, 6. All three positions (relativism, absolutism, and imperialist biblicism) were regularly criticized in Evangelical magazines. In the so-called Fundamentalist-Modernist Controversy of the 1920s and 1930s, charges of relativism were vehemently lobbed at modernist or liberal Protestants, who were accused of being beguiled by science and compromising their faith. Conversely, charges of absolutism were lobbed at Fundamentalists, who were accused of withdrawing from society in the wake of the controversy and adapting an increas-

ingly militant, separatist style. According to Evangelical historiography, a younger generation—soon to be called Evangelical—had recognized this position as folly because self-imposed exile meant that Christians were inefficient in society. The final accusation, imperialist biblicism, was leveled against overzealous leaders of the New Christian Right, who adopted an absolutist stance and black-and-white thinking. For a historical perspective on these arguments, see Sutton, *American Apocalypse*. In an opinion piece in *Moody Monthly*, Leith C. Anderson, a pastor from Minnesota, summarized the first two stances while critiquing the third. Debating how much separation from society was biblical, he criticized both the absolutist withdrawal of ascetics and the licentiousness of libertarians who appropriated biblical teachings however they saw fit. Anderson, "Separation? Who Needs It?," *Moody Monthly*, May 1982.

131. Packer, "How to Recognize a Christian Citizen," 6.
132. Henry, "Church and State: Why the Marriage Must Be Saved," 10.
133. Henry, 11.
134. In 1982, *Moody Monthly* printed a three-part series of articles from Washington correspondent Martin Mawyer asking the question, "are we losing our religious freedoms?" Late in 1983, the magazine took up the issue again, suggesting that religious freedoms, in many instances, were already lost. The November 1983 cover illustration showed a man holding an open Bible and pointing with his index finger. But a hand, sleeved in the US flag, was holding his mouth shut. Prominent New Christian Right leaders Cal Thomas and John Whitehead also contributed articles to this issue. See Mawyer, "Are We Losing Our Religious Freedoms?" The November 1983 issue included the following articles: Cal Thomas, "The Pursuit of Censorship"; Lynn R. Buzzard and Samuel E. Ericsson, "Defining Our Religious Freedom," part 1 (the second part appeared in the December issue); John W. Whitehead, "Public Education Flunks Free Speech"; and Charles E. Grassley, "A Voice in the Senate," interview.
135. Henry, "Church and State: Why the Marriage Must Be Saved," 13.
136. Stephen V. Monsma, "Windows and Doors in the Wall of Separation," *Christianity Today*, April 5, 1985. The nature of the so-called wall of separation was a much discussed theme in Evangelical magazines. In one editorial in *Christianity Today*, senior editor Terry Muck affirmed a common sentiment: "We have failed to distinguish between questions of church and state on the one hand, and questions of religion and politics on the other. We treat them as if they are the same, and in so doing put ourselves in an impossible position. Christians must affirm the separation of church and state, but not the separation of the more loosely defined attitudes and values of religion and politics." Muck, "The Wall That Never Was," editorial, *Christianity Today*, July 10, 1987, 16.
137. Monsma, "Windows and Doors in the Wall of Separation," 15.
138. Monsma, 17–18. Civil disobedience was also the theme of a long article printed in *Eternity* in January 1987: Lynn R. Buzzard, "Civil Disobedience," *Eternity*, January 1987.
139. Monsma, "Windows and Doors in the Wall of Separation," 19.

140. David L. McKenna, "A Political Strategy for the Local Church," *Christianity Today*, April 5, 1985, 19.
141. McKenna, 20.
142. For the two kingdoms, see, for example, Kenneth S. Kantzer, "Summing Up: An Evangelical View of Church and State," *Christianity Today*, April 5, 1985.
143. On the occasion of the bicentennial of the Constitution, Mark A. Noll made this point explicitly: "To recognize that the Constitution, in part, fit well with Christian beliefs is not to claim that a special divine miracle lay behind its ratification. It is rather to say that the perceptions of believers and the political experience of Americans, many of whom were not professed Christians, led the Constitution to principles conforming roughly to general Christian principles. This recognition should be an occasion, not for congratulating the United States on its special status under God, but for praising him that in his general providence a full measure of political wisdom informed the founding of the United States." Noll, "The Constitution at 200," 19.
144. Multiple Evangelical writers made the claim for patriotism. Evangelical historian Mark A. Noll set the parameters for Evangelical patriotism in his *Christianity Today* editorial "Is This Land God's Land?" Similarly, Charles W. Colson found that Christians could be patriotic: Colson, "On Waving Flags and Washing Feet," *Eternity*, July 1986. In *Moody Monthly*, Geoff Gorsuch argued that "patriotism, like politics, is neither good nor evil." Accordingly, the question was not whether one was patriotic but "what kind of patriot are you?" Gorsuch, "Patriotism to One Kingdom under God," *Moody Monthly*, October 1984.
145. Packer, "How to Recognize a Christian Citizen," 8.
146. In Matthew 13, Christians are described as "salt of the earth," a metaphor readily used in Evangelical writings. See, for example, McKenna, "A Political Strategy for the Local Church."
147. On Pat Robertson, see Balmer, *Encyclopedia of Evangelicalism*, "Robertson, Marion G(ordon) 'Pat.'" On Robertson and his organization, the Christian Coalition, see Justin Watson, *The Christian Coalition: Dreams of Restoration, Demands for Recognition* (New York: St. Martin's Press, 1997).
148. In September 1986, Pat Robertson announced that he would only run for president if three million people pledged to support his candidacy through money and activism. Beth Spring, "One Step Closer to a Bid for the Oval Office," *Christianity Today*, October 17, 1986. In February 1987, an "Americans for Robertson" committee took up work and eventually collected about $7 million in campaign contributions, a sum second only to the funds raised by the main Republican presidential contender, George H. W. Bush. McKendree R. Langeley, "Robertson's Run: Going for It?," *Eternity*, September 1987.
149. While his audience was largely Pentecostal, Pat Robertson himself is notoriously hard to categorize. His theology and preaching can be described as Pentecostal, but he also remained a member of the Southern Baptist Convention, which generally deprecates such Pentecostal gifts as speaking in tongues. From the mid-1970s onward, he called himself "Spirit-filled evangelical," and by

the 1990s he simply called himself "evangelical." Balmer, *Encyclopedia of Evangelicalism*, s.v. "Robertson, Marion G(ordon) 'Pat.'"

150. The misconduct of televangelist Jim Bakker made the cover of *Newsweek* twice in 1987: Larry Martz et al., "God and Power," *Newsweek*, April 6, 1987; Russell Watson et al., "Heaven Can Wait," *Newsweek*, June 8, 1987.

151. One report, for example, stated that "Robertson does not monopolize the evangelical vote." Kim A. Lawton, "Iowa Christians and the Race for the Oval Office," *Christianity Today*, January 15, 1988, 50. And in March 1988, "a poll taken . . . of 101 NAE [National Association of Evangelicals] board members found Robertson running last as their preferred Republican nominee, while Vice President George Bush placed first." "Pat's Big Surprise: The Army Is Still Invisible," *Christianity Today*, April 8, 1988, 44. On the label "invisible army" and those who supported the Robertson campaign, see John C. Green, "A Look at the 'Invisible Army': Pat Robertson's 1988 Activist Corps," in Green et al., *Religion and the Culture Wars*, 44–61. On the $5.4 million sought by Roberts, see McKendree R. Langeley, "Robertson's Run: Going for It?," *Eternity*, September 1987.

152. Beth Spring, "Pat Robertson for President?" *Christianity Today*, November 8, 1985.

153. Spring, 48.

154. Joseph Bayly, "On Moral Camelots and Moral Majorities," *Eternity*, November 1985, 96.

155. See, for example, "Debate: Should Pat Robertson Run for President?," *Christianity Today*, September 5, 1986.

156. Charles W. Colson, "Dear Pat: Winning Isn't Everything," *Christianity Today*, November 21, 1986, 60.

157. Colson, 60.

158. Colson, 60.

159. "The Jim Bakker Affair," *Christianity Today*, April 17, 1987.

160. "A Crackdown at PTL," *Christianity Today*, June 12, 1987.

161. Balmer, *Encyclopedia of Evangelicalism*, s.v. "Bakker, James Orsen 'Jim.'"

162. Langeley, "Robertson's Run: Going for It?," 13. *Christianity Today* also reported that televangelists across the board had suffered from the scandal, including Falwell and presidential aspirant Robertson. "A Crackdown at PTL," *Christianity Today*.

163. "The Jim Bakker Affair," *Christianity Today*.

164. "Dropping the Reins at PTL," *Christianity Today*, November 6, 1987.

165. Don McCrory, "Editor's Ink: Year of the Scandal?," *Eternity*, September 1987, 4 (emphasis in original).

166. *Christianity Today* dedicated its November 20, 1987, issue to the question of how to deal with fallen leaders. Articles included Kenneth S. Kantzer, "The Road to Restoration"; and David Augsburger, "The Private Lives of Public Leaders."

167. See, for example, "Pat's Big Surprise: The Army Is Still Invisible," *Christianity Today*; Cal Thomas, "Commentary: No Message from Super Tuesday,"

Eternity, May 1988. In a presidential year, Super Tuesday refers to the Tuesday—usually in February or March—on which the most states hold primary elections, selecting delegates for the national conventions. The national convention is the occasion used by political parties to nominate their candidate for the presidential election. Super Tuesday is thus a test run for presidential aspirants and a good indication of who has a chance to win their party's nomination.

168. Beth Spring, "Christian in the Public Square: Time to Rethink?," *Christianity Today*, November 21, 1986, 35. Also, *Eternity* from September 1987 to September 1988 printed contributions from twelve well-known Evangelical spokespersons, spelling out different aspects of an Evangelical vision of political involvement.

169. Richard Cizik, "Tweedledum and Tweedledee," *Eternity*, October 1988. New Christian Right leaders, on the other hand, eventually pooled their resources in support of George H. W. Bush and the Republican Party. Their smear tactics against Dukakis were lambasted in *Sojourners* magazine. See, for example, Vicki Kemper, "Direct-Mail Politics of the Religious Right," *Sojourners*, January 1989.

170. "Pat's Big Surprise: The Army Is Still Invisible," *Christianity Today*. Evangelical author James W. Skillen had guest contributions in both *Moody Monthly* and *Eternity* just before the presidential election. He pointed out that neither party fully represented his Evangelical position and that Evangelicals needed to continue developing their public philosophy. Skillen, "Commentary: Politics beyond the Party Lines," *Eternity*, October 1988; Skillen, "Opinion: Getting Pat Political Pragmatism," *Moody Monthly*, November 1988.

171. See, for example, Carl F. H. Henry, "Lost Momentum," interview by Beth Spring, *Christianity Today*, September 4, 1987; Kim A. Lawton, "Whatever Happened to the Religious Right?," *Christianity Today*, December 15, 1989.

172. James L. Sauer, "Robertson's Date with Destiny," book review, *Christianity Today*, March 6, 1987, 38; Pat Robertson, *America's Date with Destiny* (Nashville, TN: Thomas Nelson, 1986).

173. Rick McKinniss, "Let Christian America Rest in Peace," *Christianity Today*, February 5, 1988, 10.

174. Noll, "Is This Land God's Land?," 14.

175. Henry, "Lost Momentum," 30.

176. Lienesch, *Redeeming America*, 139.

177. Muck, "The Wall That Never Was," 17.

178. Noll, "The Constitution at 200," 23.

179. Muck, "The Wall That Never Was," 17.

180. Henry, "Lost Momentum," 31.

181. Colson, "So Much for Our 'Great Awakening,'" 72.

182. McKinniss, "Let Christian America Rest in Peace," 10 (emphasis in original).

Chapter 6

1. Jerry B. Jenkins, "The Unborn: Why the Right to Life," *Moody Monthly*, May 1980, 11. The magazine's "abortion issue" was advertised in *Moody Monthly* as

well as in other Evangelical magazines, for example: *Moody Monthly*, April 1980; *Eternity*, April and May 1980; *Christianity Today*, April 18, 1980.

2. C. Everett Koop and Dick Bohrer, "Deception-on-Demand," *Moody Monthly*, May 1980.

3. See, for example, J. C. J. Metford, ed., *Dictionary of Christian Lore and Legend* (London: Thames and Hudson, 1983), s.v. "rose."

4. On the abortion controversy, see, for example, Mark A. Graber, *Rethinking Abortion: Equal Choice, the Constitution, and Reproductive Politics* (Princeton, NJ: Princeton University Press, 1996); Karen O'Connor, *No Neutral Ground? Abortion Politics in an Age of Absolutes* (Boulder, CO: Westview Press, 1996).

5. On the WHCF, see, for example, J. Brooks Flippen, *Jimmy Carter, the Politics of Family, and the Rise of the Religious Right* (Athens: University of Georgia Press, 2011), 245-73; Leo P. Ribuffo, "Family Policy Past as Prologue: Jimmy Carter, the White House Conference on Families, and the Mobilization of the New Christian Right," *Review of Policy Research* 23, no. 2 (2006): 311-37. On "family values," see, for example, Seth Dowland, "'Family Values' and the Formation of a Christian Right Agenda," *Church History* 78, no. 3 (2009): 606-31; Michael Lienesch, *Redeeming America: Piety and Politics in the New Christian Right* (Chapel Hill: University of North Carolina Press, 1993), esp. 52-93; Ruth Murray Brown, *For a "Christian America": A History of the Religious Right* (Amherst, NY: Prometheus Books, 2002). On Reagan's use of language, see, for example, Robert C. Rowland and John M. Jones, "'Until Next Week': The Saturday Radio Addresses of Ronald Reagan," *Presidential Studies Quarterly* 32, no. 1 (2002): 84-110. One classic study of Reagan's rhetoric described it as "gospel" that morally appealed to the US people. Paul D. Erickson, *Reagan Speaks: The Making of an American Myth* (New York: New York University Press, 1985).

6. For an overview of the "abortion wars," see Rickie Solinger, *Abortion Wars: A Half Century of Struggle: 1950-2000* (Berkeley: University of California Press, 1998).

7. On "embryonic discourse," see John H. Evans, *Contested Reproduction: Genetic Technologies, Religion, and Public Debate* (Chicago: University of Chicago Press, 2010).

8. There is no lack of sociological studies into popular attitudes toward abortion, but only few studies are concerned with religion's polarizing effect in this domain. See John H. Evans, "Polarization in Abortion Attitudes in U.S. Religious Traditions, 1972-1998," *Sociological Forum* 17, no. 3 (2002): 397-422. On the abortion debate: for a secular perspective, see Dorothy E. McBride, *Abortion in the United States: A Reference Handbook* (Santa Barbara, CA: ABC-CLIO, 2008), 249-75; for the religious and moral perspective, see George F. Johnston, *Abortion from the Religious and the Moral Perspective: An Annotated Bibliography* (Westport, CT: Praeger, 2003).

9. Evans, "Polarization in Abortion Attitudes in U.S. Religious Traditions," 406. The four groups investigated were Catholics, Black Protestants, mainline Prot-

estants, and evangelical Protestants. This last category is broader in sociological analyses than is the group of self-identified Evangelical spokespersons discussed in my study.

10. John H. Evans and Kathy Hudson, "Religion and Reproductive Genetics: Beyond Views of Embryonic Life?," *Journal for the Scientific Study of Religion* 46, no. 4 (2007): 567.

11. Evans, *Contested Reproduction*, 57.

12. John P. Hoffmann and Sherrie Mills Johnson, "Attitudes toward Abortion among Religious Traditions in the United States: Change or Continuity?," *Sociology of Religion* 66, no. 2 (2005): 165.

13. The questions referring to abortion for elective reasons were "whether a woman be allowed to obtain a legal abortion if 1) she is unmarried and does not want to marry the father of the child; 2) the family has a very low income and cannot afford any more children; 3) she is married and does not want any more children." The questions referring to abortion for traumatic reasons were "whether a woman be allowed to obtain a legal abortion if . . . 4) she became pregnant as the result of rape; 5) the woman's health is seriously endangered by the pregnancy; 6) or there is a strong chance of a serious defect in the baby." Hoffmann and Johnson, 169.

14. Hoffmann and Johnson, 167. In a 1992 study focused not on religious groups but on society more generally, sociologists Elisabeth A. Cook, Ted G. Jelen, and Clyde Wilcox found that many people in the United States favored legalized abortion for traumatic circumstances. Cook, Jelen, and Wilcox, *Between Two Absolutes: Public Opinion and the Politics of Abortion* (Boulder, CO: Westview Press, 1992).

15. Evans and Hudson, "Religion and Reproductive Genetics," 575; and see Evans, *Contested Reproduction*, 56–68.

16. Treating *Roe v. Wade* and *Doe v. Bolton* as one case, the US Supreme Court legalized abortion by deciding that the right to privacy was applicable to a woman's decision to have an abortion. It handed down guidelines to the states that prohibited restrictions on abortion before the third trimester of pregnancy. States could (but did not need to) regulate and restrict abortions during the third trimester, except when doing so risked a mother's life. See, for example, McBride, *Abortion in the United States*, 19–20. Norma McCorvey, the Roe of the *Roe v. Wade* case, later converted to Catholicism and worked for the antiabortion organization Operation Rescue in the 1990s (McBride, 150). Even so, McCorvey confessed on her deathbed that she never really changed sides; she was paid off by the antiabortion groups. See, for example, Jenny Gross and Aimee Ortiz, "Roe v. Wade Plaintiff Was Paid to Switch Sides, Documentary Says," *New York Times*, May 19, 2020; Monica Hesse, "'Jane Roe,' from Roe v. Wade, Made a Stunning Deathbed Confession. Now What?," *Washington Post*, May 20, 2020.

17. Harold O. J. Brown, "Abortion and the Court," editorial, *Christianity Today*, February 16, 1973, 32. The editorial was not signed, but its author was iden-

tified as Brown, a theologian and an ethicist, by William Martin in his *With God on Our Side: The Rise of the Religious Right in America* (New York: Broadway Books, 1996), 193.

18. Martin, *With God on Our Side*, 193.

19. Kenneth S. Kantzer and Paul Fromer, "Within Our Reach," *Christianity Today*, April 19, 1985, 23. The Southern Baptist Convention's June 1971 resolution was favorably disposed toward abortion, but so was, for example, the United Methodist Church's 1972 "Statement of Social Principles" and the National Association of Evangelicals' 1971 statement on abortion. See, for example, Linda Greenhouse and Reva B. Siegel, *Before Roe v. Wade: Voices That Shaped the Abortion Debate before the Supreme Court's Ruling* (New Haven, CT: Yale Law School, 2012), 70–73; Nancy T. Ammerman, *Baptist Battles: Social Change and Religious Conflict in the Southern Baptist Convention* (New Brunswick, NJ: Rutgers University Press, 1990).

20. *Eternity*'s 1971 issue on abortion demonstrated a wide range of opinions. It included a summary of views on abortion throughout church history written by Klaas Runia, as well as a collage of opinions on abortion from different Evangelical spokespersons. Evangelical feminist Nancy Hardesty asked what the Bible had to say about abortion, concluding that (1) all life was sacred; (2) according to information and Evangelical ethical discussions currently available, abortions could be justified in rare situations; and (3) more study and discussion were needed. Finally, Carl F. H. Henry wrote a "scathing attack on abortion-on-demand." See the following articles, all in *Eternity*'s February 1971 issue: Runia, "Abortion: Can an Evangelical Consensus Be Found?"; "Fetal Life"; Hardesty, "When Does Life Begin?"; Henry, "Is Life Ever Cheap?"

21. For articles, see, for example, Jack W. Cottrell, "Abortion and the Mosaic Lay," *Christianity Today*, March 16, 1973; Harold O. J. Brown, "Abortion and Child Abuse," *Christianity Today*, October 7, 1977.

22. See, for example, Martin, *With God on Our Side*, 156, 193–94. Harold O. J. Brown became an important pro-life activist and wrote a book condemning abortion, *Death before Birth* (Nashville, TN: Thomas Nelson, 1977).

23. Francis A. Schaeffer and C. Everett Koop, *Whatever Happened to the Human Race?* (Old Tappan, NJ: Revell, 1979); Schaeffer and Koop, *Whatever Happened to the Human Race?* (Muskegon, MI: Gospel Films, 1980), VHS video, 250 min.

24. Schaeffer was a Evangelical celebrity, dubbed in *Christianity Today* as "a prophet for our time." Philip D. Yancey, "Francis Schaeffer: A Prophet for Our Time?," *Christianity Today*, March 23, 1979; Francis A. Schaeffer, "Schaeffer on Schaeffer," interview by Philip D. Yancey, 2 parts, *Christianity Today*, March 23 and April 6, 1979. Also, Schaeffer's previous book, *How Should We Then Live? The Rise and Decline of Western Thought and Culture* (Old Tappan, NJ: Revell, 1976), had been named the 1977 book of the year in *Eternity*. "1977: The Top 25 Books," *Eternity*, December 1977. On Schaeffer, see Randall Balmer, *Encyclopedia of Evangelicalism* (Waco, TX: Baylor University Press, 2004), s.v. "Schaef-

fer, Francis A(ugust)"; Barry Hankins, *Francis Schaeffer and the Shaping of Evangelical America* (Grand Rapids, MI: Eerdmans, 2008). Koop was no stranger to Evangelicals either. He was chairman of the board of the Evangelical Foundation, which published the magazine *Eternity*, in 1960, at the time of the death of Donald Grey Barnhouse, the founder of the magazine. See William J. Petersen, "The Magazine That Lived," *Eternity*, May 1975; Balmer, *Encyclopedia of Evangelicalism*, s.v. "Koop, C(harles) Everett."

25. David Singer, "'Whatever Happened to the Human Race?': A Film Preview," *Christianity Today*, August 17, 1979. A full-page ad for the speaking tour was printed, for example, in *Eternity*, May 1979; and *Christianity Today*, September 7 and October 5, 1979. Further ads appeared in *Christianity Today* on May 25, June 29, and July 20, 1979, with a full-page ad for the book appearing on September 7, 1979, and a full-page ad for the film series appearing on February 8, 1980. A subscription ad in *Christianity Today* read: "Give *Christianity Today* to your friends at special Christmas rates. And . . . we'll send you *Whatever Happened to the Human Race?* as our gift." October 5, 1979, 27.

26. Koop was cited in "Fetal Life," *Eternity*, February 1971, and was also interviewed in both *Eternity* and *Christianity Today*: C. Everett Koop, interview, *Eternity*, April 1981; Koop, "Surgeon C. Everett Koop and the Fight for the Newborn," interview by Beth Spring, *Christianity Today*, March 16, 1984. Schaeffer promoted the book *Whatever Happened to the Human Race?* in an addendum to a timely article in *Eternity*: Francis A. Schaeffer, "The Dust of Life," *Eternity*, March 1981.

27. Martin, *With God on Our Side*, 239. Also see James Risen and Judy L. Thomas, *Wrath of Angels: The American Abortion War* (New York: Basic Books, 1998), 121. Even though the importance of Schaeffer and Koop's book has been noted in the literature and Schaeffer remains a revered figure within Evangelical circles, Koop is all but forgotten outside the medical community.

28. Bruce H. Palmer, "Whatever Happened to the Human Race?," book review, *Eternity*, October 1980.

29. Risen and Thomas, *Wrath of Angels*, 122–26; and see Francis A. Schaeffer, *How Should We Then Live?*; Francis A. Schaeffer, *A Christian Manifesto* (Westchester, IL: Crossway Books, 1981).

30. In scientific literature, the term "embryo" refers to a fertilized egg and is applied to the early stages of pregnancy, up to the fourth month. After that, the unborn human organism is referred to as a "fetus." However, the periods when these terms apply are imprecise, and colloquially the terms are used interchangeably. See, for example, McBride, *Abortion in the United States*, 58–59. I use both terms to refer to prenatal life, with no pro-life or pro-choice judgment attached. Koop compared contemporary practices of abortion and infanticide to the Holocaust in, for example, his April 1981 interview in *Eternity*. As surgeon general, Koop muted his rhetoric; see Philip D. Yancey, "The Embattled Career of Dr. Koop," *Christianity Today*, October 20, 1989; Yancey, "A Surgeon General's Warnings," interview by Philip D. Yancey, *Christianity Today*, November 3, 1989. See also Balmer, *Encyclopedia of Evangelicalism*, s.v. "Koop, C(harles) Everett."

31. The "unborn child" is a term found in the sources. Although medical-technical descriptions differentiate between prenatal and born human life with terms like "fetus" as opposed to "infant," no such distinctions are made in general parlance, where expectant mothers often talk of their "baby" or "child" from the moment they know they are pregnant. While I am aware that some pro-life activists deliberately used the term to make an emotive argument, I use it where appropriate and henceforth without quotation marks. For an analysis of antiabortion violence and terrorism, see, for example, Carol Mason, *Killing for Life: The Apocalyptic Narrative of Pro-Life Politics* (Ithaca, NY: Cornell University Press, 2002); Jennifer L. Jefferis, *Armed for Life: The Army of God and Anti-Abortion Terror in the United States* (Santa Barbara, CA: Praeger, 2011). For a sociological analysis of religious-inspired terrorism, see Mark Juergensmeyer, *Terror in the Mind of God: The Global Rise of Religious Violence*, 3rd ed. (Berkeley: University of California Press, 2003), esp. 19–43.

32. George Marsden saw as Schaeffer's intention in his final book, *A Christian Manifesto*, a desire that it be read together with Franky Schaeffer's *A Time for Anger: The Myth of Neutrality* (Westchester, IL: Crossway Books, 1982) and John W. Whitehead's *The Second American Revolution* (Elgin, IL: D. C. Cook, 1982), and he took this as a sign that Francis Schaeffer was making common cause with the New Christian Right. Marsden was worried about this development in the Schaeffers' writings. The editors of *Eternity* were more cautious, pointing out that "the better half of Schaeffer will be carried on not by son Franky but by Os Guinness." (Guinness was a close Schaeffer associate and for a time lived at Schaeffer's L'Abri in Switzerland.) George Marsden, letter to Stephen Board, *Eternity*, October 18, 1982, Mark A. Noll papers (SC-116), series 2, box 4, folder 2, Buswell Library Special Collections, Wheaton College, Wheaton, Illinois; William J. Peterson and Stephen Board, letter to George Marsden, November 2, 1982, Mark A. Noll papers (SC-116), series 2, box 4, folder 2. With *A Time For Anger* and especially his follow-up book, *Bad News for Modern Man: An Agenda for Christian Activism* (Westchester, IL: Crossway Books, 1984), Franky Schaeffer alienated many Evangelicals by sidling up to political conservatives and name-calling fellow Evangelicals (neither philosophy professor Ron Sider nor *Christianity Today* met his standards, and both were subject to derision in the book), making abortion one of the touchstone issues. See Ben Patterson, "The Methods to His Madness," editorial, *Wittenburg Door*, April/May 1984; Franky Schaeffer, interview, *Wittenburg Door*, April/May 1984.

33. President Ronald Reagan appointed Koop as surgeon general, a largely behind-the-scenes position that he transformed into a visible platform. Balmer, *Encyclopedia of Evangelicalism*, s.v. "Koop, C(harles) Everett."

34. Martin, *With God on Our Side*, 238–57.

35. See Yancey, "The Embattled Career of Dr. Koop"; Koop, "A Surgeon General's Warnings."

36. Koop, interview, *Eternity*, 16.

37. Koop and Bohrer, "Deception-on-Demand," 26. In 1982, during Koop's

tenure as surgeon general, the case of "Baby Doe" brought this problematic to the fore of public discussion, as will be discussed later in this chapter.

38. Martin, *With God on Our Side*, 238; "Koop, Charles Everett," *West's Encyclopedia of American Law*, Encyclopedia.com, accessed November 16, 2015, https://www.encyclopedia.com. The Koop papers are archived and digitally available at the US National Library of Medicine: "C. Everett Koop," Profiles in Science, US National Library of Medicine, accessed November 16, 2015, https://profiles.nlm.nih.gov. On the separation of the Dominican conjoined twins Clara and Altagracia Rodriguez, see, for example, C. Everett Koop, "Separating the Siamese Twins: The Surgeon's Story," *Medical World News*, November 8, 1974; "The God-Fearing Surgeon Who Separated the Twins," *People*, October 7, 1974.

39. Koop and Bohrer, "Deception-on-Demand," 27.

40. Koop, interview, *Eternity*, 16–17.

41. Koop and Bohrer, "Deception-on-Demand."

42. Reviewing Koop's career, Philip D. Yancey opened his report with the information that one abortion clinic was "capable of eliminating 10 to 15 lives in the time it took Koop to save 1 or 2." Yancey, "The Embattled Career of Dr. Koop," 16.

43. Schaeffer and Koop, *Whatever Happened to the Human Race?*, video, episode 1.

44. Singer, "Whatever Happened to the Human Race?," 29.

45. Koop and Bohrer, "Deception-on-Demand," 28.

46. Singer, "Whatever Happened to the Human Race?," 28.

47. Palmer, "Whatever Happened to the Human Race?," 92.

48. *Moody Monthly* printed several pages of letters to the editor concerning its issue on abortion: "Shall the Unborn Live?," letters to the editor, *Moody Monthly*, August 1980. The C. Everett Koop papers at Wheaton College also contain a folder with letters in response to the film series and sometimes Koop's answers. "Correspondence, Letters re the film 'Whiter,' 1979–1981," C. Everett Koop papers (SC-58), series 2, folder 8, Buswell Library Special Collections.

49. Jim Wallis, "Coming Together on the Sanctity of Life," *Sojourners*, November 1980, 3; and see "Postmark Letters, Abortion," Sojourners records (SC-23), series 2, folder 1, Buswell Library Special Collections. For the Evangelical Left, a pro-life stance was always more encompassing than an antiabortion position. Senator Mark Hatfield, for example, has been described as taking a "'pro-life' position on abortion, capital-punishment, and poverty." David R. Swartz, *Moral Minority: The Evangelical Left in an Age of Conservatism* (Philadelphia: University of Pennsylvania Press, 2012), 84.

50. Evans, *Contested Reproduction*, 9. That the embryonic life discourse was used heavily (though not exclusively) in religious discussion of genetic research demonstrates how pervasive the discourse was. Evans, 56–68.

51. Rosalind Pollack Petchesky, "Fetal Images: The Power of Visual Culture in the Politics of Reproduction," *Feminist Studies* 13, no. 2 (1987): 268; and see Geraldine Lux Flanagan, *The First Nine Months of Life* (New York: Simon and Schuster, 1962).

52. Celeste Michelle Condit, *Decoding Abortion Rhetoric: Communicating Social Change* (Urbana: University of Illinois Press, 1990), 79–95.

53. Historian and reproductive rights activist Rickie Solinger points out that during the course of the "backlash" against the *Roe v. Wade* decision, the fetus became "enlarged," making the unborn "first-class citizens," while reducing women to "second-class citizens." Solinger, *Pregnancy and Power: A Short History of Reproductive Politics in America* (New York: New York University Press, 2005), 232–36. Of course, there were also Evangelical pro-life organizations, most prominently the Christian Action Council, founded in 1975. For social movement theory applied to evangelical Christian pro-life activism in the United States and Great Britain, see J. Christopher Soper, *Evangelical Christianity in the United States and Great Britain: Religious Beliefs, Political Choices* (New York: New York University Press, 1994), 106–14, 131–56.

54. Koop and Bohrer, "Deception-on-Demand," 24; quoted letters are from Kenneth K. Grenz Wagner and an anonymous writer, respectively, both published in "Shall the Unborn Live?," letters to the editor, *Moody Monthly*, August 1980, 5. Most of the letters were short write-ins that lauded the article; some writers confessed that reading the article led them to now oppose abortion, and a few letters included reports of women who had had abortions and regretted it. However, a few letters disagreed with Koop. None embraced abortion as a good in itself, but one anonymous letter, for example, pointed out that only a man could argue in the way Koop had, and another (from Turret T. Cox) affirmed that abortion should be an option so long as unwanted children were tortured.

55. The letters quoted here are from Kenneth K. Grenz Wagner and Larry W. Leininger, respectively. "Shall the Unborn Live?," letters to the editor, 5.

56. One crisis moment in Koop's career as surgeon general occurred when President Reagan asked him to compile a report on how abortions affected the mental health of the mother. Koop concluded that the available data was inconclusive, but the report was leaked to the press, and soon statements were published claiming that Koop had found abortion not to be detrimental to women's mental health. Even though this was never what the report said and Koop was privately convinced that abortions did have negative effects, he stuck to his report, insisting that so far there was no data to prove that abortions had a negative impact on mental health. This episode upset many pro-lifers, but Koop argued that the fight against abortion was lost if the embryonic life discourse no longer worked. Retrospectively, Koop said in an interview: "I kept telling prolife people such as Harold O. J. Brown, 'You have been magnificent in the fight against abortion by making it a moral issue, with the life of the fetus as the primary concern. Don't shift the grounds of the argument. If you have to shift to the health of the mother and the other side perceives that you've had to shift your base, you've lost it.'" Koop, "A Surgeon General's Warnings," 31.

57. For example, a strip of images indicating the development of a fetus at several stages of the pregnancy accompanied an *Eternity* news report on late-term

abortion. Russell T. Hitt, "Left to Die: When Late-Term Abortions Fail," *Eternity*, March 1985.

58. See, for example, Solinger, *Pregnancy and Power*, 232–36. And for a comparison of cultural notions of personhood, see Beth A. Conklin and Lynn M. Morgan, "Babies, Bodies, and the Production of Personhood in North American and Native Amazonian Societies," *Ethos* 24, no. 4 (1996): 657–94.

59. Petchesky, "Fetal Images," 264, 267. "Personhood" is a controversial philosophical and legal term, often used as argument for citizenship and other legal protections. Political scientist Jean Reith Schroedel, writing in 2000, provided a good overview of the legal status of the fetus across the United States. Schroedel, *Is the Fetus a Person? A Comparison of Policies across the Fifty States* (Ithaca, NY: Cornell University Press, 2000). "Fetal rights" also became a concern in campaigns against smoking and other substance use during pregnancy. See, for example,. Rachel Roth, *Making Women Pay: The Hidden Costs of Fetal Rights* (Ithaca, NY: Cornell University Press, 2000). During his term as surgeon general, Koop started the public campaign against smoking as a matter of "fetal rights." This point upset Evangelicals, who accused him of inconsistency, asking how he could advocate the fetal right to a drug-free environment but not use his position to officially denounce abortion as murder. Yancey, "The Embattled Career of Dr. Koop"; see also Anthony M. Petro, *After the Wrath of God: AIDS, Sexuality, and American Religion* (Oxford: Oxford University Press, 2015), 61–64.

60. Carl Horn, "How Freedom of Thought Is Smothered in America," *Christianity Today*, April 6, 1984, 16; and see Magda Denes, *In Necessity and Sorrow: Life and Death in an Abortion Hospital* (New York: Basic Books, 1976).

61. John R. W. Stott, "Does Life Begin before Birth?," *Christianity Today*, September 5, 1980, 50.

62. Koop and Bohrer, "Deception-on-Demand," 28.

63. Stott, on the other hand, did state this point explicitly: "By week 13, when the pregnancy is only one-third through—and when abortions usually begin—the embryo is completely organized, and a miniature baby lies in his mother's womb." Stott, "Does Life Begin before Birth?," 51. Juli Loesch, in a short article for *Sojourners*, argued that "fetus" was but the Latin word for "unborn child," and that the use of the technical term distanced people from unwanted truths. Loesch, "Fetus Is Latin for Unborn Child," *Sojourners*, November 1980.

64. Koop and Bohrer, "Deception-on-Demand," 27.

65. Doug Badger, "Divinely Knit," *Sojourners*, November 1980, 17. While Christian Action Council, Badger's organization, is frequently mentioned in the literature, there is little useful information on it. During the 1980s, it ran advertisements in Evangelical magazines, counseling against abortion, especially *Moody Monthly* (e.g., January 1984, October 1984) and *Eternity* (e.g., October 1985). J. Christopher Soper describes it as one of the most important Evangelical pro-life organizations; see Soper, *Evangelical Christianity*, 106–7, 109–11, 128. The Christian Action Council is now known as Care Net.

66. Koop and Bohrer, "Deception-on-Demand," 28.

67. Jenkins, "The Unborn," 11.

68. Van Atta used the Bible to show that there have always been hard times—because of economic reasons or war, for example—and yet women at all times had babies, and these children grew up to be no worse and often better than children born into good times and prosperity. Hard times were no excuse to justify aborting a baby. Lucibel Van Atta, "This Is No Time to Have a Baby . . . or Is It?," *Moody Monthly*, May 1980.

69. Chuck Christensen and Winnie Christensen, "If You've Aborted Your Baby," *Moody Monthly*, May 1980, 87. They repeated their advice in a similar column six years later: C. Christensen and W. Christensen, "Will God Forgive My Abortions?," *Moody Monthly*, October 1986.

70. Rodney Clapp, "Willa's Dilemma," *Christianity Today*, May 20, 1983.

71. This story starkly contrasts with templates for what fetal rights discourse was supposed to look like. Compare, for example, the description of this discourse provided by historian and reproductive rights activist Rickie Solinger: "These ways of imagining who the fetus is—and the plight of the fetus—are rarely coupled with visions of the *vulnerable* pregnant woman or the *responsible* pregnant woman. She is rarely the patient who needs medical care herself or a person who resists having a child she cannot manage." Solinger, *Pregnancy and Power*, 234 (emphasis in original). Contrary to the fetal rights template, then, fictional Willa in *Christianity Today*'s abortion issue was a visible mother and a responsible one at that.

72. Paul Fromer, "Beyond Pity: What Churches Can Do," *Christianity Today*, May 20, 1983.

73. Scott Reed and Paul Fromer, "Why Prolife Rhetoric Is Not Enough," *Christianity Today*, May 20, 1983, 19.

74. The question "what can we do?" ran through the magazines (e.g., Fromer, "Beyond Pity: What Churches Can Do") and was repeatedly asked of Koop (e.g., in his interview with *Eternity*). Asked in a *Christianity Today* interview, "What do churches need to do to restore a sense of sanctity of life to society?" Koop responded: "My message to the churches is this: You can't be against abortion, infanticide, or euthanasia without having some alternatives. If you say to a girl, 'You shouldn't have an abortion,' then I think your responsibility to her begins right then. . . . If it's a young, unmarried girl, I think you have to give her a haven of refuge while she's pregnant. Guide her to have her baby adopted, and show her what the pitfalls are of being an unmarried girl raising a child. She must be provided with good obstetric care and good legal care. . . . In addition, Christians need to think, 'What are the problems a family with a handicapped child faces?' They face financial problems and serious logistic problems. Some of them need respite. What do you do if you've been cooped up with a retarded child for a long period of time? You need some good, loving family to come in and say, 'We're going to come here on Friday night and babysit for the weekend.'" Koop, "Surgeon C. Everett Koop and the Fight for the Newborn," 37.

75. The makers of *Sojourners* lived as a Christian community in an impoverished Black neighborhood in Washington, DC, and comments about their lives and work there were interspersed in articles throughout the magazine, as for example, in an interview with Barb and Jim Tamialis on how they raised their two boys, Michael and Nathan, in this neighborhood. Barb Tamialis and Jim Tamialis, "Family, Friends, and Neighbors," interview, *Sojourners*, May 1982.

76. Marian Wright Edelman, "Suffer the Little Ones," interview, *Sojourners*, July 1981.

77. Jesse Jackson, "The Willpower to Uphold Life," *Sojourners*, November 1980, 23.

78. Spencer Perkins, "The Prolife Credibility Gap," *Christianity Today*, April 21, 1989, 21.

79. Elizabeth Moore, "A Matter of Welfare," *Sojourners*, November 1980.

80. During the 1980s, children became the focus of national and international attention. Definitions of child abuse broadened to include more than just physical violence, and US legal codes expanded in response. Richard Beck, *We Believe the Children: A Moral Panic in the 1980s* (New York: PublicAffairs, 2015). The United Nations was also concerned with children, and the Convention on the Rights of the Child was ratified on November 20, 1989. The convention can be found through the website of the UN Human Rights Office of the High Commissioner, accessed May 12, 2016, https://www.ohchr.org.

81. Rodney Clapp, "Vanishing Childhood," part 2, *Christianity Today*, June 15, 1984, 20. He borrowed the term "wanted child" from journalist Vance Packard and his new book, *Our Endangered Children: Growing Up in a Changing World* (New York: Little, Brown, 1983).

82. Clapp, "Vanishing Childhood," part 2, 19.

83. Rodney Clapp, "Vanishing Childhood," part 1, *Christianity Today*, May 18, 1984.

84. Clapp, "Vanishing Childhood," part 2, 20.

85. Harold O. J. Brown, "Not Enough Children," Speaking Out, *Christianity Today*, October 18, 1985, 10. The Speaking Out column was designed as a forum for diverse Evangelical opinions. It was printed with the disclaimer that pieces in this column did not necessarily reflect the convictions of *Christianity Today*.

86. Chuck Christensen and Winnie Christensen, "What Happened to the Joy of Parenthood?," *Moody Monthly*, April 1986, 90.

87. Robert C. Roberts, "Children: Who Needs Them?," *Christianity Today*, April 19, 1985, 34.

88. Pamela P. Wong, "No Babies?!," *Eternity*, June 1987, 12, 14.

89. On the movement for reproductive rights, see, for example, Linda Gordon, *The Moral Property of Women: A History of Birth Control Politics in America*, 3rd ed. (Urbana: University of Illinois Press, 2002). Gordon describes "voluntary motherhood," "birth control," "family planning," and "abortion" as "historical peaks of the movement for reproductive control" (296).

90. John H. White, "The Bible on Marriage and Babies," *Eternity*, June 1987, 14.

91. Roberts, "Children: Who Needs Them?," 34, 36.

92. Kelsey Menehan, "Where Have All the Babies Gone?," *Christianity Today*, October 18, 1985. The periodical *Today's Christian Woman* was targeted at women and published by Christianity Today Inc. See Glenn Arnold, "Today's Christian Woman," in *Popular Religious Magazines of the United States*, ed. P. Mark Fackler and Charles H. Lippy (Westport, CT: Greenwood Press, 1995), 463–68.

93. See, for example, the letters from Bonnie Wheeler Williams and Linda Myers Englewood that included in "Shall the Unborn Live?," letters to the editor, *Moody Monthly*, August 1980.

94. A *Moody Monthly* article singled out the Christian Action Council as the first organization to establish a Protestant abortion crisis center, doing so in Baltimore in 1981. Adoption placement was but one of the services mentioned. Martin Mawyer, "Crisis Pregnancy Centers: An Alternative to Abortions," *Moody Monthly*, December 1982. Journalist Kathryn Joyce, in her book *The Child Catchers: Rescue, Trafficking, and the New Gospel of Adoption* (New York: PublicAffairs, 2013), looks at adoption ethics and religion. She argues that it was the goal of such organizations as Christian Action Council (now Care Net) to make available for adoption the children of unwed mothers in crisis pregnancy centers.

95. Menehan, "Where Have All the Babies Gone?," 28–29.

96. Ken Myers, "Babies Having Babies," *Eternity*, March 1986.

97. Menehan, "Where Have All the Babies Gone?," 29.

98. That arguments like this could also be used to justify a practice in which the privileged preyed on and abused the plight of women in difficult situations was argued by Kathryn Joyce in *The Child Catchers*.

99. Beth Spring, *Infertile Couple* (Elgin, IL: D.C. Cook, 1987); Spring, "When the Dream Child Dies," *Christianity Today*, August 7, 1987.

100. Spring, "When the Dream Child Dies," 31. In 1983, *Eternity* printed an article on infertility that similarly delineated stages of frustration, resignation, redemptive suffering, and, hopefully, an eventual "full quiver." Timothy P. Weber, "Empty Quiver," *Eternity*, November 1983.

101. Ray S. Anderson, "God Bless the Children—and the Childless," *Christianity Today*, August 7, 1987, 28.

102. Spring, "When the Dream Child Dies," 31.

103. Beth Spring, "The Alternatives to Infertility," *Christianity Today*, August 7, 1987, 30. I return to the subject of new reproductive technologies later in this chapter.

104. Anderson, "God Bless the Children—and the Childless," 28.

105. See Petro, *After the Wrath of God*, 63–64; "Congenital Birth Defects and the Medical Rights of Children: The 'Baby Doe' Controversy," in "C. Everett Koop," Profiles in Science, US National Library of Medicine, accessed December 3, 2015, https://profiles.nlm.nih.gov.

106. "Is Every Life Worth Living?," editorial, *Christianity Today*, March 19, 1982, 12.

107. "Is Every Life Worth Living?"

108. Anita Palmer, "Foretaste," *Eternity*, January 1986.
109. Terri Graves Taylor, "Nonperson," *Eternity*, January 1986, 54.
110. Peter Leithart, "A Different Kind of Post Partum Blues," *Eternity*, September 1986, 24. Australian Peter Singer and American Michael Tooley, both philosophers, were known within the pro-life movement as advocates of infanticide.
111. Carl F. H. Henry, *The Christian Mindset in a Secular Society* (Portland, OR: Multnomah, 1984), quoted in Leithart, "A Different Kind of Post Partum Blues," 22.
112. Taylor, "Nonperson," *Eternity*, January 1986, 69. Taylor summarized the refuted argument in the following words: "As you'll recall, the distinction presupposes that we have a right to life because we are persons; that is, that the sanctity of life is grounded in personhood. Those who endorse this position argue that our right to life comes from our being made in the image of God if and only if he meets the criteria of personhood. To the degree he falls short, his right to life is suspect." Taylor, 55.
113. The health complications facing Baby Jane Doe in New York seemed substantially more severe than that of the British or Indiana infants, complicating the issue. Her doctors had predicted a possible life-span of about twenty years, and little, if any, emotional and intellectual capacities. Nonetheless, activists, including Evangelical spokespersons, advocated saving her life. See, for example, the following opinion piece: Steven Baer, "Press Skews Baby Jane Prognosis," *Moody Monthly*, February 1984.
114. Jack Resnik, "The Baby Doe Rules," *The Embryo Project Encyclopedia*, Arizona State University. Posted May 12, 2011. https://embryo.asu.edu. The Baby Doe Law is part of the Child Abuse Amendments of 1984, amendments to the Child Abuse Prevention and Treatment Act of 1974. The law, which was codified as Part B, "Services and Treatment for Disabled Infants," of Public Law 98-457, reads: "the term 'withholding of medically indicated treatment' means the failure to respond to the infant's life-threatening conditions by providing treatment (including appropriate nutrition, hydration, and medication) which, in the treating physician's or physicians' reasonable medical judgment, will be most likely to be effective in ameliorating or correcting all such conditions, except that the term does not include the failure to provide treatment (other than appropriate nutrition, hydration, or medication) to an infant when, in the treating physician's or physicians' reasonable medical judgment, (A) the infant is chronically and irreversible comatose; (B) the provision of such treatment would (i) merely prologue dying, (ii) not be effective in ameliorating or correcting all of the infant's life-threatening conditions, or (iii) otherwise be futile in terms of the survival of the infant; or (C) the provision of such treatment would be virtually futile in terms of the survival of the infant and the treatment itself under such circumstances would be inhumane." Child Abuse Amendments of 1984, Pub. L. No. 98-457, 98 Stat. 1752 (1984).
115. Beth Spring, "The Campaign to Let Retarded Children Live," *Christianity Today*, May 20, 1980, 41.

116. C. Everett Koop, "The Surgeon General Speaks Out on Baby Doe," *Christianity Today*, January 18, 1985, 27.

117. Thomas Elkins, "A Legacy of Life," interview by Harold Smith, *Christianity Today*, January 18, 1985, 18.

118. Elkins, 22.

119. Elkins, 20.

120. Koop, "The Surgeon General Speaks Out on Baby Doe," 27. Koop's remarks were interjected between the interview with Elkins and the *Christianity Today* forum on the Baby Doe cases.

121. Lewis B. Smedes, "A Biolife Perspective," *Christianity Today*, January 18, 1985, 25.

122. Harold O. J. Brown, "Our Motivation," *Christianity Today*, January 18, 1985. Brown was part of the faculty of Trinity Evangelical Divinity School in Deerfield, Illinois, but at the time he wrote this article, he was interim pastor in Klosters, Switzerland.

123. Norman B. Bendroth, "Social Schizophrenia," *Christianity Today*, January 18, 1985.

124. Koop and Bohrer, "Deception-on-Demand," 27.

125. Terry Muck, "Prolonging Life to Promote Life," *Christianity Today*, March 18, 1988.

126. V. Elving Anderson, "Genetic Engineering: Good and Harmful?," *Eternity*, April 1987, 17.

127. A 1979 decision by the Department of Health, Education, and Welfare proscribed government funding for research into human cloning. During the 1980s and 1990s, lawmakers stood by the decision. Indeed, a five-year ban on research into human cloning was proposed in 1997 by President Bill Clinton, and a voluntary moratorium was accepted by the US scientific community. During the presidency of George W. Bush, research was restricted, and the criminalization of human cloning was debated. Nonetheless, a public debate of genetics, which had been muted in the late 1980s, became virulent again in the late 1990s, when Scottish scientists successfully cloned Dolly the sheep (1997) and researchers at Johns Hopkins University produced human embryonic stem cells in the laboratory (1998). John Dombrink and Daniel Hillyard, *Sin No More: From Abortion to Stem Cells, Understanding Crime, Law, and Morality in America* (New York: New York University Press, 2007), 198; Louis J. Palmer, *Encyclopedia of Abortion in the United States* (Jefferson, NC: McFarland, 2002), s.v. "embryonic cloning."

128. Historian Myles W. Jackson describes *Diamond v. Chakrabarty* as the precedent for gene patenting. The case centered on a question of patent law, which, up until this point, had never been permitted to apply to living things. This restriction was challenged by General Electric. The firm wanted a patent for a genetically engineered bacterium invented by its researcher Ananda Mohan Chakrabarty. The bacterium could dissolve crude oil and was proposed to be used in treating oil spills. The Supreme Court granted the patent but introduced an artificial distinction between life and matter, ruling the bacterium to be mat-

ter and thus postponing a ruling on genetically altering life. See Jackson, *The Genealogy of a Gene: Patents, HIV/AIDS, and Race* (Cambridge: MIT Press, 2015), 57–58; Stephen S. Hall, *Invisible Frontiers: The Race to Synthesize a Human Gene* (New York: Atlantic Monthly Press, 1987).

129. "Life Manipulators Must Await Society's Consensus on the Limits of Science," editorial, *Christianity Today*, January 23, 1981, 13.

130. The *Christianity Today* issues on genetic engineering and medical research were dated, respectively, February 7, 1986, and March 6, 1987. The forum was published as Christianity Today Institute, "Biomedical Decision Making: The Blessings and Curses of Modern Technology," *Christianity Today*, March 21, 1986.

131. The makers of *Sojourners*, especially the editor Jim Wallis, considered genetic engineering to be detrimental human meddling in God's creation. They regarded it as potentially just as destructive as nuclear power, and just as dangerous as euthanasia and abortion. See, for example, Wallis, "Coming Together on the Sanctity of Life." An elaborate argument against genetic engineering by Jeremy Rifkin—codirector of the think tank People's Business Commission and coauthor with Ted Howard of a book on genetic engineering, *Who Should Play God? The Artificial Creation of Life and What It Means for the Future of the Human Race* (New York: Delacorte Press, 1977)—was printed in connection with the 1980 Supreme Court ruling in *Diamond v. Chakrabarty*. Jeremy Rifkin, "Playing God," *Sojourners*, August 1980.

132. Dennis Chamberland, "Genetic Engineering: Promise and Threat," *Christianity Today*, February 7, 1986; Anderson, "Genetic Engineering: Good and Harmful?"; Dave Boehi, "Where to Draw the Line?," *Moody Monthly*, June 1989.

133. "Curses or Prayers for Genetic Engineers?," editorial, *Christianity Today*, May 8, 1981; Fay Angus, "The Promise and Perils of Genetic Meddling," *Christianity Today*, May 8, 1981.

134. This was the gist, for example, of a report on a four-day conference of scientists, physicians, ethicists, and theologians at Eastern College in Pennsylvania, sponsored by the American Scientific Affiliation, an organization of Evangelicals working in science. The conference addressed the question of how Christians should deal with the prospect of genetic engineering. An informal poll showed that the participants were generally in favor of researching and applying new technologies but very careful about the reasons why they would be put to use. Most spoke out against reproductive techniques for eugenic and cosmetic reasons like a looks or intelligence. William A. Durbin, Jr., "Should Christians Oppose Genetic Engineering?," *Christianity Today*, September 4, 1987.

135. Anderson, "Genetic Engineering: Good and Harmful?," 21.

136. David B. Fletcher, "The Mandate to Heal," *Christianity Today*, February 7, 1986, 28.

137. Anderson, "Genetic Engineering: Good and Harmful?," 20.

138. Boehi, "Where to Draw the Line?," 20.

139. Christianity Today Institute, "Biomedical Decision Making," 5. The forum included a doctor, a theologian, and an ethicist: "Paul Brand served as a mission-

ary and surgeon at the Christian Medical College in India for 20 years. Currently he heads rehabilitation at the US Public Health Service leprosy hospital in Carville, Louisiana. Millard Erickson is dean and professor of systematic theology at Bethel Theological Seminary in St. Paul, Minnesota. Hans Tiefel is professor of ethics in the religion department at the College of William and Mary, Williamsburg, Virginia." The forum was facilitated by former *Christianity Today* editor Kenneth S. Kantzer. Christianity Today Institute, 3.

140. Christianity Today Institute, 5, 7–8.

141. Kenneth S. Kantzer, "Biomedical Decision Making: We Dare Not Retreat," *Christianity Today*, March 21, 1986, 15.

142. Chamberland, "Genetic Engineering: Promise and Threat," 28.

143. Christianity Today Institute, "Biomedical Decision Making," 3.

144. The legalization of abortion did not stop Evangelical opposition. Just because something was possible or legal was no guarantee of Evangelical acquiescence.

145. Christianity Today Institute, "Biomedical Decision Making," 9.

146. See, for example, Bettyann Kevles, *Naked to the Bone: Medical Imaging in the Twentieth Century* (New Brunswick, NJ: Rutgers University Press, 1997), 228–60.

147. See, for example, Evans, "Polarization in Abortion Attitudes in U.S. Religious Traditions."

148. Martin Mawyer, "So What's Wrong with Test Tube Babies?," *Moody Monthly*, September 1982, 128.

149. Mawyer, 129.

150. Robert G. Wells, "Embryo Transfer: A Woman Can Now Give Birth to Her Own Stepchild," *Christianity Today*, March 2, 1984, 31.

151. Dave Andrusko, "Fetal Tissue Transplants Suggest Pregnancy for Hire," *Eternity*, July 1988, 32. See also Kim A. Lawton, "Fetal Tissue Transplants Stir Controversy," *Christianity Today*, March 18, 1988.

152. Chamberland, "Genetic Engineering: Promise and Threat," 27; and compare Mawyer, "So What's Wrong with Test Tube Babies?"

153. Fletcher, "The Mandate to Heal," 28; and compare Anderson, "Genetic Engineering: Good and Harmful?"

154. Alan Verhey, "Society's Toolbox," *Christianity Today*, February 7, 1986, 27.

155. For example, Fay Angus wrote: "There is an enormous appeal in the right of every child to be born free of genetic defects, and bioengineered to be the most productive human possible. But what are we to do with the substandard embryo, and who is qualified to decide the acceptable standards?" Angus, "The Promise and Perils of Genetic Meddling," 27.

156. David Neff, "Abortion Rights Boomerang," editorial, *Christianity Today*, March 17, 1989, 16. Neff used the phrase "feminist boomerang" to refer to sex-selective abortions while recounting a *New York Times* story according to which doctors testified that some women used technological advances to screen the sex of the fetus and abort if it was female.

157. "Curses or Prayers for Genetic Engineers?," *Christianity Today*, 14.
158. Rifkin, "Playing God," 10.
159. Lewis B. Smedes, "Catching Up with the Revolution," *Christianity Today*, February 7, 1986.
160. Mawyer, "So What's Wrong with Test Tube Babies?," 129.
161. Law professor Elizabeth S. Scott points out that the "frames" through which surrogacy was publicly interpreted changed over time. In the 1980s, according to her, surrogacy was publicly framed as "commodification," leading most states in the 1990s to put into effect laws that prohibited the practice. Eventually, however, the "moral panic" surrounding surrogacy subsided, and a new perspective took its place. In her words, "an alternative frame has emerged, in which altruistic surrogates (contractually bound and compensated nonetheless) provide the gift of 'life' to deserving couples who otherwise would be unable to have children." Since the 2000s, there are laws in some states providing for surrogacy. Scott argues that the changed approach might be due to the changed vote of feminists: feminists who had been fiercely opposed to surrogacy during the 1980s changed their attitudes as conservative activists adopted their arguments. Scott, "Surrogacy and the Politics of Commodification," *Law and Contemporary Problems* 73, no. 3 (2009): 110.
162. See, for example, Beth Spring, "What Is the Future of Surrogate Motherhood?," *Christianity Today*, March 6, 1987; Spring, "Court Rules against Mothers for Hire," *Christianity Today*, March 18, 1988; William E. May, "Surrogate Motherhood Poses Ethical Dilemma," *Eternity*, February 1987; Paige Cunningham, "Bartering Baby M," *Moody Monthly*, June 1987.
163. Congregation for the Doctrine of the Faith, *Instruction on Respect for Human Life in Its Origin and on the Dignity of Procreation: Donum Vitae* (Boston: Pauline Books, 1987).
164. Stanley J. Grenz, "What Is Sex for?," *Christianity Today*, June 12, 1987, 22–23.
165. Spring, "What Is the Future of Surrogate Motherhood?," 42.
166. Spring reported that Smedes did not consider it adultery, for example, and theologian Millard Erickson, in the Christianity Today Institute's case discussion on surrogate motherhood, did not consider it adultery, either. Christianity Today Institute, "Biomedical Decision Making," 10. Obstetrician and gynecologist Robert G. Wells, in discussing ovum transfer, also pointed out that the practice would not constitute adultery, and, in a discussion of the article, Norman Geisler, professor of systematic theology at Dallas Theological Seminary, agreed. Wells, "Embryo Transfer," March 2, 1984; "Other Views on Embryo Transfer," *Christianity Today*, March 2, 1984.
167. May, "Surrogate Motherhood Poses Ethical Dilemma," 31.
168. Grenz, "What Is Sex for?," 23.
169. "Other Views on Embryo Transfer," *Christianity Today*.
170. Beth Spring reported that a "common presupposition of Christians who marry is that they will raise a family together. This is strongly reinforced at church,

to the point where an infertile couple may seriously question whether their marriage has any purpose." Spring, "When the Dream Child Dies," 29.

171. Grenz, "What Is Sex for?," 23. See also, for example, Fletcher, "The Mandate to Heal"; Spring, "The Alternatives to Infertility." Some even saw as acceptable artificial insemination by donor, especially when the sperm was anonymously provided by a sperm bank. Millard Erickson argued that the relational dilemma was smaller when the third party was not identifiable. Christianity Today Institute, "Biomedical Decision Making," 10. William E. May, an eminent Catholic moral theologian writing in *Eternity*, pointed out as problematic that masturbation was involved in harvesting sperm for artificial insemination. This argument seemed not to have played a role in the Evangelical discourse because it was only mentioned here. May, "Surrogate Motherhood Poses Ethical Dilemma."

172. Spring, "What Is the Future of Surrogate Motherhood?," 43.

173. Hans Tiefel formulated it this way: "What concerns me is the woman knowingly carrying a baby she has no intention of mothering—and another woman raising a baby she and her husband have arranged to have birthed from his seed but not her egg." Christianity Today Institute, "Biomedical Decision Making," 10.

174. See, for example, May, "Surrogate Motherhood Poses Ethical Dilemma"; Spring, "What Is the Future of Surrogate Motherhood?"

175. Cunningham, "Bartering Baby M," 12.

176. David Neff urged readers to forego parenthood under such circumstances; see Neff, "How to Not Have a Baby," editorial, *Christianity Today*, April 3, 1987.

177. Cunningham, "Bartering Baby M," 12.

178. Koop, "The Surgeon General Speaks Out on Baby Doe," 27.

179. Scott, "Surrogacy and the Politics of Commodification," 111.

Conclusion

1. Steve Wilkens and Donald A. D. Thorsen, *Everything You Know about Evangelicalism Is Wrong (Well, Almost Everything): An Insider's Look at Myths and Realities* (Grand Rapids, MI: Baker Books, 2010), 24.

2. Pierre Bourdieu, *Language and Symbolic Power*, ed. John B. Thompson, trans. Gino Raymond and Matthew Adamson (Cambridge: Polity Press, 2008), 236.

3. James Davison Hunter, *Culture Wars: The Struggle to Define America* (New York: Basic Books, 1991), 42.

4. Patrick J. Buchanan, "1992 Republican National Convention Speech," in *Culture Wars in America: A Documentary and Reference Guide*, ed. Glenn H. Utter (Santa Barbara, CA: Greenwood Press, 2010), 29.

5. Hunter, *Culture Wars*, 118.

6. See, for example, Alan Wolfe, *One Nation, After All: What Middle-Class Americans Really Think about God, Country, Family, Racism, Welfare, Immigration, Homosexuality, Work, the Right, the Left, and Each Other* (New York: Penguin Books, 1999); Wolfe, *The Transformation of American Religion: How We Actually Live Our Faith* (Chicago: University of Chicago Press, 2003).

7. Michael Maudlin, "Inside *CT*: Bible Study in the Trenches," *Christianity Today*, March 6, 1995.
8. John D. Woodbridge, "Culture War Casualties," *Christianity Today*, March 6, 1995, 22, 26.
9. Francis A. Schaeffer, "The Mark of the Christian," *Christianity Today*, March 6, 1995, 28.
10. Woodbridge, "Culture War Casualties," 23.
11. There was a fatal shooting at a Planned Parenthood facility in Colorado Springs in November 2015.
12. On abortion legislation, see, for example, Jennifer Ferranti, "Abortion: 'D and X' Abortion Ban Faces Clinton Veto," *Christianity Today*, December 11, 1995; Kim A. Lawton, "Abortion Pill Seems on Fast Track," *Christianity Today*, September 16, 1996; David Neff, "Mourning the Morning After Pill," *Christianity Today*, April 7, 1997; Art Moore, "Partial-Birth Abortion: States Approving Bans on Partial-Birth Abortion," *Christianity Today*, October 27, 1997; "Partial-Birth Abortion: Legislative Bans Stymied in States," *Christianity Today*, April 5, 1999; "Bitter Pills: What Does RU-486 Change about Abortion?," *Christianity Today*, December 4, 2000; "Virginia OKs Abortion Restriction," *Christianity Today*, April 2, 2001; Stan Guthrie, "RU-486: Physicians Slow to Prescribe Abortion Pill," *Christianity Today*, November 12, 2001. On politicians' positions on abortion, see, for example, Jodi Veenker, "Bush and Gore Size Up Prolife Running Mates," *Christianity Today*, July 13, 2000. On Norma McCorvey, see, for example, Mark A. Kellner, "Abortion: 'Jane Roe' Joins Pro-Life Movement," *Christianity Today*, September 11, 1995; Gary Thomas, "Roe v. McCorvey: What Made 'Roe' Betray the Pro-Choice Cause?," *Christianity Today*, January 12, 1998. Finally, the 1995 cover story was Frederica Mathewes-Green, "Why Women Choose Abortion," *Christianity Today*, January 9, 1995.
13. Frederica Mathewes-Green, "Wanted: A New Pro-Life Strategy," *Christianity Today*, January 12, 1998, 27. Further articles focused on mothers and fathers; see, for example, Mathewes-Green, "In Postabortion Interviews," *Christianity Today*, January 9, 1995; Guy Condon, "Fatherhood Aborted: The Hidden Trauma of Men and Abortion," *Christianity Today*, December 9, 1996.
14. *Time*, for example, put AIDS on its August 3, 1992, cover, titled "Losing the Battle"; proclaimed "Magic!" and offered the story of HIV-positive basketball player Magic Johnson on February 12, 1996; named AIDS researcher David Ho its 1996 Man of the Year (December 30, 1996/January 6, 1997); put television host Ellen DeGeneres on its April 14, 1997, cover with the words "Yep, I am gay"; made the devastating murder of gay student Matthew Shepard its cover story on October 26, 1998; and on February 12, 2001, featured the cover story "AIDS in Africa." *Newsweek* made "The Future of Gay America" its March 12, 1990, cover story; dedicated its July 1, 1991, issue to "Doctors with AIDS"; featured Magic Johnson's story about contracting HIV on the cover for November 18, 1991 (and made him the cover story again a few years later, February 12, 1996); ran covers

on "Teens and AIDS" (August 3, 1992), "AIDS and the Arts" (January 18, 1993), "Taming the AIDS Virus" (March 22, 1993), and "Lesbians" (June 21, 1993); asked hopefully whether we'd yet reached "The End of AIDS?" with its December 2, 1996, cover; asked "Gay for Life?" (with a story about the so-called ex-gay movement) on August 17, 1998; and, on March 20, 2000, ran the headline "Gay Today" with the drop head "How the battle for acceptance has moved to schools, churches, marriage and the workplace" and a photo of five gay professionals including a police officer, serviceman, and clergywoman.

15. Sociologist Didi Herman investigated *Christianity Today*'s attitude toward homosexuality from the 1956 inception of the magazine to 1989. She found that in the initial period, from 1956 to 1965, same-sex attraction was condemned as one among many sexual deviations. From 1965 to 1980, she observed that *Christianity Today* reported the increasing organization of gay activists into a movement. While this reporting was fairly neutral, editorials and biblical commentary made clear that *Christianity Today* opposed homosexuality. During the last period of her study, from 1980 to 1989, Herman was surprised that "*CT* showed little concern with the AIDS epidemic, and rarely articulated AIDS and homosexuality together." Herman, *The Antigay Agenda: Orthodox Vision and the Christian Right* (Chicago: University of Chicago Press, 1997), 53, and see 25–59.

16. In its "news" section, *Christianity Today* followed the developments surrounding homosexuality in Protestant denominations, such as the fight about ordaining gay individuals. See, for example, Randy Frame, "Jury Still Out on Homosexual Ordinations," *Christianity Today*, April 29, 1996; Steve Rabey, "United Methodists: Denomination Retains Homosexual Ordination Ban," *Christianity Today*, June 17, 1996; Gayle White, "Presbyterians Retain Ban on Homosexual Ordination," *Christianity Today*, August 12, 1996; Ken Garfield, "Presbyterians in Stalemate over Homosexual Ordination," *Christianity Today*, August 10, 1998. The November 11, 1996, issue of *Christianity Today* was the only issue during the 1990s when full-fledged articles on homosexuality appeared, and they were all concerned with homosexuality in the church; the section was called "Revelation and Homosexual Experience": Don Thorsen, "What Would John Wesley Have Said about This Debate in the Church?," *Christianity Today*, November 11, 1996; Wolfhart Pannenberg, "What Wolfhart Pannenberg Says about This Debate in the Church," *Christianity Today*, November 11, 1996; Thomas E. Schmidt, "A Pastoral Manifesto," *Christianity Today*, November 11, 1996.

17. Wolfe, *One Nation, After All*, 72.

18. Daniel Taylor, "Are You Tolerant? (Should You Be?)," *Christianity Today*, January 11, 1999, 43.

19. "Indiana's Mike Pence: Tolerance Is a Two-Way Street," CBN News, March 30, 2015, http://www1.cbn.com.

20. Taylor, "Are You Tolerant?," 51. For a more elaborate treatment of the topic, see, for example, Janet R. Jakobsen and Ann Pellegrini, *Love the Sin: Sexual Regulation and the Limits of Religious Tolerance* (New York: New York University Press, 2003).

21. For a short overview of Koop's career, see Randall Balmer, *Encyclopedia of Evangelicalism* (Waco, TX: Baylor University Press, 2004), s.v. "Koop, C(harles) Everett." On Koop's fight against AIDS, see, for example, William Martin, *With God on Our Side: The Rise of the Religious Right in America* (New York: Broadway Books, 1996), 238–57; Anthony M. Petro, *After the Wrath of God: AIDS, Sexuality, and American Religion* (Oxford: Oxford University Press, 2015).

22. See Anja-Maria Bassimir, "Definition—Macht—Evangelikal: Standortbestimmung zum Gegenwärtigen U.S.-Amerikanischen Evangelikalismus," *Amerikastudien/American Studies* 63, no. 3 (2018): 389–422.

23. For a list of Evangelical magazines published between 1950 and 1990, see Edith L. Blumhofer and Joel A. Carpenter, *Twentieth-Century Evangelicalism: A Guide to the Sources* (New York: Garland, 1990), 48–67. Compare Anja-Maria Bassimir and Kathrin Kohle, "Evangelikale und Massenmedien, Strukturen in den USA," in *Handbuch Evangelikalismus*, ed. by Frederik Elwert, Martin Radermacher, and Jens Schlamelcher (Bielefeld, Germany: Transcript, 2017), 409–23.

24. Additionally, *HIS* was discontinued in 1988. Blumhofer and Carpenter, *Twentieth-Century Evangelicalism*, 56, 58.

25. See Ken Waters, "Pursuing New Periodicals in Print and Online," in *Understanding Evangelical Media: The Changing Face of Christian Communication*, ed. Quentin J. Schultze and Robert H. Woods (Downers Grove, IL: InterVarsity Press, 2008), 71–84.

26. See Anja-Maria Bassimir, "Evangelical Magazines in a Digital Age," in *Religious Periodicals and Publishing in Transnational Contexts: The Press and the Pulpit*, ed. Oliver Scheiding and Anja-Maria Bassimir (Newcastle upon Tyne, UK: Cambridge Scholars, 2017), 145–67; Oliver Scheiding and Anja-Maria Bassimir, "Under the Cover of Religious Periodicals: Editorial Practice and Magazine Production," in *Periodicals in Focus: Methodological Approaches and Theoretical Frameworks*, ed. Jutta Ernst, Dagmar von Hoff, and Björn von Rimscha (Leiden: Brill, 2020) (forthcoming).

27. The magazine's survival proved wrong David Kling's prediction that "as Sojourners Fellowship goes, so goes *Sojourners*." David Kling, "Sojourners," in *Religious Periodicals of the United States: Academic and Scholarly Journals*, ed. Charles H. Lippy (Westport, CT: Greenwood Press, 1986), 481. For the *Sojourners* website, which is current as of 2021, see https://sojo.net/.

28. Waters, "Pursuing New Periodicals in Print and Online," 75, 74.

29. Rogers Brubaker, "Ethnicity without Groups," *Archives Européenes de Sociologie* 43, no. 2 (2002): 170–71.

30. Brubaker, 163–64.

31. There are notable exceptions, especially in the field of "lived religion." See David D. Hall, *Lived Religion in America: Toward a History of Practice* (Princeton, NJ: Princeton University Press, 1997).

32. Brubaker, "Ethnicity without Groups," 168.

BIBLIOGRAPHY

ARCHIVAL MATERIALS
Billy Graham Center Archives, Wheaton College, Wheaton, Illinois
Colson, Charles Wendell. Papers. CN-275.
Evangelicals for Social Action. Collection. CN-037.
Graham, Billy. Ephemera. CN-074.
Buswell Library Special Collections, Wheaton College, Wheaton, Illinois
Koop, C. Everett. Papers. SC-058.
Noll, Mark A. Papers. SC-116.
Sojourners. Records. SC-023.

PERIODICALS AND RELATED SOURCES
Aaseng, Rolf E. "Male and Female Created He Them." *Christianity Today*, November 20, 1970.
Aikman, David. "Washington Scorecard." *Christianity Today*, October 21, 1988.
Alexander, John F. "Did We Blow It?" *Other Side*, February 1981.
———. "Madison Avenue Jesus." *Post-American*, Fall 1971. First published in the *Other Side*, January/February 1971.
———. "Thinking Male." *Other Side*, July/August 1973.
Anderson, John B. "What America Needs Now." *Moody Monthly*, July 1975.
Anderson, Leith C. "Separation? Who Needs It?" *Moody Monthly*, May 1982.
Anderson, Ray S. "God Bless the Children—and the Childless." *Christianity Today*, August 7, 1987.
Anderson, V. Elving. "Genetic Engineering: Good and Harmful?" *Eternity*, April 1987.
Andrusko, Dave. "Fetal Tissue Transplants Suggest Pregnancy for Hire." *Eternity*, July 1988.
Angus, Fay. "The Promise and Perils of Genetic Meddling." *Christianity Today*, May 8, 1981.
Augsburger, David. "The Private Lives of Public Leaders." *Christianity Today*, November 20, 1987.
Babbage, Stuart Barton. "Differences of Functions." *Eternity*, January 1971.
Badger, Doug. "Divinely Knit." *Sojourners*, November 1980.
Baer, Steven. "Press Skews Baby Jane Prognosis." *Moody Monthly*, February 1984.
Barackman, Deborah. "Strange and Sane Marriage Customs." *Eternity*, March 1977.

Barcus, Nancy B. "Liberation Isn't Freedom." *Eternity*, March 1975.
———. "A Milestone for Christian Women: Letha Scanzoni and Nancy Hardesty, *All We're Meant to Be*." *Eternity*, March 1975.
Barcus, Nancy B., and Dick Bohrer. "The Humanist Builds His House upon the Sand." *Moody Monthly*, September 1980.
Barnhouse, Margaret N. "How I Think I'll Vote." *Eternity*, September 1976.
Batteau, John M. "Sexual Differences: A Cultural Convention?" *Christianity Today*, July 8, 1977.
Bayly, Joseph. "The Definition Drain." Out of My Mind. *Eternity*, January 1977.
———. "How Do We Want to Be Ruled?" *Eternity*, November 1973.
———. "On Moral Camelots and Moral Majorities." *Eternity*, November 1985.
———. "Revise Our 'Sexist' Scriptures?" Out of My Mind. *Eternity*, September 1974.
———. "Rome Fell While Moralists Slept." *Eternity*, January 1986.
———. "Senator Hatfield's Brave Words." *Eternity*, June 1973.
Beck, M. N. "The Bed Undefiled." *Christianity Today*, October 10, 1975.
Bell, L. Nelson. "A Layman and His Faith: Building Christian Homes." *Christianity Today*, October 13, 1972.
Bender, Thorwald W. "Joint Heirs of Grace." *Eternity*, January 1971.
Bendroth, Margaret Lamberts. "In Memoriam: Nancy A. Hardesty." American Academy of Religion. Accessed July 9, 2015. http://rsnonline.org.
Bendroth, Norman B. "Social Schizophrenia." *Christianity Today*, January 18, 1985.
Boehi, Dave. "Where to Draw the Line?" *Moody Monthly*, June 1989.
Boeth, Richard. "The New Activists." *Newsweek*, November 7, 1977.
Bouma, Mary. "Liberated Mothers." *Christianity Today*, May 7, 1971.
Boyd, Forrest. "Do We Really Want a Saint in the White House?" *Moody Monthly*, September 1976.
Bromiley, Geoffrey W. "Church Members First, Citizens Second." *Christianity Today*, May 16, 1986.
Brown, Harold O. J. "Abortion and Child Abuse." *Christianity Today*, October 7, 1977.
———. "Abortion and the Court." Editorial. *Christianity Today*, February 16, 1973.
———. "Evolution, Revolution or Victory." *Christianity Today*, April 10, 1970.
———. "Our Motivation." *Christianity Today*, January 18, 1985.
———. "Not Enough Children." Speaking Out. *Christianity Today*, October 18, 1985.
Buursma, Bruce. "Evangelicals Give Reagan a 'Non-Partisan' Stump." *Christianity Today*, September 19, 1980.
Buzzard, Lynn R. "Civil Disobedience." *Eternity*, January 1987.
Buzzard, Lynn R., and Samuel E. Ericsson. "Defining Our Religious Freedom." 2 parts. *Moody Monthly*, November and December 1983.

CBN News. "Indiana's Mike Pence: Tolerance Is a Two-Way Street." March 30, 2015. http://www1.cbn.com.
Chamberland, Dennis. "Genetic Engineering: Promise and Threat." *Christianity Today*, February 7, 1986.
Chang, Lit-Sen. "Old Serpent; New Strategy." *Christianity Today*, May 23, 1975.
Chapman, G. Clark, Jr. "Who Pays for Pardons?" *Post-American*, December 1974.
Chicago Tribune. "Graham Kicks Off Evangelism Congress after Seeing Hippies." September 9, 1969.
Christensen, Chuck, and Winnie Christensen. "If You've Aborted Your Baby." *Moody Monthly*, May 1980.
———. "What Happened to the Joy of Parenthood?" *Moody Monthly*, April 1986.
———. "Will God Forgive My Abortions?" *Moody Monthly*, October 1986.
Christensen, Winnie. "What Is a Woman's Role?" *Moody Monthly*, June 1971.
Christianity Today. "Bitter Pills: What Does RU-486 Change about Abortion?" December 4, 2000.
———. "Contributing Editors." September 2, 1983.
———. "A Crackdown at PTL." June 12, 1987.
———. "Curses or Prayers for Genetic Engineers?" Editorial. May 8, 1981.
———. "Debate: Should Pat Robertson Run for President?" September 5, 1986.
———. "Declaration of Evangelical Social Concern." December 21, 1973.
———. "Dropping the Reins at PTL." November 6, 1987.
———. "Farewell to the Sixties." December 19, 1969.
———. "Fifteen Turbulent Years." August 30, 1974.
———. "First at the Cradle, Last at the Cross." Editorial. March 16, 1973.
———. "Gaining Perspective after a Decade of Change." Editorial. January 4, 1980.
———. "Getting God's Kingdom into Politics." Editorial. November 2, 1979.
———. "Honor America Day." July 3, 1970.
———. "Introducing: *CT*'s Fourth Editor." October 22, 1982.
———. "Is Every Life Worth Living?" Editorial. March 19, 1982.
———. "The Jim Bakker Affair." April 17, 1987.
———. "Joe Bayly: Editor, Author, Humanist Dies at 66." September 5, 1986.
———. "Just Because Reagan Has Won . . ." Editorial. December 12, 1980.
———. "Life Manipulators Must Await Society's Consensus on the Limits of Science." Editorial. January 23, 1981.
———. "The 1969 Protestant Inaugural Prayers." February 14, 1969.
———. "Other Views on Embryo Transfer." March 2, 1984.
———. "The Pardon of Richard Nixon." September 27, 1974.
———. "Partial-Birth Abortion: Legislative Bans Stymied in States." April 5, 1999.
———. "Pat's Big Surprise: The Army Is Still Invisible." April 8, 1988.
———. "Political Cross Bearing." April 5, 1985.
———. "The Political Peak Is Also the Brink." November 19, 1976.

———. "Politics on the Ethical Periphery." November 24, 1972.
———. "Serving Singles—Don't Play Mix and Match." June 4, 1976.
———. "Should Nixon Resign?" June 7, 1974.
———. "Stacking Sandbags against the Conservative Flood." November 2, 1979.
———. "Statement of Circulation." October 20, 1978.
———. "The Top 50 Books That Have Changed Evangelicals." October 6, 2006.
———. "Virginia OKs Abortion Restriction." April 2, 2001.
———. "Why We Need Christian Think Tanks." Editorial. March 15, 1985.
———. "Young and New." Letters to the editor. June 7, 1974.
Christianity Today Institute. "Biomedical Decision Making: The Blessings and Curses of Modern Technology." *Christianity Today*, March 21, 1986.
———. "The Christian as Citizen." *Christianity Today*, April 19, 1985.
Chua-Eoan, Howard. "The Watergate Dirty Trickster Who Found God: Charles Colson (1931–2012)." *Time*, April 21, 2012.
Cizik, Richard. "Tweedledum and Tweedledee." *Eternity*, October 1988.
Clapp, Rodney. "Vanishing Childhood." 2 parts. *Christianity Today*, May 18 and June 15, 1984.
———. "Willa's Dilemma." *Christianity Today*, May 20, 1983.
Clarkson, Margaret. "Singleness: His Share for Me." *Christianity Today*, February 16, 1979.
Cleaver, Eldridge. "Soul on Grace." Interview. *Eternity*, May 1977.
Coleman, William L. "How to Be a Huggable Husband." *Moody Monthly*, February 1973.
———. "How to Be a Wonderful Wife." *Moody Monthly*, February 1973.
Coles, Robert. "The Dangers of Idol Gazing." *Christianity Today*, October 21, 1988.
Colson, Charles W. "Dear Pat: Winning Isn't Everything." *Christianity Today*, November 21, 1986.
———. Interview by Shirl Short. *Moody Monthly*, February 1976.
———. "On Waving Flags and Washing Feet." *Eternity*, July 1986.
———. "So Much for Our 'Great Awakening.'" *Christianity Today*, May 13, 1988.
———. "A View from the Evangelical Center." Interview. *Christianity Today*, April 5, 1985.
———. "Watergate or Something Like It Was Inevitable." Interview. *Christianity Today*, March 12, 1976.
———. "Who Will Help Penitents in Penitentiaries?" *Eternity*, May 1977.
Condon, Guy. "Fatherhood Aborted: The Hidden Trauma of Men and Abortion." *Christianity Today*, December 9, 1996.
Cottrell, Jack W. "Abortion and the Mosaic Law." *Christianity Today*, March 16, 1973.
Cox, Turret T. "Shall the Unborn Live?" Letter to the editor. *Moody Monthly*, August 1980.
Crabb, Lawrence J. "Counseling and Psychology of Religion." *Christianity Today*, March 1, 1974.

Cunningham, Paige. "Bartering Baby M." *Moody Monthly*, June 1987.
Dannemeyer, William E. "Who Turned the First Amendment Upside-Down?" *Christianity Today*, June 18, 1982.
Deen, Edith. "To Influence, not Command." *Eternity*, January 1971.
Dickason, C. Fred. "Where Do You Fit in the Sex Revolution." *Moody Monthly*, February 1974.
Douglass, David R. "The Total Woman: Totaled." *Moody Monthly*, September 1975.
Dugan, Robert P., Jr. "Election '84: Some Surprising Winners and Losers." *Christianity Today*, January 18, 1985.
Dunn, Bruce. "Why Vote?" *Moody Monthly*, November 1980.
Durbin, William A., Jr. "Should Christians Oppose Genetic Engineering?" *Christianity Today*, September 4, 1987.
Edelman, Marian Wright. "Suffer the Little Ones." Interview. *Sojourners*, July 1981.
Elkins, Thomas. "A Legacy of Life." Interview by Harold Smith. *Christianity Today*, January 18, 1985.
Elliot, Elisabeth. "Rebellion against God's Order." *Eternity*, January 1971.
Erickson, Millard J. "The New Birth Today." *Christianity Today*, August 16, 1974.
Erickson, R. D. Letter to the editor. *Eternity*, March 1971.
Eternity. "Armstrong, Colson, and Noll: Reviewing the Reagan Revolution." November 1988.
———. "Back to Reality." November 1973.
———. "Books of the Year 1984." December 1984.
———. "Celebrating a New Beginning." January 1979.
———. "Celebrating a New Beginning." January 1986.
———. "Does Corruption Matter?" June 1973.
———. "Fetal Life." February 1971.
———. Foretaste (regular feature). 1971–83.
———. "Friendly Persuasion." Letters to the editor. July/August 1983.
———. "The Hartford Appeal." May 1985.
———. "'Hatchet Man' Dominates Annual Poll." December 1976.
———. "Hope for the '70s." January 1971.
———. "How I Think I'll Vote." October 1980.
———. "How I Think I'll Vote." September 1976.
———. "Lincoln Inspired Hatfield's Day-of-Prayer Idea." May 1974.
———. "1981: The Winning Books." December 1981.
———. "1977: The Top 25 Books." December 1977.
———. "No Consensus." Letters to the editor. September 1983.
———. "Poll Puts Women First." December 1975.
———. "The President and Nebuchadnezzar." May 1983.
———. "72's History, 73's Issues." January 1973.
———. "The Top 25 Books: How They Ranked in *Eternity*'s Poll." December 1975.

———. "Under Conviction: Charles Colson's Damascus Road." March 1976.
———. "Watergate Logic." June 1973.
———. "The Winning List." December 1984.
Evangelicals for Social Action. "Can My Vote Be Biblical?" *Christianity Today*, November 2, 1979.
Evans, W. Glyn. "Are We Living in Post-America?" *Eternity*, December 1974.
Fager, Chuck. "The Blast at *Born Again*." *Sojourners*, December 1978.
Falwell, Jerry. "A View from Fundamentalism." Interview. *Christianity Today*, April 5, 1985.
———. "Where Is Jerry Falwell Going?" Interview by William J. Petersen and Stephen Board. *Eternity*, July 8, 1980.
Ferguson, Andrew. "Pop Goes the Culture: One Man's Quest to Preserve and Defend the Good, the True, and the Beautiful." *Weekly Standard*, January 14, 2013.
Ferranti, Jennifer. "Abortion: 'D and X' Abortion Ban Faces Clinton Veto." *Christianity Today*, December 11, 1995.
Fiske, Edward B. "The Closest Thing to a White House Chaplain." *New York Times*, June 8, 1969.
Fletcher, David B. "The Mandate to Heal." *Christianity Today*, February 7, 1986.
Flood, Robert G. "Behind the Scenes." *Moody Monthly*, December 1974.
Forbes, Cheryl. "God and Women: *All We're Meant to Be*." *Christianity Today*, December 6, 1974.
———. "Let's Not Shackle the Single Life." *Christianity Today*, February 16, 1979.
Ford, Leighton. "Revolution for Heaven's Sake." *Christianity Today*, December 4, 1970.
Frame, Randy. "Jury Still Out on Homosexual Ordinations." *Christianity Today*, April 29, 1996.
Friedrich, Robert E., Jr. "Sunday at the White House: Watchers and Worshippers." *Christianity Today*, August 22, 1969.
Fromer, Paul. "Beyond Pity: What Churches Can Do." *Christianity Today*, May 20, 1983.
Gaebelein, Frank E. "The Christian Use of the Printed Page." *Christianity Today*, January 30, 1970.
Gallagher, Sharon. "More on Women and Biblical Authority." *Sojourners*, March 1976.
Garfield, Ken. "Presbyterians in Stalemate over Homosexual Ordination." *Christianity Today*, August 10, 1998.
Gelman, David. "Is America Turning Right?" *Newsweek*, November 7, 1977.
Gilbreath, Edward. "A Prophet Out of Harlem." *Christianity Today*, September 16, 1996.
Goldin, Marion, prod. *60 Minutes*. Season 6, episode 19, "Charles Colson's Conversion." Aired May 26, 1974, on CBS.
Goldman, Peter. "The Rebirth of Hopeful Jimmy Carter." *Moody Monthly*, October 1976.

———. "The Spirit of '70: Six Historians Reflect on What Ails the American Spirit." *Newsweek*, July 6, 1970.
Gorsuch, Geoff. "Patriotism to One Kingdom under God." *Moody Monthly*, October 1984.
Graham, Billy. "An Agenda for the 1980s." *Christianity Today*, January 4, 1980.
———. Interview. *Wittenburg Door*, June/July 1974.
———. "Standing Firm, Moving Forward." Editorial. *Christianity Today*, September 16, 1996.
———. "The Unfinished Dream." *Christianity Today*, July 31, 1970.
———. "Watergate." Interview. *Christianity Today*, January 4, 1974.
Grassley, Charles E. "A Voice in the Senate." Interview. *Moody Monthly*, November 1983.
Green, Roberta. "Gender Chameleons." *Eternity*, February 1985.
Greider, William. "Colson, 'Mr. Tough Guy,' Finds Christ." *Washington Post*, December 17, 1973.
Greisch, Janet Rohler. "From College to Nursery." *Eternity*, January 1971.
Grenz, Stanley J. "What Is Sex for?" *Christianity Today*, June 12, 1987.
Gross, Jenny, and Aimee Ortiz. "Roe v. Wade Plaintiff Was Paid to Switch Sides, Documentary Says." *New York Times*, May 19, 2020.
Grounds, Vernon C. "Bombs or Bibles? Get Ready for Revolution!" *Christianity Today*, January 15, 1971.
———. "How I Think I'll Vote." *Eternity*, September 1976.
———. "Revolutions Brewing." *Eternity*, March 1971.
———. "What's Left for the Religious Right?" *Moody Monthly*, February 1988.
Gundry, Patricia. "Perhaps We Should Take a Second Look." *Moody Monthly*, May 1975.
———. "Woman Be Free!" Interview by Jon Trott. *Blue Christian on a Red Background* (blog). September 25, 2006. http://bluechristian.blogspot.com/.
Gunner, Roberta. "Well Done." Letter to the editor. *Christianity Today*, March 2, 1973.
Guthrie, Stan. "RU-486: Physicians Slow to Prescribe Abortion Pill." *Christianity Today*, November 12, 2001.
Hardesty, Nancy. "Gifts." *Other Side*, July 8, 1973.
———. "Marital Status: Single." *Daughters of Sarah*, January 1976.
———. "When Does Life Begin?" *Eternity*, February 1971.
———. "Women: Second-Class Citizens?" *Eternity*, January 1971.
Hatch, Nathan O. "Yesterday: The Key That Unlocks Today." *Christianity Today*, August 5, 1983.
Hatfield, Mark O. "Begin with Repentance." *Moody Monthly*, July/August 1973.
———. "Crisis in American Leadership." *Eternity*, July 1973.
———. "Feedback." Letter to the editor. *Post-American*, Winter 1972.
———. "Pastors and Prophets." *Post-American*, October 1974.
———. "Piety and Patriotism." *Post-American*, May/June 1973.
———. "The Vulnerability of Leadership." *Christianity Today*, June 22, 1973.

———. "Watergate: A Different View." *Christianity Today*, May 5, 1978.
Hefeley, James C. "Colson, Cons, and Christ." *Christianity Today*, July 4, 1975.
Henry, Carl F. H. "The Battle of the Sexes." Footnotes. *Christianity Today*, July 4, 1975.
———. "Church and State: Why the Marriage Must Be Saved." *Christianity Today*, April 5, 1985.
———. "Evangelicals Jump on the Political Bandwagon." *Christianity Today*, October 24, 1980.
———. "Evangelical Social Concern." Footnotes. *Christianity Today*, March 1, 1974.
———. "Friendly Persuasion." Letter to the editor. *Eternity*, July/August 1983.
———. "Further Thoughts about Women." Footnotes. *Christianity Today*, June 6, 1975.
———. "Has Democracy a Future?" *Christianity Today*. July 5, 1974.
———. "In Search of Evangelical Identity: A Ten-Piece Series." *Christianity Today*, January to October 1976.
———. "Is Life Ever Cheap?" *Eternity*, February 1971.
———. "The Judgment of America." *Christianity Today*, November 8, 1974.
———. "Lost Momentum." Interview by Beth Spring. *Christianity Today*, September 4, 1987.
———. "Out of the Closet but Going Nowhere?" *Christianity Today*, January 4, 1980.
———. "Pull the Lever Knowing Why." *Christianity Today*, October 24, 1980.
———. "Reflections of Women's Liberation." Footnotes. *Christianity Today*, January 3, 1975.
———. "Revolt on the Evangelical Frontiers." *Christianity Today*, April 26, 1974.
———. "Wavering Evangelical Initiative." *Christianity Today*, January 16, 1976.
Henry, Paul B. "Evangelicals of America, Arise!" *Eternity*, February 1974.
Hermanson, Renee J. "How Do You Know When You're Liberated?" *Daughters of Sarah*, January/February 1978.
Hertz, Todd, and Stan Guthrie. "Moody Closes Magazine, Restructures Aviation Program." *Christianity Today*, February 1, 2003. http://www.christianitytoday.com.
Hesse, Monica. "'Jane Roe,' from Roe v. Wade, Made a Stunning Deathbed Confession. Now What?" *Washington Post*, May 20, 2020.
Hitt, Russell T. "Barnhouse of Philadelphia." *Eternity*, April 1975.
———. "Capital Clout: Now What?" *Eternity*, January 1981.
———. "Editor's Ink." *Eternity*, September 1974.
———. "How I Think I'll Vote." *Eternity*, September 1976.
———. "Left to Die: When Late-Term Abortions Fail." *Eternity*, March 1985.
———. "They Come in Many Different Styles." *Eternity*, January 1980.
Horn, Carl. "How Freedom of Thought Is Smothered in America." *Christianity Today*, April 6, 1984.
Howard, Thomas. "The Yoke of Fatherhood." *Christianity Today*, June 23, 1978.

Huffman, John A., Jr. "Biblical Lessons from Watergate." *Christianity Today*, March 15, 1974.
Hunt, Gladys. "How I Think I'll Vote." *Eternity*, September 1976.
———. Letter to the editor. *Eternity*, March 1971.
Hunter, James Davidson, and Alan Wolf. "Is There a Culture War?" Moderated by Michael Cromartie. Conversation at the Pew Forum Faith Angle conference, Key West, FL, May 23, 2006. https://www.pewforum.org.
Hyer, Marjorie. "Confess Sins, Don't Implore God, Sen. Hatfield Tells Leaders." *Washington Post*, May 4 1973.
———. "Evangelist Reverses Position on God's Hearing Jews." *Washington Post*, October 11, 1980.
Irwin, James B. "How I Think I'll Vote." *Eternity*, September 1976.
Jackson, Jesse. "The Willpower to Uphold Life." *Sojourners*, November 1980.
Jackson, Neta. "Living in Community." *Eternity*, August 1972.
Jenkins, Jerry B. "Behind the Scenes." *Moody Monthly*, October 1975.
———. "75 Years at *Moody Monthly*." *Moody Monthly*, September 1975.
———. "The Unborn: Why the Right to Life." *Moody Monthly*, May 1980.
Jensen, Paul. "Humanism's Indigestion: Plop and Fizz." *Eternity*, April 1981.
Johnston, Robert K. "Submission, a Wedding Meditation." *Daughters of Sarah*, January 1977.
Kantzer, Kenneth S. "American Civil Religion." Editorial. *Christianity Today*, July 13, 1984.
———. "Biomedical Decision Making: We Dare Not Retreat." *Christianity Today*, March 21, 1986.
———. Editor's note. *Christianity Today*, March 19, 1982.
———. Editor's note. *Christianity Today*, October 22, 1982.
———. "The Issue at Hand: 'The Christian as Citizen.'" *Christianity Today*, April 5, 1985.
———. "The Road to Restoration." *Christianity Today*, November 20, 1987.
———. "The 'Separation' of Church and State?" Editorial. *Christianity Today*, May 18, 1984.
———. "Summing Up: An Evangelical View of Church and State." *Christianity Today*, April 5, 1985.
Kantzer, Kenneth S., and Paul Fromer. "Within Our Reach." *Christianity Today*, April 19, 1985.
Keim, James A. "The Search for a Christian America." Book review. *Eternity*, April 1984.
Kellner, Mark A. "Abortion: 'Jane Roe' Joins Pro-Life Movement." *Christianity Today*, September 11, 1995.
Kemper, Vicki. "Direct-Mail Politics of the Religious Right." *Sojourners*, January 1989.
Koop, C. Everett. Interview. *Eternity*. April 1981.
———. "Separating the Siamese Twins: The Surgeon's Story." *Medical World News*, November 8, 1974.

———. "Surgeon C. Everett Koop and the Fight for the Newborn." Interview by Beth Spring. *Christianity Today*, March 16, 1984.

———. "The Surgeon General Speaks Out on Baby Doe." *Christianity Today*, January 18, 1985.

———. "A Surgeon General's Warnings." Interview by Philip D. Yancey. *Christianity Today*, November 3, 1989.

Koop, C. Everett, and Dick Bohrer. "Deception-on-Demand." *Moody Monthly*, May 1980.

Kucharsky, David. "Billy Graham and 'Civil Religion.'" *Christianity Today*, November 6, 1970.

———. "The Man from Plains." *Christianity Today*, November 19, 1976.

———. "Super Salute to God and Country." *Christianity Today*, July 31, 1970.

———. "U.S. Congress on Evangelism." *Christianity Today*, September 26, 1969.

Kuhn, Harold Barnes. "Reciprocal Relationship." *Eternity*, January 1971.

LaHaye, Tim. Interview. *Wittenburg Door*, June/July 1980.

———. "What's Left for the Religious Right?" *Moody Monthly*, February 1988.

Langeley, McKendree R. "Robertson's Run: Going for It?" *Eternity*, September 1987.

Lawton, Kim A. "Abortion Pill Seems on Fast Track." *Christianity Today*, September 16, 1996.

———. "Fetal Tissue Transplants Stir Controversy." *Christianity Today*, March 18, 1988.

———. "Iowa Christians and the Race for the Oval Office." *Christianity Today*, January 15, 1988.

———. "Whatever Happened to the Religious Right?" *Christianity Today*, December 15, 1989.

Leininger, Larry W. "Shall the Unborn Live?" Letter to the editor. *Moody Monthly*, August 1980.

Leithart, Peter. "A Different Kind of Post Partum Blues." *Eternity*, September 1986.

Lindsell, Harold. Editor's note. *Christianity Today*, November 19, 1976.

Linton, Calvin D. "Dying to the God Who Is Me." *Christianity Today*, February 16, 1979.

Litfin, Diane. "Do Biblical Feminists Have a Point?" *Moody Monthly*, December 1979.

Lloyd, Joan. "Transcendent Sexuality as C. S. Lewis Saw It." *Christianity Today*, November 9, 1973.

Loesch, Juli. "Fetus Is Latin for Unborn Child." *Sojourners*, November 1980.

Lutzer, Erwin W. "The Preacher and Politics." From Pastor to Pastor. *Moody Monthly*, June 1983.

———. "Watergate Ethics." *Christianity Today*, September 13, 1974.

MacArthur, John. "Singleness as a Gift of the Spirit." *Moody Monthly*, January 1977.

MacDonald, Gordon. "How to Be an Effective Father." *Moody Monthly*, March 1976.

———. "You're the Pacesetter, Dad." *Moody Monthly*, January 1976.
MacDonald, Kenneth D. Letter to the editor. *Eternity*, March 1971.
Marsden, George M. "Current Religious Thought: America's 'Good Old Days.'" *Christianity Today*, November 25, 1983.
———. Interview. *Wittenburg Door*, December 1982/January 1983.
———. "Quest for a Christian America." *Eternity*, May 1983.
Marty, Martin E. "Adapting to the Age of Greed." *Christianity Today*, October 21, 1988.
———. "Fundamentalism Reborn: Faith and Fanaticism." *Saturday Review*, May 1980.
———. "Fundies and Their Fetishes." *Christian Century*, December 8, 1976.
———. "The Marks and Misses of a Magazine." *Christianity Today*, July 17, 1981.
———. "Points to Consider about the New Christian Right Wing." *Wittenburg Door*, June/July 1980. Reprinted from *Context*, July 15, 1980.
Martz, Larry, Vern E. Smith, Daniel Pedersen, Daniel Shapiro, Mark Miller, and Ginny Carroll. "God and Power." *Newsweek*, April 6, 1987.
Mathewes-Green, Frederica. "In Postabortion Interviews." *Christianity Today*, January 9, 1995.
———. "Wanted: A New Pro-Life Strategy." *Christianity Today*, January 12, 1998.
———. "Why Women Choose Abortion." *Christianity Today*, January 9, 1995.
Mathews, Tom. "Born Again!" *Newsweek*, October 2, 1978.
Matthews, Arthur H. "Crusade for the White House: Skirmishes in a 'Holy War.'" *Christianity Today*, November 19, 1976.
Maudlin, Michael. "Inside *CT*: Bible Study in the Trenches." *Christianity Today*, March 6, 1995.
Mawyer, Martin. "Are We Losing Our Religious Freedoms?" 3 parts. *Moody Monthly*, March to May 1982.
———. "Crisis Pregnancy Centers: An Alternative to Abortions." *Moody Monthly*, December 1982.
———. "So What's Wrong with Test Tube Babies?" *Moody Monthly*, September 1982.
May, William E. "Surrogate Motherhood Poses Ethical Dilemma." *Eternity*, February 1987.
Mayer, Allan J. "A Tide of Born Again Politics." *Newsweek*, September 15, 1980.
McAllaster, Elva. "Stunted Poplars." *Eternity*, January 1971.
McCrory, Don. "Editor's Ink: Year of the Scandal?" *Eternity*, September 1987.
McFadden, Carol Prester. "Ethics and Discipleship." *Christianity Today*, March 14, 1975.
McKenna, David L. "A Political Strategy for the Local Church." *Christianity Today*, April 5, 1985.
McKinniss, Rick. "Let Christian America Rest in Peace." *Christianity Today*, February 5, 1988.
McQuaid, Elwood. "What's Left for the Religious Right?" *Moody Monthly*, February 1988.

Menehan, Kelsey. "Where Have All the Babies Gone?" *Christianity Today*, October 18, 1985.
Michaelson, Ronald D. "What Would an Honest Politician Look Like?" *Eternity*, February 1976.
Michaux, M. J. "Female Takeover." Letter to the editor. *Christianity Today*, October 20, 1978.
Mickelsen, Berkeley, and Alvera Mickelsen. "Does Male Dominance Tarnish Our Translations?" *Christianity Today*, October 5, 1979.
——. "The 'Head' of the Epistles." *Christianity Today*, February 20, 1981.
Miller, Ella May. "Housework Doesn't Come Naturally." *Moody Monthly*, January 1976.
Miller, Ted. "Shall We Join the 'New Christian Crusade'?" *Moody Monthly*, September 1980.
Minnery, Tom. "Christianity Today Institute Focuses Evangelical Thought on the Christian as Citizen." *Christianity Today*, April 5, 1985.
Mollenkott, Virginia Ramey. "The Androgyny of Jesus." *Daughters of Sarah*, March 1975.
——. "A Challenge to Male Interpretation: Women and the Bible." *Sojourners*, February 1976.
——. "Teachers, Students, and Selfishness in the Seventies." *Christianity Today*, April 19, 1970.
Monsma, Stephen V. "The Oval Office: Three Models for a Christian." *Christianity Today*, January 21, 1977.
——. "What Makes an Ideal President?" *Eternity*, March 1980.
——. "Windows and Doors in the Wall of Separation." *Christianity Today*, April 5, 1985.
Montgomery, John Warwick. "Will an Evangelical President Usher In the Millennium?" *Christianity Today*, October 22, 1976.
Moody Monthly. "Are We Praying for Our Leaders?" February 1974.
——. "Crusaders." Letters to the editor. November 1980.
——. "Honesty Does Pay." October 1974.
——. "The Makers of America." September 1974.
——. "A National Day of Prayer." April 1974.
——. "A National Day of Prayer." May 1974.
——. "President Confers with Evangelicals." November 1976.
——. "Shall the Unborn Live?" Letters to the editor. August 1980.
——. "Was Jesus a Revolutionary?" Editorial. January 1970.
——. "Watergate: Are We Listening?" July/August 1973.
——. "What the Humanists Believe." September 1980.
Moore, Art. "Partial-Birth Abortion: States Approving Bans on Partial-Birth Abortion." *Christianity Today*, October 27, 1997.
Moore, Elizabeth. "A Matter of Welfare." *Sojourners*, November 1980.
Moran, Miriam G. "Marabel's Guide: Good despite Some Faults." *Eternity*, March 1975.

Morgan, Marabel. Interview. *Wittenburg Door*, August/September 1975.
Morris, Leon. "Conservative Evangelicals?" *Christianity Today*, November 19, 1971.
Morrow, Lance, Jason McManus, and Marion Knox. "Who Owns the Stars and Stripes?" *Time*, July 6, 1970.
Muck, Terry. "Prolonging Life to Promote Life." *Christianity Today*, March 18, 1988.
———. "The Wall That Never Was." Editorial. *Christianity Today*, July 10, 1987.
Myers, Ken. "Babies Having Babies." *Eternity*, March 1986.
Narramore, Clyde M. "Things Women Should Know about Men." *Moody Monthly*, May 1974.
Nederhood, Joel H. "Christians and Revolution." *Christianity Today*, January 1, 1971.
Neff, David. "Abortion Rights Boomerang." Editorial. *Christianity Today*, March 17, 1989.
———. "How to Not Have a Baby." Editorial. *Christianity Today*, April 3, 1987.
———. "Mourning the Morning After Pill." *Christianity Today*, April 7, 1997.
Neuhaus, Richard John. "Christianity and Pluralism in America." Interview. *Touchstone*, September 1991.
———. "The Culture War Will Continue." *Christianity Today*, October 21, 1988.
———. "How I Became the Catholic I Was." *First Things* 22 (2002): 14–20.
———. Interview. *Wittenburg Door*, February/March 1985.
———. "The Naked Public Square." *Christianity Today*, October 5, 1984.
———. "Ring of Truth." *Eternity*, May 1985.
———. "Who, Now, Will Shape the Meaning of America?" *Christianity Today*, March 19, 1982.
New York Times. "Book Ends: Call Me Mrs." June 9, 1974.
———. "Counting Souls." October 4, 1976.
———. "Honor America Day Cost Nation $68,770." July 11, 1970.
Nixon, Richard. "Inaugural Address." January 20, 1969. The American Presidency Project. Accessed June 10, 2021. https://www.presidency.ucsb.edu.
Noll, Mark A. "The Constitution at 200: Should Christians Join the Celebration?" *Christianity Today*, July 10, 1987.
———. "Counterstrike at Secularized Religion." *Eternity*, May 1985.
———. "Is This Land God's Land?" Editorial. *Christianity Today*, July 11, 1986.
———. "When 'Infidels' Run for Office." *Christianity Today*, October 5, 1984.
Nordeen, Betty Lou. Letter to the editor. *Eternity*, March 1971.
Nordland, Frances. "A Look at the Single Woman." *Moody Monthly*, January 1970.
Nystrom, Carolyn. "*HIS* Presents . . . the Competition! Other Christian Magazines You Should Know about." *HIS*, May 1979.
Olsen, Ted. "Close the Door." *Christianity Today*, April 1, 2002. http://www.christianitytoday.com.
Other Side. "Declaration of Evangelical Social Concern." March/April 1974.

Packer, J. I. "How to Recognize a Christian Citizen." *Christianity Today*, April 5, 1985.

Palmer, Anita. "Foretaste." *Eternity*, January 1986.

Palmer, Bruce H. "Whatever Happened to the Human Race?" Book review. *Eternity*, October 1980.

Pannell, Bill. "Lawlessness American Style." *Post-American*, Fall 1972.

Pannenberg, Wolfhart. " What Wolfhart Pannenberg Says about This Debate in the Church." *Christianity Today*, November 11, 1996.

Patterson, Ben. "John Wayne Lives." Editorial. *Wittenburg Door*, June/July 1980.

———. "May They Twain." *Wittenburg Door*, August/September 1975.

———. "The Methods to His Madness." Editorial. *Wittenburg Door*, April/May 1984.

People. "The God-Fearing Surgeon Who Separated the Twins." October 7, 1974.

Perkins, Spencer. "The Prolife Credibility Gap." *Christianity Today*, April 21, 1989.

Peters, George W. "What God Says about Remarriage." *Moody Monthly*, July/August 1978.

Petersen, William J. "The Magazine That Lived." *Eternity*, May 1975.

———. "25 Years of *Eternity*." *Eternity*, April 1975.

Phillips, McCandlish. "Francis Schaeffer: The Man behind the Manifesto." *Moody Monthly*, January 1982.

Pierard, Richard V. "Should We Fear the New Right?" Book Review. *Christianity Today*, October 2, 1981.

———. "What's Left for the Religious Right?" *Moody Monthly*, February 1988.

Pinnock, Clark. "The Christian as a Revolutionary Man." *Post-American*, Summer 1972.

———. "The Christian Revolution." *Post-American*, Fall 1971.

Pippert, Wes. "How I Think I'll Vote." *Eternity*, September 1976.

Playboy. "Jimmy Carter on Politics, Religion, the Press, and Sex." November 1976.

Plowman, Edward E. "An Election Year to Remember." *Christianity Today*, May 7, 1976.

———. "Ford's First Month: Christ and Conflict." *Christianity Today*, September 27, 1974.

———. "Is Morality All Right?" *Christianity Today*, November 2, 1979.

———. "News/Religion in Washington: An Act of God." *Christianity Today*, January 4, 1974.

Post-American. "Declaration of Evangelical Social Concern." January 1974.

———. "Introducing the Contributing Editors." January 1973.

———. "Man and Technocracy." Winter 1972.

———. "Signs of a New Order." March 1973.

———. "What Is the People's Christian Coalition?" Fall 1971.

Rabey, Steve. "Methodists: Denomination Retains Homosexual Ordination Ban." *Christianity Today*, June 17, 1996.

Ramm, Bernard. "A Total Way of Existing." *Eternity*, January 1971.
Rapper, Irving, dir. *Born Again*. AVCO Embassy, 1978. Film, 110 min.
Reed, Scott, and Paul Fromer. "Why Prolife Rhetoric Is Not Enough." *Christianity Today*, May 20, 1983.
Reese, Boyd. "Letha Scanzoni and Nancy Hardesty, *All We're Meant to Be*," Book review. *Post-American*, August/September 1975.
Rifkin, Jeremy. "Playing God." *Sojourners*, August 1980.
Ritchie, Daniel. "Created Equal." *Eternity*, November 1985.
Roberts, Robert C. "Children: Who Needs Them?" *Christianity Today*, April 19, 1985.
Roos, Joe. "American Civil Religion." *Post-American*, Spring 1972.
———. "Keeping the Vision Afloat." *Sojourners*, August/September 1991.
Rosenbladt, Rod. "Deprivation within the Evangelical Family and Church." *Wittenburg Door*, June/July 1973.
Rowe, H. Edward. "How I Think I'll Vote." *Eternity*, September 1976.
Runia, Klaas. "Abortion: Can an Evangelical Consensus Be Found?" *Eternity*, February 1971.
———. "Evangelical Responsibility in a Secularized World." *Christianity Today*, June 19, 1970.
Rydberg, Denny. "How I Think I'll Vote." *Eternity*, September 1976.
Ryken, Leland. "Were the Puritans Right about Sex?" *Christianity Today*, April 7, 1978.
Ryrie, Charles C. "Must Examine Scripture." *Eternity*, January 1971.
Sanders, J. Oswald. "Mary and Martha: A Study of Temperaments." *Moody Monthly*, April 1979.
Sanderson, Judith. "Jesus and Women." *Other Side*, July/August 1973.
Sauer, James L. "Robertson's Date with Destiny." Book review. *Christianity Today*, March 6, 1987.
Sayers, Dorothy L. "Are Women Human?" *Eternity*, February 1974.
Scanzoni, Letha. "Elevating Marriage to Partnership." *Eternity*, July 1968.
———. "Feminism and the Family." *Daughters of Sarah*, May 1975.
———. "The Feminists and the Bible." *Christianity Today*, February 2, 1973.
———. Interview. *Wittenburg Door*, August/September 1975.
———. "Mystique and Machismo." *Other Side*, July/August 1973.
———. "On Friendship and Homosexuality." *Christianity Today*, September 27, 1974.
———. "What Is Marriage?" *Wittenburg Door*, August/September 1974.
———. "Woman's Place: Silence or Service?" *Eternity*, February 1966.
Schaeffer, Francis A. "A Christian Manifesto." *Moody Monthly*, January 1982.
———. "Christian Revolutionaries." *HIS*, November 1970.
———. "The Dust of Life." *Eternity*, March 1981.
———. "How Should We Then Live?" Interview. *Christianity Today*, October 8, 1976.
———. "The Mark of the Christian." *Christianity Today*, March 6, 1995.

---. "Schaeffer on Schaeffer." Interview by Philip D. Yancey. 2 parts. *Christianity Today*, March 23 and April 6, 1979.
---. "Shattering the Plastic Culture." *HIS*, October 1970.
Schaeffer, Francis A., and C. Everett Koop. *Whatever Happened to the Human Race?* Muskegon, MI: Gospel Films, 1980. VHS video, 250 min.
Schaeffer, Franky. Interview. *Wittenburg Door*, April/May 1984.
Schmidt, Thomas E. " A Pastoral Manifesto." *Christianity Today*, November 11, 1996.
Shedd, Charlie, and Martha Shedd. Interview. *Wittenburg Door*, August/September 1974.
Short, Shirl. "Former Nixon Aide Heads Prison Ministry." *Moody Monthly*, January 1976.
Siddons, Philip. "Paul's View of Women." Book review. *Christianity Today*, February 10, 1978.
Sider, Ron. "Historical Context for the Declaration." Accessed July 16, 2009. http://www.evangelicalsforsocialaction.org (site discontinued).
Simon, Paul. Interview. *Wittenburg Door*, June/July 1980.
Singer, David. "'Whatever Happened to the Human Race?': A Film Preview." *Christianity Today*, August 17, 1979.
Skillen, James W. "Commentary: Politics beyond the Party Lines." *Eternity*, October 1988.
---. "Opinion: Getting Pat Political Pragmatism." *Moody Monthly*, November 1988.
Skinner, Tom. "Evangelicals and the Black Revolution." *Christianity Today*, April 19, 1970.
Smedes, Lewis B. "A Biolife Perspective." *Christianity Today*, January 18, 1985.
---. "Catching Up with the Revolution." *Christianity Today*, February 7, 1986.
Sobran, Joseph. "Bully for the Bully Pulpit." *Christianity Today*, October 21, 1988.
Sojourners. "Inside Story." August/September 1991.
Spring, Beth. "The Alternatives to Infertility." *Christianity Today*, August 7, 1987.
---. "The Campaign to Let Retarded Children Live." *Christianity Today*, May 20, 1980.
---. "Christian in the Public Square: Time to Rethink?" *Christianity Today*, November 21, 1986.
---. "Court Rules against Mothers for Hire." *Christianity Today*, March 18, 1988.
---. "One Step Closer to a Bid for the Oval Office." *Christianity Today*, October 17, 1986.
---. "Pat Robertson for President?" *Christianity Today*, November 8, 1985.
---. "Republicans, Religion, and Reelection." *Christianity Today*, October 6, 1984.
---. "What Is the Future of Surrogate Motherhood?" *Christianity Today*, March 6, 1987.

———. "When the Dream Child Dies." *Christianity Today*, August 7, 1987.
Sroka, Barb. "The Single, and Living Happily Ever After." *Moody Monthly*, December 1976.
Stagg, Frank. "Keep Pace with Jesus." *Eternity*, January 1971.
Stott, John R. W. "Does Life Begin before Birth?" *Christianity Today*, September 5, 1980.
Strauss, Richard L. "The Family Church: Any Place for Singles?" *Christianity Today*, July 29, 1977.
Sullivan, Joseph F. "Falwell Warns Jersey Liberals at Capitol Rally." *New York Times*, November 11, 1980.
Sweeting, George. "Give Your Wife a Happy Husband." *Moody Monthly*, December 1975.
———. "Happy Birthday, America." *Moody Monthly*, July 1975.
———. "An Open Letter to President Carter." *Moody Monthly*, January 1977.
———. "Talking It Over: Godly Citizenship." *Moody Monthly*, August 1980.
Tamialis, Barb, and Jim Tamialis. "Family, Friends, and Neighbors." Interview. *Sojourners*, May 1982.
Taylor, Daniel. "Are You Tolerant? (Should You Be?)." *Christianity Today*, January 11, 1999.
Taylor, Terri Graves. "Nonperson." *Eternity*, January 1986.
Tengbom, Mildred. "Ten Guidelines for a Happy Marriage." *Moody Monthly*, October 1977.
Thiessen, Lois. "What If You Don't Get Married . . ." *Moody Monthly*, April 1974.
Thomas, Cal. "Commentary: No Message from Super Tuesday." *Eternity*, May 1988.
———. Interview. *Wittenburg Door*, December 1983/January 1984.
———. "The Pursuit of Censorship." *Moody Monthly*, November 1983.
Thomas, Gary. "Roe v. McCorvey: What Made 'Roe' Betray the Pro-Choice Cause?" *Christianity Today*, January 12, 1998.
Thornton, Zeda. "Dare to Be Liberated." *Moody Monthly*, November 1972.
———. "*The Total Woman*: An In-Depth Look at the Recently Released Book." *Moody Monthly*, December 1973.
Thorsen, Don. "What Would John Wesley Have Said about This Debate in the Church?" *Christianity Today*, November 11, 1996.
Time. "Back to That Old Time Religion." December 26, 1977.
———. "The Confrontation of the Two Americas." October 2, 1972.
———. "The New Housewife Blues." *Time*, March 14, 1977.
———. "Richard John Neuhaus." *Time*, February 7, 2005.
———. "The Two Americas. Is It Still a Contest?" October 2, 1972.
Tinder, Donald. "Sexuality: A New Candor in Evangelical Books." *Christianity Today*, March 18, 1977.
Townder, Jason. "Single Men and Hasty Conclusions." *Eternity*, January 1979.
Van Atta, Lucibel. "This Is No Time to Have a Baby . . . or Is It?" *Moody Monthly*, May 1980.

Veenker, Jodi. "Bush and Gore Size Up Prolife Running Mates." *Christianity Today*, July 13, 2000.
Verhey, Alan. "Society's Toolbox." *Christianity Today*, February 7, 1986.
Wagner, Kenneth K. Grenz. "Shall the Unborn Live?" Letter to the editor. *Moody Monthly*, August 1980.
Wallis, Jim. "Babylon." *Post-American*, Summer 1972.
———. "Biblical Politics." *Post-American*, April 1974.
———. "Coming Together on the Sanctity of Life." *Sojourners*, November 1980.
———. "The Lesson of Watergate." *Post-American*, January 1974.
———. "The Move." *Post-American*, August 1975.
———. "The Movemental Church." *Post-American*, Winter 1972.
———. "The New Regime." *Post-American*, October 1974.
———. "Post-American Christianity." *Post-American*, Fall 1971.
———. "'Revolt on Evangelical Frontiers': A Response." *Christianity Today*, June 21, 1974.
———. "Ten Years." *Sojourners*, September 1981.
———. "A View from the Evangelical Left." Interview. *Christianity Today*, April 5, 1985.
———. "What's Left for the Religious Right?" *Moody Monthly*, February 1988.
Wallis, Jim, and Wes Michaelson. "The Plan to Save America." *Sojourners*, April 1976.
Watson, Russell, Ginny Carroll, Lynda Wright, Daniel Pedersen, and Rich Thomas. "Heaven Can Wait." *Newsweek*, June 8, 1987.
Weber, Timothy P. "Empty Quiver." *Eternity*, November 1983.
Weigel, George. "The Public Square Is Still Naked." *Christianity Today*, October 21, 1988.
Wells, Robert G. "Embryo Transfer: A Woman Can Now Give Birth to Her Own Stepchild." *Christianity Today*, March 2, 1984.
White, Gayle. "Presbyterians Retain Ban on Homosexual Ordination." *Christianity Today*, August 12, 1996.
White, John H. "The Bible on Marriage and Babies." *Eternity*, June 1987.
Whitehead, John W. "Public Education Flunks Free Speech." *Moody Monthly*, November 1983.
———. "A Response." *Eternity*, May 1983.
———. "The Secularizing of America." *Moody Monthly*, July 1981.
Willoughby, William. "Inauguration amid Religious Trappings." *Christianity Today*, February 14, 1969.
Wilson, Marvin. "What D'ya Say, Dear?" *Eternity*, January 1971.
Wittenburg Door. "I Was a Teenage Fundamentalist." December 1982/January 1983.
Wong, Pamela P. "No Babies?!" *Eternity*, June 1987.
Woodbridge, John D. "Culture War Casualties." *Christianity Today*, March 6, 1995.
Woodward, Kenneth L. "Billy Graham and the Surging Southern Baptists." *Newsweek*, July 20, 1970.

Woodward, Kenneth L., John Barnes, and Laurie Lisle. "Born Again." *Newsweek*, October 25, 1976.
Wooten, James T. "Nixon Hears War Called a 'Sin.'" *New York Times*, February 2, 1973.
Yancey, Philip D. "The Embattled Career of Dr. Koop." *Christianity Today*, October 20, 1989.
———. "Francis Schaeffer: A Prophet for Our Time?" *Christianity Today*, March 23, 1979.
Zernike, Kate. "George Gallup Jr., of Polling Family, Dies at 81." *New York Times*, November 22, 2011.

BOOKS AND SECONDARY SOURCES

Abelman, Robert, and Stewart M. Hoover. *Religious Television: Controversies and Conclusions*. Norwood, NJ: Ablex, 1990.
Allitt, Patrick. *Religion in America since 1945: A History*. New York: Columbia University Press, 2003.
Nancy T. Ammerman, Nancy T. *Baptist Battles: Social Change and Religious Conflict in the Southern Baptist Convention*. New Brunswick, NJ: Rutgers University Press, 1990.
Anderson, Benedict R. *Imagined Communities: Reflections on the Origin and Spread of Nationalism*. London: Verso, 1991.
Arnold, Glenn. "Today's Christian Woman." In Fackler and Lippy, *Popular Religious Magazines of the United States*, 463–68.
Balmer, Randall. *Encyclopedia of Evangelicalism*. Waco, TX: Baylor University Press, 2004.
Bartkowski, John P. "Debating Patriarchy: Discursive Disputes over Spousal Authority among Evangelical Family Commentators." *Journal for the Scientific Study of Religion* 36, no. 3 (1997): 393–410.
———. *Remaking the Godly Marriage: Gender Negotiation in Evangelical Families*. New Brunswick, NJ: Rutgers University Press, 2001.
Bassimir, Anja-Maria. "Combating Caustic Communication with Truth and Beauty: Christianity Today, Beautiful Orthodoxy, and US Culture." In *Strong Religion and Mainstream Culture: Opposition, Negotiation, and Adaption*, edited by Stefan Gelfgren and Daniel Lindmark, 213–37. Basingstoke: Palgrave, 2021.
———."Definition—Macht—Evangelikal: Standortbestimmung zum Gegenwärtigen U.S.-Amerikanischen Evangelikalismus." *Amerikastudien/American Studies* 63, no. 3 (2018): 389–422.
———. "Evangelical Magazines in a Digital Age." In Scheiding and Bassimir, *Religious Periodicals and Publishing in Transnational Contexts*, 145–67.
———."Religiöse Zeitschriften am Beispiel von *Christianity Today*." In *Zeitschriftenforschung: Eine Einführung*, edited by Oliver Scheiding and Sabina Fazli. Leiden: Brill, forthcoming.
Bassimir, Anja-Maria, and Kathrin Kohle. "Evangelikale und Massenmedien, Strukturen in den USA." In *Handbuch Evangelikalismus*, edited by Frederik

Elwert, Martin Radermacher, and Jens Schlamelcher, 409–23. Bielefeld, Germany: Transcript, 2017.

Bates, Stephen. *God's Own Country: Religion and Politics in the USA*. London: Hodder, 2008.

Beck, Richard. *We Believe the Children: A Moral Panic in the 1980s*. New York: PublicAffairs, 2015.

Bellah, Robert N. "Civil Religion in America." *Daedalus* 96, no. 1 (1967): 1–21.

———. "Habits of the Heart: Implications for Religion." Lecture, St. Mark's Catholic Church, Isla Vista, CA, February 21, 1986. Robert N. Bellah (website), Hartford Institute for Religion Research, accessed June 10, 2021, http://www.robertbellah.com.

Bellah, Robert N., and Phillip E. Hammond. *Varieties of Civil Religion*. New York: Harper and Row, 1980.

Bendroth, Margaret Lamberts. *Fundamentalism and Gender, 1875 to the Present*. New Haven, CT: Yale University Press, 1993.

———. "The Search for 'Women's Role' in American Evangelicalism, 1930–1980." In Marsden, *Evangelicalism and Modern America*, 122–34.

Bercovitch, Sacvan. *The American Jeremiad*. Madison: University of Wisconsin Press, 1978.

Berger, Peter L., and Thomas Luckmann. *The Social Construction of Reality: A Treatise in the Sociology of Knowledge*. Garden City, NY: Anchor Books, 1967.

Berkley, Kathleen C. *The Women's Liberation Movement*. Westport, CT: Greenwood Press, 1999.

Berman, Harold J. "Law and Religion in the West." In Eliade, *The Encyclopedia of Religion*, vol. 8, 472–75.

Berneburg, Erhard. *Das Verhältnis von Verkündung und Sozialer Aktion in der Evangelikalen Missionstheorie*. Wuppertal, Germany: R. Brockhaus Verlag, 1997.

Bernstein, Carl, and Bob Woodward. *All the President's Men*. New York: Simon and Schuster, 1974.

"Billy Graham: Pastor to Presidents." Billy Graham Evangelistic Association. May 17, 2021. http://billygraham.org.

Bloesch, Donald G. *The Evangelical Renaissance*. Grand Rapids, MI: Eerdmans, 1973.

Blumhofer, Edith L., and Joel A. Carpenter, eds. *Twentieth-Century Evangelicalism: A Guide to the Sources*. New York: Garland, 1990.

Bourdieu, Pierre. *Language and Symbolic Power*. Edited by John B. Thompson. Translated by Gino Raymond and Matthew Adamson. Cambridge: Polity Press, 2008.

Brænder, Morten. "Justifying the Ultimate Sacrifice: Civil and Military Religion in Frontline Blogs." PhD dissertation, Aarhus University, 2009.

Brands, H. W. *American Dreams: The United States since 1945*. New York: Penguin Books, 2010.

Brown, Candy Gunther. *The Word in the World: Evangelical Writing, Publishing, and Reading in America, 1789–1880*. Chapel Hill: University of North Carolina Press, 2004.

Brown, Harold O. J. *Death before Birth*. Nashville, TN: Thomas Nelson, 1977.

Brown, Ruth Murray. *For a "Christian America": A History of the Religious Right*. Amherst, NY: Prometheus Books, 2002.

Brubaker, Rogers. "Ethnicity without Groups." *Archives Européenes de Sociologie* 43, no. 2 (2002): 163–89.

Bruce, Steve. *Pray T.V.: Televangelism in America*. London: Routledge, 2020.

———. *The Rise and Fall of the New Christian Right: Conservative Protestant Politics in America, 1978–1988*. New York: Oxford University Press, 1988.

Bruns, Roger A. *Billy Graham: A Biography*. Westport, CT: Greenwood Press, 2004.

Buchanan, Patrick J. "1992 Republican National Convention Speech." In *Culture Wars in America: A Documentary and Reference Guide*, edited by Glenn H. Utter, 26–31. Santa Barbara, CA: Greenwood Press, 2010.

Bungert, Heike, and Jana Weiß. "Die Debatte um 'Zivilreligion' in Transnationaler Perspektive." *Zeithistorische Forschung/Studies in Contemporary History* 7, no. 3 (2010): 454–59.

Burch, Maxie B. *The Evangelical Historians: The Historiography of George Marsden, Nathan Hatch, and Mark Noll*. Lanham, MD: University Press of America, 1996.

Campbell, Heidi. *Exploring Religious Community Online: We Are One in the Network*. New York: Peter Lang, 2010.

———. "Understanding the Relationship between Religion Online and Offline in a Networked Society." *Journal of the American Academy of Religion* 80, no. 1 (2012): 64–93.

———. *When Religion Meets New Media: Media, Religion and Culture*. London: Routledge, 2010.

Carlisle, Rodney P., and J. Geoffrey Golson, eds. *America in Revolt during the 1960s and 1970s*. Santa Barbara, CA: ABC-CLIO, 2008.

Carpenter, Joel A. "Fundamentalist Institutions and the Rise of Evangelical Protestantism, 1929–1942." *Church History* 49, no. 1 (1980): 62–75.

———. Introduction to Blumhofer and Carpenter, *Twentieth-Century Evangelicalism*, ix–xv.

———. "Moody Monthly." In Lora and Longton, *The Conservative Press in Twentieth-Century America*, 103–11.

Carroll, Peter N. *It Seemed Like Nothing Happened: America in the 1970s*. New Brunswick, NJ: Rutgers University Press, 2000.

"C. Everett Koop." Profiles in Science, US National Library of Medicine. Accessed November 16, 2015. https://profiles.nlm.nih.gov.

Christianity Today (home page). Accessed June 10, 2021. https://www.christianitytoday.org.

Cochran, Pamela D. H. *Evangelical Feminism: A History*. New York: New York University Press, 2005.

Coffman, Elesha J. *The Christian Century and the Rise of the Protestant Mainline.* New York: Oxford University Press, 2013.
Colson, Charles W. *Born Again.* Old Tappan, NJ: Chosen Books, 1976.
———. *Kingdoms in Conflict.* Grand Rapids, MI: Zondervan, 1987.
Colson, Charles W., and Richard John Neuhaus, eds. *Evangelicals and Catholics Together.* Nashville, TN: Thomas Nelson, 1994.
Condit, Celeste Michelle. *Decoding Abortion Rhetoric: Communicating Social Change.* Urbana: University of Illinois Press, 1990.
Congregation for the Doctrine of the Faith. *Instruction on Respect for Human Life in Its Origin and on the Dignity of Procreation: Donum Vitae.* Boston: Pauline Books, 1987.
Conklin, Beth A., and Lynn M. Morgan. "Babies, Bodies, and the Production of Personhood in North America and a Native Amazonian Society." *Ethos* 24, no. 4 (1996): 657–94.
Conover, Pamela Johnston, and Virginia Gray. *Feminism and the New Right: Conflict over the American Family.* New York: Praeger, 1983.
Convention on the Rights of the Child. Ratified November 20, 1989. UN Human Rights Office of the High Commissioner. Accessed May 12, 2016. https://www.ohchr.org.
Cook, Elisabeth A., Ted G. Jelen, and Clyde Wilcox. *Between Two Absolutes: Public Opinion and the Politics of Abortion.* Boulder, CO: Westview Press, 1992.
Cottrell, Robert C. *Sex, Drugs, and Rock 'n' Roll: The Rise of America's 1960s Counterculture.* Lanham, MD: Rowman and Littlefield, 2015.
Critchlow, Donald T. *Phyllis Schlafly and Grassroots Conservatism: A Woman's Crusade.* Princeton, NJ: Princeton University Press, 2005.
"CTAdvertising." *Christianity Today.* Accessed December 1, 2014, http://www.christianitytodayads.com.
Davis, Nancy J., and Robert V. Robinson. "Religious Orthodoxy: An Army without Foot Soldiers?" *Journal for the Scientific Study of Religion* 35, no. 3 (1996): 249–51.
Davis, Thomas W. "Babylon." In *Baker's Evangelical Dictionary of Biblical Theology*, edited by Walter A. Elwell. Grand Rapids, MI: Baker Books, 1996. Bible Study Tools. Accessed June 10, 2021. https://www.biblestudytools.com.
Dayton, Donald W. "Some Doubts about the Usefulness of the Category 'Evangelical.'" In *The Variety of American Evangelicalism*, ed. Donald W. Dayton and Robert K. Johnston, 245–51 (Knoxville: University of Tennessee Press, 1991).
DeBerg, Betty A. *Ungodly Women: Gender and the First Wave of American Fundamentalism.* Macon, GA: Mercer University Press, 2000.
Denes, Magda. *In Necessity and Sorrow: Life and Death in an Abortion Hospital.* New York: Basic Books, 1976.
Denton, Melinda Lundquist. "Gender and Marital Decision Making: Negotiating Religious Ideology and Practice." *Social Forces* 82, no. 3 (2004): 1151–80.

DeRogatis, Amy. "What Would Jesus Do? Sexuality and Salvation in Protestant Evangelical Sex Manuals: 1950 to the Present." *Church History* 74, no. 1 (2005): 97–137.
Diamond, Sara. *Not by Politics Alone: The Enduring Influence of the Christian Right*. New York: Guilford Press, 1998.
Doan, Alesha E. *Opposition and Intimidation: The Abortion Wars and Strategies of Political Harassment*. Ann Arbor: University of Michigan Press, 2010.
Dochuk, Darren. *From Bible Belt to Sunbelt: Plain-Folk Religion, Grassroots Politics, and the Rise of Evangelical Conservatism*. New York: W. W. Norton, 2012.
Dochuk, Darren, Thomas S. Kidd, and Kurt W. Peterson, eds. *American Evangelicalism: George Marsden and the State of American Religious History*. Notre Dame, IN: University of Notre Dame Press, 2014.
Dombrink, John, and Daniel Hillyard. *Sin No More: From Abortion to Stem Cells, Understanding Crime, Law, and Morality in America*. New York: New York University Press, 2007.
Domke, David, and Kevin M. Coe. *The God Strategy: How Religion Became a Political Weapon in America*. New York: Oxford University Press, 2010.
Dorgan, Howard. *The Airwaves of Zion: Radio and Religion in Appalachia*. Knoxville: University of Tennessee Press, 1993.
Dowland, Seth. "'Family Values' and the Formation of a Christian Right Agenda," *Church History* 78, no. 3 (2009): 606–31.
Eck, Diana L. *A New Religious America: How a "Christian Country" Has Now Become the World's Most Religiously Diverse Nation*. San Francisco: Harper San Francisco, 2001.
Eells, Robert, and Bartell Nyberg. *Lonely Walk: The Life of Senator Mark Hatfield*. Chappaqua, NY: Christian Herald Books, 1979.
Eliade, Mircea, ed. *The Encyclopedia of Religion*. 16 vols. New York: Macmillan, 1987.
Engdahl, Sylvia, ed. *The Women's Liberation Movement*. Detroit, MI: Greenhaven Press, 2012.
Erickson, Paul D. *Reagan Speaks: The Making of an American Myth*. New York: New York University Press, 1985.
Evans, Colleen Townsend, and Louis H. Evans. *My Lover, My Friend*. Old Tappan, NJ: Revell, 1976.
Evans, John H. *Contested Reproduction: Genetic Technologies, Religion, and Public Debate*. Chicago: University of Chicago Press, 2010.
———. "Polarization in Abortion Attitudes in U.S. Religious Traditions, 1972–1998." *Sociological Forum* 17, no. 3 (2002): 397–422.
Evans, John H., and Kathy Hudson. "Religion and Reproductive Genetics: Beyond Views of Embryonic Life?" *Journal for the Scientific Study of Religion* 46, no. 4 (2007): 565–81.
Fackler, P. Mark, and Charles H. Lippy, eds. *Popular Religious Magazines of the United States*. Westport, CT: Greenwood Press, 1995.

Falwell, Jerry. *The Fundamentalist Phenomenon*. Garden City, NY: Doubleday, 1981.

Farber, David R., and Beth L. Bailey. *The Columbia Guide to America in the 1960s*. New York: Columbia University Press, 2001.

Finger, Reta Halteman, and S. Sue Horner. "Euro-American Evangelical Feminism." In Keller and Ruether, *Encyclopedia of Women and Religion in North America*, 467–76.

Flanagan, Geraldine Lux. *The First Nine Months of Life*. New York: Simon and Schuster, 1962.

Flippen, J. Brooks. *Jimmy Carter, the Politics of Family, and the Rise of the Religious Right*. Athens: University of Georgia Press, 2011.

Foster, Gaines M. *Moral Reconstruction: Christian Lobbyists and the Federal Legislation of Morality, 1865–1920*. Chapel Hill: University of North Carolina Press, 2002.

Fowler, Robert Booth. *A New Engagement: Evangelical Political Thought, 1966–1976*. Grand Rapids, MI: Eerdmans, 1982.

Fuller, Daniel P. *Give the Winds a Mighty Voice: The Story of Charles E. Fuller*. Eugene, OR: Wipf and Stock, 2014.

Gallagher, Sally K. *Evangelical Identity and Gendered Family Life*. New Brunswick, NJ: Rutgers University Press, 2003.

———. "The Marginalization of Evangelical Feminism." *Sociology of Religion* 65, no. 3 (2004): 215–37.

Gallagher, Sally K., and Christian Smith. "Symbolic Traditionalism and Pragmatic Egalitarianism: Contemporary Evangelicals, Families, and Gender." *Gender and Society* 13 (1999): 211–33.

Gardella, Peter. "Sex and Submission in the Spirit." In *Religions of the United States in Practice*, edited by Colleen McDannell, vol. 2, 173–93. Princeton, NJ: Princeton University Press, 2002.

Gardner, Christine J. *Making Chastity Sexy: The Rhetoric of Evangelical Abstinence Campaigns*. Berkeley: University of California Press, 2011.

Genovese, Michael A. *The Watergate Crisis*. Westport, CT: Greenwood Press, 1999.

Giardina, Carol. *Freedom for Women: Forging the Women's Liberation Movement, 1953–1970*. Gainesville: University Press of Florida, 2010.

Girolimon, Michael T. "Eternity." In Fackler and Lippy, *Popular Religious Magazines of the United States*, 221–26.

Gloege, Timothy E. W. *Guaranteed Pure: The Moody Bible Institute, Business, and the Making of Modern Evangelicalism*. Chapel Hill: University of North Carolina Press, 2017.

Gordon, Linda. *The Moral Property of Women: A History of Birth Control Politics in America*. 3rd ed. Urbana: University of Illinois Press, 2002.

Graber, Mark A. *Rethinking Abortion: Equal Choice, the Constitution, and Reproductive Politics*. Princeton, NJ: Princeton University Press, 1996.

Graham, Billy. *How to Be Born Again*. 1977. Dallas, TX: Word, 1989.

Gray, Patrick. "'God Is Dead' Controversy." *New Georgia Encyclopedia*. April 1, 2003. https://www.georgiaencyclopedia.org.
Green, John C. "A Look at the 'Invisible Army': Pat Robertson's 1988 Activist Corps." In Green, Guth, Smidt, and Kellstedt, *Religion and the Culture Wars*, 44–61.
Green, John C., James L. Guth, Corwin E. Smidt, and Lyman A. Kellstedt, eds. *Religion and the Culture Wars: Dispatches from the Front*. Lanham, MD: Rowman and Littlefield, 1996.
Green, John C., Mark J. Rozell, and Clyde Wilcox, eds. *The Christian Right in American Politics: Marching to the Millennium*. Washington, DC: Georgetown University Press, 2003.
Greenhouse, Linda, and Reva B. Siegel. *Before Roe v. Wade: Voices That Shaped the Abortion Debate before the Supreme Court's Ruling*. New Haven, CT: Yale Law School, 2012.
Griffin, Leslie C. "Religious Sanctity and Political Power." In *The Legacy of Billy Graham: Critical Reflections on America's Greatest Evangelist*, edited by Michael G. Long, 107–21. Louisville, KY: John Knox Press, 2008.
Griffith, Ruth Marie. *God's Daughters: Evangelical Women and the Power of Submission*. Berkeley: University of California Press, 2000.
Groothuis, Rebecca Merrill. *Women Caught in the Conflict: The Culture War between Traditionalism and Feminism*. Grand Rapids, MI: Baker Books, 1993.
Grounds, Vernon C. *Revolution and the Christian Faith: An Evangelical Perspective*. Philadelphia, PA: Lippincott, 1971.
Gundry, Patricia. *Woman Be Free: Biblical Equality for Women*. Grand Rapids, MI: Ministry Resources Library, 1977.
Guth, James L. *The Bully Pulpit: The Politics of Protestant Clergy*. Lawrence: University Press of Kansas, 1997.
———. "The Bully Pulpit: Southern Baptist Clergy and Political Activism, 1980–92." In Green, Guth, Smidt, and Kellstedt, *Religion and the Culture Wars*, 146–73.
Guth, James L., and John C. Green. "The Moralizing Minority: Christian Right Support among Political Contributors." In Green, Guth, Smidt, and Kellstedt, *Religion and the Culture Wars*, 30–43.
Gutjahr, Paul C. "The Perseverance of Print-Bound Saints: Protestant Book Publishing." In *A History of the Book in America*, vol. 5, *The Enduring Book: Print Culture in Postwar America*, edited by David Paul Nord, Joan Shelley Rubin, and Michael Schudson, 376–88. Chapel Hill: University of North Carolina Press, 2009.
Haberski, Raymond J. *God and War: American Civil Religion since 1945*. New Brunswick, NJ: Rutgers University Press, 2012.
Hall, David D. *Lived Religion in America: Toward a History of Practice*. Princeton, NJ: Princeton University Press, 1997.
Hall, Stephen S. *Invisible Frontiers: The Race to Synthesize a Human Gene*. New York: Atlantic Monthly Press, 1987.

Hammill, Faye, Paul Hjartarson, and Hannah McGregor. "Magazines and/as Media: Periodical Studies and the Question of Disciplinarity." *Journal of Modern Periodical Studies* 6, no. 2 (2016): iii–xiii.

Handy, Robert T. *A Christian America: Protestant Hopes and Historical Realities.* 2nd ed. New York: Oxford University Press, 1984.

Hangen, Tona J. *Redeeming the Dial: Radio, Religion, and Popular Culture in America.* Chapel Hill: University of North Carolina Press, 2002.

Hankins, Barry. *Francis Schaeffer and the Shaping of Evangelical America.* Grand Rapids, MI: Eerdmans, 2008.

Harding, Susan Friend. *The Book of Jerry Falwell: Fundamentalist Language and Politics.* Princeton, NJ: Princeton University Press, 2000.

Harris, Jane. "American Evangelical Women: More Than Wives and Mothers—Reformers, Ministers, and Leaders." In Keller and Ruether, *Encyclopedia of Women and Religion in North America*, 447–57.

Hase, Thomas. *Zivilreligion: Religionswissenschaftliche Überlegungen zu einem Theoretischen Konzept am Beispiel der USA.* Würzburg, Germany: Ergon Verlag, 2001.

Hatfield, Mark. *Between a Rock and a Hard Place.* Waco, TX: Word Books, 1976.

Henry, Carl F. H. *The Christian Mindset in a Secular Society.* Portland, OR: Multnomah, 1984.

———. *The Uneasy Conscience of Modern Fundamentalism.* Grand Rapids, MI: Eerdmans, 1947.

Herman, Didi. *The Antigay Agenda: Orthodox Vision and the Christian Right.* Chicago: University of Chicago Press, 1997.

Hibbs, Ben, ed. *White House Sermons.* New York: Harper and Row, 1972.

Hipps, Shane A. *The Hidden Power of Electronic Culture: How Media Shapes Faith, the Gospel, and Church.* Grand Rapids, MI: Zondervan, 2005.

Hochgeschwender, Michael. *Amerikanische Religion: Evangelikalismus, Pfingstlertum und Fundamentalismus.* Frankfurt: Verlag der Weltreligionen, 2007.

Hoffmann, John P., and Sherrie Mills Johnson. "Attitudes toward Abortion among Religious Traditions in the United States: Change or Continuity?" *Sociology of Religion* 66, no. 2 (2005): 161–82.

Hofrichter, Peter. "Haupt." In *Bibeltheologisches Wörterbuch*, edited by Johannes Baptist Bauer, 285–87. Graz, Austria: Styria, 2001.

Hoover, Stewart M. "The Culturalist Turn in Scholarship on Media and Religion." *Journal of Media and Religion* 1, no. 1 (2002): 25–36.

———. *Mass Media Religion: The Social Sources of the Electronic Church.* Newbury Park, CA: Sage, 1988.

———. *Religion in the News: Faith and Journalism in American Public Discourse.* Thousand Oaks, CA: Sage, 1998.

Howard, Ted, and Jeremy Rifkin. *Who Should Play God? The Artificial Creation of Life and What It Means for the Future of the Human Race.* New York: Delacorte Press, 1977.

Huff, Peter A. *What Are They Saying about Fundamentalisms?* Mahwah, NJ: Paulist Press, 2008.
Hunter, James Davison. *Culture Wars: The Struggle to Define America.* New York: Basic Books, 1991.
———. *Evangelicalism: The Coming Generation.* Chicago: University of Chicago Press, 1987.
———. "Religion and Political Civility: The Coming Generation of Evangelicals." *Journal for the Scientific Study of Religion* 23, no. 4 (1984): 364–80.
Ingersoll, Julie. *Evangelical Christian Women: War Stories in the Gender Battles.* New York: New York University Press, 2003.
"InterVarsity and IFES History." InterVarsity. Accessed June 10, 2021. https://intervarsity.org.
Isserman, Maurice, and Michael Kazin. *America Divided: The Civil War of the 1960s.* New York: Oxford University Press, 2000.
Jackson, Myles W. *The Genealogy of a Gene: Patents, HIV/AIDS, and Race.* Cambridge: MIT Press, 2015.
Jacoby, Kerry N. *Souls, Bodies Spirits: The Drive to Abolish Abortion since 1973.* Westport, CT: Praeger, 1998.
Jakobsen, Janet R., and Ann Pellegrini. *Love the Sin: Sexual Regulation and the Limits of Religious Tolerance.* New York: New York University Press, 2003.
Jefferis, Jennifer L. *Armed for Life: The Army of God and Anti-Abortion Terror in the United States.* Santa Barbara, CA: Praeger, 2011.
Johnson, Eithne. "Dr. Dobson's Advice to Christian Women: The Story of Strategic Motherhood." *Social Text* 57 (1998): 55–82.
Johnson, Stephen D., and Joseph B. Tamney. "The Christian Right and the 1980 Presidential Election." *Journal for the Scientific Study of Religion* 21, no. 2 (1982): 123–31.
Johnston, George F. *Abortion from the Religious and the Moral Perspective: An Annotated Bibliography.* Westport, CT: Praeger, 2003.
Jorstad, Erling. *The Politics of Moralism: The New Christian Right in American Life.* Minneapolis: Augsburg, 1981.
Joyce, Kathryn. *The Child Catchers: Rescue, Trafficking, and the New Gospel of Adoption.* New York: PublicAffairs, 2013.
Juergensmeyer, Mark. *Terror in the Mind of God: The Global Rise of Religious Violence.* 3rd ed. Berkeley: University of California Press, 2003.
Keely, Charles B. "Effects of the Immigration Act of 1965 on Selected Population Characteristics of Immigrants to the United States." *Demography* 8, no. 2 (1971): 157–69.
Kehrer, Günter. "Bürgerliche Religion/Civil Religion." In *Handbuch Religionswissenschaftlicher Grundbegriffe*, edited by Hubert Cancik, Burkhard Gladigow, and Matthias Laubscher, vol. 2, 176–80. Stuttgart, Germany: Kohlhammer, 1990.
Keller, Rosemary Skinner, and Rosemary Radford Ruether, eds. *Encyclopedia of*

Women and Religion in North America. Vol. 1. Bloomington: Indiana University Press, 2006.
Kevles, Bettyann. *Naked to the Bone: Medical Imaging in the Twentieth Century*. New Brunswick, NJ: Rutgers University Press, 1997.
Kiecolt, K. Jill, and Hart M. Nelsen. "Evangelicals and Party Realignment, 1976–1988." *Social Science Quarterly* 72, no. 3 (1991): 552–69.
Killeen, Alison J. "Finding Aid for the Nancy A. Hardesty Papers." Archive of Women in Theological Scholarship, Burke Library, Union Theological Seminary. Accessed July 9, 2015. http://library.columbia.edu.
Killen, Andreas. *1973 Nervous Breakdown: Watergate, Warhol, and the Birth of Post-Sixties America*. New York: Bloomsbury, 2008.
Kintz, Linda, and Julia Lesage, eds. *Media, Culture, and the Religious Right*. Minneapolis: University of Minnesota Press, 1998.
Kling, David. "Sojourners." In *Religious Periodicals of the United States: Academic and Scholarly Journals*, edited by Charles H. Lippy, 479–82. Westport, CT: Greenwood Press, 1986.
Kling, David W., Michael E. Pregill, Antonio D. Sison, Janet E. Spittler, Greg Sterling, Jay Twomey, Andrew Wingate, and Zvi Zohar. "Conversion." *Encyclopedia of the Bible and Its Reception*. Accessed June 10, 2021. https://doi.org/10.1515/ebr.conversion.
"Koop, Charles Everett." *West's Encyclopedia of American Law*, Encyclopedia.com. Accessed November 16, 2015. https://www.encyclopedia.com.
Krämer, Felix. *Moral Leaders: Medien, Gender und Glauben in den USA der 1970er und 1980er Jahre*. Bielefeld, Germany: Transcript, 2015.
Krapohl, Robert H., and Charles H. Lippy. *The Evangelicals: A Historical, Thematic, and Biographical Guide*. Westport, CT: Greenwood Press, 1999.
Kruse, Kevin M. *One Nation under God: How Corporate America Invented Christian America*. New York: Basic Books, 2016.
Kutler, Stanley I. *Watergate: A Brief History with Documents*. Malden, MA: Wiley-Blackwell, 2010.
LaHaye, Tim. *The Battle for the Mind*. Old Tappan, NJ: Revell, 1980.
Larson, Edward J. *Summer for the Gods: The Scopes Trial and America's Continuing Debate over Science and Religion*. New York: Basic Books, 1997.
Latham, Sean, and Robert Scholes. "The Rise of Periodical Studies." *PMLA* 121, no. 2 (2006): 517–31.
Levy, Peter B., ed. *America in the Sixties—Right, Left, and Center: A Documentary History*. Westport, CT: Greenwood Press, 1999.
Lewis, C. S. *Perelandra: Voyage to Venus*. London: Harper Collins, 1943.
Liebman, Robert C., and Robert Wuthnow. *New Christian Right: Mobilization and Legitimation*. New York: Aldine, 1983.
Lienesch, Michael. "Family." In *The New Christian Right: Political and Social Issues*, edited by Melvin I. Urofsky and Martha May, 296–352. New York: Garland, 1996.

———. *Redeeming America: Piety and Politics in the New Christian Right*. Chapel Hill: University of North Carolina Press, 1993.

Linder, Robert D. "The Resurgence of Evangelical Social Concern." In *The Evangelicals: What They Believe, Who They Are, Where They Are Changing*, edited by David F. Wells and John D. Woodbridge, 189–210. Nashville, TN: Abingdon Press, 1975.

Lindsell, Harold. *The Battle for the Bible*. Grand Rapids, MI: Zondervan, 1976.

Lora, Ronald, and William Henry Longton, eds. *The Conservative Press in Twentieth-Century America*. Westport, CT: Greenwood Press, 1999.

Lorenz, Konrad. "Die angeborenen formen möglicher Erfahrung." *Zeitschrift für Tierpsychologie* 5, no. 2 (1943): 235–409.

Lovin, Robin W. "Reinhold Niebuhr (1892–1971)." In *Makers of Christian Theology in America*, edited by Mark G. Toulouse and James O. Duke, 413–19. Nashville, TN: Abingdon Press, 1997.

Luhr, Eileen. "A Revolutionary Mission: Young Evangelicals and the Language of the Sixties." In Schäfer, *American Evangelicals and the 1960s*, 61–80.

Luker, Kristin. *Abortion and the Politics of Motherhood*. Berkeley: University of California Press, 1984.

Magruder, Jeb Stuart. *From Power to Peace*. Waco, TX: Word Books, 1978.

March, Charles. *Wayward Christian Soldiers: Freeing the Gospel from Political Captivity*. Oxford: Oxford University Press, 2007.

Marsden, George M., ed. *Evangelicalism and Modern America*. Grand Rapids, MI: Eerdmans, 1984.

———. *Fundamentalism and American Culture*. Oxford: Oxford University Press, 2006.

———. *Reforming Fundamentalism: Fuller Seminary and the New Evangelicalism*. Grand Rapids, MI: Eerdmans, 1995.

———. *Understanding Fundamentalism and Evangelicalism*. Grand Rapids, MI: Eerdmans, 1991.

Martin, William. *With God on Our Side: The Rise of the Religious Right in America*. New York: Broadway Books, 1996.

Martschukat, Jürgen, and Olaf Stieglitz. *Geschichte der Männlichkeiten*. Frankfurt, Germany: Campus Verlag, 2008.

Marty, Martin E. "Pluralism." *Annals of the American Academy of Political and Social Science* 612 (July 2007): 14–25.

———. "The Protestant Press: Limitations and Possibilities." In *The Religious Press in America*, edited by Martin E. Marty, John G. Deedy Jr., David Wolf Silverman, and Robert Lekachman, 5–63. New York: Holt, Rinehart and Winston, 1963.

Mason, Carol. *Killing for Life: The Apocalyptic Narrative of Pro-Life Politics*. Ithaca, NY: Cornell University Press, 2002.

McBride, Dorothy E. *Abortion in the United States: A Reference Handbook*. Santa Barbara, CA: ABC-CLIO, 2008.

McConkey, Dale. "Whither Hunter's Culture War? Shifts in Evangelical Morality, 1988–1998." *Sociology of Religion* 62, no. 2 (2001): 149–74.
McGirr, Lisa. *Suburban Warriors: The Origins of the New American Right.* Princeton, NJ: Princeton University Press, 2001.
Metford, J. C. J. ed. *Dictionary of Christian Lore and Legend.* London: Thames and Hudson, 1983.
Mettele, Gisela. *Weltbürgertum oder Gottesreich? Die Herrnhuter Brüdergemeine als globale Gemeinschaft, 1760–1857.* Göttingen, Germany: Vandenhoeck and Ruprecht, 2009.
Miller, Steven P. *The Age of Evangelicalism: America's Born-Again Years.* Oxford: Oxford University Press, 2014.
———. *Billy Graham and the Rise of the Republican South.* Philadelphia: University of Pennsylvania Press, 2009.
Modica, Joseph B. "Daughters of Sarah." In Fackler and Lippy, *Popular Religious Magazines of the United States,* 202–6.
Mollenkott, Virginia Ramey. *Women, Men and the Bible.* Nashville, TN: Abingdon Press, 1977.
Morgan, Marabel. *Total Joy.* Old Tappan, NJ: Revell, 1977.
———. *The Total Woman.* Old Tappan, NJ: Revell, 1973.
Morrow, Richard A. "Door." In Fackler and Lippy, *Popular Religious Magazines of the United States,* 212–18.
Munson, Ziad W. *The Making of Pro-Life Activists: How Social Movement Mobilization Works.* Chicago: University of Chicago Press, 2008.
Murphy, Andrew R., and Thomas Wortmann. "Jeremiad." *Encyclopedia of the Bible and Its Reception.* Accessed June 10, 2021. https://doi.org/10.1515/ebr.jeremiad.
Neuhaus, Richard John. *The Naked Public Square: Religion and Democracy in America.* Grand Rapids, MI: Eerdmans, 1984.
Noll, Mark A. *American Evangelical Christianity: An Introduction.* Oxford: Blackwell, 2001.
———. "Evangelicals Past and Present." In *Religion, Politics, and the American Experience: Reflections on Religion and American Public Life,* edited by Edith L. Blumhofer, 103–22. Tuscaloosa: University of Alabama Press, 2002.
Noll, Mark A., Nathan O. Hatch, and George M. Marsden. *The Search for Christian America.* Westchester, IL: Crossway Books, 1983.
Ockenga, Harold John. Introduction to C. Henry, *The Uneasy Conscience of Modern Fundamentalism,* 13–14.
O'Connor, Karen. *No Neutral Ground? Abortion Politics in an Age of Absolutes.* Boulder, CO: Westview Press, 1996.
Olson, Keith W. *Watergate: The Presidential Scandal That Shook America.* Lawrence: University Press of Kansas, 2003.
Olson, Roger E. *The Westminster Handbook to Evangelical Theology.* Louisville, KY: Westminster John Knox Press, 2004.

Packard, Vance. *Our Endangered Children: Growing Up in a Changing World.* New York: Little, Brown, 1983.
Padgett, Alan G. "The Bible and Gender Troubles: American Evangelicals Debate Scripture and Submission." *Dialogue* 47, no. 1 (2008): 21–26.
Palmer, Louis J. *Encyclopedia of Abortion in the United States.* Jefferson, NC: McFarland, 2002.
Petchesky, Rosalind Pollack. "Fetal Images: The Power of Visual Culture in the Politics of Reproduction." *Feminist Studies* 13, no. 2 (1987): 263–92.
Petro, Anthony M. *After the Wrath of God: AIDS, Sexuality, and American Religion.* Oxford: Oxford University Press, 2015.
Phillips, Anne. *Democracy and Difference.* Oxford: Oxford University Press, 1993.
Pierard, Richard V., and Robert D. Linder. *Civil Religion and the Presidency.* Grand Rapids, MI: Academic Books, 1988.
Pierce, Ronald W. "Contemporary Evangelicals for Gender Equality." In Pierce and Groothuis, *Discovering Biblical Equality,* 58–75.
Pierce, Ronald W., and Rebecca Merrill Groothuis, eds. *Discovering Biblical Equality: Complementary without Hierarchy.* 2nd ed. Downers Grove, IL: InterVarsity Press, 2005.
Preston, Andrew. *Sword of the Spirit, Shield of Faith: Religion in American War and Diplomacy.* New York: Anchor Books, 2012.
Prison Fellowship (home page). Accessed January 25, 2014. http://www.prisonfellowship.org.
Quebedeaux, Richard. *The Young Evangelicals: Revolution in Orthodoxy.* New York: Harper and Row, 1974.
"Religion in America." Special issue, *Gallup Report,* nos. 201–2 (June/July 1982).
Resnik, Jack. "The Baby Doe Rules." *The Embryo Project Encyclopedia.* Arizona State University. Posted May 12, 2011. https://embryo.asu.edu.
Ribuffo, Leo P. "Family Policy Past as Prologue: Jimmy Carter, the White House Conference on Families, and the Mobilization of the New Christian Right." *Review of Policy Research* 23, no. 2 (2006): 311–38.
Rice, John R. *Bobbed Hair, Bossy Wives and Women Preachers: Significant Questions for Honest Christian Women Settled by the Word of God.* Wheaton, IL: Sword of the Lord, 1944.
Risen, James, and Judy L. Thomas. *Wrath of Angels: The American Abortion War.* New York: Basic Books, 1998.
Robertson, Pat. *America's Date with Destiny.* Nashville, TN: Thomas Nelson, 1986.
Roth, Rachel. *Making Women Pay: The Hidden Costs of Fetal Rights.* Ithaca, NY: Cornell University Press, 2000.
Rousseau, Jean-Jacques. *The Social Contract.* 1762. New York: Wallachia, 2015.
Rowland, Robert C., and John M. Jones. "'Until Next Week': The Saturday Radio Addresses of Ronald Reagan." *Presidential Studies Quarterly* 32, no. 1 (2002): 84–110.

Ruether, Rosemary Radford. *Sexism and God-Talk: Toward a Feminist Theology.* Boston: Beacon Press, 1993.
Ryan, Mary P. *Mysteries of Sex: Tracing Women and Men through American History.* Chapel Hill: University of North Carolina Press, 2009.
Ryrie, Charles C. *The Place of Women in the Church.* New York: Macmillan, 1958.
Saletan, William. *Bearing Right: How Conservatives Won the Abortion War.* Berkeley: University of California Press, 2003.
Scanzoni, Letha. *Letha's Calling* (blog). Accessed June 10, 2021. http://www.lethadawsonscanzoni.com.
——. *Sex and the Single Eye.* Grand Rapids, MI: Zondervan, 1968.
——. *Why Am I Here? Where Am I Going? Youth Looks at Life.* Westwood, NJ: Revell, 1966.
——. *Youth Looks at Love.* Westwood, NJ: Revell, 1964.
Scanzoni, Letha, and Nancy Hardesty. *All We're Meant to Be: A Biblical Approach to Women's Liberation.* Waco, TX: Word Books, 1974.
Schaeffer, Francis A. *A Christian Manifesto.* Westchester, IL: Crossway Books, 1981.
——. *The Church at the End of the Twentieth Century.* London: Norfolk Press, 1970.
——. *The God Who Is There.* Downers Grove, IL: InterVarsity Press, 1968.
——. *How Should We Then Live? The Rise and Decline of Western Thought and Culture.* Old Tappan, NJ: Revell, 1976.
Schaeffer, Francis A., and C. Everett Koop. *Whatever Happened to the Human Race?* Old Tappan, NJ: Revell, 1979.
Schaeffer, Franky. *Bad News for Modern Man: An Agenda for Christian Activism.* Westchester, IL: Crossway Books, 1984.
——. *A Time for Anger: The Myth of Neutrality.* Westchester, IL: Crossway Books, 1982.
Schäfer, Axel R., ed. *American Evangelicals and the 1960s.* Madison: University of Wisconsin Press, 2013.
——. *Countercultural Conservatives: American Evangelicalism from the Postwar Revival to the New Christian Right.* Madison: University of Wisconsin Press, 2011.
Scheiding, Oliver, and Anja-Maria Bassimir, eds. *Religious Periodicals and Publishing in Transnational Contexts: The Press and the Pulpit.* Newcastle upon Tyne, UK: Cambridge Scholars, 2017.
——. "Under the Cover of Religious Periodicals: Editorial Practice and Magazine Production." In *Periodicals in Focus: Methodological Approaches and Theoretical Frameworks,* edited by Jutta Ernst, Dagmar von Hoff, and Björn von Rimscha. Leiden: Brill, 2020 (forthcoming).
Schroedel, Jean Reith. *Is the Fetus a Person? A Comparison of Policies across the Fifty States.* Ithaca, NY: Cornell University Press, 2000.
Schultze, Quentin J. *Televangelism and American Culture: The Business of Popular Religion.* Grand Rapids, MI: Baker Books, 1991.

Scott, Elizabeth S. "Surrogacy and the Politics of Commodification." *Law and Contemporary Problems* 73, no. 3 (2009): 109–46.
Sharlet, Jeff. *C Street: The Fundamentalist Threat to American Democracy*. New York: Little, Brown, 2010.
———. *The Family: The Secret Fundamentalism at the Heart of American Power*. New York: Harper Collins, 2008.
Shedd, Charlie, and Martha Shedd. *Celebration in the Bedroom*. Waco, TX: Word Books, 1979.
———. *How to Stay in Love*. Kansas City, KS: Andrews and McMeel, 1980.
———. *Praying Together: Making Marriage Last*. Grand Rapids, MI: Zondervan, 1985.
Shermer, Elizabeth Tandy. *Sunbelt Capitalism: Phoenix and the Transformation of American Politics*. Philadelphia: University of Pennsylvania Press, 2015.
Shipps, Kenneth W. "Christianity Today." In Lora and Longton, *The Conservative Press in Twentieth-Century America*, 171–80.
Shorris, Earl. *The Politics of Heaven: America in Fearful Times*. New York: W. W. Norton, 2007.
Smidt, Corwin E. *American Evangelicals Today*. Lanham, MD: Rowman and Littlefield, 2013.
———. "Evangelicals within Contemporary American Politics: Differentiating between Fundamentalist and Non-Fundamentalist Evangelicals." *Western Political Quarterly* 41, no. 3 (1988): 601–20.
———. "'Praise the Lord' Politics: A Comparative Analysis of the Social Characteristics and Political Views of American Evangelical and Charismatic Christians." *Sociological Analysis* 50, no. 1 (1989): 53–72.
Smith, Christian. *American Evangelicalism: Embattled and Thriving*. Chicago: University of Chicago Press, 1998.
———. *Christian America? What Evangelicals Really Want*. Berkeley: University of California Press, 2002.
Smith, Gary Scott. *Religion in the Oval Office: The Religious Lives of American Presidents*. New York: Oxford University Press, 2015.
Smith, Leslie Dorrough. *Righteous Rhetoric: Sex, Speech, and the Politics of Concerned Women for America*. New York: Oxford University Press, 2014.
Smith, Timothy L. "The Evangelical Kaleidoscope and the Call to Christian Unity." *Christian Scholar's Review* 15 (1986): 125–40.
Solinger, Rickie. *Abortion Wars: A Half Century of Struggle: 1950–2000*. Berkeley: University of California Press, 1998.
———. *Pregnancy and Power: A Short History of Reproductive Politics in America*. New York: New York University Press, 2005.
Soper, J. Christopher. *Evangelical Christianity in the United States and Great Britain: Religious Beliefs, Political Choices*. New York: New York University Press, 1994.
Sperling, S. David. "Jeremiah." In Eliade, *The Encyclopedia of Religion*, vol. 8, 1–6.
Spring, Beth. *Infertile Couple*. Elgin, IL: D. C. Cook, 1987.

Stasson, Anneke. "The Politicization of Family Life: How Headship Became Essential to Evangelical Identity in the Late Twentieth Century." *Religion and American Culture* 24, no. 1 (2014): 100–138.
Stout, Daniel A., and Judith M. Buddenbaum. "Genealogy of an Emerging Field: Foundations for the Study of Media and Religion." *Journal of Media and Religion* 1, no. 1 (2002): 5–12.
Sutton, Matthew Avery. *American Apocalypse: A History of Modern Evangelicalism*. Cambridge, MA: Belknap Press of Harvard University Press, 2017.
Swartz, David R. "The Evangelical Left and the Move from Personal to Social Responsibility." In Schäfer, *American Evangelicals and the 1960s*, 211–30.
———. *Moral Minority: The Evangelical Left in an Age of Conservatism*. Philadelphia: University of Pennsylvania Press, 2012.
Sweeney, Douglas A. "Christianity Today." In Fackler and Lippy, *Popular Religious Magazines of the United States*, 144–51. Westport, CT: Greenwood Press, 1995.
———. "The Essential Evangelicalism Dialectic: The Historiography of the Early Neo-Evangelical Movement and the Observer-Participant Dilemma." *Church History* 60, no. 1 (1991): 70–84.
Sweet, Leonard I. "Wise as Serpents, Innocent as Doves: The New Evangelical Historiography." *Journal of the American Academy of Religion* 56, no. 3 (1988): 397–416.
Tavard, George H. *Woman in Christian Tradition*. Notre Dame, IN: University of Notre Dame Press, 1996.
Thomson, Irene Taviss. *Culture Wars and Enduring American Dilemmas*. Ann Arbor: University of Michigan Press, 2010.
Vaca, Daniel. *Evangelicals Incorporated: Books and the Business of Religion in America*. Cambridge, MA: Harvard University Press, 2019.
VanDrunen, David. "The Two Kingdoms Doctrine and the Relationship of Church and State in the Early Reformed Tradition." *Journal of Church and State* 49, no. 4 (2007): 743–63.
Ward, Anna E. "Sex and the Me Decade: Sex and Dating Advice Literature of the 1970s." *Women's Studies Quarterly* 43, no. 3–4 (2015): 120–36.
Warner, Rob. *Secularization and Its Discontents*. New York: Continuum, 2010.
Waters, Ken. "Evangelical Magazines." In *Evangelical Christians and Popular Culture: Pop Goes the Gospel*, edited by Robert H. Woods Jr., vol. 3, 195–211. Santa Barbara, CA: Praeger, 2013.
———. "The Evangelical Press." In *The Oxford Handbook of Religion and the American News Media*, edited by Diane Winston, 551–64. New York: Oxford University Press, 2012.
———. "Pursuing New Periodicals in Print and Online." In *Understanding Evangelical Media: The Changing Face of Christian Communication*, edited by Quentin J. Schultze and Robert H. Woods Jr., 71–84. Downers Grove, IL: InterVarsity Press, 2008.
———. "Religious Magazines: Keeping the Faith." In *The Routledge Handbook of*

Magazine Research: The Future of the Magazine Form, edited by David Abrahamson and Marcia R. Prior-Miller, 308–22. New York: Routledge, 2015.

———. "Vibrant, but Invisible: A Study of Contemporary Religious Periodicals." *Journalism and Mass Communication Quarterly* 78, no. 2 (2001): 307–20.

Watson, Justin. *The Christian Coalition: Dreams of Restoration, Demands for Recognition*. New York: St. Martin's Press, 1997.

Watt, David H. *A Transforming Faith: Explorations of Twentieth-Century American Evangelicalism*. New Brunswick, NJ: Rutgers University Press, 1991.

Webber, Robert E. *The Moral Majority: Right or Wrong?* Saint Louis, MO: Cornerstone, 1981.

Weber, Max. *Economy and Society: An Outline of Interpretive Sociology*. 1922. Edited by Guenther Roth and Claus Wittich. Berkeley: University of California Press, 1978.

Weiß, Jana. *Fly the Flag and Give Thanks to God: Zivilreligion an U.S.-Amerikanischen, Patriotischen Feiertagen, 1945–1992*. Trier, Germany: Wissenschaftlicher Verlag Trier, 2015.

Wells, Tom. *Wild Man: The Life and Times of Daniel Ellsberg*. New York: Palgrave, 2001.

Wenzel, Knut. *Kleine Geschichte des Zweiten Vatikanischen Konzils*. Freiburg im Breisgau, Germany: Herder, 2005.

Whitehead, John W. *The Second American Revolution*. Elgin, IL: D. C. Cook, 1982.

Wilcox, Clyde. "Premillennialists at the Millennium: Some Reflections on the Christian Right in the Twenty-First Century." In *The Rapture of Politics: The Christian Right as the United States Approaches the Year 2000*, edited by Steve Bruce, Peter Kiviston, and William H. Swatos Jr., 21–40. New Brunswick, NJ: Transaction, 1995.

Wilcox, Clyde, and Carin Robinson. *Onward Christian Soldiers? The Religious Right in American Politics*. Boulder, CO: Westview Press, 1996.

Wilentz, Sean. *The Age of Reagan: A History, 1974–2008*. New York: Harper Perennial, 2008.

Wilkens, Steve, and Donald A. D. Thorsen. *Everything You Know about Evangelicals Is Wrong: (Well, Almost Everything): An Insider's Look at Myths and Realities*. Grand Rapids, MI: Baker Books, 2010.

Williams, Daniel K. "Sex and the Evangelicals: Gender Issues, the Sexual Revolution, and Abortion in the 1960s." In Schäfer, *American Evangelicals and the 1960s*, 97–120.

Wilson, Bryan R. "Secularization." In Eliade, *The Encyclopedia of Religion*, vol. 13, 159–65.

Wimberley, Ronald C. "Testing the Civil Religion Hypothesis." *Sociological Analysis* 37, no. 4 (1976): 341–52.

Wimberley, Ronald C., Donald A. Clelland, Thomas C. Hood, and C. M. Lipsey. "The Civil Religious Dimension: Is It There?" *Social Forces* 54, no. 4 (1976): 890–900.

Wittenburg Door (home page). Accessed June 10, 2021. http://www.wittenburgdoor.com.

Wolfe, Alan. *One Nation, After All: What Middle-Class Americans Really Think about God, Country, Family, Racism, Welfare, Immigration, Homosexuality, Work, the Right, the Left and Each Other.* New York: Penguin Books, 1999.

———. *The Transformation of American Religion: How We Actually Live Our Faith.* Chicago: University of Chicago Press, 2003.

Worthen, Molly. *Apostles of Reason: The Crisis of Authority in American Evangelicalism.* New York: Oxford University Press, 2016.

Wuthnow, Robert. *After Heaven: Spirituality in America since the 1950s.* Berkeley: University of California Press, 1998.

———. "Religious Commitment and Conservative: In Search of an Elusive Relationship." In *Religion in Social Perspective: Essays in the Empirical Study of Religion*, edited by Charles Y. Glock, 117–32. Belmont, CA: Wadsworth, 1973.

———. *The Restructuring of American Religion: Society and Faith since World War II.* Princeton, NJ: Princeton University Press, 1988.

Young, Neil J. "'A Saga of Sacrilege': Evangelicals Respond to the Second Vatican Council." In Schäfer, *American Evangelicals and the 1960s*, 255–79.

INDEX

Aaseng, Rolf E., 109, 111–12
abortion, 134–35, 177–81, 186, 199, 205, 210, 224, 305n89, 310n156; and culture war rhetoric, 229–30; for elective reasons, 180, 196–97, 224, 297n13; as family problem, 194–98; legalized, 140, 178, 181, 205, 245n26, 263n175, 310n144; as murder, 178, 180, 184, 186, 189, 204, 229; polarized attitudes toward, 296n8, 296n9; and poverty, 196–98; and race, 197–98; for traumatic reasons, 180, 297n13. *See also* antiabortion activism
abortion alternatives, 196, 201. *See also* adoption
abortion clinic, 191
abortion crisis center, 306n94
abortion procedure, 191–92, 191 (Fig. 6.5)
"abortion war," 281n31
absolutism, 291n130
academic Evangelicalism, 253n47
Adam and Eve (first persons), 110
adoption, 201–2, 306n94
advice literature, 112, 279n163
agency, women's, and submission, 99–100
Agnew, Vice President Spiro, resignation of, 50, 259n128
AIDS (Acquired Immune Deficiency Syndrome), 184, 232, 313n14
AIH (artificial insemination by husband), 221
Aikman, David, 134
Alexander, John F., 16, 31, 48, 103, 128, 130. *See also Other Side* (magazine)
Allitt, Patrick, 130
Alternative to Abortion hotlines/centers, 201–2

Ambrose (saint, bishop), 51
American Coalition for Traditional Values, 133
American Council of Christian Churches, 235n3
Americanism, 257n100
American Scientific Affiliation, 309n134
Anderson, Benedict R., 240n39
Anderson, John B., 65, 128
Anderson, Leith C., 292n130
Anderson, Ray S., 203–4
Anderson, V. Elving, 214–15
androgyny, 105–7, 110; psychological, 106–7
Andrusko, Dave, 217
Angus, Fay, 310n155
antiabortion activism, 123, 134–35, 182, 188, 197, 229, 281n31, 297n16
antiabortion terrorism, 184
artificial insemination by donor, 312n171
Augustine of Hippo (saint, bishop), 266n4

Baby Doe cases, 205–12
Baby Doe Law, 307n114
baby-for-spare-parts narrative, 217
Baby M case, 219–21, 223
Back to God Hour (radio program), 35
Badger, Doug, 194, 303n65
Bakker, Jim, 169–70, 172–73, 294n150
Bakker, Tammy Faye, 173
Balmer, Randall, 236n5, 284n29
Barabbas (New Testament figure), 37, 253n38
Barackman, Deborah, 13
Barcus, Nancy B., 91, 108–9, 120, 158
Barnhouse, Donald Grey, 12–13
Barnhouse, Margaret N., 68

Bartkowski, John P., 247n40
Bayly, Joseph, 13, 31, 53, 56, 70, 105, 109, 141, 171, 261n158
Beers, V. Gilbert, 12, 291n116
Bell, L. Nelson, 11
Bellah, Robert N., 29–30, 248n7, 249n8, 256n80
Bendroth, Margaret Lamberts, 23, 25, 76, 246n40, 272n62
Bendroth, Norman B., 211
Bentley, Ruth L., 77
Berger, Peter L., 160, 240n38
Bernstein, Carl, 50
"better together," 109–12, 122
Bible Belt, 19
Biblical/Christian feminists, 246n34
biblical citations: 1 Cor. 11, 81, 86; 1 Cor. 11:3, 118; 1 Peter 3:7, 82; 1 Sam., 117; 1 Tim. 2, 81; 2 Chron. 7:14, 65; Eph. 5, 75; Eph. 5:23, 118; Exod. 20:13, 194; Gal. 3:28, 86; Gen. 1, 81, 86; Gen. 1:26–27, 267n16; Gen. 1:26–28, 194; Gen. 1:27, 104, 106; Gen. 2, 77, 81, 86; Gen. 2:21–22, 267n16; Gen. 3, 78; Jer. 14:11, 60; Lev. 19:18, 230; Luke 1:41–44, 192; Luke 9:23–24, 262n165; Luke 10:38–42, 119; Mark 12:17, 49; Matt. 13, 293n146; Matt. 25:14–30, 34–35, 90; Matt. 25:31–46, 34–35; Prov. 31, 115; Ps. 139, 192; Rom. 16:1, 86; Rom. 16:3–4, 118
biblical inerrancy, 11
biblical parables and passages: creation account, 81, 104, 106, 109, 114; "Give to the emperor . . .," 49; Mary and Martha, 119–20, 279n174; Parable of the Talents, 34–35, 90; Priscilla and Aquila, 118; Sheep and the Goats, 34–35; Wife of Noble Character, 115
biblicism, 81, 277n151, 291n130
Billy Graham Crusade (University of Tennessee, Knoxville, 1970), 45
Billy Graham Evangelistic Association, 38, 46, 255n68

biomedical developments, 135, 212–16, 224–25
birth control, 198–201, 305n89
Black Evangelicalism, 31, 36–37, 48, 197–98, 253n38
Black liberation movement, 36–37
Bloesch, Donald G., 235n4
Board, Stephen, 13
Boehi, David, 215
Bohrer, Dick, 158, 177, 185
Boice, James Montgomery, 13
Boorstin, Daniel J., 250n20
born again, 30, 64, 70–72, 128, 261n158, 264n191. *See also* conversion, notion of; political conversion
Born Again (film, dir. Irving Rapper, AVCO Embassy Pictures, 1978), 261n159
Bourdieu, Pierre, 8–9, 227
Brand, Paul, 215, 309n139
Brands, H. W., 5, 146
Bray, Michael, 184
Brown, Harold O. J., 36, 181, 199–200, 211, 308n122
Brown, Ruth Murray, 24
Brubaker, Rogers, 233–34
Brushaber, George K., 12
Bryant, Anita, 92
Buchanan, Pat, 227–28
Burch, Maxie B., 289n89
Bush, President George H. W., 227
Bush, President George W., 308n127
Buursma, Bruce, 147

Calvin, John, 78, 266n4
Care Net, 306n94
Carpenter, Joel A., 14, 19, 21, 236n5, 239n27, 241n49, 264n191
Carroll, Peter N., 4, 33
Carter, President Jimmy, 19–20, 30, 67–70, 128, 130, 263n178; election of, 63, 67, 74; White House Conference on Families, 123, 178
CBN (Christian Broadcasting Network), 170, 173

INDEX

Chakrabarty, Ananda Mohan, 308n128
Chamberland, Dennis, 215-16
Chang, Lit-Sen, 64-65
Chapman, G. Clark, Jr., 259n129
Charisma (magazine), 233
child abuse, 187, 305n80
Child Abuse Amendments (1984), 307n114
Child Abuse Prevention and Treatment Act (1974), 209, 307n114
childhood, changing concept of, 198-201
child-rearing manuals, 92-93
children, 123, 135, 177, 198-204, 223-26, 305n80. See also unborn child
children, desire for, 221, 225
Children's Defense Fund, 197
children's rights movement, 199
Christensen, Charles, 194-95, 200
Christensen, Winnie, 78, 104, 109, 114, 194-95, 200
Christian Action Council, 181-82, 194, 201-2, 211, 302n53, 303n65, 306n94
Christian America, 10, 137, 139-40, 149-55, 152 (Fig. 5.2), 168, 175-76, 237n8
Christian Century (magazine), 10, 134, 142, 271n61
Christian citizens, 147-49, 162-69, 175-76
Christian communities, 39-40, 253n51, 253n52, 305n75. See also L'Abri
Christian foundations, debate over, 155-62
Christian History, 11
Christianity Today Institute, 10-11, 162-69, 309n130, 309n139; forum on biomedical decision-making, 214-15
Christianity Today (magazine), 2, 6, 8, 10-12, 21, 31-32, 43, 67, 70, 72, 90, 141, 147, 184, 203 (Fig. 6.8), 239n27, 255n68, 261n159; on abortion, 179, 181, 182 (Fig. 6.3), 183 (Fig. 6.4), 188, 195-98, 229-30, 304n71; articles, 34-35, 38, 47-48, 56, 60-62, 64, 91-92, 104, 107, 109-11, 118, 142, 144, 159-60, 170-71, 181, 186, 191, 197-200, 218, 220, 264n188, 277n141; on books, 94, 98; cartoons, 95-96, 95 (Fig. 3.1), 128, 129 (Fig. 4.1), 140; covers, 35-38, 63 (Fig. 2.5), 131, 132 (Fig. 4.2), 195-96, 195 (Fig. 6.7), 209-12, 209 (Fig. 6.9); on culture war, 228; editorials, 33, 50-51, 57, 69, 87-88, 127, 129, 181, 206-7, 212-13, 259n129, 292n136; on feminism, 78, 85-89, 268n22; on genetic engineering and medical research, 213-14, 309n130; and Hatfield's speech at Chicago Mayor's Prayer Breakfast (1973), 54-55; on homosexuality, 231-32, 314n15, 314n16; and Honor America Day, 45-47; interviews, 51, 157, 304n74; on New Christian Right, 127-28; online archive, 240n32; publication history, 233, 291n116; on Reagan Revolution, 131-34; retrospective on 1970s and forecast for 1980s, 140; Speaking Out column, 305n85; and *Whatever Happened to the Human Race?*, 182; "Willa's Dilemma" (story), 196-97
Christian Liberation Front (Berkeley, CA), 77, 253n51, 268n19
Christian Realism, 265n203
Christian revolution, 33-43
Christian Right, 20. See also New Christian Right
Christians for Biblical Equality (CBE), 246n34, 246n40, 278n154
Christians for Social Action, 266n9
Christian Statesman (magazine), 153-54, 288n81
citizenship, theology of, Christianity Today Institute and, 162-69
civil disobedience, 184, 292n138
civil religion, 10, 25, 27, 29-30, 44, 47, 69, 72, 141, 232, 248n7, 249n7, 256n80; Graham and, 47-48, 51-52;

Hatfield and, 54–56, 58; Rousseau and, 248n7
Clapp, Rodney, 198–99
Cleaver, Eldridge, 64
Clinton, President Bill, 134, 227, 308n127
Cochran, Pamela D. H., 24, 245n34, 246n40, 277n151
coins and currency, addition of wording "In God We Trust" to, 44
Coleman, William L., 114–15, 116 (Fig. 3.4)
Coles, Robert, 133–34
collective suicide, 200
Colliton, William Jr., 219
Colson, Charles W., 30, 62–64, 63 (Fig. 2.5), 73, 163, 176, 260n151, 260n156, 261n158, 261n159, 262n166, 286n45, 293n144; *Born Again*, 64; on Reagan Revolution, 131–32; on Robertson candidacy, 171–72
compassion, importance of, 205–6, 210–12, 223
complementarian view, 109–12, 114, 122, 245n33. *See also* "better together"; marriage
Concerned Women for America, 20
Condit, Celeste Michelle, 189
Congress on Evangelism (1969), 255n68
Conover, Pamela Johnston, 265n3
conscientious objectors, in Vietnam War, 59
Conservative Baptist Theological Seminary (Denver), 34, 69
conservative politics and conservative Christianity, alliance of, 43–49, 147
constructivist theory, 240n38
contemporary crisis, sense of, and New Christian Right, 140–42, 150
contraception. *See* birth control; procreation
conversion, notion of, 25, 62–70, 261n162, 262n165, 262n166
conversion, private, 73, 262n166

conversion experience, Evangelical, 62–70. *See also* born again
conversion politics, 10, 128, 232
Cook, Elisabeth A., 297n14
cooperation, as feminist principle, 25–26
corruption, official, 29; Evangelicals and, 51–58
Council on Biblical Manhood and Womanhood, 246n34
counterculture, 20, 25, 33–43, 139, 251n20
CT, 11
Culbertson, William, III, 14
cultism, 55–56
cultural evangelicalism, distinguished from Evangelicalism, 236n5
culture war, 5, 147–49, 228–29
Cunningham, Paige, 223

Daniel (prophet), 32
Dannemeyer, Rep. William E., 161
Daughters of Sarah newsletter, 8, 24, 75–77, 119, 278n154
Dayton, Donald W., 77, 235n4
Dayton, Lucille Sider, 77, 85
Dean, John, 258n111
DeBerg, Betty A., 23
Declaration of Evangelical Social Concern, 16, 22, 31–32, 76, 242n72, 250n16, 266n8
Deen, Edith, 83
Denes, Magda, 191
denomination/church, use of term, 235n3
Densen-Gerber, Julianne, 272n75
DeRogatis, Amy, 273n79, 277n141
Dickason, C. Fred, 111–12, 278n163
digital archives, 7
disability, 185, 205–12, 223
Dobson, Ed, 232
Dobson, James, 123
Dochuk, Darren, 244n10
Dombrink, John, 282n31

Douglass, David R., 96
Down syndrome, 208–10
Durkheim, Émile, 141

Eck, Diana L., 251n23
Edelman, Marian Wright, 197
editors, as representatives of Evangelicalism, 9
Eells, Robert, 258n110
Ehrlichman, John, 258n111
Eli (biblical figure), 117
Elkins, Thomas, 210
Elliot, Elisabeth, 24, 82, 84
embryonic life discourse, 135, 179, 184, 187–98, 217, 299n30, 301n50, 302n56
endangered species, 187
end times, approaching, 60
envisioning, use of term, 9
Erickson, Millard J., 64, 262n165, 310n139, 311n166, 312n171
Escobar, Samuel, 61
establishment, the, 39–40
establishment Evanglicalism, 31, 46, 49
Eternity (magazine), 12–13, 25, 49, 53, 61 (Fig. 2.4), 66 (Fig. 2.6), 67–69, 78, 127, 141, 261n159, 271n61, 295n168, 302n57; on abortion, 179, 181, 188, 207, 298n20; articles, 60, 128, 160, 200, 213, 220, 306n100; book award, 98; cartoons, 222–23, 222 (Fig. 6.10); closure of, 233; covers, 101–3, 102 (Fig. 3.3), 170, 170 (Fig. 5.4); editorials, 34–35, 50, 56, 202, 260n153; and Hatfield's speech at Chicago Mayor's Prayer Breakfast (1973), 54–55; interviews, 138–39; Out of My Mind columns (Bayly), 13, 31, 261n158; and quest for Christian America, 151–53, 152 (Fig. 5.2); reviews, 91–92, 157, 183; on Robertson candidacy, 173; on *Whatever Happened to the Human Race?*, 184; on women, 80–85, 108, 268n22

eugenics, 205, 208, 218–19
euthanasia, 185
evangelical (term), 138, 236n5–236n6, 249n11, 264n191
Evangelical (term), 2, 70–71, 236n6, 292n130
Evangelical and Ecumenical Women's Caucus, 278n154
Evangelical Foundation, 299n24
Evangelical identity crisis of 1970s, 9–10
Evangelicalism, 1–2, 19, 236n5, 244n18, 264n196; distinguished from cultural evangelicalism, 236n5; distinguished from Fundamentalism, 20–21, 143–44, 285n30; lack of institutional structures, 235n3; and New Christian Right, 142–44; transcending of denominational boundaries, 235n3; as "unity of disparate people," 227
Evangelical Left, 16, 22, 31, 42–43, 45, 73, 78, 127, 253n47, 268n19, 278n151, 280n21; distrust of political Left, 144–45; focus on social concern, 140–42. *See also Post-American/Sojourners* (magazine)
Evangelical magazines, 2–4, 6. *See also individual magazine titles*
Evangelical narratives, 8–9
Evangelical politics, 27–30
Evangelical renaissance, 235n4
"Evangelicals for McGovern," 50
Evangelicals for Social Action, 77, 127, 266n9, 267n11. *See also* Christians for Social Action
Evangelical Theological Society, 12
Evangelical Women's Caucus, 16, 24, 76–77, 88, 246n34, 278n154. *See also* Evangelical and Ecumenical Women's Caucus
Evans, Colleen Townsend, 276n139
Evans, John H., 179–81, 188, 282n34
Evans, Louis H., 276n139
Evans, W. Glyn, 61 (Fig. 2.4)

Faith Theological Seminary, 39
Falwell, Jerry, 71, 138-39, 142-43, 147-48, 284n27; and Christianity Today Institute, 162-63; *The Fundamentalist Phenomenon*, 143; and New Christian Right, 284n29; and PTL, 173; visit to South Africa, 171. *See also* Moral Majority
family, concept of, 122-24, 203, 222-23, 222 (Fig. 6.10)
family life, politicization of, 98
family manuals, Christian, 247n40
family of God, 203-4, 224
family planning, 200, 305n89. *See also* birth control
family relations, as context for fetus, 194-98
family values, 74, 178
feminism, 22-25
feminism, biblical, 85-89, 275n111, 278n154
feminism, evangelical, 25-26, 31, 36, 77-78, 98-101, 120-24, 246n34, 246n40, 247n40; development of, 23-25; and gender roles, 112-20; Scanzoni and, 85-89. *See also Daughters of Sarah* newsletter
feminism, traditionalist, 24-26, 76-78, 87, 98-101, 120-24, 245n34, 246n40, 247n40; and gender roles, 112-20
"feminist boomerang," 218, 310n156
fetal rights, 303n59, 304n71
fetal screening, 218
fetal tissue transplants, 217
fetus: image of, 188, 190-93, 193 (Fig. 6.6); as unborn child, 184, 188-98, 206
Finger, Reta Halteman, 278n154
First Things (magazine), 290n103
Flanagan, Geraldine Lux, *The First Nine Months of Life*, 188
Fletcher, David B., 215
Flippen, J. Brooks, 74
Focus on the Family, 123

Forbes, Cheryl, 91
Ford, Leighton, 38
Ford, President Gerald, 50, 59, 259n128; pardon of Nixon, 57, 59, 68, 259n129, 260n154
Fowler, Robert Booth, 24, 38-39, 85, 93, 95
Friedan, Betty, *Feminine Mystique*, 22
Fromer, Paul, 197
Fuller Theological Seminary, 2, 11, 19, 21, 203, 211
Fundamentalism, 1-2, 19, 71, 244n18, 264n196, 291n130; distinguished from Evangelicalism, 20-21, 143-44, 285n30; and New Christian Right, 142-44
Fundamentalist-Modernist controversy, 1-2, 291n130
Fundamentals: A Testimony to Truth (1910-15), 1

Gaebelein, Frank E., 4, 31
Gallagher, Sally K., 246n40, 269n29
Gallagher, Sharon, 31, 77, 85, 121-22, 274n111
Gallup, George, Jr., and Year of the Evangelical, 63, 261n161
Gardella, Peter, 273n77
Gardner, Christine J., 100
gay rights, 140, 231. *See also* homosexuality
Geisler, Norman, 311n166
gender, use of term, 107, 270n48
gender equality, 76-77, 85, 89, 98-99, 112-20; and "better together," 109-12; "equal but different," 105-9. *See also* feminism, evangelical; sexual differences
gender hierarchy, 112-20
gender relations, 101-20, 247n40
gender roles, 23-24, 76, 112-24; and Morgan's "Total Woman," 92-98
gene patenting, 213, 308n128
genetic research and engineering,

135, 205, 212–16, 218–19, 224–25, 308n127, 309n131, 309n134
genetic screening, 216
Genovese, Eugene D., 250n20
Gish, Art, 31
Goldman, Peter, 263n174
Gordon-Conwell Theological Seminary, 64, 250n13
Graham, Billy, 1–2, 14, 21, 24, 45, 64, 73, 140, 256n78, 256n87, 257n100, 258n110; and Christian Action Council, 181–82; and *Christianity Today*, 6, 10–11; and Honor America Day (1970), 43–49; *How to Be Born Again*, 64; and pastoral politics, 32–33; relationship with President Nixon, 22, 43–49, 51–52, 255n67
Granberg-Michaelson, Wes, 53
Gray, Virginia, 265n3
Green, Roberta, 275n114
Greisch, Janet Rohler, 82
Grenz, Stanley J., 220–21
Griffin, Leslie C., 255n67
Griffith, Ruth Marie, 99, 120–24, 273n80
Groothuis, Rebecca Merrill, 247n40
Grounds, Vernon C., 31, 34, 68–69, 133–34, 280n21; *Revolution and the Christian Faith*, 42
"groupness," 234
Guinness, Os, 300n32
Gundry, Patricia, 78–79; *Woman Be Free*, 269n23
Gundry, Stan, 269n23
Guth, James L., 286n45

Hacker, Andrew, 250n20
Haldeman, R., 258n111
Handy, Robert T., 149–50
Hardesty, Nancy, 31, 77, 79, 85, 118, 270n30, 271n61, 272n62, 275n131, 298n20; *All We're Meant to Be* (with Scanzoni), 89–92, 98; and *Eternity* forum on women, 80–85
Harding, Susan Friend, 283n5

Hartford Appeal, 160–61, 290n111–290n112
Hase, Thomas, 249n7–249n8
Hatch, Nathan O., 151, 154, 241n49, 288n72
Hatfield, Sen. Mark, 15, 31–32, 51, 69, 250n18, 257n103, 257n104, 258n122, 301n49; and *Post-American*, 52–53; proposed national Day of Repentance, 63, 260n153; speech at Chicago Mayor's Prayer Breakfast (May 1973), 54–55, 58, 258n110
headship, 113, 118, 122, 230–31, 237n8, 279n165. *See also* feminism, traditionalist; submission
Henry, Carl F. H., 1–2, 9, 11, 15, 31, 57, 60–62, 140–41, 153–54, 175, 242n72, 259n130; on abortion, 298n20; and Christianity Today Institute, 162, 164–66; and Declaration of Evangelical Social Concern, 32; on the fetus, 208; on New Christian Right, 176; on presidential election (1980), 128; quarrel with Wallis, 77; on theology of marriage, 112; *The Uneasy Conscience of Modern Fundamentalism*, 21; on woman question, 104–5, 109, 119. *See also Christianity Today* (magazine)
Herman, Didi, 314n15
Hermanson, Renee J., 119
heterosexuality, as divine intention, 111–12
hierarchy, 24, 26, 77, 99, 114. *See also* feminism, traditionalist
Hillyard, Daniel, 282n31
Hippocratic Oath, 205, 212, 216–17, 230
HIS (magazine), 8, 14, 16, 39, 315n24
Hitt, Russell T., 13, 67–69, 127, 130, 260n156
HIV (human immunodeficiency virus), 313n14
Hoffmann, John P., 180, 282n31
Hofstadter, Richard, 250n20

360 INDEX

Hollinger, Dennis P., 250n13
homosexuality, 184, 231–32, 277n141, 314n15, 314n16
"honest politician," figure of, 66, 66 (Fig. 2.6)
Honor America Day (1970), 43–49
Horn, Carl, 161, 191
Horner, S. Sue, 278n154
Howard, Thomas, 110–11
Hudson, Kathy, 180–81
Hughes, Sen. Harold, 64, 260n157
human cloning, 213, 308n127
humanism, 156–59, 286n40. *See also* secular humanism
Humanist Manifesto II (1973), 158
human/person distinction, 207–8
Hunt, Gladys, 68, 84
Hunter, James Davison, 5, 21–22, 147–49, 227–28

Ignite Your Faith, 11
imagined community (Anderson), 240n39
imago dei, 104–5, 136, 207, 215, 224, 231
impeachment, Nixon and, 56
imperative to heal, 205–7
incest, 189–90
infanticide, 184–85, 199, 205–7
infertility, 201–4, 203 (Fig. 6.8)
Ingersoll, Julie, 246n40
Institute Tie, 13–14
Internet, 4, 233
InterVarsity Christian Fellowship, 16, 233
in vitro fertilization, 216–18
Irwin, James B., 68
Isserman, Maurice, 5

Jackson, Jesse, 197
Jackson, Myles W., 308n128
Jacoby, Kerry N., 281n31
Jarman, W. Maxey, 11
Jehovah's Witnesses, 236n5
Jelen, Ted G., 297n14
Jenkins, Jerry B., 6, 14, 177

jeremiads, 29, 73, 248n6
Jeremiah (prophet), 32, 41, 60, 248n6
Jesus Christ, life of, 36–37, 100, 253n38
John Chrysostom (saint), 266n4
Johnson, Eithne, 123
Johnson, President Lyndon B., 44
Johnson, Sherrie Mills, 180, 282n31
Johnson, Stephen D., 286n48
Johnson, Virginia, 92
Johnston, Robert K., 75–76
Jorstad, Erling, *The Politics of Moralism*, 72
Joseph, Ray, 153–54
Joyce, Kathryn, 306n94, 306n98

Kantzer, Kenneth S., 11–12, 15, 141, 151, 159, 161–63, 181, 215, 291n116, 310n139
Kazin, Michael, 5
Kent State massacre (1970), 34
Killen, Andreas, 4
Kinlaw, Dennis F., 12
Kleindienst, Richard, 258n111
Kling, David, 58–62
Koop, C. Everett (US surgeon-general), 177, 178 (Fig. 6.1), 179 (Fig. 6.2), 211–12, 225, 232, 299n24, 299n26, 299n27, 300n33, 302n56, 303n59, 304n74; on abortion, 184, 299n30; and Baby Doe cases, 208–11; and Christian Action Council, 181–82; on disability, 185; and embryonic discourse, 193–94; on euthanasia, 185; on infanticide, 184–85; issue of insensitivity to pregnant woman, 189–90; and neonatal care, 185–86; as pediatric surgeon, 185; on sanctity of life, 193–94; *Whatever Happened to the Human Race?* (book and film, with Schaeffer), 182–87, 299n25
Kroeger, Catherine, 246n34, 278n154
Kruse, Kevin M., 20, 22, 45
Kucharsky, David, 47–48, 69, 255n68
Kuhn, Harold Barnes, 82

INDEX

labour of representation (Bourdieu), 3, 9–10
L'Abri community, 39–40
LaHaye, Tim, 14, 133, 137, 144; *The Battle for the Mind*, 157
Lawing, John, 129 (fig. 4.1)
Leadership Journal, 11
Left Behind book series, 14
Leithart, Peter, 207–8
Lewis, C. S., 107; *Mere Christianity*, 262n166; *Perelandra*, 107, 275n116
Lienesch, Michael, 175, 274n94, 283n10, 287n64
Linder, Robert D., 45
Lindsell, Harold, 11, 69, 241n50
Litfin, Diane, 277n151, 278n152, 278n154
Lloyd, Joan, 107
Loesch, Juli, 303n63
Louisville Institute, 12
Luckmann, Thomas, 240n38
Luhr, Eileen, 35, 38
Luker, Kristin, 281n31
Lundquist, Melinda, 79–80
Luther, Martin, 78, 266n4, 291n128
Lutzer, Erwin, 146
Lynd, Staughton, 250n20

MacDonald, Gordon, 117
Machen, J. Gresham, 39
magazine closures, of 1990s and later, 233
magazine market, of 1970s and 1980s, 233
Magruder, Jeb Stuart, 64
marriage, 75–77, 111, 225; as "better together," 109–12, 122
marriage manuals, 93–94, 276n139
Marsden, George M., 20–21, 139, 143, 151–54, 241n49, 300n32
Martin, William, 181–82
Marty, Martin E., 4, 92, 134, 142, 238n11, 239n27, 272n75, 286n40
Masters, William, 92, 272n75
Mathewes-Green, Frederica, 229–30
Maudlin, Michael, 228
Mawyer, Martin, 141–42, 217, 292n134

May, William E., 312n171
Mayers, Kenneth A., 13
McAllaster, Elva, 83
McCorvey, Norma ("Jane Roe"), 229, 297n16
McCrory, Don, 173
McFadden, Carol Prester, 98
McGirr, Lisa, 24
McIntire, Carl Thomas, 31
McKenna, David L., 164, 167–68
McKinniss, Rick, 174–75
McMillan, Herb, 242n71, 250n13
McQuaid, Elwood, 134
media: and New Christian Right, 137–38; and rediscovery of Evangelicalism, 19–20. *See also titles of publications*
Melnik, Glen, 242n71, 250n13
membership issue, Evangelicalism and, 235n3
men: as defining humanity, 103; as husbands and fathers, 109–12
Menehan, Kelsey, 201–2
mercy killings, 205–7
Michaelson, Ronald D., 66 (Fig. 2.6), 257n104
Mickelsen, Alvera, 118
Mickelsen, Berkeley, 118
Miller, Steven P., 43, 255n67, 257n105
Miller, Ted, 145
Minnery, Tom, 162
misogyny, in Christian tradition, 78
Modernist Journals Project, 239n31
Modernists, 1
Mollenkott, Virginia Ramey, 36, 85, 106, 113, 274n111
Monsma, Stephen V., 69, 128, 164, 166–67
Montgomery, John W., 263n175
Moody, Dwight L., 13
Moody Bible Institute (Chicago), 13–14, 19, 65, 69, 242n63, 269n23
Moody Magazine, 14
Moody Monthly (magazine), 6, 8, 13–15, 33, 57, 59, 65, 78, 98, 260n151,

260n153, 263n174, 268n22; abortion issue, 177–79, 193–95, 295n1; advice columns, 112, 200; articles, 96, 104, 111, 114–15, 116 (Fig. 3.4), 128, 142, 184–85, 217, 219, 223, 292n130, 292n134, 306n94; closure of, 233; covers, 131, 133 (Fig. 4.3), 158, 158 (Fig. 5.3), 292n134; and Hatfield's speech at Chicago Mayor's Prayer Breakfast (1973), 54–55; letters to the editors, 145, 301n48; on loss of religious freedoms, 141–42; From Pastor to Pastor column, 146; and Reagan Revolution, 131–34; review of Morgan's *Total Woman*, 93–94

Moore, Elizabeth, 198

moral issues, as focus of New Christian Right, 140–42

morality politics, 68–70, 136–40

Moral Majority, 20, 72, 133, 137–39, 142, 144, 148, 168, 232, 285n37

"moral minority," 29

moral relativism, 54, 141

Mordecai (biblical figure), 117

Morgan, Marabel, 24, 98–101, 272n75, 273n80, 276n139; and "Total Woman," 92–98

Morris, Leon, 5, 30–31, 41

Moynihan, Sen. Daniel Patrick, 65

Muck, Terry C., 12, 175, 292n136

Munson, Ziad W., 281n31

Murphy, Miriam, 261n161

mutual submission, 75–76, 100, 113, 118, 122

Nathan (prophet), 51

National Association of Evangelicals, 2, 21, 127, 235n3

National Council of Christian Churches, 235n3

national decay, and conversion, 64–67

National Organization for Women, 22

National Prayer Breakfast, 44, 53, 254n66

Nederhood, Joel H., 35

Neff, David, 310n156

neoconservatives, 160–61

neo-evangelicalism, 20–22, 241n49

neonatal medicine, 185

Neuhaus, Richard John, 142, 144, 150–51, 160, 285n38, 290n103; *The Naked Public Square*, 159–61

New Christian Right, 19–20, 22, 24, 30, 46, 71–72, 74, 127–28, 135–40, 164, 166, 174–76, 232, 247n40, 253n47, 274n94, 280n2, 283n10, 286n40, 286n48, 287n64, 289n82, 292n134, 300n32; and absolutism, 292n130; and Christian America, 153; and civil religion, 72; emergence of, 19–20, 142–46, 148–49; Evangelicals and, 142–44, 148–50; and family values, 178; and imperialist biblicism, 292n130; and moral issues, 140–42; and Reagan Revolution, 129–30, 133–34, 146–47; and Robertson candidacy, 169–74; Schaeffer and, 184; and secular humanism, 157; and traditional family values, 123. *See also* Christian America

New Left, 40

Newsweek (magazine), 2, 10, 30, 47, 70–72, 142, 148, 250n20, 265n203

New York Times, 45, 92, 148, 256n78, 263n174, 310n156

Niebuhr, Reinhold, 265n203

Nixon, President Richard M., 22, 27, 43, 50, 254n66, 255n66; appointment of Ford, 259n128; nonadmission of guilt and lack of repentance, 63, 260n154; pardoned by Ford, 57, 59, 68, 259n129, 260n154; relationship with Billy Graham, 43–49, 51–52, 255n67; resignation, 29, 50, 56–57, 59; and Watergate crisis, 49–58

Noll, Mark A., 20–21, 139, 151, 154, 160, 175–76, 241n49, 288n72, 293n143, 293n144; *The Search for Christian America*, 154–55

nonpartisanship, and Honor America Day, 45–46
nostalgic vision of a better past, 46–47
Nyberg, Bartell, 258n110

Ockenga, Harold John, 11, 21
Olson, Roger E., 101, 236n5, 249n11
online publishing, 11, 16
Operation Rescue, 183, 297n16
Other Side (magazine), 8, 16, 48–50, 78, 90, 103–4
ovum transfer, 217

Packard, Vance, 305n81
Packer, J. I., 12, 164–65
Padgett, Alan G., 245n33
Palmer, Bruce H., 183
Pannell, Bill, 48
parenthood, 198–201, 225
Parsons, Talcott, 249n8
pastoral politics, 32–33, 250n18
Patterson, Ben, 16, 107, 109, 144–45, 147
Pence, Mike, 232
Pentecostalism, 71, 172–73, 264n196, 293n149
People's Christian Coalition, 15, 27, 31, 40, 250n13, 253n52
periodicals, Protestant, 25, 238n11
periodical studies, 7
periodicity, 7
Perkins, John M., 31
Perkins, Spencer, 197–98
personal-morality model, 69
personhood, 124, 207–12, 303n59; fetal, 191–95
Petchesky, Rosalind Pollack, 188, 190–91
Peterson, William J., 13
Pew, J. Howard, 11
Pew Charitable Fund, 236n8
Phillips, Anne, 270n47
Phillips, Tom, 262n166
Pierard, Richard V., 31, 45, 72, 133, 280n21
Pinnock, Clark, 15, 41–42

Pippert, Wes, 68
Pledge of Allegiance, addition of "under God" to, 44
pluralism, 33, 140, 150, 251n23
policy-transformation model, 69–70
political activism, 19–21, 25, 32, 127–34, 137–40, 145–46. *See also* Declaration of Evangelical Social Concern; Moral Majority; New Christian Right
political conversion, 30, 62–70, 73–74, 260n156, 261n158, 261n159, 262n166
political office, calling to, 169–74
politics, US, in wake of Watergate crisis, 58–72
politics and religion. *See* civil religion
Pontius Pilate (historical and biblical figure), 37
post-American perspective, 58–62
Post-American/Sojourners (magazine), 8, 15–16, 27, 31, 40–42, 50, 52–53, 58–62, 141, 147, 214, 219, 233, 242n75, 250n13, 257n103, 305n75, 309n131, 315n27; abortion issue, 188, 194, 197; articles, 41, 106; covers, 28 (Fig. 2.1)–28 (Fig. 2.2), 29 (Fig. 2.3); and feminism, 78; on Graham, 48–49; and Honor America Day, 45; publication history, 247n1, 257n104; reviews, 91–92
Post-Americans/Sojourners, 58–62, 233, 268n19
potential person, 207–8, 224
poverty, and abortion, 196–98
prenatal life, 177, 186, 299n30
prenatal medicine, 205
presidential campaign: of 1980, 127–34; of 1988, 169–74
Preston, Andrew, 255n67
Prison Fellowship, 62, 163
procreation, 110, 198–201, 220–23, 311n170. *See also* children; family; reproductive technologies
pro-life movement, 135, 180–204, 281n31

prophetic politics, 32–33, 45–46, 250n18
Protestantism, as American faith, 149–50
PTL (Praise the Lord) imperium, 169–70, 172–73

qualtiy-of-life argument, 211
Quebedeaux, Richard, 268n19

race, and abortion, 197–98
race suicide, 200
radio, 2–4
Ramm, Bernard, 83–84
rape, 189–90
reading audience, 3
Reagan, President Ronald, 74, 123, 128, 131, 170, 178, 209, 227, 255n66, 263n178; election, 129–34, 146–47
Reagan Revolution, 129–34, 132 (Fig. 4.2), 133 (Fig. 4.3), 146–47
reconciliation, Evangelicals and, 40
Reconstructionism, 289n82
Reed, Scott, 197
Reese, Boyd, 91, 242n71, 250n13
Relevant online periodical, 233
religious bookstores, 93
religious freedom, 168, 176, 292n134; perceived loss of, 141–42
Religious Right, 142. See also New Christian Right
Religious Roundtable, 137, 147
repentance: Nixon's lack of, 63, 260n154; and regeneration, 261n162
reproductive rights movement, 200, 305n89
reproductive technologies, 135, 204–5, 216–23, 309n134
Revelation (magazine), 12
reversal, and conversion, 66–67, 73–74
revolution, as original Christian concept, 64–65
revolutionary spirit, of 1960s US, 33–43
Ribuffo, Leo, 123
Rice, John R., 24
Rice, Wayne, 16

Rifkin, Jeremy, 219, 309n131
Right On! tabloid, 77
Risen, James, 183, 281n31
Roberts, Oral, 170, 170 (Fig. 5.4)
Roberts, Robert C., 200
Robertson, Pat (Marion Gordon Robertson), 71, 293n149; presidential candidacy (1988), 169–74, 170 (Fig. 5.4), 174–75, 232, 293n148, 294n151
Robison, James, 137, 146–47
Rockefeller, Nelson, 59–60
Roman Catholicism, 252n25; and new reproductive technologies, 220
Roos, Joe, 27, 49
Roosevelt, President Franklin D., 44
Rosenbladt, Rod, 107–8
Rousseau, Jean-Jacques, 29, 248n7
Rowe, H. Edward, 263n178
Ruether, Rosemary Radford, 266n4
Runia, Klaas, 46, 298n20
Rushdoony, R. J., 289n82
Ryan, Mary P., 23, 123, 265n2, 270n48
Rydberg, Denny, 16, 263n178, 263n181
Ryrie, Charles C., 24, 81–82

Sabath, Bob, 15, 242n71, 250n13
Saletan, William, 282n31
salvation, Evangelical theology of, 261n162
sanctity of life, 10, 135–36, 186, 189, 193–94, 214, 223–26
Sanderson, Judith, 103–4
Sayers, Dorothy L., 102–3
Scanzoni, Letha, 25, 79, 97–101, 112, 114, 117–18, 271n61, 272n62, 275n131; *All We're Meant to Be* (with Nancy Hardesty), 89–92, 98; "Feminists and the Bible," 85–90
Schaeffer, Edith, 24
Schaeffer, Francis A., 39, 139, 186, 228, 253n47, 289n89, 298n24, 299n27; *A Christian Manifesto*, 151, 183, 300n32; *The Church at the End of the Twentieth Century*, 39–40; *The God Who*

Is There, 156; *How Should We Then Live?*, 156, 183; on secular humanism, 156–57; *Whatever Happened to the Human Race?* (book and film, with Koop), 182–87, 299n25
Schaeffer, Franky, 183, 289n89; *A Time for Anger*, 151, 300n32
Schäfer, Axel, 20–21, 35, 73–74, 255n68
Schlafly, Phyllis, 23, 71
Schlesinger, Arthur M., Jr., 250n20
Schroedel, Jean Reith, 303n59
Scopes Trial, 1–2
Scott, Elizabeth S., 225, 311n161
Second Coming, of Jesus Christ, 60
Second Vatican Council (1962–65), 251n25
secular humanism, 144–45, 155–62
secularism/secularization, 159–61, 252n25
self-help books, 93–94, 99
"separate spheres," 23–24
separatism, 39, 59, 292n130
seriality, 7
700 Club, 170, 173
sex, theology of, 111–12
sexism, statement on, 76
sex manuals, 92–93, 95, 111, 273n79
sexual abstinence, 100
sexual differences, 83, 91, 105–12, 276n141
shared vision, use of term, 9
Shedd, Charlie and Martha, 111, 276n137
Short, Shirl, 268n22
Sider, Ron, 76–77, 266n9
Siegel, Mark, 71
silent majority, 39–40, 43, 251n20
Silent Scream (short film, 1984), 188–89
Simon, Paul, 285n37
Singer, David, 186
single life, 92, 109, 275n131
situational ethics, 54
Skillen, James W., 295n170
Skinner, Tom, 36–37, 253n38
Smedes, Lewis B., 211, 219, 221

Smidt, Corwin E., 143–44, 235n3, 285n30
Smith, Christian, 79–80, 121–22, 149, 244n13, 269n24, 269n29, 287n62
Sobran, Joseph, 133
social concern, 21–25, 32, 134–36; Evangelical workshop on (Chicago, 1973), 76–77; as focus of Evangelical Left, 140–42. *See also* antiabortion activism; Declaration of Evangelical Social Concern
social unrest, of 1960s US, 33–43
Sojourners (magazine), 6. *See also Post-American/Sojourners* (magazine)
Solinger, Rickie, 302n53, 304n71
Soper, J. Christopher, 303n65
Southern Baptist Convention, 181, 293n149
sperm donation, 216
spokespersons, Evangelical, 3, 9–10, 72–74, 227, 234; on Christian citizenship, 168–69; on gender norms, 25–26; on gender relations, 101–20, 247n40; and political engagement, 127–34; on women's issues, 76, 84–85, 120–24
Spring, Beth, 131, 170–71, 173–74, 202–4, 209, 220, 311n170
Stasson, Anneke, 269n29
stem cell research, 308n127
Stern, Elizabeth and William, 219–20
Stott, John R. W., 192, 303n63
Stout, Harry, 241n49
Stowell, Joseph, 14
Strang, Cameron, 233
submission, 10, 75–76, 92–101, 108–9, 115, 120–24, 230–31, 273n80. *See also* mutual submission
surrogacy, 216, 219–23, 225–26, 311n161, 311n166
Sutton, Matthew Avery, 20–21, 241n49, 244n18
Swartz, David R., 29, 47, 50, 52–53, 268n19
Sweeting, George, 14, 65, 69, 115–17, 140
Sword of the Lord (magazine), 24

Tamney, Joseph B., 286n48
Taylor, Daniel, 231–32
Taylor, Terri Graves, 207, 307n112
televangelists, 169–70, 172–73, 232, 249n162, 294n150
television, 2–4
Terry, Randall, 183
test-tube babies, 217, 219
Thomas, Cal, 139, 142–44, 232, 284n26, 292n134
Thomas, Judy L., 183, 281n31
Thomson, Irene Taviss, 147–48
Thornton, Zeda, 78, 93–94, 109, 119, 268n22
Thorsen, Donald A. D., 227
Tiefel, Hans, 215–16, 310n139, 312n173
Time (magazine), 5, 229, 250n20, 272n75, 313n14
Today's Christian Woman, 11, 201, 306n92
tolerance, 231–32
Topliff, John, 242n71, 250n13
"Totaled Woman," 96–98, 97 (Fig. 3.2)
totalitarianism, perceived risk of, 40, 42
"Total Man," 95–96, 95 (Fig. 3.1)
"Total Woman" (Morgan), 92–98; workshops, 92, 272n76
transformative power, Christian, 33–43
Trinity Evangelical Divinity School (Deerfield, IL), 15, 27, 30–31, 41, 242n71
Trump, President Donald, 233
Turner, Barry, 242n71, 250n13
two-kingdom doctrine, 291n128

ultrasound imaging, 216
unborn child, 187–98, 300n31
UN Convention on the Rights of the Child (1989), 178, 305n80
UNESCO International Year of the Child (1979), 178
US Constitution, 293n143
US House of Representatives Committee on the Judiciary, 50
US Senate Watergate Committee, 50

US Supreme Court: *Diamond v. Chakrabarty* (1980), 213, 308n128, 309n131; *Roe v. Wade* (1973), 23, 181, 297n16; and Watergate crisis, 50

Vaca, Daniel, 4
value of life, 205–7
values crisis, 141–42, 155–62
Van Atta, Lucibel, 194–95, 304n68
vanishing children, 198–201
Verhey, Alan, 218
Victorian gender norms, 23–24
Vietnam War, 27, 59
vision, use of term, 8–9, 227, 240n39

Wacker, Grant, 241n49
Wallis, Jim, 15, 27, 31, 40, 48, 52, 57, 73, 77, 133, 188, 242n71, 242n72, 250n13, 260n154, 280n21; and Christianity Today Institute, 162–63; and "Post-American Christianity" project, 58–62. *See also* People's Christian Coalition; *Post-American/Sojourners* (magazine)
wall of separation, 292n136
wanted child, 198–201, 305n81
Washington Post, 50
Watergate crisis, 29, 49–60, 63, 68, 139, 260n151
"Watergate logic," 54, 258n113
Waters, Ken, 6, 16, 233
Webber, Robert E., *The Moral Majority*, 72
Weber, Max, 250n18
Wells, Robert G., 311n166
Weyrich, Paul, 71
White, John H., 200
Whitehead, John W., 153, 289n89, 292n134; *The Second American Revolution*, 151, 300n32
Whitehead, Mary Beth, 219–21
White House Conference on Families (WHCF), 123, 178
Wilcox, Clyde, 19–20, 150, 297n14

Wilentz, Sean, 5
Wilkens, Steve, 227
Wilson, Marvin, 83
Wittenburg Door (magazine), 3, 8, 16, 233, 240n32, 285n38; and concept of "submission," 98–101; cover (June/July 1980), 137, 138 (Fig. 5.1); on Fundamentalism, 143–44; interviews, 111, 139, 159; on "Totaled Woman" (1975), 96–98, 97 (Fig. 3.2)
Wolfe, Alan, 149, 228, 231, 287n62
womanhood: changing Evangelical views of, 79–101; question "are women human?," 101–5; traditional Christian models of, 77–78
women: as "full persons," 92; and submission, 120–24; as wives and mothers, 109–12
women, liberated, 112–20
Women's Aglow Fellowship, 273n80
women's liberation movement, 22–25, 76–79, 119–24, 230–31, 271n48. *See also* feminism
women's mental health, abortion and, 302n56
Wong, Pamela P., 200
Woodbridge, John D., 228–29
Woodward, Bob, 50
World Council of Churches, 164
World Relief organization, 22, 127
World Vision organization, 22, 127
Worthen, Molly, 241n49
Wuthnow, Robert, 30, 287n55

Yaconelli, Mike, 16
Yancey, Philip D., 301n42
Year of the Evangelical (1976), 30
Young, Neil J., 251n25
Young Evangelicals, 31, 253n47, 253n51, 268n19. *See also* Evangelical Left